Public Finance in Australia

THEORY AND PRACTICE

Third edition

Public Finance in Australia

THEORY AND PRACTICE

Third edition

Peter Groenewegen
Professor of Economics, The University of Sydney

Prentice Hall

New York London Toronto Sydney Tokyo Singapore

Typeset by Keyboard Wizards, Harbord, NSW.

Printed and bound in Australia by Impact Printing, Brunswick, Vic.

Cover design: Kim Webber

1 2 3 4 5 94 93 92 91 90

ISBN 0 7248 0918 X

National Library of Australia
Cataloguing-in-Publication Data

Groenewegen, P. D. (Peter Diderik)
Public finance in Australia: theory and practice.

3rd ed.
Bibliography
Includes index.
ISBN 0 7248 0918 X.

1. Finance, Public – Australia. I. Title.

336.94

Prentice Hall, Inc., *Englewood Cliffs, New Jersey*
Prentice Hall Canada, Inc., *Toronto*
Prentice Hall Hispanoamericana, SA, *Mexico*
Prentice Hall of India Private Ltd, *New Delhi*
Prentice Hall International, Inc., *London*
Prentice Hall of Japan, Inc., *Tokyo*
Prentice Hall of Southeast Asia Pty Ltd, *Singapore*
Editora Prentice Hall do Brasil Ltda, *Rio de Janeiro*

PRENTICE HALL

A division of Simon & Schuster

Contents

Preface to the Third Edition

A third edition of this text was long overdue. The second edition was prepared during 1983 and in the intervening six years Australian public finance arrangements underwent a great deal of change. At the same time the changes made in the second edition revealed that the book's division into chapters had become a disadvantage in terms of structure. Apart from updating statistical material, and incorporating the many changes which have occurred in Australia's public finance arrangement, the book's contents have also been significantly restructured by turning the ten chapters of the first and second editions into twenty. Much of this restructuring has involved subdividing the former chapters and incorporating former appendices into the text. Those familiar with the first and second editions will easily see that these structural transformations have been made by turning the previous two chapters on government spending into four, three tax chapters into eight and the chapter of fiscal federalism into three, one of which, dealing with State and local finance, is almost completely new. The other largely new chapter, Chapter 19, deals with international aspects of public finance.

Reorganisation and revisions have allowed the shifting of capital gains tax to income tax and the addition of sections on fringe benefits tax, superannuation tax and imputation to business taxation, while allowing more detailed treatment of broad-based consumption taxes. Material on expenditure has also expanded by distinguishing more clearly the theory from the practical considerations in Chapters 4 and 5 respectively. The same was done with fiscal federalism arrangements in Chapters 14 and 15. The two substantive chapters which appear to have survived this restructuring unscathed — those on the public debt and stabilisation respectively — have been considerably shortened. Presentation of contents has also been remodelled and now includes a summary of major points, and notes for further reading, as well as the notes at the end of each chapter.

Some of these changes were suggested by colleagues who were using the text in their courses. I acknowledge the helpful suggestions from the five anonymous referees provided by my publisher. Thanks are also due to David Collins who encouraged the restructuring plan finally adopted; to Judy Yates for her useful comments on some of the earlier chapters; and to Warren Hogan who commented on Chapter 17, saving me from some errors. Once again, Valerie Jones had the enormous task of processing a neat manuscript from my untidy and sometimes illegible manuscripts, tolerating many alterations and revisions which she completed in her usual excellent and efficient manner. Jack Towe provided research assistance in preparing some tables and graphs and obtaining relevant material.

Extracts from the Preface to the first edition indicate the philosophy and general objectives on which this book was produced in the mid-1970s and the general debt I owe to my students in its preparation.

Peter Groenewegen,
Sydney, February 1990.

Extract from Preface to the First Edition

The title of this book betrays its intentions. The major part of the title — *Public Finance in Australia* — indicates the strength and limitations of this text. This is an *Australian* text, designed for Australian students, presenting Australian institutions, giving Australian examples, and providing Australian references. That there is a need for such a book for students (and teachers) of public finance in Australia needs little emphasis (I personally experienced it in teaching public finance at Sydney University for over a decade). It was this need which made me accept the offer to write this book. This primary aim should be kept in mind when interpreting the second half of the title.

Theory and Practice — the subtitle — requires a caveat. In the trade-off between the two (and within the budget constraint implied by the availability of space and ultimate cost, of which my publishers constantly reminded me), practice has gained at the expense of theory. The reason for this is not my dislike for theory. It is that there are excellent textbooks available on the theory of public finance, some of which also present the background for other countries. The book should therefore be supplemented by the further reading given in the endnotes.

In fact, the book is "littered" with notes to provide guides for further reading not only on the theory but also for further investigation of the Australian material. Most of the more important Australian official and unofficial public finance sources are documented in this way.

The subject-matter in the book covers the major areas of public finance with a strong institutional slant. Chapter 1 defines the scope of the subject; Chapters 2 and 3 deal with aspects of the budget process and with the public expenditure decision-making process; Chapters 4 to 6 deal with taxation; Chapter 7 with the public debt; Chapter 8 with intergovernmental financial relations; and Chapter 9 with fiscal policy for stabilisation (but not with income determination and inflation theory). Chapter 20 looks at the future and investigates some public finance issues likely to become relevant to the 1980s.

In completing this project, I have incurred many intellectual debts. Bob Wallace read the whole of the manuscript through two successive drafts and made so many suggestions for improvements that it is sometimes difficult to tell what is his contribution and what is mine in the construction of many paragraphs. Peter Saunders also read the whole of the manuscript and gave me many constructive comments. Other individual chapters were read by specialists in the field.

I owe this book to my public finance students of the past few years on whom segments of it were tried out in lectures. Without their help my learning through teaching would not have been achieved.

Peter Groenewegen,
Sydney, September 1978.

Figures

Tables

1

Introduction

DEFINITION OF PUBLIC FINANCE

Public finance, as its name indicates, is concerned with matters related to the finance of the public sector. This definition is at once too narrow and too broad. It is *too narrow* because the financial matters are primarily the means for affecting the more fundamental issues, namely the transfer of real resources from the private to the public sector and between the individuals, firms, and classes who comprise the private sector. The definition is *too broad* because some of the financial aspects of the work of the public sector are not covered; for example, the techniques for ensuring that public revenues raised are spent effectively and in accordance with the Parliament's intentions have long been the special province of public administration. More recently, the issue of how the Budget deficit is to be financed (or the surplus disposed of) has been largely incorporated into discussions of monetary theory and policy. Finally, public sector economics, as distinct from public finance, in addition examines the economics of public enterprises, a topic largely excluded from this text.

To some extent the meaning of public finance can be described in terms of the subject matter it deals with. As Adam Smith, one of the first comprehensive writers on the economics of public finance, put it, the subject is concerned with the expenses and the revenue of the sovereign or Commonwealth; that is, with the analysis of government expenditure, of taxation and of the public debt. Although the emphasis on these three components of public finance has shifted in the 200 years since the publication of his *Wealth of Nations*, their analysis has remained the major concern in the study of the subject.

Be that as it may, it is clear that public finance involves the public sector, or, more specifically, the economic transactions of the public sector. This in itself needs some definition. The public sector has been defined by one author as being "engaged in providing services (and in some cases goods) whose scope and variety are determined not by the direct wishes of the consumers, but by the decision of government bodies, that is, in a democracy, by the representatives of the citizens".[1] As shown in Chapter 2, this traditional allocative function needs to be extended to incorporate redistributional and stabilisation functions.

This defines the public sector by the *functions* which it performs, namely the provision of goods and services, the nature and extent of which are decided upon not through the market but through government bodies. The definition necessarily raises questions about the nature of publicly provided goods, about the government bodies which make up the public sector, and about the nature of the State and the political process. It also raises the issue of the proportion of the public sector relative to the private sector in a mixed economy such as Australia. These issues are important and should be clarified at the outset.

THE NATURE OF PUBLICLY PROVIDED GOODS

When different countries are examined, or even when State or local government practice in the same country is looked at, many goods and services can be found which are both privately and publicly supplied. Education, transport, telephone services, broadcasting, television are examples that spring readily to mind. At the same time, there are some services which are rarely supplied privately. External defence is the leading example, and it is interesting to note that this is the major function assigned to government by the political philosophers of the seventeenth century and by Adam Smith, in his early writings on public finance.

At this stage the distinction between *public provision* and *public production* must be drawn. Many goods which are privately sold in the market may be publicly produced; for example, the bricks produced by State brickworks and the electricity sold by county councils and produced by State electricity commissions. At the same time, a publicly provided good such as defence may consist of many *privately produced* goods. Examples include trucks and other motor vehicles made by enterprises within the private sector. Publicly provided goods mean goods whose provision is financed through the Budget; they do not refer to how or where they are produced.

Because there is considerable variety in the nature and scope of goods and services provided by the public sector in different countries, the question arises as to whether there are any characteristics which make goods or services *public* goods provided through the Budget as against *private* goods provided through the market. To put it another way, are the reasons why some goods are supplied by the private sector and some by the public sector dictated by purely political and ideological considerations, or do they derive from more objective sources which lie outside the political arena?

The answer to this question is not clear-cut, although in the past many economists have tried to indicate that it was.[2] Part of the argument was based on the notion of "collective goods", that is, goods which cannot generally be purchased by *individuals* because supply is frequently indivisible. Such goods (lighthouses and public health measures were frequent examples) as well as the more traditional government services of defence and the administration of justice have these characteristics and were, it was argued, the preserve of government. All other goods, that is, those capable of being privately marketed, were to be the domain of the private sector.

This theory of the functions of the public sector is vulnerable on two major grounds. First, it cannot be more robust than is the definition of public goods. Second, even if public goods could be unequivocally defined, "it is not true that the economic activity of the State is designed to satisfy all collective needs and only collective needs" as Barone has argued in opposition to this claim.[3]

A more pragmatic approach was therefore frequently used to describe the scope and nature of publicly provided goods and services and to assign limits to the size of the public sector. John Stuart Mill, the nineteenth century liberal political philosopher and economist, devoted much attention to this question in his *Principles of Political Economy*. He offered the general principle of *laissez faire*, namely that "the great majority of things are worse done by the intervention of government, than the individuals most interested in the matter would do them, or cause them to be done, if left to themselves",[4] but he listed so many exceptions to this rule that its practical significance was severely eroded. It is of interest, however, that the exceptions cited by Mill in 1848, such as education, public charity, hospitals and public works (roads, docks, harbours, canals and irrigation) provide the justification for nearly all the items of expenditure undertaken by governments in mixed economies, including those of the modern welfare state.

This pragmatic approach has remained a feature of the discussion of the nature of public goods. Although much has been written on the theory of public goods, this literature does not pose the question of whether there are natural limits on government in the provision of goods and services. These theories can only provide the basis for a distinction between private and public goods, and a rationale for the application of efficiency criteria to the decision-making about the supply of these public goods.[5] This matter will be looked at in more detail in Chapter 4.

In general, public goods are distinguished from private, marketable goods on the basis of their characteristics. Goods can be described as private on two grounds. First, the *exclusion principle* must apply; that is, consumers can obtain exclusive rights over the object of their satisfaction and, what is more important, the seller can exclude specific individuals from its consumption. Second, private goods are *rival* in consumption; individual benefits from their consumption are reduced if their consumption is shared by somebody else. For "pure" private goods both these conditions must apply. Public good or social characteristics appear as soon as the exclusion principle cannot be applied as is the case in the provision of external defence; they also appear as soon as consumption is non-rival, as in the case of a television program where my enjoyment is not diminished when my neighbour switches on, to take an example of a service provided by both the public and private sector. Before cable television could be introduced and paid for by individual consumers, technology to exclude non-payers had to be available.

None of this helps solve the question whether there are "natural limits" to the public sector. Barone's view is that public-goods characteristics are largely irrelevant to the question of which goods are to be supplied by the public sector because this is determined by political decisions. Both the privatisation debate and the steps taken by the Federal Government to commercialise the activities of public enterprises such as Telecom, Qantas, Australian Airlines and Australia Post, illustrate the relevance of Barone's proposition to contemporary conditions. Furthermore, some non-rival consumption goods where the exclusion principle can be applied, such as cinema performances, football matches and, increasingly, television transmission, can be privately marketed. Finally, the application of the exclusion principle is sometimes cumbersome or administratively expensive, as it would be if the use of all individual roads was to be separately paid for. Toll roads are infrequent exceptions, though the expedient of a tollway is more widely used in times of fiscal stringency.

The possibility of applying the exclusion principle and/or the attribute of rival consumption are not necessarily exclusive features of any particular goods. In the case of many goods and services, part of the benefit may be exclusively appropriated by a particular consumer, whereas another part of the benefit may accrue to others, if not to the public at large. In spraying my fruit trees for fruitfly, I also benefit the trees of my neighbour, or, to take an example more in the public domain, the education of an individual person may benefit society at large as well as the particular individual. The right to consumption of the private benefit from education can in principle be marketed, but it is impossible to apply the exclusion principle to the consumption of the social benefit. Charging for education, particularly at the tertiary level, is therefore not a simple matter of reintroducing student fees on a simple full cost recovery basis. Current Australian practice in this regard is looked at in Chapter 9.

These two examples illustrate the importance of *externalities* or *spill-over effects* in the theory of public finance. Such externalities are not necessarily beneficial; pollution caused by the smoke of public or private incinerators or the noise from jets and motor-mowers involve adverse spill-over effects. The examples also illustrate *spatial aspects* of externalities. Fruitfly spraying in my garden may affect only a small geographical area; the externalities provided by education may affect the nation as a whole. These spatial aspects of social benefits are discussed in Chapter 14 in the theory of intergovernmental financial relations where they can be used to delineate the functions to be assigned to the various levels of government.

It is relatively easy to distinguish *pure* private goods from *pure* public goods. The first are completely *rival* in consumption and susceptible to easy application of the *exclusion* principle. The second are goods which all people enjoy in common in the sense that each individual's consumption leads to no subtraction from any other individual's consumption of those goods. However, the pure cases are, generally speaking, abstract constructions at the polar extremes. In practice, nearly all publicly provided goods have *both* public *and* private good characteristics.[6]

Finally, and this is of particular importance to modern public finance analysis, governments increasingly provide goods whose supply is not determined directly or indirectly by individual preferences but by the preferences of government bodies. Musgrave[7] uses the term "merit goods" to describe goods which are provided through the Budget because some authority considers they are "socially desirable". Such merit goods are specifically designed to interfere with consumer preferences on the ground that the government knows better what is good for individuals and therefore they contain an element of coercion (for example, compulsory wearing of seat-belts). Other examples of merit goods mentioned by various writers include the broad socially desirable "goods" of full employment and the elimination of poverty, as well as narrower categories such as education (or perhaps even more narrowly, primary education only); free milk for schoolchildren; art galleries; participation by a national team in the Olympic Games; and support for training of athletes in government-funded sport institutes. The concept of merit goods is so elastic that, once admitted, no limit can in principle be placed on the size of the public sector.

The size of the public sector is largely decided through the political framework and this necessitates a brief examination of the institutions of the public sector as well as discussion of the different notions of the State and different types of society. Apart from the subsequent material in this introduction, such issues are examined in Chapter 2. Factors influencing the growth of the public sector in theory and practice are examined in Chapter 3. Such institutional features must be grasped for a proper understanding of public finance problems.

GOVERNMENT BODIES

In the discussion of public goods, reference has been made to such concepts as "representatives of the people", "government bodies", the "State", the "public sector" and the "political framework". These concepts are frequently used in the literature of public finance, though their specific meaning for the purpose at hand is often not explained. To some extent, this gives the theory a greater air of generality than it actually has, since in practice the usefulness of the theory, either as explanation, or as a guide to policy decisions, varies quite markedly according to how accurately it reflects the institutions of the country concerned.

These variations in the nature of the institutions relevant to the study of public finance among different countries are not minor difficulties that can be easily overcome. In many cases, the different institutions raise problems in one country which are not encountered in another. An important example of such a difference for the study of public finance is whether the country in question is a federation or a more unitary State.[8] Another example, at a more theoretical level, is the conception of the State (the "theory of the State") which provides the basis for a theory of Budget determination. For instance, the two polar views of the State derive, at one extreme, from the individualistic, democratic notion of the State and, at the other, from the organic and more authoritarian view. It should be noted that the view of the "proper" scope of public finance differs substantially when considered in the context of a capitalist economy compared with an advanced socialist society or with a developing nation in the Third World. This book is primarily concerned with Australian public finance, that is, with the public finance of a federal system in a capitalist economy with representative government, but these institutional issues are too important to be left unexplored. In order to get an adequate view of the scope of this study of public finance, some of the implications of this decision must be illustrated. Other peculiarities of the Australian public sector are examined in this introduction and in subsequent chapters, particularly Chapters 2 and 16.

THE AUSTRALIAN PUBLIC SECTOR

The Australian National Accounts,[9] prepared by the Australian Bureau of Statistics, offer a definition of the public sector in Australia. This definition is, of course, of intrinsic interest and it also gives an excellent illustration of the complexities of the meaning to be given to the public sector in a modern economy. The definition is:

> The public authority sector in the Australian National Accounts covers the activities of government (Australian, State and local), semi-government authorities, and other bodies (e.g. universities, public hospitals, public libraries etc.) carrying out defined functions on behalf of the government. The current operations of public trading enterprises are represented in the accounts of the public authority sector by their net income . . .[10]

Figure 1.1 illustrates the interrelationships between these various institutions within the Australian public sector. It also reveals a number of important classifications in the Australian public sector. First of all, it indicates that Australia is a federation divided into three tiers of government: Federal, State, and local. Second, it shows quite clearly that government proper is only part of the public sector, and that there are other institutions in the public sector whose activities fall wholly or partly inside or outside the Budget. Some of

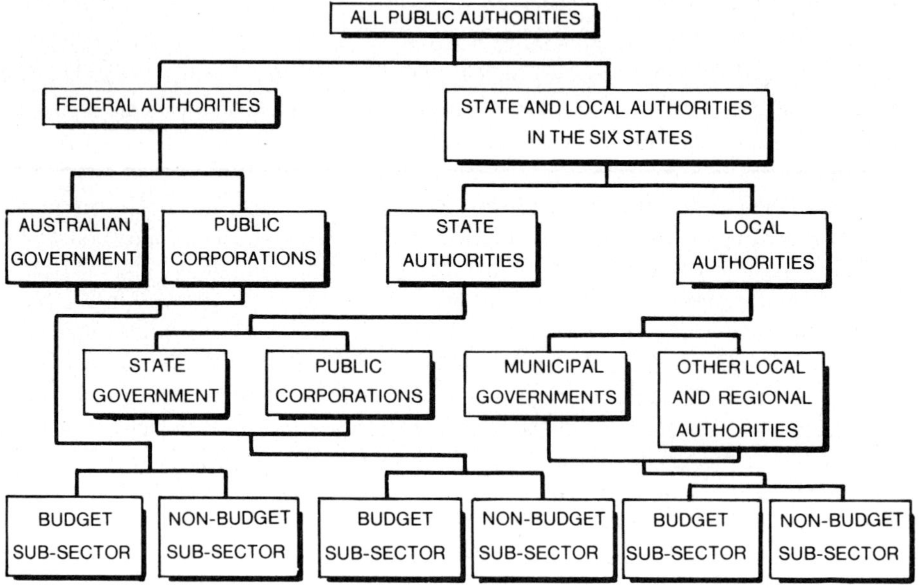

Figure 1.1 The Australian public sector

these institutions are almost totally financed from within the Budget; for example, the Australian Broadcasting Corporation. The transactions of other public authorities such as Qantas Airways Ltd and Telecom have, in general, only marginal impact on the Budget. Their links to the government come via the ministerial appointment of the Boards which control these institutions, and via the capital injections the government makes to such enterprises within and without the Budget (as further discussed in Chapter 17).

The fiscal implications of the fact that Australia is a federation are discussed in Part III, but in this introduction some important characteristics may be emphasised. Unlike England, Australia has seven *sovereign governments* (eight, perhaps nine, if the Northern Territory and the self-governing Australian Capital Territory are included), seven (nine) Parliaments, and hence seven (nine) Budgets, seven (nine) tax systems, and seven (nine) areas of public expenditure and public endeavour to be investigated. This is something which can be easily forgotten when attention is invariably focused on the national parliament and on the national Budget because of the predominant financial powers of the Commonwealth Government. The study of public finance is therefore much more complicated in Australia than in England, since it cannot be assumed that the economic behaviour of the State governments is unimportant, or that this behaviour is more or less uniform among the States. From 1978–79 onwards, the Northern Territory has been treated as part of State and local government, although it does not have the full legal status of a State, while the Australian Capital Territory became self-governing in 1989.

In addition to the Federal and State governments, Australia has over 800 local governments. These governments are not sovereign entities but derive their powers, including their fiscal powers, from the governments of the States in which they are situated. Local government also prepares its annual budgets, which, on aggregate, account for approximately 6 per cent of total public expenditure. In addition, there are other local or regional authorities such as the county councils, local government business enterprises, and local semi-government authorities such as the Melbourne and Metropolitan Board of Works and the New South Wales Metropolitan Water, Sewerage and Drainage Board. Issues of State and local government finance are canvassed in more detail later in this book, especially in Chapter 17.

The second distinction of importance in the Australian public sector indicated in Figure 1.1 is the division between government and public corporations and between the Budget and non-Budget sub-sectors. This distinction applies to both the Federal and the State governments and should be explained. Broadly speaking, the Budget sector comprises all departments and authorities whose transactions are recorded in detail in the public accounts, that is, within the Consolidated Revenue Fund, the Loan Fund, and the trust funds which form the basic accounts of Australian governments. A discussion of these funds is presented in Chapter 2. The non-Budget sub-sector then comprises those public authorities, mainly trading or business enterprises, only part of whose financial transactions are reflected in the public accounts.

Examples drawn from the Commonwealth public sector will make this clearer. The Commonwealth Budget sector consists of most of the general government and administrative departments responsible for public administration, defence, social welfare activities including health, education and housing. A number of authorities whose detailed financial transactions are not recorded in the public accounts (such as the ABC and CSIRO) are off-budget, but because they are largely dependent on government funding they are not included with the public trading enterprises sector. Together with the Budget sector they form the general government sector. The Commonwealth public trading enterprises sector includes Telecom, Australia Post, Qantas and Australian Airlines. Public financial enterprise transactions are all off-budget apart from contributions they make to Commonwealth revenue as rent, dividends and royalties. At the State level, the general government level includes the provision of health, education and community services while State public trading enterprises include electricity, gas and most public transport. On these definitions, the general government sector accounts for about 95 per cent of Commonwealth outlays, the corresponding proportion at the State/local level is around 80 per cent.[11]

The distinctions raised in this type of classification have important implications for the study of public finance, as well as for the preparation of the national accounts. For example, measurement of the size of the public sector over time and international comparisons of the relative size of a country's public sector require that these distinctions be tightly drawn. More important, a model of public expenditure decision-making which only involved the role of Parliament would be a most inadequate model.

The standard theories of Budget determination[12] suggest that both the nature and the scope of public expenditure are determined by the representatives of the people in Parliament. The distinctions between public sector institutions used in the National Accounts classification indicate the inadequacy of this view. In the first place, the non-Budget sub-sector, which includes many large public enterprises, is in many cases independent from Parliament in its decision-making, even though their boards of directors are appointed by the government and there is a duty upon them to report annually to the Parliament. The degree of their independence varies. Trends in recent years, particularly as a result of initiatives taken by the Commonwealth in May 1988 and the corporatisation initiatives in State governments from the late 1980s, have increased the commercial independence of public trading enterprises. Secondly, within the Budget sector there are many virtually independent commissions and institutions which are wholly or partly financed from budgetary appropriations but where the detailed spending decisions are made by non-elected officials. These are subject to the usual Budget scrutiny and the Budget appropriates the Commission's allocation. The matter of Commissions is further examined in Chapter 4 but it is important to note at this stage that not all public sector spending decisions are decided within the parliamentary framework.[13]

If the public sector were to be defined as that part of the economy which provides goods and services whose nature and scope is determined by the representatives of the people, then this discussion makes it clear that such a definition has implications for measuring the size of the public sector. On that definition, the non-Budget sector would clearly be excluded, while it could also be argued that parts of the Budget sub-sector should be eliminated from the public sector proper. It should also be noted that these classifications if applied in a narrow sense could give quite arbitrary results. For example, up to the end of the 1950s the Australian Post Office was fully within the Budget sector; today, as Australia Post, it is almost completely outside it. It would be difficult to maintain that the size of the Australian public sector has been altered as a result of such changes in the status of these entities.

Such changes in classification do, however, affect the measurement of the size of the public sector over time, and also its size as measured for the purpose of making international comparisons. A difference in the treatment of the receipts and outlays of public enterprises in the public authority accounts could result in quite a significant change in the proportion of GDP defined as going to the public sector; this proportion is the indicator most frequently used to make comparisons about public sector size. For this reason, the United Nations has published a national accounting framework to make practice in its member countries more uniform, but where the institutions are vastly different, such "uniformity" can become quite spurious and hide significant differences in the size of the public sector between countries. This problem is examined further in Chapter 3 where the growth of the Australian public sector over time is discussed.

In public finance discussion, the treatment of the public sector is generally confined to the Budget sector and sub-sector so that for Australia, public finance concerns itself with the transactions included in the annual Federal Budget, the six State government Budgets and that of the Northern Territory, (and Australian Capital Territory to a lesser extent) as well as the Budgets of over 800 local government units where much of the decision-making about expenditure, borrowing, and taxation is made by elected representatives of the people. The economics of public enterprises, which for practical purposes would include a large number of the commissions and other agencies of the Budget sub-sector, has now become a separate specialisation (dealing with such issues as investment decisions and pricing policies) and is outside the scope of this book.

NATURE OF THE STATE

The nature of the State is a subject of considerable importance in the study of public finance and unfortunately it is all too frequently forgotten that this subject is viewed quite differently in various parts of the world from both a philosophical and political standpoint. Most of the public finance theories in the English-speaking world are based on the philosophical views of nineteenth century liberalism in representative government, while the public finance of some European countries, and of socialist countries and those in the Third World, may be based on a quite different political philosophy.

The theory of public expenditure contained in many English and American textbooks is predicated on the assumption that only individuals can experience wants or express needs and that society as a whole cannot have any wants separate from the wants of the individuals of which it is composed. In other words, it is argued that two individuals *A* and *B* can express wants but that it is nonsense to speak of $(A + B)$ together as being capable of expressing a want separate from that expressed by *A* and *B* individually. This view, that the whole can be no more than its separate parts and that therefore there can be no group views as such, is an important assumption in the public expenditure analysis based on voluntary exchange theory, where individuals acting together offer to exchange part of their resources (taxes) for a certain quantity of some collectively provided product or service. Increasingly, the simplicity of such views is realised and many textbooks now emphasise the role of pressure groups in public finance decision-making. Aspects of this are further explored in Chapter 4.

The market-oriented public finance rests on the view that there is a definite demand for public goods which is the sum of individual demands, while the supply of the demanded goods is regulated by the price (tax) individuals are willing to offer for any particular quantity of them. When the number of individuals in the "market" for public goods is particularly large, the wishes (demand functions) of the individual members of society are reflected in the wishes (demand functions) of their elected representatives who are able to interpret these wishes precisely and accurately. This sort of mechanism lies behind the public finance theories of Wicksell, Lindahl, Bowen, Samuelson, Musgrave, Buchanan, and many others.[14]

These theories, on which excellent discussions are available in the textbooks[15], have not only grave theoretical shortcomings, but also imply a rather naive political philosophy. The liberal model of representative government on which they are based and the institutional framework on which they rely have no counterpart anywhere in the world of the twentieth century, where representation of constituents by parliamentarians is far from perfect, where voting in most countries (the United States is an exception) is conducted completely on party lines, and where the budgetary process and framework precludes in the presentation of the Budget the individual combination of expenditure items with the alternative means of financing them, on which the theory relies.[16] When the Australian Budget process is briefly examined in Chapter 2, it will be seen that such bargaining theories have little relevance to the explanation of Budget determination.

Apart from these practical and theoretical shortcomings, this approach to the theory of Budget determination has also been challenged by other views on the wants of the State. One such criticism is well illustrated in the work of Hans Ritschl,[17] who distinguishes *communal economy* from *market economy* by separating individual desires and self-interest — which regulate goods supply in the market economy — from the "communal spirit" which merges, "especially when the nation is in the most desperate straits" into "one great single will". Here, to revert to a previous example, $(A + B)$ is depicted as the collective, national will, which is different from and greater than the sum of the desires of *A* and *B* considered individually. It is interesting though not surprising that this view that the State or rather its ruling élite can express the national will better than a democratic government especially in a period of crisis, was written during the rapid rise of National Socialism in Germany in the early 1930s. The organic view of the State on which it is based is therefore frequently associated with totalitarianism.

Another view of the State and of public finance based on the notion that groups have aims and desires which transcend the wishes of individual members of society is the Marxist view of the State.[18] In this analysis, attention is focused on socio-economic classes, and on the way in which the dominant class manipulates the State apparatus to promote its own ends. Thus in private enterprise economics, the capitalist class and the economic élites in general are portrayed as utilising the State to aid the private accumulation of capital, to provide a stable environment for the expansion of capitalist production, and to maintain the social *status quo* by providing the rules of the game, and thereby to prevent the peaceful overthrow of the social system.

In the Marxist approach to public finance analysis, particular attention is paid to the effects of government expenditure and of taxation on particular class interests, and this gives a special twist to their theory of tax and expenditure incidence. Furthermore, a Marxist analysis examines, at least for societies like Australia, the class purpose of public endeavour and not only the immediately apparent individual purpose. Social service payments are thus regarded as having the individual aim of alleviating poverty by meeting particular needs, while at the same time they are shown to have the class aim of preventing civil disorder, and of maintaining political, social, and economic stability. Such a viewpoint sheds light on a wider range of issues than does the more traditional analysis.[19]

Before leaving the discussion of the significance of the different views of the State for the study of public finance, some reference should be made to two other views of the State: those expressed by the right-wing libertarians and by the anarchists. For anarchists the need to study public finance is virtually non-existent, since the State is to be abolished and with its abolition, its functions (including the traditional ones of defence and law and order) will disappear. As Proudhon, the influential French anarchist, expressed it:

> In place of political powers we will put economic forces . . . In place of standing armies, we will put industrial associations. In place of police we will put identity of interests. In place of political centralisation, we will put economic centralisation.[20]

In such a society there is little need for government and, consequently, no need for public finance except through very small voluntary contributions for minor public works.

Right-wing libertarian opinion, on the other hand, still sees a positive role for government, but argues that to preserve freedom this role should be kept to a minimum by leaving decisions, particularly economic decisions, as much as possible to the market. The role of government is therefore defined as maintaining law and order, defining property rights and the rules of the game, acting as arbiter in disputes, and providing such goods and services as the market cannot provide because of the presence of market failure. This view, epitomised by the writings of Milton Friedman and the new Right in American economics,[21] has gained a substantial following in the Western developed world. It increasingly seeks to roll back the activities of government, because of a rising appreciation and elucidation of government failure. Chapter 20 examines the policy implications of this perspective in terms of United States, United Kingdom and increasingly Australian experience as well.[22]

It is necessary to stress that this libertarian view should not be confused with that of American liberalism in most of the post-war period. This liberal view, characterised by the work of Galbraith[23] stresses the need for a growing public sector not only for the provision of merit wants in larger amounts, but also because it sees the need for greater government co-operation with industry and the trade unions either in a consultative role or in the more active manner as in the indicative planning framework used for some time in France. Such views continue to be put forward in Australia by sections of the trade union movement and others[24] but at the official level they are now on the decline in many parts of the world.

Public finance in socialist economies

The discussion so far has dealt exclusively with capitalist countries, and it is now necessary to give a brief indication of the basic differences that arise when the public finance of socialist economies is considered. One frequent misunderstanding on this matter can be cleared up straight away; the fact that the means of production are virtually completely state-owned in countries such as the USSR, East Germany, and Bulgaria, does not mean that therefore the whole of their economic activity is covered by the study of public finance. By using the distinction between public provision of goods and services and public production which was made earlier, it can be shown that there is still a distinctive public sector which provides public goods and which is financed through a government budget by taxation and sometimes by public borrowings. The ratio of collective goods to GDP could be less in a socialist country than in a mixed economy. Nevertheless, there are important differences between a socialist public finance and one that is relevant to capitalist countries. These differences appear on both the expenditure and the taxation side.

The three major differences on the expenditure side relate to the provision of merit wants, the provision of social security cash benefits, and the role of public capital formation. Socialist states have often been more interested in providing for merit wants — such as public education, public health, public housing, recreation, the arts, and sport — than have governments in capitalist economies, but this factor cannot be stressed too much. For example, at the start of the 1960s the adjusted Budget expenditures excluding military expenditure relative to GDP varied from 15 to 27 per cent in a sample of seven market economies and from 15 to 30 per cent in seven Eastern European countries.[25] In capital formation, an exceedingly important part of the economic decisions to be made in a centrally planned economy, the vast proportion is channelled through public institutions and this presents a sharp contrast to the practice in capitalist economies. Differences in social security provision should also not be exaggerated since socialist countries, like capitalist countries, also have the aged, the sick, widows, and dependent children, and the benefits provided vary more with national wealth than with ideology.[26] Different approaches to distribution problems are crucial for understanding the different taxation structures in socialist and capitalist countries. Concern with achieving a more equitable income distribution dictates the relatively high proportion of revenue raised by a progressive income tax in many capitalist countries. In socialist countries where property income has been largely eliminated — though there are substantial inequalities in earnings — there is less emphasis on income redistribution and therefore on the income tax. The bulk of government revenue in socialist countries is raised through sales taxation, turnover taxes, and through the State's share in the profits of its enterprises. However, increased focus on small-scale private initiatives and the restoration of market forces in many sectors of the economy have altered perspectives on taxation policy in socialist countries, particularly in China, Hungary, but from 1989 increasingly throughout much of the Communist world.

From these considerations it can be seen that the public finance of the socialist world can differ substantially from that of the capitalist nations; there are different problems and therefore, different solutions. This is not to say that public finance in general cannot offer some principles which would apply to both forms of society; it is rather to argue that the differences are substantial, as is indicated by the small but separate literature dealing with the public finance of socialist countries. For this reason the subject will not be further pursued,[27] while increased adoption of market principles in the economic management of such countries, including privatisation of much public property, has meant that in many respects these alternative systems are coming closer together.

Public finance and developing countries

It should also be stressed that there are substantial differences between the public finance for developed countries and that for developing countries. Again, as in the case of socialist countries, it can be said that the public finance of developing countries has become a quite separate subject from the general public finance of the capitalist developed world, because of the vastly different problems facing these two types of countries.[28] These differences arise on both the expenditure and the taxation side but here broad generalisations are not so easy to make because of the tremendous diversity among the developing countries themselves.

For this reason, one example of such differences will have to suffice. It is well known that in many developing countries the distribution of income and wealth is much more unequal than in the United States and Australia. The introduction of a progressive income tax, perhaps supplemented by a wealth tax, would achieve even less in such countries than in developed nations, because of the ease with which such taxes would be evaded. Many developing countries lack a good tax administration and there is also generally a greater prevalence of corruption in such countries. If some income redistribution is desired, the most effective taxes are likely to be import duties and excise on luxury goods, which are relatively easy to administer and more difficult to evade. Such commodity taxes are usually not seen as instruments for redistributive purposes in developed countries. It is interesting to note that these types of taxes were extensively used to raise revenue in England in the thirteenth and fourteenth centuries (when England itself was a relatively underdeveloped nation) because of the ease of their administration and the difficulty of evading them. However, the income distribution motive was not present at the time.

As this book is basically concerned with Australian public finance, this discussion cannot be taken further. This does not mean that growth considerations will be ignored in what follows. In expenditure as well as in taxation policy, Australia's growth and development needs are major considerations. However, the devices and institutions Australia is able to use to promote policies are substantially different from those used in countries such as Indonesia, the Philippines and Thailand, not to mention the developing nations of Africa, the Pacific and Latin America.

AN ECONOMICS OR A POLITICAL ECONOMY OF PUBLIC FINANCE?

The broad conclusion of the issues surveyed in this introduction is that the problems raised in public finance inevitably have political as well as economic aspects. The tools of economic analysis can and will be used in the explanation of public expenditure determination and in the discussion of taxation. However, it should be stressed at the outset that there is no positive economics of public finance in the sense of value-free science. This is the case as much in the theory of taxation as in the theory of public expenditure. Behind the traditional Anglo-Saxon approach to public finance analysis lies a particular ideology and a particular set of political judgements, as Myrdal showed a long time ago in his classic study, *The Political Element in the Development of Economic Theory*. This has been made abundantly clear in the previous discussion on the role of government. The notions of public goods and merit wants, the premise of a democratic, totalitarian, or anarchist society, the question of the distinction between individual and communal wants, and the different views on the structure of society all clearly indicate that the economic problems raised by public finance quite frequently have "political answers". Politics and economics are firmly related in this field as is shown in the following parts on public expenditure, taxation, fiscal federalism, public debt and stabilisation policy.

SUMMARY

1. Public finance deals with matters relating to the finance of the public sector, a definition in some respects both too narrow and too wide.

2. Functions of the public sector relate to real resource transfers and reallocation of such resources, the task of the traditional allocational function of the Budget. In addition there are concerns with redistribution and stabilisation functions.

3. The public sector covers general government functions like health, education, and law and order, fully contained in the Budget as well as the activities of public authorities and trading enterprises. The last in particular raise questions outside the scope of this book.

4. Although the public sector is concerned with the provision of public goods, or providing goods with a high degree of public good characteristics (non-rivalness in consumption and non-excludability), its role need not be confined to such provision. The scope of the public sector depends on past history, institutional factors and political as well as economic choices, as is already implied in the notion of merit wants.

5. The nature of the public sector is made more complex in a federal system with its two sets of sovereign governments (Federal and State) though many fiscal federalism issues arise also in countries with unitary systems of government and sizeable local and regional government sectors.

6. Public finance, dealing as it does with the state, thereby implies a theory of the State. In much traditional public finance, this theory is the liberal vision of the state as a collection of individuals where democratically elected representatives reflect what the community wants of individuals. Other theories of the state are possible and use different mechanisms for explaining community wants.

7. Public finance often has different functions and objectives in socialist economies and the developing world, as compared with the mixed private enterprise world of which Australia is a part. This highlights the continuing evolving nature of public finance theory and the institutional background which needs to be appreciated before theory can be satisfactorily applied.

NOTES

[1] U.K. Hicks, *Public Finance* (Walwyn: James Nesbit, 1958), p. 1.

[2] This is well illustrated in many of the readings from the work of nineteenth-century economists included in R.A. Musgrave and A.T. Peacock (eds.), *Classics in the Theory of Public Finance* (London: Macmillan, 1958); for example, U. Mazzola, "The Formation of the Prices of Public Goods", pp. 42–3, and Giovanni Montemartini, "The Fundamental Principles of a Pure Theory of Public Finance", esp. pp. 137–8.

[3] E. Barone, "On Public Needs", in R.A. Musgrave and A.T. Peacock (eds.), *Classics*, p. 165.

[4] J.S. Mill, "Principles of Political Economy", Book 5, ch. 2, 5, in *Collected Works of John Stuart Mill* (Toronto: University of Toronto Press, 1965), vol. 3, p. 941. It is interesting to note that Book 5, which deals with public finance, starts with the statement, "One of the most disputed questions both in political science and in practical statesmanship at this particular period, relates to the proper limits of the functions and agency of governments" (p. 799).

[5] This topic is discussed in all the leading textbooks. See for example, R.A. and P. B. Musgrave, *Public Finance in Theory and Practice* (New York: McGraw Hill, 1984), chs. 3 and 4; and for a more extensive treatment, J.M. Buchanan, *The Demand and Supply of Public Goods* (Chicago: Rand McNally, 1968).

[6] The material quoted is from P.A. Samuelson, "The Pure Theory of Public Expenditure", in R.W. Houghton (ed.), *Public Finance* (Harmondsworth: Penguin, 1973), p. 181. This approach to public expenditure theory has been criticised by J. Margolis on the ground stated in the last sentence of the paragraph. See his "A Comment on the Pure Theory of Public Expenditure", in *Public Finance*, pp. 186-90, esp. pp. 187–8. Samuelson's theory is discussed in more detail below in Chapter 4.

[7] R.A. Musgrave, *Fiscal Systems* (New Haven, Conn., Yale University Press, 1969), ch. 1, esp. pp. 7–13.

[8] In his inaugural lecture at the London School of Economics given in November 1972, Professor A.R. Prest went so far as to argue that in a federation, the study of public finance is much more developed because it it more important than in a country like England with a unitary system of government.

[9] Reference should be made to the most recent edition of the annual Australian Bureau of Statistics publication, *Public Authority Finance: State and Local Authorities*, and to Budget Statements, Statement No. 7, "Transactions of the Public Sector as a Whole", in Budget Paper No. 1, 1987–88, for example, esp. pp. 404-5.

[10] Department of the Treasury, 1974–75 Budget Paper No. 11, *National Accounting Estimates of Receipts and Expenditure of Australian Government Authorities* (Canberra: AGPS, 1974), p.17. A more detailed definitional statement can be found in Australian Bureau of Statistics, *Classifications Manual for Government Finance Statistics Australia*, Canberra: Australian Bureau of Statistics, 1984 (Cat. No. 1217.0), ch. 2.

[11] Budget Statements 1987-88, Budget Paper No. 1, pp. 404-5, and see also Statement 8.

[12] For example, P.A. Samuelson, "A Pure Theory of Public Expenditure", in R.W. Houghton (ed.), *Public Finance*, Reading 9a and the readings which follow this paper; R.A. and P.B. Musgrave, *Public Finance in Theory and Practice* (see Note 5), ch. 6. See Chapter 4 below for further discussion.

[13] The precise proportion is not easy to calculate. It should also be noted that each year the annual appropriation voted on by Parliament is only a small part of total Budget outlays, for much government expenditure is a carry-forward of funds appropriated by earlier legislation.

[14] See K. Wicksell, "A New Principle of Just Taxation" and E. Lindahl, "Just Taxation —A Positive Solution", in *Classics in the Theory of Public Finance*; see also R.A. Musgrave, *Theory of Public Finance* (New York: McGraw Hill, 1959), chs. 4 and 6, and J.M. Buchanan, *The Demand of Supply of Public Goods* and the references cited in Note 12.

[15] See for example, R.A. and P.B. Musgrave, *Public Finance in Theory and Practice*, ch. 3. For further details, see Chapters 4 and 7 below.

[16] Wicksell's analysis of voting for the Budget (in *Classics in the Theory of Public Finance*, pp. 91–4) relies on linking particular expenditure proposals with a variety of methods of finance. For example, a particular proposal such as increasing pensions by 5 per cent could be financed alternatively by a certain rise in income tax, sales tax, property tax, etc. Each of these alternatives would be voted on, and that alternative chosen which gained the highest number of votes, provided that the majority was of the required magnitude. Wicksell himself realised the practical difficulties involved in this procedure (p. 92, note d) and it is not exaggeration to say that these difficulties have increased more than proportionately with the rise in public expenditure experienced in the twentieth century.

[17] Hans Ritschl, "Communal Economy and Market Economy", in *Classics in the Theory of Public Finance*". The quotation comes from p. 237. See also the comments of the editors of this work in the Introduction, pp. vii-viii.

[18] A Marxist view of the State in relation to public finance has not yet been developed to any large extent, largely because Marx himself did not discuss this subject in detail. Reference should be made to R. Miliband, *The State in Capitalist Society* (London: Weidenfeld and Nicolson, 1969), esp. chs. 4, 6 and 9, and for some specific writings on public finance to Rudolf Goldscheid, "A Sociological Approach to Problems in Public Finance"; in *Classics in the Theory of Public Finance*; M. Kalecki, *Selected Essays in the Dynamics of the Capitalist Economy* (Cambridge University Press, 1971), essays 4, 12, and 14; and James O'Connor, *The Fiscal Crisis of the State* (New York: St. Martins Press, 1973).

[19] For a critical view of Marxist public finance, see Richard Musgrave, "Theories of Fiscal Crisis: An Essay in Fiscal Sociology", in H.J. Aaron and M.J. Boskin (eds.), *The Economics of Taxation* (Washington, D.C.: The Brookings Institution, 1980), pp. 361-90.

[20] P. J. Proudhon, *The General Idea of the Revolution*, cited in G. Woodcock, *Anarchism* (Harmondsworth: Penguin, 1962), pp. 124–5.

[21] See Milton and Rose Friedman, *Free to Choose* (Harmondsworth: Penguin, 1980).

[22] Such right-wing policies on the public sector have been articulated by the Monash Centre of Policy Studies in their now annual studies, edited by John Freebairn, Michael Porter and Cliff Walsh, *Spending and Taxes: National Economic Priorities* (Sydney: Allen and Unwin, 1987); *Spending and Taxes: Taking Stock* (Sydney: Allen and Unwin, 1988); *Savings and Productivity* (Sydney: Allen and Unwin, 1989).

[23] See particularly Galbraith's *The Affluent Society* (Boston: Houghton Mifflin, 1958); *The New Industrial State* (Harmondsworth: Penguin, 1969); and *Economics and the Public Purpose* (Harmondsworth: Pelican, 1975).

[24] See *Australia Reconstructed, ACTU/TDC Mission to Western Europe* (Canberra: Australian Government Publishing Service, 1987), especially chs. 2 and 3; Labour Resource Centre, *The Role of the Public Sector*, December 1987; H.V. Evatt Foundation, *The Capital Funding of Public Enterprise in Australia* (Sydney: H.V. Evatt Foundation, 1988); H.V. Evatt Foundation, *State of Siege* (Sydney: Pluto Press, 1989); and for a general theoretical discussion, Kerry Schott, *Policy, Power and Order, the Persistence of Economic Problems in Capitalist States* (New Haven: Yale University Press, 1984).

[25] The data which applies to 1962 is from F. L. Pryor, *Public Expenditure in Communist and Capitalist Nations* (London: Allen & Unwin, 1968), p. 61, Table 2–1. The seven market economies are the United States (14%), West Germany (25%), Austria (27%), Ireland (17%), Italy (12.4%), Greece (16%), and Yugoslavia (20%); the Eastern European countries are Czechoslovakia (26%), East Germany (30%), Soviet Union (18%), Hungary (15%), Poland (16%), Romania (16%), and Bulgaria (16%).

[26] For a detailed discussion of this subject see F. L. Pryor, *Public Finance Expenditure in Communist and Capitalist Nations*, ch. 4.

[27] Pryor's comprehensive study has unfortunately not been updated. For more recent discussion

of Soviet state budgeting see Igor Birman, *Secret Incomes of the Soviet State Budget* (The Hague: Martinus Nijhoff, 1981), especially chs. 2–5; and on the situation in Yugoslavia, Bruce McFarlane, *Yugoslavia* (London: Pinter Publishers, 1988), esp. ch. 6. However, the rapid economic changes from 1989 in Eastern Europe, the Soviet Union and China, make it difficult to expound further on this subject.

[28] See for example, Stephen R. Lewis Jr., *Taxation for Development* (New York: Oxford University Press, 1984); Richard Goode, *Government Finance in Developing Countries* (Washington: 1983); P. Shome (ed.), *Fiscal Issues in South-East Asia* (Singapore: Oxford University Press, 1986), and David Newbery and Nicholas Stern, *The Theory of Taxation and Developing Countries* (New York: Oxford University Press for the World Bank, 1987).

FURTHER READING

Introductions to other widely used texts are recommended to see the differences in perspective open to students of public finance. Useful are:

Richard A. Musgrave and Peggy B. Musgrave, *Public Finance in Theory and Practice*, 4th edn. (New York: McGraw Hill, 1984), ch. 1.

C. V. Brown and P. M. Jackson, *Public Sector Economics*, 3rd edn. (Oxford: Basil Blackwell, 1986), ch. 1.

Joseph E. Stiglitz, *Economics of the Public Sector*, 2nd edn. (New York: W.W. Norton and Company, 1988), chs. 1 and 2.

By way of further introduction to the subject, students with an interest in the historical development of public finance, may like to read:

Richard A. Musgrave, "A Brief History of Fiscal Doctrine", in Richard A. Musgrave, *Public Finance in a Democratic Society* (Brighton: Wheatsheaf Books, 1986), vol. 2, ch. 23.

Richard A. Musgrave and Alan T. Peacock (eds.), *Classics in the Theory of Public Finance* (London: Macmillan for the International Economic Association, 1958), Introduction and particularly the extract from E. Barone, "On Public Needs", pp. 165–7.

An overview of the Australian public sector can be obtained from the chapter on public finance in the most recent issue of the *Year Book Australia* published in Canberra by the Australian Bureau of Statistics. This also provides useful data on a wide variety of traditional government functions.

2

The scope of government activity and the Budget process

In 1988–89 the Australian governments consumed under one-fifth of the national output (GDP) in the exercise of their many functions. In addition, their welfare payments, subsidies and other transfers redistributed a further 15 per cent of national output. Total government outlays by the three tiers of government rose steadily until the mid-1980s after which they started to decline relative to GDP. More precisely from about 30 per cent of national output by the end of the 1960s, the governments' share in GDP peaked in 1984–85 and 1985–86 at 36.9 per cent. Changes in the growth of the public sector are investigated further in Chapter 3 while the use by government of these vast resources is discussed more fully in Chapters 4 and 5. This chapter investigates the general functions of government for which these resources are appropriated and puts them in the perspective of government accounting and the budget process.

GOVERNMENT FUNCTIONS AND BUDGETARY FUNCTIONS

At the outset, a distinction has to be made between the budgetary functions and government functions in general. The budgetary functions are only one component of government functions in the sphere of economic policy, and in turn, economic policy-making is but one category of total government functions.[1] The classification of economic policy instruments available to the government typically utilises the following five headings:

1. *Fiscal or budgetary policy*: taxation and expenditure policy.
2. *Monetary policy*: debt management, credit, and banking policy.
3. *External policy*: Exchange rate policy, tariffs, and bounties.
4. *Wages policy*: through the Accord, linked with fiscal policy through tax/wage trade-offs and the importance of public expenditure in determining the social wage.
5. *Direct regulation through legislation*: for example trade practices legislation, Industrial Relations legislation, consumer protection legislation.
6. *Government business activity*: prices and output policies of the public utilities and public corporations.

Although there are difficulties separating aspects of budgetary and monetary policy,[2] broadly speaking this classification clarifies the meaning to be given to the scope of government activity in a book concerned with public finance. Apart from some discussion in Chapter 17 of the financing of the Budget by means of borrowing, the functions of government relevant to the discussion are expenditure and taxation policy. The discussion in this and the next three chapters are mainly concerned with public expenditure; the subject matter of the subsequent eight chapters (Chapters 6 to 13) is the function of government as the taxing authority.

The distinction between expenditures and taxation

What is expenditure and what is taxation is not always clear-cut. For example, the price and output policies of the government business sector have been excluded from consideration in this book; nevertheless they raise some issues which are virtually indistinguishable from expenditure or tax policy. Some public utility charges — water rates are an apt example — have virtually the same characteristics as local government taxes, though excess water charges introduce an element of pricing based on use. Many other fees, fines, and licences included among tax revenues fall within the grey area between public utility prices and what are generally understood to be taxes. The levy imposed on incomes to finance Medicare can be either regarded as a tax or as a price for the use of medical services. Likewise the Higher Education Contribution Scheme or graduate tax can be seen as a deferred fee for services rendered.[3]

Furthermore, the magnitude of the operating surplus or loss of the public enterprise often reflects the political choice of whether the enterprise is to be seen as a community service or as a self-financing business. Traditionally, Australians have tended to see public transport, postal services, and other means of communication as falling in the first rather than the second category. This dual aspect inherent in the treatment of public enterprise introduces expenditure and tax policy considerations into public utility prices in addition to the general principle of covering costs. At the State government level this can be illustrated with the pricing of specific transport services which frequently embody subsidies of a social welfare nature in the form of concessional fares for pensioners and school children; alternatively the subsidies (and penalties) in the setting of freight charges may be designed to stimulate (or inhibit) the growth of particular industries or regions. Similarly, the pricing policies of Australia Post and Telecom have reflected a redistributional bias towards the rural community through a well-entrenched system of cross-subsidisation. These examples illustrate how public utility prices can hide specific tax or expenditure measures. More recent perspectives on government business enterprises stress the commercial elements and the need to utilise general business practices to enhance the efficiency of such state-owned enterprises.[4]

The lack of distinction between tax and expenditure instruments is also made clear from the increased use of the terminology of tax expenditures.[5] The Australian income tax system has always contained disguised expenditures of a social nature, such as rebates for health expenditures. In addition, it has provided subsidies to a wide variety of industries ranging from life insurance to mining and primary producers and, more selectively, to the Australian film and horse-breeding industries. Sales tax has also been used extensively to subsidise primary industry and to achieve more general objectives such as the conservation of fossil fuels.[6]

On the negative side the treatment of many social service cash benefits as negative taxes illustrates a similar difficulty. With continuing interest in negative income tax, tax credits, and other forms of guaranteed income schemes (a discussion postponed until Chapter 20) the difference between some transfer payments and taxes has become increasingly blurred. For example, if cash transfers for social security and subsidies were treated as negative taxes, the share of revenue in GDP in 1987–88 would fall from 27.7 to 18.5 per cent for the Commonwealth Government while its share of public outlays in GDP would fall from 26.9 to 17.7 per cent. If tax rebates were introduced as a full replacement for social security benefits and all subsidies to industry were given through the tax system, this relative fall in taxation and public expenditure would be recorded in the statistics and such a "nominal" change would alter the relative size of Australia's public sector quite drastically. On the other hand, when tax concessions are replaced by direct subsidies, the size of the public sector and that of tax revenue statistically increases. This happened quite strikingly in May 1976 when the Government introduced a family allowances system which combined the tax rebates for dependent children with child endowment payments. This change raised welfare expenditure by approximately $750 million and personal income tax collections by approximately $700 million.

How the line is drawn depends on the purpose at hand. For example, if the impact of taxes on incentives to work is being discussed, it is the gross tax collected which is relevant. For another purpose, we may want to draw the tax-expenditure line quite differently. Other difficulties in measuring public sector size for international and other comparisons are discussed in Chapter 3.

The lack of a clear-cut distinction between expenditure and taxation underlines the fact that the two are highly interdependent and that for many practical purposes they are only the opposite sides of the same coin. It also emphasises that in the analysis of the effects of government budgetary interference in the distribution of income[7] both the "incidence"[8] of taxation and expenditure must be considered. An analysis of taxation by itself, or of taxation and selected items of government expenditure by itself, is insufficient for this important purpose. Even though the next four chapters treat expenditure and tax instruments separately, it must be remembered that this procedure can only be defended on the ground that not everything can be covered at the same time.

THE BUDGETARY FUNCTIONS OF AUSTRALIAN GOVERNMENT

Some constitutional issues

Australia is a federation and the functions of the Australian Federal Government are prescribed by the Constitution. The States have residual powers, that is, those powers not exclusively granted to the Federal Government. Some knowledge of the Constitution is therefore required to appreciate the division of functions between the sovereign tiers of government. The economic principles of such a division are discussed in Chapter 14. The third tier of government, the hundreds of local government units, are not sovereign entities and derive their powers from State legislation, such as the New South Wales *Local Government Act* 1919. Their finances are examined in Chapter 16.

Broadly speaking, the major economic powers of the Federal Government are contained in section 51 of the Constitution. These include foreign and inter-State commerce; taxation;

bounties on production and exports; borrowing on the credit of the Commonwealth (a power widely extended under the terms of the financial agreement which established the Loan Council, a topic discussed in Chapters 15 and 17); postal, telegraphic, telephonic communications, and other like services which now also include radio and television broadcasting; defence; civil aviation; social security (largely by virtue of one of the few successful constitutional amendments, passed in 1946); immigration and emigration; money, banking and insurance; the acquisition, with the consent of a State, of railways from that State, as well as railway construction with the consent of a State; and finally, any matter referred to the Federal Parliament by the State governments.

Section 51(ii) gives the Federal Government a general power to tax, sections 86, 90 and 114 provide further details of this power, including the exclusive power over customs and excise. This exclusive power over customs and excise has been interpreted by the High Court to include all commodity taxation but not the taxation of consumption. This distinction has allowed some of the States to tax the "consumption" of excisable commodities through liquor licences and business franchise taxes.[9] These sections also provide for the exemption of federal property from State and local taxation though Commonwealth-owned trading enterprises are now liable for such taxes as a result of decisions taken at Premiers' Conferences in 1988 and designed to put them on a more even competitive footing with private enterprise. Section 96, a small but very important section for Australian students of public finance, gives the power to make conditional grants to the States; sections 105 and 105A provide the basis for Federal-State financial relations in the matter of loan raisings. The sections of the Constitution mentioned in this and in the preceding paragraph are well worth reading since they explain many of the difficulties in Federal financial relations.[10]

The functional classification of government spending

A simple way of grasping the functions of government in Australia is to look at the functional classification of public authority spending as presented by the Australian Bureau of Statistics in the National Accounts. Table 2.1 presents a summary of the outlays of Australian governments and indicates the relative importance of each of the areas of spending; not only relative to aggregate government outlays, but also in terms of the three tiers of government.

An examination of Table 2.1 quickly illustrates the following points:

1. The exclusive power of the Federal Government over defence and foreign aid (foreign transfers).
2. The predominance of the States in fields such as education and health.
3. The predominance of the Federal Government in cash benefits to persons such as pensions, unemployment, and sickness benefits.
4. The far greater importance of State and local government purchase of goods and services as compared with the Federal Government.
5. The relative burden of interest and debt charges by level of government (this issue is further discussed in Chapter 17).
6. The relative magnitude of government outlays (that is, purchases of goods and services *and* transfer payments) for the three tiers of government as compared with their purchases of goods and services and, more interestingly, their revenue raising capacity.

Table 2.1 Outlays of Australian governments 1986–87: by function

	Current government outlays C'wealth $m	State [a] $m	Local $m	Total $m	*Percentage of total outlays* %	*Percentage of total outlay on each function* C'wealth %	State %	Local %
Expenditure on goods and services								
Defence	6,850	—	—	6,850	6.0	100.0	—	—
Public order and safety	493	2,600	85	3,178	2.8			
Health, social security welfare	8,777	8,626	280	17,683	15.5	49.6	48.8	1.6
Education	4,695	11,498	20	16,213	14.2	29.0	70.9	0.1
Housing and community amenities (includes water supply)	131	419	501	1,051	0.9	12.5	39.9	47.7
Culture and recreation	807	762	604	2,173	1.9	37.1	35.1	27.8
General public services	4,442	2,038	704	7,184	6.3	61.8	28.4	9.8
Economic services								
Transport and communication	354	2,784	666	3,804	3.3	9.3	73.2	17.5
Fuel and energy	178	150	1	329	0.3	54.1	45.6	0.3
Other	1,636	1,780	81	3,497	3.1	46.8	50.9	2.3
All other	1,286	692	20	1,998	1.8	64.4	34.6	1.0
Total expenditure on goods and services	29,649	31,349	2,962	63,960	56.1	46.4	49.0	4.6
Transfer payments [b]	1,352	2,658	—	4,010	3.5	33.7	66.3	—
Cash benefits to persons	24,101	791	—	24,892	21.8	96.8	3.2	—
Grants for private capital purposes	346	137	—	483	0.4	71.6	28.4	—
Transfers overseas	824	—	—	824	0.7	100.0	—	—
Other public debt transactions	14,873	3,594 [c]	793 [c]	19,260	16.9 [d]	77.2	18.7	4.1
Other	16	584	–74	526				
Total government outlays	71,161	39,113	3,681	113,955	100.0	62.4	34.3	3.2

Notes:

a. State governments include State authorities and enterprises and the Northern Territory.
b. Excluding intergovernment transfers.
c. Includes interest paid to Commonwealth Government ($2,433 million).
d. If State interest payments to Commonwealth excluded, the percentage becomes 14.8.

Source: Australian Bureau of Statistics, *State and Local Government Finance Australia 1986–87* (Cat. No. 5504.0), Canberra, 1988. *Commonwealth Government Finance, Australia, 1986–87* (Cat. No. 5502.0), Canberra, 1988.

As already indicated, the process of government expenditure decision-making is examined more fully in Chapters 4 and 5, following the discussion of public sector growth in Chapter 3. In the remainder of this chapter the discussion of the functions of government is continued by looking at some related topics. First the Australian Budget process is examined, including in that discussion relevant aspects of government accounting, how the Budget is framed, and the role of the various government agencies in that process. In this discussion the functions of the Budget and the objectives of budgetary policy are briefly outlined.

THE BUDGET

The discussion of the public sector in the previous chapter (Chapter 1) showed that budgetary decision-making involved political factors through the parliamentary process. The Budget, in many respects the most important single document for students of public finance, must therefore be carefully examined to show the interaction of social, political and economic factors in the formation of government policy. This section examines the Budget process to show briefly how and by whom these decisions are made and to discuss the functions of the modern Budget. In later chapters, specific aspects of this budgetary process will be discussed in more detail. For example, in Chapters 4 and 5 the picture of the actual process of Budget determination is contrasted with some theories of Budget determination which have been offered by economists.

The Budget process[11]

The Budget process in Australia, whether at Commonwealth, State, or local level, is essentially a process of determining government expenditure priorities together with the methods of supplying the revenue from which these expenditures are to be met. These decisions are made in the context of the current economic situation, such as the rate of inflation, the level of unemployment and the balance of payments, as well as in the light of government policy on income distribution. In this process of actual Budget formation, the decisions are made by a variety of agencies which, for the Commonwealth Government are as follows:

1. The various government departments which assist in the provision of forward estimates.
2. The Finance Department, which is in control of the public accounts and the continuing financial evaluation of expenditure proposals and appropriations. It supervises the collection, preparation and financial analysis of these forward estimates prepared by the departments. Treasury combines expenditure estimates and revenue estimates, examines all matters relating to them and to the Budget outcome in the light of the economic situation and government budgetary policy objectives in order to prepare its brief on budgetary policy for consideration by Cabinet.
3. Cabinet, in particular its Expenditure Review Committee, consisting of senior ministers and senior permanent advisers, examines the Budget strategy as a whole in the light of the overall economic and political situation.
4. The Premiers' Conference and the Loan Council, which determine loan allocations and loan raisings, as well as the revenue transfers from the federal to State and local governments.

5. Sometimes, special outside advisers (such as the 1973 Coombs Task Force, the 1976 Bland Committee, the 1981 "Razor Gang") review old expenditure policies to eliminate waste and duplication in the light of current government priorities, while from 1983, the Economic Planning Advisory Council (EPAC) is a further body involved in Budget advice.

The functions of the Budget

Before looking at the Budget process in more detail by means of an examination of the Budget cycle, this process must be put in the perspective of the functions and objectives of the Budget. As was indicated earlier, in the Australian federation the budgetary functions and objectives are divided among the three levels of government by means of legislation, in particular, the Constitution, by the financial power of the levels of government, and by tradition. This subject is pursued further in Chapter 15. Broadly speaking, the Budget functions of the seven Australian governments include the following:

1. An evaluation of total government and public authority receipts and expenditures within the Budget sector.
2. An ordering of priorities in expenditure and revenue items to determine the scale of public services and also to implement government objectives on income and wealth distribution and on the allocation of resources within the public and private sectors.
3. To act as the Parliament's instrument of accountability and control over government in its handling of financial matters.
4. To provide a means of control over the level of economic activity of the nation as a whole in order to secure a rate of economic growth adequate to provide rising living standards and the job opportunities required to employ a growing population and subject to a constraint of price stability. (As shown in Chapter 14, this function is assigned to the central government in a federation.)

Functions 2 and 4 describe what are generally regarded as the economic functions of the Budget: the allocation function, the distribution function and the stabilisation function.[12] These functions are discussed in considerably more detail in subsequent chapters; the discussion here is a summary.

The allocation function

This function relates to both the relative size of the public sector (share of output appropriated by the public sector) and the allocation of these resources among the various functions and programs carried out by the government. The subsequent three chapters look at various aspects of this dimension of the Budget allocation function. Because both government expenditure and taxation policies influence the allocation of resources in the private sector (both in the present and the future), the Budget decision-making process must take account of the allocation consequences. For example, a decision to raise public expenditure on road construction will have widespread effects on the private sector.

Until recently, Australian budgetary practice rarely stressed the allocation function of the Budget explicitly. This has changed with the increased emphasis on allocational efficiency in government decision-making. Examples are the greater emphasis on program budgeting and the establishment in 1987 of the Structural Adjustment Committee of Cabinet whose task is the consideration and resolution of issues affecting the efficiency of resource use in the economy. Its importance is reflected in the May 1988 Economic Statement; for example, the announcements flowing from the Business Tax Review. Such initiatives stress the importance of the Budget's allocational function as compared with the past. It needs also to be stressed that all budgetary decisions have allocation consequences and these should always be anticipated and assessed by the policy-makers. At the same time it should be remembered that resource allocation is not the only objective of budgetary policy; and that there are other government instruments such as the tariff which can alter resource allocation. The allocation function may conflict with other political, social, and economic functions of the Budget, and such conflict possibilities are discussed later.

The distribution function

In most democracies, Australia included, the government accepts some responsibility for the degree of inequality in wealth and income distribution and it attempts to alter this distribution by means of budgetary and other policies. Apart from budgetary policy, the government has a variety of other instruments at its disposal to influence distribution objectives. These include incomes policy particularly in connection with public service salaries, price surveillance and competition policy, attitudes to public utility pricing and the charging for government services in general, land tenure policy and advice on wages policy through its negotiations with the Trade Unions under the Prices and Incomes Accord and in its submissions to the wage hearings conducted by the Industrial Relations (formerly Arbitration) Commission. This book concentrates on the Budget's direct influence on income and wealth distribution.

All budgetary policy decisions have distributional implications, that is, they have an impact on the pattern of real disposable incomes among the various social and economic groups. This is indicated in the discussion of expenditure incidence in Chapter 5, in that of tax incidence in Chapter 8, in the analysis of the various tax instruments in Chapters 9–13, of the system of revenue transfers from one level of government to other levels of government in Chapter 15, and of debt policy in Chapter 17. Again, in this context it should be clear that the design of distributional policy is not only influenced by economic factors such as considerations about incentives to work and to save, but also by political and social factors such as the degree of poverty and the range between the lowest and highest incomes which is considered acceptable.

Distributional policy in Australia is frequently confused with social welfare policy, but that is only a small part of the total distribution function of the Budget. All expenditure, tax, and other financing decisions have distributional consequences, and not just those explicitly aimed to directly impinge upon the incomes of specific social groups. For example, a Budget may contain specific social welfare measures such as an increase in means-tested family allowances and the family income supplements which are specifically targeted to low-income families. Other Budget measures — those relating to education or health, for instance — affect the real incomes of all families. Distribution policy obviously raises controversial political and social issues, on which there seems to be little agreement in contemporary Australian society. It is also clear that distributional policy will often conflict with other budgetary objectives.

The stabilisation function

The adoption of the White Paper on full Employment in 1945 heralded a long period during which Australian governments explicitly accepted responsibility for promoting full employment, price stability, economic growth, and external balance. These involved the adoption of appropriate budgetary and other economic policy such as monetary and wages policy as well as more direct controls. Through the impact of the Budget on economic activity, a subject discussed in more detail in Chapter 18, the objectives espoused in 1945 were promoted. During the 1970s, as indicated subsequently, some of these traditional fiscal policy aims have been diluted. The Federal Government has the primary role in this area; the States, although they pledge co-operation with the Federal Government in this matter, are less effective in connection with stabilisation policy.

Stabilisation policy is not just a technical economic matter, its specification contains political and social judgements. Such judgements are already required for the interpretation of the policy objectives; an "adequate level" of employment and "a reasonable degree" of price stability are difficult to define. Trade unions and the unemployed prefer high levels of employment for rather obvious reasons; employers and Treasury officials may prefer higher unemployment because it makes labour discipline easier, because it is easier to expand activity if there are no labour shortages, and, though this is debatable, because they claim it facilitates the control of wage-push inflation. Similarly, the distributional effects of inflation make higher rates of inflation attractive to some, and unattractive to others. Higher rates of inflation facilitate government revenue raising in the absence of tax indexation, and thereby lead to "painless" increases in the public sector. They favour debtors as against creditors and they favour those with a degree of power over their incomes through wage bargaining and price setting as against people on less flexible incomes. In addition, the stabilisation instruments selected to deal with these problems themselves affect the distribution of income and wealth, thereby leading to further potential social and political conflict.

Budgetary policy in post-war Australia has also aimed at encouraging sustainable economic growth. From the early 1970s this has carried the proviso that high growth rates should not affect the environment too adversely nor impair the quality of life. Broadly speaking, the growth policy of the Budget is effected by the instruments which affect the sources of economic growth such as the labour supply and labour productivity (for example, immigration policy and education spending); capital formation (taxation policy and public investment); technical progress (government aid to and participation in research and development); and a whole series of more specific policies to aid particular industries or sectors of industry.

The government can also aid the growth objective through the planning potential of the Budget. Although general economic planning has never been an important consideration in the Australian budgetary process,[13] it is argued by at least some economists that private sector growth can be substantially aided if businessmen are informed in advance of government intentions on spending and taxation. Indeed, the essence of French "indicative planning" was the collation and dissemination of knowledge about the intentions of the public sector and of the major investors in the private sector. Since the public sector, as has been shown earlier, accounts for such a large proportion of total national output and because through its purchases of goods and services it makes up a large part of the total demand for private production, the utilisation of the Budget as a general planning instrument would be as potent a factor in the encouragement of economic growth as the more traditional policies outlined in the previous paragraph.[14]

From the mid-1970s there have been substantial changes in the manner of looking at budgetary policy and the specification of its stabilisation objectives. A number of examples may be given but a more detailed discussion is left to Chapter 18. First, with the much bigger unemployment levels of this period, the traditional full employment objective appears to have been redefined. Much of this reflects theoretical debate about the desired stance of fiscal policy and the causes of unemployment. Secondly, growth and development objectives have increasingly been affected by environmental considerations. This is illustrated by the creation of special government departments dealing with the environment, conservation, and preservation of the national estate and by the legal requirements to have environmental impact studies for major private and public development projects such as new mines, airport extensions and freeway construction. Environmental considerations impose constraints on development policies and hence create the potential for conflict. There are further conflict possibilities inherent in the growth objective. The pursuit of an expansionary immigration policy for example, in times of considerable unemployment may lead to conflict with the unions and with those who advocate low population growth on environmental grounds. Thirdly, the Government's 1983 decision to float Australia's foreign exchange rate has removed the constraint imposed by adequacy of the level of international reserves and altered that imposed by the balance of payments.

Conflicts and trade-offs in the government objectives

When governments attempt to achieve these economic objectives, conflicts can arise from three sources: from inconsistencies between the economic objectives themselves; from inconsistencies between the economic and the social and political objectives of the government; and, in a federation, from inconsistencies between the implementation of policies by the central government and the policies pursued by the State governments.

The conflict between the objectives themselves was commonly illustrated by the so-called trade-off between inflation and employment, where it is argued that a little less inflation can be purchased at the cost of a little more unemployment. Many other illustrations of conflicts between the objectives can be given. The distributional objective may require increases in social security cash benefits to compensate their recipients for higher prices; anti-inflationary policy may require curtailment of aggregate demand and sacrifice of the employment objective; the growth objective may require a higher savings ratio whereas distributional considerations may require the introduction of a capital gains or a wealth tax, which have their major impact on the high-income, large-saver groups.

Some illustrations of the conflicts between political and social objectives and the economic objectives have already been given. In Australian practice, such policy conflicts become particularly noticeable as elections approach, and when this is the case it is the electoral strategy that often triumphs.[15] When more efficient resource allocation over greater equality in income distribution demands the curtailment or abolition of certain expenditures, taxes or tax concessions, there are always lobbies which often can successfully resist such changes. As was argued in Chapter 1, to many of these apparently economic questions there are only political answers.

A final source of conflict in budgetary policy arises in a federal system in which there may be substantial short-run policy differences between the federal government and the governments of the State. In connection with allocational objectives, differences may arise over the division of functions between the levels of government, which may lead to duplication and waste; in connection with the distributional objective, tax policy in the States may conflict with that of the federal government; while the taxation and spending policies of the States may also cause serious problems for federal stabilisation policy. These implications of a federal system for budgetary policy decision-making are, however, becoming more widely recognised, as is the need for federal fiscal co-operation in order to reduce these conflicts to a minimum.

Other functions of the Budget: the control and managerial functions

Apart from the economic functions of the Budget, there are two further functions: the evaluation of total government receipts and expenditure, and the accountability and control function. The second of these is the oldest function of the Budget. It reflects the concern over the accountability of the executive branch of government in its handling of the "public purse" to the representatives of the people. The form and contents of the financial documents presented with the Budget, and a great deal of the parliamentary procedure surrounding the Budget have been influenced by this particular function. The traditional guardians of the Parliament's rights in this matter, the Auditor-General, the Joint Committee of Public Accounts, the Senate Estimates Committee and the House of Representatives Standing Committee on Expenditure, have been mainly concerned with seeing that this accountability function is satisfactorily performed.

The meaning and purpose of the other, or "managerial" function as it is frequently called, are also well defined. It is concerned with the efficient use of resources within the government services and is partly exercised by the government departments themselves, partly by the Department of Finance when it scrutinises the expenditure estimates, and partly by the previously mentioned parliamentary watchdogs, the Auditor-General, the Public Accounts Committee, the Senate Estimates Committee and the House of Representatives Standing Committee on Expenditure. Procurement regulations and policy, administrative procedures in the handling of public moneys, manpower policy in the public service, and technical improvements in the provision of public services come under this heading. The classifications and divisions in the Estimates and in the public accounts are largely geared to facilitate this type of control.[16]

Like the accountability and control function, the managerial function takes the objectives, size, and specifications of the program embodied in the expenditure items as given. Both functions are concerned with the efficient use of resources appropriated by the government for the specific purposes indicated; they are not involved with an efficient allocation of resources to the various functions of government. In this manner, they have so far represented the traditional role of the Budget and its associated financial procedures and conventional accounting methods.

In its discussion of the role of the Auditor-General, the 1973 Royal Commission on Australian Government Administration suggested the introduction of efficiency auditing, that is, a systematic inquiry into the efficiency with which government objectives are met through the programs for which funds are appropriated. After the investigation by a working party of the feasibility of efficiency auditing, the system was adopted and enacted in the *Audit Amendment Act* 1979. Since then a considerable number of efficiency audits have been conducted by the Auditor-General's Department and all of these have been subsequently examined by the Standing Committee on Expenditure.[17] The role and office of the Auditor General itself was investigated in 1988 by the Joint Committee of Public Accounts, in the context of charges by the Auditor-General that cutbacks in public expenditures and ceilings on staff salaries had meant inadequate resources were being made available for his important office.[18]

Conventional government accounting

The accountability, management, and control functions of the Budget are exercised internally by the Department of Finance through the preparation of the conventional public accounts; external control is exercised mainly by the Auditor-General but also by parliamentary committees. To a large extent, a discussion of these matters falls outside the scope of public finance[19] but some background on these matters should be given, in particular on the meaning of the three funds — the Consolidated Revenue Fund, the Trust Fund, and the Loan Fund — into which the public accounts have been traditionally divided.

The Consolidated Revenue Fund, the most important of these three funds, is authorised for the Commonwealth by section 81 of the Constitution. Its sources of funds include most of the revenue collected in taxation as well as other departmental revenue, and these are used to make payments to or for the States, for departmental and running expenses, for the payment of social security benefits to pensioners and others, for public works and other services and for Interest and Sinking Fund contributions. At the end of the financial year, this fund is balanced by the transfer of any surplus revenue to the Trust Fund or from the transfer of loan funds for defence purposes from the Loan Fund. The State governments also have consolidated revenue funds, which have broadly similar purposes.

The Trust Fund is not established by the Constitution but by section 60 of the *Audit Act*. Part of its purpose, as mentioned in the previous paragraphs, is to receive surplus Commonwealth revenue, which, under the original terms of federation agreed upon, otherwise would have to go to the States. Many other trust accounts have since then been established by other Acts of Parliament for a variety of reasons. Some details of Trust Fund expenditure and investments are presented in the supplement to the *Treasurer's Statement of Receipts and Expenditure* and in the *Report* of the Auditor-General, which are presented annually to Parliament.

Finally, there is the Loan Fund, also established by the *Audit Act*, for the receipt of loan moneys raised on the credit of the Commonwealth. There are no rules about which types of expenditure are to be made from the Fund; in recent years it has been used largely for the purchase of defence equipment, for financing the works and program of the States and for advances for housing. Details of loan expenditure are given in an annual Budget Paper, *Estimates of Receipts and Summary of Estimated Expenditure*.

The accounts which are included within these three funds are called conventional accounts or "line item"[20] budgets because their overriding purpose is the control of public receipts and expenditure by matching the inputs purchased by departments — for wages and salaries, material, and equipment — with the appropriation for the department approved by parliament. This conventional accounting approach is contrasted with two other forms of public accounting: the public accounts in national accounting form, and the functional or program accounting which emphasises the function of the expenditures rather than the purchases of particular departments. These two additional forms of public accounting have been developed for use in implementing the economic functions of the Budget, because for the analysis of the allocation, distribution, and stabilisation functions of the Budget they present the data in a more useful form than do the conventional accounts. Reasons for using the Budget in functional form are discussed in Chapter 5.

THE ANNUAL BUDGET CYCLE [21]

Co-ordination of the various functions of the Budget by the decision-making agents in the Budget process is illustrated by a brief examination of the annual Budget cycle. This topic is not only of considerable importance in itself for students of public finance, but it also allows integration of the various topics which have been discussed in this chapter and allows for some comments on the relative importance of the Budget's decision-makers — that is, the heads of government departments, the departments of Treasury and Finance, the Premiers' Conference and the Loan Council, Cabinet and the Parliament. It will also make it possible to illustrate how the subsequent chapters on public expenditure, taxation, public debt, inter-governmental relations, and stabilisation policy, fit into the actual governmental framework of decision-making.

The Commonwealth Budget Process now generally starts before the Budget which forms the conclusion of the previous Budget cycle has passed through the Parliament. It begins with the preparation of the forward estimates, intended to provide the government and the public with the level and composition of public outlays over the following three years in the absence of policy changes. Such estimates are the basis for developing a budget strategy for the coming year and in 1988 were published in November for the three years 1989–90 to 1991–92. It is a rolling planning program in which each year a new third year is added while the first year's estimates provide the initial input for the coming Budget's estimates of expenditure. In addition, it is a powerful tool for expenditure control and restraint. In January or February there are consultations on additional estimates for the current financial years whose implications for future financial years are incorporated into the forward estimates. In February or March there is a ministerial strategy review covering the economic and budgetary position, the broad budgetary parameters and priorities and decisions are made on detailed guidelines for preparing the Budget. This is assisted with detailed Treasury submissions. Additional estimates are finalised in readiness for the submission of Draft Estimates for the coming financial year in April. During May there is a general review of outlay proposals by the Expenditure Review Committee after the meeting of EPAC and officials' consultations on portfolio expenditures,[22] following which there are consultations between the Minister for Finance and individual Ministers on budget options. These take on extra importance, and are conducted earlier, whenever there is a commitment to present a May Economic Statement, as was the case in 1985, 1987 and 1988, or sometimes earlier, as in April 1989. June sees a Cabinet review of Budget outlays, followed by the Premiers' Conference and Loan Council meetings which finalise the following year's federal financial assistance to other governments. In July, again after a meeting with EPAC, the Expenditure Review Committee gives final consideration of Budget revenues and outlays, Budget cabinet finalises the Budget decisions and the Budget is presented, traditionally on the third Tuesday of August. A Treasury depiction of the Timetable is reproduced as Figure 2.1.

At the same time, a critical review of the current Budget is undertaken by officers of the

Figure 2.1 Timetable of Budget processes in a typical year

Aug. Sept. Oct. Nov. Dec. Jan. Feb. Mar. Apr. May Jun. July Aug.

Current year's processes

BUDGET tabled in Parliament

Regular internal reviews update budget estimates

Budget outcome published in June

Outlays & receipts monitored & reported in public monthly statements

Next year's processes

Forward estimates of outlays prepared

ERC & Cabinet consider possible budget timetable and processes

Treasurer's economic outlook & policy submissions to ERC and Cabinet

ERC decisions endorsed by Cabinet

Budget Cabinet

Reviews and possibly some savings papers on specific programs commissioned

ERC and Cabinet consideration of budget strategy

PREMIERS' CONFERENCE/ LOAN COUNCIL

BUDGET tabled in Parliament

Additional outlays papers commissioned

POSSIBLE MAY STATEMENT

ERC consideration of savings papers if there is a May Statement

Preparation and consideration of further savings options

Budget Revenue Committee of Cabinet considers revenue options as required

Estimates updated for parameter and policy changes

Aug. Sept. Oct. Nov. Dec. Jan. Feb. Mar. Apr. May Jun. July Aug.

Source: Christopher Higgins and David Borthwick, "The Treasury", *Economics Papers* 7 (4) December 1988, p. 74. Reproduced with kind permission of the authors and the Economic Society of Australia.

Finance Department. These reviews are continual for financial control purposes, but major reviews are generally undertaken three times during the financial year in November, January and May. These reviews are not only to implement the accountability, control, and managerial functions of the Budget, they also aid the preparation of the forthcoming Budget and thereby serve important planning purposes. The review of the old and the planning of the new Budget are complementary activities. Revenue estimates are obtained by the Department of the Treasury with assistance from the Taxation Office, the Australian Bureau of Statistics, and customs and excise officials. Treasury also carries major responsibilities for advice on the economic impact of the Budget.

Final Budget recommendations are scrutinised by Cabinet on the basis of Treasury memoranda dealing with economic conditions such as the level of employment and prices, the balance of payments, economic growth, monetary conditions, and other relevant aspects, including the Treasury view of the required overall Budget strategy. The Budget proposals are therefore discussed in Cabinet in the light of political and economic considerations, during which conflicts may arise between the need in an election year to maintain or increase expenditure programs and to lower taxes while economic policy may demand expenditure decreases and a rise in taxation. Other conflicts may arise over the priorities adopted by the government in its decisions and the priorities of specific government departments. These conflicts are often real and further underline the fact that many basic decisions about Budget strategy are often made on political grounds, but then, in turn, are influenced and tempered by the economic effects of various policies.

It should be noted in this context, that unlike the practice in some other countries, particularly the United States, parliamentary backbenchers and the public have little say in the framing of the Budget. However, the establishment of EPAC permits formal pre-Budget discussions between leading Ministers and various interest groups, such as employers' organisations, trade unions, consumer groups and so on, while the Party room occasionally influences the budgetary stance of the government on issues of expenditure and tax policy. These types of pressures tend to have a long-term rather than an immediate effect on the outcome of the Budget under consideration, which remains the prerogative of executive government.

As indicated below, the complete Budget is generally brought down in August when the Treasurer delivers his Budget Speech to Parliament and presents the associated Budget Statements and papers.[23] It is subject to formal debate for several months before the Appropriation Bills are finally passed in the two Houses, generally in November. In line with Westminster practice, the government stands or falls with its Budget proposals. However, with the strict discipline obtained by the Party system, such events are not likely to occur in the House of Representatives though Senate retains and occasionally has used its right to reject supply.[24]

It is difficult to say which are the more important government departments in the Budget process apart from the general statement that the Department of Finance now has a major role in Budget preparation and control on the public expenditure side, with crucial economic inputs from Treasury and the economic section of Prime Minister and Cabinet. Although EPAC's importance was stressed in the Government's 1984 strategy for Budget Reform, its role seems to be confined to that of an institutional device allowing simultaneous consultation with the business interests, trade unions, consumer groups and State governments traditionally consulted in the Budget decision-making framework. Treasury dominance in this area disappeared from the mid-1970s when many of its Budget functions were allocated to a Department of Finance created in 1976.[25]

One further issue related to the annual Budget cycle must be discussed. Is such an annual cycle useful for all the functions of the Budget? It seems clear that there is nothing wrong with this annual cycle in so far as the traditional Budget functions of accountability, control, and financial management are concerned. It is different with the economic functions. For stabilisation purposes, more frequent variations, especially in the tax instruments, can be useful and Chapter 18 shows how much more use has been made of mini-budgets in Australia during the 1980s to achieve this greater flexibility. The government's revealed preference for greater reliance on monetary policy is partly explained by this factor. At the same time, for planning purposes, a longer cycle is required. Chapter 5 discusses whether the three-year forward estimates first introduced in 1971 are adequate for this purpose. Longer-term budgetary planning tends, however, to be constrained by the electoral cycle of a maximum three years, in practice often much shorter. An annual Budget can, and does in Australia, incorporate both these features and thereby allows a shorter, as well as a longer, time horizon. During the 1960s, defence spending was planned on the basis of a five-year rolling program within the annual Budget cycle; similarly, much of federal education spending has usually been planned on a three-year basis. The forward estimate procedures in force from the mid-1980s likewise provide for more effective expenditure planning mechanisms on a three-year rolling basis.

Implicit in this discussion of the Budget cycle has been the view already encountered in Chapter 1: the Budget summarises the scope of the study of public finance. Subsequent chapters on expenditure evaluation (Chapter 5), taxation (Chapters 6 to 13), debt policy and management (Chapter 17), intergovernmental financial relations (Chapter 15) and stabilisation policy (Chapter 18), investigate the principles underlying the decisions made in connection with the functions of the Budget in detail.

SUMMARY

1. Government functions in general need to be carefully distinguished from budgetary functions in order to grasp the institutional and classificatory divisions of economic policy.

2. The distinction between taxation and expenditure, although often straightforward, is made more complex by the notion of tax expenditures or subsidies to households and industry groups given through the tax system. In addition, the distinction between taxes and user charges and prices is not always clear-cut.

3. The budgetary functions of the Australian Government are constrained by their assignment in the Constitution. Section 51 defines the major expenditure powers of the Commonwealth Government, as well as its general taxing powers while its exclusive tax and conditional grants power are given by Sections 90 and 96.

4. The Budget is the most important single document for students of public finance, hence the Budget process needs to be clearly grasped. This includes a need for knowledge on

the various agencies involved in budget decision-making such as Departments of Treasury and Finance, Cabinet, and its Expenditure Review Committee, Premiers' Conference and Loan Council and external advice from special committees or more permanent institutions like EPAC.

5. The Budget functions include an allocation, redistribution and stabilisation function, as well as more traditional accountability, control and planning functions. Such functions are subject to change over time, as illustrated by the variation in the attitudes to the unemployment objective in Australian policy discussion. There can also be important conflicts and trade-offs between the objectives.

6. The Budget's control and management functions rely on external agencies such as the Auditor-General, the Joint Committee of Public Accounts as well as on internal (departmental) controls, particularly from the Finance Department. Such control is assisted by conventional and government accounting.

7. The annual Budget cycle illustrates the interaction between agencies and functions in the Budget process. Examples are the use of forward estimates as planning and expenditure restraint devices, the importance of general economic forecasting for revenue estimates and the setting of fiscal policy stance, the role of Premiers' Conferences and Loan Council in determining a significant proportion of federal budgetary outlays, as well as the political constraints generated by the government's desire to get re-elected.

NOTES

[1] In a narrow sense the Budget does embrace all the functions of government because all these functions require *some* spending of money which is channelled directly or indirectly through the Budget. For a useful discussion of the institutional division of labour in Australian economic policy in the 1980s see Michael Keating and Geoff Dixon, *Making Economic Policy in Australia 1983–1988* (Melbourne: F.W. Cheshire, 1989), pp. 5–8, and for an institutional glossary, pp. 73–5.

[2] For a discussion of the demarcation between fiscal and monetary policy see L. Johansen, *Public Economics* (Amsterdam: North Holland Publishing, 1971), pp. 23–5; Alan S. Blinder and Robert Solow, "Analytical Foundations of Fiscal Policy", in *The Economics of Public Finance* (Washington, D.C.: The Brookings Institution, 1974), esp. p. 4.

[3] Chapter 7 discusses the benefit principle which argues that all taxes are prices for benefits received. It therefore completely eliminates a distinction in principle between public utility prices and taxes. In another sense, public utility prices are nothing but earmarked taxes. Chapter 9 discusses the implications of the Higher Educational Contribution Charge for income taxation.

[4] See *Economic Statement May 1988* (Canberra: AGPS, 1988), pp. 151–4 for Commonwealth Government reforms of their business enterprises on such lines; New South Wales Commission of Audit, *Focus on Reform* (Sydney: New South Wales Commission of Audit, 1988), chs. 3, 10, 16 for the proposals of a State government on this subject. For a general discussion see Michael Keating and Geoff Dixon, *Making Economic Policy in Australia*, pp. 54–5.

[5] For a general discussion of the concept of tax expenditures see H.J. Aaron and M.J. Boskin (eds.), *The Economics of Taxation* (Washington, D.C.: The Brookings Institution, 1980), Part II.

[6] For an Australian analysis, see Treasury, *Tax Expenditures Statement* (Canberra: AGPS, 1986) which replaced the previous practice of providing such information with the Budget Paper No. 1, Budget Statements, Statement No. 4.

[7] Government influence on income distribution arises from many types of policy: the arbitration process, restrictive trade practices legislation, exchange rate policy, interest rate policy, and so on. Budgetary policy designed to influence income distribution is confined to taxation and expenditure instruments.

[8] In this context, the term "incidence" refers to the increase or reduction in income resulting from expenditure or taxation measured as a proportion of total household income in various ranges. Expenditure incidence and tax incidence are discussed in Chapters 5 and 8 respectively.

[9] For discussions of the constitutional position with respect to State taxation, see Cheryl Saunders, "Constitutional Limits on State Taxation", in *Tax Reform and the States*, R.L. Mathews (ed.) (Canberra: Centre for Research on Federal Financial Relations, 1985), ch. 2; Report of the Advisory Committee to the Constitutional Commission, *Trade and National Economic Management* (Canberra: AGPS, 1987), pp. 151–66; New South Wales Tax Task Force, *Review of the State Tax System* (Sydney, 1988), ch. 3.

[10] The Constitution is very accessible to students of economics since it is reprinted in all volumes of the *Official Year Book of Australia*, which are regularly published by the Australian Bureau of Statistics. See, for example, *Yearbook Australia 1988* (Canberra: Australian Bureau of Statistics, 1988), pp. 115–36. Reference can also usefully be made to Attorney-General's Department, *The Australian Constitution Annotated* (Canberra: AGPS, 1980) and in the context of constitutional reform of the economic and financial clauses, the Report of the Advisory Committee to the Constitutional Commission, *Trade and National Economic Management* (Canberra: AGPS, 1987). Australian fiscal federalism arrangements are examined in detail in Chapter 15.

[11] More detailed discussion is provided in *Budget Reform* (Canberra: AGPS, 1984), esp. section 2; *Financial Administration Handbook* (Canberra: AGPS, 1985), esp. chs. 2, 8, 11; M.N. Johnston and D.S. Harrison, *Modelling the Interactions between the Economy and the Budget*, Department of Finance Discussion Paper No. 1, November 1985, esp. pp. 2–7.

[12] This classification, which is widely used, is that of Musgrave. See R.A. and P. B. Musgrave, *Public Finance in Theory and Practice*, ch. 1.

[13] Attitudes to planning in Australia in the 1950s and 1960s are discussed by Bruce McFarlane in *Economic Policy in Australia*, chs. 3 and 10–12. The 1972–75 federal Labor government did not alter these attitudes substantially. For a discussion of the planning experience of the Labor government from 1972 to 1975 see P.P. McGuinness, "Planning the Relationship between Industrial Structure and Government", *Economic Papers*, No. 57 (January 1978). Reference can also be made to the Symposium on the Market and the State in the *Australian Journal of Public Administration*, 48(2) June 1990, particularly the contribution by Greg Whitwell.

[14] EPAC was designed originally as a vehicle for this type of planning, under its charter disclosed by the Treasurer to the 1983 Economic Summit, but by August 1985 it was generally conceded that these initial expectations of its role were not fulfilled. For a general discussion of attitudes to planning by the Labor government of the late 1980s see Ian Ward and A. Kulkarni, "The Rise and Fall of National Allocative Planning in Australia", *Australian Economic Review*, 2/87, pp. 37–48.

[15] See F.H. Gruen, "The Federal Budget: How much Difference do Elections Make?", *Australian Economic Review*, 3/85, pp. 36–52.

[16] See Australian Public Service Board, *Financial Administration Handbook*, op.cit., chs. 2–5, 10; and at the State level, Victorian State Government, Economic Budget Review Committee, *Discussion Papers on the Review of Budget Estimates by Parliament* (Melbourne: F. Atkinson, Government Printer, 1987), esp. ch. 2.

[17] See *Report of Royal Commission on Australian Government Administration* (Canberra: AGPS, 1976), ch. 11, esp. p. 378 and Appendix, vol. 4, pp. 153–89; Report of Working Party on Efficiency Audits (Canberra: AGPS, 1977); and, for details about the reports on efficiency audits conducted, Annual Reports of the Australian Audit Office, for example, that for 1987–8 (Canberra: AGPS, 1988), ch. 3, Appendix 6. These have been reviewed by the House of Representatives Standing

Committee on Expenditure on a regular basis. See for example, Parliament of the Commonwealth of Australia, *An Efficient Organisation, or an Efficient Audit?* (Canberra: AGPS, February 1987), especially ch. 8.

[18] Joint Committee of Public Accounts, Report No. 296, Reform of the Australian Audit Office (Canberra: AGPS, 1989). Its 78 recommendations include funding increases for the Audit Office, in part to facilitate a greater use of its resources in the area of efficiency audits.

[19] See Public Service Board, *Financial Administration Handbook*, op.cit., chs. 1, 6, 7, 10–11; for a discussion of the relationship between these accounts and the coverage and classification of information in the Budget statements, see *Budget Statements 1988–89*, 1988–89 Budget Paper No. 1 (Canberra: AGPS, 1988), pp. 405–25. This also discusses the precise relationships between the non-budget sector and budget sector, general government and public trading enterprise sector (discussed above in Chapter 1) and the information contained in the Budget papers.

[20] "Above the Line" items comprise outlays and revenue — the difference between them is the budget balance (surplus or deficit); "below the line items" are undertaken to finance the deficit or utilise the surplus. See *Budget Statements 1988–89*, op.cit., p. 407.

[21] See *Budget Reform*, op.cit., ch. 2, esp. p.6; H.N. Johnston and D.N. Harrison, "Modelling Interactions between Economy and the Budget", op.cit., pp. 2–7 and Attachment A; C. I. Higgins and D. Borthwick, "The Treasury", *Economic Papers* 7(4) Dec. 1988, Appendix 3, reproduced as Fig. 2.1. Recent developments in the use of forward estimates are discussed in Michael Keating and Geoff Dixon, *Making Economic Policy in Australia*, pp. 18–19.

[22] Portfolio classification refers to the outlay classification by Ministry with the overall administrative responsibility for the outlay. See *Budget Statements 1988–89*, pp. 419–25.

[23] From the 1960s onwards the Budget Speech has been accompanied by an increasing number of documents while the statements originally appended to the speech have lengthened considerably. These documents known as the Budget Papers, in 1988 numbered four main papers, and eleven related papers. Paper No. 1, *Budget Statements* and Paper No. 4, *Commonwealth Financial Relations with other Levels of Government* can be regarded as the more important of the major Budget papers for Public Finance students. Related Paper No. 1, *Government Securities on Issue*, is also referred to in this book (Chapter 17).

[24] For a brief discussion of the parliamentary Budget process see David Solomon, *Inside the Australian Parliament* (Sydney: Allen & Unwin, 1978), pp. 76–9. See also *Budget Reform*, ch. 3.

[25] For a detailed history of the role of Treasury see Greg Whitwell, *The Treasury Line* (Sydney: Allen and Unwin, 1986); see also Christopher Higgins and David Borthwick, "The Treasury", *Economic Papers* (7) 4, December 1988, pp. 60–74.

FURTHER READING

For a general discussion of the Budget functions and institutions discussed in this chapter, reference should be made to introductory textbook material such as:

R.A. and P.B. Musgrave, *Public Finance in Theory and Practice*, 4th edn. (New York: McGraw Hill, 1984), ch. 1, pp. 7–20; ch. 2.

C.V. Brown and P.M. Jackson, *Public Sector Economics*, 3rd edn. (Oxford: Blackwells, 1986), ch. 7, esp. pp. 178–189.

Joseph E. Stiglitz, *Economics of the Public Sector* (New York: W.W. Norton and Company, 1988), ch. 2.

David Heald, *Public Expenditure* (Oxford: Martin Robinson, 1982), chs. 5–8.

Useful Australian discussions of the subject raised in this chapter are:

Christopher Higgins and David Borthwick, "The Treasury", *Economic Papers*, 7(4), December 1988, pp. 60–74.

Michael Keating and Geoff Dixon, *Making Economic Policy in Australia 1983–1988* (Melbourne: Longman Cheshire, 1989), esp. chs. 2, 5, 7.

3

The growth of the public sector

Although drastic changes in public spending in the short-term have been few and far between, over the twentieth century as a whole the change in government spending has been dramatic. In virtually all countries, the State has absorbed a steadily increasing share of national output, and Australia, as will be shown later, is no exception to this phenomenon. Only from the mid-1980s has the size of Australia's public sector (measured in terms of outlays relative to GDP) started to decline but it is too early to indicate whether this is a trend towards smaller government or a short-term change induced by policy responses to harsh economic circumstances. The search for explanations of this rising share of output going to the public sector has caused considerable debate among economists and economic historians and has shed considerable light on the question.[1] These explanations are not only intrinsically important; they are also important because they indicate changing attitudes of the public to government expenditure and government intervention in the economy.

Before looking at the growth of the Australian public sector in more detail, a number of other issues need to be canvassed. These include statistical problems associated with measuring the size of the public sector, examination of the various theories of public sector growth, and an attempt to assess the view, often put by various economists, that there are "natural limits" to public sector growth.

A suitable starting-point for such a discussion is Wagner's law of "expanding State activity", which was formulated at the end of the nineteenth century. Broadly speaking, this law stated that with rising per capita incomes in industrialising nations, the relative share of the public sector in national output would rise. Wagner offered three reasons to explain this phenomenon. First, with industrialisation there would be increased need for the administrative and protective functions of the State. Secondly, the cultural and welfare functions of the State should expand, especially those connected with education and income distribution; while thirdly, with the changes in technology accompanying industrialisation and the increasing capital requirements of many industries, the State would have to nationalise many such industries to prevent consumer exploitation by private monopolies, while the direct investment role of the government would also expand. Curiously, Wagner did not see war and defence as playing a role in the growth of the public expenditure, largely because of the widely held view at the time that the growth and progress of civilisation would reduce the number of wars and their duration. In this matter Wagner was unfortunately proven wrong and war and defence expenditure, in some countries at least, proved to be one of the more important causes of growth of public expenditure in the twentieth century.[2]

Although Wagner's Law is broadly supported by the empirical evidence of public sector growth in the twentieth century, some of his reasoning has to be modified to make the theory fit the facts. Current knowledge suggests that there are several reasons for the phenomenon of public sector growth, which can be summarised as follows:

1. The effect of economic growth on public sector outlays (Wagner's Law proper).
2. The high income elasticity of demand for public goods at certain stages of development (public goods as "luxury" goods).
3. Productivity differentials between the public and private sector (the productivity lag or relative price effect).
4. The effects of national crises on public sector growth (the displacement effect).
5. Inflation.
6. Bureaucrats.

As a preliminary to this discussion, some statistical problems in public sector measurement should be noted.

STATISTICAL PROBLEMS IN PUBLIC SECTOR GROWTH MEASUREMENT [3]

As has already been indicated, the most convenient measure of public sector growth is the change in public expenditure relative to GDP over time. This immediately raises two difficulties. First, is public expenditure to be measured in terms of goods and services actually used for government consumption and capital purposes, or are transfer payments to be included in the measure as well? Second, and with respect to the denominator in the measure, is this GDP at market prices or GDP at factor cost? Both difficulties raise issues of principle and are therefore important.

Take first the items to be included when estimating public expenditure. If the size of government is conceived in terms of its actual use of resources taken from the private sector, then something is to be said for measuring it in terms of expenditure on goods and services relative to national output as a whole. Transfer payments such as social security benefits do not directly involve government use of resources; such transfers affect resources from one section of the community to another. However, such transfers contain a coercive element, as, for example, in the case where they involve taxing the rich to pay means-tested pensions or family assistance. This is a reflection of the redistributive function of government activity, a function ignored if transfer payments were excluded in measuring public sector size. In short, leaving transfer payments out of consideration means that the full range of public sector activity is not included in the index of public sector size adopted.

Focusing on government outlays in the numerator also raises the question of what part of the public sector is to be measured. In terms of the classification of the public sector used in Chapter 1, is general government expenditure only to be included, or should expenditure on goods and services by public trading enterprises be included as well? In other words, is the public sector synonymous with the budget sector, and to what extent should the transactions of the non-budget sector be included in the public sector? No simple answers are available to this problem which to some extent raises the distinction between public provision and public production in the context of defining the public sector.

There is a further difficulty in using public expenditure which arises from the practice of tax expenditures. As indicated in Chapter 2, paying subsidies or welfare benefits through the taxation system makes the public sector look smaller by reducing the relative size of outlays and taxation collections (which can be used as a proxy for outlays or as an index of public sector coercive activity). Such changes, for example, the transformation of tax rebates for dependent children into family allowances, raise difficulties in interpreting conclusions when comparisons of public sector size over time made in terms of public expenditure relative to GDP. Likewise, variations in the treatment of the transactions of public authorities or public business enterprises may distort inter-temporal comparisons of public outlays relative to GDP.

An arithmetical example illustrates the importance of choosing between GDP at market price or GDP at factor cost. Two countries A and B both have GDP at factor cost of $200 and public expenditure of $100. Country A finances its public expenditure by $10 of direct and $90 of indirect taxation, Country B levies $90 in direct and $10 in indirect taxation. Subsidies from public expenditure are $20 in A and $30 in B. This means that GDP at market prices for A equals $270 ($200 + $90 – $20) while for B it equals $180 ($200 + $10 – $30). Hence measured in terms of GDP at factor cost, the public sectors of A and B are of equal size (50 per cent); in terms of GDP at market prices, the difference is substantial. A's public sector then takes up 37 per cent of national output, B's 56 per cent, a difference only explicable in terms of the different tax mix used in the two countries and variations in the relative importance of subsidies in their fiscal systems. This rather extreme example is useful because it highlights the dangers in uncritical international comparisons of public sector size or inter-temporal comparisons for a country which has experienced a substantial change in its tax mix between direct and indirect taxation. However, not too much can be made of it because of its simplifying assumption that factor costs levels are independent of tax-mix, an assumption difficult to sustain in practice.

Alternative approaches to public sector measurement

Some of these measurement problems can be eliminated by the careful selection of more specific measures of public sector size. Given the various roles which can be assigned to the public sector as consumer, as producer, as employer, as redistributor, as re-allocator, as borrower and as regulator, specific measures can be designed to reflect these different attributes to government activity.

1. *Government as consumer of resources.* This is measured by the value of goods and services absorbed by government from national output measured at market prices, that is, the percentage of government current and capital expenditure on goods and services as GDP at market prices. In 1987–88 this was estimated at 18.5 per cent for the general government component of the public sector; 21.6 per cent for the public sector incorporating public authorities.

2. *Government as producer*. In its role of provider of public services, some of which are in fact marketed, the government can be seen as producer as well. To measure the public sector in this capacity, the final output attributable to government or its value added is compared to GDP at factor cost. For 1987–88 this gives an estimate of 19.9 per cent.
3. *Government as employer* in theory measures government use of factors relative to the total supply of these factors, that is, incomes of factors such as labour employed in the government sector relative to national factor incomes. This cannot be easily measured from available income data, but in physical terms it can be approximated by the percentage of government employees in the national labour force. (See Table 3.2). If average government wages and salaries differ substantially from those in the private sector, the physical measure departs significantly from the measure in value terms. For the financial year ending June 1987 the physical terms percentage can be estimated at 30.8 per cent.
4. *Government as distributor*. With transfer payments interpreted as a mechanism by which the government redistributes within the private sector, government transfers relative to national or, in some cases, household income, can give an indication of the relative importance of this government function. For 1987–88 government transfers relative to household income can be estimated at 11.8 per cent.
5. *Government as re-allocator* looks at the weight of taxation relative to national output because the weight of taxation measures the amount of resources the government coercively transfers to itself from the private sector. Rather than using GDP, national income can be selected as the denominator because that more adequately reflects disposable resources in the private sector. For 1987-88 this ratio is estimated at 39.5 per cent.
6. *Government as borrower*. This can be measured in terms of new loan raisings, in which case it is partially reflected in the Public Sector Borrowing Requirement. Alternatively, it can be measured in terms of the relative size of the public debt. Both of these are now generally measured relative to GDP. Measured in this way, they were 0.7 per cent for the net public sector borrowing requirement of the aggregate public sector and 21.7 per cent for the Commonwealth public debt in 1987–88 .
7. *Government as regulator*. Regulatory activity and its impact on the private sector is not easily reflected in expenditure measures relative to some index of private sector economic activity. No measures of this facet of Australian public sector activity are readily available. Canada and the United States measure federal regulatory expenditure (in money terms) relative to both total public expenditure and to GDP, or in physical terms of public servants employed in regulatory activity relative to total public sector employment at the federal level. Both these measures are useful for inter-temporal comparisons but are not particularly useful as absolute indices of regulatory activity.
8. *Real versus nominal measures*. If different deflators are available for government consumption expenditure, government investment expenditure and their private counterparts, different results arise in inter-temporal comparisons depending on whether measures use current or constant price data. As shown subsequently in the discussion of the relative price effect or productivity lag explanation for public sector growth, the changes in price movements reflected in the different rates of change in the deflators may imply serious over-statement of public sector size relative to GDP if public sector prices rise faster than private or market output prices.

These difficulties in public sector measurement need to be recalled in the discussion of public sector growth which follows, particularly in the evaluation of Australian public sector growth at the end of the chapter. It needs to be understood that comparisons over time of public sector size are hazardous for reasons explained in this section. It is therefore never easy to draw conclusions from past experience in public sector growth, or to make firm propositions about acceptable levels of public sector size whether in terms of limits of taxation or some other way.

THE GROWTH OF THE PUBLIC SECTOR: SOME EXPLANATIONS

The growth of the public sector in terms of public expenditure relative to GDP was a phenomenon increasingly statistically visible from the late nineteenth century in many of the world's developed and industrialised countries. Explanations were quickly forthcoming. As indicated earlier, Wagner's law of expanding state activity was the first of such explanations and one which is still discussed despite the fact that it was originally formulated during the 1890s. During the 1970s and 1980s, other attempts have been made to explain the phenomenon. These draw on the large expansion of OECD country public sectors disclosed in the comparable data the OECD has been publishing. More contemporary explanations have generally focused on particular aspects of the problem which only surfaced after World War II.

The effects of economic growth on public sector outlays

As stated previously, Wagner's argument gave three reasons to explain the effects of economic growth on public sector outlays and thereby his law of expanding State activity. The first of these concerns the need for an expansion of the protective and administrative agencies of government as a result of industrialisation, partly because of the conflict potential in the development of capitalist society which requires the protection of one section of the society from that of another. That this has taken place is easy to demonstrate. Examples of such agencies include the following: the provision of arbitration and conciliation machinery to mediate in conflicts between capital and labour, consumer protection legislation; policies designed to safeguard rural interests from the demands made on the government by the manufacturing sector, such as subsidies to compensate rural producers for the cost disadvantage they suffer through the tariff protection of manufacturing industry; protection of workers against unemployment, a consequence of the inevitable trade cycle which accompanies industrialisation; and, a more modern example, the protection of the environment against the demands of motorists and manufacturing and mining enterprises.

The growth of defence spending, an aspect that Wagner did not think particularly significant, can also be related to industrialisation. In the first place, technology played a major role in increasing the cost of war, not only through the use of more sophisticated hardware but also in the use of manpower on a giant scale as compared with the nineteenth century. The whole concept of total war, developed in the twentieth century, rests on a massive industrial complex, as World Wars I and II clearly showed. Secondly, the growth of industrialisation in Europe in itself spawned international conflicts. The growth of industry and commerce fostered pressures for territorial expansion, as well as the need to safeguard foreign investments, trade routes, the supplies of essential materials; these considerations provided some of the reasons why governments sought increased military preparedness. Such external conflicts among the leading developed nations are explained by the modern theories of imperialism.[4]

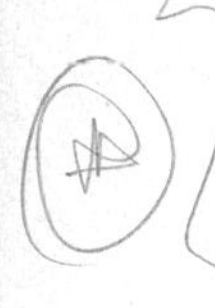

The second explanation which Wagner found for his law was based on the increased need for industrialising nations to spend on culture and welfare. General and popular education was one such need which became vested in the hands of the State because it alone could organise resources for supplying a skilled workforce to the more and more complex machinery of industry and commerce. At the same time welfare spending had to increase as a State activity, since industrialisation and the urbanisation that went with it destroyed the informal welfare system based on families and private charity. The growth of the welfare State was not only the product of more enlightened liberal thinking, it was also a necessity caused by the disruption of social relations brought about by industrial capitalism.

These social aspects of the industrial revolution and the process of industrialisation are only now being fully investigated by economic and social historians in research on the changing concept of the family, its duties and responsibilities, in history. Early findings suggest it is reasonable to assume that the disruptions caused to family life by industrialisation in all its aspects created a wide variety of welfare problems, just as the dissolution of the monasteries created poverty in Tudor England as a result of the economic reorganisation of agriculture to which it led. A further aim of State welfare expenditure was to disarm some of the propaganda of the growing labour movement; for example, Bismark's policy of social security in the 1880s in Germany which led the world at that time was largely designed to pacify the demands of workers who were flocking to support the Social Democratic parties.

Urbanisation also brought other public costs in the form of public health, sanitation, transport, and waste disposal, all of which have become important items in government budgets.

Finally, Wagner linked the growth of public activity to the new technology and the growth of natural monopolies[5] which this entailed. These natural monopolies became important, especially in the area of transport (roads, railways, and later aviation), of communications (postal, telegraphic, and telephonic as well as radio and television), and in connection with public utilities for the supply of water, gas, and electricity. In all these areas public investment began to predominate, either to safeguard consumers against private monopolies or because the initially huge capital investment required could not easily be provided by private enterprise.[6] From the 1980s concerns with public sector efficiency have reversed this trend with privatisation of many of these instrumentalities, an issue further explored in Chapter 20.

Variations in the income elasticity of demand for public services

In his study of fiscal systems, Musgrave found variations in the income elasticity of demand for public services in three ranges of per capita income. At low levels of per capita income, associated generally with pre-industrial society in the developing nations, demand for public services was generally very low because nearly all income was devoted to satisfying primary needs. When per capita income starts to rise above these low levels, a demand for services supplied by the public sector (such as public health, education, and transport) becomes more important. Hence over this middle range of income, public sector outlays expand at a faster rate than private expenditure. In this manner, relative public sector growth, that is relative to

GDP, is related to the rising living standards associated with industrialisation. Finally, at the high levels of per capita income associated with developed economies, the rate of public sector growth will decline as the more basic public wants are satisfied. At this stage of development, public and private expenditure were expected to grow at much the same rate because of complementarities between public and private goods. Musgrave's cross-sectional data therefore lends some support to the analysis of Wagner's Law in the middle ranges of income, the income range associated historically with the most rapid economic development.[7] However, increasing concerns with government failure in the 1980s in developing and less-developed countries, and subsequent privatisation of much government activity, has made such associations between growth levels of income and public spending less clear-cut, and in some countries, reversed them.

The "productivity lag" or "relative price effect"

A further effect of economic growth on public sector outlays is associated with productivity differentials in the public and in the private sector which cause measurement problems — the so-called productivity lag. If the productivity of resources used in the public sector rises less sharply than that of similar resources used in the private sector, then there is a greater relative need for inputs to produce a given output in the public sector, which tends to increase over time. Since the size of the public sector is invariably measured by its inputs, that is, its purchases of goods and services especially labour, the size of the public sector in terms of output values becomes very difficult to measure. Furthermore, with labour costs of greater importance in the public than in the private sector, input costs will also expand more rapidly in the public sector, since wages rise generally at a faster rate than the prices of produced inputs. The public sector may therefore have grown at a much lower rate than conventional measurement suggests, though with the present statistical information available this is not easy to verify.

The best way to illustrate the "productivity lag" or "relative price effect" is by taking a striking example provided in a seminal paper on the subject by Baumol.[8] A Schubert trio scored for a half-hour's performance requires one-and-a-half person-hours to produce. It is not easy to speed the performance without affecting its quality nor can a trio be performed by two musicians. Baumol used this example to demonstrate that some productive sectors are liable to slow, or in some cases even zero productivity growth, particularly in the case of labour intensive personal services where time and personal contact are essential parts of the product. This will affect the relative costs of providing the low productivity growth services, as is shown by the following example where there is only a small productivity differential.

Assume manufacturing sector productivity rises annually at a rate of 3 per cent, while in public sector services productivity increases only by 1 per cent per annum, which suggests a productivity lag between the two sectors of 2 per cent. Wages are geared to productivity growth in the manufacturing sector, hence increase annually at the rate of 3 per cent. At any point of time, which may be called year 1, take the examples of two goods, one from the manufacturing sector and one from the public sector which both cost \$1.00 to produce. Since costs match productivity in the manufacturing sector, this price will stay at \$1.00 over time, other things remaining equal. However, costs exceed productivity in the public sector by 2 per cent, so that at the beginning of year 2 the price of its good has to rise to \$1.02 if it is to match costs. After ten years, the cost differential from the productivity lag is 22 cents; after twenty years 67 cents if costs are to be covered. A productivity differential in this way implies a bias in favour of public sector growth as conventionally measured since maintenance of the same quantity of public goods in physical terms will cost more in terms of inputs relative to the (private supplied) manufactured goods which enjoy a productivity growth advantage. A 2 per cent productivity differential over twenty years enhances costs in the low productivity sector by 67 per cent or, if public outlays on such goods required 25 per cent of national output in year 1, the proportion of resources required would rise to 36.5 per cent in year 21 if the same physical quantity of public goods was to be provided.

This productivity lag which produces a relative price effect is widely accepted as explaining a substantial proportion of observed public sector growth. For example, over two decades a 1 per cent lag or relative price effect can increase the size of the public sector from 30 to 37 per cent of GDP without in any real sense adding to public goods provision. In their study of OECD experience, Saunders and Klau[9] tested for the importance of this relative price effect for the period from 1971 to 1982. Using the price deflators for public and private consumption as a proxy for the relative price effect, they found an average productivity lag of 0.7 per cent per annum for the OECD as a whole, with several countries well above this average. Australia experienced a 1.1 per cent lag for example, while France, New Zealand, the United Kingdom and Luxembourg experienced a lag of 2.0 per cent or more. However, given the fact that other things do not necessarily remain equal, they correctly stressed that these data cannot provide simple inferences on public sector growth.

The displacement effect and the concentration process

In their research of British government expenditure growth,[10] Peacock and Wiseman noted changes in the rate of growth of British public expenditure, which they especially associated with wars. Relative to GNP, the growth rate of British public expenditure accelerated during the Boer War, the Korean War, but especially during the two world wars. What was important in this context was not the rise in public expenditure associated with the war years, but rather the fact that post-war expenditure levels did not return to their pre-war level but remained significantly above them. War expenditure appeared to have what they called a "displacement effect".

This displacement effect is explained as follows. Public expenditure is largely financed from taxes, especially in normal circumstances. Over the years people build up a certain degree of tolerance to what they regard as acceptable levels of taxation; this taxation threshold is not easily passed, except in times of national crisis such as war. Under such circumstances people will accept rises in taxation out of the ordinary; during the period of conflict they grow used to these new tax burdens and, although in the immediate post-war period tax levels are reduced, they do not fall back to pre-war levels. In this way, the level of public expenditure for civilian purposes which can be supported by taxation has been displaced upwards, by the greater tax effort of the public necessitated by the war. In addition, the sacrifices made by the public during the war raise its expectations about the type of post-war society they want — and this will increase the social expenditure of the government.

The research of Peacock and Wiseman points to a further characteristic of public expenditure growth in the United Kingdom. The process of economic development tends to concentrate government responsibilities in the hands of the higher levels of government and away from the lower levels such as local government, and State or provincial governments in a federal system. This arises partly out of the need for uniformity in planning in an emergency, which naturally goes to the central government. The planning of the war economy is not the only example of this; anti-cyclical action, which became a major government responsibility after the Depression of the 1930s, is also usually in the hands of the central government. Another reason for this concentration process arises from improved transport and communications, which make people more aware of different standards in public services in various parts of the country. The consequent desire for greater uniformity and standardisation of these services generally requires central government intervention through the provision of equalisation grants to State, and sometimes to local governments, to remedy the situation. The concentration process is therefore partly associated with the displacement effect, but is also explained by other factors. This is further discussed in Chapter 15.

Inflation and public sector growth

Inflation has been seen as an increasingly important influence on public sector growth from the 1970s. Ease of financing expenditure growth is part of the explanation. This flows from the now well-recognised effects of inflation on tax revenues, particularly income tax (as discussed more fully in Chapters 9 and 10), and on the real costs of debt servicing. In addition, the increasing practice of indexing government expenditure — such as the automatic adjustment of most social security benefits — and of maintaining the *real* value of expenditure for purposes such as education, facilitates growth of public outlays on aggregate. However, empirical research suggests no strong association between inflation and public sector growth.[11]

Bureaucrats as an influence on public sector growth

Some economists[12] have also suggested that growing public servants' influence and power may partly explain the acceleration in public sector growth during the post-war period. This is a simple inference from the self-interest of public sector bureaucrats, since their incomes are favourably affected by an expansion of the activities on which they are engaged by raising the demand for their services and by opening up new opportunities for promotion. The rising relative importance of public servants among the total number of voters may also make the electorate as a whole more amenable to a larger public sector, although there is little empirical evidence of this.

The research on public sector growth has so far not generated simple explanations for the phenomenon which can be clearly supported by the empirical evidence. One interesting finding from the major OECD empirical study on the subject is the linkage between public sector growth and the degree of openness of the economy, a matter explicable by the need for greater government intervention to remedy more substantial instability potential in such economies.[13]

ARE THERE NATURAL LIMITS TO PUBLIC SECTOR GROWTH?

The argument of continued public sector growth and, consequently, growing government power, has been challenged in the past on many occasions by people who have tried to define a "natural limit" to the public sector. In Chapter 1 it was indicated that the attempts of the nineteenth-century public finance theorists to find such a natural limit to public sector activity by means of their classification of public goods ended in failure, largely because of Barone's dictum that "it is not true that the economic activity of the State is designed to satisfy all collective needs and only collective needs".[14] Nevertheless, and for a variety of reasons, economists have continued to try to define a natural limit to the public sector.

One of the more celebrated attempts at such a limitation was produced by Colin Clark in an article published in 1945. From data on inflation and levels of taxation relative to national income in many European countries and other developed countries between the two world wars, he concluded that "excessive" government spending was the basic cause of inflation, though not the only one, and that the truth of this hypothesis was supported by the data he had collected. In fact, he stated the argument more strongly:

> The data appears to give very considerable support to the hypothesis that once taxation has exceeded 25 per cent of the national income (20 per cent or less in certain countries), influential sections of the community become willing to support a depreciation of the value of money; while so long as taxation remains below this critical limit, the balance of forces favoured a stable, or occasionally an increasing value of money.[15]

This argument cannot be sustained in the light of world experience. OECD studies of revenue statistics for member countries clearly indicate that most countries had exceeded this tax threshold by the end of the 1960s. By the mid-1980s only Turkey among OECD countries had a tax ratio to GDP of less than 25 per cent while over a third of OECD member countries had tax ratios in excess of 40 per cent, with Australia's ratio in excess of 30 per cent for the whole of the 1980s. However, the economic problems of inflation and growing unemployment experienced by many of these countries from the end 1970s onwards have been blamed by some economists on these massive increases in taxation and government spending.[16]

One important example of such recent analysis has attempted to show by theoretical argument rather than statistical inference that the British problem of high inflation and unemployment of the 1960s and 1970s was due to an ever-increasing public sector, growing too large relative to a private sector which had to produce the marketable goods and services on which sustainable economic activity depends.[17] The theoretical argument behind this hypothesis is relatively simple.

Broadly speaking, the analysis bases itself on classical growth models which stress the surplus product potential of an economy, that is, that product obtained from production over and above the necessary expenses of production including the replacement of capital. This surplus product is disposable in the sense that it can be utilised in "unproductive" consumption — that is, goods and services which are not marketed and therefore not creating surplus — without affecting the potential for the same amount of production in the following period. If part of this surplus is invested, the economy will have a positive growth rate but if unproductive consumption exceeds the surplus for a period of time, the economy's growth rate will become negative and it will stagnate. For continual economic growth, the difference between the surplus product and unproductive consumption and investment must be sufficiently large to finance increases in productive investment and, in a trading nation, a rising level of exports to ensure a healthy balance of payments.

How well this model applies to the public sector depends on whether public spending is the major area of "unproductive spending" and therefore the cause of the depletion of the surplus at the expense of private investment and exports and therefore, of sustainable economic growth. Although Bacon and Eltis do not include *all* public spending in the "unproductive" category, the inference which most readers of their book have made, and which is fostered in the more popular versions of their theory, is that the too rapid growth of the public sector is the cause of the trouble. The higher and higher taxation required by public sector growth has in turn led to higher and higher wage adjustments and inflation, a profits squeeze, and then low investment and high unemployment. Only a reduction in the size of the public sector can, by implication, restore economic growth, increase employment and reduce inflation.

Some of these conclusions cannot be sustained. Although the theoretical aspects of their analysis, founded on classical theory, are quite satisfactory, it is rather difficult to interrelate these theoretical concepts with particular items of expenditure, whether public or private. Education expenditure, for example, which is largely "unmarketed" and therefore "unproductive" on their criteria, does enhance productivity and therefore contributes to the disposable surplus. As the brief discussion of education spending evaluation in Chapter 5 indicates, this is not to say that all education expenditure is productive nor that there are no wasted resources in education. The education example can be supplemented with other examples of non-marketed, public spending, such as investment on roads which has undoubted productivity effects. This means that for the purpose of the Bacon-Eltis analysis it is difficult to separate the unproductive public expenditure from the non-marketed public goods.

It is on these types of difficulties of application of the analysis that the model breaks down. Unless the division between "productive" and "unproductive" expenditures can be clearly established, *in concrete cases*, the analysis is somewhat of an "empty box". In fact, it can be said that their model, despite the very many useful insights it contains, is very difficult to apply to actual situations and cannot be accepted as providing the key to *the* cause of economic problems whether in the United Kingdom or in Australia. Other attempts to blame the economic problems experienced by many developed countries on excessive public sector size are equally unsatisfactory even though in many such countries, including Australia, reduction in the size of the public sector is often advanced as a satisfactory policy response to such economic problems. Failure to establish high correlations between public sector size and stabilisation policy performance in terms of inflation and unemployment supports this conclusion. This issue is pursued further in Chapter 20.

THE GROWTH OF PUBLIC EXPENDITURE IN AUSTRALIA

Can the growth of public expenditure in Australia be explained by these hypotheses about the growth of the public sector? That such growth has occurred relative to national output (GDP) cannot be doubted: the statistical evidence for the last fifty years is quite clear. The data is graphed in Figure 3.1, not only for total public expenditure as a percentage of GDP but also for the relative shares in output of defence spending.

Various features of Figure 3.1 may be commented on. In the first place there is a noticeable rise in government expenditure relative to GDP during the period 1930 to 1935 which is explained not by any great rise in public expenditure but rather by the dramatic fall in the level of output during the Great Depression. Figure 3.1 also clearly illustrates the effect of World War II on the Australian public sector. It is obvious that most of the increased

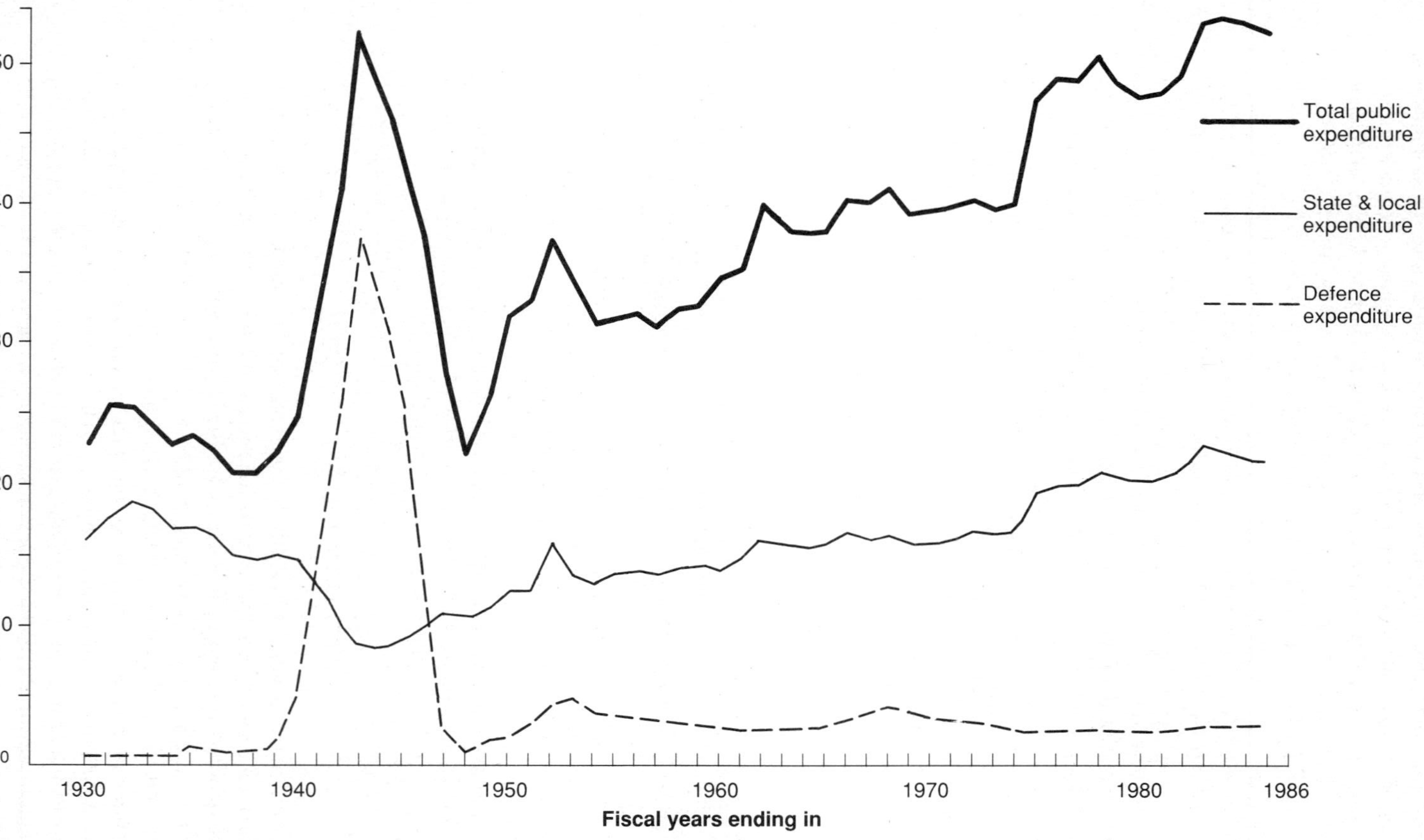

Figure 3.1 The growth of public expenditure in Australia 1929–30 to 1985–86

Note: From 1978–79 State and local expenditure shares are affected by inclusion of Northern Territory, which was formerly treated as part of the Commonwealth sector.

Source: 1929–30 to 1948–49, R. L. Mathews, *Public investment in Australia* (Melbourne: Cheshire, 1967), ch. 1; 1949–50 to 1985–86, Reserve Bank of Australia, Occasional Paper No. 8A, *Australian Economic Statistics 1949–50 to 1986–87*, pp. 33 and 43.

spending was devoted to defence purposes, and that civilian expenditure — especially State and local expenditure — actually fell, in relative terms, during most of the war. Some displacement effect undoubtedly occurred; after the war public expenditure relative to GDP was greater than in the period before the war. A similar effect on aggregate public spending in the public sector during the 1960s and 1970s cannot, however, be really explained in terms of the displacement of the Vietnam War.

Perhaps a better indication of the strength of such displacement can be obtained from the behaviour before and after wars of civilian public outlays (that is, government purchases of goods and services excluding defence but including transfer payments). In the five years before World War II, civilian public outlays on average were 20.6 per cent of GDP; after the war they rose to 23.6 per cent of GDP, a sizeable displacement effect. At the end of the 1950s, the five-year average (1955–56 to 1959–60) of civilian outlays stayed at 23.6 per cent of GDP so that the Korean War (1950–54) had no clear displacement effect on civilian government spending. In the following five-year period (1960–61 to 1964–65), the average share of civilian outlays in GDP rose to 16 per cent, while in the first five years of the 1970s (1970–71 to 1974–75) it rose to 29.8 per cent. It is doubtful whether this last shift in the size of the public sector can be attributed to Australia's military involvement in the Vietnam War, since defence spending during the 1960s remained relatively small; even at the height of the Vietnam conflict Australia's defence spending reached a peak of only 4.1 per cent of GDP, as compared with the more normal share of defence spending of approximately 2.5 to 3 per cent of GDP before and after that conflict. It seems therefore that for Australia the displacement effect of wars on public outlays for civilian purposes was only important in the case of the two world wars, while it was not significant in connection with Australia's participation in wars in Asia in the 1950s and 1960s. From the mid-1970s total public expenditure has been above 30 per cent of GDP, though as indicated in Figure 3.1, after peaking in 1984-85, it has gradually declined in the following years on a net basis. Much of this relative decline in Australian public sector size is explicable in terms of tight fiscal policy needed to lower demand, hence imports and overseas indebtedness.[18]

The foregoing theoretical discussion of public sector growth suggests several other explanations for the growth of Australian public spending from the 1960s. The effects of economic growth, including the population growth largely achieved by the post-war immigration program were undoubtedly important, since such growth requires the provision of public services. The impact of inflation on government revenue, and hence on ease of financing, likewise may have played a part in public sector growth of the 1960s and 1970s. Table 3.1 presents data on the growth of public consumption spending, public investment, cash transfer payments, and taxation relative to GDP for selected years in the post-war period.

Table 3.1 reveals a steady growth rate in government outlays, which in the case of public consumption expenditure on goods and services and cash benefits including those for social services, accelerated in the mid-1970s, partly a reflection of the differing social philosophy of the Labor government which was in office from 1972 to the end of 1975. The particularly rapid growth of the public sector in this period can be partly attributed to political factors. Whether the whole period covered in Table 3.1 reflects a rising income elasticity of demand for public services is more difficult to say. The data from this table, after all, is consistent with a constant income elasticity, provided that it is greater than unity. The figures also disclose some "productivity lag"; this is apparent in the relative shift to consumption

Table 3.1 Indicators of public sector growth: 1949-50 to 1987-88 (selected years)

	Government outlays on goods and services				
	Consumption	Investment	Cash transfers	Personal income tax	Total taxation
	As a percentage of Gross Domestic Product				
1949–50	5.8	8.2	6.2	7.3	22.8
1954–55	6.0	8.7	5.8	7.4	22.8
1959–60	6.8	8.3	6.2	6.4	22.2
1964–65	7.8	9.2	6.9	8.2	23.6
1969–70	9.0	9.1	7.1	9.5	26.0
1974–75	13.0	9.2	9.3	13.2	30.3
1979–80	13.8	7.6	10.2	13.1	29.8
1984–85	18.9	7.1	10.1	13.8	30.8
1987–88	17.9	6.2	9.5	15.8	31.6

Note: Government consumption expenditure on goods and services excludes defence expenditure.
Source: Australian Bureau of Statistics, *Yearbook of the Commonwealth of Australia* (Canberra 1954), Australian Bureau of Statistics, *Australian National Accounts 1953–54 to 1966–67* (Canberra: ABS, 1968), Australian Bureau of Statistics, Time Series Service Data Tape, 1989.

expenditure on goods and services, the area of public expenditure where productivity rises are more difficult to detect. It would require a detailed econometric analysis of the statistics to give more precise answers to the questions of public sector growth in Australia, but such analysis is unfortunately not available, though a study prepared for EPAC shows the importance of the relative price effect in assessing the relative growth of public consumption over the period in question.[19]

The picture is a little different for taxation. For the first fifteen years covered by Table 3.1, total taxation revenue remained remarkably steady as a percentage of GDP. From the early 1970s it started to rise appreciably but this rate of increase slowed considerably during the 1980s. The acceleration of taxation from 1969–70 to 1974–75, largely attributable to that on personal income, illustrates the effects of inflation on government revenue, and perhaps its consequent effects on public expenditure. The stabilisation of taxation and public expenditure from the late 1970s onwards suggests that it is difficult to reduce the public sector once a relative increase has occurred, but experience after 1984–85 shows it is not impossible.

The explanation of public sector growth in Australia is therefore a complex one; no single cause can be regarded as dominant in this process. As in most comparable countries, World War II caused a displacement effect in Australia's public expenditure, which raised public expenditure relative to GDP above pre-war levels. During the 1950s and 1960s, the public sector continued to grow and this growth can be largely explained by the demands for public services and investment from a steadily expanding economy. Finally, political factors arising from the change in government in 1972, combined with the effects of inflation on tax revenue, explain the accelerated rate of growth of the public sector in the mid-1970s, which since then has been partially reversed.[20]

Australian public sector growth experience in the post-war period has not been unique since similar growth has been experienced by many of the OECD countries. In fact, Australia's public sector and relative tax burden are still relatively small. For example, in

Table 3.2 Share of public sector employment in civilian workforce and relative shares of public sector employment by level of government: 1901–88 (selected years)

Years ending 30 June	Shares in civilian labour force			Civilian employment by level of government						
	Government %	Private %	Unemployment %	Federal 000	State 000	Local 000	Total 000	Federal %	State %	Local %
1901	8.7	87.4	3.9	18.2	102.4	13.1	133.8	13.5	76.5	9.8
1911	10.8	86.4	2.8	29.8	157.2	15.7	202.6	14.7	77.6	7.7
1921	13.4	80.8	5.8	44.8	225.9	18.7	289.4	15.4	78.1	6.5
1931	12.5	68.9	18.6	47.7	235.1	39.8	322.6	14.8	72.9	12.3
1941	16.2	78.5	5.3	111.1	285.8	49.1	446.1	24.9	64.1	11.0
1951	19.4	79.5	1.1	208.7	402.9	66.8	678.3	30.8	59.4	9.8
1961	19.0	78.6	2.4	230.6	497.9	84.1	812.6	28.4	61.3	9.8
1971	19.8[a]	78.8	1.4	336.0	641.2	106.1	1083.2	31.0	59.2	10.3
1981	22.8	71.3	5.9	401.3	1010.7	130.3	1542.3	26.0	65.6	9.8
1988	22.1	70.2	7.7	438.1	1139.7	156.2	1734.1	25.3	65.7	8.4

Note: Figures may not add due to rounding.

(a) After 1971, data not strictly comparable with earlier data because of different public sector employment classifications used.

Source: 1901–71, Institute of Applied Economics and Social Research, *The Australian Economic Review*, first quarter, Melbourne, 1977, Tables 2 and 4, pp. 50–1.
1971–88, Australian Bureau of Statistics, Time Series Service, Canberra, 16 December, 1988.

1985,[21] Australia ranked with the last quarter of OECD countries with respect to taxation as a proportion of GDP if this measure includes social security contributions; if such contributions are excluded, Australia ranks pretty well in the middle. Much of the public sector growth of the 1970s and 1980s Australia experienced, was therefore a catch-up phenomenon, since during the 1950s and 1960s Australia had been lagging behind the rest of the world in this regard. However, international comparisons on the subject are difficult to interpret, and provide few clear guides for policy guidance in themselves.[22]

An alternative method of measuring public sector growth

Another useful method of measuring the size of the public sector is to look at the relative importance of public sector employees in the total labour force. Table 3.2 provides data on this for selected years from 1901, which reveals the increase in public employment which has taken place especially after World Wars I and II. It should also be noted that the relative shares in the public sector work force of the three levels of government have altered considerably. What is particularly striking in this table is the rise in the relative importance of the federal government and the relative decline of the work force of the State governments, ignoring in this context the abnormal conditions of World War II.This trend, which Peacock and Wiseman called the concentration process, is examined in more detail in Chapter 15. Nevertheless Table 3.2 shows that more than two-thirds of public sector employment is in State and local government, a proportion which is broadly comparable to the shares in expenditure on goods and services of these three governments shown in Table 3.1. The relative decline after 1981 of Commonwealth public servants has been due to the more rigid public service ceilings at the federal level from the mid-1970s onwards, a policy increasingly imitated by State and local governments during the 1980s.

CONCLUSIONS

Irrespective of the difficulties in funding explanations for public sector growth, or predicting the extent to which the phenomenon can continue, the large proportion of resources utilised in the public sector raises problems for the public finance economist about the efficiency and effectiveness with which these resources are used. Some theoretical answers to the questions are discussed in Chapter 4; Chapter 5 examines problems of public expenditure evaluation in more detail; while Chapter 20 discusses privatisation and some other potential factors inducing reversal of continual twentieth century public sector growth.

SUMMARY

1. The growth of the public sector is generally measured in terms of public expenditures/outlays in relation to GDP. This raises the problem of whether expenditures/outlays are broadly or narrowly defined, and whether to use GDP at market prices or at factor costs. Real versus nominal measures may also affect the outcome depending on price deflators used.

2. The twentieth century in general has seen very substantial growth in the size of the public expenditure, a phenomenon explained by various hypotheses in terms of the relationship between public sector growth and economic growth, productivity differentials between public and private sectors, displacement effects induced by a need to expand public sector activity in times of national crisis like war or depression, as well as by inflation and the actions of bureaucrats to expand their sphere of influence.

3. Not only how to measure but what to measure is important to testing the growth of the public sector. Government can be measured as consumer of resources, as producer, as employer, as distributor, as re-allocator, as borrower and as regulator.

4. Several economists have linked economic growth with public sector growth. Wagner did this in terms of the growing need for government intervention in conflict resolution, social welfare, investment in public utilities induced by industrialisation and urbanisation. Musgrave linked varying values for the income elasticity of demand for public services with different stages of economic growth. Experience of the 1980s has reversed some of these trends, as concern with government failure in equitable and effective goods and service delivery started a wave of privatisation and reduction in public sector size.

5. Other factors used to explain public sector growth are the relative price effects associated with productivity differentials between public and private sectors; inflation which facilitates financing of expenditure growth and induced nominal growth in outlays when many of them are indexed by annual CPI movements; as well as bureaucratic self-interest in encouraging public sector growth. The significance of some of these effects has proved difficult to capture statistically.

6. Various limits to public sector growth have been suggested by economists from the end of the nineteenth century. Colin Clark in 1945 suggested 25 per cent of national income as such a limit; if governments exceeded it inflation and other economic problems would follow. But this prediction has not been matched by OECD experience. Empirical evidence suggests in fact no straightforward relationship between public sector size and economic performance.

7. Australian public sector growth, virtually continuous for the period for which good data are available, illustrates many of these factors explaining public sector growth. The reversal in such expansion of relative public sector growth in Australia from the mid-1980s can be explained by a growing concern over government failure to efficiently and fairly deliver government serices but, more importantly, by the fiscal policy imperative of demand restraint for the sake of securing external balance.

NOTES

[1] International comparisons, now rather dated, are in R.A. Musgrave, *Fiscal Systems* (New Haven, Conn: Yale University Press), ch. 3, and R.A. and P.B. Musgrave, *Public Finance in Theory and Practice* (New York: McGraw Hill, 1984), ch. 7. A detailed study of the post-war phenomenon in industrialised countries is given in Peter Saunders and Frederick Klau, *The Role of the Public Sector: Causes and Consequences of the Growth of Government* (Paris: OECD, 1985). The initial discussion of this phenomenon dates back to the work of Adolph Wagner in the 1890s, and more recently, to the study of A.T. Peacock and Jack Wiseman, *The Growth of Public Expenditure in the United Kingdom* (London: Allen and Unwin, 2nd rev. edn., 1967).

[2] This paragraph is largely based on Richard M. Bird, "Wagner's Law of Expanding State Activity", *Public Finance/Finances Publiques*, vol. 26 (1971), pp. 1–24. For a contrary view on the growth of expenditure see Ronald W. Crawley, "Long Swings in the Role of Government: An Analysis of Wars and Government Expenditure in Western Europe Since the Eleventh Century", *Public Finance/ Finances Publiques*, vol. 26 (1971), pp. 17–41.

[3] Detailed discussion of such statistical problems can be found in R.M. Bird, *The Growth of Government Spending in Canada* (Ottawa: Canadian Tax Foundation, 1970), especially Appendix A; Saunders and Klau, *The Role of the Public Sector*, op.cit., esp. ch. 2, and see Jack Diamond and Alan A. Tait, "The Growth of Government Expenditure: A Review of Quantitative Analysis", *IMF Working Paper* 88/17, Washington, 1988.

[4] See for example, M. Barratt Brown, *The Economics of Imperialism* (Harmondsworth: Penguin Modern Economic Texts, 1974). It has also frequently been suggested that large-scale military expenditure has been an important device to keep up the level of aggregate demand and thereby maintain stable economic growth. For a critical discussion of this hypothesis, see R.P. Smith, "Military Expenditure and Capitalism", *Cambridge Journal of Economics*, vol. 1 (March, 1977), pp. 61–76 and the references cited therein.

[5] A natural monopoly can be defined as one where for reasons of technology, namely large indivisibilities in investment outlays and increasing returns to scale, costs of supplying the service are greater if there is more than one producer in a particular location. Railway tracks, airports, electricity, gas and water supply all fall into this category.

[6] There are wide differences here between various countries which frequently reflect differing political attitudes. In Australia, the communications industry is largely a State monopoly with the exception of broadcasting. In the United States, telephonic communications are operated by private enterprise. The 1980s, as mentioned earlier, have seen various attempts to privatise natural monopolies in the United Kingdom. In Australia, the matter remains on the political agenda though both the Labor and Conservative parties in Australia have strong supporters of privatisation, particularly in transport and communications.

[7] See R.A. Musgrave, *Fiscal Systems*, ch. 4. On strict logical grounds Musgrave's cross-sectional data cannot support Wagner's Law, because cross-sectional evidence is irrelevant to a law dealing with the development of economies over time. Strictly speaking, Wagner's Law can therefore only be tested by time series analysis — the procedures used here in discussing the growth of the Australian public sector.

[8] W.J. Baumol, "Macroeconomics of Unbalanced Growth: the Anatomy of Urban Crisis", *American Economic Review*, June 1967, pp. 415–26.

[9] Saunders and Klau, *The Role of the Public Sector*, op.cit., pp. 57–61.

[10] Alan T. Peacock and Jack Wiseman, *The Growth of Public Expenditure in the United Kingdom* (London: Allen & Unwin, 2nd edn., 1967). This book is well worth reading, especially the introduction and the first three chapters. For a more contemporary statement of their theory see A.T. Peacock and J. Wiseman, "Approaches to the Analysis of Public Expenditure Growth", *Public Finance Quarterly*, vol. 7, no. 1, January 1979, pp. 3–23. Their thesis has been criticised on the empirical evidence in OECD, *Public Expenditure Trends* (Paris: OECD, 1978).

[11] See Alan T. Peacock and Martin Ricketts, *The Growth of the Public Sector and Inflation*, Institute of Social and Economic Research, University of York, Reprint Series No. 268, 1978, and Saunders and Klau, *The Role of the Public Sector*, pp. 114–17. On the merits of

indexing public expenditures see EPAC Council Paper No. 23, *Flexibility in Government Spending: Issues in Efficiency and Control* (Canberra: AGPS, 1986, pp. 20–6); a reflection of the relative importance of index-ation influenced outlays is given on p. 8, while the impact on demographic factors is evaluated on pp. 17–18.

12 See C.V. Brown and P. M. Jackson, *Public Sector Economics* (Oxford: Martin Robertson, 1986), ch. 5, esp. pp. 104–14; K.V. Greene and V.G. Munley, "Generating Growth in Public Expenditures: The Role of Employee and Constituent Demand", *Public Finance Quarterly*, vol. 7, no. 1, January 1979, pp. 92–109; Saunders and Klau, *The Role of the Public Sector*, op.cit., pp. 114–18.

13 Saunders and Klau, *The Role of the Public Sector*, ibid.

14 E. Barone, "On Public Needs", in R.A. Musgrave and A.T. Peacock (eds.), *Classics in the Theory of Public Finance*, p. 165.

15 Colin Clark, "Public Finance and Changes in the Value of Money", *Economic Journal*, vol. 55, December 1945, pp. 371–89. The quotation comes from p. 380.

16 The Australian data are from 1988–89 Budget Paper No. 1, Budget Statements 1988–89, Statement No. 7; the OECD data from *Revenue Statistics of Member Countries 1965–1986* (Paris: OECD, 1987). See also EPAC Council Paper No. 4, *The Size of Government and Economic Performance — International Comparisons* (Canberra: EPAC, 1985).

17 Robert Bacon and Walter Eltis, *Britain's Economic Problem: Too Few Producers* (London: Macmillan, 1976), especially ch. 5. The subsequent three paragraphs provide a brief summary and critique of their interesting argument.

18 See Michael Keating and Geoff Dixon, *Making Economic Policy in Australia* (Melbourne: Longman Cheshire, 1989), ch. 2, esp. pp. 17–19.

19 EPAC Council Paper No. 5, *Public Sector Expenditure in Australia* (Canberra: EPAC, October 1985), pp. 7–8 and Table 1.

20 For a detailed historical discussion of public sector growth up to the early 1980s, see A. Barnard, N.G. Butlin and J.J. Pincus, *Government and Capitalism* (Sydney: George Allen and Unwin, 1982), and P.D. Groenewegen, *Problems and Prospects of Public Sector in Australia* (Canberra: Centre for Research on Federal Financial Relations, 1983), Occasional Paper no. 27, esp. pp. 10–20. For more recent statistical analysis, see EPAC Council Paper No. 5 (referred to in Note 18); EPAC Council Paper No. 17, *Growth in Australian Social Expenditures* (Canberra: EPAC, March 1986) and 1988–89 Budget Paper No. 1, Budget Statements 1988–89, Statements No. 6, 7.

21 OECD, *Revenue Statistics of Member Countries 1975–1986* (Paris: OECD, 1987), Tables 1 and 2.

22 P. Saunders, "Understanding Government Expenditure, Trends in OECD Countries and their Implications for Australia", *Australian Quarterly*, Autumn 1987, pp. 34–43.

FURTHER READING

Comparative public sector growth experience in Australia, the United States and the United Kingdom, can be studied by referring to other major texts:

R.A. and P.B. Musgrave, *Public Finance in Theory and Practice*, 4th edn. (New York, McGraw Hill, 1984), ch. 7.

Joseph Stiglitz, *Public Sector Economics*, 2nd edn. (New York: W.W. Norton, 1988), pp. 41–6.

C.V. Brown and P.M. Jackson, *Public Sector Economics*, 3rd edn. (Oxford: Blackwells, 1986), ch. 6.

A detailed historical study of the role of the public sector in Australia in the twentieth century is:

N.G. Butlin, A. Barnard and J. J. Pincus, *Government and Capitalism* (Sydney: Allen and Unwin, 1982), esp. Part 1, introduction.

An exhaustive survey of the quantitative evidence with a useful bibliography is:

Jack Diamond and Alan A. Tait, "The Growth of Government Expenditure: A Review of Quantitative Analysis", *IMF Working Paper* 88/17, Washington, February 1988.

4

The pure theory of public expenditure

In Chapter 1 public goods were defined in terms of the characteristics which distinguished them from private, marketable goods. The basis for this distinction was the exclusion principle and the degree of rivalness in their consumption. Pure public goods are completely non-rival in consumption and are perfectly non-excludable, hence a polar case in the classification of goods exploited in theories of public expenditure of the type to be examined in this chapter. In other words, this chapter looks at the implications of public goods for economic theory by examining several of the approaches used by economists to explain the determination of public goods supply. These range from the voluntary exchange or supply and demand models of public finance which were already mentioned in Chapter 1, to models more specifically designed to address the optimality conditions in resource allocation decision-making with respect to public goods relying on the tools of modern welfare economics. They also include theories of social choice, which have evolved as solutions to problems arising from applications to Pareto optimality to public expenditure decision-making.

Several aspects of public expenditure analysis were raised in the subsequent two chapters. Chapter 2 examined the functional classification of public expenditure and set it within the framework of federalism, the framework in which public expenditure decisions in Australia are made. Examination of the pure theory of local public goods is postponed, however, to Chapter 14. The discussion of public sector growth in Chapter 3 placed public expenditure in a dynamic setting and raised issues of limits on public sector size which supplement those presented in this chapter. Finally, the introductory chapter also stressed the state-theoretic considerations on which public expenditure theories are inevitably based, thereby drawing attention to the limitations of much of the theorising in this area of public finance.

A SEQUENTIAL VIEW OF PUBLIC EXPENDITURE DECISIONS

The issues involved in public expenditure analysis can be briefly described by listing four separate aspects of the public expenditure decision-making process. Following Steiner[1], these can be summarised as follows. Decisions have to be made about:

1. The *total level* of public expenditure.
2. The *relative size* of the major programs of public expenditure, such as defence, welfare, health, and education.
3. The set of specific projects which will constitute a *program* (and the necessary counterpart of the rejection or postponement of other projects).
4. The designs of accepted projects which are to be implemented, and the alternative designs which must be rejected or postponed.

It is convenient to investigate these inter-related decisions *as if* they were made separately; the theory and practice of the decision-making process for each of them will be analysed, as well as the practical constraints under which they operate. In this manner, the theory of public expenditure in general and its more particular aspects, such as cost/benefit analysis and planning-programming-budgeting techniques, can be put into perspective. The first two phases of this sequence are examined in this chapter, the other two in Chapter 5.

THE TOTAL LEVEL OF PUBLIC EXPENDITURE

This first aspect of the problem has received a great deal of attention in the theories of public expenditure put forward by economists, especially in the post-war period. As already indicated there have been three types of theoretical models of overall Budget determination in the literature: the voluntary exchange models, the maximum welfare models, and the models which determine the optimum size of the Budget through an analysis of the voting process.[2] In addition, and with particular reference to the problem of inflation, there have been arguments presented about the optimum size of aggregate public expenditure relative to GDP, the most famous of which was presented by the Australian economist Colin Clark, as discussed in Chapter 3.

The voluntary exchange models utilise the tools and concepts of the micro-economics of the private market in their solution to the problem of optimum Budget determination. Broadly speaking, they pose this problem in the following way: the private, competitive market promises efficiency in production and exchange; hence, if market criteria can be applied to the public sector, efficiency, in the sense of maximum public satisfaction at minimum cost, may be achieved in the sphere of government-provided goods and services. The supply and demand apparatus is applied to the public sector in the following way: the demand for public goods comes from the individual members of the public — either directly or through their elected representatives — and is expressed by their willingness to pay a price in the form of taxation for a certain quantity of these goods. The total supply of public goods will then be determined by the public demand for them as measured by what contribution to the cost of that supply they are willing to bear. The determination of the Budget is therefore a special case of the theory of exchange: it is the voluntary exchange of resources given up by individuals in the form of taxes in return for a supply of goods and services offered by the government. Given the supply functions of the public goods, as based on the cost of providing the goods in question, and the demand schedules of the public suitably aggregated, the equilibrium Budget is determined at the intersection of supply and demand. Many theories derived from these simple propositions — but with considerably greater sophistication — have been put forward.[3] One of the most prominent of these theories — Samuelson's pure theory of public expenditure — is examined in more detail.

An exposition of Samuelson's pure theory

Samuelson's "pure theory of public expenditure" is based on the voluntary exchange approach to Budget determination.[4] This analysis of public expenditure was carried out initially by Samuelson to fill a gap in his general equilibrium analysis in his *Foundations of Economic Analysis*, which largely ignored the role of the State, but it provides only a starting-point in which private and public want satisfaction are strongly distinguished. This approach is defended on the ground that doctrinal history shows that theoretical insights often come from considering strong or extreme cases. Furthermore, this approach, although based on highly unrealistic assumptions, emphasises some generally valid points about the nature of public want satisfaction. In what follows, only the much simpler geometrical version of the theory will be discussed, because it is spelt out in more detail, is easier to understand, and makes exactly the same points as the more general algebraic solution published earlier by Samuelson.

Assumptions

Assume that there are two goods — a private good and a collective good — and two individuals (or groups of individuals), A and B. If X_1 is the total supply of the private good, X^A_1 and X^B_1 the respective consumption of persons A and B, it can be said that the total supply equals the sum of the separate consumption, i.e. $X_1=X^A_1+X^B_1$. This implies the usual characteristics of pure private goods, that is, divisibility of supply and demand, and the fact that an increase in the consumption of person A means a reduction in the consumption of person B, given the supply of X_1. (Consumption is rival.) The supply of X_1 can, of course, be varied.

A public good, X_2 is also available (in a variable supply). It differs from the private good in that each person's consumption is related to the supply of the public good by a condition of equality rather than a condition of summation. That is, $X_2=X^A_2=X^B_2$. This implies the usual characteristic of a collective public good, that is, consumption is non-rival, or the want satisfaction of person A is not influenced by that of person B, given the supply.

The diagrammatic exposition

The first three figures posit the relevant information relating to the tastes of persons A and B (Figures 4.1 and 4.2) and the technical possibilities in the economy relating to the production of the public and private good, given the stock of resources (Figure 4.3).

The difference in slope of the indifference curves on the two indifference maps indicates different preferences of the two individuals. Person A has a relatively greater preference for public goods than person B, so that they can be taken as representative individuals reflecting community tastes. In Figure 4.3, AB is the production possibility curve drawn on the usual assumption of increasing relative marginal costs or generalised diminishing returns.

Because of the nature of the public good, Figures 4.1 to 4.3 are not independent but must be lined up with the same horizontal scale. A supply of public goods in any one diagram determines the supply of the public good in the other two diagrams, since by definition, $X_2 = X^A{}_2 = X^B{}_2$ (that is, OM in Figures 4.1 to 4.3). Furthermore, once X_2 is determined, with the given technical possibilities posited in the shape of the production possibilities curve (AB in Figure 4.3), X_1 is determined. Variations can, of course, occur in the distribution of X_1 between A and B, that is, in $X^A{}_1$ and $X^B{}_1$ without violating the condition, $X_1 = X^A{}_1 + X^B{}_1$. This brings aspects of income distribution implicitly into the diagram.

The necessary efficiency (Pareto optimal) condition is obtained in the following manner. Select a position for person B anywhere on his indifference map, say E_2 on the indifference curve CD in Figure 4.2. What is the highest possible indifference curve which person A can reach? To obtain the solution, copy the indifference curve CD of person B on Figure 4.3 (shown as C'D'), subtract C'D' vertically from AB, and plot the algebraic result (cd) on Figure 4.2. Person A is best off where cd is tangential to the highest possible indifference curve, that is, U_1' at point E_1. (It should not have to be pointed out that at point E (Figure 4.3), E_1 (Figure 4.1) and E_2 (Figure 4.2), the characteristics defining X_1 and X_2 are satisfied, that is, $X_1 = EM = X^A{}_1 + X^B{}_1 = E_1M + E_2M$ and $X_2 = X^A{}_2 = X^B{}_2 = OM$.)

The same procedure can be carried out with points G, G_1 and G_2, which yields a large public goods supply and a different distribution of the private good X_1 among A and B. If points E_1 and E_2 are compared with G_1 and G_2 respectively, it can definitely be said that at the G points, A is better off than at the E points, and vice versa for B. (At G_1 person A is on a higher indifference curve than at point E_1, while the opposite applies to B). It is also clear that both E and G points are Pareto optimal positions. It cannot therefore be concluded that E is better or worse than G without engaging in interpersonal comparisons of utility.

Because there is an infinite number of positions where A or B can be placed on their indifference maps and then the best possible situation calculated for the other person, there are also an infinite number of Pareto optimal positions among which no choice can be made without introducing normative considerations through interpersonal comparisons of utility. The analysis therefore does not provide a solution to the problem of Budget determination because there are an infinite number of Pareto optimal Budget outcomes.

The optimum Budget allocation in the model

Figure 4.4 provides the additional (normative) information which allows a unique Budget determination. It is derived partly from the information contained in Figures 4.1 to 4.3 since pp is the utility frontier constructed from all the possible Pareto optima (with the E, G positions indicated as e and g). The shaded area contains the non-Pareto optima which are rejected as inefficient solutions. The shape of the pp utility frontier reflects the conflict possibilities of any contract locus of Pareto optima in the sense that as you move from left to right (right to left) along the curve, the position of person B (person A) continually worsens, the social welfare function (U', U", U"') provides the means to obtain a unique Budget determination by the usual tangency condition. The optimum optimorum (the optimum of the Pareto optima) is given at point g, where pp is tangential to U", the highest possible social welfare contour. This unique solution is artificial in the sense that an objective welfare function can never be found; if the social welfare function had a different shape it could easily have been tangential at e, the better position for person B.

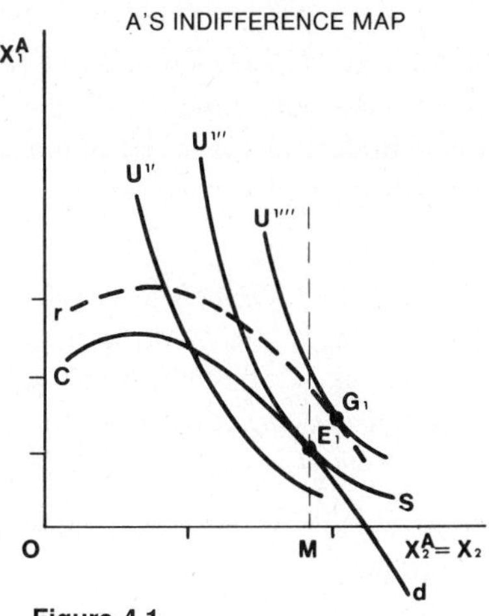

Figure 4.1

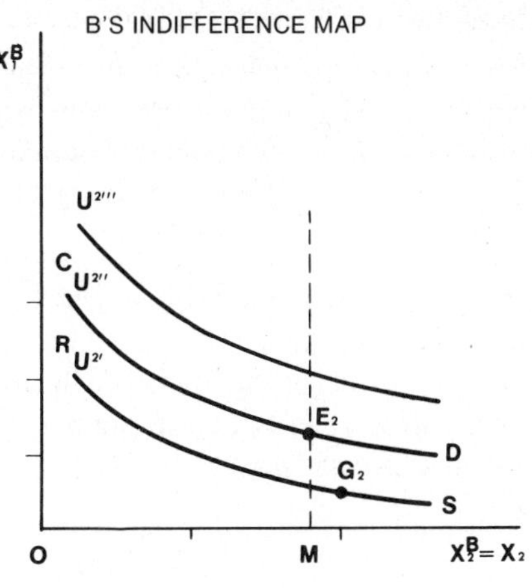

Figure 4.2

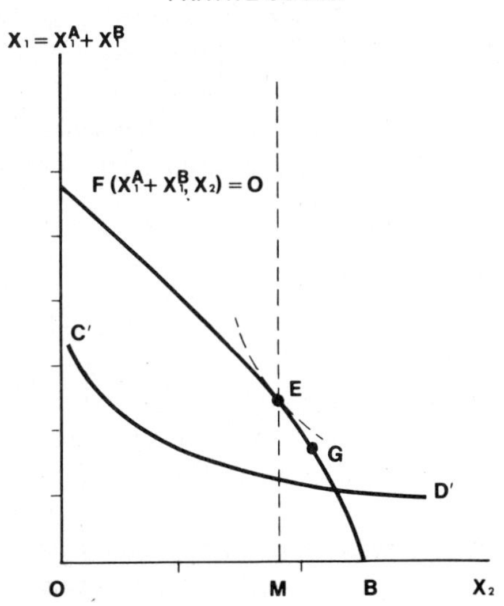

Figure 4.3

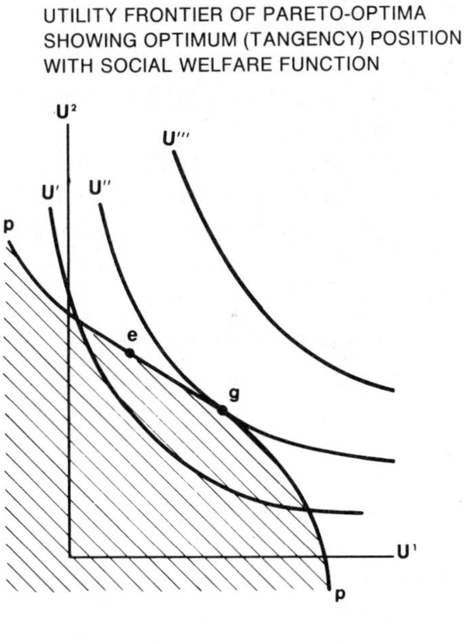

UTILITY FRONTIER OF PARETO-OPTIMA SHOWING OPTIMUM (TANGENCY) POSITION WITH SOCIAL WELFARE FUNCTION

Figure 4.4

Figures 4.1 - 4.4 Geometrical exposition of Samuelson's theory of public expenditure

Source: P. A. Samuelson, "Diagrammatic Exposition of a theory of Public Expendutuure", *Review of Economics and Statistics*, vol. 37 (1955), pp. 350–6. (Reproduced with kind permission of the author.)

Some conclusions from the model

Samuelson's major conclusion from his theory is as follows: "No decentralised pricing system can serve to determine optimally the levels of collective consumption . . .", that is, a free market pricing system, cannot determine an optimum Budget allocation. He continues, in criticism of the voting school of Budget determination (a theory discussed subsequently in this chapter):

> Utopian voting and signalling schemes can be imagined . . . But there is still this fundamental technical difference going to the heart of the whole problem of social economy: by departing from his indoctrinated rules, any one person can hope to snatch some selfish benefit in a way not possible under the self-policing competitive pricing system of private goods.[5]

In other words, the "free rider" problem makes it impossible to have a "grand optimising solution" in the nature of private market general equilibrium.

Other useful conclusions are derivable from the Samuelson model. In the first place, it clearly illustrates the normative aspect of optimum Budget determination: a *positive* solution to the problem of Budget determination is impossible. Secondly, it illustrates the strong possibility of conflict in Budget determination when there are two classes of society with sharply differing preferences for public as against private goods. This point is reflected in the shape of the pp curve in Figure 4.4; it emphasises the point that Budget determination in the final analysis is a political process which tries to resolve in a more or less fair manner, the conflicting interests of various groups. Finally, the theory indicates that benefit taxation (which is discussed and fully defined in Chapter 7) cannot be used to obtain a solution to Budget determination. These are useful results because they emphasise that in much of the discussion of public finance, the economic questions asked generally have political answers. (Or is it that economists cannot provide answers to political questions?)

Criticism of the theory

Much of the philosophical foundation of this type of theory was criticised by Myrdal in the 1930s,[6] and in the short discussion of the theory of the State, which was given in Chapter 1. Samuelson's model is based on the liberal political philosophy of the State where the demands for public goods are no more and no less than the sum of the individual demands for public goods. There is no room for government or State-initiated demands for the provision of public goods and services, while, as was indicated in Chapter 3, both the government bureaucracy and the politicians can generate demands for public goods in their own interests. In Samuelson's theory, the whole analysis is conducted in terms of consuming households; others[7] have tried to develop a theory of government expenditure in which the four parties to the expenditure decision-making process (that is, government, public servants, private consumers, and private producers) all interact.

The polar nature of the model is another important weakness. The analysis is conducted in terms of pure public and pure private goods; in practice, most goods, whether publicly or privately provided, have both public and private goods characteristics. If real goods were introduced, the model could not work. It was also indicated earlier (in Chapter 1) that merit goods, a very important item in modern budgets, cannot be fitted into the theory unless room is made for a third interest group, the legislators, whose interests in some respects differ from those of some of the citizens in the State.

A further limitation of the voluntary exchange approach is that within the framework of this type of analysis, expenditure must always equal taxation, so that stabilisation functions of the Budget are automatically excluded. The analysis also provides little scope for distributional consideration in the process of Budget determination. This aspect of optimal budget determination theory fits uneasily with the theory of fiscal federalism as well. In most federations, and Australia is no exception, national governments have revenue in excess of their own expenditure needs, while state governments have revenue sources inadequate for the expenditure responsibilities assigned to them. This problem of vertical fiscal imbalance is examined in Chapters 14-16. In spite of such shortcomings, voluntary exchange theories have some use: they serve as a constant reminder that public goods are not free goods, that is, that they must be paid for through taxation. They also emphasise the need for resource allocation efficiency in Budget decision-making.

THE MAXIMUM WELFARE APPROACH

A brief account of the maximum welfare approach is now considered. This theory is based on two simple propositions. First, resources should be distributed among different public uses so as to equalise the marginal return of satisfaction for each type of outlay; second, public expenditure should be taken to the point where the satisfaction obtained from the last dollar spent is equal to the satisfaction lost from the last dollar taken in taxes, thereby equalising the marginal satisfaction derived in the public and private sectors. This model is illustrated in Figure 4.5.

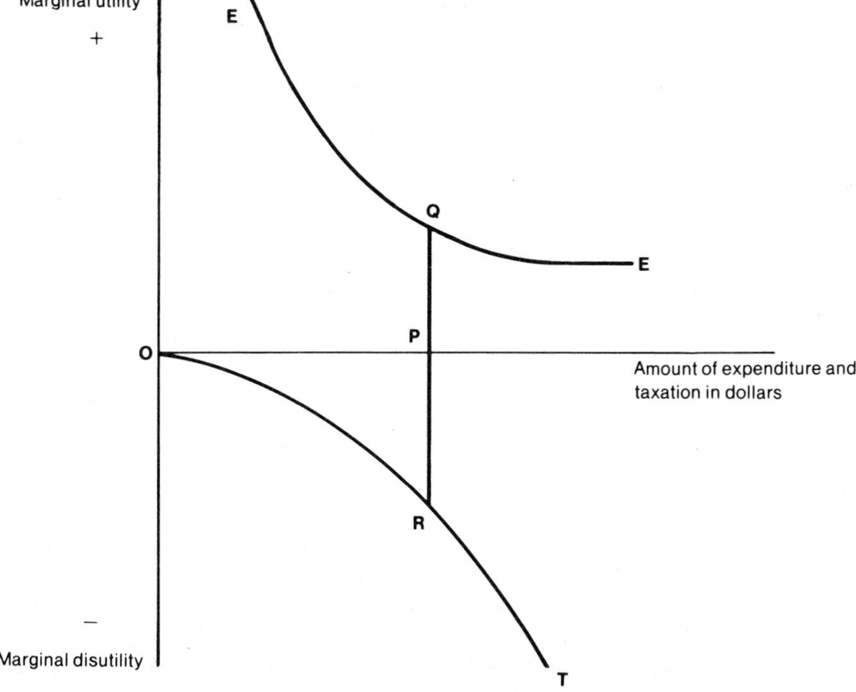

Figure 4.5 The maximum welfare approach to budget determination

The size of the Budget in dollars is measured on the horizontal axis, the marginal utility of public expenditure (positive) and the marginal disutility (negative) of taxation are measured on the vertical axis. EE shows the declining utility of successive dollars of public expenditure on the assumption that each dollar is optimally allocated within the public sector, while OT shows the rising disutility of each additional dollar taken in taxes, imposed to cause least total sacrifice by individual taxpayers. The optimum Budget (OP dollars) is determined when the marginal utility (QP) of OP dollars in public expenditure equals the marginal disutility (PR) of OP dollars taken in taxes. The neatness of the diagram obscures the great difficulties inherent in the construction of both the OT and EE curves.[8] At best, it reiterates the interdependence of taxation and expenditure decisions, and the fact that allocational efficiency is important in budgetary planning. In determining the *total level* of public expenditure, economic theory has still little to offer.

What about the actual determination of the budgetary aggregates? At the end of Chapter 2, in the discussion of the annual Budget cycle, it was indicated that the actual process of Budget determination involves bids for resources made by departments in their preliminary expenditure estimates for the coming financial year. The Treasury, the officials of the Finance Department, and the Cabinet, scrutinise these estimates separately and in aggregate in the light of current economic as well as political circumstances.

Much of the expenditure embodied in these estimates is predetermined by commitments enacted in existing legislation; for example, existing social welfare legislation and the promise to adjust many cash social security benefits regularly according to movements in the Consumer Price Index (CPI) determine the expenditure with respect to social security benefits for those entitled to them. There are also contractual obligations which make much public expenditure unavoidable: interest must be paid on the public debt; wages and salaries must be paid to public servants who have permanent positions and who cannot therefore be easily dismissed if it is decided to abandon a program or abolish a department. Finally, as the beneficiaries of much existing public expenditure have a strong vested interest in its continuation, this creates a powerful political constraint on the removal of such expenditure; for example, subsidies or concessions to industry groups, to the arts, expenditure on health and education, and so on.

In general, it can therefore be said that control can only be exercised over *new areas* of expenditure, unless a conscious decision has been made to review and repeal legislation in order to reduce or remove past spending commitments. The absolute cutbacks in spending which can be effected by such committees are marginal; their impact is upon the future growth rate of government spending and upon the share of GDP absorbed by the government.[9]

There are two further constraints on the overall size of the Budget. The first of these is its impact on the stability of the economy, that is, on objectives such as full employment and sustainable rates of growth. These issues are explored in Chapter 18. Second, ideological and political fears about a threat from vastly increased government expenditure to the viability of the private sector may mean that the overall size of the Budget becomes an important objective of government policy in itself. As a result of the relatively poor performance of the Australian economy in the 1970s which coincided with the substantial public sector growth during the period of the Whitlam Labor government of 1972–75 (see Chapter 3), many economists and even more politicians argued that the huge transfer of resources from the private sector which this growth of public expenditure implied, was the cause of the poor growth performance of the private sector and therefore of the recession and its accompanying unemployment. This issue is further explored in Chapter 20.

THE RELATIVE SIZE OF THE BUDGET PROGRAMS

The second phase of the sequential expenditure-decision model — the relative size of the major Budget program — may be approached by examining the departmental estimates, which show the amount of resources required for carrying out their functions (Budget outlays classification by portfolio) or, as available from the early 1970s, outlays by function. The last is of much greater interest, as it allows the identification of resources allocated by broad program either in monetary terms, or, by staff resources devoted to their achievement. Outlays by functional classification or portfolio classification can also be subdivided by economic type, that is, with respect to its components in terms of expenditure on goods and services, transfer payments, including personal benefits payments, interest and inter-governmental transfers, asset sales and so on.[10] Outlays on specific programs relative to total federal outlays for selected years from 1965–66 to 1988–89 are shown in Table 4.1.

Table 4.1 Outlays on specific programs as a percentage of total Federal outlays, selected years from 1965–66 to 1988–89 (estimated)

	1965–66 %	1970–71 %	1975–76 %	1980–81 %	1983–84 %	1988–89 %
Defence	14.1	13.5	8.5	9.8	9.3	9.3
Education	2.3	3.7	8.7	8.1	7.4	7.6
Health	6.2	6.9	13.5	10.1	7.6	13.1
Social security and welfare	18.6	17.0	23.0	27.3	29.7	28.7
Urban and regional development and the environment	0.3	0.4	1.9	0.3	0.3	0.2
Housing	3.6	2.5	2.6	0.9	1.6	1.5
Culture and recreation	1.1	1.1	1.2	1.1	1.1	1.3
Economic services	14.1	14.7	9.4	6.5	7.3	6.1

Source: Budget Speech 1975–76, p. 132; Budget Speech 1977–78, p. 164 Budget Statements 1982–83, p.330; Budget Statements 1983-84, p. 72; Budget Statements 1988–89, pp. 69, 181.

Economic theory has little to offer on this topic except for the general rule, made explicit in the maximum welfare model which was discussed earlier in this chapter, that the degree of social satisfaction derived from the last dollar spent on each function should be equal for all these functions. But how can an objective comparison be made between the satisfaction obtained from the last dollar spent on defence and that spent say, on culture and recreation?

It is much more realistic to say that the allocational priorities implicit in Table 4.1 were largely determined by the past commitments of ongoing expenditure, together with the political and social judgements of the ruling political party.

That these priorities can be substantially varied by changes in the political complexion of the government is also illustrated in Table 4.1. The first two periods shown in this table reflect the priorities of Liberal-Country Party governments, the third those of the last Budget of the Whitlam Labor government, the fourth the priorities of the Fraser-Liberal-National Party coalition in office from 1975 to 1983. The final two columns show expenditure estimates of the first Hawke government Budget, and its most recent Budget available at the time of writing, that of 1988–89.

As indicated by relative spending levels, the Whitlam Labor government favoured health (the introduction of Medibank in 1975), urban and regional development, education, and social security and welfare at the expense of defence spending and expenditure on economic services. The return of a non-Labor government in 1975 altered this public expenditure pattern considerably. Spending on housing and on urban and regional development was decimated, that on health and education reduced, the beneficiaries being defence and social security and welfare. Defence however has not been restored to its pre-Whitlam (and Vietnam War) importance, and a substantial part of the relative increase in social security spending is explained by the replacement of child endowment and child dependent rebates for income tax by family allowances in 1976. The Hawke government followed the Whitlam government in devoting much more resources to health (Medicare) and housing, but it followed its conservative predecessors in giving low spending priorities to urban and regional development and the environment, as well as to economic services.[11]

The relative size of the major Budget programs depends then on the priorities assigned to them by the government in office, on the vigour with which particular programs are supported by individual ministers and individual departments, which implies that public servants are also strongly involved in this decision-making process. The mechanism through which these individual decisions are made is complex and influenced by particular circumstances. Important general factors which influence it are the political platform of the government in office, particularly as translated into a policy speech for electoral purposes, the forcefulness of departments and of their ministerial and permanent heads in the Budget deliberations in Cabinet, and sometimes the influence of backbenchers in the party room. In programs such as industry assistance, the role of specific industry lobbies and pressure groups is often influential. For other programs, such as health and education, organised occupational groups and groups within the public service will exert pressure of a more subtle kind; for example, seeking to identify the general public interest with expanded programs in an area where they have a special interest. This last point is further examined in Chapter 5.

One further aspect of this stage in the sequential expenditure-decision model must be commented on. This is the use and role of special commissions in the Australian Budget process. The best way to examine this is to look at how the major programs are subdivided in the Budget, the details of which are provided in the statements appended to the Budget Speech. Consider, for example, the subdivision of the cultural and recreational program; much of this spending is appropriated by the Australian Broadcasting Corporation, the Australia Council, and the Australian Heritage Commission. Until their abolition in 1987 much Budget spending on education was based on recommendations by the Tertiary Education Commission and Schools Commission. Such commissions, once they receive their Budget allocation, can use it with a substantial degree of independence in pursuit of the purposes for which they are established by statute.

This widespread use of commissions means that many *detailed* expenditure decisions are taken outside the sphere of government departments. This procedure is justified as follows. In the first place, by appointing experts to the particular commissions, resource allocation can be assumed to increase in efficiency, since these experts would be familiar with the major problems and needs in the area of public service over which their commission has jurisdiction. Secondly, the independent status of the commissioners would result in a minimum amount of political interference in the administrative and allocational decision-making process in their area of responsibility, which was felt to be particularly desirable in fields such as broadcasting, education, and government financial assistance to industry and the arts. Whether these desirable objectives are always realised in practice is a different matter.

The commissions are independent spending decision-makers but are constrained by the allocation of funds contained in the general appropriation made for their function in the Budget. In addition, their action is sometimes curtailed by detailed guidelines as to the areas of spending within their field of responsibility. Furthermore, government exercises some control over their spending through the general requirement that they present an annual report on their activities to the investigatory powers of the Auditor-General and the Joint Commission of Public Accounts.

The role of these commissions in public expenditure decision-making in Australia emphasises the inadequacy of conventional public-expenditure theory (the voluntary exchange model, for example) which discusses only the elected representatives as translators of the people's demand for public goods. When the role of public servants in the actual decision-making process is taken into consideration, the picture presented by conventional theory becomes even less realistic. There is plenty of evidence that public servants exert tremendous influence on what programs should be proceeded with, what programs are, if possible, to be stopped, and what programs are to be starved of funds. This is not only because of political prejudices in the public servants concerned. The public service bureaucracy has a vested interest in the size and scope of programs, for reasons of power and prestige, as well as promotional opportunities and job security. The abolition of the federal education commissions in 1987 is explicable both in terms of the vested interests of the education bureaucracy in the new Department of Employment, Education and Training, and the political ambitions of its then Minister.

Social choice and fiscal politics

The problem stated

As indicated in this and earlier chapters, many of the theories of public expenditure attempt to deal with the problem of social or public choice in a manner analogous to choices in the market. In practice, public expenditure and more generally, Budget decisions, are made through voting in a democratic society. Since public finance by its very nature is therefore involved in political issues, some of the aspects of social choice seen as particularly relevant for public finance students are briefly investigated. These include problems of majority voting and other paradoxes arising from the theory of social choice. This section canvasses some of the more frequently encountered problems in social choice such as Arrow's famous impossibility theorem, areas of theoretical welfare economics which can therefore be seen as posing some interesting problems for the student of public finance.

Voting and Pareto optimality

In a comment on the Tiebout model of optimal local expenditure determination, Samuelson[12] demonstrated that in the rather trivial case of two boys, A and B, and two girls, 1 and 2, out of the four possible pairing outcomes derived from simple ordinal preference patterns only one is Pareto optimal. This set of combinations is Pareto optimal because its implementation would give all of the four their first choice so that none of them would be disadvantaged by this outcome. Samuelson adds that this set of combinations would also be Bergson-optimal[13] that is, would maximise any social welfare function respecting individual tastes. The optimal outcome is the situation where A prefers 1 and B prefers 2, while 1 prefers A and 2 prefers B. Two other possible cases, for example those where the two girls both prefer the same boy and the two boys both prefer the same girl, would not yield Pareto optimal outcomes, nor would the case of perfect unrequited love where A prefers 1 and B prefers 2, but 2 prefers A and 1 prefers B.

Take further the case where 1 and 2 both prefer A, and A and B both prefer 1. A and 1 who are agreed in their preferences will presumably pair off, leaving 2 and B to make their own arrangements. However, whether this is an optimal outcome depends on other considerations. For example, 2 may have an enormous preference for A while 1 is almost, but not quite, indifferent to choosing between A and B. With cardinal utilities (discussed briefly later under the heading of point voting) this would make the combinations of 1 and B plus 1 and A a superior outcome in terms of aggregate social welfare. Samuelson concludes this simple analysis of the mathematics of marriage with the following important finding: "there remain many important analytical problems of public good determination that still need investigation at every level of government".[14] Even *revealed* preferences do not invariably produce optimum outcomes in social choices.

Resolution of social choices through the political process

The dilemmas in obtaining satisfactory outcomes from preference orderings in social choices, inherent even in Samuelson's simple example which has just been examined, are in practice solved by the political process. Except for the few cases where all citizens still have the right to directly participate in local decision-making (preserved in some New England towns in the United States and in some Swiss local communities), public expenditure decisions are made indirectly by political representatives elected by the people, or, as occurs more frequently in practice, by their advisors in the public service. As indicated in Chapter 1, this considerably complicates public expenditure analysis based on individual preferences since it can now be argued that the supply of public goods is no longer solely determined by the preference patterns of the potential consumers. Public goods supply is now shown to be influenced, at least in principle, by the preference patterns of possibly three additional parties to the public expenditure decision-making process. As already suggested on a number of occasions in this chapter, public expenditure determination in practice involves:

1. *the politicians*, whose preferences for public goods are partly influenced at least by their desire to get re-elected;
2. *the bureaucrats*, whose preferences for public goods are partly influenced by their own promotion opportunities, power-seeking through empire-building and so on;
3. *producers of public goods in the private sector* who have an interest in extending public expenditure if it means substantial and profitable contracts;

as well as the consumers of the public service, on which traditional analysis has focused.

From this wider perspective, the public choice theories based on analogies with the perfectly competitive private market start to break down since the division of benefits from public goods provision is very much different from the appropriation of benefits from private goods. (In the context of the incidence of public expenditure, this is discussed in Chapter 5.)

Majority voting, peaked preferences and Arrow's impossibility theorem

The political process, including that in Australia, in practice reconciles the many possible conflicting preferences on public goods supply through majority voting. However, in the context of the notion of Pareto efficiency which underlies the mainstream discussion of public expenditure determination (recall the Samuelson theory discussed earlier in this chapter) majority voting can give rise to many non-Pareto efficient outcomes. For example, Wicksell's important analysis of justice in taxation, which has been referred to on a number of occasions, implied that only his unanimity rule of voting would ensure Pareto optimality since anyone who expected to be worse off in the proposed public expenditure program would vote against it and thereby veto it. In small committees and small communities, unanimity can generally be ensured through compromise and bargaining but in modern government, even that of small municipalities, unanimity would often be difficult if not impossible to achieve. It would also be very time- consuming and therefore costly so that majority voting, although not Pareto-efficient, is probably the most cost-efficient of the various ways of collective decision-making.

The development of an alternative set of rules which transform individual preferences into ethically acceptable social choices was attempted by Arrow.[15] In this analysis, he developed a set of five assumptions or necessary conditions on which to base an internally locally consistent constitution into social choices. These five necessary conditions are summarised as follows:

1. *The assumptions to secure rational choices.* The necessary social choice rule must produce a social ordering which is complete and transitive. Completeness here refers to preference or indifference being expressed for each pair of alternative social states; transitivity requires that if X is preferred to Y, and Y to Z, then X is of necessity preferred to Z.
2. *Independence of irrelevant alternatives.* This condition requires that social choice depends only on the ordering of the alternatives by individuals and not on anything else. This means that preferences by some ruling élite are excluded and that the individual preferences transformed into social choices only relate to the same alternatives.
3. *The Pareto principle.* If every individual prefers X to Y, then social choice must prefer X to Y. Secondly, if one person prefers X to Y and all others are indifferent between X and Y, then a social choice must prefer X to Y.

4. *The condition of an unrestricted domain.* Social ordering must be produced in such a way that the domain from which it is derived includes all logically possible individual orderings. No social ordering can be generated which effectively restricts the domain of individual orderings. This condition ensures that the social choice is a genuine transformation of individual choices.
5. *Non-dictatorship.* This condition excludes the possibility of the presence of an individual "I" who by preferring X to Y thereby determines the social choice of preferring X to Y irrespective of all the other individual preferences in society.

When Arrow combined these five conditions for the transformation of individual choices into social choice, he derived both his possibility and his impossibility theorems. Take first his impossibility theorem. This states that in combination, the five conditions involve a logical contradiction which can be expressed as follows. Condition 5 of non-dictatorship postulates that no individual preference shall be decisive; the second implication of the Pareto principle stated (condition 3) suggests one possibility in which one individual preference is decisive. Arrow's possibility theorem puts this matter in another way. It indicates that

> . . . if we exclude the possibility of interpersonal comparisons of utility, then the only method of passing from individual tastes to social preferences which will be satisfactory and which will be defined for a wide range of sets of individual orderings are either imposed or dictatorial.[16]

Put differently, the possibility theorem suggests that majority voting is not a satisfactory way to translate individual preferences into social choices unless these preferences can be expressed in terms of cardinal utility, that is, by the explicit introduction of interpersonal comparisons of utility. Only in this way can consistent social choices arise in a non-dictatorial manner.

Peaked preference and the voting paradox

Part of this dilemma in majority voting can be illustrated by the Condorcet voting paradox named after the French mathematician and philosopher who discovered it in the eighteenth century. This example examined the preference patterns of three voters, A, B and C choosing from three alternative policies 1, 2 and 3. The data of their preference patterns relevant to this paradox are given in Figure 4.6.

The first pattern of preferences, which (to use the term coined for this type of preference pattern) displays single-peaked preferences, yields a clear outcome from majority voting. Alternative 2 is clearly the majority social choice since it is twice preferred to both alternatives 1 and 3.

The second pattern of preferences, which is multiple-peaked, provides no clear social choice preferred by the majority opinion since no alternative scores a clear majority of preferences. Option 1 is twice preferred to option 2, option 2 is twice preferred to option 3, and option 3 is twice preferred to option 1. To revert back to the language of the first condition of Arrow's social choice analysis, the preference pattern in the second set of data is intransitive, since a majority of persons prefer alternative 1 over alternative 3 and vice versa. Intransitive preference patterns, it can be concluded in general, do not yield consistent social choices.

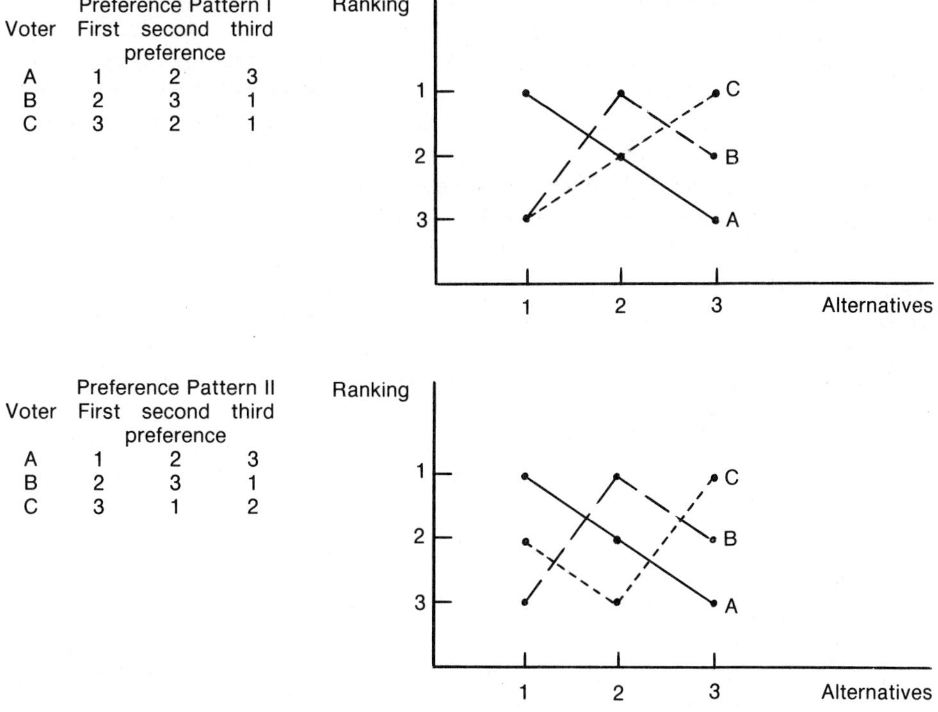

Preference Pattern I

Voter	First	second preference	third
A	1	2	3
B	2	3	1
C	3	2	1

Preference Pattern II

Voter	First	second preference	third
A	1	2	3
B	2	3	1
C	3	1	2

Figure 4.6 Peaked preferences and the voting paradox

Majority voting, plurality voting, and point voting

Intransitive or multiple-peaked preferences may not be very common in practice so that a non-satisfactory outcome in social decision-making is not a strong possibility. This is even more so when it is recalled that most parliamentary voting is in terms of a simple choice between supporting or voting against a particular proposal. More important, as Arrow's possibility theorem indicates, solutions can be obtained if preferences are weighted and then aggregated, a procedure which implies interpersonal comparisons of utility. The preference patterns are then no longer ordinally expressed but imply a cardinal ranking since that gives quantitative expression to the amount of utility expected to be derived by individual voters from the various alternatives. As indicated in the earlier example from Samuelson's mathematics of marriage, at least some deadlocks can be resolved in this fashion.

The voting paradox inherent in simple majority voting has led to the development of two alternative forms of voting. The first, plurality voting, assigns weights to the ranking by giving the first out of ten alternatives, for example, 9 points, the second 8 points and so on. When the vote has been completed, adding the total points gained in this manner by the various alternatives may yield a unique result. For example, applying the technique of plurality voting to the data in preference pattern 1 of Figure 4.6 gives the outcome of 4 points for alternative 2, 3 points to alternative 3 and 2 points for alternative 1, thereby confirming the outcome of simple majority voting. Applying plurality voting to the data in the second preference set once again yields no outcome, since all three alternatives end up with the same number of points.

A point system explicitly weights the alternatives by asking voters to assign a number of points from a total of say 10 points allotted to them. Summing these across the various choices, yields, generally speaking, a unique social choice. For example, if the three voters in the second set of preferences of Figure 4.6 had been asked to allocate a total of 10 points among the three alternatives, an outcome such as the following may have resulted. A is assumed to have such a strong preference for 1 that all 10 points are given to it, while B and C have less well-defined preferences for any particular one of the alternatives. They therefore assigned 5, 3 and 2 points to their respective preference listing. Alternative 1 in this case is the preferred social choice with 15 points, the other alternatives 2 and 3 gaining 7 and 8 points respectively.

This example illustrates the importance of strategies in voting on a number of alternatives by which individual voters can influence the outcome and achieve the one which they prefer. The key to the voting pattern, which made alternative 1 win in the example just given, was the first voter's inordinately strong support for it which gave no points whatsoever to the other alternatives. In point voting, tactical considerations may therefore lead voters to disguise their real preferences by voting in this manner for the option they prefer. If all three voters had followed this pattern of voting, the result would once again have been a deadlock since each of the three alternatives would have scored 10 points.

Median voter analysis and fiscal decision-making

Figure 4.6 also allows identification of the "median voter", who prefers the medium size program among the three alternatives, the preference which "wins" in the simpler voting systems outlined in the preceding section (that is, excluding the point system of voting where voting strategies can easily influence the outcomes away from median voter "wins"). Simple voting models based on median voter behaviour form the basis for many empirical studies of fiscal decision making. Their reliance on single-peaked preferences is applicable to cases of choice about the size of a public program where additional units of the program can be obtained at constant costs and the costs are shared among the three consumer/voters in equal lump sum tax amounts (poll taxes). More generally, the nature of fiscal choices is such that single-peaked preferences cannot readily be presumed, hence median voter models relying as they do on simple majority voting and single-peaked preferences, are flawed by this simplification when they form the basis for empirical work.[17]

An economic theory of democracy?

This kind of economic exposé on the social choice problems associated with public expenditure decision-making has given rise to a substantial literature on what is called the economic theory of democracy after its major originator.[18] Although this writing has close and important connections with the public finance literature on public spending in the sense that the latter inspired the former, this material is more closely related to the literature of political science and cannot be further pursued here. The discussion of this section has, however, reinforced the position taken in much of this book, namely that economics by itself cannot really provide complete answers to the problem of public finance. As shown in the discussion of the criteria for taxation in the next chapter, there are no precise answers to many social choice problems, unless the preferences are clearly specified in a quantitatively precise manner, that is, are assigned weights in a cardinal manner.

In short, the theories of public expenditure examined here although informative in a variety of ways, also entail considerable limitations. It seems unlikely that complete adequately economic solutions will ever be forthcoming, so what is required are supplementary politico-sociological discussions of public expenditure, which examine why some public goods are provided free of charge, why some are rationed, why some are made compulsory, and how their quantities are determined. Where possible, the economic consequences (for resource allocation, income distribution, stabilisation, and growth) of the resulting public expenditure patterns can then be analysed and discussed. This is *not* elegant pure theory, but it provides a realistic starting-point and foundation for the theoretical discussion of public expenditure. This procedure may also assist us to see whether we are consistent in our treatment of different types of expenditure.

SUMMARY

1. The sequential model of public expenditure decision-making examines the public expenditure decision-making process in the following four stages.

   i The total level of expenditure.
   ii The relative size of the major programs of public expenditure such as wealth, welfare, education, defence.
   iii The set of specific projects which will constitute a program.
   iv The design of accepted projects which are to be implemented and the alternative designs which must be rejected or postponed.

2. Three types of theoretical model attempt to explain overall Budget determination: the voluntary exchange model, the maximum welfare model and voting analyses of Budget determination.

3. The first of these develops efficiency conditions for public goods supply determination using the conventional micro-economic tools of indifference curves (consumer preferences) and production possibility frontiers (techniques of production). The nature of public goods and the free rider problem inherent in the provision of such goods requires an omniscient dictator (social welfare function) to solve the problem of optimal Budget allocation. The famous Samuelson public expenditure theory serves as a model illustration for this approach.

4. The model is criticised because

   i It fails to explicitly account for State-initiated projects or bureaucratic influence on the Budget process.
   ii It fails to deal with the non-polar cases of goods with both private and public goods characteristically.

iii It presumes a balanced Budget, hence ignoring stabilisation functions and the vertical fiscal imbalance possible in federations.

5. The maximum welfare model depicts optimum Budget outcomes in terms of equating benefits of outlays at the margin with their marginal tax costs, hence highlighting the optimum allocational rule of equalising benefits from all Budget outlays at the margin.

6. The maximum welfare model assists therefore also in explaining the relative size of individual Budget programs by its rule of equalising marginal benefits from each program.

7. Budget determination in practice involves social choice and voting procedures. Majority voting or other voting rules may imply difficulties for reaching Pareto optimal outcomes.

8. One of these difficulties is highlighted by Arrow's impossibility theorem which shows that the five conditions required for rational social choice involve a logical contradiction only resolved by the explicit introduction of inter-personal comparisons of utility.

9. This is illustrated by solutions to social decision-making problems from different voting rules, which shows point voting is generally required to overcome the voting paradox when intransitive preferences exist.

10. By-products of this analysis are median voter analysis in fiscal decision-making and development of an economic theory of democracy.

NOTES

[1] P.O.Steiner, "Public Expenditure Budgeting", in Alan S. Blinder and Robert M. Solow *et al.*, *The Economics of Public Finance* (Washington, D.C.: The Brookings Institution, 1974), p. 300.

[2] For a discussion of this literature, see R.A. Musgrave, *Theory of Public Finance* (New York: McGraw-Hill, 1959), pp. 73–89; 113–15, and ch. 6; more recent surveys of such theories are presented in Agnar Sandmo, "Public goods" in John Eatwell, Murray Milgate and Peter Newman (eds.), *The New Palgrave, A Dictionary of Economics*, (London: Macmillan, 1987), vol. 3, pp. 1061–6; William H. Oakland, "Theory of Public Goods", in Alan J. Auerbach and Martin Feldstein (eds.), *Handbook of Public Economics* (Amsterdam: North Holland, 1987), vol. 2, pp. 485–535. For useful textbook references, see R.A. and P.B. Musgrave, *Public Finance in Theory and Practice* (New York: McGraw Hill, 4th edn., 1984) chs. 3, 4 and 6; C.V. Brown and P.M. Jackson, *Public Sector Economics* (Oxford, Basil Blackwell, 3rd edn., 1986), chs. 3 and 4.

[3] For example, K. Wicksell, "A New Principle of Just Taxation", and Erik Lindahl, "Just Taxation — a Positive Solution", in R.A. Musgrave and A.T. Peacock (eds.), *Classics in the Theory of Public Finance* (London: Macmillan, 1958); James M. Buchanan, *The Demand and Supply of Public Goods* (Chicago: Rand McNally, 1968), and the articles by Samuelson referred to in Note 4 below.

[4] See P.A. Samuelson, "The Pure Theory of Public Expenditure", *Review of Economics and Statistics*, vol. 36 (1954), pp. 387–9, "Diagrammatic Exposition of a Theory of Public Expenditure", *Review of Economics and Statistics*, vol. 37 (1955), pp. 350–6; "Aspects of Public Expenditure Theories", *Review of Economics and Statistics*, vol. 40

(1958), pp. 332–8. These three articles are reprinted in R.W. Houghton, *Public Finance*, 2nd edn., Reading 9, pp. 181–5, 190–204, 218–31. See also P.A. Samuelson, "Pure Theory of Public Expenditure and Taxation", in J. Margolis and H. Guitton (eds.), *Public Economics* (London: Macmillan, 1969), rep. in R.W. Houghton (ed.), *Public Finance*, pp. 231–60. The first part of this section draws heavily on Samuelson's second article.

5 See P.A. Samuelson, "The Pure Theory of Public Expenditure", in R.W. Houghton (ed.), *Public Finance*, pp. 184–5.

6 See G. Myrdal, *The Political Element in the Development of Economic Theory*, ch. 7.

7 R. Bartlett, *Economic Foundations of Political Power* (New York: The Free Press, 1973). This aspect is discussed subsequently in this chapter in the context of social choice theory.

8 For a discussion of these difficulties see R.A. Musgrave, *The Theory of Public Finance*, pp. 114–15; C.V. Brown and P.M. Jackson, *Public Sector Economics*, p. 49.

9 For a discussion see EPAC Council Paper No. 4, "The Size of Government and Economic Performance — International Comparisons" (Canberra: EPAC, October 1985) and EPAC Council Paper No. 23, "Flexibility in Government Spending: Issues in Efficiency and Control" (Canberra: EPAC, November 1986).

10 For illustrations of these various classifications see Budget Paper No. 1, *Budget Statement 1988–89* (Canberra: AGPS 1988), pp. 77–85, 423–5.

11 A detailed discussion is provided in A. Patience and B. Head (eds.), *From Whitlam to Fraser* (Melbourne: Oxford University Press, 1979), esp. chs. 5–9; in R.B. Scotton and Helen Ferber (eds.), *Public Expenditure and Social Policy in Australia*, vol. I, "The Whitlam Years 1972–75", vol. II "The First Fraser Years 1976–78" (Melbourne: Longman Cheshire, 1978 (vol. I), 1980 (vol. II)); and in A. Patience and B. Head (eds.), *From Fraser to Hawke* (Melbourne: Longman Cheshire, 1989), esp. chs. 11–15.

12 P.A. Samuelson, "Aspects of Public Expenditure Theories", *Review of Economics and Statistics*, vol. 40, pp. 332–8, reprinted in R.W. Houghton (ed.), *Public Finance*, Penguin Modern Readings in Economics, 2nd edn. (Harmondsworth: Penguin, 1973), pp. 218–31, esp. pp. 228–31.

13 P.A. Samuelson, ibid., p. 230. The Bergson optimal situation refers to Bergson's famous "Reformulation of Certain Aspects of Welfare Economics", *Quarterly Journal of Economics* (52), 1938, pp. 310–34 reprinted in K.J. Arrow and T. Scitovsky (eds.), *Readings in Welfare Economics* (London: Allen & Unwin, 1969) pp. 7–25.

14 P.A. Samuelson, ibid., p. 231; this indicates that the free rider problem is not the only problem in theoretical public expenditure determination.

15 See K.J. Arrow, *Social Choice and Individual Values*, 2nd edn., (New Haven: Yale University Press, 2nd edn., 1951). A condensed version, "A Difficulty in the Concept of Social Welfare" appeared in the *Journal of Political Economy* (58), 1950, pp. 328–46, reprinted in Arrow and Scitovsky (eds.), *Readings in Welfare Economics*, pp. 147–68.

16 K.J. Arrow, ibid., p. 59.

17 There is now a substantial literature on this subject, which cannot be pursued here. Some preliminary discussion and further references are provided in R.A. and P.B. Musgrave, *Public Finance in Theory and Practice*, ch. 6, and C.V. Brown and P.M. Jackson, *Public Sector Economics*, ch. 4. An Australian investigation of the median voter in budget determination with special reference to tax policy is H.G. Brennan, "Taxation and Policy Change: A Median Voter Model for Australia 1968–69 to 1981–82", *Australian Economic Review*, 3/85, pp. 20–33.

18 See Anthony Downs, *An Economic Theory of Democracy* (New York: Harper and Row, 1957); Gordon Tullock, "Problems of Majority Voting", *Journal of Political Economy* (67), 1959, pp. 571–9; Duncan Black, "On the Rationale of Group Decision Making", *Journal of Political Economy* (56), 1958, pp. 23–4, both reprinted in Arrow and Scitovsky (eds.), *Readings in Welfare Economics*.

FURTHER READING

The standard texts all provide full elaboration of the contents of this chapter. See for example,

R.A. and P.B. Musgrave, *Public Finance in Theory and Practice*, 4th edn. (New York: McGraw Hill, 1984), chs. 3, 4, 6.

C.V. Brown and P.M. Jackson, *Public Sector Economics*, 3rd edn. (Oxford: Blackwells, 1986), chs. 3,4.

J.E. Stiglitz, *Economics of the Public Sector*, 2nd edn. (New York: W.W. Norton, 1988), chs. 5–7.

On the specific models and issues discussed in this chapter, students may also find the following reading helpful:

P.O. Steiner, "Public Expenditure Budgeting", in A.S. Blinder and R.M. Solow, et al., *The Economics of Public Finance* (Washington D.C.: The Brookings Institution, 1974), ch. 3, esp, pp. 241–310.

R.W. Houghton (ed.), *Public Finance*, 2nd edn. (Harmondsworth: Penguin Books, 1973), Reading 9, *A Pure Theory of Public Expenditure* which reprints the Samuelson Theory and important commentary literature.

More advanced reading is provided by:

William H. Oakland, "Theory of Public Goods" in A.J. Auerbach and M. Feldstein (eds.), *Handbook of Public Economics* (Amsterdam: North Holland, 1987), vol. 2, ch. 9.

5

Public expenditure evaluation and incidence

The third and fourth phases of the sequential public expenditure decision framework introduce a more limited but at the same time more practical aspect in public expenditure decision-making. It will be recalled from Chapter 4 that these two phases were concerned with two of the more specific aspects of public expenditure decisions. The first of these is associated with the set of specific projects which will constitute a program and, the essential counterpart of this choice, the rejection or postponement of other projects. The second phase to be discussed in this chapter, but the fourth and last of the sequential decision-making framework, concerns the design of accepted projects which are to be implemented and the alternative designs which must of necessity be rejected or postponed. Much of this chapter is therefore devoted to examination of choosing between alternatives by which government objectives can be achieved.

The limited *and* practical nature of the aspects of public expenditure evaluation to be canvassed in this chapter need to be addressed at the outset. Take first the practical nature. The concerns about growth of public expenditure and excessive public sector size expressed by what are by no means confined to conservative circles, have raised demands for ensuring that the substantial resources appropriated by government are effectively and efficiently used. A Report on the New South Wales State Finances focusing on financial reform stressed the need "to require cost benefit analysis of all major capital works" adding the requirement that resumes of such analyses should be published as part of the budget for capital works costing in excess of $50 million, and, in such cases where the results from the cost benefit analysis do not justify a decision to go ahead, the reasons which made the government persevere with the project, ought to be clearly stated.[1] One of the limitations of cost benefit analysis and similar decision rules is indicated in this report: governments may often choose not to act according to their findings. More important, and as explained subsequently in this chapter, such rules themselves have inherent limitations which must be understood if their value for public expenditure decision-making is to be fully grasped.

Some definitional issues in public expenditure evaluation

Before proceeding to the examination of some of the major techniques of public expenditure evaluation, some definitional issues need to be clarified. In Planning-Programming-Budgeting, in cost benefit analysis and even in expenditure incidence analysis, reference is made to programs, to projects and the inputs and outputs involved in their achievement. A program can initially be defined in terms of a broad government function (for example, welfare, education, health) as was discussed in the previous chapter. These can be subdivided into general programs (for example, day-care service for children) and into specific activities within the program (for example, licencing, funding and advising pre-schools, to continue within the general program of pre-schools). Detailed specification of the activities in which governments are involved enables more precise identification, and hence more careful scrutiny, of their costs or inputs and of the benefits they are designed to yield in terms of their objectives (outputs).

Efficiency should also be distinguished from effectiveness with respect to program evaluation. *Efficiency* is the target of Planning-Programming-Budgeting and cost/benefit analysis. It involves relationships between inputs and outputs, which are evaluated in terms of cost minimisation for a given required output, or the maximum output achievable from a specific allocation of inputs. *Effectiveness* of a program refers to the degree of success by which this program meets the government objectives. It compares actual output with desired output from the program and these may not always be identical. For example, a particular program of cash benefits designed to cater for a particular class of need may in fact be largely appropriated by persons not within that specific need category. Targeting social security payments in a more accurate manner is a matter associated with the effectiveness of social welfare programs. Reviews to test the effectiveness of programs require various stages. Identification of the program's desired objectives is required first of all, and this has to be followed by a detailed review of how program delivery meets these desired objectives; and finally, stage three in the process, the findings of the review should be implemented if they indicate problems with the specific program being evaluated for its effectiveness. As discussed later in more detail, tertiary education provision was scrutinised as to its efficiency and effectiveness in 1986 by the then Tertiary Education Commission, with its findings providing grounds for many of the changes the Federal Government introduced in the management of the tertiary education sector during the late 1980s.[2]

THE SET OF SPECIFIC OBJECTIVES WITHIN A PROGRAM

The broad functional classification which indicates the relative size of the major programs, although useful as an indication of the broad priorities of the government, is not sufficient for planning purposes or for the analysis of expenditure or its evaluation. The third stage of the sequential public expenditure decision-making process divides these broad categories into more specific projects and objectives of government policy, thereby identifying explicitly the purposes for which the expenditure is to be made. It is at this stage that the strength of a functional classification in budgeting comes into its own, and that the techniques of expenditure evaluation embodied in planning-programming-budgeting systems can be fruitfully introduced.

As discussed in Chapter 2, the *conventional accounting system* serves the *control* and *audit* functions of the Budget, which are basically concerned with checking that expenditures are made in accordance with the law, that they are properly recorded, and that they do not involve misappropriations and waste. In these accounts, the emphasis is on departmental *inputs* or costs, such as wages and salaries, procurement of equipment, and not on the objectives or functions of the department as characterised by the specific services it provides. There is therefore little concern with the efficient allocations of resources to the various functions and projects, since that would involve a discussion of the objectives, or outputs of the government department as well as the inputs.

This last point illustrates the crucial difference between the traditional functions of the Budget in so far as resource use is concerned, and the planning, analysis and evaluation of public expenditure from the economist's point of view. The economist is concerned with the successful achievement of objectives, by which is generally meant either the achievement of the specific objectives by least cost, or the maximum return in terms of benefits derived from the objectives obtainable from a given Budget outlay. It is this interrelationship between inputs and outputs, or between costs and objectives, that lies at the heart of the third stage of the decision-making process, that is, the specification of projects within a broad program such as defence, health, and education. The identification of specific projects or outputs is the third stage of the sequential expenditure model; the evaluation of ways of achieving the objectives by techniques such as cost/benefit analysis or cost effectiveness studies is the fourth stage.

Planning-programming-budgeting

The process of relating specified objectives to costs is the basis for the technique of planning-programming-budgeting.[3] Such a form of systematic expenditure analysis requires that government departments clearly identify and list the specific purposes of their expenditure programs and that they check that they are still in line with government policy. This procedure will disclose duplications between the objectives of individual government departments or the economies to be reaped from interdepartmental co-operation. The detailed breakdown of the program into specific objectives also allows an investigation of superior alternatives and, more important, a calculation of the time period over which the objectives are to be achieved, thereby extending the time horizon of the traditional Budget cycle. The more precise interrelationship between costs and objectives which underlies the choices available for achieving the designated objectives forms the fourth stage of the decision-making process.

Although this sounds deceptively simple in theory, it is quite difficult in practice, since the outputs of many government programs are not easily defined, and if defined, are not easily quantified. What for example, is the objective of the education program? If it is defined as the "achievement of equality of opportunity for all Australians", then it would be very difficult if not impossible to quantify. On the other hand, in primary and secondary schools, the various tertiary institutions, and the adult and migrant education programs, outputs can be quantified but not in a manner easily commensurable with costs.

In the interest of developing funding systems of tertiary education responsive to institutional performance and the achievement of mutually agreed goals, the 1988 Government White Paper on Higher Education Policy stressed the importance of output or performance indicators. Although advances have been made in the development of such indicators, the White Paper acknowledged the many problems involved in this task. In the first place, "the range of indicators to be developed should cover such issues as student demand and course completion rates, quality of teaching and curriculum design, relative staffing provision and measures of academic staffing performance in various aspects of research, publication, consultancy and other professional services. Indicators of performance against equity goals and measures of organisational efficiency should also be included in this process".[4] Secondly, estimation on comparable basis of such indicators is not easy, and their amalgamation into performance (output) indices is a formidable if not impossible task. Furthermore, the design of such performance indicators and their use in monitoring the efficiency of the organisation may induce precisely the sorts of problems for which the centralised Soviet planning process is rightly criticised.[5]

Although there are therefore substantial difficulties in the specification and quantification of "outputs" in education, such a search for a quantifiable output in this field is made easier by the fact that most of the outputs are internal to the education departments and institutions. If, to take another example, the program objective is poverty eradication, many departmental boundaries would be crossed because achievement of the objective involves social security, health, education, law reform, Aborigines, and primary industry. In such a case, the construction of a program Budget is a much more complicated affair and exceedingly difficult to construct in practice. Such difficulties are enhanced by interdepartmental rivalries, which often can considerably impede the free flow of information.

If, in addition to departmental boundaries, government boundaries have to be crossed, the difficulties become even greater. This of course happens in a federation like Australia. To return to the earlier example of education: it is clear that in Australia a program Budget specifying educational objectives would require considerable federal-State co-operation if it is to be properly constructed. Some of these reasons explain why PPB is not highly regarded by many Australian treasuries and by other government departments.[6]

Although over the last two decades governments have made a substantial number of improvements in the formulation and presentation of their Budgets, the results from these innovations in terms of improved efficiency in decision-making about priorities can be questioned. The following improvements were seen as the more important in the previous discussion of Chapter 2. Three-year forward expenditure estimates, first required from all Commonwealth departments in 1971, are now prepared in the context of State Budgets as well. Functional classification of Budget data was introduced in the Commonwealth Budget in 1973 and this practice has likewise been adopted by State governments. In addition, there have been improvements in capital budgeting at the State level, an important improvement since States are responsible for the greater part of public investment in Australia. From 1979, the Federal Government has widened the powers of the Auditor-General to include efficiency auditing and this practice is also spreading among the States. Finally, during the 1980s all Australian governments regularly issue budget information by programs and have greatly enhanced the quality and comprehensibility of the information provided in their financial statements.

Unfortunately, the benefits of these changes appear to have been smaller than originally expected. Forward estimates have not been the exercise in forward planning which some had anticipated. However, their value and continuing improvement as part of the Budget-making process are now fully recognised. Similarly, although the merits of the actual efficiency audits prepared by the Auditor-General have been questioned, their benefits in suggesting improvements in administration should be recognised. In short, there should be a greater realisation that reforms aimed at securing greater efficiency in public spending are slow to be implemented and gradual in their results.[7]

The need to recognise the difficulties in rapidly increasing efficiency in public spending and of reversing priorities is all the more important in a climate of general public expenditure restraint. Some exercises of expenditure-cutting in the early 1980s have been predicated more on the ease of reducing the item in question than on the longer-term efficiency consequences at the cut. As is so often the case in economics, there are no simple solutions here.

Some solutions to the problem which smack of over-simplification have been suggested in the United States. These include "zero-based budgeting" — the attempt to evaluate and justify *the whole* of an appropriation rather than the addition to it — and the more specific sunset legislation proposals which limit the life of a program to a specific number of years, so that its continuation after that time will have to be justified afresh. Both strategies to enhance public-sector efficiency appear rather gimmicky. As one Australian practitioner has commented on these types of proposals: "Their most obvious result appears to have been a doubling of the amount of paperwork involved in evaluating programs."[8]

The design of accepted projects to be implemented: cost benefit analysis

The final part of the public expenditure decision-making model evaluates the *specific* Budget outputs or programs desired in terms of their costs, thereby providing information on the best way to implement a certain project or the best manner in which a certain Budget appropriation for a specific purpose can be spent. In general, this procedure is nothing but a means of comparing the advantages and disadvantages of a given course of action, by way of evaluating the benefits and costs of a project or a set of projects.[9]

To illustrate this problem take, as an example, a Road and Traffic Authority which has a variety of projects for highway construction which it wants to carry out and for which the costs and benefits are fully known. Its appropriation (Budget constraint) for the period in question does not allow it to achieve all of these objectives in the Budget period; it has to decide which of the projects to adopt and which to forgo or postpone. If it is assumed that the total Budget allocation to the department is $42 million, and that the data on costs and benefits of the seven alternatives are as shown in Table 5.1, the problem has a simple solution.

The total cost of the seven projects ($75 million) exceeds the budget of $42 million and prevents all of them from being completed during the period. Since the costs of the various projects are different, they cannot be ranked in terms of benefits alone; in order to obtain an efficiency ranking and make a choice, they must be ranked according to the benefit/cost ratio, or, what leads to the same ranking, the ratio of net benefits to costs, i.e., $\frac{B}{C}$ and $\frac{B-C}{C}$ respectively. On this criterion, if the four best projects are chosen (i.e., G, A, F, and E in Table 5.1) the total budget of $42 million will be exhausted and maximum benefits are obtained from the expenditure.

If there was no Budget constraint, the issue is decided on similar criteria, that is, the benefit/cost ratio or the ratio of net benefits to costs. The latter rate (i.e., $\frac{B-C}{C}$) in fact reflects a rate of return over costs, which can be expressed as a percentage (for example, A's net rate of return in Table 3.3 is 50 per cent, B's 20 per cent, and so on). If it is assumed that before projects can be adopted by Road Traffic Authority, such projects must return at least 25 per cent over their lifetime – that is, they must have a ratio of net benefits to costs greater than or equal to 0.25 – then A, D, E, F, G will be acceptable projects while B and C will be rejected as inefficient.

Table 5.1 Cost/benefit analysis data

	Costs C *\$m*	*Benefits* B *\$m*	*Benefits-Costs* B – C *\$m*	$\frac{B}{C}$	$\frac{B-C}{C}$	*Project Ranking*
A	20	30	10	1.5	0.5	2
B	15	18	3	1.2	0.2	6
C	10	11	1	1.1	0.1	7
D	8	10	2	1.25	0.25	5
E	12	16	4	1.33	0.33	4
F	5	7	2	1.4	0.4	3
G	5	10	5	2.0	1.0	1

Internal rate of return rule

An alternative method of testing the efficiency of projects is to estimate their internal rate of return. Instead of determining the net value of the project (discounted to present values) in order to rank alternative projects, projects can be ranked according to their internal rate of return or the discount rate which equates the present value of the benefit stream with the cost of the project. By setting the present value of benefits equal to the present value of costs, an expression is obtained from which the discount rate which equalises them (the internal rate of return) can be estimated. That is, using the expression,

$$\sum_{i}^{n} \frac{B_i - C_i}{(1 + r)^i} = 0$$

"r" can be calculated, provided the net benefits of the project are known for the appropriate time period of the project.

There are problems associated with the internal rate of return rule. If the net benefit stream fluctuates over time, with net benefits alternating between positive and negative, the equation above may yield more than one value for "r". In addition, ranking by internal rate of return may differ from ranking obtained with a common discount rate. For example, two investments of differing maturities may yield the same internal rate of return, but their ranking can be altered if benefit streams are discounted with a market rate such as the long term bond rate. If the bond (market) rate exceeds the internal rate, the shorter investment will rank first while longer term investments gain preference when the market rate lies below the internal rate of return.

Some problems in cost/benefit evaluation

In the discussion so far, a number of crucial difficulties in cost/benefit analysis were assumed away, while the criticism of the internal rate of return rule drew attention to the importance of the selection of a rate of discount by which costs and benefits are discounted to their present value. In the order in which they are discussed to provide an indication of the difficulties involved, these problems in cost/benefit analysis are: (1) the selection of the relevant costs and benefits; (2) the evaluation of the costs and benefits; (3) the rate of interest at which costs and benefits are to be discounted to their present value; (4) the constraints under which the analysis operates and (5) the uncertainty problem.[10]

1. *Which costs and benefits are to be included?* The *direct* costs of a project can usually be quite easily found; they include the labour costs, material costs and capital costs; there may, however, be *intangible* direct costs which are more difficult to handle, because such intangible direct costs have no market evaluation and by some may not be regarded as "costs" at all (for example, the loss of urban bushland as a site for the construction of a freeway). There are usually also various *indirect* costs of the project, which similarly can be tangible or intangible, that is, have or not have a market value. Indirect costs are secondary costs or by-products of the project: an example of a tangible indirect cost is that the project may bid up local labour costs and thereby raise the local cost structure; the creation of environmental nuisances such as smoke or other forms of pollution and the destruction of wildlife would be classed as indirect intangible costs.

The benefits of a project can similarly be direct or indirect, tangible or intangible. Generally speaking, the direct benefits are the easiest to include, intangible and indirect benefits more difficult. The example of an irrigation project may illustrate some of these detrimental effects. The direct benefit is the increase in farm output resulting from the completion of the project, this is *tangible* and easily evaluated. An *intangible direct benefit* might be the beautification of the area by the creation of the lake which supplies the irrigation water. *Indirect benefits* of the project might be the reduction of soil erosion as well as the use of the lake for water sports and thereby as the basis for establishing a thriving tourist industry. An *indirect tangible benefit* from such a project may be decentralisation and the support of rural society. From these examples, it can be seen that for particular projects the list of costs and benefits can be immense and the *choice* of which to include and which to leave out can be agonising.

2. *How are they to be valued?* Having selected which costs and benefits to include, they have to be valued. In the case of intangible costs and benefits (direct or indirect) such valuation is a matter of judgement because market values are not available. This does not imply that the evaluation of tangible costs and benefits is easier. For example, in the evaluation of costs, are current market costs to be used, that is, are these estimates to be made in terms of constant prices, or are expected price rises to be taken into account? Are labour and material costs to be valued at market prices or at social opportunity cost, which may be lower or higher depending on the degree of unused capacity in the economy or in the region where the project is to be situated? In connection with benefits, the problems of evaluation are just as great, if not greater. If the output of the project is not to be sold, how is it to be valued? If it is to be sold, what pricing policy will the project adopt?[11] If the project (as in the irrigation example) is designed to increase agricultural output for export, what price and market expectations are built into the evaluation of the future benefits? It is therefore easy to conclude that the evaluation of costs and benefits is fraught with difficulties.

3. *The choice of the discount rate.* In most large-scale public investment projects, costs are incurred over long periods while benefits will frequently accrue over far longer periods. In order to make costs and benefits commensurable, the future costs and benefits streams will have to be reduced to their present value by means of a discount rate. The choice of such a

discount rate is very important because it has repercussions on the choice of the technique and the capital intensity of the project, a low discount rate favouring capital-intensive projects and vice-versa. Is the proper criterion for such a choice the private market rate (as reflected in the rate of long-term debentures or the long-term bond rate)? A case can be made for each of these, and there is no consensus as to which is best.[12]

4. *The relevant constraints.* There are several constraints which have to be taken into account in cost/benefit analysis. These include the physical constraints imposed by whatever techniques are available; various legal constraints such as local, State and federal laws and regulations; distributional constraints in the sense that public investment projects should harmonise with the government's policies on income distribution; balance of payments constraints if the project would absorb large amounts of scarce foreign exchange; and lastly, the Budget constraint relating to the total resources which can be appropriated for the project. This Budget constraint was illustrated in the Roads Authority example given in Table 5.1.

Distributional constraints in project evaluation can be dealt with by placing constraints on important variables in the analysis: a minimum level of wages for the labour employed, a minimum number of people employed, services provided by the project to be targeted sections of the community such as ethnic minorities, Aboriginals and the handicapped, while pricing policy of these services may likewise attempt to target appropriate social groups for distributional reasons. Balance of payments constraints may be important in comparing alternative transport projects, where facilities for modes of transport such as motor vehicles relying on imported fuels are deliberately handicapped when compared with projects based on rail links using domestically produced energy. Social and environmental policies may likewise constrain decisions.

5. *The uncertainty problem.* The outcomes of many projects are uncertain, and for those with long construction periods, the same uncertainty may attach to costs. If there are wide differences in the degree of uncertainty attached to net benefit streams of particular projects whose worth is to be compared, it is clearly important to make allowance for this. However, it is just as obvious that this cannot be easily done in an objective manner and that there are no simple valid rules for taking uncertainty into consideration. Where uncertainty about net benefits increases with time, the more distant net benefits may be weighted by a progressively higher discount rate, or by omitting those future benefits altogether. However, such omissions may have important consequences, for example when potentially important but uncertain negative environmental consequences are ignored in this way. Likewise, the analytical constraints may involve uncertainties. The degree of importance of imported motor fuel for the Australian balance of payments in the 1990s is uncertain, but ignoring it, as the New South Wales Road and Traffic Authority is doing, could have serious implications for the calculation of net benefits from road projects. Likewise, high variability in market rates of interest increases the uncertainties and risks attached to choice of the appropriate discount rate.

From this catalogue of difficulties, it can be seen that cost/benefit analysis, or, for that matter, any other technique of project evaluation, is far from simple. In spite of this, these are useful techniques because they bring into the open the information on which the decision is to be made. In addition, the analysis can bring out possible areas of disagreement about the project, while it frequently can lead to the rejection of inferior alternatives, or, in some cases, completely uneconomic projects. On the other hand, such analysis is itself not without cost, since it takes valuable manpower, but this expense can generally be justified in the case of large projects.[13]

In Australia, although cost/benefit analysis and cost effectiveness studies have been frequently used in project appraisal, and are in fact part and parcel of the Treasury evaluation of new expenditure submissions, some further difficulties should be noted. One of the advantages of these techniques, as was indicated earlier, is that they bring the relevant information into the open, but this is only the case where the study is published or otherwise made available to general scrutiny. Unfortunately, there are many examples in Australia where the results of cost/benefit studies have been suppressed, not infrequently because they have been adverse to projects on economic grounds while political expediency suggests their adoption. As Professor Mathews has graphically described the situation:

> The Australian countryside is littered with monuments to past follies perpetrated by Australian governments in the name of development... Irrigation is a major area where it seems necessary to remind governments that technical feasibility needs to be tempered with careful economic evaluation.[14]

There are plenty of other Australian examples where political considerations and occasionally, technical incompetence, have resulted in the selection of wrong public investment projects from the point of view of economic criteria.

The application of resource-allocation efficiency criteria to public expenditure determination and evaluation is exceedingly difficult as the brief discussion in this and the previous chapter of the sequential public expenditure decision-making model has shown. Apart from the fact that there is no really satisfactory theory of budget determination to act as a guide for the solution of this resource allocation problem, it was noted that techniques of program evaluation such as cost/benefit analysis, are difficult to apply in practice. These difficulties reflect the economic and political problems in Budget decision-making, but these problems should not be used as an excuse to abandon the search for efficiency in public expenditure decisions.

PUBLIC EXPENDITURE AND INCOME DISTRIBUTION: INCIDENCE ANALYSIS

In Chapter 2 it was stated that both expenditure programs and taxation policy affect the distribution of income. So far, little has been said on the distributional aspects of public expenditure decision-making though it is clear that this important subject cannot be ignored.[15] In general, it can be said that public expenditure confers benefits on its consumers, directly, as in the case of pensions or education or, less directly, to larger groups in the community, as in the provision of collective goods such as parks and defence. In addition, the government provides benefits in the form of employment and income to producers; directly, in the case of public servants and other government employees such as teachers, and indirectly, to those who supply goods and services subsidised by the government such as doctors and superphosphate producers. Sometimes these benefits can be transferred, or snatched from the original recipients. The discussion of the allocation and shifting of public expenditure benefits to groups or individuals is called the incidence analysis of public expenditure.

Before giving some examples of public expenditure incidence analysis, the basic theoretical problem of such an analysis must be outlined. In the first place, it is important to differentiate between the various types of government outlays which confer benefits, that is, to distinguish between transfer payments and between the provision of goods and services which may be either divisible or indivisible in supply. The first two of these confer benefits which can be privately appropriated, while the last confers a collective benefit which has to be *allocated* to individual groups. Secondly, the types of beneficiaries have to be identified, which requires a distinction between consumers and producers, and the conscious choice of whether a personal or a class distribution of income is to be considered.[16] Thirdly, the time period of the analysis must be discussed; finally, there is the economic analysis of the shifting or the snatching of the benefits from the original recipients, which is open to considerable difficulties.

To illustrate these points, some examples of the problem of incidence analysis of particular classes of government outlays may be given. A good starting-point is to take the example of transfer payments (social service cash benefits, assistance to industry in the form of subsidies and bounties and so on) where it is easy to identify *legal incidence*, that is, the effects on the income of the people who receive the payments in the first instance. These payments can therefore easily be allocated to their individual recipients, classified by income groups: social service payments increase the income position of consuming households or individuals[17] while bounties and subsidies increase the incomes of the producers employed in the subsidised industries.

It is during the next stage of the analysis that the difficulties start. When the recipients start to spend their additional income, it can be shown that the benefit derived from these transfer payments may be shifted. In the case of social service payments, part of the benefit may be transferred to the producers of the consumer goods on which the transfer payments are spent, while the assistance to industry may benefit the consumers of the commodities produced – including foreign consumers through the lower prices which may result from the subsidy or bounty.[18] Negative benefits may accrue to industries whose products compete with those of the subsidised industry but which themselves are not subsidised. For example, a subsidy to butter producers has adverse effects on manufacturers of margarine. These longer-term considerations in expenditure incidence analysis introduce the problem of the time period of the analysis and require assumptions about the supply and demand elasticities which underlie the examination of the shifting process.

To illustrate this, take the example of rent subsidies to pensioners or cash subsidies to low income tenants. The first impact of such a measure is to raise the incomes of the beneficiaries of such a policy. However, if the supply of rented accommodation is inelastic, as it generally is in the short-run, the additional demand for rented accommodation caused by the subsidy may force up rents so that the benefits are wholly or partly transferred to the owners of the rented premises, the precise impact depending on the elasticities of supply and demand. These higher rents will also affect the tenants who do not get the government subsidy; they therefore will experience negative benefits from the government's policy. If a longer period is taken for the analysis, the raising of the rate of return on existing accommodation for rent may cause an increase in the supply, with favourable consequences for the subsidised tenants. An important consideration in incidence analysis is where to draw the line: at the immediate stage when the real incidence is the same as the legal incidence; or at the intermediate stage when the benefit may be largely shifted to "high income" landlords, or at the final stage, when the benefit may be more evenly shared. In general, economists tend to favour short-period incidence analysis, since the longer period adjustments give rise to widely diffused effects and may make the problem indeterminate.[19]

In the case of publicly provided goods and services, the difficulties are as great, if not greater. This may be illustrated by the example of education expenditure, a very important part of total Budget outlays. The usual solution[20] to the problem of estimating the incidence of education expenditure is to add the average cost of education per student (which varies according to whether the student is in primary, secondary or tertiary education) to the incomes of households with such students in the various income groups. This procedure has a variety of shortcomings.

In the first place, it ignores the social benefits of education expenditure which are reflected, for example, in the benefits conferred on employers in being able to draw on a well-educated workforce, while there may also be important benefits for the whole of society of well-educated population. These more or less intangible benefits arising from education are very difficult to distribute as additions to income to individual households. Secondly, it can be argued that the real benefits of education only accrue to its recipients through the higher future income which they can reasonably expect to earn[21] and which therefore does not accrue as additional income to their current households. In this case, it is not the cost of the education but the future additions to income resulting from it (discounted to their present value) which should be allocated to household income. This is a very difficult procedure. Finally, it can be shown that increases in education expenditure may not always lead to an extension of educational facilities but may lead to large increases in the salaries of teachers and thereby confer little, if any, benefit on the families with students. In this case, the incidence is on the producers rather than on the consumers of the government service.

Some of the difficulties of expenditure incidence analysis are clearly illustrated in the example of education expenditure. First of all, it shows that the beneficiaries of expenditure are not easily or uniquely identifiable in practice. Individual benefits may go either to the producers of the service (the teachers in the education example), or to the immediate consumer (the households with students). Public expenditure also frequently confers social, indivisible benefits (the effects on economic growth of education, and so on) which are impossible to allocate accurately to the benefiting households. The example also shows the difficulties of valuation involved: should the benefits be valued at cost (the usual manner of making such calculations in education expenditure incidence analysis) or should they be valued, as was suggested in the education example, by the net benefit in the form of future income of the student. If the benefits are valued as in the latter case, the value of the benefits may greatly exceed the cost value of the total expenditure.

These difficulties are, of course, not confined to expenditure on education. They apply to many other classes of government expenditure such as that on health,[22] roads,[23] defence, general public administration and the provision of law and order.[24] If the allocation of the benefits from this type of expenditure is only made to *consuming households*, a misleading picture may be presented since such allocation is then made on the most arbitrary assumptions. It can be argued, for example, that very substantial property owners benefit mainly from the provision of law and order, an assumption which would greatly affect the incidence of this type of expenditure. Similarly, if the effects of defence expenditure on the actual recipients of that expenditure are considered—that is, on the producers of military hardware and the members of the armed services—a completely different distributional pattern results from that obtained by allocating the benefits (that is, the costs) of this service in equal amounts to all "consuming" households in the nation. These problems are difficult to resolve and there is no single clear answer.

It is therefore easy to show that the problems of public expenditure incidence analysis are many as well as formidable. Questionable assumptions have to be invoked in order to make a start on the analysis, and these assumptions frequently reflect the values of the researchers. Unhappily, most of the analyses put forward in the literature provide doubtful guides to the policy-makers. This does not mean that the problem is unimportant or that it can be ignored. Any estimate of the distributional impact of the government's budgetary policy must take account of expenditure considerations; furthermore, the whole approach of this type of analysis brings into focus the importance of the distributional issues in the planning and evaluation of public expenditures.

PUBLIC EXPENDITURE, STABILISATION, AND GROWTH

It has already been indicated that expenditure decisions are also influenced by stabilisation considerations and by consideration of growth. This is especially true in Australia, where much of budgetary policy from the 1950s onwards has been predicated on the twin objectives of stability and growth. The general analysis of the interrelationship between public expenditure, stabilisation and growth is the analysis of income determination which lies behind most of macroeconomic theory. A discussion of issues in Australian fiscal policy is given in Chapter 18; all that can be said in this context is evaluation of public expenditure projects and that in the case of some expenditure programs, such as the post-war immigration in Australia, growth considerations may be of paramount importance.

The economist and public expenditure analysis

This, and the previous chapters have indicated the many difficulties facing the economist in analysing public expenditure. These problems, as was seen, arise partly out of inadequate theory but, above all, out of the fact that the public expenditure decision-making process is a complex one involving politicians and public servants, as well as the producers and consumers with whose behaviour economists feel so much more at home. This difficult mixture of political and economic considerations explains the failure so far to construct a *general economic* theory of public expenditure, but this failure does not mean that public expenditure analysis cannot be carried out. As has been shown, it is possible to evaluate public expenditure by a variety of techniques such as cost/benefit and incidence analysis, imperfect though they may be. In the interest of better decision-making on the expenditure side of the Budget, more research and applied work is urgently required if these shortcomings are to be removed.

SUMMARY

1. Efficiency needs to be distinguished from effectiveness in program evaluation. Efficiency (the target of PPB analysis and C/B analysis) evaluates programs in terms of cost minimisation for given output or output maximisation from a given budget. Effective-

ness is concerned with assessing the success by which government programs meet the objectives for which they were introduced.

2. The PPB technique involves the process of relating specified objectives to costs. It requires clear specification of programs and their costs, sometimes a very difficult procedure.

3. C/B analysis provides information on the best way to implement a certain project by comparing the advantages and disadvantages of a given course of action through evaluation of benefits and costs of alternative ways of achieving a certain objective.

4. An alternative way of ranking is provided by the *Internal Rate of Return* rule of the discount rate which equates the present value of the benefit stream with the cost of the project.

5. Five problems are associated with evaluation of projects using C/B analysis:

   i selection of relevant costs and benefits;
   ii evaluation of the costs and benefits;
   iii the rate of discount used to estimate present value of costs and benefits;
   iv constraints of the analysis such as physical, legal, distributional, balance of payments and environmental constraint;
   v uncertainty of outcomes and costs.

6. Public expenditure incidence analysis is likewise crucial to public expenditure decision-making because of the information it supplies on the distributional consequences of Budget programs.

7. Problems in such an analysis arise from:

   i the allocation of collective benefits to society at large inherent in publicly provided goods with public good characteristics;
   ii identification of the beneficiaries: consumers, producers, providers;
   iii time period of the analysis;
   iv possibilities for shifting or snatching of benefits.

NOTES

[1] New South Wales Commission of Audit, *Focus on Reform. Report on the State's Finances* (Sydney: Government Printer, 1988), p. 87.

[2] EPAC Paper No. 23, *Flexibility in Government Spending: Issues in Efficiency and Control* (Canberra: EPAC, November 1986), pp. 23–4; Commonwealth Tertiary Education Commission, *Review of Efficiency and Effectiveness of Higher Education* (Canberra: AGPS, 1986). An interesting example of the difficulties in such studies is the Finance Department Discussion Paper, *What Price Heritage? The Museums Review and the Measurement of Museum Performance* (Canberra: Finance Department, 1988).

[3] There is a large literature on the theory and practice of planning-programming-budgeting. Reference should be made to J. Burkhead and J. Miner, ch. 6; R.A. and P.B. Musgrave, *Public Finance in Theory and Practice*, pp. 210–11, and in more detail to F.J. Lyden and E.G. Miller (eds.), *Public Budgeting, Program Planning and Implementation* (Englewood Cliffs: Prentice Hall, 1982). For early Australian discussion, see K.W. Knight and K.W. Wiltshire, *Formulating Government Budgets* (Brisbane: University of Queensland Press, 1977), ch. 4; Review of New South Wales Government Administration, *Further Report, Unfinished Agenda* (Sydney: N.S.W. Government, 1982), Part B, Section 3 and Appendices 1 and 2.

[4] Minister for Employment, Education and Training, *Higher Education, A Policy Statement* (Canberra: AGPS, 1988), pp. 85–6; cf. OECD, *Evaluation of Research* (Paris: OECD, 1987), esp. chs. 1, 4.

[5] See Michael Bleaney, *Do Socialist Economies Work?* (Oxford: Basil Blackwell, 1988), pp. 47–50.

[6] See Royal Commission on Australian Government Administration, Appendix, vol. I, Program Budgeting, esp. pp. 102–12, and for more recent comment, P. Weller, " The Commonwealth Budget System: An Evaluation", in David Shand (ed.), *Making Government Budgets Work* , p. 24. However, despite these criticisms, the Federal Government and some State governments have introduced Budget estimates classified by programs from 1983 onwards. See for example, "Program Presentation of Appropriations and Outlays — Departmental Estimates 1983–84", presented by the Minister for Finance for the information of members, (Canberra: AGPS, 1983); "New South Wales Budget Estimates classified by Program 1983–84", presented by the Treasurer for information only (Sydney: New South Wales State Treasury, 1983), esp. pp. 1–16.

[7] For general evaluation of these matters in an Australian context see R.L. Mathews (ed.), *Recent Developments in Budgeting* (Canberra: Centre for Research on Federal Financial Relations, 1979); David Shand, *Making Government Budgets Work*, particularly the papers by Weller, Wiltshire, and Sheehan; Review of New South Wales Government Administration, *Further Report*, Part B, Section 3, 7–9. Initial enthusiasm about these techniques has evaporated; though, as illustrated in the context of higher education evaluation, the search for performance indicators as tools for such evaluation continues.

[8] B.W. Fraser, "Recent Developments Affecting the Outlay Side of the Commonwealth Budget", in R.L. Mathews, *Recent Developments in Budgeting*, p. 4; and for past optimistic Australian appraisals, Senate Standing Committee on Social Welfare, *Through a Glass, Darkly: Evaluation in Australia's Health and Welfare Services* (Canberra: AGPS, 1979). See also F.J. Lyden and E.C. Miller (eds.), *Public Budgeting*, introduction and chs. 17 and 19, and EPAC Paper No. 23, *Flexibility in Government Spending: Issues in Efficiency and Control*, esp. pp. 22–5.

[9] If the outputs can be quantified in physical terms but not in money terms, the technique for evaluating the project is called a cost-effectiveness study; if both the costs and benefits can be measured in money terms, the technique is called cost/benefit analysis. The principles underlying the two techniques are the same. For a discussion of some of the differences, see Neil M. Singer, *Public Micro-Economics*, ch. 12.

[10] A classic survey of the issues, despite its age, is that by A.R. Prest and R. Turvey, "Cost Benefit Analysis: A Survey", *Economic Journal* (December 1965), pp. 683–735; and for more detailed textbook discussions, see R.A. and P.B. Musgrave, chs. 8 and 9 (which

gives some interesting examples of applications); C.V. Brown and P.M. Jackson, *Public Sector Economics*, ch. 8, and for a more advanced treatment, Jean Drèze and Nicholas Stern, "The Theory of Cost-Benefit Analysis", in Alan J. Auerbach and Martin Feldstein (eds.), *Handbook of Public Economics*, ch. 14.

11 For a thorough discussion of the valuation problem see Peter Bohm, *Social Efficiency: A Concise Introduction to Welfare Economics* (London: Macmillan Press, 1979), pp. 95–106 and the references cited in the previous footnote. A very useful Australian official contribution is Department of Finance, *Guidelines for Costing of Government Activities* (Canberra: Department of Finance Discussion Paper, 1988).

12 The social time preference rate has been defined as the rate "which reflects the government's judgement about the relative value which the community as a whole is believed to assign, or which the government feels that it ought to assign, to present as opposed to future consumption of the margin" (P.D. Henderson, "Investment Criteria for Public Enterprises", in R. Turvey (ed.), *Public Enterprise* (Harmondsworth: Penguin, 1968), p. 97). See also Peter Bohm, *Social Efficiency*, pp. 106–110. Sensitivity analysis can test for the degree of importance to be attached to small changes in discount rate, by estimating the consequences, for example, of discount rates varying between 4 and 10 per cent when 7 is the preferred rate. Other problems associated with the choice of discount rate were encountered in the discussion of the Internal Rate of Return Rule above.

13 Appreciation of such difficulties is most easily gained from studying actual cost/benefit analysis or from looking at the difficulties involved in evaluating the costs and benefits of particular projects. For examples see Peter Abelson, *The Economic Evaluation of Roads in Australia* (Mosman: Australian Professional Publications, 1986) and his earlier *Cost Benefit Analysis and Environmental Projects* (Westmead: Saxon House, 1979). Some useful British examples are included in Leslie Wagner, (ed.), *Readings in Applied Micro-Economics* (Oxford University Press, 1981), Readings 15, 16 and 17.

14 R.L. Mathews, *Public Investment in Australia* (Melbourne: F.W. Cheshire, 1967), pp. 306–7. The quotation from the Report on New South Wales State Finance in the opening paragraph of this chapter shows that this problem has as yet not been overcome.

15 For a discussion of some of the distributional problems in connection with the allocational decision-making framework, see Robert Millward, *Public Expenditure Economics* (London: McGraw Hill, 1971), pp. 346–58.

16 In most incidence studies, personal distribution effects are analysed with the emphasis on consumption aspects of public expenditure. See for example, Rufus S. Tucker, "The Distribution of Government Burdens and Benefits", *American Economic Review* (May 1953), pp. 518–34; W.J. Gillespie, "Effects of Public Expenditure on the Distribution of Income", in R.A. Musgrave (ed.), *Essays in Fiscal Federalism* (Washington, D.C.: The Brookings Institution, 1965) and R.A. and P.B. Musgrave, *Public Finance in Theory and Practice*, ch. 12, esp. pp. 261–3. The difference between individual and social incidence is further discussed in Chapter 8.

17 An example of the impact of some of these transfer payments on the distribution of income by households in Australia is given by Ann Harding, *Who Benefits? The Australian Welfare State and Distribution* (Sydney: University of New South Wales, Social Welfare Research Centre, Report and Proceedings No. 45, April, 1984).

18 Most incidence analyses only consider domestic distributional effects. Where assistance is given to industry to lower export prices, the benefits are frequently snatched by foreign consumers as occurred, for example, in the export of Australian dairy products to the United Kingdom and elsewhere.

19 These time period considerations are just as important in the analysis of tax incidence, as is shown in Chapter 8.

20 See W.J. Gillespie, "Effects of Public Expenditure on the Distribution of Income", pp. 146–7.

21 Interrelationship between educational attainment and future income prospects have been well documented. For recent discussions see Tai-Tee Chia, "Has the Value of A Degree Fallen?", paper presented to 1988 Australian Economics Congress, 29 August 1988, and B.J. Chapman and Tai-Tee Chia, "Financing Higher Education. Private Rates of Return and Externalities in the Context of a Tertiary Tax" (Canberra: Australian National University, Centre for Economic Policy, Research Discussion Paper, June 1989).

[22] See J.R. Richardson and T.J. Philips, "An Analysis of Medical Practice using before and after Medibank Data", a paper given at 48th ANZAAS Congress, Melbourne, September 1977, where the authors argue that part of the increased health expenditure attributable to Medibank went to sharp increases in doctors' fees rather than increases in services. This suggests incidence on producers rather than consumers.

[23] See P. Bentley, D.J. Collins and D.J.S. Rutledge, "The Distributional Impact of Road Expenditure and Finance in Australia" (Macquarie University, School of Economic and Financial Studies, Research Paper No. 140, 1977). This is one of the few detailed Australian public expenditure incidence analysis available.

[24] See R.A. and P.B. Musgrave, *Public Finance in Theory and Practice*, pp. 261–3.

FURTHER READING

The information in this chapter can be usefully supplemented by reading the relevant chapters of other texts:

R.A. and P.B. Musgrave, *Public Finance in Theory and Practice*, 4th edn. (New York: McGraw Hill, 1984), chs. 8 and 9.

C.V. Brown and P.B. Jackson, *Public Sector Economics*, 3rd edn. (Oxford: Blackwells 1986), ch. 8.

J.E. Stiglitz, *Economics of the Public Sector*, 2nd edn. (New York: W.W. Norton, 1988), Part III, esp. ch. 10.

Much more advanced recent surveys in public expenditure evaluation are:

Peter Hammond, "Principles for Evaluating Public Sector Projects", in Paul G. Hare (ed.), *Surveys in Public Sector Economics* (Oxford: Blackwells, 1988), ch. 2.

J. Drèze and N. Stern, "The Theory of Cost-Benefit Analysis", in A.J. Auerbach and M. Feldstein (eds.), *Handbook of Public Economics* (Amsterdam: North Holland, 1987), ch. 14.

A useful Australian case study is:

Peter Abelson, *The Economic Evaluation of Roads* (Sydney: Australian Professional Publications, 1986).

and more generally:

Department of Finance, *Guidelines for Costing of Government Activities* (Canberra: Department of Finance, Issues for Discussion, May 1988).

Taxation: an introduction

The financing of government expenditure, that is, the revenue side of the Budget, will now be considered. Broadly speaking, government expenditure is financed from three basic sources: taxation revenue; charges and fees, including the contributions made by government enterprises to consolidated revenue; and government borrowing. This, and the subsequent seven chapters, examine the most important of these revenue sources, namely taxation. Chapter 17 treats government borrowing and issues relating to the public debt. (As indicated earlier, this book will not deal with issues relating to public enterprises.)

Because Chapters 6 to 13 deal with taxation, a brief summary of their contents may be found helpful at the outset. In this chapter the Australian tax structure is examined: its historical development since federation, and its classification by level of government and by tax base. The chapter also provides some international comparisons of tax structures, partly to allow identification of potential problem areas in Australia's tax system from the differences such comparisons disclose. A definitional glossary concludes the chapter. Chapter 7 deals with the principles of taxation, not only with the current guiding principles of "equity", "efficiency", "neutrality" and "simplicity" but also with the earlier "ability-to-pay" and "benefit" principles, and the reasons for good taxation systems put forward by Adam Smith and other classical writers of tax analysis. Such principles of taxation provide the foundation for tax reform discussion as it has taken place in Australia over the last two decades. Chapter 8 examines the incidence of taxation, both from a theoretical and empirical perspective. The final five chapters devoted to taxation successively examine personal income tax (Chapter 9), company tax and business taxation (Chapter 10), wealth and property taxes (Chapter 11), broad-based consumption taxes (Chapter 12) and other transaction taxes (Chapter 13). The last of these chapters covers many of the State taxes, while issues in local taxation are examined more fully in Chapter 16.

THE DEVELOPMENT OF THE AUSTRALIAN TAX STRUCTURE

The growth of public expenditure since federation was examined in Chapter 3. The

Australian tax structure has exhibited a comparable growth both in its scale and complexity. There have been transfers of major taxes from one level of government to another. The uniform income tax legislation of 1942 is the most important example of this; others include the transfer of payroll tax from the federal government to the States in 1971 and the vacation of land and entertainment tax by the federal government in the 1950s. These issues are discussed further in Chapter 15 on governmental financial relations. In addition, new taxes were added to the tax structure as it existed at Federation in 1901. These include sales tax added in 1930, payroll tax in 1941; financial institutions duties and other financial transaction taxes in 1983,[1] while to effectively broaden the income tax base, a separate capital gains tax and fringe benefits taxation were introduced in 1985. Table 6.1 presents taxation data for the federal government and the States (including local government) for selected years since 1901–2. This table also portrays the growth of taxation both in absolute amounts and relative to GDP.

The most obvious feature of Table 6.1 is that the total weight of taxation has steadily increased over this long period from 6.8 per cent of GDP in 1901–02 to approximately 31 per cent in 1980–81. The more recent data (presented in Table 6.3 which classifies taxes on the system devised by the OECD) shows that relative to GDP taxation has continued to rise during the 1980s, despite the relative curtailment of government outlays documented in Chapter 3. In 1984–85 total taxation accounted for 31.1 per cent of GDP, in 1987–88 for 31.7 per cent.

Table 6.1 also shows that the shares of State and federal taxes in total taxation revenue have fluctuated widely since Federation. The major source of nineteenth-century tax revenue was customs and excise revenue which in 1901–2 raised 63 per cent of total taxes. At federation, the central government acquired exclusive power over customs and excise; the States could utilise the remaining sources of tax revenue. The central government entered land taxation in 1910, estate duty in 1914 and income taxation in 1915. Nevertheless, the State governments greatly expanded their tax revenue in the period between the two world wars, largely through their increased use of income taxes. These raised half of State tax revenue in 1929–30, at which time total State and local taxation amounted to 46 per cent of all tax revenue. As a result of the effective transfer of income tax from the States in 1942, the federal share of total tax revenue rose to close to 90 per cent in the post-war period but from the 1950s stabilised at approximately 80 per cent. In 1987–88, for example, Commonwealth tax revenue amounted to 80 per cent, State taxation to 16 per cent and local government for the remaining 4 per cent, proportions which have remained remarkably stable over the last two decades.

Table 6.1 (supplemented by the data in Table 6.3 to reflect more recent experience) also sheds light on the changing structure of the Australian taxation system through the introduction of new taxes such as sales tax, taxation of motorists, gambling taxes and from 1983 onwards, new financial transaction taxes. It likewise reveals changes in the relative importance of particular tax instruments over the twentieth century. For example, income taxes, which were insignificant in 1901–2, gradually increased in relative importance from 26.1 per cent in 1929–30 to 50.6 per cent in 1948–49, 55.3 per cent in 1980–81, the proportion at which they have more or less stabilised during the 1980s. Customs and excise duties as well as death duties have gradually declined in relative importance; in fact, death duties were eliminated from both federal and State tax structures in the decade following 1976 when Queensland abolished such taxes (see Chapter 11). Customs and excise duties raised

63 per cent of taxation revenue in 1901–2,[2] 38.9 per cent in 1929–30, 23.4 per cent in 1940–49 and 19.1 per cent in 1980–81. By 1987–88 they had further declined to 15.3 per cent, reflecting in part the growing sophistication of tax administration which permits the introduction of more complex tax instruments, more easily attuned to the achievement of policy objectives now demanded from tax systems. Changes in the relative importance of taxes arise from various causes, and their study can inform the discussion of broad issues of tax reform, including that of whether the tax system has a balanced structure with respect to the use it makes of the three tax bases of income, property and outlays or transactions.

THE CLASSIFICATION OF TAXATION

Table 6.1 presents a classification of taxation by types of tax and by level of government. Although useful in many respects, this table has some shortcomings which largely arise from the fact that in it the tax structure of the States and local government are amalgamated. For example, the substantial differences between these tax systems are disguised. For local government, most of the differences in local government rates between States are related to the differences in tax base but there are also substantial variations in the tax rate for individual local government units. Such issues of local government finance are postponed until Chapter 16. State tax structures show substantial differences in tax mix, in the rate at which the various taxes are levied, and in details of the legislation by which these taxes are assessed and collected. Some of these differences are illustrated in Table 6.2 but their more detailed exploration awaits the discussion of specific tax instruments in Chapters 11 and 13. Problems from the degree of tax decentralisation which separate State and local tax systems imply, are raised in Chapters 14 and 15. From the variations in tax structures it discloses, Table 6.2 reveals the inaccuracy of a frequently held opinion that States have no discretion in taxation policy.

Apart from the methods of tax classification by type of tax and by level of government, there are two others; the traditional and popular classification of taxes into direct and indirect taxation and the more modern classification of taxes according to tax base of which the taxes, fees and fines classification currently in use by the Australian Bureau of Statistics is the major form. As illustrated in Table 6.3, this subdivides taxes into those on income, on employers' payrolls, on property, on the provision of goods and services and on the use of goods and performance of services. This classification enables reporting of Australian data to international agencies (particularly the OECD), hence facilitating more reliable international tax comparisons of the type discussed at the end of this chapter.

Classification according to tax base

A first variant of this classification is to draw a distinction between *narrow-based* and *broad-based taxes*, which is useful for analysing their economic effects. For example, for a narrow-based and relatively minor tax, partial equilibrium incidence analysis would suffice whereas for broad-based taxes on income and consumption expenditure a more general analysis is required. In some cases this classification is easy: a personal income tax clearly falls into the second category, while the excise on canned fruit clearly falls into the first. In other cases, say the sales tax on motor vehicles or the excise on beer, which raises a large amount of revenue, the distinction is less clear-cut.[3]

Table 6.1 Australian tax structure 1901–02 to 1980–81 by Federal, State and local taxation and by type of tax (selected years)

	1901–02						*1929–30*					
	States		*Federal*		*Total*		*States*		*Federal*		*Total*	
	$m	%	*$m*	%	*$m*	%	*$m*	%	*$m*	%	*$m*	%
Income taxes on persons	} 1.3	12.6			} 1.3	4.6	33.9	34.5	} 22.2	19.1	} 56.1	26.1
Income taxes on companies[a]												
Customs duties			} 17.8	100	} 17.8	63.4			60.3	51.8	60.3	28.1
Excise duties									23.3	20.0	23.3	10.8
Sales taxes												
Payroll tax												
Estate and gift duties	2.4	23.3			} 2.4	8.5	8.0	8.1	4.2	3.6	12.2	5.7
Stamp duties n.e.i.							7.2	7.3			7.2	3.3
Motor vehicle taxation							9.0	9.2			9.0	4.2
Taxes on gambling							2.8	2.8			2.8	1.3
Land taxes							3.7	3.8	5.7	4.9	9.4	4.4
Entertainment tax	1.0	9.7			1.0	3.6						
Local government rates	5.0	48.5			5.0	17.8	30.8	31.3			30.8	14.3
Other taxes	0.5	4.8			0.5	1.8	2.9	3.0	0.8	0.7	3.7	1.7
Total	10.3	100.0	17.8	100	28.1	100.0	98.3	100.0	116.5	100.0	214.8	100.0
Percentages of Federal/State	%		%		%		%		%		%	
and local taxes of total taxation	36.7		63.3				45.8		54.2			
Taxation as a percentage of GDP	2.5		4.3		6.8		6.3		7.4		13.7	

Table 6.1 (continued)

	1948–49						1980–81					
	States		*Federal*		*Total*		*States*[c]		*Federal*		*Total*	
	$m	*%*	*$m*	*%*	*$m*	*%*	*$m*	*%*	*$m*	*%*	*$m*	*%*
Income taxes on persons			399	42.0	399	37.0			17,543	53.5	17,543	43.4
Income taxes on companies[a]			146	15.4	146	13.6			4,800	14.6	4,800	11.9
Customs duties			127	13.4	127	11.8			1,884	5.7	1,884	4.7
Excise duties			125	13.2	125	11.6			5,834	17.8	5,834	14.4
Sales taxes			78	8.2	78	7.2			2,102	6.4	2,102	5.2
Payroll tax			40	4.2	40	3.7	1,923	25.3	14		1,937	4.8
Estate and gift duties	20	15.7	11	1.2	31	2.9	158	2.1	17	0.1	175	0.4
Stamp duties n.e.i.	14	11.0			14	1.3	1,242	16.3	8		1,250	3.1
Motor vehicle taxation	21	16.5			21	1.9	842	11.1	7		849	2.1
Taxes on gambling	17	13.4			17	1.6	633	8.3	1		634	1.6
Land taxes	3	2.3	6	0.6	9	0.8	325	4.3			325	0.8
Entertainment tax			11	1.2	11	1.0	b					
Local government rates	42	33.1			42	33.1	1,508	19.8	19	0.1	1,527	3.8
Other taxes	10	7.9	7	0.7	17	1.6	974	12.8	546	1.7	1,520	3.8
Total	127	100.0	950	100.0	1,077	100.0	7,605	100.0	32,776	100.0	40,380	100.0
	%		%		%		%		%		%	
Percentages of Federal/State and local taxes of total taxation	11.8		88.2				18.8		81.2			
Taxation as a percentage of GDP	2.8		21.3		24.1		5.8		25.1		30.9	

Totals may not add due to rounding.

Notes:

a Includes interest and dividend withholding tax in 1980–81.
b. No State levied entertainment tax in 1980–81.
c. State and local taxation includes Northern Territory taxation.

Source: 1901–02 — R.L. Mathews and W.R.C. Jay, *Federal Finance* (Melbourne: Nelson, 1972), Table 6;
1929–30 — ibid., Table 18;
1948–49 — ibid, Table 24;
1980–81 — Australian Bureau of Statistics, *Taxation Revenue, Australia*, 1980–81, Cat. Ref. 5506.

Table 6.2 State taxation[a] by State and type of tax: 1987–88

	New South Wales		*Victoria*		*Queensland*		*South Australia*		*Western Australia*		*Tasmania*		*Northern Territory*	
	$m	*%*	*$m*	*%*	*$m*	*%*	*$m*	*%*	*$m*	*%*	*$m*	*%*	*$m*	*%*
Estate, gift, probate and succession duties[b]	1.6	0.0	0.7	0.0	—	0.0	—	0.0	—	0.0	0.1	0.0	—	0.0
Land tax	412.8	6.5	209.5	4.7	62.5	3.3	56.7	5.3	63.0	4.4	12.0	3.4	—	0.0
Taxes on gambling	601.9	9.5	385.4	8.7	162.7	8.5	90.6	8.4	80.9	5.6	32.7	9.3	2.1	1.9
Taxes on ownership and operation of motor vehicles[c]	745.7	11.8	407.8	9.2	344.5	17.9	153.6	14.3	181.9	12.7	42.5	12.1	8.8	7.9
Payroll tax	1592.9	25.1	1231.6	27.9	462.8	24.1	249.5	23.2	360.3	25.1	88.6	25.1	48.3	43.4
Stamp duties (n.e.i.)	1461.8	23.1	978.8	22.1	495.1	25.8	176.1	16.3	238.2	23.5	40.0	11.3	17.4	15.7
Business franchise taxes[d]	405.3	6.4	361.3	8.2			116.8	10.8	156.1	10.9	63.1	17.9	19.6	17.6
Liquor taxes	169.3	2.7	94.4	2.1	71.5	3.7	36.1	3.4	51.9	3.6	12.5	3.6	9.3	8.4
Other	950.6	15.0	750.6	17.0	323.6	16.8	198.1	18.4	204.1	14.2	61.1	17.3	5.7	5.1
Total	6340.0	100.0	4420.1	100.0	1922.7	100.0	1077.5	100.0	1436.4	100.0	352.6	100.0	111.2	100.0
Per capita taxation	1120.30		1044.05		710.48		768.98		945.06		787.41		709.64	
Index of per capita tax Aust. average = 100.0	115.3		107.5		73.2		79.2		97.3		87.1		73.1	

Totals may not add due to rounding.

Notes:

a. Including Northern Territory.
b. Abolished in Queensland from 1976, South Australia and Western Australia from 1980, New South Wales from 1982. Northern Territory never had death duties.
c. Included $0.1 million levied by local authorities in Western Australia.
d. Includes levies on public corporation, liquor franchise only in Queensland.

Source: Australian Bureau of Statistics, *Taxation Revenue Australia 1987–88* (Canberra: 1989); Australian Bureau of Statistics, *Australian Demographic Statistics*, September Quarter 1988, Cat. No. 3101.0, Canberra, March 1989.

Table 6.3 Taxes, fees and fines by types of tax base: 1980–81, 1984–85 and 1987–88

	1980–81	*1984–85*	*1987–88*
		Percentage of total taxation	
1. Taxes on income	54.9	53.6	54.8
1.1 Income taxes levied on individuals	43.1	44.4	44.7
1.2 Income taxes levied on enterprises	11.2	8.2	9.2
1.3 Income taxes levied on non-residents	0.6	0.9	0.9
2. Employers' payroll taxes	5.6	4.7	5.3
2.1 General taxes (payroll tax)	5.6	4.7	4.4
2.2 Selective taxes (Stevedoring industry charge)	..	..	..
2.3 Fringe benefits tax	—	—	0.9
3. Taxes on property	8.0	7.7	9.0
3.1 Taxes on immovable property (land tax and local rates)	4.6	4.6	4.4
3.2 Estate, inheritance and gift duty	0.4	..	..
3.3 Taxes on financial and capital transactions	2.9	3.1	4.7
4. Taxes on provision of goods and services	27.2	28.4	25.7
4.1 General taxes (sales tax)	5.2	7.5	8.1
4.2 Excises	15.2	14.1	11.3
4.2.1 Crude oil and LPG	7.6	6.4	2.2
4.2.2–4.2.7 Other excises	7.6	7.7	9.1
4.3 Taxes on international trade	4.7	4.5	4.0
4.4 Taxes on gambling	1.5	1.6	1.5
4.5 Taxes on insurance	0.6	1.0	0.9
5. Taxes on use of goods and performance of activities	3.2	4.1	3.9
5.1 Motor vehicle taxes (n.e.i.)	2.0	2.0	2.0
5.2 Business franchise taxes	1.0	1.7	1.7
5.3 Other taxes on use of goods and performance of activities	0.1	0.1	0.2
9. Fees and fines	1.0	1.1	1.2
Total taxation	100.0	100.0	100.0
As percentage of GDP at market prices	29.6	31.1	31.7

Source: Australian Bureau of Statistics, *Taxation Revenue Australia*, various issues, Cat. No. 5506.0; *National Income and Expenditure 1987–88*, Cat. No. 5204.0 (Canberra: ABS,1989).

The second method is to classify taxation according to type of tax base, that is, whether it falls on income, on property, or on expenditure on goods and services. Here again there are several conceptual difficulties but despite these, this method of classifying taxes is useful since it sheds light on the balance of the tax structure as measured by the degree of utilisation of these three types of tax base which in turn reflect the three indexes of capacity to pay. Table

6.3 presents data on Australia's taxation system for the 1980s based on this type of classification now used by the Bureau of Statistics in its annual publication on tax revenue in Australia.[4]

Table 6.3 highlights some important structural features of the Australian tax system in the 1980s. As mentioned earlier, its use in conjunction with Table 6.1 allows comment on tax structure changes for the whole of the post-war period. Before making such observations, the type of taxes within the various classifications on which Table 6.3 is based, have to be clearly identified.[5]

Taxes on income, the first group in the classification is a relatively straightforward group. Its sub-group 11 largely consists of personal income tax including the Medicare levy from 1984, and the Higher Education Contribution Charge (HECS) levied from January 1989. Income taxes on enterprises include company income tax[6] and income tax paid by superannuation funds, while non-resident income taxes are confined to the interest and dividend withholding taxes levied by the Federal Government. More detailed discussion of these income taxes is presented in Chapters 9, 10 and 19.

The second group consists of State payroll taxes, also levied in the Australian Capital Territory and Northern Territory (sub-group 21). Selective payroll taxes, of which the stevedoring industry charge is the only Australian example, are another group in this category though a training levy on business payrolls (proposed during 1988–89)[7] would likewise fall within it. The fringe benefits tax levied on business enterprises with respect to fringe benefits they pay to their employees is a third Australian tax in this group (sub-group 23).[8]

The third group of taxes, those on property, covers taxes on both the ownership and the transfer of property. The former are now confined in Australia to taxes on immovable property in the form of land taxes and the various types of local rates. The latter formerly included taxes on the transfer of property at death (sub-group 32) but is now confined to stamp duties and the financial transactions taxes and bank cheque account debit taxes levied from 1983 at State and federal level. The taxes referred to in this and the preceding paragraph are discussed in more detail in Chapters 11 and 13.

The fourth and fifth group of taxes cover taxes on goods and services, based either on their provision (group 4) or on their use and performance of associate activities (group 5). The first of these groups covers sales taxation (sub-group 41), excises (sub-group 42) of which sub-divisions 422-427 cover excise on petroleum products, beer and potable spirits, tobacco products, agricultural production taxes and levies on statutory corporations. Sub-group 43 (taxes on international trade) includes customs duties on both imports and exports, as well as specific agricultural produce export taxes. Taxes on gambling (sub-group 44) covers taxes on all forms of betting, lotteries, poker machines, casino games, mainly levied at the State level. It excludes individual gains from gambling, for reasons discussed in Chapter 9. Sub-group 45 (taxes on insurance) covers levies to finance fire-fighting authorities, third party charges and stamp duties together with any other stamp duties levied on insurance contracts. Finally, there are taxes on the use of goods and the performance of activities. These include taxes on the use of motor vehicles (drivers licence fees, vehicle registration and road maintenance taxes) and business franchise taxes levied on suppliers of gas, petroleum products and tobacco products and liquor, by means of a licence fee whose size is determined by turnover values. It also includes broadcasting licences, such as those charged to listeners and viewers until their abolition in 1974 by the Australian Federal

Government, the overseas departure tax and similar levies. More detailed discussion of these taxes is presented in Chapters 12 and 13.

Specific listing of the items within the tax classification categories is necessary to highlight problems in identifying the relative importance of certain classes of taxes to which reference is often made in popular discussion. For example, the category consumption tax has to be constructed from a substantial variety of sub-groups in classifications 3, 4 and 5 such as sales tax, excises, franchise taxes, gambling taxes, and taxes on motorists, but only in so far as they fall on personal final consumption. In short, taxes falling on intermediate goods or inputs in the production process have to be excluded. Likewise, to give an example of another category frequently encountered in popular discussion, taxes on motorists include not only the taxes of which sub-group 51 is composed; they include the substantial proportion of sales tax levied on motor vehicles and parts, excise on petroleum products, and the petroleum products portion of business franchise taxes. Their aggregation is not easily accomplished from published tax data of the type discussed in this chapter. Finally, it should be noted that stamp duties, one of the more important revenue sources of State governments, feature in sub-groups 33, 45, 51 and 53, hence illustrating that these duties are a tax group comprising many different species.

Bearing these aspects of tax classification in mind, some tax structure implications of Tables 6.1 and 6.3 can be given. First, these Tables reveal the tremendous importance of income taxation in the Australian tax system. However, for the 1980s, while personal income taxation has shown slight increases in its relative importance as a revenue raiser, company taxation has fluctuated widely and over this decade as a whole exhibited a downward trend. Secondly, with respect to property taxes, taxes on financial transactions and those on property transfers for consideration have rapidly increased in relative importance. General wealth taxes on transfers by bequest and/or gift, on the other hand, have disappeared. Even taxes on real property ownership are gradually declining. Taxes on provision of goods and services have remained stable in revenue-raising importance but their composition has changed. The relative importance of sales tax has steadily risen, that of customs and excise has declined, continuing the century-old trend previously noted. The fall in excise is largely explicable in terms of reduced revenue from locally produced crude oil and LPG as the Bass Strait oil wells are further depleted, a position reversible if new important local oil discoveries are made and exploited in the future, for example, those on the North-West Shelf. The relative position of other taxes has remained remarkably steady, with the exception of payroll tax. After its rapid relative growth in the 1970s when the states exploited it as a new tax base, the tax has steadily declined in importance for the whole of the 1980s. The high proportion of income taxes in Australia's tax structure, combined with the very selective nature of its goods and services taxation, differentiate it from many other OECD tax structures and have inspired tax reform scenarios designed to boost the role of general consumption taxation.[9]

Direct and indirect taxation

Although this is the more usual form of tax classification, its usefulness has been questioned on the ground that the distinction is largely meaningless.[10] This is shown by an examination of the definition of direct and indirect taxation. Those taxes paid by the people on whom they are levied are to be classed as *direct*, while those which are in any degree shifted to others are to be classed as *indirect*. As it is now agreed that all taxes can in some way be "shifted", the distinction has lost its meaning since all taxes in use are on this definition classed as indirect.

When the distinction persists, as it does in the national accounting framework, for example, where indirect taxes are an important element in differentiating GDP at factor cost from GDP at market prices, it is made on administrative fiat rather than on principles. In the Australian national accounts, indirect taxes are defined as "taxes assessed on producers, i.e. enterprises and general government, in respect of the production, sale, purchase or use of goods and services, which are charged to the expenses of production". The remaining taxes are classified as income taxes (on individuals and companies) and "other direct taxes", which include estate and gift duties, "and other taxes, fees for services of a regulatory character, fines and gifts paid by persons to general government".[11] If income and some of these other taxes are shifted to the expenses of production, this distinction can only be described as arbitrary.

The terminology of direct and indirect taxation is difficult to eradicate, largely because it is associated with so many popular prejudices. In political rhetoric, for example, direct taxes are generally advocated because they are progressive while indirect taxes are condemned as regressive, despite the fact that such conclusions are frequently unwarranted. Similarly, the literature of traditional welfare economics argued that indirect (excise) taxes entailed large excess burdens while direct (income) taxes did not, and that therefore the latter should be preferred. This argument has been shown to be fallacious. In this context, something would also be gained if the distinction was abolished.[12]

INTERNATIONAL TAX COMPARISONS

A different perspective on Australia's tax system can be obtained by comparing it with the tax systems of the developed nations which are members of the OECD. Such comparisons are facilitated by the regular data on revenue statistics of member countries the OECD publishes as well as the more detailed comparative analyses of income, property and consumption taxes which it prepares on a less regular basis. Such a perspective allows the identification of differences in tax systems from which the particular country in question can learn, and hence assists the process of tax reform. However, tax comparisons and the lessons to be derived therefrom require care in interpretation. For example, being out of step with the rest of the world in tax matters need not necessarily indicate there is something wrong and may in fact suggest a superior tax system. The example of New Zealand's single rated general goods and services tax with few exemptions is one which many OECD countries who likewise use a value added tax could easily follow.

Three types of comparisons are illustrated in this section. The first relates to the relative burden of taxation in the various OECD countries. Table 6.4 shows total tax revenue (exclusive of social security contributions) relative to GDP for various years after 1965 for the OECD member countries. For 1986 this shows Australia in the top half of those countries with respect to relative tax burdens, but when social security contributions are included, Australia's position drops to nineteenth. However, in 1965 Australia's relative position was considerably lower. Relative to Scandinavian countries, and a substantial number of countries of Western Europe, Australia has always been a relatively lightly taxed country.

Table 6.4 Total tax revenue (including social security) as percentage of GDP: 1965–86 (selected years)

	1965	*1970*	*1975*	*1980*	*1985*	*1986*
Australia	23.5	24.2	27.8	29.0	30.8	31.4
Austria	26.0	26.6	28.0	28.4	29.4	29.0
Belgium	21.1	24.5	28.0	30.3	31.2	30.1
Canada	24.0	28.3	29.1	28.3	28.5	28.6
Denmark	28.3	38.8	40.8	44.7	46.9	49.0
Finland	28.6	29.9	32.0	29.8	33.5	34.9
France	23.0	22.3	21.9	23.9	25.2	25.3
Germany	23.1	22.9	23.8	24.9	24.1	23.6
Greece	15.0	17.7	17.9	19.0	22.6	24.7
Ireland	24.3	28.6	27.2	29.2	33.3	34.5
Italy	15.6	15.1	13.6	18.6	22.7	23.8
Japan	14.3	15.3	14.9	18.0	19.5	20.2
Luxembourg	20.6	21.6	27.6	29.0	32.0	31.6
Netherlands	23.0	24.4	26.9	28.4	25.1	26.2
New Zealand	24.7	27.4	31.3	33.0	33.8	32.9
Norway	29.3	33.0	33.7	37.2	37.7	38.7
Portugal	14.4	17.5	16.2	20.2	23.3	23.3
Spain	10.6	10.8	10.3	12.4	16.9	18.5
Sweden	31.1	34.2	35.3	35.1	38.0	40.1
Switzerland	16.1	18.2	21.0	21.3	21.8	22.3
Turkey	14.1	16.5	18.8	18.6	16.9	19.8
United Kingdom	25.9	32.0	29.3	29.5	31.3	32.0
United States	21.6	23.6	21.9	21.8	20.6	20.3
Unweighted average						
OECD total	21.7	24.1	25.1	26.5	28.0	28.7
OECD Europe	21.7	24.2	25.1	26.7	28.4	29.3
EEC	20.4	23.0	23.6	25.8	27.9	28.6

Source: OECD, *Revenue Statistics of OECD Member Countries*, 1965–1987 (Paris: OECD, 1988), p. 84.

A second type of comparison examines different tax structures in terms of composition by major types of tax. Table 6.5 does this for 1986 with reference to income, payroll, property and goods and services taxation; in short, on the basis of the tax classification which was discussed in the context of Table 6.3.[13] Table 6.5 places Australia second to Finland in the relative importance of income tax as a revenue raiser in terms of total tax revenue (but only eighth in terms of the importance of income taxes relative to GDP). It is sixth (or seventh in terms of GDP) with respect to property taxation, and eleventh (sixteenth relative to GDP) with respect to taxes on goods and services. Although not discernible from this table, Australia levies no really general sales taxation. As shown in Chapter 12, Australia's wholesale sales tax is a rather selective instrument, and quite unlike the widely used broad based consumption taxes in other OECD countries. Australia's property taxes (as shown in Chapter 11) exclude taxes on the ownership and/or transfer of wealth by gift or bequest. Australia's heavy reliance on income taxation which was noted earlier in the context of comparing changes in its tax structure over time, remains an unusual feature when compared to OECD practice.

A final international tax comparison which is frequently made is with reference to tax burdens measured by disposable income as a percentage of gross earnings for an average

Table 6.5 Tax revenue of main headings as percentage of total taxation — 1986

	1000 Income & profits	*2000 Social security*	*3000 Payroll*	*4000 Property*	*5000 Goods & services*	*6000 Other*
Australia	55.6	—	5.9	8.0	30.5	—
Austria	26.8	31.9	5.8	2.4	32.1	1.1
Belgium	40.4	33.6	—	1.9	24.0	0.1
Canada	45.9	13.7	—	9.4	29.7	1.3
Denmark	56.2	3.1	0.5	4.7	35.4	0.2
Finland	51.9	9.0	—	3.1	35.8	0.2
France	18.2	42.7	2.0	4.8	29.4	2.9
Germany	34.5	37.2	—	3.1	25.2	—
Greece	17.5	32.6	1.6	2.7	45.4	0.1
Ireland	36.1	14.2	1.7	3.9	44.1	—
Italy	37.9	34.3	0.5	2.7	24.6	—
Japan	45.7	29.8	—	10.9	13.4	0.3
Luxembourg	43.2	25.6	0.6	6.2	24.5	—
Netherlands	27.7	42.5	—	3.6	26.0	0.3
New Zealand	70.5	—	1.0	1.7	26.9	—
Norway	36.1	22.2	—	2.1	38.8	0.6
Portugal	21.2	28.1	—	1.9	48.0	0.9
Spain	25.2	39.1	—	3.2	32.0	0.6
Sweden	42.8	25.0	4.5	2.8	24.8	0.2
Switzerland	41.2	31.6	—	8.4	18.8	—
Turkey	39.0	12.8	—	3.3	31.5	13.4
United Kingdom	38.2	17.9	—	12.9	30.9	—
United States	42.4	29.8	—	10.3	17.5	—
Unweighted average:						
OECD total	38.9	24.2	1.0	4.9	30.0	1.0
OECD Europe	35.2	26.9	1.0	4.1	31.7	1.1
EEC	33.0	29.2	0.6	4.3	32.6	0.4

Source: OECD, *Revenue Statistics of OECD Member Countries* 1965–1987 (Paris: OECD, 1988), Table 7, p. 85.

production worker in a one-earner family. On OECD data prepared for a study on the tax benefit position of selected income groups in OECD member countries, Australia ranked twelfth in severity of taxation on this measure; a subsequent study ranked Australia among the top ten in tax severity measured in terms of personal income tax relative to gross earnings (but excluding the effects of non-standard tax reliefs and cash benefits for households with an employed breadwinner.)[14] Many other types of more detailed tax comparisons are possible, but, as already implied in the type of comparisons mentioned in this paragraph, the greater the detail, the greater the risk of potential incompatibility between the things being compared.

The discussion of this chapter has focused on the anatomy of tax systems, with specific reference to how tax systems can change over time and how they can differ between countries. Apart from providing thereby some background of real tax systems to the generally more abstract discussion of the two subsequent chapters on taxation, this discussion of tax systems has laid the foundations for the discussion of some Australian fiscal federalism and tax reform problems to be discussed in Chapters 15 and 20.

GLOSSARY OF TAX TERMINOLOGY

To avoid scattered definitions, and the need to repeat them unduly, a glossary of frequently used tax definitions concludes this introductory chapter.[15]

Ability-to-pay-principle — The view that taxes should be levied according to income and/or wealth ownership, those with the highest income and/or wealth, paying relatively most (see Chapter 7 for further discussion).

Accelerated depreciation — Allowing the cost of a capital asset to be written off against tax liability more quickly than would be indicated by the actual year-by-year fall in the asset's value during its working life.

Assessable income — All income derived by a taxpayer not exempt from tax. Taxable income is assessable income less all allowable deductions.

Avoidance — Legal rearrangement of affairs to minimise tax liability.

Benefit principle — The view that taxes should be levied in accordance with the benefits received from the services financed by these taxes (see Chapter 7 for further discussion).

'Black' or 'underground' economy — The aggregate of unrecorded activity which escapes economic measurement and tax assessment, due generally to its reliance on cash transactions.

Broad-based consumption tax (BBCT) — The term broad-based consumption tax is a generic term used to describe both multi-stage taxes such as the Value Added Tax and single-stage taxes such as the retail sales taxes applied in the United States and Canada. In the 1985 Draft White Paper on Tax Reform the term referred to a single-stage retail tax.

Capital gains: — Increase in value of an asset.
- *Nominal* — Monetary increase in value of an asset, that is, without adjusting for inflation.
- *Real* — Increase in value of an asset after adjusting for inflation.
- *Accrued* — Estimated annual increase in value of an asset.
- *Realised* — Increase in value of an asset as determined when asset is sold.

Classical company tax system — System where a company and its shareholders are taxed as separate entities with no allowance given to shareholders, when assessed on their dividend income, for tax paid at company level.

Deduction

Item allowed as offset against assessable income; for example, work-related expenses, donations to approved charities.

Dependent spouse rebate

Amount subtracted from personal income tax liability if taxpayer has dependent spouse. Rebate is reduced if dependent spouse has income above specified amount. Higher rebate applies if taxpayer also has one or more dependent children.

Direct tax

Tax paid by the individuals on whom it is levied: personal income tax, company tax, local rates on owner-occupied house are taxes classed as direct for national accounting purposes.

Double taxation of dividends

Situation where a company's distributed profits are subject to both company tax and personal income tax.

Economic depreciation

Actual year-by-year fall in value of an asset during its working life.

Equity:

Horizontal

Similar tax treatment of individuals in similar circumstances.

Vertical

Different tax treatment of individuals in different circumstances, with better-off bearing a greater tax burden than less well off.

Evasion

Illegal arrangement of affairs so as to eliminate or reduce tax liability, for example, understatement of taxable income, over-statement of deductions.

Excise

Tax imposed on value or quantity of production of particular commodity (e.g., cigarettes, alcohol and petroleum). In Australia, all excises are imposed on quantity of production.

Foreign tax credit

System under which foreign source income of residents is subject to domestic tax and credit given for foreign tax paid on that income.

Fringe benefits

Material rewards for employment over and above wages and salaries paid. Usually take the form of non-money income (e.g., company car for private purposes) but sometimes involve cash (e.g., expense allowance which remains partly unspent).

Gearing
Use of borrowings to acquire assets. Used to magnify tax deductions in tax sheltering arrangements.

Incidence of a tax:

Legal incidence
Point where tax is legally assessed, for example, formal incidence of company tax is the company.

Effective incidence
Ultimate bearer of tax following adjustments to economic behaviour after tax is imposed.

Indirect tax
Comprise taxes assessed on producers, in respect to the production, sale, purchase or use of goods and services, charged to expenses of production and ultimately passed on to final consumers.

Income-splitting
Artificial increase in number of individuals deriving a given income in order to lower tax liability otherwise payable on that income.

Input-taxing
Taxing inputs (e.g., raw materials, machinery, services) used in production of a commodity, but not sales of that commodity.

Investment allowance
Income tax deduction additional to depreciation. In June 1985 applied at rate of 18 per cent of initial expenditure on eligible new plant and equipment incurred under contract entered into (or where construction commences) before 1 July 1985 provided plant is first used or installed ready for use by 30 June 1987.

Negative gearing
Investment (e.g., in rental property) structured so that deductible expenses in early years exceed income from property, with excess being offset against, and thus reducing tax on, income from other sources.

Neutral tax system
Tax system with minimal impact on the economic behaviour of economic entities, or one with no excess burden.

Pay as you earn (PAYE)
Tax instalment deduction system requiring tax to be deducted by employer from salary and wages and remitted to Tax Office on behalf of employee.

Poverty trap — Situation where, due to interaction between income taxation and income tests on social security benefits, beneficiaries are exposed to very high effective withdrawal rates.

Prescribed payments system (PPS) — Deduction of tax at source in respect of certain payments (in prescribed industries where tax evasion known to be significant) for work and services not subject to existing PAYE system.

Rebate — An amount by which tax liability is reduced.

Regressive tax — Where average rate of tax falls as income rises.

Tax base — Object to which tax rate applies, for example, income, wealth or consumption.

Tax expenditure — Reliefs or concessions in tax system (not being a basic component of the taxation structure) which reduce tax liability and have effect on the Government's Budget similar to direct expenditures.

Tax havens — Countries with very low, or nil, tax rates on some or all forms of income, together with accommodating financial institutions and other arrangements favourable to tax avoidance or evasion activities.

Tax rates:

Average — Tax payable divided by taxable income expressed as a percentage. (Synonymous with effective tax rate.)

Marginal — Percentage of extra dollar of income paid in tax.

Tax unit — Entity recognised by law as responsible for paying tax, for example, individual income earner, company, wholesaler.

Threshold:

Tax-free threshold — Level of taxable income at or below which tax is levied. The personal income tax-free threshold in June 1989 is $5,100 per annum.

Effective tax threshold — Level of taxable income, after taking into account tax rebates, below which no tax is payable.

Trust — Money or property entrusted to a person (the trustee) to administer in the interests of others (the beneficiaries).

Unearned income — Income derived from assets rather than work, for example, interest from bank deposits, dividends from shares. (Sometimes called property income.)

Value-added tax (VAT) Multi-stage sales tax on consumer goods and services, levied on amount of value added (excess of firm's sales over purchases of inputs) at each stage in production and distribution process.

Withholding at source Arrangements whereby tax is withheld at source and credit is given against taxpayer's final liability at end-of-year assessment (e.g., the PAYE and PPS arrangements).

Withholding tax Arrangement for withholding tax payable at source where it is a final tax (e.g., in relation to dividend and interest payments to non-residents.)

SUMMARY

1. Taxation is the major source of government finance. Other sources include charges and fees and fines, including operating surpluses (or the contribution therefrom to the Budget) from government business enterprises and government borrowing.

2. Tax instruments can be classified by

   i level of government
   ii type of tax or tax base or whether they are direct or indirect, or narrow-based or broad-based.

3. The direct and indirect tax classification is now only useful for national accounting purposes (it is used in distinguishing GDP at factor cost from that at market prices) and in the context of international agreements on appropriate policy behaviour such as the GATT rules. It remains a popular distinction in public discussion.

4. International tax comparisons are a useful mechanism by which to learn from the practice of other countries.

NOTES

1 For a discussion of pre-Federation (colonial) taxation, see Alan Barnard, "Government Finance", in Wray Vamplew (ed.), *Australia's Historical Statistics*, (Sydney: Fairfax, Syme and Weldon Associates, 1987), ch. 15., esp. pp. 282–3.

2 Just prior to Federation, customs and excise duties accounted for approximately 75% of State tax revenue. See R.L. Mathews and W.R.C. Jay, *Federal Finance* (Melbourne: Nelson, 1972), Table 6. The federal financial relations issues discussed in this and the next paragraph are discussed in more detail in Chapter 15.

3 This classification was introduced by C.S. Shoup, *Public Finance* (London: Macmillan, 1969), ch. 1. For a critical discussion of this method, see A.R. Prest, "On the Distinction Between Direct and Indirect Taxation", in W.L. David (ed.), *Public Finance, Planning and Economic Development Essays in Honour of Ursula Hicks* (London: Macmillan, 1973), pp. 53–4.

4 That is *Taxation Revenue Australia*, Cat. No. 5506.0 annually published.

5 For details see Australian Bureau of Statistics, *Classifications Manual for Government Finance Statistics Australia*, Cat. No. 1217.0, (Canberra: ABS 1984), pp. 78–99, as well as the introductions to *Taxation Revenue Australia* with respect to taxes subsequently introduced.

6 Capital gains tax are taxed under personal income tax or company income tax, depending in whose hands the capital gains are taxable. Capital gains tax issues are discussed in more detail subsequently in Chapter 9.

7 EPAC Discussion Paper 88/13, Enterprise Based Training (Canberra, EPAC, November 1988), "Policies for Skill Formation" by W.J. Bailey and E.A. Mayer, esp. pp. 12–16.

8 For details of fringe benefit taxation, see Chapter 10.

9 See Taxation Review Committee, *Full Report* (Canberra: AGPS, 1975), pp. 511, 520–2; Commonwealth of Australia, *Reform of the Australian Tax System*, Draft White Paper (Canberra: AGPS, June 1985), introduction, and for academic discussion of these points, R.L. Mathews, "The Structure of Taxation" in John Wilkes (ed.), *The Politics of Taxation* (Sydney: Hodder & Stoughton, 1980) and Peter Groenewegen, "Rationalising Australian Taxation Revisited", *Economic Record* 60 (169) June 1984, pp. 113–27. This issue of tax reform is further pursued in Chapter 20.

10 See A.R. Prest, "On the Distinction Between Direct and Indirect Taxation", R.A. and P.B. Musgrave, *Public Finance in Theory and Practice* (New York: McGraw Hill, 1984), pp. 223–4, substitute personal and *in rem* taxation which they prefer to the ambiguous direct versus indirect classification. Personal taxes must be placed on persons (households), *in rem* taxes may be placed on households or firms.

11 For a discussion of the direct/indirect classification with respect to the OECD classification by type of tax used in Table 6.3, see *Classifications Manual for Government Finance Statistics Australia*, pp. 78–99. On this basis approximately 60 per cent of taxation in Australia in 1987–88 was direct, 40 per cent indirect, with 90 per cent of direct taxation in the form of income taxation.

12 For a survey of this long debate in welfare economics see D. Walker, "Direct v Indirect Taxation", in R.W. Houghton (ed.), *Public Finance* (Harmondsworth: Penguin, 1973), Reading 16. If the distinction between direct and indirect taxes was dropped, few problems would arise. These relate to the validity of a factor cost concept of GDP; the use of ratios incorporating GDP in cross-section or time series analysis; the validity of a notion of the Consumer Price Index discounted for "indirect taxes" for the purpose of wage hearings or personal income tax indexation; the GATT rules about the remission of "indirect taxes" on exports. Most of these problems can be easily solved, with the additional advantage from the abolition of this terminology that a misleading distinction has been removed from official and popular usage.

13 Because Australia does not use the social security contributions included as group 2000 in the OECD classification, group 3000 in Table 6.5 is the equivalent of group 2 in Table 6.3; group 4000 of group 3, group 5000 of group 4 and group 6000 covers groups 5 and 9 of the Australian classification.

14 OECD, *The Tax Benefits Position of Selected Income Groups in OECD Member Countries* (Paris: OECD, 1980), p. 42; OECD, *Taxation in Developed Countries* (Paris: OECD, 1987),

Attachment A, p. 79. As indicated in the text, these results reported in the two studies are not comparable, predicated as they are on different measures of tax burdens.

[15] This glossary draws heavily on that provided as part of the Draft White Paper, *Reform of the Australian Tax System*, pp. x–xiv.

FURTHER READING

Again, the other leading textbooks provide a useful perspective. See, for example:

R.A. and P.B. Musgrave, *Public Finance in Theory and Practice*, 4th edn. (New York: McGraw Hill, 1984), ch. 10.

C.V. Brown and P.M. Jackson, *Public Sector Economics*, 3rd edn. (Oxford: Blackwells, 1986), ch. 10.

J.E. Stiglitz, *Economics of the Public Sector*, 2nd edn. (New York: W.W. Norton, 1988), ch. 16, pp. 386–8.

On tax classification see:

A.R. Prest, "On the Distinction between Direct and Indirect Taxation", in W.L. David (ed.), *Public Finance, Planning and Economic Development: Essays in Honour of Ursula Hicks* (London: Macmillan, 1973).

Australian tax data and international tax data can be regularly updated by using the latest issue of:

Australian Bureau of Statistics, *Taxation Revenue Australia* (Canberra: ABS, Cat. No. 5506).

OECD, *Revenue Statistics of Member Countries* (Paris: OECD).

IMF, *Government Finance Statistics* (Washington, DC: IMF).

7

Principles of taxation

In discussions of tax reform or, more generally, examination of tax policy issues, reference is invariably made to principles of taxation. Taxation is such an important part of organised human existence, arising as it did as soon as government and social order were established,[1] that principles of tax justice developed relatively quickly. Having examined the structure of Australian taxation, and compared it with its counterparts in the developed world, general tax criteria can be examined. At the outset it needs to be stated that many of these principles and criteria are imprecise, that they are often difficult to define clearly, so that their application is frequently hazardous. Nevertheless, their meaning must be as clearly grasped as possible, because many of the tax criteria draw attention to principles which students of taxation neglect at their peril.

Given its social importance, it is not surprising that the topic of taxation was one of the first subjects studied by economists. Early economic writers were especially eager to see whether rules could be found whereby to judge if taxes were good, or harmful, to society. One of the earliest important English contributions to this subject is Sir William Petty's *A Treatise of Taxes and Contributions* published in 1662.[2] The search for taxation criteria was greatly advanced when Adam Smith in 1776 introduced his discussion of the subject by laying down four maxims of taxation which remain relevant. These maxims are as follows:

> The subjects of every State ought to contribute toward the support of the government, as nearly as possible, in proportion to their respective abilities; that is, in proportion to the revenue which they respectively enjoy under the protection of the State . . . The tax which each individual is bound to pay ought to be certain and not arbitrary . . . Every tax ought to be levied at the time, or in the manner, in which it is most likely to be convenient for the contributor to pay it . . . Every tax ought to be contrived as both to take out and to keep out of the pockets of the people as little as possible over and above what it brings into the public treasury of the State.[3]

The last three maxims are hardly debatable. There should be economy in the administration and collection of taxation to ensure that the bulk of the revenue goes to finance government expenditure; taxes which are expensive to administer should be avoided as much as possible. Taxes should also be levied in a manner convenient to the taxpayer; for example, the PAYE (pay as you earn) instalment deductions by which most personal income tax is collected make it far easier for the average person to pay income tax liability than if a lump sum had to be paid at the end of the year. Finally, taxes should not be arbitrary; the taxpayer should know tax liability and when and where to pay it. A corollary to this important tax maxim is a plea for simplicity in the law by which taxation is assessed and collected.

Smith's administrative maxims were elaborated on by Sir Josiah Stamp in the 1920s. These added several desirable qualities which tax systems needed to have, given the experience of nineteenth-century tax administrations. Administrative feasibility was one principle Stamp explicitly took into account. In this context, he stressed ease of evasion and incentive to dishonesty as matters needing particular attention. In introducing new tax measures, he emphasised the need to avoid both political unrest and international conflicts involving other tax jurisdictions.[4] All these principles are still to be kept in mind when formulating tax policy proposals.

Returning to Smith's four tax maxims, the first is the most interesting from the *theoretical* point of view. It contains elements of the two great modern principles of tax justice — the benefit principle and the ability to pay principle — developed in the second half of the nineteenth century. The benefit principle states that people should contribute to taxation according to the benefits they receive from government expenditure, while the second principle argues that people should pay taxes according to their taxable capacity as measured by their "revenue", that is, their income or their property or both.

For Smith, these two principles led to the same conclusion: proportional taxation of income and wealth. His first maxim linked personal tax contributions proportionally to personal revenue, thereby indicating the ability to pay principle. His comments about State protection of the enjoyment of this revenue, links the maxim to the benefit principle because the protection of property (defence, law, and order) was the major function of the government of the day. The result of both the principles was that the rich should pay more in taxes. In the nineteenth century it was argued, among others by John Stuart Mill, that the poor gained more from State expenditure so that the benefit principle resulted in a tax rule opposite to that derived from ability to pay.[5] Neither of these conclusions holds as simply for the twentieth century. These principles need, therefore, to be interpreted in the light of contemporary tax issues.

Before discussing them further, it should be pointed out that these nineteenth-century principles have a close affinity to the more modern criteria of taxation, that is, the criteria of "efficiency", "equity", and "simplicity". Although there are many difficulties in their application to practical tax problems unless their meaning is very precisely defined, they nevertheless embody much of what is fruitful in the more traditional approach to tax principles.

The ability to pay principle

The ability to pay principle is now one of the most widely accepted principles of taxation, though its practical application is frequently disputed. It is concerned with the "just distribution" of the tax burden. Once the level of public expenditure is exogenously determined by the workings of the political process, the task is to distribute the resulting tax burden in conformity to this principle. Two problems immediately arise in its application:

what is the index of ability to pay, and what type of rate structure is suggested by the principle?

The index of ability to pay

According to Smith's first maxim, a person's ability to pay taxes is reflected in the amount of revenue enjoyed. There are a variety of practical difficulties in this concept of revenue. If revenue is taken to mean money income, several problems arise. In the first place, money income by itself without any regard to wealth ownership does not fully reflect taxable capacity. For example, does a person with $10,000 a year have a greater ability to pay taxes than a person with property worth $50,000 from which an annual income of $4,000 is derived? Secondly, money income should be related to the time taken to earn it. A person who earns $10,000 with six months work has a higher taxable capacity than the person who earns the same amount over a full year. The problem of leisure in connection with taxation to which this aspect of ability to pay measurement draws attention, is unfortunately more far-reaching, as discussed subsequently in the context of efficiency. Finally, as Kaldor argued in particular,[6] actual consumption expenditure can be regarded as a better index of capacity to pay taxes since it provides the real measure of a person's economic well-being by utilising the income actually enjoyed.

The issue of what is the best measure of capacity to pay taxes is not easily resolved in practice, though the working solution that most countries have adopted is to impose a major tax on personal income, perhaps supplemented by a tax on personal wealth. Even if as a working solution it is decided that income is the generally preferred index of ability to pay, some difficult problems have to be solved. First, the *meaning of income* should be clearly defined, and this raises many legal and conceptual difficulties. Secondly, should all *forms of income* be treated equally, for example, should property income be treated differently from income from personal exertion? Furthermore, should there be a level of minimum exempt income? Should individual or household income be the measure of ability to pay? Finally, should income be calculated on an annual basis or over the whole life-cycle? These questions are examined in more detail in Chapter 9 where the concept of income for personal income taxation is discussed.

The rate structure

Once the index of ability to pay has been decided, there is still the problem of the rate structure. Should taxation be progressive, that is, levied at rates which rise as income rises, or should it be levied at proportional rates or at regressive rates, that is, at rates which fall as income rises? Many attempts have been made in the past to provide a "scientific foundation" for the correct degree of progressive taxation, but none was successful.[7] The *principle* of progressive taxation is therefore an *ethical* judgement while the degree of progression is largely a matter of *social and political choice*.[8]

The benefit principle

The benefit approach views taxation as a price for the individual services produced by government and argues that "tax justice" requires that those who benefit from government services should pay the cost in the form of taxation. This view, as mentioned in Chapter 4, underlies the voluntary exchange models of Budget determination. The benefit principle therefore stresses resource allocation efficiency and has little to say on the distributional issues involved in taxation policy. This is in contrast to the ability-to-pay principle which emphasises distributional issues, largely ignores allocation, and is not inconsistent with stabilisation objectives because it leaves government expenditure undetermined.

In the discussion of the voluntary exchange model in Chapter 4, it was concluded that although the benefit principle has a number of advantages — such as strongly interrelating public expenditure decisions and taxation policy — it is difficult to apply in practice. This does not mean that the benefit principle is useless and irrelevant; in Australia, for example, it is often applied to local government taxation.[9] It can also be applied to the case of so-called earmarked taxes and it also has some relevance to the problem of public utility prices. Each of these will be briefly considered in turn.

The benefit approach and earmarked taxes[10]

The earmarking of the proceeds of certain taxes for particular public expenditures is an extension of the principle that those who benefit should pay. An example of earmarking taxes is provided by the frequent suggestions made by motorists, that revenue from the excise on petrol should be directed to roadworks.[11] According to motorist organisations such as the National Roads and Motorists Association of New South Wales, this would be more equitable than paying this revenue into consolidated revenue fund. At first sight this seems to be a fair argument and easy to apply in practice. In fact, although it is of course easy to earmark the revenue of a specific tax for a specific purpose,[12] it is very difficult to *match* the benefits enjoyed by users and the tax incidence upon those users. The difficulties associated with the latter are frequently not stressed.

In the first place, to apply the theory of earmarked taxes to motorists, all taxes on motorists and all government services provided for their benefit would have to be identified. These are by no means confined to the excise on petrol and the provision of road space. Taxes on motorists on the whole can be fairly easily identified. As shown in Chapter 6, apart from those on petrol, they include sales tax on motor vehicles and parts, and the registration and other licence fees imposed by State governments on the ownership and use of vehicles. The public services provided for them are more difficult to define; they include not only road space and all that goes with it, but parking facilities, traffic police and other forms of traffic control, hospital and ambulance services in connection with road accidents, and a variety of other general administrative costs. To estimate the total money value for all these services would be a major research undertaking, yet this would be required if taxes on motorists were to be genuinely earmarked for the provision of services to them.

The difficulties do not stop there. Some of the services for motorists are provided from taxes which do not only fall on motorists. Local government rates which finance a large proportion of road expenditure are a good example. In addition, there are problems of incidence arising from both the taxes on and the services provided for motorists. A good deal of these taxes and benefits are shifted through changes in the prices of goods transported by road; while there is also an externalities problem which in much of the expenditure on motorists would be difficult to handle. Furthermore, many of the charges on motorists are flat charges independent of the consumption of the services provided; this creates more problems. Finally, the whole procedure ignores distributional questions, and the taxation of motorists is far too large a portion of total taxation revenue to do this with impunity.

There is, however, a more fundamental difficulty with earmarking taxes as an application of the benefit principle. The discussion in the previous two paragraphs about the matching of benefits to taxes on motorists suggests a one-for-one trade between the tax cost of the motorist and the expenditure by the government on services for motorists. In fact, the actual benefit from these services derived by the motorist may far exceed the cost of providing them, as is recognised in the theory of consumer surplus.[13] Even if the problems raised in the previous discussion can be solved, it could eventuate that "true tax" contribution of the motorists is valued at $100 million, the spending on roads and other services is valued at only $50 million but this spending generates benefits valued at $200 million by road users. The major problem of the benefit approach therefore is that it does not make clear whether it is the Budget cost of providing the benefit or the utility of the benefit received by users which is the proper basis for its application.

The benefit approach and public utility pricing

The pricing of public utilities at first sight seems to be a fruitful area for the application of the benefit principle, since here the consumer is frequently, but not always, required to pay the full cost of the service. This, however, is more apparent than real. When public utilities are run at a loss, as is the case, for example, with all State railway systems, the principle does not apply, since non-users pay part of the cost. Even when the public utilities break even or make a profit, there are difficulties. For instance, Australia Post which on the adoption of the user-pay principle has generally made profits, does not really apply the benefit principle strictly in its pricing policies, since this would involve a highly complex differential tariff system. For example, the standard letter rate would have to vary according to distance and handling costs, and would not be set at the flat charge per letter which generally applies to Australia as a whole. Likewise, Telecom's tariff structure includes a wide array of cross-subsidisation between users in the interest of meeting its community obligations.

In spite of such problems, increased concerns about accountability for the providers of public services matched with the alleged efficiency benefits from the application of commercial principles to public service provision, the benefit principle in the guise of user-pay is increasingly being adopted as the superior public services pricing principle in public policy discussion.[14] Pursuing this matter further would take the discussion into the realms of public sector economics which were explicitly excluded from this book.

The essence of the benefit approach is therefore the attempt at applying market principles to the government sector and thereby to bring the theory of government finance and taxation within the theory of resource allocation applicable to a competitive market system. Where a government can readily identify beneficiaries, this suggests a strong case for transferring the activity out of the Budget sector and closer to the market. This happened with the provision of postal, and telecommunication services and, increasingly, transport services in Australia from the mid-1970s. Removing these activities from the Budget sector, and their commercialisation or corporatisation is designed to increase their efficiency by placing them under the discipline of the market and the profit motive. The fact that these types of services have social as well as private aspects — for example, subsidised prices for certain classes of customers for welfare and other reasons — creates difficulties for such removal and the need for special analysis of the economics of public enterprises. As indicated earlier, this field lies outside the scope of this book.

THE MODERN CRITERIA OF TAXATION: EQUITY, EFFICIENCY, SIMPLICITY

The two traditional principles of taxation do not fully meet all the purposes of modern economic policy, which are partly achieved through the Budget, that is, the allocational, distributional, and stabilisation functions. For this reason, three broader criteria of taxation: equity, efficiency, and simplicity, are more frequently cited in current writings on taxation and tax reform.[15] These three criteria embody what is fruitful in the two more traditional approaches to taxation principles, and their meaning must therefore be carefully specified.

Equity or fairness

The benefit and ability-to-pay principles were both proposed as principles of just or fair taxation, but the modern principle of equity invariably relies upon ability to pay considerations. The difficulties in applying that principle — particularly the measure of capacity to pay taxes and the rate structure to be imposed — have already been mentioned, so how then is fair or equitable taxation defined? There is no simple definition of this principle but the following is generally accepted. Fairness in the tax system implies equal treatment for people with equal capacities to pay; it also implies that those with different capacities to pay taxes should be treated differently, that is, the proportion of income they pay in taxes should rise with capacity to pay. These two implications of tax fairness are called "horizontal equity" and "vertical equity" respectively. Their arbitrariness is indicated by the fact that both depend on the measure and definition of capacity to pay taxes, which, as shown earlier, is not straightforward. Some examples will illustrate this.

Horizontal equity

From the definition of horizontal equity, it follows that if income is used as the measure of ability to pay, then two people earning $50,000 per annum should also pay the same amount in taxation. This raises several anomalies. For example, $50,000 per annum for a single person implies a different capacity to pay tax than the same amount of income for a person with a dependent spouse and three dependent children. Furthermore, $50,000 largely obtained from property income by one person implies a different capacity to pay than $50,000 paid as wages to a worker who has worked a great deal of overtime or who works at a dangerous job. A variety of circumstances may therefore drive a wedge between income and capacity to pay. In such circumstances tax authorities have tried to maintain fairness in the system by allowing special treatment for taxpayers with dependants, for example. This is discussed in more detail in Chapter 9 in the context of income tax.

Different tax treatment between income from work (personal exertion) and property has also been abolished in most income tax systems, despite the obvious horizontal equity issues involved. These are discussed further in Chapter 11 in the context of wealth taxation. No tax system has been able to take account of the time spent in earning income or the arduousness of the work. In fact, many adjustments for horizontal equity reasons are based on social or political judgements and are constrained by what is administratively feasible. They likewise provided much opportunity for "pork-barrelling" at election time by giving specific concessions to crucial sections of the community for electoral purposes. [16]

Horizontal equity issues are not confined to income tax. Broadening the consumption tax base can also be justified on horizontal equity grounds. Selective consumption taxation as used in Australia, discriminates between households with equal economic capacity in terms of income purely on the ground of their consumption preferences.[17]

Vertical equity or the progressivity of taxation

Vertical equity embodies the principle that those with a higher capacity to pay should pay *relatively* more in taxation, and therefore sanctions a progressive rate structure. What that progressive rate structure should be, is a key question. The degree of progression adopted in setting income tax rates will be influenced by consideration of the expected effects of high marginal tax rates[18] on incentives to work and to save, as well as by political factors such as the tolerance of taxpayers to such high rates. The question of what is the "proper degree of progression in taxation" is not exclusively resolved by economic analysis.

Given such vertical equity considerations, often exclusively linked with the degree of progression in personal income tax, it is useful to recall the inclusion of prevention of avoidance and evasion among Josiah Stamp's set of tax principles. Failure to enforce compliance with the provisions of a progressive income tax by enabling the well-to-do to escape intended liability through legal loopholes, is hardly conducive to vertical equity. This was stressed in the Federal Government's 1985 *Draft White Paper on Tax Reform*[19] in the context of a widespread, and justifiable, belief that the personal income tax had become a voluntary tax for many taxpayers, because of the ease with which many non-wage and salary earners could evade or avoid its provisions.

Efficiency

Tax systems should also be "efficient". Like the attribute of equity, the meaning of efficiency in connection with taxation is complex. One efficiency aspect in taxation is that tax structures should be suitable and flexible to achieve budgetary objectives of resource allocation, income distribution, stabilisation, and economic growth. In this sense, an efficient tax structure implies that suitable tax instruments are available for altering the allocation of resources redistributing income and wealth, changing aggregate demand levels to secure desired unemployment and inflation rates. When the various tax instruments are discussed in Chapters 9–13, their efficiency will be looked at from this point of view.

Efficiency in connection with taxation is more frequently defined[20] in terms of neutrality with respect to consumer or business decisions. Any tax interference in these decisions results in an "excess burden" for the taxpayer. Further examination of the excess burden concept helps to explain the notion of tax neutrality.

The notion of excess burden is most easily demonstrated in terms of a partial equilibrium analysis of the effects of an excise tax on a commodity in perfectly elastic supply. The imposition of a tax levied at a specific rate then raises the supply curve from SS to S'S' (as shown in Figure 7.1) with the consequence that price rises from OS to OS' and quantity sold is reduced by EC to OC. The tax levied at the rate SS'/OS raises SS'AB revenue. Prior to the tax, consumers paid OEFS to purchase OE of the commodity priced at OS but would have paid OEFP, so that the consumer surplus before tax is the triangle SFP. After tax, the same consumers pay OCAS' to purchase OC of the commodity at the after-tax price of OS', which entails a reduction in their consumer surplus to S'AD. The difference between pre-tax and post-tax consumer surplus of SFAS' is partly explained by the revenue transferred to the

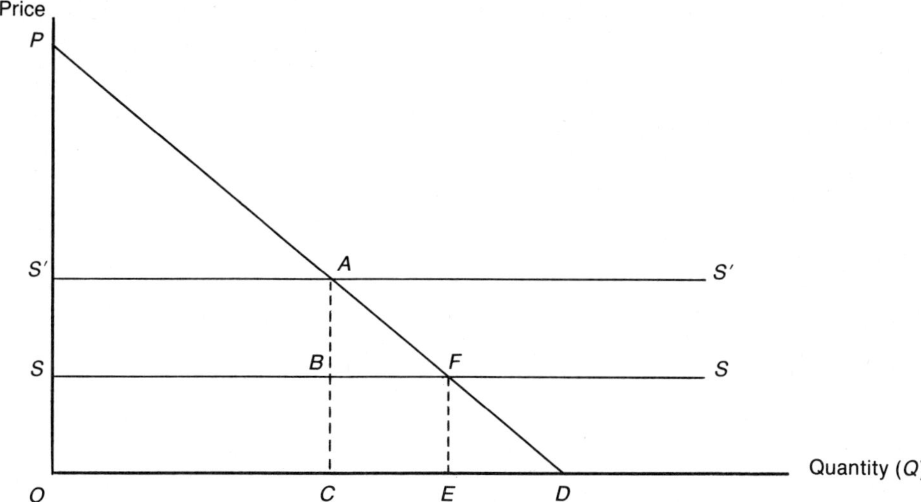

Note: The formula in the text is derived from the fact that the area of the excess burden triangle *BFA* equals ½.Δ*P*.Δ*Q*, and since t equals Δ*P*/*P* and E = Δ*Q*/*Q*.*P*/Δ*P* substitution achieves the relationship between excess burden size, tax rate and price elasticity of demand.

Figure 7.1 Excess burden of an excise on a commodity produced under conditions of perfectly elastic supply

government (that is, SBAS') but this leaves an excess burden of the tax measured by the difference between the aggregate loss of consumer surplus and the revenue collected by the government, or the little triangle BFA.

A number of conclusions can be derived from this simplified analysis. First, the size of the consumer loss in this simple case can be estimated by the area of the triangle which is given by the formula, $^1/_2$ E.t.^{2}.P.Q. where E is the price elasticity of demand, t the tax rate and P and Q stand for price and quantity. Excess burden is therefore greater the greater the elasticity of demand and the greater the tax rate. This leads to a second conclusion. The more inelastic the demand for the commodity taxed, the lower will be the excess burden, *ceteris paribus*. Thus commodities exhibiting low price elasticities of demand, that is, necessities, produce less excess burden for any rate of tax than taxes on luxuries with higher price elasticities of demand. This proposition forms the foundation for the optimal tax rule that efficiency is increased in a tax regime which concentrates on the taxation of necessities.[21]

Excess burdens do not of course arise only from taxes. They can arise from any interference in choices exercised by consumers or producers. Confining ourselves to taxation, however, it can easily be shown that all taxes involve alterations of choices and thereby induce excess burdens. The one exception is the poll tax or head tax levied irrespective of ability to pay. Since such a tax is undesirable on distributional grounds, this is another illustration of the potential conflict between equity and efficiency already noted in general in Chapter 2. A practical policy conclusion which can be derived from the excess burden concept is that taxes should discriminate as little as possible between commodities and activities, unless a specific alteration in spending or other behaviour is desired by the government. This issue is further examined in the chapters dealing with specific tax forms, especially Chapters 10 to 13.[22]

Some further aspects of efficiency may be addressed in this context. The excess burden or "dead weight welfare losses" aspects of taxation have given rise to attempts to measure such losses. When partial equilibrium approaches were used in such measures they tended to yield relatively modest estimates of welfare losses. General equilibrium approaches to their measurement have yielded more substantial losses, though such estimates should be regarded as tentative and controversial. For the United States, excess burdens of the tax system as a whole have been estimated at 30 per cent of the revenue collected, or approximately ten per cent GDP.[23] However, as the Musgraves have pointed out, the estimated extent of such "excess burden" cannot be used to justify very substantial curtailment of the public sector on general efficiency grounds.[24]

As mentioned earlier, optimal tax rules have been developed for commodity and income taxes in the context of an excess burden analysis. It needs to be explicitly noted here that tax distortions do not only apply to consumption decisions as the simple example given in Figure 7.1 may suggest. Income taxes can distort the work/leisure choice in favour of leisure, the saving/consumption choice in favour of consumption; inter-industry allocation of capital may be distorted by both company tax and property taxation, while many specific tax concessions produce distortions in the industrial sectors to which they apply. These efficiency aspects are discussed when examining the specific instruments of taxation to which they are most relevant. Given the substantial costs which empirical estimates have attributed to such distortions, it is not surprising that rules have been developed for optimal taxes which minimise or eliminate such costs.

From the example of excess burden in Figure 7.1 it was shown that a tax regime concentrating on necessities tends to minimise excess burden, *ceteris paribus*, because of their low price elasticity of demand. In a general equilibrium framework, where the demand for commodities is interdependent with that for leisure, such a view no longer suffices. Minimisation of excess burden then involves heavier taxation on goods complementary to leisure. Such a tax strategy enables the indirect taxation of leisure thereby ending its effective tax exemption which distorts work and consumption choices under commonly used tax regimes.

With respect to income taxation, optimal tax literature has attempted to solve the problem of the appropriate rate of progression. This takes into consideration the distortions in work/leisure (labour supply) choices and consumption/saving (intertemporal allocation) choices high marginal tax rates involve, thereby offsetting the vertical equity advantages of tax progression. The complex solutions to this problem involve detailed knowledge about the distribution of earnings capacities in the population, the behaviour patterns of workers with respect to leisure choices as influenced by net wage earnings, together with knowledge about the social welfare function the society under consideration wishes to apply. This highly sophisticated analysis, although directed to a crucial social choice question for modern developed (and even developing) nations has so far not produced practical solutions to the problem for which it was designed.[25]

Simplicity

Tax systems should also be as administratively simple as possible in order to minimise the cost of assessment and collection not only for the Taxation Department but also for the individual taxpayers in so far as their cost of compliance is concerned. For example, much of the motivation in personal income tax reform over the last decade has come from a desire to simplify this complex tax for as many taxpayers as possible. Likewise, single rating with no exemptions simplifies administration and compliance in a broad based consumption tax. The removal of concessional rebates to enhance simplicity involves a loss of horizontal equity; single rating and no exemptions in broad-based consumption taxes enhances horizontal equity but, in the absence of compensatory measures for certain low-income groups in the community, is certain to have adverse vertical equity consequences.

Costs of compliance are largely related to the cost of record-keeping by the taxpayers and their agents in the form of solicitors and tax accountants. Such costs can be substantial for individual taxpayers with respect to personal income tax and, prior to their abolition, with respect to death duties. For business, compliance costs are usually greater, particularly in those cases where business acts as the tax collector for government. Small business, generally speaking, is particularly badly affected. For example, a commissioned study for the Taxation Review Committee found that compliance costs became more important the smaller the firm. For most small unincorporated enterprises the study found that tax compliance costs exceeded 2.5 per cent of the wage and salary bill whereas this only applied to one-third of incorporated business. Unfortunately, research on this subject has only just begun in Australia.[26]

As the "economy maxim" of Adam Smith indicated, government costs of assessment and collection should also be kept to a minimum. This leads to possible conflicts between fairness in taxation on the one hand, and administrative efficiency on the other. For example, it is possible to introduce a progressive sales tax by discriminating against those luxuries which feature almost exclusively in the consumption budgets of high income groups but such a procedure would be administratively prohibitively expensive. Furthermore, fairness in personal income taxation as far as possible requires elimination of tax evasion and avoidance opportunities. This requirement generally results in rather complex tax legislation. As the Taxation Review Committee pointed out, the general notion of a fair tax system frequently suggests a tax system which is far from simple.[27]

Two ways of increasing the simplicity of the tax system in Australia — and hence lowering administrative and compliance costs — may be briefly mentioned. The first is to reduce the number of taxes and the number of taxpayers liable to any particular tax. The second is to introduce greater uniformity in tax legislation especially in the area of State taxes where the law with respect to these taxes varies from State to State. The lack of uniformity in State taxes is further discussed in Chapters 14 and 15.

Other considerations in tax policy

As noted on several occasions, the Draft White Paper on Tax Reform prepared by Treasury in 1985 listed other considerations of relevance in evaluating a tax system. The need to prevent avoidance and evasion has already been referred to, as has the need to consider the inevitable interaction of tax and social security systems for both efficiency and distributional considerations. In addition, the effects of inflation on tax burdens cannot be ignored in designing tax proposals for countries like Australia where inflation seems to be a continuing problem. Last but not least, the ability of a tax system to raise the required revenue for the exercise of public expenditure responsibilities, should always be kept in mind in tax policy discussion. As this book has already emphasised on many occasions, taxation is only the other side of the public expenditure coin.[28]

The principles of taxation and tax reform

The principles which have been discussed in this chapter, despite many shortcomings arising from their imprecise meaning and their difficulty of application, are nevertheless important for the study of taxation and for the development of proposals for tax reform. No matter what political party is in office in Canberra or in the State capitals, and no matter what tax reforms they envisage, the drafting and implementation of tax reform proposals requires careful application of these principles to study their effect on the distribution of income, on the use made of resources in the private sector, on the fairness of the system as a whole, and on their suitability to act as instruments in stabilisation and growth policy. Although there can be no general agreement on the precise meaning of these principles or an objectively satisfactory manner in which they can be applied, these principles do introduce the relevant considerations which cannot be avoided if meaningful discussion of tax reform is to take place.

The point to be grasped is that there is no system of taxation that contains the "optimal" trade-offs between the various "principles". Taxation systems can only be more or less workable, more or less tolerable, more or less "efficient" and more or less "equitable". The tax principles, as *specified* by our political and social prejudices, or judgements about the need for more or less inequality, more or less neutrality, more or less active interference by governments, and so on, can be used to criticise the existing tax structure or to advance proposals for its reform. As was stated in Chapter 1, an "objective", "value-free" public finance is impossible; any pretensions that such a system of theory could exist, is intellectual fraud. This applies to taxation reform as much as it does to other areas of the subject.

SUMMARY

1. From the introduction of taxation, an introduction concomitant with the beginning of organised society, economists have searched for tax principles of good and just taxation.

2. To Adam Smith's four maxims of tax justice — in terms of capacity to pay, certainty, economy and convenience — Stamp added administrative feasibility, elimination of avoidance and evasion opportunities and prevention of domestic political disturbance and international conflict in judging tax measures.

3. Smith's first maxim of tax justice contains both the ability-to-pay and benefit principles of taxation, the forerunners of the modern tax criteria trinity of equity, simplicity and efficiency.

4. Ability-to-pay as a tax principle concerns itself with just distribution of the tax burden. This principle requires an index of ability-to-pay and the appropriate rate structure to apply to the tax base suggested by that index. Income, but also consumption and wealth have been suggested as appropriate measures of ability to pay tax, sometimes in combination.

5. The benefit approach argues that those who benefit from government services should pay their cost in the form of taxation. This view emphasises resource allocation efficiency but ignores redistribution and stabilisation functions.

6. The modern tax criteria are equity, efficiency and simplicity.

7. Equity can be interpreted vertically or horizontally. Horizontal equity refers to the equal tax treatment of those with equal capacity to pay; vertical equity to the unequal treatment of those with different capacity to pay tax, namely that those with greater taxable capacity should pay proportionally more in tax.

8. Efficiency in taxation likewise has two dimensions. Traditionally, it was applied to the degree of efficiency with which particular taxes could assist in achieving budgetary functions. At present, it is more often identified with neutrality in decision-making and minimising excess burden.

9. Excess burden is the welfare loss from a tax distortion and varies directly with the square of the tax rate involved. Empirical estimates of such welfare losses suggest they are significant for all taxes which distort consumption and production decisions.

10. Simplicity in taxation requires minimum compliance and administration costs.

NOTES

[1] A useful history of taxation starting at the beginning of organised society and within the perspective of expenditure and budgeting is Carolyn Webber and Aaron Wildavsky, *A History of Taxation and Expenditure in the Western World* (New York: Simon and Schuster, 1986). This frequently illustrates the need for tax rules for effective tax systems.

[2] Reprinted in C.H. Hull (ed.), *Economic Writings of Sir William Petty* (New York: Kelly, 1963), vol. 1, pp. 1–97.

[3] Adam Smith, *Wealth of Nations*, Modern Library edn., pp. 777–8.

[4] Sir Josiah Stamp, *The Fundamental Principles of Taxation in the Light of Modern Developments,* new and rev. edns. (London: Macmillan, 1936), pp. 103–4.

[5] See R.A. Musgrave, *Theory of Public Finance*, pp. 63–8. For a detailed discussion of the development of these principles in the literature of public finance, see ibid. Chapters 4 and 5.

[6] N. Kaldor, *An Expenditure Tax* (London: Allen & Unwin, 1955), esp. ch. 1.

[7] See R.A. Musgrave, *The Theory of Public Finance*, pp. 95–110. Since the early 1970s, new attempts have been made to answer this question in the optimal income tax literature. For a discussion see C.V. Brown and P.M. Jackson, *Public Sector Economics*, ch. 20; and N.H. Stern, "Optimal Taxation", in *The New Palgrave. A Dictionary of Economics* (London: Macmillan, 1987), vol. III, pp. 734–8, esp. pp. 736–7.

[8] Henry Simons, *Personal Income Taxation* (Chicago: Chicago University Press, 1938), ch. 1, esp. pp. 18–19. For an Australian discussion of this issue, see Taxation Review Committee, *Full Report*, ch. 4; and for a review of past attitudes and policies on progressive taxation, Peter Groenewegen, "The Progressive Personal Income Tax in Historical Perspective", in J.G. Head (ed.), *Flattening the Tax Scales: Alternative Scenarios and Methodologies* (Melbourne: Longman, 1990), ch. 1.

[9] For a discussion, see John Howard, "Local Government Revenue Raising", in *National*

Inquiry into Local Government Finance, Research and Consultancy Reports (2), (Canberra: AGPS, 1985), pp. 229–31.

[10] For a discussion of the theoretical issues see J.M. Buchanan, "Earmarked Taxes", in R.W. Houghton (ed.), *Public Finance*, Reading 11.

[11] This was partly done in Australia under the system of Road Assistance Grants of the Federal Government between 1931 and 1959, when a fixed proportion of customs and excise duties on petrol determined the size of the overall grant. See *Payments to or for the States and Local Government Authorities 1974–75* (Canberra: AGPS, 1974), pp. 184–6. For a general argument in favour of treating petrol taxes as benefit taxes see Taxation Review Committee, *Full Report*, paragraph 17.15. Many State governments utilise the proceeds from motor registration fees and other charges for road construction purposes. The NSW State government in 1989 doubled its rate of business franchise taxes on petroleum products, assigning the increase to road expenditure.

[12] This is in fact frequently done by Australian State governments. For example, the revenue of the New South Wales poker machine tax is earmarked for hospital expenditure, while the revenue collected from a special lottery was earmarked for the construction costs of Sydney's Opera House. A more recent example is given in Note 11 above.

[13] For a discussion of this concept, see A. Marshall, *Principles of Economics*, 8th edn. (London: Macmillan, 1920), book 3, ch. 6 and appendix K. For a more accessible version see David Laidler, *Introduction to Micro-economics* (London: Phillip Allen, 1981), ch. 4, or any other intermediate micro-economics text.

[14] Examples can be given from both the federal and State level. For the former, see Treasurer, *Economic Statement May 1988*, (Canberra: AGPS, 1988), p. 18; for the States see *Focus on Reform, Report on the State's Finances* (Sydney: New South Wales Government Printer, 1988), esp. ch. 10, and with special reference to taxation, New South Wales Tax Task Force, *Review of the State Tax System* (Sydney: New South Wales Government Printer, 1988), ch. 23, esp. pp. 307–12; *Report of the Committee of Inquiry into Revenue Raising in Victoria* (Melbourne: Victorian Government Printer, 1982), ch. 12.

[15] See, for example, *Reform of the Australian Tax System, Draft White Paper*, ch. 1, "Criteria for Tax Reform", pp. 14–17.

[16] The 1989 Federal Opposition tax policy designed to assist families is a good example.

[17] This is not to say there is no room for discriminatory consumption taxes. As shown in the context of efficiency, tax discrimination may sometimes be seen as a useful instrument for improving the overall resource allocation in the economy.

[18] See the definitions provided in the glossary at the end of Chapter 6.

[19] *Reform of the Australian Tax System, Draft White Paper*, pp. 15–16.

[20] See Taxation Review Committee, *Full Report*, p. 10; *Reform of the Australian Tax System. Draft White Paper*, p. 5; R.A. and P.B. Musgrave, *Public Finance in Theory and Practice*, pp. 291–311.

[21] See R.A. and P.B. Musgrave, *Public Finance in Theory and Practice*, pp. 302–3, and for an Australian discussion in the context of policy formation, P.L. Swan, "An Optimum Business Tax Structure for Australia", in Australian Financial System Inquiry, *Commissioned Studies and Selected Papers*, Part 3 (Canberra: AGPS, 1982), pp. 37–43.

[22] For a strong defence of an active discriminatory role for taxation, see Kaldor, "The Reform of Personal Taxation", in N. Kaldor, *Essays on Economic Policy*, (London: Duckworth, 1964), vol. I, esp. p. 203; see also Peter Groenewegen, "Rehabilitating the Classical Notions of 'Productive' and 'Unproductive' with Special Reference to their Relevance to Taxation", in *Taxation and Fiscal Federalism*, Geoffrey Brennan et al. (eds.) (Canberra: Australian National University Press, 1988), esp. pp. 96–8.

[23] R.A. and P.B. Musgrave, *Public Finance in Theory and Practice*, p. 307; for Australian research in this area, see J. Piggott, "Economic Effects of Changing the Tax Mix", in J.G. Head (ed.), *Changing the Tax Mix* (Sydney: Australian Tax Research Foundation, 1986), pp. 95–113, and J. Piggott, "Tax Reform: Do Numerical Estimates Help?", in J.G. Head (ed.) *Australian Tax Reform in Retrospect and Prospect* (Sydney: Australian Tax Research Foundation, 1989), pp. 431–43.

[24] R.A. and P.B. *Musgrave, Public Finance in Theory and Practice*, pp. 307–8. For an Australian attempt to do just that see John Freebairn et al. (eds.), *Spending and Taxing.*

Australian Reform Options (Sydney: Allen and Unwin, 1987), chs. 5 and 11, esp. pp. 67–9.

25 See the references in Note 9 above, and for an application of this type of theory to developed nations, David Newbery and Nicholas Stern (eds.), *The Theory of Taxation for Developing Countries* (New York: Oxford University Press for the World Bank, 1987), esp. chs. 1–3.

26 See B.L. Johns, W.C. Dunlop, and W.J. Sheehan, "Taxation and the Small Firm in Australia", Taxation Review Committee, *Commissioned Studies*, esp. pp. 327–35. Until recently there have been no empirical studies in Australia similar to those conducted by Sandford. See Cedric Sandford, Michael Godwin and Peter Hardwick, *Administration and Compliance Costs of Taxation* (Bath: Fiscal Publications, 1989), and for a general discussion of the issue, C. Sandford, "Administrative and Compliance Costs of Taxation", in G.S. Cooper and R.J. Vann (eds.), *Decision Making in the Australian Tax System* (Sydney: Australian Tax Research Foundation, 1986), Appendix 1, pp. 187–98. A large Australian empirical study of the problem commenced in 1988. See Jeff Pope, "The Compliance Costs of Personal Income Taxation — A Review of the Issues", *Australian Tax Forum* 6(2), 1989, pp. 125–42.

27 Taxation Review Committee, *Full Report*, ch. 5. Administrative and compliance issues are raised in the context of specific instruments below in Chapters 9 to 13.

28 There are several specific dimensions to this aspect of tax principles, including the dimension of federalism examined subsequently (in Chapters 14 to 16) and the need to review the tax expenditure content of the existing tax structure on a regular basis as part of a con-tinuing review of public expenditure, efficiency and effectiveness. The Draft White Paper discussion refers to *Reform of the Australian Tax System*, pp. 15–17.

FURTHER READING

Tax principles are discussed in all major textbooks. The classical treatment of the ability-to-pay and benefit principles is R.A. Musgrave, *The Theory of Public Finance* (New York: McGraw Hill, 1959), chs. 4–5.

Other useful textbook treatments are:

R.A. and P.B. Musgrave, *Public Finance in Theory and Practice*, 4th edn. (New York: McGraw Hill, 1984), chs. 11,14.

C.V. Brown and P.M. Jackson, *Public Sector Economics*, 3rd edn. (Oxford: Blackwells, 1986), pp. 241–22.

J.E. Stiglitz, *Public Sector Economics*, 2nd edn. (New York: W.W. Norton, 1988), chs. 16, pp. 390–408.

For Australian discussions of these tax principles, see:

Taxation Review Committee, *Full Report* (Canberra: AGPS, 1975), chs. 3 and 5.

Draft White Paper, *Reform of the Australian Tax System* (Canberra: AGPS, 1985), ch. 1, reprinted in Peter Groenewegen (ed.), *Readings in Australian Tax Policy*, 2nd edn. (Melbourne: Longman Cheshire, 1987), Reading 1.

On optimal taxation see:

C.V. Brown and P.M. Jackson, *Public Sector Economics*, ch. 20.

J.E. Stiglitz, *Public Sector Economics*, ch. 20.

For a more advanced treatment see:

A.J. Auerbach, "The Theory of Excess Burden and Optimal Taxation", in A.J. Auerbach and M. Feldstein (eds.), *Handbook of Public Economics* (Amsterdam: North Holland, 1987), ch. 2.

The incidence of taxation

In discussing the distinction between direct and indirect taxation in Chapter 6, tax shifting and the problem of tax incidence was explicitly raised. Incidence was also seen in Chapter 5 as a crucial aspect in public expenditure evaluation, and its analytical difficulties were briefly canvassed in that context. The subject of tax incidence is also an important one. Apart from its substantial impact on the formulation of tax policy and schemes for tax re form, its controversial nature in economics[1] requires a separate chapter to be devoted to its discussion.

In his commissioned study for the Taxation Review Committee, Brennan has tentatively defined tax incidence in the following manner: "The incidence of a budgetary operation [in the sphere of taxation] is its effect on the levels (and distribution) of individuals' incomes, defined in real terms, in the short and long run".[2] This definition, despite its imperfections, focuses on three very important aspects of incidence analysis, which are as follows:

1. The effects of the tax or its impact. This raises questions about the difference between the initial impact of the tax (its legal incidence) and its final impact — that is, questions about the shifting of the tax.
2. Incidence is concerned with effects on income, namely the levels of income and the distribution of income.
3. The time period of the analysis. As noted in the discussion of expenditure incidence in Chapter 5 the time period assumptions are crucial.

Before continuing the discussion on incidence, some of the terminology that has been used must be clarified. Legal incidence refers to the immediate impact of the tax: for instance, the legal incidence of the Australian sales tax is on the wholesaler who pays the tax to the government. *Final impact* or *economic incidence* refers to the shifting of the tax; in the sales tax example the consumer may pay the whole or part of the tax if it is shifted forward in the form of higher prices, or producers may effectively pay part of the tax if the tax influences the level of output of the affected industry. Incidence can be discussed in terms of *individuals*, that is, in terms of effects on individual consumers, households, and producers, or it can be discussed in terms of effects on *social classes* such as workers and capitalists. In the last case it is known as *social incidence* analysis; this was the technique developed by the classical economists such as Smith and Ricardo and resurrected by Kalecki and his followers.[3] The notion of "tax burden" frequently used in the literature, is defined in the next section.

The nature of "tax burdens"

In incidence analysis, the notion of a "tax burden" is often seen as important,[4] because this is what is shifted in a manner analogous to the benefit-snatching of expenditure incidence analysis. Unfortunately, the term "burden" is not unambiguous, nor should it be understood in the sense that taxation is bad or harmful. The term "burden" in fact has a variety of meanings which can be distinguished as follows:

The resources burden. This is the amount transferred by the tax from the private to the public sector. It is usually expressed in money terms. Referring to the data presented in Table 6.1, the sales tax burden for 1980-81 amounted to $2102 million.

Excess burden. This arises from distortions in economic choices resulting from the effects of taxes on relative prices. As was shown in Chapter 7, this concept of welfare loss has become important in discussions of efficiency in taxation and "estimates" of such burdens have been made.

Output effects. The imposition of taxes may lead to changes in work and saving habits which may affect the supply of labour and investment and thereby the level of output. Such micro-economic changes in output induced by tax changes are not reflected in the resources burden and are also different from the macro-economic effect of tax changes on output via the level of effective demand.

Employment and other output effects. The imposition of taxes will generally affect aggregate demand and hence the level of employment and output as a whole. Such effects cause great difficulties in the interpretation of the effects of taxation on the distribution of income.

In empirically estimating the incidence of taxation by means of the shifting of tax burdens, the resource burden impact on individual households is most generally used. The output effects caused by changes in habits of work and saving are frequently a longer-run phenomenon and are therefore often ignored. The short-term output and employment effects are important, and must, where possible, be included in the analysis. Excess burden estimates have been prepared to assess the efficiency gains and losses of tax policy changes, and are now also being used in the statistical estimates of tax incidence.

THREE CONCEPTS OF INCIDENCE: ABSOLUTE, DIFFERENTIAL, AND BUDGET INCIDENCE[5]

If the distributional effects of a tax are examined by themselves, that is, while holding public expenditure and other taxes constant, the analysis deals with the *absolute incidence* of the tax. This is a reasonable procedure when the tax analysed is a minor one and the charge in question is small, because in that case the partial equilibrium assumptions are warranted. When the tax change is more significant, say a 5 per cent surcharge or rebate on income tax — such as those formerly used for stabilisation purposes in Australia — partial equilibrium assumptions can no longer be sustained. The tax change will not only have a distributional impact, but will also have substantial output and employment effects which cannot easily be ignored. General equilibrium incidence analysis, discussed subsequently in this chapter, does not experience this type of problem to the same extent.

To overcome this difficulty, the concept of *differential incidence* is employed. This looks at the distributional effects of a tax change whose revenue effects are compensated for by an opposite change in another tax, thereby holding total tax revenue constant. Differential incidence analysis is applicable to examine the distributional consequence of a reduction in income tax and the simultaneous introduction of a general value-added tax which will raise the same amount of revenue. This procedure neutralises a significant part of the output and employment effects. For some income groups disposable income would not be drastically changed by such a tax substitution; for low and high income groups there would be substantial losses or gains respectively.[6]

Finally, there is the concept of *Budget incidence*. In this case what is examined is the effects of a tax change and a compensatory expenditure change, so that the aggregate Budget position remains unchanged. An example of the relevance of such analysis is the abolition of dependent children's rebates for income tax purposes and the compensatory increases in family allowances which were implemented in 1976.[7] Basically, this measure favoured the lower income groups whose incomes were so low that they could only qualify at most for part of the income tax rebates for dependent children because their tax payable was smaller than the value of these rebates.

The time period of the analysis

As in the case of expenditure incidence analysis, the time period is crucial in determining the distributional consequences of a tax change. This is not surprising, since a longer time period allows supply conditions to change substantially, something which is frequently ruled out in a short-period analysis.[8] An example will illustrate the difficulties involved.

Take the case of the introduction of an excise on wine, a commodity previously untaxed. The initial result will be a rise in price because the wine producers will attempt to pass the excise on to the consumers. The rise in price will lead to a fall in demand, the extent of which will depend on the elasticity of demand for wine, which partly depends on the availability of close substitutes. If the demand is inelastic, the consumers will bear the greater part of the tax, since the wine output will hardly be affected. If the demand is elastic, the effects of the tax will be different. In the first place, the output of wine will be affected and this result will be partly transferred to the grapegrowers in a falling demand for their product. This will shift part of the excise backwards[9] to grapegrowers in the form of lower grape prices. In the even longer run, this fall in income may cause grapegrowers to leave the industry, raise the price of grapes through the diminution in supply, and shift the excise once more to the consumers of wine. Some of the distributional effects will therefore depend on the time period chosen for the analysis. If wine consumers shift their demand to substitute products, for example, beer, its relative price may be affected and this will transfer part of the burden to beer consumers. This example clearly shows some of the difficulties in tax incidence analysis.

THE INCIDENCE OF SPECIFIC TAXES[10]

Subject to the difficulties in the assumptions about the relevant supply and demand elasticities, the market structure of the industry, and the time period of the analysis, the incidence of commodity taxation can be made relatively straightforward provided that *ceteris paribus* clauses are allowed. It can be argued, however, that these difficulties are so great, particularly with respect to supply elasticities, that the analysis of commodity tax incidence is worthless for practical purposes. It is no different with a tax on personal income, company taxation, payroll taxes, and local rates. For example, it is now accepted in principle that personal income taxes can be partially shifted forward, either directly through the wage bargain or through higher charges for professional services such as those of doctors and dentists, or indirectly through the effects of income tax on the supply of labour. The importance of these effects is often disputed. In connection with the pay-roll tax there is considerable dispute as to whether the tax is passed forward in the form of higher prices or shifted backwards to the employees.

The major controversies arise over the incidence of company taxes. Here the various analyses suggest backward shifting either to the shareholder, or to the employees, or to both; while, particularly under the assumption of mark-up pricing and less than competitive conditions, a substantial portion of the tax may be shifted forward in the form of higher prices. Despite the empirical studies on this subject, the evidence is inconclusive.

ALTERNATIVE APPROACHES TO THE THEORY OF TAX INCIDENCE

This chapter so far has only presented a brief, partial equilibrium analysis of the incidence of an excise on wine, while the introductory paragraph to the various concepts of incidence raised the limitations of such partial equilibrium incidence analysis. Reference has also been made to divergence of opinion on the subject, including the different results derivable from neo-classical as against Post Keynesian analysis of tax incidence. This section presents the major version of general equilibrium incidence theory in the literature, known as the Harberger-Mieszkowski general equilibrium analysis, subsequently comparing its results with those from Post Keynesian incidence analysis, with special reference to its foundations in the tax incidence analysis presented by Kalecki.[11]

The general equilibrium approach to tax incidence theory

If most taxes used in the world are general rather than specific taxes, it is argued that partial equilibrium analysis is inappropriate because it neglects the complex interrelationships of modern economic systems. General equilibrium analysis must therefore be used to study tax incidence. The earliest of these general equilibrium tax incidence models is that by Harberger[12] further developed by Mieszkowski and by McLure.[13] These modern neo-classical models are based on the marginal productivity theory of distribution, which assumes that firms choose factor proportions so as to minimise costs, and set commodity prices at levels which maximise profits. In addition, the following assumptions are generally made: *fixed aggregate factor supplies*, to eliminate tax effects on the supply of labour, on saving, and on investment; *perfect factor mobility*; *perfect competition* in factor and product markets with fully flexible prices — this ensures, among other things, full employment;

closed economy, linear homogeneous production functions; homogeneous marginal propensities to consume, needed to ensure that distribution of income cannot affect relative prices; and *no fixed money assets* so that relative price changes only have economic consequences.

In such a constant-returns-to-scale, perfectly competitive economy, prices will equal average costs, and factors of production will receive their marginal products. Factor returns are therefore fully determined by the given resource endowments and the technical factors underlying the production functions. These assumptions have rather straightforward and simple implications for the incidence of general taxation, that is, taxes imposed at the same general rate on all commodities or factor incomes. In such an economic system the *real* incidence of a general tax will be the same as its *legal* incidence. This result must follow from the fact that relative prices are not affected and that the general tax on wages, on profits, or on commodity consumption, will therefore fall fully on wages, on profits, and on consumers.

The story is different with *partial* commodity and *partial* taxes on factor incomes. These will affect relative prices, and thereby cause factor substitution. If capital, for example, is taxed at a differentially higher rate in a particular industry or sector, the relative price of commodities produced by this industry or sector will increase. Moreover, the increase in cost of the taxed factor will encourage substitution of the untaxed factor thereby affecting relative factor prices. The taxed factor will be released from the taxed sector, partly because of the output effect caused by the change in relative prices of the output in the taxed sector and partly because of the relative factor price change caused by the tax. Output will diminish in the taxed sector, thereby freeing resources for use by the untaxed sector, while the taxed factor will move to sectors of the economy where it is untaxed. With partial taxes, the *real* incidence is not the same as the *legal* incidence, because relative prices, including relative factor prices, change.

Many of these aspects of incidence analysis are illustrated in the general showpiece of this type of analysis: the Harberger corporation tax incidence analysis. Harberger treats this tax as a *partial* factor income tax, since it taxes profits in the corporate sector but not in the non-corporate sector. Under conditions of perfect competitive equilibrium, after-tax rates of return on capital must be equal in the two sectors. Consequently, because initially after-tax rates of return are lower in the corporate sector, capital will move into the non-corporate sector. This will lower the relative factor price of capital (or its rate of return) in the non-corporate sector and will raise it in the corporate sector. Furthermore, as a result of these capital movements, non-corporate output will expand at the expense of the corporate sector, and corporate product prices will rise relative to non-corporate prices. Finally, the decline in corporate output will cause workers to move from the corporate to the non-corporate sector, the impact of this output effect on workers' movement depending on the production functions in the two sectors.

Whether the tax is shifted to labour or to capital depends on the elasticities of substitution between capital and labour in the two sectors, and on the degree of labour intensity in the corporate production process. If, for example, the corporate sector is highly labour-intensive and there is limited substitutability of labour for capital in the non-corporate production function, wage rates would have to fall significantly until the non-corporate sector had fully employed the large number of released workers from the corporate sector. The shifting of the corporation tax to labour would be complete if the difference between the after-tax wage bill and the before-tax wage bill exactly equals the legal incidence of the corporation tax.

If, on the other hand, the elasticities of substitution between capital and labour are equal in the two sectors, and equal to the elasticity of substitution in consumption between the two sector outputs, then wage rates will not be affected by the tax, and capital (in both sectors) effectively bears the burden of the corporation tax as a result of the change in rates of return to capital following the movement of capital from the corporate to the non-corporate sector. From his econometric research on the parameters in the analysis, Harberger concluded that the elasticities of substitution were such that the corporation tax was most likely paid by all capital, that is, by capital in both the corporate and the non-corporate sector.

The extent to which this result can be accepted must not be exaggerated. To a large extent it depends on the assumptions and on theory which can be regarded as suspect. One unrealistic set of assumptions on which the argument is based is the amalgam of perfect competition, homogeneous and linear production functions, and marginal productivity-determined factor prices. Some of the validity of this type of analysis has been questioned in the Cambridge controversies over capital theory.[14] The assumptions of a closed economy (particularly for the United States with its small foreign sector), and of perfect mobility of factors are less damaging to the theory, particularly since analyses with partial factor mobility have been presented. More important, however, is the fact that the model *assumes* full employment, obtained through the absorption of released factors from the taxed sector in the non-taxed sector by means of the changes in relative factor prices. This type of analysis and assumption is attacked especially by the Post Keynesians where employment is determined by aggregate demand and *not* by relative factor price changes.

Some other aspects of the analysis must be emphasised. These concern the time factor in the analysis, which, as discussed earlier in this chapter, is crucial in tax incidence analysis. The general equilibrium tax incidence analysis is exceedingly *long-term*. In the example of the incidence of the corporation tax, a great deal of time is required for the factors to be released from the taxed sector. Although with the usual neo-classical assumptions of capital malleability it could be assumed that the past can be undone in an instant, experience suggests that the movement of capital from one sector to another, let alone similar movements of labour, takes considerable time to be effected. In short, general equilibrium incidence analysis analyses only the long-period incidence of taxation. In the short-period, the same result applies to partial taxes as does to general taxes, the *real* incidence is the same as the *legal* incidence, because the changes required to make real incidence diverge from legal incidence take a very long time to complete.

Two other significant weaknesses of this general equilibrium tax incidence analysis are indicated by Break.[15] In the first place, these types of incidence models analyse changes in terms of differentials, and implicitly assume the absence of other taxes. The analysis can therefore only be applied to the imposition of infinitestimally small taxes in a zero-tax world. Tax changes in a non-zero tax world are likely to involve significant excess burdens and there is still no agreement on whether these should be analysed separately as additional economic effects of tax changes or incorporated into the general incidence analysis. Secondly, by neglecting the effects of taxation on factor supplies, the analysis cannot deal with a growing economy for which dynamic incidence analysis is required.[16] These major shortcomings of general equilibrium incidence analysis have led to the development of alternative approaches to incidence theory, which escape these pitfalls at the expense of introducing some others.

The post Keynesian (Kaleckian) tax incidence analysis

This analysis differs substantially from the neo-classical general equilibrium analysis in a variety of respects, some of which have already been indicated. In the first place, the analysis deals with *social* incidence of taxation because it is conducted in terms of social classes (capitalists and workers) though sometimes the capitalists are subdivided into rentiers (shareholders who draw dividends) and profit-making firms who retain part of the profits for investment. Secondly, the analysis does *not* generally assume full employment and frequently assumes excess capacity in the producing sector. In any case, full employment is not obtained by movements in relative factor prices (wage rates and profit rates) but by changes in aggregate demand which depend on income and expenditure by the social classes. Thirdly, and most important, the analysis is short-period, which requires that investment is *given* as determined by past decisions, so that output can only vary from working *existing* resources (including unemployed labour) more intensively. This analysis, not surprisingly, does *not* conclude that legal and real incidence are the same thing in the short-period.

The examples of this analysis which are given here are essentially those developed by Kalecki in 1937.[17] In addition to the assumptions mentioned in the preceding paragraph, we assume a closed economy, excess capacity of labour and equipment, workers spending all their wages on consumption and unemployed workers all their doles, so that only rentiers and firms (capitalists) save; and a balanced Budget with all State expenditure financed from taxation. An elastic money supply is also assumed to be accommodating itself to changes in the price level, given money wages levels, and the insensitivity of capitalists' propensity to consume according to expectations of changes in income.

Gross profit in such a system is the difference between the value of sales and prime costs, and is maximised when marginal prime cost is equated with marginal revenue. National income is defined as wages plus profits, and is, of course, equal to the value of consumption and investment output in a closed economy. With no saving by workers, this means that profits (P) are equal to capitalist consumption (C) plus investment (I), or

$$P = C_c + I$$

If $C_c + I$ (capitalists' spending) increases or decreases, a shift in the marginal revenue curve takes place, employment or prices change as a result of this change in demand until P is once more equal to the increased or decreased spending of the capitalists. $P = C_c + I$ is therefore the fundamental equation of the analysis, and the causality in it runs from right to left, that is, capitalists' spending determines profits because they can influence their spending decisions but not their incomes. In the short-period analysis which is assumed here it is not likely that changes in capitalist spending will occur; changing investment takes longer than the short-period, and capitalist consumption is only influenced by past, not by expected, changes in income.

A tax on wage goods or workers' consumption to finance State expenditure on salaries and on doles for the unemployed is now introduced. The tax is a general *ad valorem* tax on all wage goods at the same rate. The imposition of such a tax constitutes a new prime cost for the firms in the wage goods industry. National income is now equal to wages, profits *plus* the revenue from the tax on wage goods, but it still equals the value of consumption and investment output. Wages still equal the value of workers' consumption on wage goods, the revenue from the tax on wage goods equals salaries to public servants and doles to unemployed workers (which are also assumed to be spent in total on wage goods), so that the condition $P = C_c + I$ still holds.

Assume an increase in the rate of this general sales tax on wage goods from 3 to 5 per cent, the increase to be spent on doles for unemployed workers. As (C_c and I) do not change by assumption, P remains constant, and employment will remain the same. Since employment and the wage bill have not changed (the constant money wages assumption), but doles have increased by the amount of the new tax revenue, the total demand for wage goods rises by 2 per cent. Marginal cost has also risen by 2 per cent so that prices (constant output assumed) rise also by 2 per cent. In the new short-period equilibrium, prices of wage goods have therefore risen by 2 per cent, real wages have fallen by 2 per cent (on the assumption of constant money wages), profits remain constant, so that the incidence of the tax change is on the workers whose incomes are reduced to the same extent as the increase of tax.[18]

A flat rate income tax on profits is now introduced. This is not a prime cost but the tax forms part of gross profits. Capitalists will continue to maximise gross profits in order to maximise after-tax profits. It is easy to see that the profits equation now alters. The national income is still equal to wages, profits and the tax revenue from the tax on wage goods and this still equals output of consumption and investment goods but gross profits, P, now is equal to capitalists' spending *plus* the profit tax, that is, $P = (C_c+I) + T_i$, where T_i is the income tax paid from gross profits. The State now takes T_i from gross profits (again for the payment of doles) while the part received by the capitalists is equal to $(C_c + I)$ as before.

Assume now that T_i is raised from 15 per cent to 25 per cent. No change will occur in $(C_c + I)$ by assumption but demand is increased by ΔT_i through the spending of the recipients of the increase in revenue (that is, the unemployed workers on the dole) on wage goods. The result of this increase in demand is a shift in the marginal revenue curve, prices of wage goods will therefore rise, the rise in price increasing profits by ΔT_i so that P is still equal to $(C_c + I) + T_i$ at the higher tax rate. The incidence of the income tax on profits is therefore on the consumers of wage goods, that is, on the workers and on the unemployed recipients of the dole, whose real incomes have fallen as a result of the price change in wage goods. The short-period[19] consequence of a profits tax increase in this model is therefore a fall in real wages with profits remaining constant.

The results of the Kaleckian tax incidence are therefore quite different from the general equilibrium incidence analysis considered earlier. Under the new set of assumptions and with the different way in which the model is set up, the real incidence can diverge from the legal incidence even in the short-period. These different results arise, of course, from the different assumptions; in particular the assumption that relative "factor prices" are no longer determined by marginal products; that prices are determined by mark-ups over prime cost instead of by supply and demand under perfect competition, and that there is now excess capacity in the system instead of full employment of all resources achieved by flexible prices in the factor and goods markets. At the same time, the assumption of the closed economy is here more important, since the simplicity of the national income identities on which the crucial relation between profits and capitalists' spending depends, would disappear if the balance of trade was in surplus or deficit.

The major difficulties with Kalecki's analysis arise therefore from the assumptions he uses. Apart from the assumption of a closed economy, to which we have already referred, there is the assumption of the fixity of capitalist spending. If this spending is influenced by *expected* profits (income) then different results can arise because the important relation $P = C_c + I$, is broken. As Asimakopulos and Burbidge have shown, this shortcoming can be overcome by expanding the analysis, but this more complex Kaleckian tax incidence analysis cannot be developed here. The strength of the Kaleckian approach to incidence theory is illustrated when its assumptions are compared with the assumptions required by neo-classical general equilibrium incidence analysis, as was done in the previous paragraph. In that context, Kalecki's assumptions are far more realistic, and the results of the model, by implication, therefore more realistic.

Enough has been said, however, in this chapter to show that the complexities and difficulties in tax incidence are many, and that the results of such analysis vary a great deal with the assumptions used. In Chapters 9 to 13, when aspects of the incidence of specific taxes are further discussed, the importance of these difficulties will be re-emphasised. For tax policy formation in particular, this question is very important, as has already been indicated. It can also be stated here that most of the incidence models developed by public finance theorists have serious weaknesses, which makes the application of their results and their econometric testing a very hazardous procedure. To conclude this chapter, the fiscal incidence of Australia's tax system is examined. This puts some numbers on the broad distributional consequences of Australian taxation as a whole.

THE FISCAL INCIDENCE OF THE TAX STRUCTURE

The analysis of the impact of aggregate taxation on the distribution of income is called the fiscal incidence of the tax structure. In Australia, several attempts at such an analysis are now available,[20] the broad results of which are illustrated in Figure 8.1. The analysis reveals that as income rises the proportion of income paid in taxes first falls, then remains more or less proportional for the substantial majority of taxpayers until it gradually starts to rise at high income levels. Figure 8.1 reveals the distinct change in pattern of that proportionality for middle income earners (deciles 4 to 8) between 1975-76 and 1984-85.

Table 8.1 partly illustrates how these results are obtained. Each type of tax — Federal, State, and local — is apportioned to the various ranges of household income into which taxpayers are divided for the analysis. This procedure is fairly straightforward for income taxes if forward shifting is excluded. It is much more difficult for other types of taxes. Take for example, the case of an excise on tobacco products on the assumption that it is fully shifted forward to consumers. This should then be apportioned to the various household income ranges in proportion to their expenditure on tobacco. Similar procedures apply in analysing the impact on the income from consumers of other excise duties, sales tax, and many of the State taxes. If, like the excise on petrol, the impact is on producers, the effect of the tax must be traced through the input-output tables before its incidence can be reasonably allocated to income groups. The empirical analysis therefore requires detailed knowledge of the consumption expenditure patterns of the various household income groups and data on industry use of taxed commodities from the input-output tables.

In the case of local rates, the distribution of the tax burden depends on the assumed relationship between income and property ownership; the specific assumption used can be deduced from the data in Table 8.1. If company income is assumed to be distributed according to the ownership of shares of the various income groups, the incidence analysis

8.1A

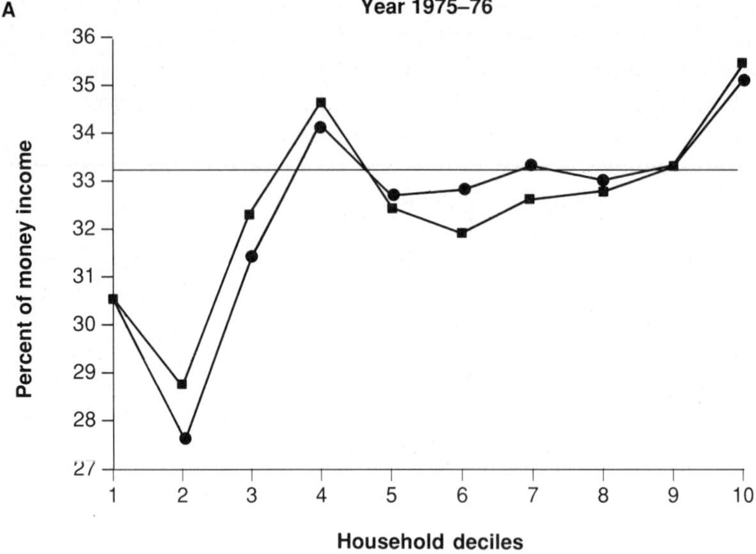

8.1B

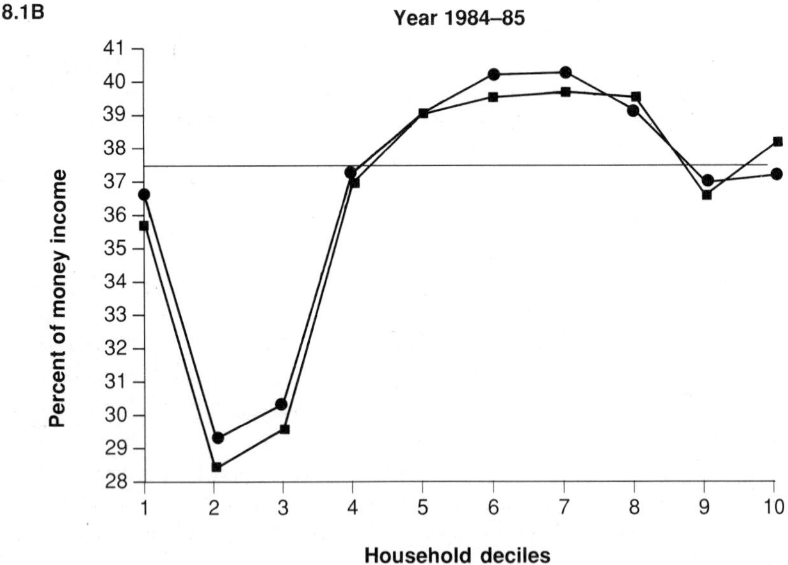

Figure 8.1 Differential tax incidence: Australia 1975–76 and 1984–85

Source: N. A. Warren, "Changes in Australian Tax Incidence 1975–76 and 1984–85", in *Australian Tax Reform in Retrospect and Prospect* (Sydney: Australian Tax Research Foundation, 1989), p. 462, Figure 2. Reproduced with kind permission of the author and the Australian Tax Research Foundation.

Table 8.1 Incidence of Australian taxes on domestic households: 1984–85

	Household deciles										
	1	*2*	*3*	*4*	*5*	*6*	*7*	*8*	*9*	*10*	*All*
Average number per household											
Adults	1.14	1.60	1.84	1.84	1.90	1.97	2.09	2.17	2.36	2.79	1.97
Children	.16	.44	.76	.90	1.12	1.13	1.09	1.04	.97	1.02	.86
Persons	1.31	2.04	2.60	2.74	3.02	3.10	3.18	3.21	3.33	3.81	2.83
Per cent of money income											
Federal taxes:											
Personal income	5.6	3.7	5.7	13.2	16.3	18.6	20.1	19.8	19.6	21.5	17.7
Corporation	2.8	2.6	3.0	2.8	2.5	2.2	2.1	2.5	2.0	3.0	2.5
Wholesale sales	3.9	3.4	3.4	3.3	3.3	3.0	3.0	2.9	2.6	2.4	2.8
Excise — petrol	4.8	4.1	4.1	4.0	4.0	3.6	3.4	3.3	2.9	2.6	3.3
— other	2.0	1.6	1.7	1.8	1.6	1.6	1.4	1.3	1.1	.9	1.3
Customs duty	2.5	2.0	2.0	1.9	1.9	1.7	1.6	1.6	1.5	1.5	1.6
Other federal	.8	.6	.6	.7	.6	.6	.5	.5	.4	.5	.6
All federal	22.3	18.1	20.5	27.6	30.1	31.3	32.1	31.9	30.1	32.3	29.9
State taxes:											
Payroll	3.2	2.5	2.3	2.2	2.2	2.0	1.9	1.9	1.6	1.6	1.9
Stamp duties	2.1	1.6	1.2	1.3	1.5	1.2	1.0	1.2	.9	.9	1.1
Motor vehicle	1.3	1.1	1.1	1.0	1.0	.9	.9	.8	.7	.6	.8
Gambling	.7	.5	.6	.7	.5	.7	.7	.6	.6	.6	.6
Franchise	1.0	.8	.8	.9	.8	.8	.7	.6	.6	.5	.6
Other state	1.9	1.4	1.3	1.3	1.2	1.1	1.0	1.0	.9	.8	1.0
All state	10.1	7.9	7.2	7.3	7.2	6.6	6.1	6.2	5.3	4.9	6.1
Local — rates	3.4	2.3	1.9	1.9	1.8	1.6	1.5	1.4	1.1	.9	1.4
ALL TAXES	35.8	28.4	29.5	36.9	39.1	39.6	39.7	39.5	36.5	38.1	37.4

Source: N.A. Warren, 'Changes in Australian Tax Incidence 1975–76 and 1984–85', in J.G. Head (ed.), *Australian Tax Reform in Retrospect and Prospect* (Sydney: Australian Tax Research Foundation, 1989), Table 5, p. 461. Reproduced with the kind permission of the author and the Australian Tax Research Foundation.

would reveal different proportions of company tax for various household income groups if it was assumed that company tax was passed forward in the form of higher prices. The distribution pattern of the company tax would then resemble that shown for the various sales taxes and customs duties.

Not surprisingly, the precise results of the incidence analysis of the total tax structure depend on the assumptions made about the incidence of individual taxes, on the accuracy of the consumer expenditure survey data, and on the definition of income used. For example, a more comprehensive definition of income which includes forms of income such as realised capital gains which are concentrated at the high income levels, would alter the incidence results as shown in Table 8.1.[21]

The results of such empirical studies are often queried on other grounds as well. A classical criticism has been that by Prest[22] which pointed to a potential inconsistency between the assumptions frequently employed in such analyses. Perfectly inelastic commodity demands are usually assumed to enable all indirect taxes to be attributed to consumption. Perfectly inelastic factor supplies are assumed to attribute all income taxes to labour. However, criticisms like this do not reduce the potential value of empirical incidence studies, but point only to their limitations.

With increased general equilibrium modelling of fiscal incidence, much of the "ad hocery" in the treatment of tax shifting has disappeared. Larger general equilibrium models also permit lifetime incidence results, based on estimates of lifetime rather than annual income or expenditure patterns. Results from such studies[23] differ from the more usual annual results. As would be expected, lifetime income tax becomes less progressive, lifetime sales tax incidence more progressive as compared with annual results. Lifetime incidence studies also turn out to be less sensitive to shifting assumptions than studies reflecting annual estimates.

Other general equilibrium studies[24] have enabled emphasis on the difference between average and marginal net fiscal incidence. This points to the fact that only marginal analysis can include dead-weight losses (the excess burden of taxation examined in Chapter 7) in the analysis of measuring the impact of tax burdens. As indicated in that chapter, such welfare losses have been found to be substantial, and hence modify the quantitative results from more traditional work. Theoretical problems like this ensure continuing work on the analysis of this important problem of trying to determine the distributional consequences of a national tax system.[25]

In the next five chapters, the specific taxation forms in use in Australia are surveyed together with some other relevant tax instruments. In the discussion, the principles analysed in this and the previous two chapters will be frequently utilised, thereby further illustrating the relevance of these principles to tax analysis. In this examination of specific taxes, the *tax base* will invariably be considered first, secondly, the *rate structure*, and thirdly, the *economic effects* and other issues associated with the particular tax, such as its effects on incentives to work and to save, its incidence and other related matters. These chapters are an essential adjunct to the discussion of the general principles in Chapters 6–8.

SUMMARY

1. Incidence, defined as the effect of a budgetary operation on the level and distribution of income in the long and short run, is a crucial concept in public finance analysis.

2. Since incidence of taxation refers to shifting of tax burdens, the various notions of tax burden need to be carefully distinguished. These are:

   i the resources burden
   ii excess burden
   iii micro-economic incentive output effects
   iv macro-economic employment and output effects.

3. Various concepts of incidence need to be distinguished, that is, absolute, differential and budget incidence where the first refers to an incidence of a tax change in isolation; the second, of a tax change with a revenue compensating change in another tax; the third where the revenue effect of the tax change is offset by a compensatory expenditure change.

4. Time period of the incidence analysis is crucial because of substantial variations in adjustment times for responses to the tax.

5. Effective incidence of specific taxes is controversial.

6. Partial equilibrium incidence analysis is generally inappropriate because it neglects the complex inter-relationships of modern economic systems. General equilibrium incidence analysis is therefore more appropriate, but it too has its shortcomings.

7. Incidence results, not surprisingly, depend on the assumptions on which the analysis is based. This can be illustrated by contrasting the analysis of profit tax incidence under a neo-classical Harberger model and a Post Keynesian (Kaleckian) model.

8. Empirical incidence analysis has been widely used to inform tax policy. Its major problems arise from both theoretical weaknesses and the income and household expenditure data which they require.

NOTES

[1] For a good indication of the current level of disagreement on this subject, see Peter Mieszkowski, "Tax Incidence Theory", *Journal of Economic Literature* (December 1969), pp. 1103–24; A Asimakopulos and J.B. Burbidge, "The Short Period Incidence of Taxation", *Economic Journal* (June 1974), pp. 267–88; G. Break, "The Incidence and Economic Effects of Taxation", in A.S. Blinder and R.M. Solow, *Economics of Public Finance* (Washington, D.C.: The Brookings Institution, 1974), pp. 119–240; and C.V. Brown and P.M. Jackson, *Public Sector Economics*, chs. 11 and 12. A good introduction to the subject is in R.A. and P.B. Musgrave, *Public Finance in Theory and Practice* (New York: McGraw Hill, 1984), ch. 13. A theoretical discussion highlighting some of these disagreements is presented below in this chapter.

[2] H.G. Brennan, "A Policymakers Guide to Incidence", in Taxation Review Committee, *Commissioned Studies*, reprinted in P.D. Groenewegen (ed.), *Australian Taxation Policy* (Melbourne: Longman Cheshire, 1987), p. 55.

[3] See Adam Smith, *Wealth of Nations* (New York: Random House, 1937), Book 5, ch. 2; David Ricardo, *Principles of Political Economy and Taxation* (Cambridge: Cambridge University Press, 1951), chs. 8–18; M. Kalecki, *Selected Essays in the Dynamics of the Capitalist Economy*, essay 4. A social incidence analysis, as developed by Kalecki, is presented below.

[4] The classification is that of R.A. and P.B. Musgrave, *Public Finance in Theory and Practice*, pp. 248–49, on which this section has drawn heavily.

[5] These concepts were introduced by R.A. Musgrave. See R.A. and P.B. Musgrave, *Public Finance in Theory and Practice*, pp. 251–3.

[6] For a discussion of such matters see the contributions by John Piggott and Neil Warren to a volume on changing the tax mix, as was contemplated in Australia in 1985, that is, J.G. Head (ed.), *Changing the Tax Mix* (Sydney: Australian Tax Research Foundation, 1986) chs. 5 and 6; and N.A. Warren, *The Distributional Impact of a Change in the Tax Mix in Australia* (Sydney: Australian Tax Research Foundation, 1987), esp. ch. 8.

[7] See "Fiscal Policy Decisions", Ministerial Statement, House of Representatives, *Hansard* No. 10, 1976, pp. 2,342–3. This policy was based on a recommendation of the Henderson Commission of Inquiry into Poverty, Interim Report, *Poverty in Australia* (Canberra: AGPS, 1974), pp. 11-12. The longer-term

distributional consequences of this decision were influenced by the fact that family allowances were not indexed until 1989 while they were means-tested from 1987.

[8] One of the differences between Post Keynesian and neo-classical incidence analysis arises from the short-period supply assumptions. Post Keynesian analysis allows for unused capacity so that short-period supply changes are sometimes consistent with its assumptions, in neo-classical analysis full employment is assumed so that short-period supply is inelastic. These different approaches to incidence analysis are examined in more detail later in this chapter.

[9] Forward shifting is the term used in incidence analysis to describe the shifting process through price rises to consumers, backward shifting that of price falls for the producers of the taxed commodity.

[10] For a more detailed discussion of this subject see the discussion of the specific taxes in use in Australia in Chapters 9–13.

[11] See Peter Mieszkowski, "Tax Incidence Theory: The Effect of Taxes on the Distribution of Income", *Journal of Economic Literature* (December 1969); and George F. Break, "The Incidence and Economic Effects of Taxation" in A.S. Blinder and R.M. Solow et al., *The Economics of Public Finance*, esp. pp. 129–34, 140–1; M. Kalecki, "A Theory of Commodity, Income and Capital Taxation", in *Selected Essays on the Dynamics of the Capitalist Economy*, ch. 4; A. Asimakopulos and J.B. Burbidge, "The Short-Period Incidence of Taxation", *Economic Journal* (June 1974); J.L. Eatwell, "On the Proposed Reform of Corporation Tax", *Bulletin of the Oxford University Institute of Economics and Statistics* (November 1971), pp. 267–74. For a general comparison of the two approaches see A. Asimakopulos and J.B. Burbidge, "Harberger and Kalecki on the Incidence of Taxation: A Critical Comparison", *Greek Economic Review* 1(2), December 1979, pp. 70–81.

[12] A.C. Harberger, "The Incidence of the Corporate Tax", *Journal of Political Economy*, (June 1962), pp. 215–40.

[13] P.M. Mieszkowski, "On the Theory of Tax Incidence", *Journal of Political Economy* (June 1967), pp. 250–62; C.E. McLure, "The Theory of Tax Incidence with Imperfect Factor Mobility", *Finanzarchiv*, vol. 30 (1971), pp. 27–48. Further references are provided in the Mieszkowski survey cited in Note 1 above. Useful text book accounts of general equilibrium incidence analysis are R.A. and P.B. Musgrave, *Public Finance in Theory and Practice*, pp. 280–6, C.V. Brown and P.M. Jackson, *Public Sector Economics*, ch. 12.

[14] See G.C. Harcourt, *Some Cambridge Controversies in the Theory of Capital* (Cambridge: Cambridge University Press, 1972) and L.L. Pasinetti, *Growth and Income Distribution* (Cambridge: Cambridge University Press, 1974), pp. 122–39.

[15] See G. Break, "The Incidence and Economic Effects of Taxation, pp. 132–4.

[16] For a discussion of dynamic incidence, see G. Break, "The Incidence and Economic Effects of Taxation", pp. 134–7, and the references cited.

[17] That is, Kalecki, "A Theory of Commodity, Income and Capital Taxation", pp. 35–42. In the analysis which follows, his treatment of capital taxation is neglected.

[18] The elasticity of money supply assumption neutralises the effects of the changed price level on investment, output, and employment. If capitalists also consume wage goods, the rise in their price may cause shifts in their consumption patterns, and consequently shifts in the output of wage goods and of capitalists' luxury consumption output. It can be shown that a tax on wages at the same rate of the commodity tax will have exactly the same effect. When workers do not save, a flat tax on consumption is the equivalent of a flat tax on the income of workers.

[19] This argument stops short of Kalecki's analysis of the effects of the income tax on profits, in which the effect of the tax on interest rates is analysed, and then, via the rise in interest rates on the inducement to investment. In the final part of the argument, the analysis thereby shifts out of the short period, since investment is affected. The result as stated in this paragraph conforms to the results of Asimakopulos and Burbidge, "The Short Period Incidence of Taxation", *Economic Journal* (June 1974), p. 276. Reference should also be made to D. Mair, "The Incidence of Business Rates: Preliminary Estimates", *Environment and Planning C: Government and Policy* 5(1) February 1987, pp. 99–103.

[20] The pioneering study is that by P. Bentley, D.J. Collins and N.T. Drane, "The Incidence of Australian Taxation", *Economic Record*

50 (132) December 1974, pp. 489-504. Other studies are by Neil Warren. See his "Australian Tax Incidence in 1975–76: Some Preliminary Results", *Australian Economic Review* 3/79, pp. 19–30; "Changes in Australian Tax Incidence between 1975–76 and 1984–85" (Sydney: Centre for Applied Economic Research, Working Papers No. 94, December 1986), revised version published in J.G. Head (ed.), *Australian Tax Reform in Retrospect and Prospect* (Sydney: Australian Tax Research Foundation, 1989), ch. 17.

21 Sensitivity analysis, both here and overseas, has shown that altering the specific incidence assumptions has little effect on the overall results. See for example, P. Bentley, D.J. Collins, and D.J.S. Rutledge, *Incidence of Australian Taxation: Some Further Results*, Figures 1–5. For a discussion of the effect of changes in the definition of income on such incidence results, see Neil Warren, "Changes in Australian Tax Incidence Between 1975–76 and 1984–85", pp. 451–3 and for the potential impact on these results of widespread avoidance and evasion, see P.D. Groenewegen, "Distributional and Allocational Effects of Tax Avoidance", in D.J. Collins (ed.), *Tax Avoidance and the Economy* (Sydney: Australian Tax Research Foundation, 1984), pp. 23–37.

22 See A.R. Prest, "Statistical Calculations of Tax Burdens", *Economica*, No. 22(2), August 1955, pp. 234–45.

23 See J. Davies, F. St. Hilaire and J. Whalley, "Some Calculations of Life Time Tax Incidence", *American Economic Review*, 74 (4), September 1984, pp. 633–49.

24 See John Piggott and John Whalley, "Net Fiscal Incidence Calculations: Averge versus Marginal Effects" (Canberra: Australian National University Working Papers in Economics and Econometrics, December 1984). For a general discussion of general equilibrium computation in this and other public sector issues, see John Piggott, "General Equilibrium Computation Applied to Public Sector Issues", in Paul G. Hare (ed.), *Surveys in Public Sector Economics* (Oxford: Basil Blackwell, 1988), ch. 9.

25 See, for example, Andrew Dilnot, John Kay and Michael Keen, "Allocating Taxes to Households: A Methodology" (Colchester: University of Essex, Economics Discussion Paper Series, No. 344, April 1989).

FURTHER READING

Detailed references to the relevant literature useful as additional reading are given in the notes section of this chapter, especially Notes 11 and 13.

A useful introduction to the subject is:

H.G. Brennan, "A Policy Maker's Guide to Incidence" in Taxation Review Committee, *Commissioned Studies* (Canberra: AGPS, 1975) reprinted in Peter Groenewegen (ed.), *Readings in Australian Tax Policy* (Melbourne: Longman Cheshire, 1987), Reading 3.

Reference can also usefully be made to:

J.E. Stiglitz, *Public Sector Economics*, 2nd edn. (New York: W.W. Norton, 1988), ch. 17.

and, at a far more advanced level,

Laurence Kotlikoff and Lawrence Summers, "Tax Incidence", in A.J. Auerbach and M. Feldstein (eds.), *Handbook of Public Economics* (Amsterdam: North Holland, 1987) vol. 2, ch. 16.

On empirical tax incidence studies, the pioneering Australian study remains a useful study, that is:

P. Bentley, D.J. Collins and N.T. Drane, "The Incidence of Australian Taxation", *Economic Record* 50 (132), December 1974, pp. 489–504.

Reference should also be made to:

N.A. Warren, "Australian Tax Incidence in 1975–76: some Preliminary Results", *Australian Economic Review* 3/79, pp. 19–30, reprinted in Peter Groenewegen (ed.), *Readings in Australian Tax Policy*, Reading 4;

and

N. A. Warren, "Changes in Australian Tax Incidence between 1975–76 and 1984–85", in J.G. Head (ed.), *Australian Tax Reform in Retrospect and Prospect* (Sydney: Australian Tax Research Foundation, 1989), ch. 17.

Personal income tax

Personal income tax is by far the most important tax in Australia. As shown in Table 6.3, it raised consistently in excess of 40 per cent of national taxation over the 1980s and accounted for 57 per cent of federal tax revenue in 1988–89. Personal income tax as shown in the Budget Statements is subdivided into a number of categories, of which PAYE collections remain by far the more important. In addition, it includes provisional tax paid by self-employed persons or by those with a significant proportion of property income, taxation collections from employees in a number of specific industries under the prescribed payments system and several special levies collected with personal income tax. The last include the separate Medicare levy introduced in 1984 to finance the national health care system, and the Higher Education Contribution Charge in lieu of fees for higher education students introduced in 1989 in the form of a special income tax liability. In addition, since 1985 the personal income tax system includes realised capital gains adjusted for inflation assets acquired after 19 September of that year.

Personal income tax also includes business income from partnerships, trusts, or sole traders, but it is more convenient to treat this together with company taxation in Chapter 10, because many of the issues applicable to the latter are better postponed until then. This also applies to fringe benefits tax and the tax treatment of superannuation. Issues associated with foreign income are postponed to Chapter 19.

The first personal income taxation to be imposed in Australia was that of the South Australian Government in 1884. Tasmania introduced income tax in 1894, New South Wales and Victoria in 1895, Queensland in 1902, Western Australia in 1907, and the Commonwealth Government in 1915. From 1915 to 1942 income taxation was levied by the Federal and all State governments. In 1942, as a war measure, the States were coerced to give their income tax powers to the Federal Government for the duration of the war under the uniform income tax arrangements then enacted. After the war, the Commonwealth maintained effective control over personal income taxation, but by legislation effective from 1978 to 1989 the States were given access to income tax revenue enabling them to impose income tax surcharges or rebates. This power was never used by the States. Issues of State access to income taxation are postponed to Chapters 14 and 15 concerned with fiscal federalism problems.

Income tax is levied and assessed in accordance with a number of Acts of Parliament and regulations, of which the *Income Tax Assessment Act* is the most important.[1] The tax is payable by residents and by non-residents on income which originates in Australia and which is not subject to withholding taxes. Australian residents also pay tax on income received from abroad, though this is subject to Double Taxation Agreements with other countries where these apply. (These issues of foreign taxation are discussed in Chapter 19.) Liability to tax is ascertained on the basis of an assessment made for each income year ending 30 June from the income tax return submitted by the taxpayer. Returns need generally to be submitted to the Taxation Department within two months of the close of the financial year. Tax administration issues are briefly discussed towards the end of this chapter.

THE TAX BASE

In Australia, the income tax base is known as "taxable income" which is the total of all income assessable for income tax less *allowable deductions* such as subscriptions to trade unions and professional associations, as well as other expenses incurred in the earning of assessable income, and, where applicable, certain other deductions which in 1988–89 included gifts to approved school building funds and to public institutions. It is to the *taxable* income that the rate structure is applied to calculate the amount of tax payable. This calculated tax liability is then further adjusted by a number of tax rebates.

The income tax base in Australia therefore consists of a variety of elements which must be carefully distinguished. In the first place, there is the amount of *assessable income* obtained during the income year from all sources. This is the starting-point from which *net income, taxable income,* and *income tax liability* are derived in turn. *Net income* is defined as total assessable income less expenses incurred in gaining assessable income under specific sections of the Act such as investment allowances and special primary producer deductions as applicable from time to time.[2] *Taxable income* is derived by deducting allowable deductions from net income and is the income concept from which tax liability is calculated by means of the legislated rate structure. *Net tax* payable is ascertained by deducting from the calculated tax liability the various tax rebates which were defined in the previous paragraph. These various income concepts are used in the taxation statistics published by the Commissioner and must be differentiated not only amongst themselves but also from the actual income of the taxpayer as, for example, more comprehensively defined by some of the economists' definitions of income.

The *Australian Income Tax Assessment Act* does not provide a statutory definition of assessable income but an operational definition can be obtained from the various income categories listed on current income tax returns. These, for 1988–89, included gross salary, wages, bonuses, commissions, superannuation, workers' compensation, other remunerations, royalties, honoraria, and earnings, allowances and benefits granted by the employer including those in kind, tips, and other gratuities received in connection with employment, certain lump sum payments received on termination of employment and retirement, unemployment and sickness benefits as well as other pensions and allowances paid by the Commonwealth government but excluding invalid pensions, repatriation pensions, and family allowances, income obtained from a partnership, trust, or similar institution, income from the sale of property, rent, interest, and dividend including that derived from abroad.

In short, assessable income includes all income obtained from employment and that derived from property. There are various classes of exempt income; for example, the income of charitable institutions, the income of State governors and Governors-General, electoral and other allowances provided to members of Parliament separate from their salaries, while gifts, legacies, lottery wins, and certain receipts of a capital nature are not treated as income and therefore not assessable.

As indicated previously, to arrive at taxable income, assessable income is reduced by *allowable deductions* and by certain other deductions specified in the Act, such as gifts to approved charities. Allowable deductions include losses and expenses incurred in gaining or producing assessable income or necessarily incurred in carrying on a business for that purpose, except to the extent that they are of a capital, private, or domestic nature, or are incurred in the producing of exempt income. When all appropriate deductions have been made, the resulting taxable income is used to calculate gross tax payable by applying the rate scale, but actual (or net) tax payable has to be calculated by deducting rebates from gross tax liability. The nature of these rebates has varied considerably over the years in which they have been in force.[3] Those given with respect to activities which the government in office wishes to encourage — for example, mortgage interest relief, child care expenses, basic health insurance costs — have generally had short lives not infrequently dictated by the electoral calendar.[4] Other more long-lasting ones are given with respect to specified dependants of taxpayers, as zone allowances to residents in remote areas and members of the overseas forces as well as for concessional expenditures. Since 1985, the last have been confined to net medical expenses above $1,000; the traditional concessional rebates for education expenses for dependent student children, most life insurance and superannuation contributions, rates and land taxes then disappeared.[5]

The Medicare levy and Higher Education Contribution

Tax liability as assessed by the Australian Taxation Office from 1983–84 has differed from that implied in the calculation methods described in the previous paragraph. This is caused by the introduction of separate personal income tax levies designed to defray part of the cost of specific government social welfare programs.

The first of these is the Medicare levy, designed to assist financing of the National Health Scheme. On introduction in 1984, this amounted to 1 per cent of taxable income exceeding a specific threshold (initially $6,699) and permitting exemptions for certain taxpayers such as those holding a social security health card. The levy rate was increased to 1.25 per cent from 1 December 1986 to enable more substantial recovery of federal health costs. Estimated revenue from the levy for 1988–89 was $2.3 billion or close to 5 per cent of total individual income tax collections. This accounted for approximately 30 per cent of the federal medical and hospital services outlays for that year. The effect of this user charge administered through personal income taxation is to raise the legislated personal income tax rate structure uniformly by the percentage of the levy, that is, by 1.25 per cent in 1988–89.

Similar cost recovery via the personal income tax system was applied to those directly benefiting from higher education from 1 January 1989, the date the Higher Education Contribution Scheme (HECS) began effective operation. This scheme provided for higher education students to contribute a fixed sum (in 1989 of $1800), on average equivalent to

20 per cent of tuition costs, either at the time of notification of liability (enrolment) when a 15 per cent discount applied, or, as a delayed payment through the tax system when the student's taxable income reaches $22,000. The last provides the reason for including it in a discussion of personal income taxation.

More precisely, the HECS can be defined as containing the following elements. The annual course charge (of $1800 in 1989) is to be indexed annually, (in 1990 it is $1882), with the outstanding liability for the charge for individual students likewise to be maintained in real terms. The threshold of $22,000 in 1989 at which repayment of HECS through the income tax system starts is likewise indexed while the rate at which the accumulated HECS liability is to be repaid, has the form of a progressive rate structure. Repayment in the year of introduction is calculated at 1 per cent where taxable income reaches $22,000 (in 1990, $23,583) at 2 per cent where it reaches $25,000 (in 1990, $26,799) and at 3 per cent where it reaches $35,000 (in 1990, $37,514). A number of HECS exemptions apply with respect to fee paying students, students in TAFE, students with post-graduate scholarships and (at least until 1993) students in basic nurse education courses. For 1989–90, the HECS contribution channelled through the tax system has been estimated at less than $10 million, or approximately 9 per cent of the total revenue contribution of the charge. However, this proportion can be expected to increase considerably from early 1992 when students in first year at the commencement of the scheme enter the workforce in substantial numbers as graduates.[6]

The design of these levies reflect equity and efficiency considerations. Linking charges to taxable income thresholds introduces the equity characteristics of these user charges or benefit taxes. The efficiency consequences arise from tying tax costs to public good benefits at the margin, as suggested in the conventional theory of public expenditure discussed in previous chapters.[7]

Some theoretical issues of the income tax base

As shown earlier, the *Australian Income Tax Assessment Act* does not provide a concise definition of income for income tax purposes. This is not because a concise and acceptable definition is impossible. The definition based on the "accretion" principle and first popularised by Henry Simons in the 1930s has long been widely accepted by tax economists as a starting point for discussion. This definition is as follows:

> Personal income may be defined as the algebraic sum of (1) the market value of rights exercised in consumption and (2) the change in the value of the store of property rights between the beginning and the end of the period in question. In other words, it is merely the result obtained by adding consumption during the period to "wealth" at the end of the period and then subtracting "wealth" at the beginning.[8]

In symbols,

$$Y = C + W_t - W_{t-1}$$

where Y is income for the period, C is consumption for the period, and W_{t-1} and W_t stand for wealth at the beginning and at the end of the period respectively.

This very comprehensive definition of income has been put forward by some as the "ideal" to which the actual base used in income tax should move. However, actual income tax systems have never proceeded that far partly because various types of receipts defined as income on this definition would be politically or administratively impossible to tax by a personal income tax. A number of the more important "income" items under the Simons accretion concept which normally are exempt under actual income tax systems (including Australia's) are the following:

1. Some *non-pecuniary* parts of income such as home-grown vegetables, do-it-yourself repairs, services of the housewife, and services rendered by consumer durables are not easily measurable and in Australia are generally ignored for tax purposes. However, in the case of residential dwellings, an imputed rent is easily calculated — such an imputed rent for instance was included in income for British income taxation purposes — but in Australia it has not been included in assessable income since the 1930s. This may lead to some unfairness in the taxation of the rent-paying taxpayer, as compared with the home owner.

This favourable treatment of home owners can be explained by the fact that the encouragement of home ownership is an important objective of both major political parties. Such an objective is, however, in conflict with the objective of fairness, not only because of the different treatment of rent paying as against home-owning taxpayers, but also because home ownership is an important factor in the assessment of economic capacity to pay taxes, the principle which underlies the personal income tax in Australia. For this reason, the taxing of the imputed rent of an owner-occupied dwelling is frequently advocated in Australia.[9]

2. A taxpayer's *leisure* is also an important part of non-pecuniary income. Its value is not easily measured for income tax purposes, however. The omission of the value of leisure from income tax purposes makes for less fairness in the tax system, as was seen when horizontal equity was briefly discussed in Chapter 7. There the question was asked whether $5,000 per annum earned by means of a twenty-hour week was equivalent to the same amount earned by a forty-hour week. The question of the treatment in taxable capacity of the difficulty of work or the enjoyment derived from it was also raised in that context. For example, is the $5,000 earned annually by a street-sweeper the equivalent of $5,000 earned by a poet? The fact that leisure is excluded from the comprehensive income base in principle makes it a non-general tax. This has potentially important efficiency consequences as shown in a subsequent section on income tax and incentives.

3. Receipts of *income in kind* from employment (for example, the company car, the expense account lunch, subsidised housing or housing loans for employees, and discounts on sales from a firm to its employees) may be hard to evaluate. Even if the cost incurred by the firm can be identified, it does not follow that this cost is identical to the value placed by the employee on this privilege. For example, it would be harsh to treat a $40 lunch as an addition of $40 to taxable income if the consumer of the lunch preferred say, $10 in cash, to the lunch. The Fringe Benefits Tax introduced in Australia in 1986 (discussed in Chapter 10) was designed to tackle this difficult assessment problem indirectly.

4. *Windfall gains* such as gifts and bequests, gambling winnings, are generally not included in income tax, the former frequently taxed separately under capital transfer taxes such as estate and gift duty discussed in Chapter 11.

5. *Capital gains*, or the appreciation of assets as they accrue are clearly also included in the "accretion" concept of income together with accrued capital losses. The capital gains tax measures introduced in 1985 are in terms of realised gains, while other features of this income

tax innovation, such as the exemption of the principal residence from the ambit of its provisions, make it conform even less to the comprehensive income "ideal". These issues are discussed subsequently.

Further issues relating to the income tax base

Neither Australia's pragmatic definition of income for income tax purposes nor Simons' definition can adequately solve the administrative difficulties associated with the various types of income just enumerated. There are, however, several issues which actual tax systems must resolve in one way or another, but which raise interesting questions for the tax economist through the equity, efficiency, and other anomalies they create in the tax system actually adopted. The first of these issues relates to the income tax paying unit, that is, whether *household or individual income* is to be used for tax purposes, the second relates to the *time period* over which the income accrues; and the third is the issue whether *money income or real income* is the appropriate income measure for tax purposes.

Household or individual income

Income accrues to individuals, but frequently it is utilised by a household with more than one person. In Chapter 7 it was seen that this raised questions for horizontal equity when the question was asked, "Is an annual income of $10,000 equivalent from the point of view of taxable capacity if it is earned by a person with no dependants, by a man with a wife and children to support, or by a working couple, earning say, $5,000 each?" It can be easily argued that these equal nominal amounts of income imply differing taxable capacities for the income-earning taxpayer(s). Tax systems usually provide explicit tax concessions for taxpayers with dependants which may take various forms, or assistance to households with dependants may be provided through the social security, as is the case in Australia with family allowances.

In Australia the taxpaying unit is the individual income earner, not the household. Table 9.1 illustrates the effects of such a system on tax payable as well as the average tax rate on household income for four different households which all have an annual household income of $25,000.

Table 9.1 clearly illustrates the differing tax liabilities of these various types of households. The single person, for example, pays the largest proportion of income in tax, which seems fair because this income is not shared with other, non-income earning people. Table 9.1 also illustrates the advantages of income-splitting in an individual tax unit system with a progressive rate structure. The working couple who earns $12,500 each (household 3) pays less tax than household 4 where the earnings are not equally distributed between spouses. In the last household it would pay the high income recipient to reduce assessable income by passing it to the low income recipient till both incomes were equal. The tax saving from this income-splitting equals $449. If full income-splitting between husband, wife, and children were allowed, household 2 would pay more than 90 per cent less in tax on aggregate (that is, $276) or an average rate of only 1.1 per cent. In Australia, general income-splitting is not allowed but in practice it is possible for those with property income through the device of trusts, partnerships, and other forms of property settlements which allow the shifting of income from the taxpayer with a high income (and high marginal tax rate) to those with low marginal tax rates.

Table 9.1 Tax liability for various forms of households with annual income of $25,000

		Tax payable $	*Average rax rate* $
1.	Single person	6 001	24.0
2.	Husband with non-working wife and two children *	4 971	19.9
3.	Working couple, no children earning $12,500 each	3 552	14.2
4.	Working couple, one spouse earning $20,000, the other $5,000	4 001	16.0

* Maximum spouse rebate of $1030 but excludes family allowance. If these are included, the average tax rate falls to 17.2 per cent.

Source: Calculated from 1988–89 personal income tax rates.

These examples show that the choice of the tax unit is of considerable importance. Unfortunately, the decision to adopt individual or household taxation is difficult to make in practice, because that choice depends on the objectives of the tax system envisaged, as well as on other considerations. Household taxation is useful, for example, if it is desired to eliminate income-splitting. It is also useful if it is desired to supplement the income tax with an annual tax on wealth, a subject discussed further in Chapter 11. On the other hand, individual taxation avoids the very considerable practical difficulties of defining a household for tax purposes, it gives working wives a greater right of disposal over their incomes (an issue of particular importance to the women's movement), and it is said to provide greater incentives for women to enter the workforce. Without clear and precise specification of the objectives of the tax system (which, as was seen in Chapter 7, is a matter for political and social judgement) it is impossible to provide a simple conclusion on this matter.[10]

The time period of income implicit in the tax base

In Australia the time period of income for income tax purposes is the twelve months from 1 July to 30 June. With a progressive rate structure, this levy of tax upon the income of *each year* is of little importance for a person with a steady income, but where incomes fluctuate widely (as is the case, for example, with primary producers), it can make considerable difficulty to tax liability. This is illustrated in Table 9.2.

From Table 9.2 it can be seen that although the aggregate income for the five-year period is the same for both taxpayers, taxpayer A pays less tax than taxpayer B over the five-year period because of the annual assessment of tax liability. If the assessment period was five years, the tax liability of A and B would be equal as would be the case if five-year income averaging was allowed to B in period 5. Some specific categories of fluctuating incomes are provided for in the Australian Income Tax Assessment Act by special allowances including averaging.[11]

Table 9.2 Different tax liabilities of persons with fluctuating incomes and steady incomes for five-year period: 1988–89 Australian income tax rates*

	Taxpayer A			Taxpayer B		
Income period	*Taxable income* $	*Tax payable*	*Average tax rate* %	*Taxable income* $	*Tax payable*	*Average tax rate* %
Year 1	25,000	6,001	24.0	20,000	4,001	16.0
Year 2	25,000	6,001	24.0	70,000	27,151	35.8
Year 3	25,000	6,001	24.0	5,000	—	—
Year 4	25,000	6,001	24.0	—	—	—
Year 5	25,000	6,001	24.0	30,000	8,001	26.7
TOTAL	125,000	30,005		125,000	39,153	
Yearly Av.	25,000	6,001	24.0	25,000	7,830.6	31.3

* Single taxpayer with no rebates.
Source: Calculated from 1988–89 income tax rates.

Real or money income as the income base

The third important issue is whether money income or real income should be used as the tax base. This issue has received a great deal of attention in Australia since the 1970s. Inflation may push some income earners into higher income tax brackets (higher marginal tax rates) and invariably raise their tax liability, even though higher money incomes reflect much smaller rises in real income. Taxation of income from capital, particular interest income on fixed nominal debt, likewise implies higher real income tax rates, particularly when inflation rates are high. In short, in the absence of specific adjustments, inflation distorts the legislated distributional intentions within the income tax scale particularly where much of that income is from interest receipts.[12]

From the mid–1970s Australian governments have experimented with a variety of measures to adjust for the effects of inflation on personal income taxation. For the 1976–77 income year, Australia adjusted for inflation by the procedure of indexing the income tax brackets at which different marginal tax rates become applicable. Figure 9.1 illustrates this principle of indexation by graphing the marginal tax rates of 1975–76 and 1976–77. In addition, there were provisions for increasing some of the tax rebates then in force by the proportional change in the Consumer Price Index. For a number of years afterwards only partial indexation was applied to the rate scales. This was sometimes justified, as in May 1977, by the need to remove government-induced changes in the CPI from the indexation factor, but on other occasions it was simply argued that full indexation was too costly to the revenue. In 1981, indexation of personal income tax scales was abolished altogether for political reasons. Governments since then have preferred to reap the political kudos of discretionary tax cuts to providing the automatic adjustment of the scales for inflation, the benefits of which are not nearly as visible to the voting public.[13]

As indicated in the earlier discussion of HECS, both the accumulated liability incurred under it, and the thresholds of taxable income determining the rates of repayment are annually adjusted for inflation. Likewise, as discussed more fully when examining the current provisions for capital gains taxation, such gains are adjusted to remove the contribution which inflation has made to them. Differential inflation adjustments in this

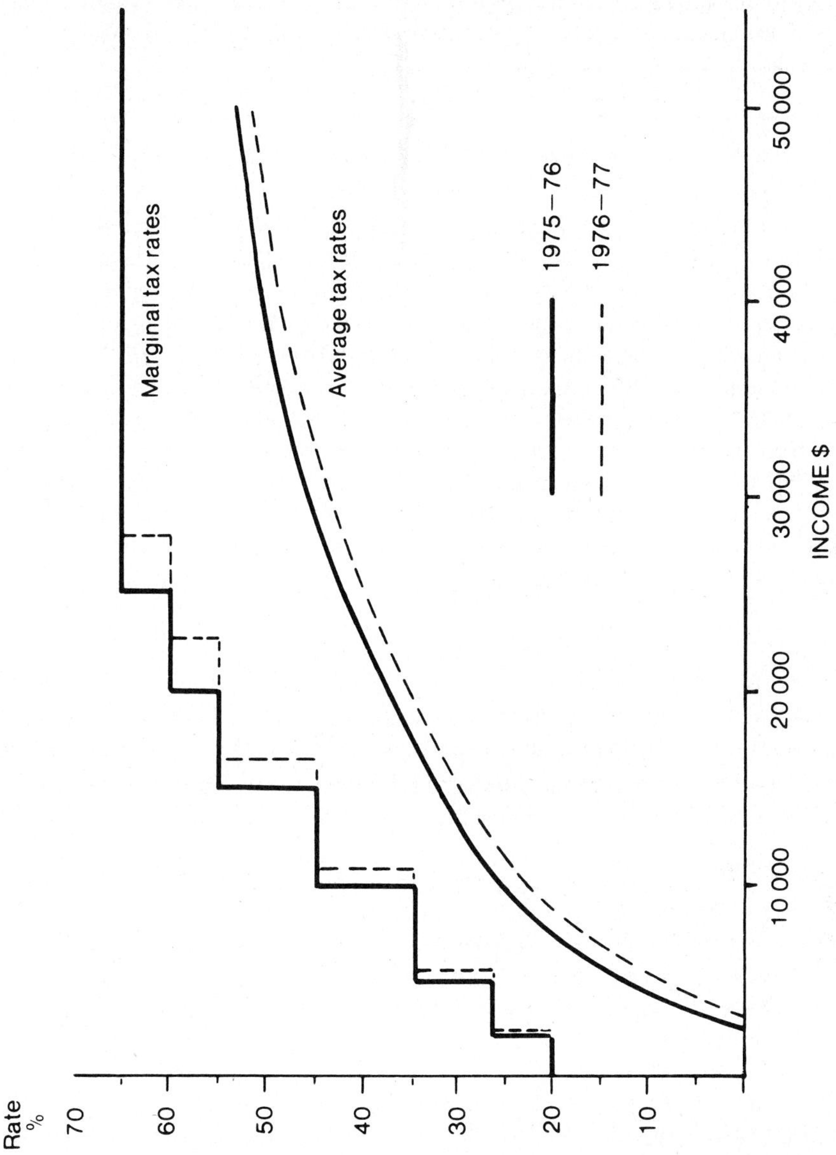

Figure 9.1 Indexed rate scales: Australian income tax 1975–76 and 1976–77

manner distorts investment choices by altering after-tax-rates of return, hence contravening the neutrality criterion. Other aspects of this are examined subsequently in the context of the economic effects of personal income tax.

Differences between the Australian income tax base and the Simons' accretion concept of income

It was shown earlier that Simons' definition for income tax purposes was wider than the definition implicit in the *Australian Income Tax Assessment Act*. The Australian income tax base excludes gifts, inheritances, and bequests, all lottery and other gambling winnings, non-pecuniary income from property in dwellings, all accrued capital gains (though from 1985 there is provision for the systematic inclusion of realised real capital gains among taxable income). In addition, since 1985 a substantial number of fringe benefits are now taxed in the hands of the employer (as discussed more fully in Chapter 10), both income base broadening measures which have brought Australia's income tax closer (but nevertheless still far removed) from the Simons' income tax ideal. Such base broadening, by enabling a substantial increase in tax yields, permits rate reductions with matching benefits for those previously taxed on their full income. The important base broadening measure of capital gains tax can be briefly examined in this context.

CAPITAL GAINS TAXATION

From the 1985–86 income year, Australia has taxed realised capital gains on most assets acquired after 19 September 1985 as part of income, but with the gain adjusted for inflation from the period of acquisition to the period of disposal. This description of Australia's capital gains tax draws attention to three specific features of its base, which it shares with all such taxation.

The first of these is the nature of the asset liable to capital gains. Although in principle a capital gains tax should cover the disposal of all owned assets, in practice assets are excluded for political, social or administrative reasons. Exempt assets for Australian capital gains tax purposes include the taxpayer's principal residence, most personal-use assets, most motor vehicles (because their value tends to decline over time with use), most superannuation and life insurance policies, casual gambling winnings, some compensation payments (those related to a wrong or injury suffered by a person) and one-fifth of the goodwill from a business for persons whose interests in business undertakings on a net value basis aggregate to less than $1 million. Taxable assets therefore include: real estate other than the principal residence, leases, shares in companies,[14] rights to acquire shares, company-issued options to shareholders to take up shares, convertible notes, and amounts received as consideration for restrictive covenants, exclusive trade tie agreements, variations of contracts and giving up amateur status. Personal use assets (with an acquisition value in excess of $100) are also taxable on disposal if they are works of art, rare books or manuscripts, antiques, coins or stamps. The relative importance of these classes of assets for capital gains tax purposes in the first two years of its operation are given in Table 9.3. These show the overwhelming importance of the disposal of shares and real estate in generating capital gains, though gains generated from the distribution made by non-corporate business are also very significant.

Table 9.3 Taxable capital gains by type of asset 1986–87 and 1987–88

	1986–87		*1987–88*	
	$m	*%*	*$m*	*%*
Shares	81.1	81.8	191.7	58.4
Real estate	2.2	2.2	51.5	15.7
Other property	2.0	2.0	12.1	3.7
Personal use assets	0.9	0.9	3.0	0.9
Distribution from partnerships and trusts	12.9	13.0	70.0	21.3
	99.1	100.0	328.3	100.0

Note: Figures may not add due to rounding.
Source: Commissioner of Taxation, *Annual Report 1987–88* (Canberra: AGPS, 1988), p. 183; *Income Tax Statistics 1987–88 Income year,* 1988–89 Budget Related Paper No. 3 (Canberra: AGPS, 1989), p. 12.

Acquisition of the asset giving rise to the capital gain has to be after 19 September 1985, a provision intended to prevent retrospectivity when the tax was introduced. Acquisition can be by purchase (hence implying a disposal) but also by gift, bequest, construction or creation and can apply to the whole of the asset or part thereof. Date of acquisition is either the date of contract or the date of effective transfer. Disposal is by sale, by gift, by loss or destruction, but not by death unless disposed of by the representative of the estate or by a beneficiary. The last provision, which can be seen as a provision enabling substantial tax deferral, was designed to allay fears that the tax was a substitute death duty (see Chapter 11).

Since capital gains (offset by capital losses), are included with taxable income, the Australian rate structure is the same as the personal income tax rate structure, examined subsequently in this chapter. Where capital gains are taxed separately, as in the United States, a flat rate, generally lower than the maximum marginal income tax rate, tends to apply. Other capital gains taxes apply lower rates of tax depending on the length of time over which the asset disposed of has been held.[15]

Other considerations in capital gains taxation

The case for capital gains taxation is generally made on ability-to-pay principles. When capital gains are untaxed, the tax base does not cover the whole taxable capacity of individual taxpayers. In addition, such an exemption itself provides an opportunity for wealthy taxpayers to convert taxable income into tax-exempt capital gains, thereby avoiding personal income tax. This opportunity is reduced but not eliminated when capital gains are taxed separately from income at a proportional rate. The vertical equity dimension of this is indicated by the fact that capital gains are concentrated in the hands of those with annual incomes in excess of $50,000. Horizontal equity is violated by the non-taxation of capital gains *per se*. These are major reasons why comprehensive capital gains taxation was introduced in Australia in 1985.[16]

Opportunities for tax avoidance arising from the exemption of capital gains from taxation should be given some emphasis, since they are increasingly seen as not only distorting the desired distributional consequences of personal income tax, but also as an important distorting influence on the investment decision. Since the potential of capital gains and prospective tax liability both affect the after-tax rate of return which an investor generally seeks to maximise, the non-taxation of capital gains substantially affects the after-tax rate of return of certain assets. This non-neutrality influences investment decisions unfavourably by steering investors to those assets which yield capital gains rather than taxable income and these are generally assets of a less productive nature from the social point of view.

Other resource allocation effects of the tax should also be briefly considered. It is easy to show, for example, that a tax on capital gains lowers the effective rate of return on certain investments and that this may affect the supply of saving or risk-taking. It is, however, difficult to state with any precision how large this effect actually is. Another effect of the tax, frequently mentioned when only realised gains are taxed, is the "locking-in" effect. When the decision to sell an asset has been made on general economic grounds, the existence of a capital gains tax involving a substantial tax liability may induce the owner to hold the asset for a longer period, for example, until sufficient losses to offset the gain have been accumulated. This has the effect of reducing the mobility of investible funds, and therefore the choices open to investors. Further, the introduction of a capital gains tax may enlarge the problem of share price fluctuations on the stock exchange, increasing the instability of the share market. Exemption of particular assets, such as the principal residence in Australia's capital gains tax makes investment into that type of asset even more attractive than it already is.

Because asset values can frequently fluctuate over the course of the trade cycle, some people consider the tax a useful automatic stabiliser because it will siphon off excess spending power during periods of strong economic activity while capital losses will reduce tax liability in periods of recession. With the yield of the tax generally rather small, this cannot be an important effect overall, but the tax can be seen as a useful addition to the other automatic stabilisers of the fiscal system. In the context of the growth objective, it is frequently argued that capital gains tax should be abandoned because it is inimical to saving through both its income effect and its effect on the rate of return on investment.[17]

The disincentive effects ascribed to capital gains tax induced an Opposition proposal during the 1990 election campaign to replace it by a speculative gains tax. This would tax the full capital gain if realised within a year of acquisition, 80 per cent of the gain if realised during the second year, 60 per cent if realised during the third year so that gains on assets held for more than five years would be tax-free. Such a speculative gains tax would reduce the efficiency and equity benefits reaped from the present tax.

Finally, there is the problem of administration. In many countries, capital gains taxation has proved to be an expensive tax to administer and the yield has been rather small. This has been the experience in the United States and in the United Kingdom, an experience now replicated in Australia. In their attempts to eliminate administrative problems, tax legislators have frequently introduced compromises which have seriously weakened the impact of the tax, including that on income distribution, which is often the major reason for introducing a capital gains tax. In addition, the compliance costs of the taxpayer are generally large. In short, the capital gains tax provides a good illustration of the conflict between equity and simplicity in the construction of a tax system, though Australia's experience shows that the vertical equity gains from having it are substantial.

THE RATE STRUCTURE

When discussing fluctuating incomes and tax averaging, the tax unit and income-splitting, and the effects of inflation on taxation, the realistic assumption was made in the Australian context that income tax is levied under a progressive rate structure. The meaning of progressive rate structure — and of a proportional and regressive rate structure — was discussed in Chapter 7 in connection with the ability to pay principle. In this section on the Australian income tax rate structure elements of this discussion will be drawn together, the debate between those favouring and those against progressive taxation will be examined, as will the rationale for rate scale simplifications such as those which took place in the 1970s.

Before proceeding with this discussion some of the formal properties of a progressive rate structure should be reiterated. These concern the relationship between average and marginal tax rates, the effective changes in the average rates brought about by a system of selective tax rebates, and the association between average rates and the tax base. Examples of these relationships, based on the 1988–89 personal income tax rate schedule, are given in Table 9.4.

The first example in Table 9.4 shows the relationship between average and marginal tax rates in a progressive tax structure. As income rises from $5,000 to $200,000 the marginal tax rates rise in discontinuous steps from 0 to 49 per cent but the average rates rise smoothly from 0 to 45.4 per cent. More specifically, average tax rates rise continually with income, and asymptotically approach the maximum marginal rate at very high income levels. It will be recalled from Chapter 7 that the rise of average tax rates as income rises is a necessary condition for progressive taxation and this is assured when there are two marginal tax rates (which may include one equal to zero, giving rise to the concept of linear income tax discussed later).

The second example is designed to show how a system of selective tax rebates as currently in force in Australia alters the effective average tax rates and thereby the degree of progression built into the formal rate structure. Despite the equality of the taxable income of the four taxpayers used in the example, which means that they are all confronted with the same marginal tax rate, their differing personal circumstances give rise to different access to tax rebates and hence differing average rates. This shows that the apparent degree of progression embodied in the average tax rate structure (and derived from the marginal tax rate schedule) can be very significantly altered by tax rebates when these are selectively applied.[18]

The last example in Table 9.4 shows the effects of alterations in the tax base — that is, in the various income concepts discussed earlier in this chapter — on the marginal and average tax rates. Although all three taxpayers in the example start with equal actual incomes, their tax liability in absolute terms varies considerably and as a consequence so do their average tax rates. Taxpayer A either illegally (by not declaring $10,000 as income) or legally (by converting that $10,000 into tax exempt income) reduces actual income to $15,000 of assessable income, reduced by a further $2,000 of allowable deductions. Taxpayer B either has no opportunity (being a wage or salary earner) or no inclination to avoid or evade tax but likewise reduces assessable income by $2,000 in allowable deductions. Taxpayer C has no opportunity at all for reducing actual income. The effects on tax rates of these differing

Table 9.4 Actual income, assessable income, taxable income, tax rebates, average and marginal tax rates: 1988–89 income tax rates

Example (i) Single taxpayer

(1) Taxable income $	(2) Tax payable %	(3) Marginal tax rate %	(4) Average tax rate %
5,000	—	—	—
10,000	1,176	24	11.4
15,000	2,496	29	16.7
20,000	4,001	40	20.0
25,000	5,396	40	21.6
50,000	17,351	49	34.7
100,000	41,851	49	41.9
200,000	90,851	49	45.4

Note: Average tax rate (column 4) = column 2 as a percentage of column 1.

Example (ii) The effect of tax rebates on average tax rates

	Taxable income $	Tax payable $	Marginal average tax rates %	%
Single taxpayer	20,000	4,001	40	20.0
Taxpayer with dependent spouse	20,000	3,171	40	15.9
Taxpayer with dependent spouse and dependent children*	20,000	2,971	40	14.9
Concessional expenditures of $3,500	20,000	2,246	40	11.2

* Excludes family allowance for dependent children.

Example (iii) Actual, assessable, and taxable income and average tax returns

Taxpayer	(1) $	(2) $	(3) $	(4) $	(5) %	(6)	(7)	(8)
A	25,000	15,000	13,000	1,916	29	7.7	12.8	14.7
B	25,000	25,000	23,000	5,201	40	20.8	20.8	22.6
C	25,000	25,000	25,000	5,396	40	21.6	21.6	21.6

Notes: (1) actual income (2) assessable income (3) taxable income (4) tax payable (5) marginal tax rate (6) average tax rate with respect to actual income (7) average tax rate with respect to assessable income (8) average tax rate with respect to taxable income.

Source: Calculated from 1988–89 personal income tax rate schedule.

opportunities for transforming actual income into lower taxable income for the three taxpayers are clearly shown in the table. One general conclusion can be derived from this example. Where actual incomes diverge greatly from taxable incomes, the degree of progressivity of the rate structure is drastically altered from that shown in the legislated tax scale. The actual degree of progression must be interpreted with a great deal of care. A further difficulty also clearly illustrated is that the term "average tax rate" becomes ambiguous (with respect to the type of income to which actual tax liability is applied). Because average tax rate behaviour provides the generally accepted measure of progressivity, this means that measure becomes also less clear-cut.

Proportional or progressive income taxation?

When discussing the ability to pay principle in Chapter 7, Simons' view that progressive taxation is a desirable feature of a nation's taxation structure, not because there are economic arguments to suggest that this is the case, but because general public opinion appears to support this notion, was approvingly quoted. The case for progressive taxation and for the degree of progression is largely a matter of ethical and political judgement. Australia is one of the many countries in the world which has accepted this judgement and which has therefore applied a progressive rate structure with varying degrees of progression to its personal income taxation for the greater part of this century.

From the 1970s onwards, arguments in favour of progressive personal income taxation, particularly when achieved by frequent changes in marginal tax rates, have been challenged for a variety of reasons. The deleterious effects of inflation on such a rate scale — through altering its legislated distributional consequences — provided one reason. In addition, there was growing concern about the encouragement such rate structures gave to tax avoidance and tax evasion, as well as the more traditional worry about the effects of high marginal tax rates on incentives to work, save, and invest. These factors, discussed in more detail later, together with the continuing rise in the relative importance of personal income tax as a revenue raiser (shown in Table 6.3) and the unfavourable comparisons in this respect which can be drawn with the practice in most OECD countries, sparked proposals for rate scale simplification of which the most extreme suggested a fully proportional rate structure.

In the wake of this debate, substantial rate simplification has taken place in Australia.[19] The 29 steps in the 1973 marginal rate scale were reduced to 3 in 1977, with a subsequent increase in 1984 to 5, the number of steps in force in 1990. The maximum marginal rate was gradually lowered over this period from 67 per cent in 1973 to 49 per cent from January 1990. However, the real value of the threshold at which this rate comes into operation has declined even more, and by 1990 approximated average annual earnings. Initial marginal tax rates rose steadily from 7 per cent in 1974 to the 21 per cent applicable from 1989, with a 1977 maximum of 32 per cent. Such high initial rates are required in rate scale simplifications to maintain the revenue potential of the tax. They raise the initial average tax rate and maintain it at a reasonable level for higher income groups. A fourth feature of the rate simplification has been a rise in the tax threshold from $1040 in 1974 to the $5100 applicable from 1989, because a high threshold lowers the impact of high initial marginal tax rates on low income groups. The consequences of these rises in the tax threshold is to exempt increasing numbers of low taxable income taxpayers from income tax. In February 1990 the Government introduced a new rate scale to take effect from July 1990 as part of a wage-tax trade-off under its Prices and Incomes Accord. This raised the threshold to $5400 and introduced a new maximum marginal tax rate of 47 per cent for incomes in excess of $50,000.

Although it may seem progressive at first sight, exempting "low income" taxpayers by high tax thresholds may introduce a variety of anomalies into the tax structure. Many of these low income taxpayers are not necessarily "poor"; they include, for example, married women with property income, or with part-time jobs yielding a high hourly rate of pay; students with holiday earnings and "split income" parcelled out to dependent children by wealthy taxpayers as a tax avoidance device. To eliminate this last anomaly, the threshold for property income for dependent children at which penalty rates apply was lowered first to $1040 in 1978, and then to $416 in 1983.[20]

There are several reasons for simplifying the rate structure. One is the simplification of tax administration and the reduction of compliance costs for a substantial number of taxpayers. Secondly, it simplified indexation of the rate scale somewhat when this was in force. Thirdly, reductions in maximum marginal rates were defended because of their alleged favourable incentive effects. Lastly, the 1980s saw a veritable avalanche of rate simplification in OECD countries in which one country's rate simplification led to that of another. Before examining these aspects further in the next section, two other forms of rate scale simplification discussed in Australia must be looked at.

Linear income tax

The linear income tax maintains income tax progression through continuous rises in average tax rates up to a maximum and takes the rate scale simplification to its logical conclusion by reducing the number of tax brackets to two. There is a generally substantial tax threshold at which a zero marginal tax rate applies, and one non-zero marginal tax rate which applies to all other income. For reasons already discussed, a high non-zero marginal tax rate is required in order to raise substantial revenue when there is a high tax threshold. This will also ensure a reasonable degree of progression.

The linear income tax was first proposed in the context of negative income taxes and guaranteed minimum income schemes (discussed in more detail in Chapter 20) but other advantages independent from this use have also been claimed for it. It has been argued for example, that many of the complexities, inequities, and inefficiencies of the current income tax structure would largely disappear on the adoption of a linear income tax. Its introduction eliminates the need for income averaging, resolves the problem of the tax unit and income-splitting, removes the need to distinguish between tax deductions and tax rebates, reduces incentives to tax avoidance and evasion, involves smaller disincentives to work and save, and facilitates company tax reform to remove the double taxation of dividends (discussed in Chapter 10) if the company tax rate and the linear income tax rate are equalised.[21] The extent to which these favourable consequences are likely to eventuate is a judgement which must await the discussion of the economic and other effects of personal income tax in the next section.

Proportional or flat rate income tax

To distinguish it from the linear income tax, the proportional or flat rate tax proposal must also be briefly discussed. Such a tax eliminates the tax threshold of exempt income and thereby ensures that marginal and average tax rates are constant and equal irrespective of the level of income. This is an essential property of flat rate taxation. Such a tax definitely removes many inefficiencies and complexities from the current personal income tax system with respect to averaging, the tax unit, and indexation, as its supporters claim. It would probably also lower incentives to avoid and evade tax and reduce disincentives to work, save, invest, and take risk. However, it strongly violates the criterion of equity by totally disregarding ability to pay. Furthermore, its elimination of the threshold implies a need for considerable income support for low income earners at present untaxed and this may involve complicated new social security arrangements. Genuine proportional tax proposals have had little support in Australia and cannot really be taken seriously as tax reform options.[22] However, hybrids of these types of tax simplification have been proposed in the two-tiered tax systems supported by the Liberal-National party coalition during the 1987 and 1990 federal election campaigns.[23]

ECONOMIC EFFECTS OF THE AUSTRALIAN PERSONAL INCOME TAX

The personal income tax has many important economic effects which must be analysed. Understanding these effects is particularly important when the income tax plays such a large part in the overall tax structure, as is the case in Australia. Some of these effects are the impact of personal income tax on the *budgetary objectives*, in particular the *distributional objective*. Others relate to its *incidence*, which is affected by evasion and avoidance as well as by wage bargaining and the price setting behaviour in determining fees for professional services. There are *efficiency considerations*, such as the disincentive effects of the income tax on decisions affecting work behaviour and saving.

In Chapter 8 the possibility of shifting personal income tax was briefly referred to. This material might now be recapitulated. When wage rises are sought by trade unions to compensate for previous price rises or to increase real incomes for their members, it is now generally agreed that such wage demands frequently include an allowance for the increased tax liability resulting from higher money wages. It is the *net take home or after-tax pay* that is of importance to trade union members even though the demands are made in terms of gross pay because of the refusal of wage-fixing tribunals to consider after-tax pay. Wage demands may therefore be higher than they would be in the absence of progressive income tax. These higher wages, if granted, can be either absorbed as costs by the employers — in which case the worker's income tax liability included in the wage rise is shifted to the owners of the firm — or, what is more frequently the case, they are passed forward in higher prices and thereby shifted to consumers. In either case, part of the income tax liability is shifted by the workers to others. The validity of this type of argument is recognised in the trade-offs between tax cuts and wage-setting often proposed in the context of national policies for wage restraint.

Similar effects can occur when the prices charged for professional services are the major source of income for taxpayers, as is the case with doctors, dentists, lawyers, hairdressers, and so on. It can be argued that the rate of fee increases for such services may rise, to offset the change in income tax liability which results from such fee rises. This is especially the case for services where demand is not very responsive to rising prices. Such cost and price effects of personal income taxation are discussed further in Chapter 18 in the context of stabilisation policy.

Avoidance and evasion

A further way in which income tax can be shifted occurs when possibilities to avoid or to evade income tax are not evenly distributed among taxpayers. If there were no possibilities to avoid or evade tax, the tax rates would conceivably be lower for all taxpayers, because of the larger tax base. The practice of tax avoidance or tax evasion thereby raises the tax liability of those who cannot or do not engage in this practice, and this is equivalent to tax shifting.

For rather obvious reasons, there is little statistical evidence on the degree of tax avoidance and evasion, but it is generally agreed that it is an important problem in Australia which warrants serious attention by tax economists.[24]

Income tax is most frequently evaded by the understatement of assessable income, which is most easily done in part-time work and in connection with tradesman services for cash, where PAYE instalments are not deducted. Where PAYE instalments are deducted, as is the case of most wage and salary earners in permanent employment, evasion is virtually impossible. Other major groups of evaders are traders selling for cash such as market gardeners, small retailers, and investors. These categories figure prominently in the lists of detected tax evaders, published by the Taxation Commissioner. Tax evasion possibilities are therefore open to a variety of taxpayers and are generally independent of the level of income. *Tax evasion* is of course an *illegal* form of reducing income tax liability. The rising importance of tax evasion in the building, road transport, and several other industries was recognised in the provision for withholding tax arrangements announced in the 1982 Budget, implemented the following year as the Prescribed Payments System, and subsequently widened by covering more occupations.

Other anti-evasion measures which have been introduced are improvements in tax file numbering, as well as the system of self-assessment which the Taxation Office introduced in 1986 to enable more in-depth tax audits designed to catch tax frauds.[25]

There are, however, also *legal* ways of *avoiding* tax by reducing the level of taxable income applicable to the income taxpayer in any one income year. In general, tax can be avoided by the following expedients: taking income in kind rather than in money form; the spreading of income over time to years when low marginal tax rates are expected to apply, as in retirement, for example; income-splitting by means of partnerships, private companies, and trusts; converting income which is taxable into untaxed capital, for example, into other tax-exempt or more favourably treated capital gains; by turning capital expenditure incurred in producing assessable income, and which is not tax deductible, into current expenditure and thereby making it tax deductible; and finally, by converting private consumption expenditure into deductible business expenditures. The ingenuity of the income tax avoidance industry continually expands the range of devices by which income tax liability can be reduced for certain classes of taxpayers. Again, the frequency in which these devices are used can only be guessed at but it can be concluded for a variety of reasons that the practice grew considerably in the decade before the mid–1980s. It can also be noted that the opportunities for tax avoidance listed in this paragraph are largely confined to higher income groups, particularly to the higher ranking executives in corporations; to the self-employed, especially in the professions, and to those with substantial property income.

Since the mid–1980s several tax changes have reduced some of these tax avoidance opportunities. The fringe benefits tax has slowed, if not reduced, avoidance by payment in kind; capital gains tax has substantially reduced the benefits for avoiders from converting taxable income into capital gains; elimination of entertainment expenses as allowable deductions combined with tighter substantiation rules for expenditure from travel and other allowances, are all good examples of such reforms. Many other avoidance opportunities remain, particularly in the business income area, as disclosed by the high success rate of increasingly effective Taxation Office audits. The continuing existence of avoidance opportunities has implications for the effect of personal income tax on income distribution.

Although the distinction between *evasion* as an *illegal* act to defraud the revenue and *avoidance* as a *legal* set of tax minimisation possibilities appears to be clear-cut, this is not really the case. Two examples illustrate this. First, the artificiality of many avoidance schemes investigated in the late 1970s and early 1980s is such that they can hardly be called legal activity if that term is confined to conveying the intentions of the legislators who drafted the tax laws. Secondly, avoidance devices such as the notorious "bottom-of-the-harbour schemes" combine taking advantage of legal and intended tax exemptions with what can only be described as criminal activity. It has therefore become increasingly difficult to define undesirable tax avoidance.[26]

Some causes and effects of the growth of tax avoidance and evasion should be stressed, because they are important for tax reform policy. The rapid rise in personal tax burdens attributed partly to the high inflation rates of the mid–1970s is one frequently mentioned cause of this growth. Others include the attitude of the High Court to avoidance in its interpretation of the law, and declining tax morality in the community at large. Others have attributed this growth to faulty tax design. For example, high marginal rates of income tax are seen as major incentives to avoidance and evasion. The favoured tax treatment of capital gains, the individual tax unit and the creation of tax shelters by government, virtually invite tax avoidance. An immediate and obvious effect of this growth is loss of revenue for the government which has to be made up in alternative methods of taxing it or, as already indicated, by shifting higher burdens on those unable or unwilling to engage in such practices. There are also efficiency costs and adverse distributional consequences.

Personal income tax and income distribution

One of the reasons why progressive income taxation has so many supporters is because it is supposed to improve the distribution of income by reducing income inequalities. In earlier chapters aspects of this issue were discussed, and particular emphasis was placed on the fact that income tax is only one of many instruments affecting the distribution of income which is available to the government. From the incidence studies of Australian taxation, it can be inferred that much of the progressive impact of the personal income tax is removed by the regressive impact of other taxes. However, the progressive distributional impact of the personal income tax revealed in such studies can itself be questioned because of tax base considerations and the growth of tax avoidance and evasion discussed earlier (see Table 8.1).

What implications are there for the distributional consequences of personal income tax from the peculiarities of the Australian tax base and the incidence of avoidance and evasion? Table 9.4 illustrates how variations in the tax base — from access to tax avoidance and evasion opportunities as well as to deductions — are not evenly distributed among taxpayers, so that the distributional consequences of the personal income tax are not what they seem from its progressive rate structure. In the discussion of tax avoidance and evasion it was suggested that tax evasion is rather difficult for wage and salary earners subject to PAYE deductions, while avoidance opportunities are largely concentrated at the upper end of the scale, because they frequently require a considerable amount of property income for their successful operation. Taken together, these considerations imply that the progressive distributional results statistically attributed to the personal income tax are often exaggerated.

1984–85 statistical evidence on the progressivity of personal income tax (Table 8.1) shows that average tax rates were then no longer smoothly rising as income rises, but declined for two of the three top deciles. As Warren, the author of this study[27] indicates:

> It is this trend in the distribution of the personal income tax that has largely been the motivating factor behind the recent broadening of the personal income tax base. In particular, the introduction of fringe benefits taxation, capital gains tax, the repeal of entertainment expenses as an income tax deduction and limiting the scope for writing off losses on property investments against non-property income. It is also behind the recent call for withholding taxes on interest payments and the Australia Card (or national identification system).

Personal income tax and incentives

One of the perennial questions associated with a progressive personal income tax is the effect of such a tax on incentives to work. As was seen earlier, the proponents of proportional and linear income taxation base part of their argument on the improvement in work incentives when such a move is implemented. The theoretical argument underlying the analysis of the effect of high marginal income tax rates on incentives to work is relatively simple.

When people have some control over their work hours (for example, the self-employed or those with overtime possibilities) the marginal tax rate acts as a penalty on additional work because a larger proportion of the additional income earned goes in taxes. People compare the after-tax income against the leisure forsaken. If the marginal tax rate is sufficiently large the net income will be judged inadequate compensation for the leisure which must be given up to earn it. This is the *substitution effect* of the progressive income tax and if this was the only influence at work on incentives the disincentive effects of high marginal tax rates would be indisputable.

There are, however, other rewards from work besides money income, for example, enjoyment of the work, advancement of a career, the search for power and influence, and ambition, which are not necessarily affected by marginal income tax rates. The more important are the non-pecuniary motives for working, the less is the tax disincentive effect. In addition, there is the *income effect* of the personal income tax, which also works in the opposite direction of the substitution effect. When people aspire to a certain after-tax income (perhaps because a very high proportion is committed to mortgage and other debt repayments) an increase in tax rates will force people to work more, in order to reach their required after-tax income. The empirical evidence on this subject is not clear[28] though it is generally agreed that *very* high marginal tax rates would act as a disincentive.

Apart from these income and substitution effects on work effort, high marginal income tax rates may affect the labour supply through a variety of other factors. It may discourage immigration of skilled or professional workers because domestic tax rates are higher than those abroad. It may also affect the choice of occupation because higher paid jobs involving more work are discounted for the impact of taxation on the additional earnings. The tax system can affect decisions about actively seeking promotion or accepting promotion with higher pay and greater responsibility, and so on. High marginal tax rates, particularly if household income is the tax unit, or where there are very generous tax rebates for dependent spouses, may deter married women from entering the work force. Finally, high marginal tax rates by increasing the rate of return on tax avoidance, may draw scarce legal and accounting skills into this socially unproductive area.

A progressive personal income tax may also reduce incentives to save. In the first place, high marginal tax rates may affect individual saving schedules, perhaps shifting them downwards when tax rates rise, so that less is saved at each level of disposable income. The reason for this is that higher tax rates reduce the real after-tax rate of return to saving. "High marginal rates of income tax encourage the substitution of immediate consumption for saving, high average tax rates, especially at the upper end of the income scale where saving features more prominently, mean lower disposable incomes and hence less opportunity to save."[29] Neo-classical theory, by postulating a direct relationship between individual saving and the rate of interest, argues that since personal income taxation reduces this after-tax rate of return — a situation particularly important in periods of inflation in an unindexed income tax system — there must be disincentive effects to save from the personal income tax which become more significant the greater the interest elasticity of saving. In this context it must be remembered that the argument rests on a particular theory of saving and that, furthermore, capital formation is provided not only from personal savings but from that by governments, corporations, and other business firms, and from overseas capital inflow. The *Income Tax Act* also allows savings offsets in the form of some superannuation contributions, while the tax system as a whole provides further incentives to saving and capital formation. The issue of savings exemption in taxation is further investigated in Chapter 12 in the context of broad-based consumption taxes.

Income tax, stabilisation, and economic growth

During the 1950s, and especially during the 1960s, surcharges and rebates of personal income tax were frequently used in demand management. These changes can be made fairly quickly, particularly through the PAYE system. This use of the income tax is further discussed in Chapter 18, where it is shown that increases in personal income tax rates for the purpose of demand management also raise difficulties for stabilisation purposes in an inflationary situation through their price and cost effects.

In the context of the Prices and Incomes Accord the Government agreed with the unions in 1982, and confirmed at the National Economic Summit in 1983, income tax changes have been used directly as an instrument designed to secure lower wage growth outcomes than would otherwise be the case. The rate scale restructuring of 1984, 1985, 1989 and 1990 was part of such a wage-tax trade-off which assisted the success of Australia's wages policy in restraining real wages growth.[30]

In connection with the growth objective, personal income tax at progressive rates is frequently criticised because of its disincentive effects on saving. If economic growth and capital accumulation do depend as much on the level of savings as these theories suggest[31] a steeply progressive income tax may not be suitable if great weight is placed on the growth objective. This argument is strongly presented by the Taxation Review Committee:

> Were simplicity and efficiency the only objectives, one might aim at a system overwhelmingly dependent on revenue upon a single broad-based tax on goods and services ... set at a very high rate ... This system, too, would admirably serve the end of economic growth. With no income tax and no capital tax restraining saving ... there would be no

> direct limit on accumulation . . . But this . . . would grossly offend universally accepted interpretations of the aim of equity.[32]

This quotation forms a good conclusion for this discussion of personal income tax. It shows that the most important of Australia's taxes is generally perceived to be essential for considerations of equity and it is this feature of the tax which has made it so enduring. As shown in this chapter, the position of the income tax in the tax structure has been undermined by criticism of its traditional rate structure, by the detrimental effects on it from high rates of inflation, and by the various ways in which its impact can be avoided and evaded by sections of the community, thereby distorting its vertical and horizontal equity consequences. The significant income tax reforms which have taken place after 1985, of which the capital gains tax reform and fringe benefits tax (discussed in Chapter 10) are the more important, have redressed some of these problems. However, debate about the other problems associated with income tax is likely to continue, whether inspired by rate simplification as a way of encouraging productivity and growth, by its assistance for wage policy implementation through tax-wage trade-offs, or by its general effectiveness in achieving the income distribution which the Australian community can be said to want.

SUMMARY

1. Personal income tax covers net PAYE tax collections of wage and salary earners, provisional tax on self employed and property income recipients, prescribed payments system collection, capital gains tax as well as special levies like the Medicare levy and HECS. It also includes business income from sole traders, trusts and partnerships.

2. Assessable income — expenses incurred in gaining income specifically allowed under the Act = net income; net income — allowable deductions = taxable income. Tax liability = tax calculated by applying appropriate rate to taxable income — tax rebates.

3. Special levies collected with income tax are used to defray costs with respect to health (Medicare levy) and education (HECS). They are imposed by adding a percentage surcharge to taxable income after a specific threshold of income has been reached.

4. The comprehensive approach to income for tax purposes defines assessable income as the algebraic sum of consumption and the change in value of property rights over the period in question.

5. Actual tax systems diverge from the comprehensive ideal by excluding certain items for political, social and administrative reasons. Examples are non-pecuniary income (esp. imputed income from owner-occupied dwellings), leisure, income in kind from employment (fringe benefits), windfall gains and accrued capital gains.

6. The comprehensive income base fails to resolve questions about the appropriate tax unit, whether real or nominal income should be taxed and the time period to which tax assessment should apply.

7. Inflation particularly distorts income tax liability when rate structure and base are not appropriately adjusted. Current Australian practice adjusts only selected portions of the income base, namely capital gains, but not interest income.

8. Capital gains taxation, as part of the comprehensive income base should be taxed as part of income at the appropriate income tax rate. All other tax treatment of such gains is very much second-best. Absence of systematic capital gains taxation implies both vertical and horizontal inequity and non-neutral taxation.
9. Progressivity of personal income tax depends on base as well as rate structure depending on whether average tax rates reflect actual or taxable income.

10. Rate simplification as practised in Australia involves high initial marginal tax rates, a substantial threshold and a limited number of marginal tax rates. A linear income tax is the most progressive simple rate structure; a flat tax abandons a positive threshold and hence different average and marginal rates.

11. Distributional goals of personal income taxation can be distorted when there is significant avoidance (legal tax minimisation) and evasion (understatement of taxable income).

12. Although high marginal tax rates can be said to affect incentives, the precise extent of the response is uncertain. This conclusion applies to incentives to work, save and invest as well as the incentives to avoidance and evasion.

NOTES

[1] See Commonwealth of Australia, *Annual Report of the Commissioner of Taxation*, to which reference should be made for current information in summary form on changes in income tax legislation. Statistical information on income taxation can be obtained from this source and in more detail, from *Taxation Statistics*, the supplement to this annual report, as well as from the annual Budget Paper, *Income Tax Statistics*. Details of income tax aggregates are contained in Statement no. 4 included with the annual Budget Statements printed in Budget Paper No. 1.

[2] Commonwealth of Australia, *Taxation Statistics 1985–86* (Canberra: AGPS, 1988), pp. 6–9, which provides definitions of these and other terms used in Australian income taxation.

[3] Prior to 1974–75, tax adjustments for purposes for which rebates are now given, were provided through concessional deductions, the effective value of which rose with the marginal tax rate of the taxpayer. This was frequently criticised on the ground that it violated vertical equity considerations.

[4] Two of the examples (from 1982–83 income tax year) related to the 1982 "election" Budget. See 1982–83 (Canberra: AGPS, 1982), pp. 241–2. They were abolished by the govern-ment which won the elections for the subsequent income year and after. See Economic Statement May 1983 (Canberra: AGPS, 1983), pp. 38–9, 41. Child care expenses tax rebates were promised by the Federal Opposition in the run-up to the 1990 elections.

[5] These changes were endorsed by the Draft White Paper, *Reform of the Australian Tax System* (Canberra: AGPS, 1985), ch. 9 and implemented in the 1985–86 Budget.

[6] Details have been drawn from the relevant Budget Papers, in particular *Budget Statement*

1988–89 (Canberra: AGPS, 1988), pp. 104–5; *Budget Statements 1989–90* (Canberra: AGPS, 1989) pp. 3.70–3.71.

[7] For an economic evaluation of HECS, see B.J. Chapman, "An Economic Analysis of the Higher Education Contribution Scheme of the Wran Report", *Economic Analysis and Policy*, 18(2), September 1988, pp. 171–88.

[8] Henry Simons, *Personal Income Taxation* (Chicago: Chicago University Press, 1938) p. 50.

[9] For a discussion see Daryl Dixon and John Toms, *Housing Finance in Australia: The Impact of Taxation* (Sydney: Australian Tax Research Foundation, 1987), Occasional Paper No. 3; Joe Flood and Judy Yates, "Housing Subsidy Study" (Canberra: AGPS, 1987) for the Australian Housing Research Council, Project Series No. 160, ch.3, esp. pp. 36–46.

[10] For a discussion, see Draft White Paper, *Reform of the Australian Tax System*, ch. 6. For a discussion of OECD practice, see OECD *Personal Income Tax Systems* (Paris: OECD, 1986), pp. 17–20, 49–51.

[11] For details of such averaging as applied to particular occupations, see *Budget Statements 1986–87*, pp. 309–314; Bill Curran, Peter Minnis and Frances Freeman, "Taxation Implications of Rural Income Fluctuations" in *Taxation and the Rural Economy* (Sydney: Australian Tax Research Foundation, 1988), pp. 22–39.

[12] For a discussion of these issues, see Draft White Paper, *Reform of the Australian Tax System*, chs.12 and 18 (the last concentrating on business taxation); Peter Minnis, "Taxation, Inflation and the Measurement of Real Interest", *Australian Tax Forum* 5(3), 1988, pp. 339–57.

[13] For a discussion, see David Morgan, "Personal Income Tax Indexation: the Australian Experience", in J.G. Head (ed.), *Taxation Issues of the 1980s* (Sydney: Australian Tax Research Foundation 1983), ch. 5; John Bossons, "Capital Gains, Indexation and Imputation" in J. G. Head (ed.), *Australian Tax Reform in Retrospect and Prospect*, (Sydney: Australian Tax Research Foundation, 1989), ch. 6 and for OECD initiatives, OECD, *Personal Income Tax Systems*, ch. 3.

[14] But initially not shares disposed of within twelve months. Profit on this type of disposal is taxed in nominal terms under the provisions applying to the income (profit) from short term share transactions under Section 26AAA of the Income Tax Assessment Act. This section was repealed in 1988. See Treasurer, *Economic Statement May 1988*, (Canberra: AGPS, 1988), p. 94.

[15] For a discussion of OECD practices see OECD, *Taxation of Net Wealth, Capital Transfers and Capital Gains of Individuals* (Paris: OECD, 1988), ch. 3; the Federal Opposition's tax policy in the run-up to the 1990 election proposed such a tapered capital gains tax in the interest of encouraging saving and investment, particularly by small business.

[16] For a discussion of these reasons, see Draft White Paper, *Reform of the Australian Tax System*, ch. 7; John Head, "Australian Tax Reform — Capital Gains and Company Income Taxation", in Geoffrey Brennan, Bhajan Grewal and Peter Groenewegen (eds.), *Taxation and Fiscal Federalism* (Canberra: ANU Press, 1988), ch. 8. In 1986–87, two-thirds of capital gains tax was paid by taxpayers with taxable incomes in excess of $50,000 per annum; in 1987–88 this had dropped slightly to 62.3 per cent.

[17] OECD, *Taxation of Net Wealth, Capital Transfers and Capital Gains of Individuals*, pp. 121–8.

[18] This is not to say that such rebates have no place in a progressive income tax system. As mentioned earlier, rebates are superior to deductions on vertical equity grounds, while rebates for dependants and concessional expenditures can be generally justified on quite separate horizontal equity considerations.

[19] For a discussion, see Peter Groenewegen, "Progressive Personal Income Tax — a Historical Perspective", in J.G. Head (ed.), *Flattening the Tax Rate Scale: Alternative Scenarios and Methodologies* (Melbourne: Longman, 1990), ch. 1.

[20] Economic Statement May 1983, delivered by the Treasurer (Canberra: AGPS, 1983), pp. 40–1.

[21] The case for the linear income tax was first put by M. Friedman, *Capitalism and Freedom*, (Chicago: Chicago University Press, 1962) pp. 168–79 and has been supported by politicians and academics since then, often in the context of guaranteed minimum income schemes. See J.G. Head, " Tax Reform in Australia", pp. 215–18; R.L. Mathews, "The Structure of Taxation", pp. 112–17; and P.J. Sheehan, *Crisis in Abundance* (Melbourne: Penguin, 1980), ch. 10.

[22] For a debate on this type of tax see R.J. Tanner and D.J. Collins, *Flat Rate Tax? Pros and Cons* (Sydney: Taxation Institute Research and Education Trust, 1981). Without necessarily implying a flat tax system, there have been proposals to either eliminate or means test the threshold. For a good critique of this, see Peter Whiteford, "Income Testing the Tax Threshold" (Sydney: University of New South Wales Social Welfare Research Centre, 1988), Working Paper No. 6.

[23] Inspired by the Centre for Policy Studies proposals. See, for example, National Priorities Project 1989, John Freebairn, Michael Porter and Cliff Walsh (eds.), *Savings and Productivity: Incentives for the 1990s* (Sydney: Allen and Unwin, 1989), ch. 7.

[24] This problem was therefore accorded official recognition in the Draft White Paper, *Reform of the Australian Tax System*, part II.

[25] See Commissioner of Taxation, *Annual Report 1987–88*, esp. pp. 51–54, 62–79; Trevor Boucher, "Self-Assessment of Income Tax", *Australian Tax Forum* 3(1), 1986, pp. 45–53.

[26] For a discussion, see Peter Groenewegen, *Everyone's Guide to Australian Taxation* (Sydney: Allen & Unwin, 1985), ch. 3.

[27] N.A. Warren, "Changes in Australian Tax Incidence 1975–76 and 1984–85", in *Australian Tax Reform in Retrospect and Prospect* (Sydney: Australian Tax Research Foundation, 1989), p. 461; cf. Peter Saunders, Garry Hobbes and Helen Scott, "Income Inequality in Australia and New Zealand: Comparisons and Recent Trends" (Sydney: University of New South Wales, Social Welfare Research Centre, Discussion Paper No. 15, September 1989), esp. pp. 16–18, 30–31, 37–39.

[28] For a detailed discussion of the theoretical issues, see Michael Beenstock, *Work, Welfare and Taxation* (London: Allen & Unwin, 1987), esp. chs. 1–5; Christopher Heady, "The Structure of Income and Commodity Taxation" in *Surveys in Public Sector Economics*, P. Hare (ed.) (Oxford: Blackwell, 1988), pp. 187–96. An evaluation of the empirical evidence is in OECD, *Personal Income Tax Systems*, pp. 56–63 and EPAC, *Income Support Policies, Taxation and Incentives*, Working Papers to EPAC Council Paper No. 35 (Canberra: EPAC, 1988), pp. 48–61.

[29] Taxation Review Committee, *Full Report* (Canberra: AGPS, 1975), pp. 35–6. The empirical evidence on the subject of tax effects on saving remains an issue of considerable controversy as does the theoretical argument which postulates such effects. For a recent survey of this literature, see Roger S. Smith, "Factors Affecting Saving, Policy Tools and Tax Reform: A Review", IMF Working Papers 89/47 (Washington D.C.: IMF Fiscal Affairs Department, 1989); EPAC, *Income Support Policies, Taxation and Incentives*, pp. 55–7, OECD, *Personal Income Tax Systems*, pp. 53–6.

[30] For a general discussion of wage-tax trade-offs within the context of the Accord, see *The Indecs Economics Special Report State of Play 6* (Sydney: Allen and Unwin, 1990), pp. 66–71; for a detailed theoretical discussion, see Max Corden and Peter Dixon, "A Tax-Wage Bargain in Australia: Is a Free Lunch Possible?", *Economic Record*, 56 (154) September 1980, pp. 209–21.

[31] For a discussion see Peter Groenewegen, "Taxation: its Role in Economic Growth", *Australian Journal of Public Administration*, 49(3), September 1990.

[32] Taxation Review Committee, *Full Report*, pp. 35–6.

FURTHER READING

Useful comparative perspective can be gained from the major texts:

R.A. Musgrave and P.B. Musgrave, *Public Finance in Theory and Practice*, 4th edn. (New York: McGraw Hill, 1984), chs. 16–17.

C.V. Brown and P.M. Jackson, *Public Sector Economics*, 3rd edn. (Oxford: Blackwell, 1986), ch. 14.

J.E. Stiglitz, *Economics of the Public Sector*, 2nd edn. (New York: W.W. Norton, 1988), chs. 19 and 21.

OECD, *Personal Income Tax Systems under Changing Conditions*, (Paris: OECD, 1986).

More specialist reading:

Joseph Pechman (ed.), *Comprehensive Income Taxation* (Washington DC: The Brooking Institution, 1977).

R. Krever (ed.), *Australian Taxation: Principles and Practice*, (Melbourne: Longmans Professional, 1987), chs. 4–6.

J.G. Head (ed.), *Flattening the Tax Rate Scale: Alternative Scenarios and Methodologies* (Melbourne: Longman, 1990).

10

Company income tax and business taxation

Company income tax and personal income tax are closely linked in Australian tax practice, hence the discussion of personal income tax of the previous chapter is best followed by a discussion of company tax. The close association between personal income tax and company tax arises partly from the fact that they are assessed and collected under the same legislation. It also arises from the fact highlighted by the adoption in Australia of a full imputation system of company taxation from 1986, that in many respects company tax is nothing but a withholding tax on company income payable to individual shareholders/ income taxpayers as dividends or accruing to them as capital gains through the share value appreciation effects of undistributed profits.

Although a significant proportion of business income is directly taxed under personal income tax, as indicated in Chapter 9, business taxation issues are best dealt with under the heading of company income taxation. After all, many of these issues remain the same irrespective of the form of business organisation under which they are taxed. The annual Budget Statements refer to a number of business taxes other than company tax, but include them with the general income tax category. Discussion of withholding taxes on interest and dividends paid to non-residents is postponed to Chapter 19 on international public finance aspects. Aspects of the taxation of superannuation and the fringe benefits tax are discussed in this chapter. In 1989–90 the relative importance of these categories of business taxation was as follows. Company taxation raised 80 per cent of business taxation as here defined; superannuation funds contributed 6 per cent, as did the two withholding taxes. Fringe benefits tax raised the remaining 8 per cent of business tax revenue.

Methods of collection of company tax differ from personal income tax and have varied considerably over recent years. Company tax was initially collected on an annual basis in respect of the company income of the previous year. From 1973 it was collected on a quarterly basis, requiring instalments on 15 August, 15 November, 15 February, and the balance before 30 April. This change in collection was designed to reduce the seasonal drain on liquidity which traditionally occurred in the last (June) quarter as a result of concentrating company tax together with provisional tax in a once-a-year payment. The government financing implications of such uneven liquidity flows are examined in Chapter 17. The 1989

Budget announced proposals to end the tax deferral inherent in collecting company tax two years after the assessed income was obtained; these proposals were combined with initiatives for self-assessment of companies, to enable the Taxation Office to use its scarce personnel resources more effectively on business audits rather than on what were often routine assessments of small business income tax returns.

THE TAX BASE

The tax base of company income tax can be defined as the change in the value of the store of property rights of the company from the beginning to the end of the income period. This change in value is determined by the net income of the company which include its operating profit or loss, changes in the valuation of assets including stock of inventories, and the deductions which turn gross operating surplus into net profit. If the changes in the valuation of assets are ignored (as Australian tax law did until the application of capital gains tax to companies)[1] then the definition of the tax base becomes:

$$P = E - (V + F)$$

where P is taxable income or profit, E is the revenue or gross sales, and V and F are the variable and fixed costs of the enterprise respectively. As with personal income tax, the tax base is income earned net of the expenses incurred in producing that income.

Issues relating to the company tax base

The calculation of the company tax base in practice is complicated because it involves such difficult issues as asset valuation for depreciation, stock valuation procedures, and several other problems associated with the definition of legitimate business costs.

Depreciation[2]

One of the most difficult issues associated with the company tax base is the matter of depreciation. Allowance clearly must be made for this in calculating the net income because its definition implies that the capital stock of the company (and business) is to be kept intact. For the taxpayer, it is advantageous to depreciate as quickly as possible in order to maximise the present value of the tax saving. To protect the revenue, therefore, the Taxation Department lays down firm rules on the rates and methods of depreciation to be employed for various types of assets and these rates are invariably lower than those the taxpayer would apply.

Although economists do not agree on what is the proper rate of depreciation and on what meaning should be given to the phrase "keeping the capital stock intact", tax law and accountants have had to formulate rules for depreciation for the practical purpose of the calculation of taxable income and of net profit. In Australia, the basis for depreciation is the historical cost of the asset and not its replacement cost, and the asset must be owned by the company (business). Leased equipment or that purchased on instalment credit is depreciated by its legal owner. Two basic methods of depreciation are allowed: the diminishing value method and the prime cost method. In the first method, a higher depreciation rate than the

Table 10.1 Tax liability and depreciation methods

	Diminishing balance method depreciation rate: 15% $15 000			Prime cost method depreciation rate: 10% $15 000	
Depreciation	(1)	(2)	(3)	(4)	(5)
Year 1	2 250	2 250	50%	1 500	1 500
Year 2	1 913	4 163	38%	1 500	3 000
Year 3	1 626	5 789	29%	1 500	4 500
Year 4	1 382	7 171	19%	1 500	6 000
Year 5	1 174	8 345	11%	1 500	7 500
Year 6	998	9 343	4%	1 500	9 000
Year 7	849	10 192	–3%	1 500	10 500
Year 8	723	10 915	–9%	1 500	12 000
Year 9	614	11 529	–15%	1 500	13 000
Year 10	522	12 051	–20%	1 500	15 000

Notes: (1) Annual depreciation deduction (15% of $15,000 less depreciation already deducted given in column 2.
(2) Cumulative depreciation deduction.
(3) Column 2 relative to column 5, that is [(2)–(5)] 5.
(4) Annual depreciation deduction (10% of $15,000).
(5) Cumulative depreciation allowance.

After ten years, $2,949 of the asset has not yet been depreciated under the diminishing balance method, but the whole of the asset value has been depreciated under the prime cost or straight line method. In this example, it would only pay to use the straight line method if the expected life of the asset was greater than six years, while it would pay to use the diminishing balance method if the actual life of the asset was six years or less.

basic rate is applied annually to the value of the asset *less* the depreciation already allowed, hence the name diminishing balance. Under the prime cost method, a basic rate is applied to the cost value of the asset until the asset value is fully depreciated. Some examples of these methods are given in Table 10.1.

It can easily be seen from Table 10.1 that the tax savings under the diminishing balance method are greater than under the prime cost method but that the relative magnitude of this advantage rapidly diminishes the longer the period examined. Since the standard rates of depreciation are determined by the Taxation Office with respect to the estimated working life of the asset (but without taking account of the possibility of obsolescence or rising replacement costs), the prime cost method would only be adopted if there were considerable certainty that these assumptions were correct. If, on the other hand, there was considerable technical progress in the industry, the faster initial depreciation of the diminishing balance would be preferred, and since there is generally little certainty in this matter, most companies prefer to depreciate as quickly as possible.

This feature of company depreciation behaviour is utilised in government attempts to stimulate investment spending by altering the provisions for depreciation write-offs for tax purposes. These may take the form of *investment allowances, accelerated depreciation*, or even more generous provisions such as the double, instantaneous *write-off* allowed for certain farm improvements prior to 1973. All of these methods subsidise the cost of investment to industry, but they do so in different ways. Accelerated depreciation, as the name implies, allows more to be written off in the initial period, though the total depreciation allowed remains at 100 per cent of the initial cost. It raises the present value of the depreciation deduction when the investment is made. When the total cost of the asset can be depreciated in the first year, accelerated depreciation is the same as instantaneous write-off. An investment allowance provides for a certain proportion of the asset value to be written off in the year of installation (40 per cent in Australia under the scheme introduced in early 1976) *plus* normal depreciation of the full asset value. Under the investment allowance scheme as operated in Australia during the 1970s, 140 per cent of the asset value can be deducted for tax purposes. Prior to 1973, certain rural improvements could be written off at 200 per cent of their cost in the year in which they were made. In this last case, if the tax rate applicable was 50 per cent, the whole of the cost of the investment was passed to the Taxation Department. To encourage research and development spending and investment in the film industry, these activities were accorded favourable tax treatment during the 1980s.

Encouragement of productive investment by immediate write-off of capital expenditures has been more frequently put forward during the late 1980s to secure appropriate industry restructuring in the 1990s. In addition, this has the merit of simplifying tax administration and compliance because special depreciation rules and calculations no longer have to be devised. Instantaneous write-offs have generally been proposed in the context of cash flow company tax proposals where the benefits of immediate expensing are combined with tax disadvantages of the non-deductibility of interest payments and full taxation of capital receipts.[3]

There is considerable controversy about the effectiveness of such tax methods for stimulating actual investment spending. Methods of accelerating depreciation will influence investment activity because of a variety of factors. For example, it is clear that there will be an initial favourable effect on the cash flow of the company, the advantage of which should not be underestimated. Furthermore, if the firm has a steady and continuing policy of investment, such policies while they are in operation will ensure a permanent postponement of taxation or a permanent subsidy of the investment of such firms. There is also evidence from a number of countries that such changes in the method of calculating "depreciation" are among the more efficient methods of influencing investment activity, largely because this type of tax reduction only applies to the acquisition of real assets. This type of policy has been frequently used in Australia as a general counter-cyclical measure, or as an incentive to particular types of industry.[4]

A further problem has arisen in connection with the depreciation allowance in times of inflation. If, as Australian tax law stipulates, historical cost is to be used as the basis for depreciation calculations, the depreciation allowances provided would not be sufficient to replace the assets in question; company income would be overstated for tax purposes and companies would consequently be overtaxed. As a result, the capital stock of the company is unlikely to remain intact. This issue was explored in detail by the Committee on Taxation and Inflation which suggested alternative methods of depreciation to overcome this problem.[5]

The business tax reform of 1988 has switched depreciation rules to an effective life system of business assets subject to depreciation, for the sake of removing the favoured tax treatment of specific industries, hence "levelling the playing-field" in this aspect.[6] Some exceptions with respect to the mineral industry are to be retained. The changes that have occurred in this area suggest what economists have long realised. Objective depreciation rules are not easily applied administratively. In addition the importance of investment for sustainable growth in living standards entails a continual temptation to legislators to stimulate this activity by manipulating the tax system, whether for short-period stabilisation purposes or for longer-term restructuring.

Stock or inventory valuations for tax purposes [7]

Changes in stocks, which are part of the assets of the firm, are also reflected in its net income and here again, both the methods employed — such as LIFO or FIFO — as well as inflation, can affect the taxable profits of a firm. These two methods, FIFO (first in, first out) and LIFO (last in, first out) will, of course, give the same result when prices are stable. When prices are rising, LIFO reduces measured profits as compared with FIFO. Australian tax law uses FIFO as do many other countries.

The company tax base and inflation

Both depreciation and stock valuation consideration in company (and business) tax base calculations are influenced by inflation. In 1975 these effects of inflation on company taxation were investigated by a government committee which suggested that inflation induced gross overstatement of taxable income and hence tax liability. This required remedial measures. Depreciation on the basis of historical cost did not secure adequate provision for replacement so that the company's capital stock was not easily kept intact; inflation of stock values in the closing period raised taxable income irrespective of whether such increases were real or nominal. The committee therefore proposed valuation adjustments to depreciation and stock which corrected these effects of inflation on taxable income. In a criticism of the report it was argued that full adjustment of the tax base for inflation required adjustment of company income for the change in the value of company debt — which would be favourable to the company's financial position — and adjustment for the property of companies which tended to appreciate such as land and buildings. As in the case of "indexing" the personal income tax base, full inflation adjustment of company income introduces wide-ranging problems of capital gains and losses, and no country for that reason has therefore introduced full inflation adjustment of company income for tax purposes.[8]

Interest

Interest on borrowed funds is a deductible expense for tax purposes but dividends on share capital are not. For this tax reason (but also for other reasons) companies in Australia have frequently preferred to raise capital on the loan market rather than to issue new share capital. The consequent debt ratios can lead to financial difficulties in periods of credit shortage, and in Australia the high ratio of borrowed funds has led to some major company failures. Full dividend imputation adopted by Australia in 1986 partly redresses this situation as shown subsequently in this chapter. However, there remain substantial tax preferences for fixed interest borrowing, some of which arise from international aspects of the tax system discussed in Chapter 19.

Expense accounts

Another controversial aspect of the company tax base is the treatment of various fringe benefits for executives, such as company cars, subsidised housing, and the entertainment of clients, which frequently disguises a great deal of what is really private consumption expenditure of the employee of the company. Not infrequently, these "expenses" deductible for company tax purposes are used instead of increases in salaries, thereby implying no real cost to the company but a considerable tax saving to the executive.

A number of tax measures implemented from 1985 have substantially altered the traditional tax treatment of expense accounts and fringe benefits. From 19 September of that year entertainment expenses were no longer allowed as business deductions at an estimated revenue saving of $330 million (or 0.8 per cent of total income tax revenue). Legislation announced at the same time and enacted in 1986 introduced far more severe substantiation rules on taxpayers in the justification of work related expenses, particularly in connection with domestic and international travel. Although initial revenue from this was expected to be modest (about 0.3 per cent of income tax collections in the year of introduction), the measure substantially enhanced the equity of the tax system. Such generous travel allowances tend to predominate for employees at high income levels. Most importantly, the 1988 reforms introduced general fringe benefit taxation in the form of separate taxation "of the total taxable value of non-cash fringe benefits provided to employees (or associates)".[9]

FRINGE BENEFITS TAX[10]

A fairly comprehensive fringe benefits tax was introduced into Australia during 1986–87 to tax in the hands of employers the employment benefits they paid to employees in "kind" in the form of motor vehicles, low-interest loans and subsidised housing, to name the more important fringe benefits reached by the tax.[11] Taxing such fringe benefits in the hands of the employer rather than the employee contravenes the principle of a comprehensive income tax base (as discussed in Chapter 9) but was adopted as the only really workable approach to bringing this growing form of employee benefit into the tax system. Despite this simplification, there remain intricate problems of valuation, choice of the appropriate rate of tax as well as questions about its economic effects including incidence.

Valuation problems arise in different ways for different types of benefits. When taxed in the hands of employers, valuation procedures can legitimately use market or cost valutions which (as shown in Chapter 9) may not be appropriate for the recipient where real benefits may often be valued at considerably less than cost. Value of the low-interest loan benefit (a common feature of salary packages in financial institutions) can be estimated by the difference between interest paid and what would have been paid if the appropriate market rate had been charged. The same principle is applied to subsidised housing for employees. Motor vehicles, the payment of expenses (such as telephone accounts, health fund insurance costs and school fees expenses, rates, electricity and rent) free board, as well as goods and services, provided to employees either free or at a discount, raise more intricate valuation problems, and may sometimes make compliance with the tax complicated and costly.

The rate at which tax is charged was initially set at the company tax rate but is now aligned with the maximum marginal personal income tax rate (of 47% from 1990) excluding the Medicare levy. Its relationship with both that rate and the company tax rate (39 per cent) determines whether the use of fringe benefits in salary packages is encouraged or not. When the rate is considerably below the maximum marginal personal income tax rate, granting fringe benefits is encouraged. The alignment of these rates which took effect from 1990 is more neutral and when the tax is not deductible for company tax purposes, as is the case in Australia, the incentive to give fringe benefits to employees is substantially reduced by this practice.

The incidence of the fringe benefit tax is complex, and may in fact reduce the initially favourable distributional consequences its introduction generated. Who pays the fringe benefits tax depends in the first place on who gained from the non-payment of the tax when paying part of a salary in kind to the cost of the revenue. In general, the dominant party in a wage contract will be unaffected by the extent to which the employee's income is taken in cash or kind — the subservient party gains from exploiting the tax implications of the practice while in a competitive labour market such benefits are shared. In the first instance, the imposition of the tax will therefore fall on the beneficiary(ies) in the pre-tax situation. In the longer run, the tax can be shifted backwards to the employee by forcing them to cash-in their fringe benefits; cashing-in effectively shifts the burden of the tax from employers who then lose responsibility for paying the fringe benefits tax. This would occur only where the employer is the dominant agent in the labour contract. Forward shifting to final consumers of employers' output occurs when the tax lowers the previous benefit to employers in cost reduction and this is recovered by a price increase. Depending on the market situation faced by the employer's product, the tax will be paid by consumers of that product. In short, the effective incidence of the fringe benefit tax may be on the employees, employers or consumers, making assessment of its full equity consequence rather complex. Nevertheless, introduction of the fringe benefits tax constitutes a most useful addition to Australia's tax structure for both equity and efficiency reasons.

SUPERANNUATION[12]

A major form of fringe benefit not covered by the new fringe benefit tax is superannuation. Employees benefit not only from the part financed by deductible employer superannuation contributions but also because superannuation benefits and their own contributions may receive rather favourable tax treatment. Part of this favourable treatment may arise from the manner in which superannuation funds earnings are taxed; part of it arises from the tax treatment of the benefits when paid in lump sum, a regular pension, or both; or from the tax subsidy granted to contributions. Reasons for the favoured tax treatment of superannuation include the benefits of the additional saving it is often said to encourage, and from the public expenditure reduction advantages when more of the retired provide for their livelihood without relying on government provided age pensions.

Up to the 1980s the Australian tax treatment of superannuation was very generous indeed. Contributions by employers were fully deductible; investment income of superannuation funds was largely exempt, employees contributions deductible (or rebatable) up to a limit of $1500, while only 5 per cent of the benefits taken as a lump sum were taxed on receipt. The Campbell Committee diagnosed this tax preference as contravening tax neutrality which reduced efficiency in the capital market. Furthermore, equity problems arose because benefits of favoured tax treatment for superannuation accrued largely to the higher income groups. The majority of persons in superannuation funds fall into this category while the value of superannuation benefit conferred tended to rise with income levels. In addition, the Treasury became increasingly concerned about the rising value of this "tax expenditure" as a cost to the revenue.

Tax changes in 1983, 1988 and 1989 were designed to reduce the competitive advantage superannuation derived from the favourable tax treatment of their earnings, as well as from the tax benefits their contributors received.[13] Taxation of lump sum superannuation benefits was substantially increased in 1983. In 1988, investment earnings of funds became taxable at 15 per cent,[14] hence reducing the benefits of tax deferral to this form of investment while in addition deductible employer contributions were to be taxed at the same rate. Furthermore, benefits in excess of what were defined as reasonable benefit levels were to be taxed at the appropriate marginal tax rate of the beneficiary. Some of these measures had equity as well as efficiency objectives. Other superannuation tax measures (introduced in 1989) designed to enhance equity in tax treatment, include greater deductibility for contributions by the self-employed or those employees without access to superannuation benefits.

The impact of this array of measures is difficult to assess. In terms of equity, they may spread the benefits of superannuation over a wider section of the community, particularly when other superannuation reforms (such as those implemented under wage-fixing agreements) are included. They have also tended to lower the benefits of superannuation tax preference going to high-income groups. Efficiency gains from greater tax neutrality is another likely effect from some of these measures. Increased saving from enhanced tax preferences to superannuation contributors is a further potential benefit. However, the difficulties involved in more precise assessments of the advantages of these reforms illustrate the increasing complexity of business taxation issues in a highly sophisticated and closely integrated economy.

THE RATE STRUCTURE

In most countries which levy company taxation, the tax rates are either mildly progressive — in the sense that a certain minimum amount of income is taxed at a lower rate — or proportional. Both of these rate structures have applied in Australian company tax practice. Since 1973 a simple, proportional rate has applied in Australia. This has varied from 49 per cent to 39 per cent (the rate applicable from 1989), but for the greater part of the period since 1973 stayed at 46 per cent. The previously mildly progressive rate structure was abolished in 1973 on the grounds that it encouraged avoidance through income-splitting among companies, that it gave an unnecessary tax bonus to large companies, and that subsidies to small companies were better made by direct subsidy outside the tax system.[15] Different tax rates for different types of companies is a practice likewise greatly reduced though retained as shown in the previous section, for superannuation funds. Special rates likewise apply to friendly societies and provident funds.

Two other issues about rate structure need to be mentioned. First, to prevent the use of companies as a tax shelter, it is useful to align the company tax rate with the maximum marginal income tax rate. Apart from the two years after 1986 this policy has not been followed in Australia.[16] Secondly, the rates mentioned in the preceding paragraph are nominal tax rates which can be contrasted with the often much lower effective rates at which company tax is levied on actual company income. There are many methods for calculating effective tax rates. These vary with the tax base selected as denominator, and estimated tax liability (numerator). The last depends on the selection of tax instruments included in the calculation.[17]

FURTHER ISSUES IN COMPANY TAXATION

One question that arises with company taxation more than with any other tax is whether the tax is really necessary if a country has a comprehensive personal income tax which taxes company profits in the hands of the shareholders. This is the "integrationists" view which argues that a separate company tax is not necessary when income tax is already in operation because dividends are more appropriately taxed in the hands of their recipients as income, than at a uniform rate in the hands of a legal entity and then again as income under income tax. The last, the integrationists argue, is tantamount to "double" taxation. The issue of double taxation of dividends which arises from a classical or separate company tax system and its distorting effects on capital markets were discussed by the Australian Financial System Inquiry in the context of business taxation and neutrality in investment decision-making. This committee investigated the suitability of the various methods devised to overcome this situation in Australia[18] in 1981, as the Tax Review Committee had in 1975 and the Draft White Paper did in 1985.

Double taxation of dividends and other faults with the traditional, or "classical", company tax system can be removed in various ways,[19] of which the following four are the more common suggestions:

1. Full integration of company taxation with the personal income tax system.
2. A split rate system.
3. An imputation or tax credit system.
4. Dividend taxation relief through rebates of dividend income from personal income tax.

All four maintain a formal role for a separate company tax but in the case of a full integration its scope is reduced to that of a withholding tax analogous to PAYE instalments.

Prior to discussing these four company tax forms, the tax base has to be looked at again. Earlier, it was simply defined as operating profit of the corporate enterprise. This ignored the manner in which profit is transferred to the owners of the business, that is, the shareholders of the company. If looked at from their point of view, company income takes the form either of dividends paid out to them or of undistributed profits retained by the business which tend to increase share values. Hence undistributed profits can be turned into income by shareholders if the appreciation in share values induced by such profits is realised through the sale of these shares. Under the classical system all company income, irrespective of whether it is distributed or not, is taxed at a flat rate (in 1989, 39 per cent); profit distributed as dividends is then taxed again at the appropriate marginal rate of recipient but undistributed profits, if realised as capital gains escapes personal taxation in the absence of capital gains tax.

The different tax treatment of company income, depending on whether it is distributed as dividends or not, has a number of equity and efficiency consequences. It should be noted that for the purpose of analysing these it is assumed that the incidence of the tax is on the shareholders (that is, it is not passed forward to consumers in the form of higher prices, or passed backwards to wage earners or, as suggested in the general equilibrium model, to all owners of capital). For purposes of illustration, Australian income tax rates and company taxes as existed in 1982–83 are assumed, as well as the non-existence of a separate capital gains tax.

Equity consequences of the classical system

The equity consequences of the double taxation of dividends under the classical system arise from the fact that this affects individual shareholders differently depending on the profit distribution policy of the company, the company tax rate, and their appropriate marginal income tax rate. If r is the distribution ratio, t_c the company tax rate and t_p the appropriate marginal income tax rate, then the effective excess rates of tax arising from the double taxation of dividends applicable to individual shareholders can be calculated by the formula:

$$t_c + r(1 - t_c)t_p - t_p$$

With $t_c = 46$ per cent, t_p having possible values of 0, 30, 46 and 60 per cent and the retention ratio varying from 0 to 100 per cent, the excess rates from non-integration can vary from 46 per cent (for a taxpayer with a zero marginal tax rate and a 100 per cent distribution by the company) to –14 per cent (with zero distribution by the company and a maximum marginal tax rate shareholder). Put more generally, low income shareholders are taxed excessively under the classical system; their excess rates rising with the distribution ratio while high income earners are undertaxed, the degree of undertaxation only disappearing when the retention ratio is less than 43 per cent. Rich shareholders therefore prefer high retention ratios which allow them to take their profits in the form of lower tax capital gains and thereby avoid personal income tax.[20]

Efficiency consequences of the classical system

From the above example, it seems clear that tax considerations can affect one company management choice at least: the management decision of how much profit to distribute. In addition, the fact that dividends are taxed twice while interest on borrowed funds is a deductible cost item for tax purposes distorts the company finance choice between fixed interest borrowing and the raising of capital by share issues. This distortion is heightened in periods of inflation if real interest rates are declining.

Individual investment choices are also influenced by these company tax considerations because they alter the after-tax rates of return on various types of investment. It was for this reason that questions of company taxation and the double taxation of dividends were investigated by the committee of inquiry into Australia's financial system. The non-neutrality of classical company taxation which distorted investment decisions and hence lowered capital market efficiency was something which had to be changed.

The integration proposal

Many of these inequities and distortions would be removed if the company tax is fully integrated with the personal income tax. This requires that all company income—distributed and retained—is allocated to shareholders who then include it as assessable income for tax purposes and are therefore taxed on company profits at appropriate marginal tax rates. This solution was favoured by the committee of inquiry into Australia's financial system though not for immediate implementation. Integration has not been implemented partly because of administrative difficulties. These particularly relate to the treatment of non-resident shareholders. Its non-acceptance may also be explained because the neutrality advantages claimed for integration are exaggerated and its revenue costs may be quite substantial. The latter depends on the general profit retention policy of companies and on the marginal tax rate of the average shareholder.

A split rate system

Because excessive retentions of profits and excessive taxation of dividends are seen as the causes of equity problems in company taxation, some have proposed a split rate tax system as a solution. This penalises retention by taxing undistributed profits at a higher rate than company income paid out in the form of dividends, thereby also reducing the impact of double tax on dividends. Such a solution is deliberately non-neutral and is also difficult to implement in countries with a substantial degree of foreign investment in companies.

Other forms of dividend relief

As indicated earlier, there are several other forms of giving relief to shareholders in response to the double taxation of dividends. One of these is to make dividends deductible as a cost in raising capital, the same way as interest on borrowed funds is deductible. Another manner of giving relief to shareholders was introduced in the 1982–83 Budget. It provided for a rebate at the standard rate of tax for up to $1000 of dividend income (from resident public or private companies but excluding co-operative companies and a number of other classes of dividend payments accorded special treatment under the Act.) From the previous discussion of the inequities from the double taxation of dividends in the form of undertaxation of wealthy shareholders it can easily be seen that this proposal favoured the well-to-do. It was abolished after one year of operation.[21] The method of eliminating double taxation of dividends which Australia adopted in 1985 is the full imputation system, a system which had earlier been proposed by both the Taxation Review Committee and Draft White Paper.[22]

COMPANY TAX IMPUTATION

The manner in which an imputation system of company taxation eliminates double taxation of dividends is as follows. It imputes to the personal income taxpayer/shareholder the income from dividends together with company tax liability payable thereon, and then allows company tax actually paid as a tax rebate. The effect of this is that dividend receipts are no longer taxed twice but only once at the appropriate marginal income tax rate of the shareholder. This process of full company tax imputation is illustrated in Table 10.2.

Australia's full imputation system applies to resident shareholders only. Imputation credits can only be set off against actual income tax liability (excluding Medicare levy) and cannot give rise to cash refunds. Thirdly, to ensure that companies whose dividends are subject to imputation had paid the full rate of company tax, the government introduced measures which enabled only dividends on income which had paid full company taxation to be available for imputation credits in the hands of shareholders. Such dividends were

Table 10.2 Company tax imputation system

Corporate level		*$*
1. Profits before corporation tax		300
2. Corporation tax: 39% (1x2)		117
Shareholder level		
3. Income tax rate	24%	47%
4. Net dividend (1–2)	183	183
5. Imputed corporate tax (39/61 x 4)	117	117
6. Imputed dividend income (4+5)	300	300
7. Income tax (3x6)	72	141
8. Tax credit (5)	117	117
9. Net income tax (7–8)	–45[a]	24
Combined tax burden		
10. Total tax (2+9)	72	141
11. Effective tax rate[b] (=3)	24%	47%

Notes: a. Negative tax can be offset by shareholder against tax liability from other income.
b. Effective tax rate under full imputation equals the appropriate marginal income tax rate.

described as fully franked dividends, being paid from the Qualifying Dividend Account (QDA) to which after-tax profits which paid the full company rate were channelled. The amount of franked dividend in the QDA is calculated by the following formula.

$$\frac{1-t}{t} \text{ x } T + D$$

where t = company tax rate, T is company tax actually paid and D are the franked dividends the company in question has received from other companies. A company which paid $39,000 in company taxation in 1989 when the company tax rate was 39% and which received $9,000 in franked dividends from other companies could credit its QDA with $70,000 or:

$$61/39 \text{ x } \$39{,}000 + \$9{,}000$$

Some implications of full imputation

As shown in Table 10.2, full imputation eliminates double taxation of dividends and ensures that dividend income is taxed at the appropriate marginal income tax rate of its recipient. It also eliminates the cost disadvantage of capital raisings from shares relative to that of interest-bearing debt, with respect to resident shareholders and franked dividends only. Its benefits are largely confined to the generally high-income dividend receivers, while some low-income dividend recipients may generate insufficiently taxable income to gain advantages from imputation credits received. The general efficiency implications of full imputation are less clear-cut. The system, for example, may encourage companies with low tax rates to merge with those with high effective tax rates, in order to gain adequate franked dividend levels. The exclusion of non-resident shareholders from the system creates further non-neutralities.[23]

THE CONTINUING CASE FOR SEPARATE COMPANY TAXATION

Apart from its value as a withholding tax, there remains a strong case for a separate income tax on companies because companies are legal entities which are quite distinct from their shareholders. In addition, the legal status of incorporation confers considerable privileges on this form of business organisation of which limited liability is the prime example. Separate company taxation can then be interpreted as a benefit tax with respect to the government-conferred advantages from incorporation. Apart from the matter of the tax treatment of undistributed profits, there is an even more important reason for maintaining a separate income tax for companies in a country like Australia. This is because a large part of Australian industry is owned by foreign investors, whose incomes as a whole are not liable to Australian income tax. A general tax on company profits is one of the few methods of general taxation of the profits of overseas companies which is far superior to the essentially supplementary measures of interest and dividend withholding taxes. This aspect of income taxation will be looked at when some international aspects of taxation are discussed in Chapter 19.

Company tax and resource allocation

From the resource allocation point of view, company taxation has been frequently criticised. One reason for such criticism is that company taxation, by discriminating against various forms of business organisation, influences the choice of business organisation, while such a choice should really be made on other considerations. An example of this is the rapid growth of private companies, especially during the 1960s, which can largely be explained as induced by tax purposes.[24] Another reason is that since company taxation taxes profits, it can be regarded as a tax on efficiency because the high profit company which is taxed more heavily is usually also more dynamic and efficient. High profitability can of course also arise from other factors; for example, a high degree of protection can increase profitability and at the same time increase inefficiency, or in the case of mineral companies, temporary scarcities can lead to large windfall gains.

Business choices can also be affected by how the tax base is defined. Earlier, several of such resource allocation effects of company taxation were discussed. One which has been unfavourably commented on is the debt choice distortion which arises from the deductibility of interest charges and the non-deductibility of dividend payments. This subsidises borrowing in the market as a source of investment finance relative to share issues, which may lead to financial instability. Adoption of company tax imputation has partly addressed this problem. The investment allowance, accelerated depreciation, and similar measures of discretionary government policy, by which investment choices are intentionally influenced, were also mentioned.

RESOURCE RENT TAXATION

Although it shares efficiency advantages of the taxation of pure economic rent in land taxation, neutral mineral resource taxation in the form of a resource rent tax is most conveniently discussed as part of business taxation. This follows from the definition of its tax base. Resource rent or the base of the tax can be simply defined as the profits of an investment in a mineral project which remain after deduction of all production costs, including the minimum supply price of that investment from the proceeds of annual production. In short, a resource rent tax taxes the rent of the mine or oilfield which is being exploited. Although such a resource rent is simple to define in theory, it is more difficult to identify in practice, as should be obvious to those who followed the previous discussion on difficulties in defining the business income tax base. For instance, how is the minimum supply price of the investment (or threshold rate of return) to be determined, and will this vary from project to project? Furthermore, even if a correct resource rent tax could be imposed on a project in operation, the presence of such a tax in itself may reduce exploration investment because the existence of the resource rent tax in itself raises the risks of exploration investment. Other implementation difficulties of the tax concern the deductibility of other taxes and charges as well as the rate structure to be imposed. Technically, as suggested by the pure theory of taxation of economic rent, the whole of the rent could be taxed without affecting output levels. However, as already indicated in the case of the risks of exploration costs, a progressive rate structure raises the *ex ante* risks of investment to an inordinate extent. Other commentators have therefore suggested that an auction system for mineral leases, which takes such uncertainties into consideration, is more likely to yield optimal results.[25]

The issue of a resource rent tax has moved from one of only theoretical interest to one of practical importance with its application by the Federal Government to Australia's offshore oil industry, thereby rationalising its taxation of crude oil. After issuing a discussion paper of the proposed tax in 1983, which gave details of its base rate structure, and other relevant details which resulted in prolonged negotiations with the industry, the final form of the tax was announced in mid–1984. This provided for a tax rate of 40 per cent and a threshold determined by adding 15 per cent to the current bond rate (at the time of the announcement about 14 per cent making a total threshold rate of 29 per cent) which compared with a 45 per cent rate and a 25 per cent threshold suggested in the 1983 discussion paper.[26] It should be noted that by confining the resource rent tax to the offshore oil industry at this stage, the intergovernmental relations problems associated with its wider application have been avoided. On the other hand, its introduction in this rather limited form is a long way removed from the full rationalisation of mineral taxation which its proponents had hoped for. These issues of mineral taxation are further pursued in the chapters devoted to fiscal federalism issues and State and local finance.

Company tax and the distribution of income

The distributional consequences from the "double" taxation of dividends imposed by a separate company tax have already been discussed, though in this context it was stated that this argument depends on the backward shifting of the tax to shareholders. This is only one possibility amongst many. For example, if company tax was shifted forward to consumers through higher prices, which is a short-term possibility at least, then it would tend to be regressive as to income and its distributional effects would then resemble those of a general sales tax. As indicated in Chapter 8 there is no agreement on the incidence of this tax.

The empirical evidence from the general tax incidence studies also discussed in that chapter provide no further light, because these themselves depend on the shifting assumptions underlying the estimates. Table 8.1 reveals the fluctuating proportions of corporate income tax for various income levels, a pattern due to the fact that the estimates on which they are based assume that some company tax is passed forward to consumers and some passed backwards to shareholders. Although company tax has declined in relative importance in Australia as shown in Table 6.3, it is still important to know what its distributional consequences are with respect to resident households. Its importance in the taxation of non-residents has already been mentioned, but is further addressed in Chapter 19.

Company taxes: stabilisation and growth

The company tax is generally considered to be a relatively good automatic stabiliser as profits tend to vary with GDP over the course of the business cycle. In this context it must be remembered that company tax in Australia was until recently collected on the profits of the previous year rather than on current profits, and this could be a destabilising factor. The income effect of the tax seems to fall more heavily on investment spending than on consumer spending, but this again largely depends on the incidence of the tax. Some of these issues are further discussed in Chapter 18.

Variations in the tax base, particularly in connection with depreciation and investment spending, are frequently suggested and used as counter-cyclical instruments to influence income levels over the cycle. In many countries investment allowances or more generous depreciation allowances have been implemented to stimulate investment in periods of recession. Although the effectiveness of such measures in stimulating investment has been questioned, considerable evidence suggests that there is some stimulus to investment from such measures but that no quantitatively precise conclusion can be drawn about the strength of this effect. These issues were raised earlier in the chapter.

Company taxation has also been criticised for its effects on economic growth: largely because of its influence on the supply of saving, on the supply of risk capital, and on investment decisions. There is, of course, an impact on the rate of return to investment from the imposition of a company tax; after the tax, rates of return will be lower than in the absence of such a tax, though here again the incidence of the tax is important. This issue of company taxation and economic growth is therefore once again one on which there is no general agreement. These disagreements arise largely from theoretical differences on the theory of economic growth, but also from conflicting empirical evidence on the relative importance of the influence of company tax on the level of investment. The fundamental point that public finance analysis cannot be any stronger than the economic theory from which it derives is strikingly illustrated in the case of company tax.

SUMMARY

1. For the purpose of this chapter, business tax is here defined to include company tax, superannuation tax, fringe benefits tax and interest and dividend withholding taxes for non-residents.

2. The company tax base is net income, or gross revenue including net capital receipts less expenses incurred in producing that income.

3. Depreciation is an essential but complex part of the company tax base on the cost side. Based on nominal historical cost, depreciation can be calculated on the diminishing value or prime cost method.

4. Accelerated depreciation is a form of tax deferral and *ceteris paribus*, stimulates investment spending. Other tax measures designed to achieve this objective include investment allowances and instantaneous write-off of capital spending.

5. Depreciation cost and stock valuation aspects of the business tax are influenced by inflation, leading to overstatement of tax liability. However, full inflation adjustment of company taxation requires complex adjustments with respect to other capital gains and losses, the reason why no country has adopted full inflation adjustment in this area.

6. The treatment of interest in business taxation gives rise to distortions in the debt/equity choice in capital raising, particularly important under the classical system of company taxation with its double taxation of dividends.

7. Other problem areas in the company tax base concern fringe benefits and entertainment expense accounts. From 1985 Australia has removed deductibility of entertainment expenses and has taxed fringe benefits comprehensively from 1986.

8. The effective incidence of the tax may be on employers, employees, and even on consumers of the products of the business legally liable to pay the tax. This makes assessment of its full equity consequences complex.

9. Although favoured tax treatment of superannuation is often defended on grounds of the encouragement it gives to saving, this raises equity and efficiency issues. With superannuation particularly benefiting higher income groups, such a tax preference is vertically inequitable. Horizontal inequities arise from unequal access to superannuation benefits. There is also distortion of investment/saving decisions in this preferential treatment.

10. A single proportional rate is the best company tax rate structure. This prevents avoidance opportunities, particularly when the rate is aligned with the maximum marginal personal income tax rate. As in the case of personal income, effective rates may depart significantly from the nominal rate of tax imposed.

11. The classical system taxes dividends twice; first as part of company income under company tax, then as personal income. Undistributed profits may also be taxed twice: first as part of company income, then by a capital gains tax when the share value appreciation which they induce is captured on the sale of the shares.

12. Major remedies for this include full integration of personal income tax and company tax; an imputation or tax credit system, dividend relief or a split rate system which taxes distributed company income at a lower rate.

13. A classical system overtaxes low-income shareholders and undertaxes high-income shareholders depending on the relationship between marginal personal income tax rates, the company tax rate and the company's profit retention rate.

14. Efficiency issues are raised from the tax influence on the retention ratio and the debt/equity choice in capital raisings.

15. Company tax imputation eliminates the double taxation of dividends by giving credit for company tax paid on the dividend income. However, it has not effectively eliminated all inequities and distortions associated with the classical system.

16. Resource rent taxation, adopted for certain forms of mineral taxation, is as neutral a tax as it is possible to devise in the area of business taxation.

17. Company tax has uses as an automatic stabiliser but its impact on saving is said to be inimical growth. Adjustments to depreciation or more direct business tax concessions can be used to influence the level of investment in an economy.

NOTES

[1] Capital gains tax principles were more appropriately discussed in Chapter 9 as part of personal income tax. Companies contributed 49 per cent of capital gains tax collections in 1986–87; and 1987–88, approximately 3.6 per cent of total company taxation.

[2] For a general discussion see R.A. and P.B. Musgrave, *Public Finance in Theory and Practice*, 4th edn. (New York: McGraw Hill, 1984), pp. 400–3; Draft White Paper, *Reform of the Australian Tax System* (Canberra: AGPS, 1985), ch. 19; *The 1988 Business Tax Reform* (Canberra: AGPS, 1988), pp. 9–11.

[3] The classical discussion is E. Cary Brown, "Business Income Taxation and Investment Incentives" in Lloyd A. Metzler et al., *Income, Employment and Public Policy, Essays in Honour of Alvin H. Hansen* (New York: W.W. Norton, 1948), pp. 300–16; see also J.E. Meade et al., *The Structure of Direct and Indirect Taxation* (London: Allen and Unwin for Institute for Fiscal Studies, 1978), Chapter 12 and for an Australian proposal, National Priority Project 1989, John Freebairn, Michael Porter and Cliff Walsh (eds.), *Savings and Productivity: Incentives for the 1990s* (Sydney: Allen and Unwin, 1989), ch. 6.

[4] For recent evaluations see John Ryan, "The Implications of Taxation Incentives for Investment", in D. J. Collins (ed.), *Reform of Business Taxation* (Sydney: Australian Tax Research Foundation, 1985), pp. 141–65; John Freebairn, "An Economic Perspective on Recent Changes in the Taxation of Australian Business Income", *Australian Tax Forum* 5(4), 1988, pp. 493–521.

[5] Draft White Paper, *Reform of the Australian Tax System*, ch. 18, provides a comprehensive discussion.

[6] See Treasurer's Statement, *The 1988 Business Tax Reform* (Canberra: AGPS, 1988), esp. pp. 2, 9–11.

[7] See Draft White Paper, *Reform of the Australian Tax System*, p. 211; see also R.A. and P.B. Musgrave, *Public Finance in Theory and Practice*, 4th edn. (New York: McGraw Hill, 1984), p. 403.

[8] See Draft White Paper, *Reform of the Australian Tax System*, ch. 18 and Appendices; a summary of the recommendations of the 1975 Committee on Inflation and Taxation and the debate it generated is in Peter Groenewegen, "Taxation Policy", in F.H. Gruen (ed.), *Economic Surveys* (Sydney: Allen and Unwin, 1983), pp. 209–10.

[9] See *Reform of the Australian Tax System*, Statement by the Treasurer, September 1985 (Canberra: AGPS, 1985), pp. 32–40.

(The quotation is from p.32.) A more general discussion of these issues is Draft White Paper, *Reform of the Australian Tax System* (Canberra: AGPS, 1988), ch. 8.

[10] See the symposium on fringe benefit taxation in *Australian Economic Review*, 4/86, pp. 25–44; and D.J. Collins, "Taxation of Fringe Benefits: An Economist's Perspective", *Australian Tax Forum* 4(1), 1987, pp. 95–121 for a detailed account of the more important aspects of this type of taxation.

[11] As Collins (op.cit., pp. 109–111) points out, the fringe benefits tax is not comprehensive because it omits superannuation, sick leave, annual leave, long service leave and study leave benefits. Superannuation benefits are now taxed separately on a less favourable basis to superannuants (as discussed subsequently in this chapter). This section draws heavily on Collins' comprehensive analysis of fringe benefit tax.

[12] The tax issues involved in superannuation taxation are complex. Two useful treatments are David M. Knox, *Taxation Support of Superannuation in Australia: its Costs, Equity and Efficacy* (Sydney: Australian Tax Research Foundation, 1987); Daryl Dixon, "Retirement Savings", in J.G. Head (ed.), *Australian Tax Reform in Retrospect and Prospect* (Sydney: Australian Tax Research Foundation, 1989), pp. 185–217.

[13] See *Australian Financial System, Final Report of the Committee of Inquiry* (Campbell Committee), (Canberra: AGPS, 1981), ch. 15, Part II; Budget Statements 1983–84 (Canberra: AGPS, 1983), pp. 296–8; Budget Statements 1989–90 (Canberra: AGPS, 1989), pp. 4.6–4.10; Treasurer's Statement, *Reform of the Taxation of Superannuation* (Canberra: AGPS, 1988).

[14] In return, funds became eligible for the benefit of imputation credits from dividends received, a benefit which in some cases could offset the tax effect of taxing their earnings at 15 per cent. See *Reform of the Taxation of Superannuation,* Appendix B. The benefits of company tax imputation to dividend recipients are explained later in this chapter.

[15] See Budget Speech 1973–74, p. 26.

[16] See Draft White Paper, *Reform of the Australian Tax System*, pp. 110–11.

[17] Bureau of Industry Economics, *The Taxation of Corporate Investment Income* (Canberra: AGPS, 1988), ch. 3; Treasury Economic Paper No. 13, *International Comparisons of Business Taxation* (Canberra: AGPS, 1988), pp. 18–20, Appendix C; Treasury, *The Corporate Income Tax Base — Trends Since Late 1960s* (Canberra: The Treasury, 1989) provides another useful empirical discussion of effective company tax rates.

[18] See Australian Financial System Inquiry, *Final Report*, ch. 14, esp. pp. 210–24; *Commissioned Studies and Selected Papers, Part 3, Business Taxation and the Financing of Industry* (Canberra: AGPS, 1982), esp. pp. 1–32, 90–9, 160–5, 182–90; Taxation Review Committee, *Full Report*, ch. 16, esp. pp. 225–41; Draft White Paper, *Reform of the Australian Tax System*, ch. 17.

[19] See S. Cnossen, "Alternative Forms of Corporation Tax", *Australian Tax Forum* 1(3), September 1984, pp. 253–79, reprinted in Peter Groenewegen (ed.), *Australian Taxation Policy*, 2nd edn. (Melbourne: Longman Cheshire, 1987), pp. 202–31.

[20] High-income earners can therefore avoid tax liability if they can influence company profit distribution policy. This is generally considered to be beyond the control of individual shareholders in a public company, but it can easily be done in a private company, with its much more limited number of shareholders. Hence minimum distribution ratios as an anti-avoidance measure were forced on such companies by Division 7 of the Income Tax Act which imposed penalty rates of tax if this was not adhered to. See Australian Financial System Inquiry, *Final Report*, pp. 218–24, and its *Commissioned Studies and Selected Papers Part 3*, pp. 209–16, for a more detailed discussion.

[21] 1982–83 Budget Paper No. 1, *Budget Statements 1982–83*, Statement no. 4, p. 242; Economic Statement by the Treasurer, May 1983, pp. 41–2.

[22] Taxation Review Committee, *Full Report*, pp. 233–8; Draft White Paper, *Reform of the Australian Tax System*, pp. 192–9.

[23] See Daryl A. Dixon and Richard J. Vann, "An Examination of the Imputation System in the Context of the Erosion of Company Tax Base", *Australian Tax Forum* 491, 1987, pp. 63–93; Robert Officer, "The Australian Imputation System for Company Tax and its Likely Effect on Shareholders, Financing and Investment", mimeograph, 7 November 1989.

[24] See Taxation Review Committee, *Full Report*, p. 223; for further discussion of this issue see C. Shoup, *Public Finance*, pp. 312–13.

[25] See P. Groenewegen, *Australian Taxation Policy*, section 4.3.2, pp. 226–7 and the references there cited, and Ross Garnaut, Richard Dowell, and John Brunner on the subject in "Australian Resource Development", Autumn Forum 1981, *Economic Papers*, no. 67, August 1981, pp. 31–59 for a detailed debate on the major advantages and disadvantages of resource rent taxation.

[26] Commonwealth of Australia, *Discussion Paper on Resource Rent Tax in the Petroleum Sector* (Canberra: AGPS, December 1983), reports in *Australian Financial Review*, 28 June 1984.

FURTHER READING

Reference in the first instance should be made to these major texts:

R.A. and P.B. Musgrave, *Public Finance in Theory and Practice*, 4th edn. (New York: McGraw Hill, 1984), chs. 18–19.

C.V. Brown and P.M. Jackson, *Public Sector Economics*, 3rd edn. (Oxford: Blackwell, 1986), ch. 18.

J.E. Stiglitz, *Economics of the Public Sector*, 2nd edn. (New York: W.W. Norton, 1988), chs. 22–3.

On alternative forms of company taxation, reference should be made to:

S. Cnossen, "Alternative Forms of Corporation Tax", *Australian Tax Forum*, 1(3), September 1984, pp. 253–79, reprinted in P. Groenewegen (ed.), *Australian Taxation Policy*, 2nd edn. (Melbourne: Longman Cheshire, 1987), pp. 202–31.

Other useful references on business taxation are:

Bureau of Industry Economics, *The Taxation of Corporate Investment Income: Australia's Place in the World* (Canberra: AGPS, 1988).

Treasury Economic Paper No. 13, *International Comparison of Business Taxation* (Canberra, AGPS, 1988).

On fringe benefit tax, see:

D. J. Collins, "Taxation of Fringe Benefits: an Economist's Perspective", *Australian Tax Forum* 4(1), 1987, pp. 95–121.

OECD, *Taxation of Fringe Benefits* (Paris: OECD, 1988).

On resource rent taxation, see:

R. Garnaut and A. Clunies Ross, *Taxation of Mineral Rents* (Oxford: Clarendon Press, 1983).

11

Wealth and property taxation

Shoup[1] distinguishes five different types of wealth or property taxation. These can be classified as follows:

1. The annual tax on net wealth.
2. Death and gift duties.
3. Specific property taxes such as the land tax and local rates.
4. The capital levy.
5. Levies on the transfer of capital or property for consideration, for example, stamp duties.

Table 6.3 reveals that property taxation raised 9 per cent of national tax revenue in 1987–88, largely confined to specific property taxation or land value taxation through local rates and State land tax and a variety of levies on the transfer of capital or property, of which stamp duty and financial institutions duty are the more important.

Death duties, the form in which general property taxation was traditionally levied by State and federal governments for most of this century, was first abolished by Queensland in 1976 and by 1983 this example had been followed by the federal and the other State governments. Australia has never imposed an annual wealth tax or a capital levy.

If international comparisons are made, then on the broad definition of capital taxation employed by the OECD Australia surprisingly ranks sixth in terms of property taxation as a proportion of total tax revenue (it is only surpassed in this respect by the United States, the United Kingdom, Canada, Switzerland and Japan).[2] This high ranking is due largely to land and capital transfer taxation; if this is excluded, Australia ranks near the bottom in the OECD wealth tax scale. A comment by Shoup on wealth tax practice at the start of the 1980s should also be noted. "It is rare for a country to go to the extreme of imposing neither a transfer tax at death nor an annual net wealth tax. Australia and Mexico are examples. Canada is nearly one."[3] Even though it is likely to be long before this unique experience of Australia is altered, a discussion of general capital taxation is quite in order.

CAPITAL TAXES AND TAXES ON CAPITAL

Capital taxes are levied on a capital base, such as the capital value of property, but are frequently intended to be paid from the income derived from that property and not from the capital itself. Land taxation, although originally motivated by a desire of the federal government in 1910 to break up large rural estates, is now intended as a tax on property *income*, similar to the annual wealth taxes implemented in some European countries. A tax *on capital* in the strict sense is fully intended to be paid from capital. The prime example is the capital levy. Death duties may also be paid from capital, particularly where their payment demands the partial or total realisation of the estate on which they are levied. Whether an annual wealth tax is paid from capital depends upon the severity of the tax (as reflected in the definition of the tax base) and the rate structure imposed.

Because *taxes on capital* are inimical to economic growth, they tend to be infrequently used in capitalist countries. The context in which the use of capital levies has been suggested has usually been to appropriate large windfall gains derived by property owners either from massive currency depreciation or from war. Most economists, past and present, have opposed their implementation because of the effects on the capital stock of the nation. When such levies are anticipated, they lead to consumption and the flight of capital. Confiscatory capital taxes are occasionally advocated as a method for reducing the inequality in wealth but by and large are incompatible with the maintenance of a capitalist system. Use of capital levies has resurfaced as a policy to reduce large accumulated stocks of public debt.

The association between the aims of capital taxation and the instrument by which it is taxed is more clearly brought out by listing the three objectives generally advanced in favour of general taxation of capital. Apart from the promotion of a more equal distribution of the ownership of wealth as part of the distributional objectives of taxation, capital taxation is justified to tax the benefits conferred by wealth which are separate from the income it generates and, in addition, to discriminate against inherited wealth relative to that accumulated from personal exertion. The second of these objectives is met by taxing the ownership of wealth, the third by taxing its transfer at death or by gift. The first can be achieved by either or both of these expedients.[4]

The annual tax on net wealth

In the countries (mainly European) which impose an annual tax on net wealth, it is basically used as a supplement to the personal income tax, though some countries (Germany, Switzerland, India) have used corporate wealth taxes. The tax has never been used in Australia, although it has been advocated by several Australian economists, and it is not likely to be introduced in Australia in the near future, largely because of the general unpopularity of taxes on property in this country. In addition, a variety of administrative and other difficulties were highlighted by both the Treasury and the Taxation Review Committee in their rejection of the annual wealth tax as a suitable tax reform for Australia.[5]

The tax base[6]

The base for a net wealth tax is the value of all assets of the tax-paying unit less the value of all outstanding liabilities, hence the word "net" in its name. In other words, the base includes all the real property of the taxpayer such as land and dwellings; all personal property (furniture and fittings, vehicles and other modes of transport, art or other collections, in short, all personal belongings including clothing and jewellery), and all financial assets such as cash, bank deposits, shares, bonds, and the ownership of business assets. It has sometimes been argued that a general wealth tax base should also include the value of human capital and, perhaps more importantly, the capital value of life insurance and superannuation rights. From this aggregate value of assets owned, all debts outstanding — such as mortgage debt, hire purchase debt, bank overdrafts and personal loans — are deducted to arrive at the net value of the wealth ownership.

One of the major administrative problems of this tax — the valuation of assets — can be immediately deduced from this description of the complex nature of the tax base. For some assets and liabilities there are no great problems of valuation. There is a readily ascertainable market value for bonds, shares, and many other financial assets. In the case of real estate, valuations are frequently available for the purpose of local rating, though in many cases such valuations would have to be regularly adjusted to take account of improvements made to the land. For much of personal property, insurance valuations may be used, or values could be personally assessed by the taxpayer with the proviso that the State could acquire these assets at the stated valuations. Unincorporated businesses, particularly those associated with primary industry, pose special valuation problems, because for the former there are no share valuations by the market, while in the case of the latter, there are generally large capital asset values with low income earning capacity.

The tax is an annual one, assessed and collected generally at the same time as the personal income tax. The preferred tax unit is the household, largely for administrative and tax avoidance reasons; an individual tax unit could create administrative difficulties in the apportionment of assets among the various members of the household, and would greatly facilitate wealth-splitting for tax purposes. Because the tax base is expressed in money values, there is a good case for use of appropriate indexation to turn it into a real tax base.

The rate structure

Both proportional and progressive rates have been used for the net wealth tax. The rates imposed rarely exceed 3 per cent (and more frequently are in the vicinity of 1 per cent) irrespective of whether the rates are progressive or proportional. These apparently "low" rates are deceptive. A wealth tax of only 2 per cent on assets whose average rate of return is 8 per cent, implies a surcharge of 25 per cent on that property income and this is additional to the personal income tax payable. The lower the average rate of return on the assets, the higher is the surcharge on this property income, and this relationship between the rate of return on assets and the wealth tax rate is sometimes seen as one of the tax's advantages, as an example will make clear. If the average rate of return of the assets owned is 20 per cent and the average wealth tax rate is 3 per cent, then the wealth tax is the equivalent of a 15 per cent surcharge on property income, if the average rate of return is only 3 per cent, the same rate of wealth tax imposes a 100 per cent surcharge on the property income. In order to lower their effective tax liability, wealth owners would have a considerable incentive to shift from low-yield assets to those with high yields, in order to raise the average rate of return on their asset portfolio and thereby to lower the rate of surcharge on property income implicit in the wealth tax. Relatively high wealth tax rates where there is a low average rate of return on the assets owned could mean that the tax must, in fact, be paid out of capital.

Large exemptions are usually granted in order to minimise the total number of taxpayers liable to the tax, both for administrative reasons and also because the intention is to tax the wealthy. Some countries which impose the tax introduce a ceiling on the combined income and net worth tax liability of the taxpayer — for example, Sweden at one stage had a provision that this combined tax liability should not exceed 80 per cent of total income. Such a ceiling, or a variant thereof, would be useful if it was desired to protect the income of primary producers whose asset values (particularly in land) are frequently high relative to their income. This would protect these producers against the generally desirable effect of the tax of forcing people out of assets with a low rate of return into high-yielding ones.

Further considerations in net wealth taxation

The incidence of a net wealth tax depends largely on whether it is imposed on residents or on all forms of wealth, as well as on the degree of capital mobility which is assumed. If there is a high degree of capital mobility and all wealth is taxed (irrespective of whether it is owned by residents or not), capital will move and, on the usual neo-classical assumptions, will continue to move until the after-tax rate of return has been raised to that prevailing prior to the imposition of the tax. In this case, the tax liability is shifted by the owners of capital. If the tax only applies to residents, whose capital is generally less mobile than foreign capital, only part of the burden will be shifted by the owners of capital. In the short period, when capital can be assumed to be immobile, the tax is fully paid by the owners of capital.[7]

Reasons for introducing a net wealth tax

Where the net wealth tax is regarded as a supplement to the personal income tax, it has the following advantages. In the first place, because wealth ownership gives a taxable capacity additional to income, it is felt that this should be taxed on ability-to-pay principles. Secondly, the net wealth tax is able to tax certain non-pecuniary returns on asset ownership such as those obtained from the ownership of a residence, from art collections, and from other personal possessions. Thirdly, an annual net wealth tax provides a check on income tax avoidance by providing a double source of information on the property-owning income taxpayer, the person for whom tax avoidance is frequently the easiest.

The net wealth tax provides the equivalent of a surcharge on property income and is seen by some people as an efficient means of discriminating between income from earnings and income from property for tax purposes. This point is illustrated by the short history of the property income surcharge reintroduced by the Whitlam government in 1974–75. Between 1915 and 1953 Australian income tax had taxed property income at higher rates. This discrimination in favour of earned income was abandoned with the general simplification of the income tax scales made in 1953. In his 1974 Budget, the Treasurer reintroduced this practice on ability-to-pay grounds by means of a surcharge of 10 per cent on property income for all taxpayers whose taxable income exceeded $5,000. In the following Budget the measure was repealed because it proved to be highly unpopular. It also introduced many administrative difficulties and it was not very productive of revenue. A net wealth tax, as was seen earlier, has the same effect as a property income surcharge.[8]

Economic effects of the tax on saving, work, and investment

Because the wealth tax to some extent acts as a proxy for a surcharge on property income, incentive effects on work, saving, and investment are possible. As in the case of the disincentive effects of personal income tax, it is difficult to be precise about these, because they largely depend on the reaction of the taxpayer to the imposition of the wealth tax. There may be a normal income or substitution effect, depending on whether taxpayers seek to increase their total income to compensate for the reduction in their after-tax income, or whether they will prefer leisure or more consumption to reduce their effective tax base. The wealth tax is also likely to inhibit savings; partly because the effective rate of return on saving is lowered, partly because the total disposable income of the taxpayer is reduced. Saving may be stimulated, however, if the taxpayer is concerned with increasing assets at a certain rate.

The investment effect of a wealth tax is frequently seen as a reason in favour of the tax, because it provides an incentive to shift to high-yield assets. Earlier it was shown that the rate of surcharge on property income implied by a wealth tax depends on both the rate of the tax and the average rate of return on the assets owned, the higher the rate of return, the lower the rate of surcharge. This, it is argued, will lead to a rearrangement of asset portfolios after the imposition of a wealth tax with taxpayers shifting from low or zero yield assets to more productive, high yield assets. The overall effect would be an increase in the rate of return or the productivity of investment. Once again, the relative importance of this effect is difficult to assess, and is now generally seen as minor.

Administrative considerations

The tax is most frequently criticised because of the administrative difficulties involved in its assessment and collection, partly because of the difficulties involved in obtaining fair and accurate valuations, partly because of the ease of evasion by some taxpayers who hold certain classes of assets. These administrative difficulties can be overcome but this depends on the precise way the tax is implemented particularly in so far as exemptions are concerned. It is also often argued that the compliance costs of individual taxpayers liable to the tax would be excessive relative to the yield of the tax. On the other hand, combined with an income tax, the wealth tax provides information by which cross checks on tax avoidance can be more easily carried out. As the tax is in operation in many countries, a great deal of practical administrative experience can be drawn upon.

Some further considerations in net wealth taxation

Advocates of an annual wealth tax argue that it increases the fairness of the tax system by assessing taxable capacity of individuals or households more accurately in the light of the ability-to-pay principle and thereby has the potential to reduce the degree of inequality in wealth ownership. A second advantage of the tax is that it facilitates the compilation of wealth distribution statistics, an important item of information in connection with the formation of social policy. The tax has little significance for stabilisation purposes, largely because of its small yield. If asset values carefully reflected changes in the income from these assets, it would be useful as a minor automatic stabiliser. As was seen earlier, the effect on economic growth is uncertain; it may have unfavourable saving effects but on the other hand there may be favourable investment effects as people seek out higher-yielding assets.

Death and gift duties and inheritance taxation[9]

The taxation of property of deceased persons is one of the oldest forms of taxation; it was used as early as Roman times. Such property can, in general, be taxed in two ways: it can be taxed by an estate or death duty upon the value of the property left by the deceased persons, or it can be taxed by an inheritance tax levied on the persons who inherit the property and who thereby benefit from the estate.

The reasons for this general use of the tax are not hard to find. The taxation of legacies and inheritances was defended in the nineteenth century — despite the fact that they were frequently taxes on capital — on the grounds that they taxed an unearned increment of wealth and that they prevented the undue concentration of wealth. That is, their primary purpose was the reduction of inequality in wealth distribution. In countries which do not have other forms of wealth taxes, estate or death duty ensures that the accumulated property of a person is taxed at least once and at the administratively convenient time of death when the valuation of the estate is inevitable.[10]

In the former Australian death duties, the net value of a deceased estate was the object of taxation rather than the inheritance in the hands of the beneficiaries. As indicated earlier, federal and State death duties, more correctly called estate duty and probate and succession duties respectively, have been effectively abolished in the whole of Australia from 1983 after having been in existence for the greater part of the twentieth century. From 1914 to 1979 they were levied at both federal and State level, constituting the most serious form of tax duplication of the post-World War II period. Any reintroduction of the tax is likely to be at the national level only, thereby yielding substantial simplicity and advantages.

The tax base

The definition of the tax base appropriate to death duties depends on whether the tax is donor or donee based, to use an alternative way of distinguishing between a tax falling on the estate of a deceased person and that falling on a bequest. In the former it is the net value of the estate left by the deceased, in the latter that of the individual bequests. The definition of the base for death duties generally also requires a distinction between real and personal property since it is possible to tax the first in the case of non-residents, as was in fact done when death duties were levied by the States. In order to provide relief against the subsequent possibility of double taxation, double taxation agreements are usually in force to remedy this eventuality.

The value of the estate is calculated net of liabilities. In the former federal estate duty, liabilities included federal income tax outstanding at the time of death and liability with respect to State probate and succession duties if applicable. Gifts made in the three-year period before death are included in the tax base. As in the case of the net wealth tax, there are important problems of valuations (examples of these have already been given). These arise partly from the nature of the assets and partly from the fact that because the duty is assessed on the value at the date of death, anomalies may occur if these values change after the date of death but before the duty is paid. Shares and the value of livestock in a rural estate are assets whose values may fluctuate widely between the time of assessment and the payment of duty. Estate duty is not assessed on bequests to religious, scientific or educational institutions, or to non-profit hospitals, public benevolent institutions, public libraries, and other specified "charities".[11]

The rate structure

The rate structure of death duties is generally progressive, secured in the usual manner of rising marginal rates at discrete intervals. In the former federal estate duty, for example, the rate of duty commenced at 3 per cent on small estates, rising to a maximum of 27.9 per cent on an estate with a net value in excess of $1,000,000. In times of inflation, this imposes a requirement of indexation of the tax brackets, the absence of which is perhaps one reason why the tax became so unpopular in Australia.[12]

Both the federal and the State governments gave liberal exemptions especially to primary producers and in cases where the estate passed to the surviving spouse, to dependent children, or to other close relatives of the deceased.

Other considerations in death duties

Incidence of death duties and other economic effects. The incidence of death duties is difficult to assess because it depends largely on the reaction of both the deceased prior to death and of the beneficiaries to the existence of the tax. Although the legal incidence of the tax is on the deceased estate, the actual incidence is on the beneficiaries; it can also be said that the tax cannot easily be shifted except in so far as it is avoided or evaded prior to or at the time of death.

The effects of the tax on saving and investment depend on the manner in which the tax is anticipated by the owner of the estate prior to death, partly through its influence on the selection of specific types of assets. Death duties are often criticised for their adverse effects on savings, but such adverse effects need not necessarily arise. Anticipation of death duty may be by additional saving through insurance policies designed for the purpose of meeting death duties. Saving may also be stimulated by the existence of death duties because a person aims at leaving an estate with an after-tax value of a certain size. There is less likely to be a direct effect on the incentive to work, but there is little evidence upon the economic effects of death duties.

In the case of sizeable, but illiquid, estates such as farms and other unincorporated business enterprises, and also of some private companies, difficulties are caused because the payment of death duties may lead to the sale of business assets or part of the business, or else to a large increase in indebtedness. Although this difficulty can be overcome through careful death duty planning by the owner of the business, many owners of farms or small businesses have neither the foresight nor the ability to do this. This effect of death duties on small business may constrain the efficiency with which resources are used, because it can lead to reductions in the size of the firm below what is considered to be its economic size; for example, it may force the subdivision of a farm.

Death duties and the distribution of wealth

Although a major advantage claimed for the use of death duties is the reduction of inequality in wealth distribution and the prevention of undue concentration of wealth, there is little evidence to suggest that this objective has been successfully achieved. In countries for which evidence is available — like the United Kingdom for example — it has been shown that death duties, even where marginal rates exceed 80 per cent, have not greatly reduced the concentration of wealth. What has occurred is a redistribution of wealth from the very rich to the rich partly through the widespread practice of estate duty avoidance by gifts before death and partly through the device of generation skipping, that is, of leaving property to grandchildren rather than children. For Australia, no firm conclusion can be advanced on the effects of death duties on wealth distribution.[13]

Death duty avoidance

The United Kingdom evidence points to the importance of avoidance practices among the very wealthy; in Australia there was less empirical evidence of this but it seems likely that such practices were probably widespread. The main devices for such avoidance are as follows. First, there is the transfer of property before death by way of gift, which can lead to considerable tax savings — it is for this reason that an effective estate duty has to be integrated with a comprehensive gift duty. Secondly, there are several ways of generation skipping, either in the making of the bequests, but more effectively by means of the creation of trusts or other forms of property settlement which delay the transfer of property at death for a number of generations. It is generally accepted that such devices are more available to the very wealthy than to those with more modest estates. Nevertheless it should also be recorded that Australian estate duty statistics for 1975–76 showed that estates with a net value exceeding $500,000 which accounted for less than 1 per cent of estates assessed, contributed almost 20 per cent of the revenue and that the bottom 90 per cent of estates contributed only 30 per cent of that revenue.[14]

Administrative considerations

Like the net wealth tax, there are many problems in the administration of death duties and the associated gift duties. Valuation problems and equitable procedures in the valuation of assets are such problems, and have already been described. Secondly, there are considerable compliance costs on the taxpayer, partly in the large legal expenses incurred in the granting of probate and the assessment of the estate, but also in the hardships frequently caused to a surviving spouse and dependent children when insufficient preparation has been made for the event of the death of the breadwinner. In Australia, hardships largely arose from the long delays before probate was granted and these features of the tax, which were widely publicised, led to its unpopularity. Finally, the collection costs of these taxes are heavy; the net administrative cost (expressed as a percentage of revenue collected) for gift duty was 9.6 per cent, for estate duty, 3.2 per cent. By contrast, less than 1 per cent in the case of personal income tax is absorbed by administrative costs.[15]

Before concluding this discussion of estate duty, a comment on the associated gift duties has to be made. Although such duties were largely imposed for the purpose of preventing death duty avoidance through *inter vivos* gifts, the existence of gift duties also served an anti-avoidance purpose in connection with personal income tax. This was to impose costs on the giving of income-yielding property to close relatives for the purpose of income-splitting. The abolition of gift duty in July 1979 therefore also greatly facilitated this form of personal income tax avoidance, an illustration of some of the interdependences which can arise in taxation policy.

The capital levy

Debt management problems in countries with large public debts have brought discussion of the feasibility of a capital levy back onto the tax policy agenda. As a means of public debt reduction, particularly after major wars, capital levies have been supported by economists from Ricardo onwards, particularly in the context of the debt problems created by World War I. A recent study[16] concludes that "the imposition of such a levy can be welfare improving" but that in practice it is unlikely to gain wide popularity as a means of effectively reducing a large stock of public debt.

SPECIFIC PROPERTY TAXATION: THE TAXATION OF LAND

The taxation of land has long been important in the English-speaking world. One reason for this is that land was the major productive asset in society, and its ownership conferred political and social status. This applied to early Australia as much as to the United Kingdom. Land taxes were considered to be "fair taxes" because they taxed the "unearned increment" of land rent, which general economic development bestowed on the land owner. Economic theory traditionally argued that land tax had no detrimental effect on agricultural production if it taxed only the pure economic surplus of rent. Finally, land taxation was administratively easy since the tax was difficult to evade and because title records of this asset were usually readily available.[17]

It is therefore not surprising that for a significant part of this century, land taxation was used by all three levels of government in Australia. From 1910 to 1952 the federal government taxed land values, and most State governments have taxed land for a substantial part of the century. The relative importance of these land taxes and revenue-raisers was shown in Table 6.1. The major taxation of land is, however, by local governments in the form of rates on the capital value or rental value of land with or without the inclusion of improvements.

Local rates[18]

For the local government authorities in Australia, land taxation is the only source of tax revenue to which they have direct access. Local rates on land values are considered to be a particularly suitable tax for this level of government because they are easy to assess and collect, while in the past they have provided sufficient revenue for local government expenditure needs. More general issues about the role of local rates in local government finance are discussed in Chapter 16.

The tax base

There are several ways of utilising the local rate on land values which depend on the underlying principles of valuation. In Australia, the local government authorities in the various States have used a number of distinct variants of land values: unimproved capital value, site value, improved capital value, and assessed annual value. Unimproved capital value — usually defined as the capital value of land in its natural and original state — as a tax base is now largely confined to Queensland. Site value, which differs (generally speaking) from unimproved capital value by including the value of improvements to the site such as excavations, grading, levelling, underground draining, and clearing, is now extensively used in Australia as a more practical base for land value taxation. Assessed annual value, which is used in Tasmania and in parts of Victoria, South Australia and Western Australia, is the annual rental value of the property with or without improvements.[19]

The general preference in Australia is for unimproved capital value or site value largely because these tax bases exclude the taxation of land improvement, which is thereby encouraged. This tax base is also consistent with the general prejudice against capital taxation, which has already been noted. The four tax bases are, of course, interrelated. The assessed annual value theoretically stands in a precise relationship to the capital value, because this equals the annual return from the property capitalised at the current rate of interest. Furthermore, it should be realised that the asset value taxed is a gross value and is not reduced by the liabilities outstanding against it, such as mortgage debt.

The rate structure

Local government rates are levied at a proportional rate of cents and fractions of cents in the dollar set annually by each council on the basis of its estimated expenditure. The rate tends to fluctuate over time within local government areas, it varies substantially between councils, and generally shows as an inverse relationship with the value of the tax base, both over time and as between councils. In some cases, State local government legislation prescribes minimum or maximum rates.

In some States, local government authorities also have the power to charge differential rates to discriminate between various forms of land use. There is frequently a lower rate of tax applied to rural areas within otherwise largely urbanised council districts; similarly in the central business areas of capital cities residential property is sometimes charged a lower rate than commercial property. In addition to the general rate, some councils may levy special rates either for specific purposes in particular areas of their jurisdiction or for the general purpose of loan redemption.[20]

Other considerations in local rating

The incidence of local rates. The incidence of the local rate is still a matter of considerable theoretical dispute, and depends partly on the nature of the tax base and partly on the use to which the land is put. For example, theory suggests that if the tax is levied on the "original and indestructible powers of the soil" — for which unimproved capital value is a proxy — the tax cannot be shifted under competitive conditions. A property tax on real estate which includes improvements such as buildings can, however, be shifted in a variety of ways even under competitive conditions. In Australia there are good grounds for believing that part of the rate burden is shifted, either to tenants of rateable property or to the consumers of goods and services which are produced on rateable property, depending of course, as was shown in Chapter 8, on the supply and demand elasticities for the goods and services produced on the land. The literature on this subject is now extensive.[21]

Economic effects of the tax

The reason for the selection of unimproved capital value as the most widely used local government tax base was to encourage the improvement of the land by not taxing such improvements and to prevent the holding of large tracts of unimproved land for speculative purposes. At present, there are some disadvantages arising from this policy. For example, it can encourage the uneconomical subdivision of rural land and over-intensive land use in primary production. It has also been argued that this tax base can distort land use in the city centres of capital cities by the encouragement of improvement only in certain directions (high-rise office blocks) and thereby discouraging other activities (theatres, cinemas, restaurants) which make a less profitable use of the land. This last difficulty can be overcome by differential rating, where attention is paid to the use of the land. Also some socially desirable uses may be subsidised by the imposition of lower rates and by exemptions.

Distributional consequences of the tax

From the point of view of the distributional objective, the local rate is frequently criticised because the average tax rate relative to income falls as income rises. This phenomenon for Australia as a whole was illustrated in Table 8.1. It is doubtful whether this situation could be redressed by the introduction of a progressive rate structure in local rating, because there is no significant correlation between income and wealth in the form of unimproved capital values.

Some economists argue that since distributional policy is a national and not a local government objective, the absence of progression is not important. Instead of the ability-to-pay principle, they use the benefit principle to justify the tax because most of the benefits from the services provided by local government go to the ratepayers. This argument is not persuasive. Benefits from many local government services accrue to people other than ratepayers; this applies to the basic services derived from roads and also to recreational facilities such as beaches, reserves, and sports grounds. In these latter cases, the benefit principle suggests the use of explicit charges for users. Secondly, in larger geographical areas many of these services are unequally diffused between ratepayers. Thirdly, the possibility of tax shifting even further weakens the link between tax payable and the benefits received. As was argued in Chapter 7, the benefit principle is difficult to apply to every tax, and this includes local rates.

An unpopular tax

As a property tax, the local rate is very unpopular in Australia. This is partly because it is regressive as to income. Secondly, there is the inconvenience factor: rates are paid either in a lump sum or in quarterly instalments and this makes them most visible taxes. Thirdly, most people take local services for granted and often have a low opinion of the capabilities and integrity of the elected councillors, so that they feel they do not get value for money. Finally, and most important, there is the fact that no cash flow is generated from the asset taxed where it is the residence of the ratepayer; on the contrary, for most households, the ownership of a house involves large cash outflows for mortgage repayments. In rural areas, the disparity between rural land values and rural incomes is a major source of grievance against the tax, particularly in years of low prices of primary produce and, therefore, low incomes.[22]

Land tax[23]

All the Australian States levy land taxes, though the proportionate contribution these make to their total revenue is small and declining. In 1966–67 they raised 10.9 per cent of State tax revenues, in 1974–75 this proportion had fallen to 6 per cent, in 1987–88 it constituted only 5.2 per cent. There are wide variations in the relative importance of the tax in the tax systems of the various States. In 1987–88 land taxes raised only 3.3 per cent of tax revenue in Queensland while in Victoria, Western Australia, and New South Wales they raised approximately 5–6 per cent of State revenue. In nearly all cases, the tax is levied largely on urban land values but not on the ordinary residential building block. Land used for primary production purposes is invariably exempt.

The tax base is generally the unimproved capital value or the site value of the land alienated from the Crown, but in South Australia land from leasehold is also taxed. The rate structure is usually mildly progressive, the marginal tax rate rising — to take the example of Tasmanian land tax in 1988 — from 0.3 per cent for land values not exceeding $10,000 to a maximum of 2.75 per cent for land values over $250,000. Apart from the fact that the tax is generally levied with a progressive rate structure, it is so similar to the local rate that further discussion is unnecessary, pointing out that this similarity extends to its unpopularity. This unpopularity of the land tax is presumably the explanation why States have not used this type of taxation more extensively, despite the fact that several inquiries into State taxation have suggested such a move.[24]

CONCLUSION

Although property and capital transfer transaction taxes such as some stamp duties and financial institution duties are included with property taxes in statistical tax classification schema, their evaluation is postponed to Chapter 13, even though the base of these taxes has similarities with the bases of some of the taxes discussed in this chapter. It is likely, however, that these types of taxes which have all exhibited fast revenue growth during the 1980s will be the mainstay of Australia's property tax system during the 1990s, particularly if local rates are reduced in relative importance as a revenue source for local government, as has already happened in the United Kingdom. More general forms of wealth taxation, despite their usefulness for a balanced tax structure, are also not likely to be reintroduced in the near future.[25]

SUMMARY

1. There are five classes of wealth and property tax:

   (a) The annual tax on net wealth.
   (b) Death and gift duties.
   (c) Specific property taxes such as the land tax and local rates.
   (d) The capital levy.
   (e) Levies on the transfer of capital such as stamp duties and financial taxes.

2. A useful distinction is that between taxes on capital and capital taxes. Capital taxes use a capital value as tax base but are really taxes on the income of capital, designed to leave capital in tact. Taxes on capital are fully intended to be paid from capital.

3. There are three general objectives of wealth and property taxation: (a) to promote a more equal distribution of wealth ownership, (b) to tax benefits from wealth ownership separate from pecuniary income that ownership may generate; (c) to discriminate against inherited wealth.

4. An annual net wealth tax taxes assets less liabilities of the tax paying unit at either proportional or mildly progressive rates. It is intended as a capital tax to supplement the income tax.

5. Taxing the property of deceased persons is a very ancient form of tax. It can be donor or donee based, that is, taxed either on the value of the estate (net of liabilities) of a deceased person or on the value of an inheritance for a beneficiary. The last can be taxed cumulatively over a life time. Progressive rate structures are generally used.

6. To prevent death duty avoidance, gift duty is generally combined with an estate duty. Ease of avoidance has meant relatively little impact of the tax on the concentration of wealth ownership.

7. Land taxation has also been a long-standing government revenue raiser and Australia currently taxes land values at both the State and local level.

8. Tax base for both land tax and local rate is now generally the site value of the land (with or without improvements) or its annual rental value; rates tend to be mildly progressive in land tax and proportional in local rates. Both local rates and land taxes are capital taxes designed to tax income and/or non-pecuniary benefits from real property ownership.

9. Although property and capital transfer transaction taxes are generally classified as property taxes, their objectives fall less easily within the objectives generally ascribed to wealth taxes (see Summary point 3). Their discussion is therefore better postponed till a general discussion of specific transaction taxes (Chapter 13).

NOTES

[1] C.S. Shoup, *Public Finance* (London: Macmillan, 1969), pp. 357–8.

[2] See OECD, *Taxation of Net Wealth, Capital Transfers and Capital Gains of Individuals* (Paris: OECD, 1988), Table 0.2, p. 27.

[3] C.S. Shoup, "Wealth Taxation Today", in J.G. Head (ed.), *Taxation Issues of the 1980s* (Sydney: Australian Tax Research Foundation, 1983), p. 391. Since then, Canada has also completely abandoned general wealth taxation.

[4] See Peter Groenewegen, "Options for the Taxation of Wealth", in J.G. Head (ed.), *Changing the Tax Mix* (Sydney: Australian Tax Research Foundation, 1986), pp. 375–9.

[5] Taxation Review Committee, *Full Report* (Canberra: AGPS, 1975), ch. 26; Draft White Paper, *Reform of the Australian Tax System* (Canberra: AGPS, 1985), ch. 15 .

[6] For a detailed discussion of issues associated with a net wealth tax see OECD, *Taxation of Net Wealth, Capital Transfers and Capital Gains of Individuals*, pp. 44–73.

[7] For a detailed discussion of the incidence of net wealth taxes, see C.S. Shoup, *Public Finance*, pp. 359–62; and M. Kalecki, "A Theory of Commodity, Income and Capital Taxation", pp. 41–2.

[8] For details of this tax, see Budget Speech 1974–75, p. 26; Budget Speech 1975–76, p. 26; and especially Taxation Review Committee, *Full Report*, pp. 185–7.

[9] The complex issues relating to death duties cannot be covered here in detail. Reference should be made to OECD, *The Taxation of Net Wealth, Capital Transfers and Capital Gains of Individuals*, ch. 2; *The Structure and Reform of Direct Taxation*, ch. 15. For an Australian discussion see Taxation Review Committee, *Full Report* (Canberra: AGPS, 1975), chs. 24–5, *Report of the Committee of Inquiry into Revenue Raising in Victoria* (Melbourne: F.D. Atkinson, Government Printer, 1983), pp. 325–8; and R.L. Mathews (ed.), *State and Local Taxes* (Canberra: ANU Press, 1977), ch. 16. For a critical evaluation of death duties see Peter Groenewegen, "Options for the Taxation of Wealth", pp. 379–82.

[10] For a detailed analysis of inheritance and wealth distribution in Britain see C.D. Harbury and D.M.W.N. Hitchens, *Inheritance and Wealth Inequality in Britain* (London: Allen & Unwin, 1979) and for a similar United States study, see J.A. Brittain, *Inheritance and the Inequality of Material Wealth* (Washington, D.C.: The Brookings Institution, 1978).

[11] For a detailed discussion of the issues raised by the tax base for estate duty, see Taxation Review Committee, *Full Report*, ch. 24, pp. 442–4, and Appendix A, pp. 455–77; and from the perspective of international practice, OECD, *Taxation of Net Wealth, Capital Transfers and Capital Gains of Individuals,* pp. 112–20.

[12] For international data on rate structures, see OECD, *Taxation of Net Wealth, Capital Transfers and Capital Gains of Individuals*, pp. 81–93.

[13] For a discussion of the evidence see Peter Groenewegen, "Options for the Taxation of Wealth", pp. 380–1; John Piggott, "The Distribution of Wealth: What is it, What Does it Mean, and is it Important?", *Australian Economic Review*, 3/88, pp. 35–42.

[14] Commonwealth of Australia, *Taxation Statistics 1975–76. Supplement to the 55th Report to Parliament of the Commissioner of Taxation* (Canberra: AGPS, 1977), p. 198.

[15] Commonwealth of Australia, *56th Report of the Commissioner of Taxation* (Canberra, AGPS, 1977), p. 55. This relates to 1976–77, the last financial year during which general estate and gift duty was levied, because from 21 November 1977 estate and gift duty no longer applied to estates passing to close relatives. This effectively lowered administration cost over the two subsequent financial years prior to its complete abolition in July 1979.

[16] See Barry Eichengreen, "The Capital Levy in Theory and Practice" (Cambridge, Massachusetts: National Bureau of Economic Research Working Paper No. 3096, September 1989); Peter Groenewegen, "Options for the Taxation of Wealth", p. 388, n.4 provides details of an Australian proposal in 1916 to introduce a capital levy.

[17] See J.S. Mill, *Principles of Political Economy*, Book 5, ch. 2, sections 5 and 6, esp. pp. 819–22. Land taxation in Australia was given a great boost by the influence of Henry George's book, *Progress and Poverty,* which dealt with the programs of the more radical political parties at the end of

the 19th century. See *Papers presented in Commemoration of the Centenary of Publication of "Progress and Poverty"* by Henry George (Sydney: Australian School of Social Science, 1979); and A.R. Prest, "United Kingdom Land Taxation in Perspective" in R.W. Lindholm and A. Lynn (eds.), *Land Value Taxation* (Madison: University of Wisconsin Press, 1982), ch. 8.

[18] For a general discussion of issues in local rating see N. J. Thomson, "Issues in Local Government Rating", in Geoffrey Brennan (ed.), *Local Government Finance* (Canberra: Centre for Research on Federal Financial Relations, Occasional Paper No. 41, 1987), ch. 3.

[19] For a detailed discussion of land valuation and concepts of land value used in Australia, see M.D. Herps, *A Study of the Official Land Valuations of the Australian States*, in Commonwealth Grants Commission, *Report on State Tax Sharing Entitlements,* vol. 3, Reports of consultants (Canberra: AGPS, 1981); a more concise discussion is given in *Report of the Committee of Inquiry into Revenue Raising in Victoria*, vol. 1, pp. 285–6, New South Wales Tax Task Force, *Review of the State Tax System* (Sydney: Government Printer, 1988), ch. 19, esp. pp. 235–6.

[20] See John Howard, "Local Government Revenue Raising", in National Inquiry into Local Government Finance, *Research and Consulting Reports* (Canberra: AGPS, 1985), part 2, p. 199 and the references there cited.

[21] See for example, David Ricardo, *Principles of Political Economy and Taxation*, Sraffa edn. (Cambridge: Cambridge University Press, 1951), ch. 2 and esp. ch. 12 cf. C.S. Shoup, *Ricardo on Taxation* (New York: Columbia University Press, 1960), ch. 5; H.J. Aaron, *Who Pays the Property Tax?* (Washington, D.C.; The Brookings Institution, 1975), esp. ch. 3; H.A. Simon, "The Incidence of the Tax on Urban Real Property", in C. Shoup and R. A. Musgrave (eds.), *Readings in the Economics of Taxation*, pp. 316–435; G.F. Break, "The Incidence and Economic Effect of Taxation", pp. 154–8 and John Howard, "Local Government Revenue Raising", ch. 6, pp. 231–5.

[22] John Howard, "Local Government Revenue Raising", ch. 6, esp. pp. 236–9; ch. 13, pp. 314–17.

[23] For a good (but now also dated) discussion of land tax in Australia, see G.M. Neutze, "State and Local Property Taxes", in R.L. Mathews (ed.), *State and Local Taxation*, ch. 15; this can be updated from R.J. Mathews (ed.), *State Taxation in Theory and Practice* (Canberra: Centre for Research on Federal Financial Relations, 1981) and *Report of the Committee of Inquiry into Revenue Raising in Victoria*, vol. 1, pp. 282–314; New South Wales Tax Task Force, *Review of the State Tax System*, ch. 19.

[24] See, for example, New South Wales Tax Task Force, *Review of the State Tax System*, pp. xix–xxi, which among other things advocated the removal of the general exemption of residential land and its replacement by a value exemption. For a different reform approach to land taxation, see B.F. Reece, "Could Land Betterment be Taxed Using Resource Rent Concepts?", *Economic Papers*, 5(3), Sept. 1986, pp. 38–52.

[25] Cf. Peter Groenewegen, *Everyone's Guide to Australian Taxation* (Sydney: Allen and Unwin, 1985), ch. 9; John Piggott, "Wealth Taxation in Australia", *Australian Tax Forum* 6(3) 1989, pp. 327–46.

FURTHER READING

The general texts provide useful alternative perspectives: see, for example:

R.A. and P.B. Musgrave, *Public Finance in Theory and Practice*, 4th edn. (New York: McGraw Hill, 1984), chs. 21, 22.

C.V. Brown and P.M. Jackson, *Public Sector Economics*, 3rd edn. (Oxford: Blackwell, 1986), ch. 16.

J.E. Stiglitz, *Economics of the Public Sector*, 2nd edn. (New York: W.W. Norton, 1988), ch. 22.

See also:

The Structure and Reform of Direct Taxation, Report of a Committee chaired by Professor J.E. Meade (London: Allen and Unwin, 1978), chs. 15,16.

Sidney Carroll, "Taxing Wealth: An Accessions Tax Proposal for the U.S.", *Journal of Post Keynesian Economics* 12(1), 1989, pp. 49–69.

A useful international perspective is:

OECD, *Taxation of Net Wealth, Capital Transfers and Capital Gains of Individuals* (Paris: OECD, 1988), chs. 1, 2, 3, and 5.

Australian perspectives on wealth taxation include:

Peter Groenewegen, "Options for the Taxation of Wealth", in J.G. Head (ed.), *Changing the Tax Mix* (Sydney: Australian Tax Research Foundation, 1986), ch. 19.

John Piggott, "Wealth Taxation in Australia", *Australian Tax Forum* 6(3), 1989, pp. 327–46.

And more specifically on land taxation:

N. J. Thomson, "Issues in Local Government Rating", in Geoffrey Brennan (ed.), *Local Government Finance* (Canberra: Centre for Research on Federal Financial Relations Occasional Paper 41, 1987), pp. 31–42.

John Howard, "Local Government Revenue Raising" in National Inquiry into Local Government Finance, *Research and Consultancy Reports (2)*, (Canberra: AGPS, 1985), chs. 5–9, 13, 14.2.

New South Wales Tax Task Force, *Review of the State Tax System* (Sydney: Government Printer, 1988), ch. 19.

A.R. Prest, "Some Issues in Australian Land Taxation", (Canberra: Centre for Research on Federal Financial Relations, Reprint Series No. 5, 1983).

New South Wales State Government, *Report of Committee of Inquiry into Local Government Rating and other Revenue Powers and Resources* (Sydney: 1990) chs. 5, 6, 11.

12

Broad-based consumption taxes

Broadly speaking, there are two types of taxes on goods and services: *general outlay taxes* and *partial outlay taxes*. The former tax a wide range of goods and services and include the value added tax (VAT), the retail sales tax, and, although not applicable to the taxation of services, the wholesale sales tax. These are indirect general outlay taxes, because they are collected by the government from those not intended to pay the tax. In addition, there is a direct consumption expenditure tax, assessed and collected from individual taxpayers. The second type of outlay tax, the partial or selective tax on goods and services, taxes a limited class of transactions only. Examples are the excise on beer and cigarettes, the sales tax on motor vehicles and cosmetics, overseas departure tax, and at the State level, business franchise taxes and the various levies on gambling. Put more broadly, the tax base of all outlay taxes is therefore either general consumption outlays on both goods and services comprehensively, on goods alone, or on the purchase of specific sets of goods and services, which taxes a limited class of transactions only.

Australia levies no general outlay taxes. By contrast most European countries rely heavily on the revenue from a VAT on the consumption of goods and services. In 1975, this peculiarity was noted by the Taxation Review Committee as a shortcoming of the Australian tax structure and it therefore recommended the gradual introduction of a VAT on goods and services combined with the phasing out of some of Australia's partial outlay taxes and a reduction in the relative weight of income tax. Ten years later, the Draft White Paper on Tax Reform prepared for the National Taxation Summit proposed the introduction of a broad based consumption tax as part of the government's preferred tax reform policy option.[1]

This does not mean, of course, that Australia levies no taxes on goods and services. The Federal Government levies major forms of partial outlay taxes — excise and sales tax — customs duties on imported commodities, as well as a whole series of minor miscellaneous charges such as the wool tax, stevedoring industry charge, the tobacco charge, and so on, whose revenue is assigned to specific purposes related to the industry taxed. The States also levy a variety of partial outlay taxes such as taxes on virtually all forms of gambling, on liquor and some other commodities in the form of licence fees, and, most important, on payrolls in the form of payroll tax. The relative importance of these various partial outlay taxes in the Australian tax structure was illustrated in Tables 6.1, 6.2, and 6.3.

The major types of general taxes on goods and services have already been mentioned but of these only the value added tax will be considered in detail in this chapter. Its discussion is followed by brief examination of the retail sales tax, the wholesale sales tax, and the direct expenditure tax. The emphasis on value added tax is largely explained by the fact that this is the preferred instrument for comprehensive consumption taxation by most economists, while its introduction is recommended in Australia by most economists who seek to expand the scope of consumption taxation and its rationalisation.[2] Partial outlay taxes and other transaction taxes are examined in Chapter 13.

Value added tax (VAT)

The VAT was first suggested in 1918 as a substitute tax for the turnover tax in Germany. It was first implemented in Argentina in 1935, and France in 1948 embodied some of its principles into its general sales and turnover taxes. In 1962 the VAT was recommended as a common tax on goods and services for all countries in the European Economic Community, a recommendation which was made mandatory for all member countries by the Treaty of Rome. As a result of this, all members of the Common Market now utilise this tax. The tax is also used by many other European countries (for example, Austria and Switzerland), by some Latin-American countries and by most former French colonies in Africa. Under the name of Goods and Services Tax (GST) New Zealand introduced a VAT in 1985. The major OECD countries which do not use the tax are the United States, Canada and, of course, Australia.[3]

Following Shoup's analysis,[4] there are three types of VAT: the *product* type, the *income* type, and the *consumption* type. The latter is the one most frequently used and it is this form of the VAT to which the greater part of this discussion is confined. The income type of VAT taxes wages and profits, and it is this type of tax which resembles the pay-roll tax, particularly when profits are effectively exempted through offsets for investment.

The tax base

The tax base of the value added tax can best be appreciated in terms of the national income identities. Assuming a closed economy with two factors, and writing C for consumption, I for gross investment, D for depreciation, W for wages, and P for net profits after depreciation, Gross domestic Product = $C + I = W + P + D$. In the VAT of the product type, all expenditure is taxed without any allowance for capital expenditure, and the base is equal to GNP (= C+I). If depreciation is allowed for, the tax base becomes $C + I - D = W + P$, which is the income base for the tax. Finally, if all capital expenditure is exempt, the base becomes $GNP - I - D = C$, and the tax is a VAT of the consumption type.

For an open economy, the tax can better be defined in terms of the adjustments which are made to the value added through the various stages of production to turn the tax into a VAT of the consumption type. This yields the following definition:

> A single tax, collected in stages, upon the value of final home consumption of goods and services. This is neither gross domestic product nor is it net domestic product nor net value added (gross domestic product less the value of capital used up during the period). It is *net* value added *less* additions to capital stock, *less* exports, *less* government expenditure on wages and salaries, *plus* imports. In fact, final domestic consumption.[5]

This definition not only clearly describes the tax base of the VAT of the consumption type, it also describes the method of collection which differentiates the VAT from the general retail sales tax on goods and services. The VAT is invoiced by each firm on the sales of its final output but a credit is claimed by the firm for the VAT it has paid on its inputs. The final consumer, who cannot claim a tax credit, therefore pays the whole of the tax. This much more extensive system of collection — all producers and not only retailers are taxpayers — is considered to be one of the advantages of the tax because it prevents a large part of the tax evasion which is possible under a retail sales tax.

The definition is also based on the *destination principle*, whereby exports are excluded from the tax base and imports from abroad are included. The *origin principle*, on the other hand, exempts imports but includes the value added created by the export sector in the tax base. The destination principle taxes only those goods destined for domestic consumption; the origin principle taxes all value added created domestically. The VAT collected on the basis of the destination principle is the one used in the Common Market countries.

The purpose of the most frequently used VAT is therefore to tax all consumption of goods and services within the country in which it is imposed. In practice, this is not generally the case. Many countries have introduced exemptions for political, social or administrative reasons. The treatment of agriculture in Europe is an example of the first, the exemption of medical services and services rendered by charitable and non-profit organisations an example of the second, and the exemption of very small business in many countries is an example of the third. Other essentials, such as food, footwear, and clothing, are also frequently exempted in many countries for social reasons. This is discussed in more detail below.

Recent experience with the introduction of VAT in countries like New Zealand suggests that the administrative necessity of exempting certain goods can be greatly exaggerated. In addition, to reduce compliance costs and enhance administrative simplicity, a VAT base with no exemptions is the ideal to be aimed at, while subsequent detrimental distributional consequences can be solved outside the tax system.

The rate structure

A single proportional value added tax rate on all consumption with no exemptions considerably reduces the administrative expenses of the tax. Multiple rates introduce a more than proportionate increase in administrative costs and in compliance costs of the taxpayer. In spite of this, many of the European countries have multiple rate structures which differentiate between "basic necessities" and "luxury goods". The reason for this is that lower rates on basic necessities reduce the adverse distributional impact of the tax on low income groups. However, it is more administratively efficient and horizontally equitable to maintain a single rate on all consumption and alleviate the plight of low income groups through the social security system. This was the essence of the compensation proposal put forward by the Federal Government in its 1985 proposal for broad-based consumption taxation.[6]

Two further points on the rate structure should be made. A zero rate of VAT is not equivalent to an exemption. An exempt firm does not charge VAT to its consumers but also cannot claim a credit for the VAT paid on its inputs; a zero-rated firm likewise does not charge VAT to its consumers but because it is within the VAT system, it can claim a tax credit for the VAT paid on its inputs.

A distinction should also be made between the tax inclusive and tax exclusive manner of quoting VAT rates. For example, Finland and Sweden have tax inclusive rates, most other European countries tax exclusive rates. Tax inclusive rates have the virtue of being lower than tax exclusive rates for raising equivalent revenue from the commodities taxed. This is demonstrated by their interrelationship, expressed as

$$t_e = t_i \cdot \left(1 - \frac{1}{1 - t_i}\right)$$

where t_e and t_i are the tax exclusive and tax inclusive rates respectively. A tax exclusive rate of 10 per cent becomes a tax inclusive rate of 9.09 per cent, for example.

Economic considerations of the VAT of the consumption type

Where value added tax has been introduced, it has generally been as a substitute for other forms of taxation such as turnover taxes, sales taxes or excise, or its introduction has been combined with a reduction in personal income tax, company tax or payroll tax. The revenue potential of the tax is tremendous. A general VAT of the consumption type with no exemptions and a rate of 1 per cent would have had a gross yield of approximately $1700 million in Australia in 1987–88, a rate of 16 per cent would have raised revenue equivalent to the yield of all outlay taxes (State and federal) then levied in Australia.

Incidence of the VAT

Because the value added tax when introduced is generally part of a package deal of tax reform, it is differential tax incidence which is the appropriate tool of analysis. The national accounting assumptions on which the tax has been constructed presume a 100 per cent passing on of the tax to final consumers in the form of higher prices. This need not be the case, however, and in practice the price effects on the introduction of a VAT have been found to vary considerably. Two factors are important here. First, the type of tax for which VAT is introduced as a substitute; if this is an outlay tax then its removal will cause a drop in prices which offsets part of the price increase induced by the introduction of VAT. Secondly, the state of the economy and the degree of competition — for example, if the economy is in a recession with low levels of demand, there is a strong likelihood that producers will absorb part of the tax. It is therefore not surprising that international experience about the inflationary consequences of the introduction of VAT has shown substantial differences.[7]

Income distribution and VAT

It is generally argued that a value added tax is regressive as to income and that therefore it is not a suitable tax from the point of view of vertical equity. This is undoubtedly the case when the tax is comprehensively levied on *all* goods and services at a uniform rate. When the tax zero-rates most essentials, and taxes luxury goods and services at rates above the standard rate, the tax may become progressive. However, because of the high administrative costs associated with a multi-rated VAT, a number of countries, particularly the Scandinavian ones, have removed the adverse distribution consequences from VAT by other policy action, most frequently through adjustments of their social security benefits. As already indicated, this policy was also adopted by the Australian Government when it proposed the introduction of a broad-based consumption tax in 1985.[8]

Efficiency arguments in favour of VAT

One overwhelming efficiency advantage generally attributed to a VAT if comprehensively implemented at a uniform rate is its neutrality with respect to consumption expenditures. Generally speaking this raises welfare and horizontal equity especially when this effect of a VAT is compared with that of a highly selective commodity tax system as that used by Australia in the 1970s. This then raised 75 per cent of commodity taxation from motorists, smokers, and consumers of alcohol.[9]

Furthermore, although it is frequently implied that a VAT which exempts investment goods thereby stimulates investment, there is little positive evidence for this proposition from European experience. Such an investment effect is in any case strongly influenced by the types of taxes and their treatment of investment which the VAT is designed to replace.

Similarly, the alleged balance of payments advantages of VAT are easily overstated. The advantages in this respect from the liability of imports to VAT on the destination principle and the exemption of exports may be largely negated by the general loss of competitive advantage implied by the general rise in the price level induced by the introduction of VAT. In any case, adoption of more flexible exchange rate policy reduces the advantages, if any, from this consideration. However, because a VAT rebates indirect tax liability more effectively than is the case with other indirect tax systems like Australia's wholesale sales tax, some competitive advantage for exporters may be gained from replacing wholesale sales tax with VAT. Likewise importers lose the competitive edge they may gain from a wholesale sales tax regime as compared with a VAT.[10]

Administrative and compliance matters in relation to VAT

VAT has generally received a bad press because of its complicated collection procedures with the multi-stage invoice method and the consequent high administrative and compliance costs. Current research[11] on this subject shows that these are easily exaggerated and that, above all, they are strongly influenced by the nature of the tax adopted (that is, its comprehensiveness of ease and uniformity of rate structure). Other administrative and assessment features also influence these costs. Furthermore, when the tax is introduced to solve avoidance and evasion problems within the existing taxation system, VAT has considerable advantages through the self-policing features inherent in the invoice method of collection.[12]

Introduction of VAT

It is clear from this discussion that the introduction of VAT is most likely to be part of a package deal in tax reform; its introduction would be accompanied by the elimination or reduction of other taxes. In Australia, such a tax change could be most effectively carried out by the Federal Government, but with federal-State financial co-operation, because the States levy many important outlay taxes (especially payroll tax) which could usefully be eliminated on the introduction of VAT.

There would be other transitional problems with the introduction of VAT, particularly if the implementation of such a policy was designed to substitute consumption for income taxation to a considerable extent. The latter creates grave equity problems for those in or approaching retirement. From the point of view of administration the former requires an exhaustive education campaign in order to familiarise business with VAT procedures. The smooth introduction of the GST, New Zealand's VAT, illustrates the necessity of taking care of such transitional problems, the importance of which is now generally recognised in the literature.[13]

OTHER GENERAL FORMS OF CONSUMPTION TAXATION

In contrast with VAT, the other three forms of general consumption outlay taxes are either single stage — the retail sales tax and the wholesale sales tax — or direct — the expenditure tax. The major features of these three taxes which have all featured in Australian tax reform debate, are briefly examined in the remainder of this chapter.

The retail sales tax[14]

Retail sales taxes are now most conspicuously levied in three federations: the United States and Canada at the State and provincial level, and in Switzerland at the national level. In the rest of Europe, with the further exception of Iceland, retail sales taxes have been replaced with VAT; retail taxes are also used in some Latin American and Caribbean countries.

Tax base

The tax base of a retail sales tax is either aggregate turnover declared to the tax authority or collection on an individual transaction basis. Although in principle all goods and services can be brought within the ambit of a retail sales tax, most taxes in operation exempt producers' goods (generally including building materials) and essentials (such as food, clothing, and footwear, but more rarely furnishings, soft drinks, confectionery, and appliances) and no major retail sales tax attempts to tax services. The retail sales tax is therefore selective in practice.

Rate structure

Rates of retail taxes are invariably *ad valorem* and uniform for all transactions though Switzerland has a reduced rather than a zero rate for building materials. Rates are generally low; for example in January 1987 they varied from 2 to 8 per cent in the United States, 5 to 12 per cent in Canada, and are at 6.2 per cent in Switzerland. Rate variations in Canada and the United States are regional, not with respect to transactions. High rates in retail sales taxes, as some United States city and State experience has shown, encourages evasion of the tax and may therefore be counter-productive of revenue.

Other considerations

Retail sales tax is generally seen as a useful revenue raiser for sub-national jurisdictions in a federation but its revenue potential is limited at the national level because of ease of evasion. Being a single stage tax, it is relatively simple to implement and its compliance costs are generally speaking not high. At the moderate rates at which it is usually imposed, its regressive features and non-neutralities are minor. A single stage retail sales tax has been recommended for Australia on several occasions. Some have seen its introduction at the State level as the most appropriate solution to the revenue dependence which the States have experienced since 1942, but this, as more fully discussed in Chapter 15, requires amendment to Australia's Constitution. The broad-based consumption tax included in the preferred tax reform option of the Australian Government was likewise a tax at the retail level. As suggested earlier and discussed more fully at the end of this chapter, there is now a general consensus among tax economists that broad-based consumption taxation is best introduced by way of a VAT, particularly if the tax is to raise considerable revenue.

The wholesale sales tax[15]

The other form of single stage sales tax, levied at an earlier stage in the chain of production, is the wholesale and associated manufacturers sales tax. This form of sales tax is now mainly used in less developed countries for administrative reasons because of the simplicity advantages from a low number of tax points relative to retail sales tax. Hence its use in many African and South-East Asian countries. Among European OECD countries it is no longer in use, but it continues to be used in Australia despite its many defects, and in Canada, as a manufacturing tax, at the national level. Discussion of this tax here is confined to its Australian form where it was introduced in 1930 on the basis of Canadian experience in the 1920s.

Tax base

The tax base is the value of a wholesale transaction which invariably includes transactions of importers and manufacturers selling at the wholesale level. The Australian tax is a highly selective one, because it exempts classes of goods and classes of users while, in addition, different sets of goods are taxed at different rates. Definitional problems arising from the tax points and from goods classification add to its complexity.

Rate scale

The rate is *ad valorem* and in Australia has varied from 2.5 per cent to 66.6 per cent. Initially, the tax was levied at uniform rates but from 1940 onwards, a differential rate structure has applied which in 1951 used as many as six different rates. The rates in September 1985 were rationalised to a three rate structure of 10, 20 and 30 per cent but a new 50 per cent luxury car rate was added in 1990. As in the case of VAT, such differential rate structures greatly increase the compliance and administrative costs of the tax.

Other considerations

Distributional consequences of the sales tax are similar to those of a VAT and retail sales tax. A selective sales tax as discussed further in the subsequent section on partial outlay taxes is generally considered inefficient because of its lack of neutrality. In Australia, until the early 1970s, wholesale sales tax was frequently used as a stabilisation instrument for stimulating or reducing demand in particular sectors of the economy, especially the motor vehicle industry. It should also be noted that wholesale sales tax tends to be more inflationary than a VAT or retail sales tax since a wholesale tax (like the old fashioned turnover taxes replaced by VAT in Europe) produces a cascading effect on prices. Although in theory the tax is simple, the relatively high and differentiated rate structure combined with tax base problems have made it rather complex and subject to a considerable degree of avoidance and evasion. There is general agreement among economists in Australia that this tax should be replaced by either a retail sales tax or, preferably, a VAT. Reasons for the conclusion include the preference wholesale taxes give to backward integration of retailers, to importers and its inability to tax services.[16]

The direct expenditure tax[17]

On a number of occasions, as noted in Chapter 7, direct consumption expenditure tax has been justified on ability-to-pay grounds. Although such a tax has not been successfully implemented in any country, it has returned to public discussion in the debate of consumption versus income taxes. Its key feature is that it is directly levied on individual tax units usually by procedures which resemble personal income tax administration.

The tax base

This is often defined in terms of income with savings offsets. For practical administrative purposes the calculation of the tax base can be summarised as follows:

1. Bank balances at the beginning of the period.
2. *Plus* all receipts (from income, from borrowing, and from the sale of assets, including securities).
3. *Minus* all outgoings on non-consumption items (that is repayments of loans and purchases of securities and assets).
4. Minus bank balances at the end of the period.
5. Equals total consumption for the period in question.

In terms of the Simons/Carter comprehensive income tax base discussed in Chapter 9, the base can be expressed as $C = Y + W_t - W_{t+1}$ where C is consumption for the period, Y is income and W_t and W_{t+1} are wealth at the beginning and at the end of the period respectively.

Many economists see this tax base as a considerable simplification relative to personal income tax because it does away with the difficult distinction beween income and capital (including problems associated with capital gains and indexation).

It can be argued however, that direct expenditure tax raises the almost equally difficult problem of distinguishing consumption from saving. Reflect, for example, on the difficulty inherent in the expenditure tax treatment of housing though it should be recalled that housing creates as many, though somewhat different, difficulties, with respect to its treatment in personal income tax. In fact, as the literature on the subject abundantly demonstrates, there are as many administrative problems in this tax base as in the income base, if it is to be *comprehensively* taxed. This can be intuitively grasped from its relationship with the Simons/Carter income definition and the difficulties it encounters in tax administration.

A variation on this base was produced in 1989 by the National Priorities Project which proposed offsetting income by investment rather than saving where investment was defined as purchase of all income-earning assets except for housing and consumer durables. The latter would be financed (as under current personal income tax) from after-tax income but receipts associated with such assets, whether from imputed rental income or sales receipts (including capital gains) would be completely excluded from the tax base.[18]

Rate structure

Being a direct tax, it can be levied with a progressive rate structure and since at very high levels of income, consumption is generally speaking a relatively small fraction of total income, it is possible to have marginal tax rates greater than 100 per cent.

Other considerations in direct expenditure taxation

In principle the tax base is identical with those of the indirect comprehensive consumption taxes such as retail sales tax and VAT. The possibility of levying it at progressive rates makes it superior on distributional grounds to them, other things being equal. The efficiency advantages with respect to saving (seen as major ones by its early protagonists Irving Fisher and Kaldor) depend very much on the precise administrative definition of the tax base and the savings offsets in the income tax it is designed to replace. The major problems with the tax are associated with its administration, where in practice substantial difficulties arise. This explains why no country has successfully implemented it.

CHOICE OF INSTRUMENT FOR BROAD-BASED CONSUMPTION TAX REFORM

It is useful to conclude this chapter on broad-based consumption taxes by discussing the advantages and disadvantages of the various forms of broad-based consumption tax which have been briefly examined in it. These were:

1. The indirect multi-stage VAT of the consumption type.
2. The indirect single stage, final stage or retail sales tax.
3. The indirect single stage, higher stage or wholesale sales tax.
4. The direct consumption expenditure tax.

It may be noted immediately that only the first and the fourth of these taxes are directly defined in terms of final consumption expenditure. Single stage sales taxes (both retail and wholesale) have bases wider than consumption since both retail and wholesale sales will include sales of producers' goods (inputs) which have to be exempted. As already indicated, this is generally the case for such taxes in practice, though where producers' goods have a direct use as consumer goods as well (petrol is one prime example, but other examples are stationery, office equipment, hand tools and a wide range of other commodities), turning such sales taxes into genuine consumption taxes can be complicated and can incur very high administrative costs. The broad-based consumption tax proposed for Australia in 1985 suffered from this shortcoming. A system which comprehensively exempts inputs from single stage sales tax liability greatly increases the number of registered tax points, hence reducing the simplicity advantages of single stage over multi-stage taxes in terms of the absolute number of tax points.

As already indicated, higher stage sales taxes compare badly with the final, or retail stage sales tax. This arises from inability to tax services easily, and from the non-neutralities inherent in their implementation because of the preference they give to backward integration and imported commodities. In addition, administrative and compliance costs can be very high in selective, multi-rated wholesale sales tax systems such as those in Australia, but this feature is common to all selective multi-rated tax systems. The smaller base (wholesale values are by definition smaller than retail values) also means higher rates for a given revenue, hence higher excess burdens, *ceteris paribus*.

A retail sales tax and VAT have much in common, the advantages of the last being largely of an administrative nature. The invoice method of collecting VAT eliminates inputs automatically from the tax base, though at the cost of increasing the number of tax points. This collection method also makes evasion more difficult for a VAT, a feature of the tax which becomes all the more important, the higher the rate at which tax is collected. The last point can also be interpreted as a drawback of VAT; with its greater facility for raising revenue, it may encourage public spending growth, while the limits on retail sales tax rates (set through difficult-to-control evasion inducement) provide a barrier to such public expenditure growth. Services are likewise more easy to tax under VAT, since the many personal services sold through small retail business can at least be partly taxed on the inputs they use, as is automatically the case under the VAT system. It is these features which now provide an undisputed case in favour of VAT if broad-based consumption taxation is desired.

This conclusion continues to hold when the VAT as indirect consumption tax is compared with the direct consumption expenditure tax, irrespective of whether it is defined in terms of receipts offset by savings or investment outlays. The direct expenditure tax is administratively very complicated, which is why it has never been successfully implemented. Its attractions are its distributional potential since it can be levied at progressive rates, unlike the VAT where administrative necessity makes a single uniform rate virtually essential.

One final point can be noted in connection with this evaluation of broad-based consumption taxes. All are relatively recent taxes, that is, taxes invented and implemented during the twentieth century, when more sophisticated industrial organisation and tax administration enabled their introduction as replacements for more primitive tax forms. The progress from higher stage to final stage sales taxes and, even more, the progress to multi-stage sales taxes, illustrates this particular aspect of change in tax structures, dictated as it were by the feasibility of their administration as society advances both technologically and organisationally. More traditional and primitive forms of outlay taxes still in use are examined in the next chapter, but many of these could be eliminated on a comprehensive consumption tax reform program.

SUMMARY

1. Outlay taxes can be divided into broad-based and narrow-based, general or partial. Broad-based taxes can be direct (the expenditure tax) or indirect. Indirect taxes can be multi-stage (VAT) or single stage — either at the final retail stage, retail sales tax (RST) or higher stages, wholesale or manufacturing stage.

2. A VAT can be of three types:

   (a) product, or C + I
   (b) income, or C + I – D = W + P

(c) consumption, or $GNP - I - D = C$ in a closed economy, or $GNP - I - D - X + M$ for an open economy on the destination method. The origin method excludes import and includes exports as part of national product.

3. A VAT rate structure can have differential rating but a single rate of tax is administratively most efficient. Exemption from the tax differs from zero rating; the latter entitles the taxpayer to rebates of tax paid on inputs, the first does not.

4. The inflationary consequences of introducing VAT depends on its actual incidence, the state of the economy on introduction, and the degree of competition affecting its trade. A flat rated VAT with few, or no exemptions, is generally regressive as to income.

5. A retail sales tax levies tax (generally at a single *ad valorem* rate) either on individual retail transactions (which facilitates exemptions and multi-rating) or on aggregate retail turnover.

6. A wholesale sales tax levies tax (at an *ad valorem* rate) on the wholesale value of a transaction, implying the need for imputing a wholesale value for imports and manufactures directly sold at retail. The nature of the tax base inhibits its application to services, causes distortions from tax preferences for backward vertically integrated retailers. The smaller number of larger tax points (relative to a retail tax) makes it attractive to developing countries.

7. The direct expenditure tax levies consumption expenditure directly by taxing all outgoings from receipts over the tax period apart from those adding to wealth. Re-writing the Simons' comprehensive income definition in terms of consumption, gives the base:

$$C = Y - W_t + W_{t+1}.$$

8. The reason why introduction of general consumption taxation is often supported is the encouragement it gives to saving but this effect can be overstated.

9. The VAT is now generally regarded as the best tax to implement a broad-based consumption tax regime largely because of the administrative advantages inherent in the invoice method of assessment and collection involving all stages of production. This enables complete elimination of producer goods from the tax base, makes evasion more difficult at high rates and allows the tax to be effectively collected even from small-scale service establishments.

NOTES

1 Taxation Review Committee, *Full Report* (Canberra: AGPS, 1975), ch. 27, esp. paras. 27.1–27.2; Draft White Paper, *Reform of the Australian Tax System* (Canberra: AGPS, 1985), ch. 13.

2 See Sijbren Cnossen, "The Technical Superiority of VAT over RST", *Australian Tax Forum* 4(4), 1987, pp. 419–64; Sijbren Cnossen, "The Value Added Tax: Key to a Better Tax Mix"; Peter Groenewegen, "The Australian Indirect Taxation Regime: Targeting the Defects", both in *Australian Tax Forum* 6(3), 1989, pp. 265–302; G.M. Bascand, "A Value Added Tax for Australia", in J.E. Head (ed.), *Australian Tax Reform in Retrospect and Prospect* (Sydney: Australian Tax Research Foundation, 1989), ch. 14.

3 For a discussion of international practice, see OECD, *Taxing Consumption* (Paris: OECD, 1988), ch. 5; Alan A Tait, *Value Added Tax: International Practice and Problems* (Washington D.C.: International Monetary Fund, 1988), esp. chs. 1 and 2.

4 See C.S. Shoup, *Public Finance*, pp. 251–7. This remains one of the best short accounts of the subject. See also OECD, *Taxing Consumption*, pp. 80–3.

5 From David Stout, "Economic Aspects of the VAT in the United Kingdom", in T.M. Rybezynski (ed.), *The Value Added Tax*, pp. 2–7.

6 Draft White Paper, *Reform of the Australian Tax System*, ch. 14.

7 For a detailed discussion see Alan A. Tait, *Value Added Tax*, ch. 10.

8 See the reference in Note 6 above. For the effect of a VAT on distribution, see Alan A. Tait, *Value Added Tax*, pp. 214–20.

9 However, as mentioned in Chapter 7, a general VAT of this type would not be optimal because of its inability to tax leisure. For a general discussion of the neutrality gains attributable to VAT, see Alan A Tait, *Value Added Tax*, pp. 220–1.

10 See Peter Groenewegen, "The Australian Indirect Taxation Regime: Targeting the Defects", pp. 293–5. Other aspects of the foreign trade effects of a VAT are examined in Alan A. Tait, *Value Added Tax*, pp. 222–6.

11 Cedric Sandford, Michael Godwin and Peter Hardwick, *Administrative and Compliance Costs of Taxation* (Bath: Fiscal Publications, 1989), ch. 8; cf. Alan A. Tait, *Value Added Tax*, pp. 268–9, 351–3, 401–4.

12 S. Cnossen, "The Technical Superiority of VAT over RST", *Australian Tax Forum* 4(4), 1987, pp. 458–62; Alan A. Tait, *Value Added Tax*, ch. 14.

13 The New Zealand experience is described in Peter Groenewegen (ed.), "Tax Reform in Australia and New Zealand", in *Australian Taxation Policy*, 2nd edn. (Melbourne: Longman Cheshire, 1987), pp. 162–3, 169–70. For a general discussion of transitional problems, see Alan A. Tait, *Value Added Tax*, ch. 9.

14 For a discussion of retail sales tax see OECD, *Taxing Consumption*, ch. 4; John F. Due, "The Implications for Australia of the Experience in the United States, Canada and other Countries with a Retail Sales Tax" in J.G. Head (ed.), *Changing the Tax Mix* (Sydney: Australian Tax Research Foundation, 1986), ch. 11; and for a detailed analysis of the Canadian retail sales tax, see A.J. Robinson, *The Retail Sales Tax in Canada* (Toronto: Canadian Tax Foundation, 1986).

15 For a general discussion see OECD, *Taxing Consumption*, ch. 4; for a detailed examination of the Australian tax see Peter Groenewegen, *The Australian Wholesale Sales Tax in Perspective* (Sydney: Australian Tax Research Foundation, 1983) which can be updated from his "The Australian Indirect Taxation Regime: Targeting the Defects", pp. 286–91.

16 For a summary of the case against high stage sales taxes, see P. Groenewegen, "The Australian Indirect Tax Regime: Targeting the Defects", pp. 292–6.

17 For a detailed discussion of this type of tax, reference should be made to: N. Kaldor, *An Expenditure Tax* (London: Allen and Unwin: 1955); *The Structure and Reform of Direct Taxation: Report of a Committee Chaired by Professor Meade*, chs. 8–10; Peter Mieszkowski, "Options for Tax Reform and the Expenditure Tax", in J.G. Head (ed.), *Taxation Issues of the 1980s*, ch. 3; and George M. Bascand, "Implications of Alternative Tax Bases: with Particular Reference to Direct and Indirect Consumption Taxes" in J.G. Head (ed.), *Australian Tax Reform in Retrospect and Prospect* (Sydney: Australian Tax Research Foundation, 1989), ch. 12.

[18] John Freebairn, Michael Porter and Cliff Walsh (eds.), *National Priorities Project 1989: Savings and Productivity: Incentives for the 1990s* (Sydney: Allen and Unwin, 1989), ch. 6, esp. pp. 118–24. The suggested tax treatment of housing and durable consumer goods opens a broad range of tax avoidance opportunities and widens the tax preference given to investment in what are largely unproductive assets from the social point of view.

FURTHER READING

Again, the general texts are useful. For example, see:

R.A. and P.B. Musgrave, *Public Finance in Theory and Practice*, 4th edn. (New York: McGraw Hill, 1984), ch. 20.

C.V. Brown and P.M. Jackson, *Public Sector Economics*, 2nd edn. (Oxford: Blackwell, 1986), chs. 17, 19.

The following will also be found useful:

The Structure and Reform of Direct Taxation, Report of a Committee Chaired by Professor J.E. Meade (London: Allen and Unwin, 1978), chs. 8–10.

N. Kaldor, *An Expenditure Tax* (London: Allen and Unwin, 1955), esp. chs. 1 and 7.

OECD, *Taxing Consumption* (Paris: OECD, 1988), chs. 1, 4, 5, 6, 8, 12.

Alan A. Tait, *Value Added Tax* (Washington: D.C.: International Monetary Fund, 1988), esp. chs. 1–6, 8–9, 10–11, 14, 18.

J.G. Head (ed.), *Australian Tax Reform in Retrospect and Prospect* (Sydney: Australian Tax Research Foundation, 1989), chs. 12–14.

Australian Tax Forum 6(3), 1989: Sales and Indirect Tax Conference, pp. 265–326.

13

Miscellaneous transaction taxes

The miscellaneous transaction taxes which are the subject of this chapter include some of the oldest taxes still in use, such as the excise, various gambling taxes and a number of stamp duties. Often such taxes — the durable excise is a very good example — were imposed on only a few commodities, generally ones that were imported in order to ease the burden of tax administration. Chapter 1 mentioned the relevance of these taxes for under-developed countries, not only for this reason, but also for distributive reasons. They have other desirable qualities as well, as David Hume pointed out two centuries ago:

> The best taxes are such as are levied on consumptions, especially those on luxury; because such taxes are least felt by the people. They seem, in some measure, voluntary; since a man may chuse how far he will use the commodity which is taxed. They are paid gradually, and insensibly: They naturally produce sobriety and frugality, if judiciously imposed: And being confounded with the natural price of the commodity, they are scarcely perceived by the consumers.[1]

The force of Hume's insight into commodity taxation can be illustrated by the fact that in Australia at the beginning of the 1970s nearly 20 per cent of all commodity taxation was levied on tobacco products and alcoholic beverages at the federal level, while the Australian sales tax covers such "luxury" items as jewellery, furs, cosmetics, toys, photographic, sound, sporting and travelling equipment, as well as the "modern luxury" of the motor vehicle. Similarly, State outlay taxes have concentrated on "unnecessary" consumption such as gambling, alcohol (liquor licences), tobacco consumption and, of course, the motorist. One partial outlay tax which falls outside this category is the payroll tax and this will therefore be discussed separately. Likewise, the financial duties and capital transfer taxes classified statistically as property taxes will be given a section of their own in this discussion, after dealing more generally with these miscellaneous transaction or partial outlay taxes.

THE TAX BASE

Generally speaking, the tax base of a partial outlay tax is the purchase or selling price of a commodity, or the quantity of a commodity, or of a group of related commodities, or of a service, transaction, or activity. In Australia, the following tax bases are used:

1. *The sale of a commodity or group of related commodities.* This includes sales tax and excise, the second of which is now confined to alcoholic beverages, tobacco, and petroleum products. The Federal Government by virtue of section 90 of the Constitution has an exclusive power over excise.
2. *Services.* This includes the entertainment tax on cinema performances levied in Tasmania in the 1970s, racing taxes, and the Commonwealth overseas departure tax.
3. *Transactions.* These include a number of stamp duties, the Commonwealth Bank debits tax, and the financial institutions duties levied by the States.
4. Taxes which confer the right to engage in an activity. These include liquor licences and other business franchise (licence) taxes levied by most States, the poker machine licence tax levied in New South Wales, casino taxes in Tasmania, Queensland, and the Northern Territory, and motor vehicle registration and drivers' licence fees.

The reason why Australian taxation of goods and services must be described as partial outlay taxation is clear from this description of the tax base. By and large, Australian outlay taxes concentrate on very few items of consumption expenditure. Apart from taxing items used by motorists, the drinker and smoker, such outlay taxes have concentrated on other items of luxury spending (wholesale sales tax), gambling, and financial transactions and property transfers. Even the State business franchise taxes, introduced from the 1970s onwards, have concentrated on tobacco and petroleum products, the associated liquor licences have been a more long-standing impost. Drawing on remarks made in Chapter 12, many of these taxes are wider than consumption taxes, taxing the inputs of business, hence raising business costs particularly in the case of transport. This narrowly focused transactions tax base is one reason for the substantial interest in broad-based consumption taxes in Australia, though the tardiness of reform in the area is explicable in terms of the attractive features of selective transaction taxes noted by Hume in the quote in the opening paragraph of this chapter. Before evaluating the economic issues raised by these taxes and the rate structures at which they may be imposed, some further observations need to be made on these taxes, recalling that wholesale sales tax (rather selectively used in Australia) was discussed in Chapter 12.

Excise

In general this can refer to any toll or tax, but more particularly it denotes a duty charged on home goods either in the process of their manufacture or before their sale to the final consumer. Australian practice confines excise to petroleum products, most alcoholic beverages, tobacco products and coal. Excise is levied at specific rates but crude oil and LPG levies have a more complex rate structure. The definition of excise is important in Australia, given the exclusive power to use this type of tax assigned to the Commonwealth by the Constitution. A generally acceptable definition is not easily found but the implicit qualities ascribed to excise systems by Cnossen[2] would conform to Australian excise practice. They are "Selective taxes on goods and services" and their certain but simple tax base specified in terms of physical quantities of goods by weight or volume enables application of specific rates (see below). The Draft White Paper, however, defined excise as a tax imposed on the value or quantity of production but indicated Australian tax practice imposed excises only on the quantity of production.[3]

Business franchise taxes

These are levied by all Australian States on wholesalers and retailers of the products taxed (tobacco, petroleum products and liquor) as a licence generally comprising a fixed fee plus an *ad valorem* rate applied to the declared value of the quantity sold by the business in the period two or more month(s) prior to the month of payment. These peculiar features of business franchise taxes are designed to distinguish them from excise duty, since if this was not done, their imposition would be constitutionally invalid for the States. In practice, they resemble selective sales taxes assessed and collected on the turnover method (if the fixed licence charge element in the tax is ignored). These fiscal federalism issues associated with business franchise taxes are further mentioned in Chapter 16.[4]

Gambling taxes

Another traditional form of revenue source, gambling taxes are widely used by Australian States raising between 9 and 10 per cent of State tax revenue, with the greatest (but declining) relative importance in New South Wales. Lotteries, poker machines, horse racing and casino games are the major activities taxed, generally in the form of licence fees combined with turnover taxes, which in some cases are levied at progressive rates. Despite their relative importance in Australia they have received little careful scrutiny until the 1980s.[5]

The rate structure

The rate structure of commodity or service taxation may be either *ad valorem* or *specific*. An *ad valorem* tax rate may give rise to arguments about the nature of the value to which it is to be applied. This is especially important in the case of customs duties where the value selected as the tax base can greatly affect the degree of protection offered by the tariff rate. On the other hand, in times of inflation, the revenue from a tax with *ad valorem* rates rises with the prices of the taxed goods. With *specific* rates there can be no quarrel about the nature of the tax liability because the rate is unambiguously expressed in terms of a physical unit. With inflation, the revenue yield declines relative to the value of the commodity, unless the rates are frequently changed. For this reason, the 1983–84 Budget introduced half-yearly indexation of excise rates. Specific tax rates in general tend to fall more heavily on low quality products rather than high quality ones in the commodity groups taxed by them, such as alcoholic drinks and tobacco products. For example, an excise on wine in terms of volume falls heavily on cheap flagon and cask wines and taxes expensive vintage wines lightly relative to their value. Similarly, tobacco taxes by weight favour more expensive brands when translated into *ad valorem* rates. In Australia wine is therefore taxed appropriately at the *ad valorem* rate of 20 per cent (in 1988–89), as has also been the case with beer from 1988–89. Excise rates are now only used to tax the alcohol content of beer, for example, at the rate of $12.58 per litre of alcohol (over 1.15 per cent) applicable to beer from 1 August 1989.

As was shown earlier, sales taxes are levied at *ad valorem* rates. These also apply to State taxes such as business franchise taxes, liquor licences and a number of stamp duties. Specific rates are used mainly for excise purposes. For beer, for example, the 1989 excise rate was given in the previous paragraph per litre of alcohol, excise on tobacco products rose to $46.47 per kilogram of tobacco. States levy specific tax rates on bookmakers' betting tickets and in stamp duty on third party insurance and cheques.

Economic considerations of partial outlay taxes

It is impossible to cover all the economic considerations relevant to the detailed analysis of partial outlay taxes. In many cases, these economic considerations depend on the type of partial outlay tax being considered. To take an example: the analysis appropriate to the tax on petrol is qualitatively different from that appropriate to a minor tax on an infrequently used commodity, since in the former a general equilibrium analysis is necessary whereas in the latter partial equilibrium consideration would be appropriate. Furthermore, the discussion cannot comprehensively cover the variety of partial outlay taxes at present used in Australia, especially at the State level.

Partial outlay taxes generally speaking fare rather badly on distributional grounds. These taxes tend to fall most heavily on the lower income groups, especially when they are imposed on commodities whose consumption is widely diffused through the community irrespective of income levels. The regressiveness of these partial outlay taxes was clearly illustrated in the disaggregated data of the general incidence of Australian taxation given in Table 8.1.

The taxes on alcohol, tobacco, and petroleum products and those on motorists in general, which were seen to account for the greater part of Australia's partial outlay taxes, are frequently defended on the grounds of the benefit principle. Smokers and drinkers, it is argued, impose large social costs on the community in the form of accidents, ill health, and pollution, and these costs warrant discriminatory taxation. Chapter 7 has already considered the benefit arguments used in connection with the taxation of motorists.[6]

Incidence of partial outlay taxes

As in the case of the value added tax, the economic incidence of a partial outlay tax is frequently assumed to be fully on the consumer of the good or service taxed; these taxes are supposed to be passed on 100 per cent in the form of higher prices. This situation appears to be practically relevant in the context of an increase in the rate of excise in Australia, which is not only expected to be, but is in fact immediately passed on in the form of higher prices to the full extent of the tax increase. This may not be the case with other partial outlay taxes. As was briefly shown in Chapter 8 in the example of the tax on wine, the theoretical incidence analysis is not so simple. Whether a partial outlay tax is shifted forward to consumers or backwards to producers depends on a wide variety of considerations: the nature of the relevant supply and demand elasticities, market conditions (which in theory can range from perfect competition to oligopoly and monopoly), the time period of the analysis, and the nature of the analysis (general as against partial equilibrium). There is a large literature on these subjects.

Partial outlay taxes as efficiency taxes

Partial outlay taxes can be used as efficiency taxes to tax undesirable commodities and hence curtail their consumption. Discriminatory partial outlay taxes can also be used to encourage certain activities such as labour-intensive forms of employment, but such uses of the tax system to influence the allocation of resources usually involve administrative difficulties and may yield perverse results. Similar arguments underpin the analysis of market solutions to the pollution problem. The taxing of polluting activities is a device whereby the costs of these activities imposed on the community can be included in the market price of goods and services so that their users pay for these social costs. The rise in price induced by the tax will also frequently reduce the output of these activities. The revenue obtained from the tax can then be used to compensate the victims of the pollution.[7]

Partial outlay taxes have been used for stabilisation policy, particularly for demand management in connection with specific commodities rather than for general demand management. The sales tax on motor vehicles has been used for this purpose in Australia, both to stimulate the demand for the product of this important industry and to curtail it.

Finally, Chapter 8 indicated that selective commodity taxation can also be defended on the basis of optimal taxation rules. The difficulties in taxing leisure as a consumption good, which have already been canvassed in previous chapters, means that "second best" efficiency results require higher tax rates on commodities complementary to leisure and lower rates on leisure substitutes. Other analyses suggest that if all goods cannot be taxed, the second best requires unequal tax rates inversely related to their own-price elasticities.

STAMP DUTIES AND OTHER TRANSACTION TAXES

As capital transfer taxes, stamp duties could have been discussed under wealth and property taxation in Chapter 11, but since many stamp duties are not capital transfer taxes, and stamp duties as a whole are transaction taxes, they are more appropriately dealt with in this chapter. Stamp duties not directly related to capital transfers include the following: those levied on insurance — here the tax base is the value of the life or of the property insured — and the surcharge on motor vehicle third party insurance levied at flat rates in Victoria, South Australia, Western Australia, and Tasmania. Stamp duty legislation varies from State to State — with one exception — and as shown in Table 6.1 their overall importance in the tax structure is relatively small. Uniform State legislation in connection with stamp duties on the conveyance of marketable securities through a broker was introduced to prevent distortions in the capital market following from different stamp duties.

The tax base

The tax base is generally the capital value of the transaction involved, such as the value of the property transferred by conveyance, or the value of the mortgage, or the value of the good or service sold on an instalment purchase plan. In other cases it is the transaction itself, independent of value: for example, the stamp duty levied on a third party motor insurance policy in most States or on the transfer of a bank deposit by cheque. Under Victorian legislation applicable at the beginning of 1983, no less than 22 items were liable to stamp duties ranging from transfer of real property and securities to that of motor-boats and to gambling transactions and credit cards. Likewise in New South Wales, stamp duty constitutes a charge on a wide range of legal documents and transactions.[8]

The rate structure

This can be a simple flat charge per transaction as, for example, the 10 cents stamp duty payable in New South Wales in 1989 for each transaction by cheque. Some stamp duties are charged at proportional rates, for example, the Victorian stamp duty on the transfer of motor vehicles of $5 per $200 or part thereof of the value of the vehicle, or in the current uniform stamp duty on the conveyance of marketable securities through a broker, where the rate is 30 cents per $100 (or 0.8 per cent) for subsequent business after the first $100 of business done. The most progressive rates of stamp duty are connected with the conveyance of property by gift or settlement.

Other considerations

Stamp duties have been criticised for raising the cost structure of industry, for increasing the expenses incurred in the purchase of a home, and for hindering the mobility of funds in the capital market.

The Campbell Committee would have strongly recommended the total abolition of stamp duties in the financial area had they not been so important for State taxation revenue-raising. They therefore put forward (as a second best recommendation) the introduction of an Australia-wide uniform financial duty specifically designed not to distort financial decision-making. As shown subsequently this recommendation provided the inspiration for the introduction of a Financial Institution Duty by New South Wales and Victoria in 1982, and South Australia, Western Australia, and Tasmania a year later.

Stamp duties as the Campbell Committee rightly diagnosed are used by the States only because of their revenue-raising potential. Although not important nationally as tax revenue raisers, for most States they rank second to payroll tax in importance in this respect. In 1987–88, for example, they raised over 30 per cent in New South Wales and Western Australia, over 25 per cent in Victoria and Queensland and from 15 to 20 per cent in South Australia, Tasmania and the Northern Territory. These varying yields partly reflect the non-uniformity in stamp duty practice among the States which was noted earlier. Part of this non-uniformity is explained by a desire in some States to attract financial business to their urban centres by providing stamp duty relief for certain transactions or total exemption from this tax. This has occurred particularly in Queensland and the Northern Territory and has created various stamp duty avoidance possibilities. Consequently, stamp duty avoidance has become a more serious matter particularly for New South Wales and Victoria, the States where Australia's major financial centres are situated.

Stamp duties are also inequitable, being often regressive with respect to income. This is partly because they are sometimes levied at flat proportional rates, but also because they fall on transactions, such as hire purchase, which are mainly used by low-income earners as frequently the only credit source open to them. Apart from their revenue-raising attractions for the States, stamp duties are therefore best described as "nuisance taxes", an undesirable consequence of the unsatisfactory state of intergovernment financial relations.[9]

FINANCIAL TRANSACTION TAXES

Financial institutions duty

Partly in response to the Campbell Committee's suggestion for uniform duty on financial transactions as a replacement for non-uniform stamp duties, Victoria and New South Wales in 1982 (followed in 1983 by all other States except Queensland) introduced a duty on the receipts of nearly all financial institutions. At the same time, these States also abolished some but by no means all of the more important stamp duties, and different ones in different States. The neutrality objective which provided the basis for the Campbell Committee's suggestion for such duties was therefore not achieved. This partly arose from the desire for tax competition by some States.[10]

The tax base

The tax base is defined as receipts by financial institutions or, in other words, all financial transactions engaged in by such institutions for the credit of their customers from both business and households. Such receipts therefore cover deposits, subscriptions and loan repayments, interest payments from their customers, as well as transfers between financial institutions themselves. Financial institutions are broadly defined to include not only banks, building societies, finance companies, credit unions, money market operators, cash management, and other unit trusts, but also credit card providers including retailers as well as stockbrokers and trustee companies. There are exemptions of certain receipts—for example, from banking by charitable institutions, by government and government authorities—while institutions with annual dutiable receipts of less than $5 million are also exempt. Additional exemptions apply to some further transactions such as clearing-house settlements between banks and for constitutional reasons, proceeds from the sale of goods. Special provisions apply to the receipt of short-term money market operators, as indicated below.

The rate structure

At 30 June 1988 and from introduction, a general rate of 0.03 per cent applied in New South Wales, Victoria and the ACT subject to a maximum of $300 per transaction. A lower preferential rate is provided for short-term money market dealers: this is 0.005 per cent calculated on the daily average liability per month of the operator's short-term dealings. In 1983 Western Australia introduced a rate of 0.05 per cent, but by 1988 this had been lowered to 0.02 per cent. Tasmania and South Australia have a rate of 0.04 per cent.

Other considerations in financial institutions duty

As compared with the stamp duties it replaced, the new duty is more neutral since it is more uniform. It is also more equitable, arising particularly from its less regressive treatment of hire purchase contracts. However, the exemptions provided for, and its absence in Queensland and the Northern Territory, mean that neutrality in financial transaction taxation has not been achieved. There appear also to be avoidance problems associated with the tax, largely arising from its non-uniformity. It has been suggested that the tax should be administered nationally, the revenue to be shared among the States.

Bank account debits tax

Neutrality in financial transactions was further diminished with the almost simultaneous introduction of a bank account debits tax by the Commonwealth Government in 1983. The base of this tax is all debit entries in a cheque (current) account with a trading bank, except debits reversing a credit and debits of the bank account debits tax but not debits such as the payment of Financial Institutions Duty. Accounts exempt from the tax are those of non-profit organisations, religious and charitable organisations, governments including foreign government organisations, and diplomatic and consular personnel.

The rate structure of the tax is progressive: 15 cents for all debits up to $100; 35 cents for those from $100 to $499, 75 cents on those from $500 to $4999, $1.50 from $5,000 to $9,999, and $2.00 on those of $10,000 and over in 1988–89.

The effects of this tax are clearly discriminatory by penalising users of cheque accounts, hence subsidising financial transactions through savings bank accounts, building societies, and credit unions. This distorts neutrality and horizontal equity. Vertical equity consequences — despite the progressive rate structure — are probably rather doubtful since the average rates of tax are relatively high on small transactions. Banks had special administrative problems on the introduction of the tax, and despite computerisation of current account transactions, the multiple rate structure makes it rather expensive to administer (0.5 per cent of revenue in 1987–88).

Its combination with financial institutions duty increases the distortionary impact of the tax, especially when the non-uniform stamp duties on cheques are also taken into consideration. The rationale of the tax — apart from its revenue potential and the need to widen the indirect tax base — has not really been explained by the Government, particularly since a further effect of the tax is encouragement of the cash economy. Tasmania, alone among the States, uses a similar tax but extended it to building societies and credit unions and charged it at a flat rate of 15 cents per $100.[11]

Payroll tax

The last important tax to be considered in this chapter is the payroll tax. This tax was introduced in Australia in 1941 as a concomitant to the *Child Endowment Act* 1941, because the revenue of this tax was to be earmarked for the payment of this particular cash social security benefit. The linking of payroll tax with social security conformed with United States practice and that of many European countries. By 1952 this link was completely abolished and payroll tax revenue was paid into the Consolidated Revenue Fund. In 1971, the Federal Government transferred the tax to the States, which since then have used it extensively by turning it into their major revenue source. The tax remains as a federal tax in the territories of the Commonwealth.[12]

The tax base

The tax base is the payroll or wage bill paid by employers in both the public and the private sector, but with certain types of employers exempt. These exempt wage bills include those paid by vice-regal and diplomatic establishments, public hospitals, religious or public benevolent institutions, and those Commonwealth authorities whose wages are paid from Consolidated Revenue Fund. The number of exempt employers has been increased at various times, mainly to include certain newly created international bodies operating in Australia and some further non-profit organisations.

A number of aspects of the base must be clarified. First, the wage bill is generally defined to include not only wages and salaries paid by the firm in question, but also commissions, bonuses, allowances and remunerations, and benefits in cash or in kind, now frequently described as the fringe benefits from employment. Although such fringe benefits have been rapidly growing in relative importance from the end of the 1970s, with practice varying considerably between industries, they have been difficult to include in the payroll tax base. Attempts by the Victorian Government to deal with the avoidance potential of fringe benefits in this manner proved eventually successful. Secondly, apart from the exemption of specific classes of employers, there is a general exemption of payrolls below a certain size. On introduction of the tax this amounted to $2,080 per annum; by 1975, the last year of uniformity in this respect, it had risen to $41,600. By January 1988 exemptions varied from $299,000 in the ACT to $400,000 in New South Wales. The declared aim of this exemption is to aid small businesses but it also yields administrative savings. In a period of rapidly rising money wages, the exemption has to be continuously raised and preferably should be indexed with reference to the annual wage bill incurred for, say ten male employees, paid at average wage rates. States have preferred more discretionary adjustments to automatic indexation. In its 1983–84 Budget, for example, the Victorian exemption limit was raised from $140,000 to $200,000 but this increase was designed to encourage increased employment offers by firms and not by the rise in money wages of the previous year. To prevent payroll-splitting for tax avoidance purposes, States have provided for group taxation of payrolls by combining those of all related and associated parts of an organisation.

From the mid-1970s on, exemptions from payroll tax have also been given for certain classes of employees, partly as a method of short-term employment creation. For example, in 1977 New South Wales introduced a general exemption in connection with the employment of young, inexperienced workers from the payroll tax with respect to their wages for a period of one year. Policies to exempt the wages of apprentices in whole or in part from payroll tax have likewise been introduced. Exemptions are also frequently given for firms establishing business in remote areas as part of decentralisation policy.

The rate structure

The rate at which payroll tax is levied was initially a single, proportional rate, which on its introduction in 1941 and until its transfer to the States remained at 2.5 per cent. When the States took over the tax it was quickly raised to 3.5 per cent, then to 4.5 per cent and from 1 December 1974 to 5 per cent. Since then, States have increasingly departed from rate uniformity. The Northern Territory levies the tax at 4.5 per cent. In 1981 New South Wales and Victoria introduced a surcharge of 1 per cent on payrolls in excess of $1,000,000. In 1983 this surcharge affected 11 per cent of Victorian employers, but these employers contributed 89.1 per cent of payroll tax. Victoria abolished this surcharge in 1987–88 to introduce a general rate restructuring based on a sliding scale. Western Australia, Tasmania and the Northern Territory likewise imposed surcharges by 1987–88, the first as part of a generally progressive rate scale with steps of 3.75 and 4.75 per cent before a maximum 6 per cent was reached. Apart from such explicit departures from uniformity in rate structure it should be noted that the uniformity of rates for all States had long been only nominal. The diversity in exemption limits and shading-in provisions gives substantial differences in *average* rates for pay-rolls of equal size in the various States irrespective of the surcharge, reflected in the substantial variations in marginal rates which faced employers at different levels of annual payroll.[13]

Other considerations in payroll tax

The payroll tax is a much criticised tax and many have advocated its abolition,[14] particularly since the emergence of severe unemployment in the 1970s when it has come to be regarded as a tax on employment. The validity of this last argument is examined later, when the incidence of the tax is examined, as is the criticism of the tax based on the fact that it is "inflationary", due to its "cascading" effect on prices in a system of mark-up pricing. A further criticism of the tax is that it is inequitable because it taxes firms irrespective of their capacity to pay. Even if the firm makes a loss, it is still liable to pay the tax. This argument applies, of course, to all other outlay taxes and charges which are paid by the firm and not only to payroll tax.

The incidence of payroll tax

The incidence of payroll tax is still very much a disputed matter. It is generally concluded that the tax payment is shared by employers, workers, and consumers, but it is difficult to determine proportions; in short, the tax is capable of being shifted forwards or backwards or both. The empirical evidence on the subject, as is usual in the case of tax incidence, is not conclusive.

There are several theoretical arguments to support such a broad conclusion. The neo-classical argument on the incidence of payroll tax is based on the marginal productivity theory of employment: rational behaviour and competition lead an employer to employ additional labour up to the point where the wage rate is recouped by the marginal value product of the labourer. When a tax is placed on the payroll, the marginal worker(s) either take a cut in real wages or face unemployment. The incidence of the tax therefore impinges fully on the worker. Other economists, particularly in the post-war period, have argued that the tax is treated as part of the variable costs by the firm, and that this cost will be passed forward in the form of higher prices, subject to the state of demand and the degree of competition in the market. In slack periods, for example, an increase in the tax would be absorbed, thereby leading to a short-run reduction in profits; in the longer run it would lead to curtailment of production and unemployment. This second type of analysis suggests that there are several possibilities open, that is, changes in the tax can affect prices, profits, employment and wages.[15]

Efficiency considerations

The payroll tax was used as an "efficiency" tax by the Federal Government to encourage the export sector. During the 1960s and the early 1970s, the Federal Government gave payroll tax rebates to exporters, the amount of rebate depending on the growth in their export sales. This system ceased to operate in 1974. It was shown earlier that many States use payroll tax exemptions for a variety of purposes ranging from decentralisation to the encouragement of apprenticeship training and employment creation. Like all selective outlay taxes, the payroll tax can be used to influence resource allocation. This last proposition has taken on particular significance in the context of the association between payroll tax and unemployment. Prior to the high unemployment rates which commenced during the mid-1970s it was frequently argued that the payroll tax was an efficiency tax since by taxing the employment of labour it encouraged the adoption of more mechanised processes, thereby raising labour productivity. With high rates of unemployment, this substitution effect attributed to the tax was seen as its major deficiency and increased the clamour for its abolition. As indicated by the Victorian State Committee into revenue-raising which attempted to probe the economic consequences of payroll tax, it is very difficult to determine the extent of importance of such a substitution effect. An answer to this question requires "extensive theoretical and applied" analysis in which the "nature of the assumptions will most probably determine the results" and where "even the most sophisticated analysis is unlikely . . . to provide a universally accepted answer".[16]

Other economic considerations

On distributional grounds the payroll tax fares as badly as most partial outlay taxes though this conclusion depends on the incidence assumptions used. The lack of uniformity and hence of regional neutrality has already been noted but its importance for distorting interstate investment decisions can easily be exaggerated. Finally, although the tax appears simple and easy to administer, this statement no longer applies with its former force. Compliance costs can now be high particularly for firms operating across borders. Furthermore, avoidance opportunities and incentives to take advantage of them appear to be increasing thereby making it less easy to administer. However, the high revenue contribution of payroll tax for the States together with its low collection costs make its abolition unlikely except as part of a general reform of outlay taxation and intergovernmental financial relations.[17]

SUMMARY

1. The base of selective transaction taxes include:

   (a) the sale of a commodity or group of related commodities;
   (b) specific services;
   (c) specific transactions;
   (d) the right to engage in a specific activity.

2. Excise, a tax on domestic production, is generally levied on quantities of production by specific rates.

3. Business franchise taxes are levied for constitutional reasons on turnover of the dealers in the taxed commodities in some previous specified period and may embody a fixed element or licence to trade in the taxed commodity.

4. *Ad valorem* rates (expressed as a percentage of the tax base) are distinguished from *specific* rates (expressed as a fixed money sum per unit of weight, or volume of the item taxed). Indexation of specific rates is required to preserve the revenue in times of inflation.

5. Selective taxes, despite their non-neutrality, are useful as a means to internalise externalities, such as those involved in alcohol and tobacco consumption, and more generally, in the context of polluting activities.

6. Stamp duties are levied on a variety of legal documents and transactions, largely for revenue reasons. In Australia they are particularly important revenue raisers for the States.

7. Basically for revenue reasons, Australian governments also levy a number of financial transaction taxes.

8. The base of a payroll tax is the wage and salary bill, though in Australia with a value exemption to exempt small business. Specific exemptions to certain classes of employees have sometimes been used as a means of short-term employment creation.

9. The incidence of payroll tax is said to be on consumers if the tax is shifted forward through higher prices, or on producers (lower profits or reduced wages or employment) if shifted backwards. The possible employment consequences of the tax have induced considerable criticism of its use in Australia, and explain its relative decline as a State tax revenue raiser.

NOTES

[1] David Hume, "Of Taxes" (1752) reprinted in T.H. Green and T.H. Grose (eds.), *Essays Moral, Political and Literary*, (London: Longmans 1875), vol. I, p. 358.

[2] S. Cnossen, *Excise Systems: A Global Study of the Selective Taxation of Goods and Services* (Baltimore: Johns Hopkins University Press, 1977), pp. 1 and 4. A useful history of excise is Graham Smith, *Something to Declare. 1000 Years of Customs and Excise* (London: Harrap, 1980). The simplicity and certainty of the base made the tax easy to assess and collect.

[3] Draft White Paper, *Reform of the Australian Tax System* (Canberra: AGPS, 1985), p. xi, cf. Chapter 6 above, p.106. See also B.J. Gordon, "What is an Excise Duty? Nineteenth Century Literature and the Australian Constitution", *HETSA Newsletter* No. 11, Winter 1989, pp. 22–42.

[4] New South Wales Tax Task Force, *Review of the State Tax System* (Sydney: Government Printer, 1988), ch. 21, pp. 273–4; Peter Groenewegen, "Innovation Possibilities in State Business Taxation", in *Review of the State Tax System*, vol. 2, *Commissioned Study* (Sydney, 1989), pp. 309–13.

[5] Jim Johnson, "Gambling as a Source of Government Revenue in Australia", in G. Caldwell, M. Dickerson, B. Haigh and L. Sylvan (eds.), *Gambling in Australia* (Sydney: Croom Helm, 1985), pp. 78–93; T. Alchin, "Gambling Taxes: The Milch Cow of New South Wales", *Economic Papers* 2(1), May 1983, pp. 74–83; New South Wales Tax Task Force, *Review of the State Tax System*, ch. 22. Details of rates and base can be obtained from Commonwealth Grants Commission, *Annual Reports*, Appendix on State and Territory Taxation.

[6] As the Taxation Review Committee, *Full Report* (Canberra, AGPS, 1975) paragraphs 27.14–17.18 pointed out, such selective taxation is corrective of the externalities imposed on the rest of the community by the activities taxed. For a recent United States estimate of these costs see Michael Crossman, "Health Benefits of Increases in Alcohol and

Cigarette Taxes" (Cambridge, Massachusetts: National Bureau of Economic Research, Working Paper No. 3082, August 1989).

[7] "Developing Government Responses to the Threat of the Greenhouse Effect", *Economic Roundup*, The Treasury, Canberra, November 1989, esp. pp. 12–13.

[8] See *Report of the Committee of Inquiry into Revenue Raising in Victoria* (Melbourne: Victorian Government Printer, 1983), pp. 329–50, esp. p. 331 which lists the various duties used in the early 1980s; New South Wales Tax Task Force, *Review of the State Tax System*, ch. 20. Information on State stamp duty systems can be obtained from the appendix on State and territory taxation included with the Annual Reports of the Commonwealth Grants Commission.

[9] Such incidence matters are raised by the Committee of Inquiry into Revenue Raising in Victoria, vol. 1, pp 184–5; New South Wales Tax Task Force, *Review of the State Tax System*, pp. 84, 86. The description of these taxes as "nuisance taxes" is from P.D. Groenewegen, "Tax Assignment and Revenue Sharing in Australia", in Charles McLure Jr. (ed.), *Tax Assignment in Federal Countries*, (Canberra: Centre for Research on Federal Financial Relations, 1983), p. 309. For a good theoretical treatment of stamp duties, see C.S. Shoup, *Public Finance*, pp. 402–6.

[10] *Report of the Committee of Inquiry into Revenue Raising in Victoria*, vol. 1, pp. 381–8, on which much of this section is based. See also New South Wales Budget Speech 1982–83 (Sydney: Government Printer, 1982), pp. 21–2. The Queensland Government announced in April 1983 that it would not introduce such a duty, and at the same time announced stamp duty reductions to attract business to the State. This unilateral decision violated the aims of tax neutrality desired by the Campbell Committee.

[11] 1982–83 Budget Speech (Canberra: AGPS, 1982), p. 32; 1982–83 Budget Paper no. 1, Budget Statements 1982–83 (Canberra: AGPS, 1982), p. 243. ACT rates are higher because of the initial absence of a Financial Institutions Duty in the Capital Territory (which ended in 1987).

[12] Details of these can be found in Commonwealth Year Books for the relevant years. In 1971–72, States raised 21.6 per cent of their tax revenue from payroll tax. This was raised to 35.6 per cent in 1974–75 but by 1981–82 had fallen to 33.8 per cent, and by 1987–88 had fallen further to 25.8 per cent.

[13] See New South Wales Tax Task Force, *Review of the State Tax System*, Table 18.3, p. 211; while the whole ch. 18 is worth studying as a useful analysis of current problems with Australian payroll tax. State variations in payroll tax can be monitored from the Appendix on State and Territory taxation in the *Annual Reports* of the Commonwealth Grants Commission.

[14] See P.D. Groenewegen, "Taxation Policy", in F.H. Gruen (ed.), *Surveys of Australian Economics* (Sydney: Allen and Unwin, 1983), vol. 3, p. 233 and the literature there cited.

[15] For a discussion of the incidence of the payroll tax, see R.A. and P.B. Musgrave, *Public Finance in Theory and Practice*, 4th edn. (New York: McGraw Hill, 1984), pp. 495–7. For a more detailed discussion of both theory and empirical evidence, see J. A. Brittain, *The Payroll Tax for Social Security* (Washington, D.C.: The Brookings Institution, 1972), chs. 2 and 3, and for an Australian discussion, Neil Warren, "Spatial Incidence of Selected New South Wales Taxes", in New South Wales Tax Task Force, *Commissioned Studies*, ch. 7, pp. 94–118.

[16] *Report of the Committee of Inquiry into Revenue Raising in Victoria*, vol. 1, p. 261, cf. pp. 262–3. See also D. McDonald, "A Review of the Payroll Tax from a Labour Market Perspective", in New South Wales Tax Task Force, *Commissioned Studies*, pp. 160–81.

[17] *Report of the Committee of Inquiry into Revenue Raising in Victoria*, vol. 1, pp. 242–5, 269, vol. 2, pp. 550–5. Payroll collection costs remain very low at 0.24 per cent as compared with 1.08 per cent for total State taxation (ibid., vol. 2, p. 641). The finding of the New South Wales Tax Task Force which reported five years later in 1988 appears to be similar. See *Review of the State Tax System*, ch. 18 and esp. pp. 213–19. Collection costs in 1986–87 were 0.1 per cent (ibid., p. 90).

FURTHER READING

For many of the taxes discussed in this chapter, the basic texts provide little information, apart from payroll tax and excise analysis. See, for example:

R.A. and P.B. Musgrave, *Public Finance in Theory and Practice*, 4th edn. (New York: McGraw Hill, 1984), ch. 23.

S. Cnossen, *Excise Systems: A Global Study of the Selective Taxation of Goods and Services* (Baltimore: Johns Hopkins University Press, 1977).

For the other taxes, reference should be made to more specialist Australian literature, namely:

Report of the Committee of Inquiry into Revenue Raising in Victoria (Melbourne: Government Printer, 1983), esp. ch. 8, sections A, D, F, H, I, J.

New South Wales Tax Task Force, *Review of the State Tax System* (Sydney, 1988), esp. chs. 4–7, 18–23; *Commissioned Studies* (Sydney, 1989), esp. Studies 2, 3 and 5.

Jim Johnson, "Gambling as a Source of Government Revenue in Australia", in G. Caldwell, et al. (eds.), *Gambling in Australia* (Sydney: Croom Helm, 1985), pp. 78–93.

14

Fiscal federalism: theoretical considerations

Some of the most publicised questions in Australian public finance relate to intergovernmental financial relations. Premiers complain of "insufficient revenue" for their States and demand "more adequate revenue sharing arrangements"; ratepayers are discontented with rising rate burdens, and councillors stress the need to "stabilise" rates by giving local government greater access to national tax revenue; federal politicians defend or decry "central government interference" in State domains on the grounds of efficiency or the national interest; there are demands for regional government as a fourth tier of government in the federation, and proposals for the wholesale reform of the federal system. In later chapters it will be shown that the federal structure creates difficulties in such matters as tax reform, public borrowing and stabilisation policy in Australia.

This, and the following two chapters are devoted to issues of fiscal federalism. Theoretical issues of fiscal federalism, the relevance of which Australia shares with other federations and even with countries with unitary forms of government[1], are the subject-matter of this chapter. The subsequent chapters deal with problems of Australian fiscal federalism (Chapter 15) and more generally, with issues of State, local and regional finance (Chapter 16).

THE MERITS OF DECENTRALISED GOVERNMENT

The case for a federation can be made by listing the advantages which decentralised government is said to possess. Historically, such a case relies on the motivations of those who formed the federation by adopting a federal Constitution. In Australia in the 1890s the case for a federal union was based on the attempt to secure the advantages of a national union in foreign affairs — particularly with respect to defence and immigration — and even more in trade and commerce through eliminating the internal trade barriers and other forms of protective arrangements which characterised the commercial relations of the six founding colonies.

In addition there are a set of economic rationales for a federal system of government, but as is so often the case in public finance, these also reflect the political and social values of the economists who put them forward. The more important ones are briefly described in this section because they provide the foundation for the theory of fiscal federalism.[2]

As mentioned in Chapter 1, the benefits of some government services affect people in a restricted geographical location only, whereas those of many others are diffused over large areas. When the first type of service is provided by smaller units of government, there are important advantages to be reaped. People's tastes for public services differ. A number of decentralised governments can, by providing different goods and services, and by prescribing different by-laws (concerning such diverse matters as the standards of building, tree preservation, and the keeping of domestic pets), give the people a wider pattern of choice about their environment. At the same time, decentralised government brings government closer to the people by providing more contact between the electorate and their representatives. Finally, the more levels of government there are, the greater the possible diversity in the public expenditure/taxation mix and the greater the degree of choice that people have in these matters. If there is a wide diversity, and if there is considerable mobility in the population, then people can move to those areas whose range of taxes and services they prefer.[3]

It is also argued that decentralisation allows more effective collective decision-making. Fewer people are involved, there is more information available on the problems faced in the area; and there is greater chance of homogeneity of interests in a smaller area. Furthermore, in small decentralised areas, politicians have to be more specific in their programs and thus are more easily questioned on them by their constituents. In such situations, there is a much greater chance that the wishes of the people are met than in the case of large centralised government.

Finally, decentralised government provides opportunities for experimentation and innovation in the provision of services. Successful ideas introduced by one body will be copied by other bodies and the less successful innovations will involve waste in only a small area. Experiments are less frequent in a centralised system of government.

To some extent these listed advantages claimed for decentralised government have substance, but their merit can be easily exaggerated. For example, Australian local government units have powers which are too limited to permit them to be really innovative and original, as discussed more fully in Chapter 16. Uniformity rather than diversity is the rule, both at the State and local government level. Public services are highly centralised and there are considerable pressures to impose uniform or minimum standards of services on all the States. The drive towards "equal capacity" to provide services among the States, for example, is partly ensured through the special financial assistance provided to some States on the recommendations of the Commonwealth Grants Commission. The latter is discussed in Chapter 15.

Federal institutions have been aptly described as a compromise between the two principles of independence and nationality, between diversity and uniformity. The need for compromise implies the possibility of conflict and the relations between States and the Federal Government, particularly their financial relations, provide plenty of illustrations of both. This chapter examines the basic issues of the economics of federalism, starting with a more formal analysis of the benefits of decentralisation, before looking at the important issue of allocating budgetary functions in a federation, the associated question of tax assignment and revenue sharing in a federal system, and the rationale for intergovernmental grants.

The optimal fiscal community

In the previous section, attention was drawn to the geographical dimension of benefit diffusion in the case of some public goods, which suggests that service delivery units other than national government may be a more efficient allocational device. With the possibility of spatial benefit diffusion, there is, as the Musgraves [4] put it, "an *a priori* case for multiple jurisdictions". From this proposition, it is a simple step to argue that for each public good, or group of public goods, there must be a community or government level whose size in terms of population (or population density in some cases) is optimal with respect to provision of that good.

A simplified approach to this complex issue initially assumes one pure public good, the benefit incidence of which is limited to a given geographical area, that is, it yields no benefits outside that area. Incomes and preferences of residents are assumed to be homogenous, so that there is unanimity on the virtue of providing the public good in question. It will be recalled from Chapter 4, that with a pure public good, per capita benefit is not affected by the number of persons involved in its consumption. Cost savings from cost sharing, or the technical conditions of production of the public good, are therefore a crucial factor in determining a solution, which, in the absence of other factors, and on the assumption of increasing returns to scale, suggests the largest possible[5] size as optimal. Diminishing returns in production of the public good then becomes one limiting factor on size. Another is the disadvantage of crowding. The optimal community size can then be initially determined by equating at the margin per capita service costs for a given level of public service with the cost of crowding. This is shown in Figure 14.1.

Given a particular service level of the public good, say Q_1, the cost per capita continually declines but at a decreasing rate as N, the number of persons in the community increases. This is the basis for C_a in Figure 14.1. Cost savings from each additional unit of population (the marginal curve, C_m) therefore likewise declines. With increased size of the community, costs of crowding rise as shown in curves R_a and R_m. Optimal size for service level Q_1 is determined at N_1 when marginal congestion costs equal the benefits in cost savings from cost sharing. If service size was expanded to Q_2 the cost saving curves would shift outwards, to Ca_2 and Cm_2, and optimum community size would expand to N_2.

The next step in the argument is to determine the optimal service level for any particular group size. This is illustrated in Figure 14.2 which shows service levels Q on the horizontal axis, unit cost per capita on the vertical axis on the assumption of a given community size, N. The shape of the unit cost (supply) schedule, depends on the technical conditions of production (production function) of the public good in question as well as on community size; the supply schedule for a community with double the number (N_2) being vertically half below the supply schedule pertaining to community N. If costs are shared equally, a demand schedule DD determines the optimum service level for each community size.

Optimum size and service level can be determined simultaneously by combining the results from Figures 14.1 and 14.2. Figure 14.1 enables the construction of a relationship between service level costs C and community size N. (C_1 for N_1, C_2 for N_2, and so on). This is graphed as NN in Figure 14.3. Likewise, Figure 14.2 enables a linking of community sizes with optimum service levels (Q_1 for N_1, Q_2 for N_2 and so on), a relationship graphed as QQ in Figure 14.3. This, in combination enables determination of optimal service level and community size as an overall optimum for the public good in question.

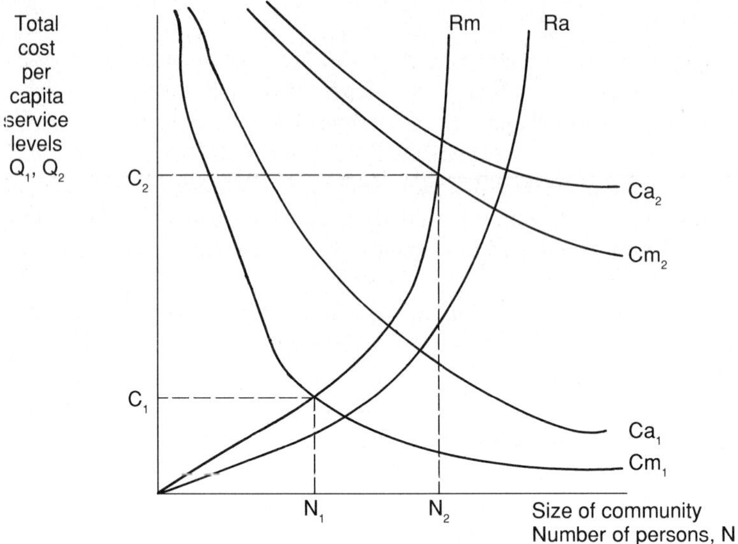

Figure 14.1 Optimum size of community for given service levels Q_1, Q_2

C_{a1}, C_{a2} curves: average (per capita) service cost for service levels Q_1, Q_2 (i.e. Q_1/N, Q_2/N).

C_{m1}, C_{m2} curves: marginal savings in per capita service costs (i.e. Q_1/N^2, Q_2/N^2, or the negative slopes of the C_{a1}, C_{a2} curves).

R_a curve: average (per capita) crowding cost.

R_m curve: marginal per capita crowding cost.

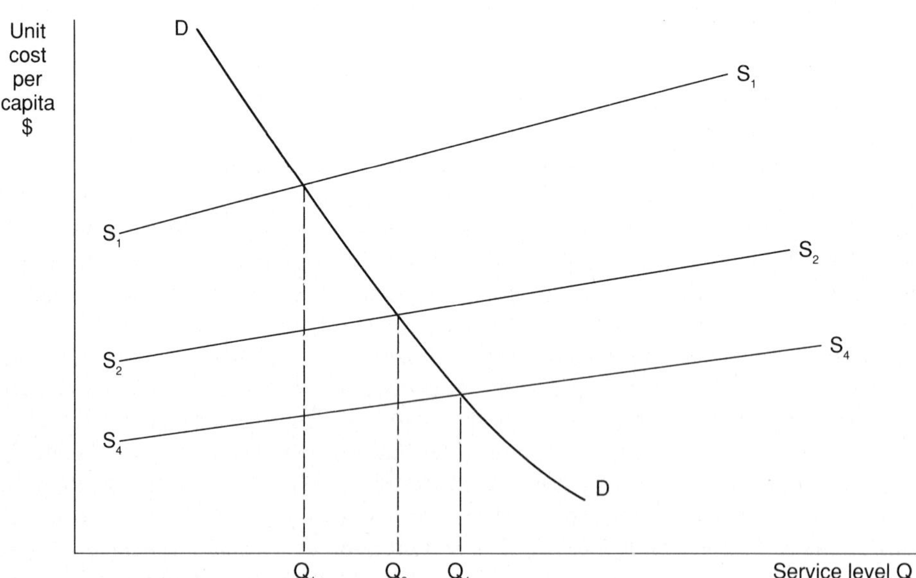

Figure 14.2 Optimum service level for given community size

Note: S_1S_1 reflects unit costs for community N, S_2 S_2 for community N_2, S_4S_4 for community N_4 where N_4 is double N_2, N_2 double numbers of N.

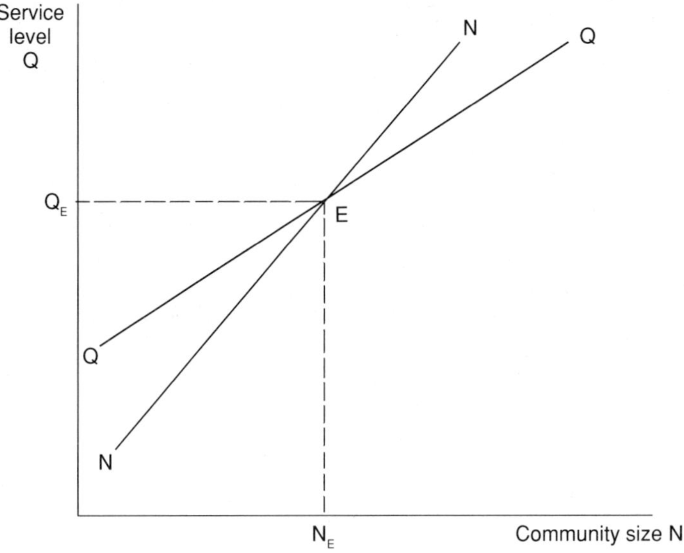

Figure 14.3 Optimum community size and optimum service level

This simple model of efficient design suggests the efficiency for multiple fiscal units differing in size and regional scope, depending on tastes, the production function and the congestion costs for each particular public good, about each of which it made quite specific assumptions.

Differing tastes among members of the community will alter the result, efficient outcomes being secured when people with similar tastes are grouped together in specific communities. The importance of taste differences can be intuitively grasped from Figures 14.2 and 14.3 since the demand curve shift implied in differing tastes will alter the relationship between Q and N and hence the shape and position of the QQ curve in Figure 14.3. Likewise, abandonment of the pure public good assumption will raise congestion costs for the particular service in question, hence altering the relationship between Q and N reflected in the NN function in Figure 14.3 derived from Figure 14.1. Furthermore, economies of scale affect the relationship by invalidating the independence between service level per capita costs and community size (assumed in the construction of Figure 14.2). Last, but not least, if benefits from a particular public good are not uniformly diffused, but vary with distance, spill-overs between jurisdictions may occur, particularly in the case where some of the benefits have a wider geographical dispersion than others.

All of these considerations modify the efficiency case for decentralisation in public goods supply; enhancing it in situations where tastes are different, congestion costs are real, diffusion of benefits is spatially non-uniform; and reducing this case when technical economies of scale in production or distribution exist. To enable revelation of preferences by voting by feet (moving) as discussed in Chapter 4, sufficient local communities must be available to satisfy fully the optimal levels of service demanded for particular public goods by particular sections of the community. This suggests a higher level of decentralisation than practised in most countries, and the value of tying particular public service provision (such as water supply, fire protection, police, and education) to quite specific levels (and sizes) of jurisdictions. An aspect of this is examined at the end of Chapter 16.

ALLOCATION OF FUNCTIONS IN A FEDERATION

In Chapters 1 and 2 it has already been shown that the Australian Constitution, in particular, section 51, apportions the functions of the Federal and the State governments and that the States' local government legislation designates the functions and powers of local government. The Constitution makes no explicit mention of the budgetary functions, however, and it is therefore useful to discuss how these budgetary functions might rationally be divided among the various levels of government. As also shown in Chapter 2, these functions are generally classified into three, namely the allocational, the distributional and the stabilisation functions.

The allocational functions

If the view is accepted that the functions of providing specific services should be allocated to the various levels of government according to the area over which their benefits are diffused, then national defence, foreign affairs, and international trade policy, for example, are clearly the responsibility of a federal government, whereas street lighting, kerbing and guttering are highly localised benefits and therefore fall under the aegis of local government. The analysis of the previous section devoted to optimal community size and service levels shows that this type of assignment is more complex in practice, resting as it does on factors other than the diffusion of benefits. Some of these can now be briefly reiterated.

In the first place, a large number of government services cannot be so easily allocated on this principle, because some of their benefits are localised while others cross local government and State boundaries. For example, the education provided by a local school has an obvious benefit to its immediate local recipients, but there are also the wider benefits derived from an educated workforce which will spill over to the entire community. As shown in Chapter 5 in the discussion of the incidence of education expenditure, the difficulties in apportioning such benefits between "consumers" and "producers" of education services are considerable. It is just as difficult to separate the localised from the external benefits as a basis for practical cost sharing arrangements. This issue is of special relevance when examining the rationale for specific purpose payments.

In transport, the multi-level funding of roads is partly founded on this principle. Local government finances local urban roads, the State departments of main roads finance the highways which link the different provincial localities, while the national highways and some parts of the inter-State network are funded by the Federal Government. This division of responsibilities according to whether the road is a "local", "intra-State", or "national" one is of course rather simplistic, for in practice it is difficult to say of any road whether it fulfils a "local", a "State", or a "national" purpose, and many roads fulfil more than one function.

In addition to these spill-over effects, economies of scale provide a second reason why services with primarily localised benefits are carried out by larger instrumentalities than local government. An example is provided by the New South Wales county councils which distribute, and Elcom which produces electricity. Electricity supply also provides an example of federal-State co-operation: the Snowy Mountains Hydro-Electric Authority provides electricity to several States as well as to the Australian Capital Territory. The scale of operations made this a national project. The same justification can be used for the allocation of a wide range of functions to State governments or to the larger semi-government authorities, rather than to local government.

The aim of a federal system claimed by its supporters as its major advantage, that is, providing diversity and public choice, is best secured through supplying as many public goods as possible at the local and regional government level. This implies decentralisation and lack of uniformity in public goods supply. From a libertarian perspective, such local and regional freedom fosters local pride, enhances the welfare of local residents and improves the responsiveness of government to residential demands. This is argued to raise the efficiency and quality of public goods provision. The cost of such diversity is a lack of uniformity and unequal access to the provision of public services. In the developments of the Australian federation, equality of opportunity in education, health, transport and other publicly provided services has generally been seen as more important than diversity and has hence fostered a high degree of centralisation.[6]

The tax assignment issue

In theory, the principle of matching benefits to government areas can be extended to the division of taxing powers, so that those taxes whose impact is mainly local (the tax base is immobile) and whose assessment and collection involves no great economies of scale are assigned to local and State governments. This is why local rates are considered to be a useful local government tax, but the argument is difficult to apply to many other taxes and their distribution among the other two levels of government in Australia.

More generally, tax assignment rules have been put forward which suggest broader possibilities for the allocation of specific tax instruments to sub-national jurisdictions. On the basis of fair access to revenue and efficient resource use, implicit in his subdivision of the budgetary functions into allocational, distributional, and stabilisation branches, Musgrave[7] has argued that the following six principles of tax assignment can be put forward:

1. Middle and especially lower-level jurisdictions should tax those bases which have low inter-jurisdictional mobility.
2. Personal taxes with progressive rates should be used by those jurisdictions within which a global base can be implemented most efficiently.
3. Progressive taxation, designed to secure redistributional objectives, should be primarily central.
4. Taxes suitable for purposes of stabilisation policy should be central, while lower-level taxes should be cyclically stable.
5. Tax bases which are distributed highly unequally among sub-jurisdictions should be used centrally.
6. Benefit taxes and user charges are appropriate at all levels.

Taken together, these six principles provide justification for integrated and comprehensive income and expenditure taxes, natural resource taxes and user charges at the national level; income tax, destination-based commodity taxes, natural resource taxes, and user charges at the middle or State-provincial level, while at the local government or regional level there is room for property and payroll taxes as well as user charges.

The implicit case for tax centralisation to which this type of argument leads can be questioned and modified on a variety of grounds. First, it relies substantially on the exclusive assignment of distributional and stabilisation functions to the central government. Secondly, it ignores the diversity which federalism requires to ensure the efficiency consequences of decentralisation. It also eliminates the benefits of competition between jurisdictions in public goods supply and its financing. The case for tax centralisation is likewise advanced by a frequently unwarranted belief in the economies of scale associated with national tax administration. The fiscal problems associated with combining revenue raising are an important issue in practical discussions of intergovernmental financial relations in federations and countries with unitary levels of government.[8]

The distributional functions

It is generally agreed that the major explicit distributional policies should be carried out by the national government. A State government, for example, which either placed on, or removed, taxes from the wealthy would encourage their migration to or from other States. The abolition of death duties in Queensland in 1976 provides an example of the need for co-operation between the federal and State governments in distribution policy through taxation. Queensland's move initially led to some migration of wealthy and aged persons (and companies) to that State with the consequence that revenue losses through death duties were partly compensated by the increased tax revenue collected from these migrants, particularly in the form of stamp duties revenue from real estate transactions. These effects induced the other States to follow Queensland's example and, as noted in Chapter 11, has left Australia without any form of general capital taxation. This illustrates the wisdom of assigning such distributionally oriented taxes to the national government, as the Taxation Review Committee argued in the case of death duties.[9]

Similarly, more generous social service provision in one State would attract migrants from other States. Social security became primarily a federal function after the passing in 1946 of one of the few successful referenda in Australia's constitutional history. During the referendum campaign, it was argued that all Australians should enjoy uniform standards of social services. The lower levels of government continue to have an influence on distributional objectives through their taxation and expenditure policies. However, the policies with the most explicit distributional impact — progressive income taxation and social security income maintenance schemes — are federal matters.

The public choice proponents of federalism basing their case on the benefits of diversity secured through federation by differing tax and spending mixes at the regional level, argue that since all taxes and expenditures have distributional consequences, this central assignment of distributional responsibilities would destroy revenue and expenditure independence for sub-national governments. It can also be argued that distribution, particularly in expenditure policy, has a spatial dimension. This partly arises when benefits are diffused over a small area (for example, child care provision and local library services) but also because lower levels of government may be more sensitive to local distributional needs and tastes. It is therefore argued that the chances of Pareto optimal distribution can be said to be greater at the local than at the national level.[10]

The stabilisation and growth functions

Stabilisation policy is now accepted as a national responsibility though in Australia it was recognised as such only as a result of the Great Depression in the 1930s. Some major instruments of stabilisation policy such as money supply growth must be a national responsibility in a federation. In the evolution of federalism, the central government has also managed to gain control over the major source of taxation and over government borrowing. The experience of the 1970s has shown, however, that like the distribution objective, stabilisation policies require some federal-State co-operation if their objectives are to be successfully achieved. But, as in the case of distribution responsibility assignment, this conclusion has been questioned by a number of economists partly because some stabilisation problems, particularly those associated with unemployment, are best tackled by regional policies. Some of these matters are further pursued in Chapter 18.

The growth objective is perhaps the most difficult to allocate in a federation, because here inter-State and local rivalries predominate and may conflict with national priorities. Part of the achievement of the growth objectives is the formal responsibility of the national government—for example, immigration policy and control over national resources, but the State governments seek to encourage economic development within their own States. Accordingly, they endeavour to influence the flow of migration by such measures as their housing policies and charges set by public authorities for power, water-supply, and so on, and attract foreign investment to their States by means of delegations and agents permanently established abroad. The States also do not accept federal autonomy in the area of natural resources policy, as evidenced by the stopping of sand-mining on Fraser Island by the Federal Government (contrary to the wishes of the Queensland Government), and more recently, by federal intervention to prevent the damming of the Franklin River in Tasmania for electricity generation, the development consequences of which had been supported by Tasmanian voters in a referendum conducted by their State government. Similar conflicts over growth priorities between State and federal governments have arisen over offshore control of mineral resources, logging in State forests, Aboriginal landrights, uranium mining, the price of coal for export, the possibility of resource taxation, and so on. Even at the level of local government, development policies conflict with those of State planning authorities, for example, in connection with freeway construction, zoning regulations for building, commercial development, and so on.

Conflicts in the budgetary objectives under federalism

Under a federal system, the possibility for conflict in achieving the budgetary objectives is therefore considerably increased. Some examples have already been given of how some States can snatch a momentary advantage at the expense of other States and to the detriment of national objectives. In a federation, such conflicts can be partly overcome by increased co-operation such as the exchange of information between the various governments, through the co-ordination of such activities as transport planning, and by the active intervention of the central government through the funding of national priorities by specific purpose grants. The last is discussed later in this chapter.

FURTHER FISCAL PROBLEMS IN A FEDERATION

Two further specific problems in intergovernmental financial relations which must be considered are the "vertical" and "horizontal" imbalance between revenue-raising powers and expenditure needs. *Vertical imbalance* is concerned with disparities between revenue sources and expenditure requirements among the various levels of government, and *horizontal imbalance* is concerned with such disparities among the various units within the same level of government.

Vertical imbalance occurs when for efficiency, or other reasons, decentralisation of expenditure functions has been more vigorously practised than decentralisation of revenue instruments including borrowing powers. This is the most frequent cause of the actual imbalance between expenditure responsibilities and revenue-raising powers exhibited in the practice of all major federations and even in that of many unitary governments.[11] Such imbalance is in practice resolved by grants from levels of government with spare revenue raising capacity to those with inadequate access to revenue sources.

Horizontal fiscal imbalance among members of a lower level of government in a federation arises both from cost disabilities in the provision of public services and from differences in their revenue-raising capacity. In turn, these are largely influenced by the different geographic, demographic and economic characteristics of the various units as reflected in the cost of services (for example, as in the comparative cost of providing a transport system in a densely, as compared with a sparsely, populated region) and in their relative capacity to raise revenue (for example, the possibility of extracting mining royalties can vary considerably between government units in practice).

Expenditure differentials originate from a great variety of factors. Some arise from population characteristics. A high proportion of schoolchildren in the population entails above average expenditure on education; a high proportion of aged people calls for greater social welfare and health expenditure; with increasing density of population, the cost of services at first falls through economies of scale but then, higher concentration of population, in the case of very large cities, may lead to diseconomies of scale. Resource endowment differences may influence the cost of providing services such as road and railway construction, the provision of water supply, electricity supply, and the construction and maintenance costs of public buildings and other public works.

The taxable capacity of a government unit is also influenced by these factors. A high proportion of people of working age in the population, low unemployment and above average earnings all enhance personal income per capita, and therefore enhance taxable capacity. The resource endowment of the government unit will influence the revenue obtainable from mining royalties, land taxes, and land sales. There are other, less obvious factors which influence the taxable capacities of individual jurisdictions. Population density influences the number of motor vehicle registrations; climatic factors influence the consumption of alcohol; disparate influence of religious groups may inhibit gambling and so on. Such factors affect the size of a jurisdiction's actual tax base and hence its taxable capacity. The first of these indicators, per capita income, may be called a global measure of taxable capacity; the others are more partial measures.

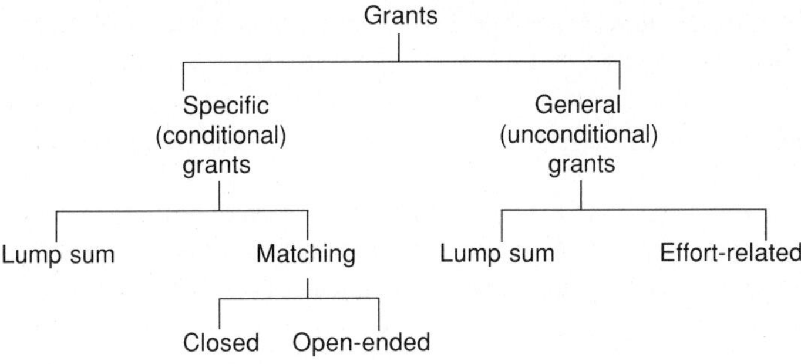

Figure 14.4 A hierarchy of grants in a multi-unit government system

Horizontal fiscal imbalance is likewise remedied by intergovernmental financial flows, either from the national government units or by an agreement among units of a government at a particular level to transfer resources from units fiscally well-endowed to less-well endowed fiscal units.

HIERARCHY AND THEORY OF GRANTS

Considerations of fiscal imbalance, both horizontal and vertical, suggest the important role of intergovernmental revenue flows or grants in a federal system. Earlier discussion, such as the funding of national priorities or the need for cost sharing where public good benefits cross sub-national government unit boundaries, suggested a further rationale for financial flows between levels of government in multi-government systems like a federation. The former problems of fiscal imbalance call for general revenue assistance; the latter type of problem implies grants tied to a specific purpose. This suggests a hierarchy of grants which are possible in multi-unit government structures, with different objectives and consequences for the various types of grant. This hierarchy is depicted in Figure 14.4.

General grants: objectives and consequences

The notion of fiscal imbalance provides the rationale for general grants from one unit of government to another. An imbalance between assigned expenditure responsibilities and revenue capacity of assigned tax instruments between levels of government (vertical fiscal imbalance) and between different units of the same level of government because of fiscal capacity differences (horizontal fiscal imbalance) can be solved by such general revenue grants. If the size of the grant is determined independently of the revenue-raising policies of the grantee government, it is a lump-sum grant; an effort-related general grant takes revenue-raising policy of the grantee government or, less frequently, its spending performance, into account in a specific way.

Although it could be argued that the size of general revenue grants designed to eliminate vertical fiscal imbalance should be determined by the extent of the inherent revenue gap, this is clearly not feasible. Such a revenue gap cannot be objectively measured since its extent as indicated by practice is subject to far too much influence by the grantee. This is one reason why effort-related general grants are often contemplated when such grants ensure that the grantee government is raising revenue at some generally accepted standard. Generally speaking, the size of annual revenue assistance tends to be fixed by specific historical circumstances, such as the conditions under which such grants were first paid. Some Australian illustrations of such determination are presented in Chapter 15. Once determined, the grant's growth can be regulated by a variety of factors, such as the rate of growth of wages and prices, sometimes grossed up by a percentage to permit improvement in the standard of services the grantee government can provide.

Equalisation grants

General revenue grants designed to alleviate horizontal fiscal imbalance can be designed either to ensure fiscal capacity equalisation or to ensure the equalisation of fiscal outcomes. The first determines grants by compensating for fiscal disabilities arising from assessed differences in revenue-raising ability and the costs involved in providing services to residents at a standard level. The second seeks to secure minimum standards of service level for all citizens in the country without particular sub-national jurisdictions having to resort to excessively high tax rates.

Questions of the standard, or the degree of equalisation to be aimed at, constitute a first problem in determining equalisation assistance. Should this standard be set at some arbitrary minimum level, which all States should reach; or should it be the national average achieved in the absence of equalisation; or should it be more ambitiously targeted at the level which the more well-endowed government units have reached in the absence of equalisation?

Secondly, what is to be equalised influences how the appropriate equalisation grant is determined and hence its outcome. Fiscal capacity equalisation requires a careful estimate of differences in taxable capacity and the cost disabilities in providing various services. As discussed more fully in Chapter 15 in the context of Australian fiscal equalisation practice, the taxable capacity measure may be global (income level per head to take a frequently used index of taxable capacity which was discussed in Chapter 7) or specific, that is, the relative size of the tax base of all taxes actually in use in the jurisdictions whose capacity is being equalised. In cost disability calculations, careful estimates have to be made about cost per unit, eligible population for the service (such as school-age children for education services) where the first require technical judgements not only about the cost function of providing the service in question but also on effects thereon of the degree of dispersion of eligible population and specific factors such as climate, terrain and like factors.

The consequences of general grants

Two factors may here be mentioned. If general grants for fiscal imbalance are provided, will they stimulate increased services? Or will they partly restrain tax revenue growth, because the grantee government uses the grant to curtail tax increases, perhaps in combination with a smaller degree of service growth than the size of the grant may have warranted. There is a large American literature on the impact of such grants on grantee behaviour, the results of which are not easy to summarise. Stimulus to increased spending by the grantees tends to increase with the degree of effort required by the grantees in maintaining or raising their spending levels from pre-grant levels.[12]

In equalisation grants, a major potential economic consequence is the degree to which such equalisation interferes with the right of the sub-national jurisdiction to make its own expenditure and tax-raising decisions. Fiscal outcome equalisation clearly tends to reduce this freedom. Supporters of fiscal capacity equalisation argue that its operation is neutral with respect to grantee fiscal decision-making. The last outcome, as Australian debate on the issue is demonstrating, is not independent of the precise manner in which fiscal equalisation is implemented.[13]

Specific purpose payments

Grantor governments may attempt to influence the spending patterns of other jurisdictions by making conditional or specific purpose grants. As shown in Figure 14.4 such grants may be lump-sum or matching. If matching, they may be closed, that is, limited to a maximum amount of subsidy by the grantor, or open-ended. Generally speaking, and in line with what intuition suggests, the success in stimulating spending on the preferred objective is considerably affected by the type of specific grant used; it is greatest with open-ended matching grants, and least with lump-sum specific purpose grants.

The imposition of grantor preferences inherent in the making of specific purpose grants can be justified in several ways. Where benefits from a generally locally provided good cannot be fully localised, cost-sharing through specific purpose grants can prevent the otherwise inefficient curtailment of the public good supply in question. Secondly, new initiatives in public good provision can be centrally fostered by such grants, particularly in the case of merit wants whose value is less appreciated in certain sub-national juris-dictions for social or cultural reasons.

Where, as in past Australian fiscal federalism arrangements, there are institutional rigidities from a necessity to apply allocation formulas in some circumstances without any flexibility whatsoever, provision of specific purpose grants may supply a means of correcting the subsequent misallocation. The Loan Council's rigid formula distribution of loan funds to individual States (referred to in Chapter 17) is an example.

Hence, although often criticised as incompatible with the spirit of federalism, specific purpose grants are able to enhance efficiency in resource allocation by the internalisation of externalities, providing "seed" money for new initiatives, and flexibility in resource transfers where traditional mechanisms can provide none.

The decentralisation advantages inherent in federal, or more generally, all multi-unit government structures, entail problems some of which are reflected in the fiscal imbalances apparent in most inter-governmental financial relations. Grants, with varying degrees of success, provide solutions to such problems. The theoretical approach to this fiscal federalism problem given in this chapter can now be illustrated and applied to Australian experience.

SUMMARY

1. Decentralised government has advantages in efficient public service provision arising from different preferences for such public goods, cost savings in signalling such preferences and a variety of other factors which make diversity in public good supply an important advantage of multi-unit government structures.

2. In theory an optimal fiscal community can be determined in terms of a single pure public good whose benefits are uniformly diffused over a limited geographical area in terms of congestion costs, per capita cost from cost sharing, the demand for the public good in question given uniform tastes, and the production function of the public good.

3. Optimal size becomes less specific to particular public goods when tastes are allowed to vary; outcomes allow for spillovers across jurisdictional boundaries; congestion costs become variable when rivalry in consumption is introduced (reducing the purity of the "publicness" of the service under analysis); while economies of scale introduce complex interdependencies between community size and service level.
4. The analysis suggests that specific spending (allocational) functions can be assigned to national, State or local levels depending on the specific characteristics of the goods in question in terms of benefit diffusion, homogeneity of preferences, conditions of production, and liability to congestion. Many of these suggest the desirability of a high degree of decentralisation in public goods provision.

5. When applied to tax assignment, these principles produce a more centralist outcome, since many tax effects are diffused nationally while tax assessment and collection is said to be subject to substantial economies of scale. When distributional and stabilisation budget functions are exclusively assigned to the central government, the case for tax centralisation becomes even stronger. However, much of a federation's quality for diversity is lost if it cannot have diversity in financing expenditure through choice of tax instruments.

6. Avoidance of national distributional intent at sub-national levels through migration makes central assignment of the distributional function a generally accepted principle. However, if distributional outcomes are regarded as societal objectives subject to varied preferences, central assignment of this function need not follow.

7. Spill-over effects of most macro-economic policy instruments make stabilisation a central government function. Its effective implementation requires sub-national government co-operation in certain cases.

8. Different degrees of decentralisation of expenditure and revenue-raising responsibilities can induce vertical fiscal imbalances by creating a disparity between revenue sources and expenditure responsibilities. Horizontal fiscal imbalance arises from different resource endowments yielding difference in fiscal capacity and costs of actual service levels.

9. Fiscal imbalances can be, and are, in practice, generally redressed by grants.

10. Grants can also be used to fund national priorities, to internalise external benefits from sub-national provided public goods. Specific purpose (conditional) grants best address this type of problem, general revenue assistance grants are used to solve both vertical and horizontal fiscal imbalances.

11. Grants to remedy vertical fiscal imbalance can be only imperfectly determined with respect to the revenue gap to be covered; their growth is generally determined by either keeping their real value intact in terms of purchasing power or costs, or sometimes marginally above this rate, to enable increased service provision.

12. Equalisation grants to remedy horizontal fiscal imbalance attempt to equalise fiscal outcomes or fiscal capacity. Both involve judgements about the standard of equalisation to be aimed at.

13. Grants have been criticised since their outcomes may have unintended consequences: general revenue assistance may not stimulate service levels to the desired levels, but lower tax burdens instead; equalisation grants may distort the efficient resource

NOTES

[1] For a discussion of the background to Australian federation see R.L. Mathews and W.R.C. Jay, *Federalism* (Melbourne: Nelson, 1972), ch. 2. See also Reports of the Advisory Committee to the Constitutional Commission, especially those on *Distribution of Powers* and on *Trade and National Economic Management* (Canberra: AGPS, 1987).

[2] There is an extensive literature on this subject, largely derived from the United States. For an excellent collection see B.S. Grewal, G. Brennan and R.L. Mathews (eds.), *The Economics of Federalism* (Canberra: ANU Press, 1980). A good summary is B.S. Grewal, *Economic Criteria for the Assignment of Functions in a Federal System*, in Advisory Council for Inter-Government Relations, Towards Adaptive Federalism, Part A (Canberra: AGPS, 1981), and in more detail, David King, *Fiscal Tiers, The Economics of Multi-Level Government* (London: Allen and Unwin, 1984).

[3] See B.S. Grewal, G. Brennan, and R. Mathews (eds.), Part 2, especially the essay by C. Tiebout, "A Pure Theory of Local Expenditure".

[4] R.A. and P.B. Musgrave, *Public Finance in Theory and Practice*, 4th edn. (New York: McGraw Hill, 1984), p. 303. Much of this section draws on their excellent account of this issue, and that in David King, *Fiscal Tiers, the Economics of Multi-Level Government*, chs. 1 and 2.

[5] Largest possible in terms of geographical or political, but not economic, limits of size.

[6] For a discussion, see C. Walsh, "Economic Aspects of Multi-level Government and the Distribution of Fiscal Responsibilities", in R.L. Mathews (ed.), *Responsibility Sharing in a Federal System* (Canberra: ANU Press, Centre for Research on Federal Financial Relations, Research Monograph, no. 4, 1975), ch. 1, esp. pp. 20–1. Whether Australian States public services provision is uniform rather than diverse has been investigated by E.M. Gramlich, " 'A Fair Go': Fiscal Federalism in Australia", in *The Brookings Survey of the Australian Economy* (Washington, D.C.: The Brookings Institution, 1984).

[7] See Richard Musgrave, "Who Should Tax, Where and What", in C.E. McLure Jr. (ed.), *Tax Assignment in Federal Countries*, pp. 2–19, esp. pp. 11 and 13. This whole volume is devoted to the subject and in Part 3 includes case studies of particular federations.

[8] For a detailed discussion, see Peter Groenewegen, "Taxation and Decentralisation: A Reconsideration of the Costs and Benefits of a Decentralised Tax System" (Sydney: University of Sydney Department of Economics Working Papers, No. 104, March 1988), in R.J. Bennett (ed.), *Decentralisation, Local Government and Markets*, (Oxford: Oxford University Press, 1990), ch.6.

[9] Taxation Review Committee, *Full Report*, paras. 24.7, 29.76, p. 453.

[10] For a percepive discussion of this matter see B.S. Grewal, "Economic Criteria for the Assignment of Functions in a Federal

System", op.cit., pp. 27–32 and the references there cited.

[11] A statistical analysis of such imbalances in the six major OECD federations is in Peter Groenewegen, "Taxation and Decentralisation", pp. 6–9.

[12] This is discussed in more detail in Chapter 15, in the context of an evaluation of debate on the resource allocation implications of Grants Commission equalisation methodology.

[13] This matter is discussed in some detail in Chapter 15.

FURTHER READING

The leading textbooks provide interesting additional perspectives on this topic:

R.A. and P.B. Musgrave, *Public Finance in Theory and Practice*, 4th edn. (New York: McGraw Hill, 1984), chs. 24–6.

C.V. Brown and P.M. Jackson, *Public Sector Economics*, 3rd edn. (Oxford: Blackwells, 1986), ch. 9.

J.E. Stiglitz, *Economics of the Public Sector*, 2nd edn. (New York: W.W. Norton, 1988), ch. 26.

More specialised treatment of the issue is given in:

B.S. Grewal, "Economic Criteria for the Assignment of Functions in a Federal System", in Advisory Council for Inter-Government Relations, *Towards Adaptive Federalism* (Canberra: AGPS, 1981), pp. 1–57.

In more detail:

David King, *Fiscal Tiers, The Economics of Multi-Level Government* (London: Allen and Unwin, 1984), esp. chs. 1–6.

For a useful collection of readings, see:

B.S. Grewal, Geoffrey Brennan and R.L. Mathews (ed.), *The Economics of Federalism*, (Canberra: ANU Press, 1980).

Tax Assignment issues are canvassed in detail in:

C.E. McLure Jr. (ed.), *Tax Assignment in Federal Countries* (Canberra: Centre for Research on Federal Financial Relations, 1983), esp. chs. 1, 3 and 4.

15

Australian fiscal federalism

Having examined the underlying theoretical principles which inform Australian fiscal federalism discussions, these principles can now be applied to an evaluation of Australian fiscal federalism issues. In this chapter, the assignment of functions in the Australian federation is briefly reiterated, partly to focus on the substantial vertical fiscal imbalance which has been present in the Australian federation for the greater part of the century. The solutions which have been, and can be, adopted to this imbalance are also investigated. A discussion of horizontal fiscal imbalance and equalisation grant procedures, followed by an examination of Australia's use of specific purpose grants concludes this chapter. Issues of State, local and regional finance are postponed to Chapter 16, while some fiscal federalism aspects of the Loan Council are raised in Chapter 17.

FUNCTION ASSIGNMENT IN AUSTRALIA'S FEDERATION

The nature of Australia's federal system as a three-tier structure of federal government, States and territories, and local government was described in Chapter 1. This description indicated, as did subsequent discussion in Chapter 2, that Australia's Constitution divides functions, including tax powers, between the Federal Government and the six sovereign State governments which formed the original federation, by naming specific powers assigned to the Commonwealth (Federal) Government and leaving residual powers to the States. Local government has no specific part in the federal compact, its limited powers derive from the relevant state legislation. Federal territories, now largely self-governing, share the characteristics both of States and local government; the Northern Territory since 1978 being fully statistically integrated with State financial data.

In combination, these general considerations and the actual assignment of functions in the Australian Constitution as interpreted over the years,[1] seem to have little resemblance to the theoretical assignment principles developed in Chapter 14. Much public service delivery has not been decentralised to the degree warranted by the specific aspects of the public good in question, that is, the preferences of its potential consumers, the technical conditions of its production, to name some of the more important variables which in theory determine optimum community size. Exceptions at the extremes of the spectrum are the national functions of defence, immigration, external affairs and trade and, at the local level, garbage disposal, sanitation, footpaths and access roads with their kerbing/guttering and lighting. Similarly, the actual division of taxing powers (historically illustrated in Table 6.1) has only limited resemblance to the tax assignment principles developed in Chapter 14. The exceptions, likewise, are at the national and local extremes: local rates as a tax on an immobile base are properly assigned to local government; while the integrated income tax has been assigned to the national level, as have other taxes required to secure effective stabilisation policy. However, contrary to what the conventional tax assignment principles indicate, Australian States no longer have effective access to income tax while they have never really enjoyed a right to levy destination based product or sales taxes.[2]

VERTICAL FISCAL IMBALANCE IN THE AUSTRALIAN FEDERATION

It is not as a consequence of applying traditional assignment rules that Australia experiences vertical fiscal imbalance. Vertical imbalance arises because the Federal Government has revenue resources far in excess of its expenditure needs, while the States and local government have insufficient independent revenue sources to finance their expenditure commitments. The nature of this vertical imbalance for Australia in 1988–89 is illustrated in Table 15.1.

Table 15.1 illustrates two situations of surplus or deficit for the three tiers of government; one before, and one after intergovernmental transfers have been taken into account. It can be seen that in the first case, the Federal Government has a sizeable surplus while the States and local government have a substantial deficit, thereby indicating a situation of vertical imbalance. When intergovernmental transfers and advances from one level of government to another are included, the situation changes: the federal surplus and the deficits of the States and of local government are likewise reduced. As explained in the notes to Table 15.1, the net deficit of the aggregate public sector which eliminates intergovernmental transfers approximates the public sector borrowing requirement, the importance of which is raised in Chapter 17.

Vertical imbalance in Australia can be simply explained by the constitutional position on taxing powers and expenditure functions for the States and federal governments, and the interpretations placed thereon by the High Court. The Court gave the Federal Government an exclusive power over taxation of the sale of goods (more specifically, customs and excise) and confirmed the effective powers which the Commonwealth gained over income taxation as a result of the Uniform Income Tax legislation of 1942. The historical perspective on vertical imbalance was illustrated by Table 6.1. It was shown that only in the period when the States could effectively use income tax for themselves (that is, the period between the two world wars), was there vertical balance with the States and the Federal Government raising revenue from taxes sufficient for their own expenditure requirements.

The vertical fiscal imbalance depicted in Table 15.1 is less marked than it was before the mid-1980s. Then States relied on revenue from grants for financing over 50 per cent of outlays, whereas by 1987–88 this had declined to 42.3 per cent. Own revenue sources rose from 39 per cent of outlays to 46.5 per cent over the same period. Local government's share

Table 15.1 Vertical fiscal imbalance in the Australian Federation 1987–88

	Federal $m	State [a] $m	Local $m
Net expenditure on goods and services			
Current	16 426	27 521	2 960
Capital	2 982	10 557	2 547
Transfers (net of inter-governmental transfers)	38 007	14 593	943
Total (own purpose) outlays	57 415	52 771	6 450
Taxation revenue	74 688	15 662	3 287
Other revenue	7 620	8 890	1 344
Total revenue	82 308	24 552	4 631
Surplus (+), Deficit (–) before intergovernmental transfers	+24 893	–28 219	–1 819
Net grants received (+) and (–)	–23 819	+22 339	+1 480
Surplus (+) Deficit (–) after intergovernmental transfers	+ 1 074	– 5 880	– 339
Net borrowing [b]	– 3 163	4 961	243
Increase in provisions	1 683	2 171	297
Advances	—	– 48	3
Net financial requirement [c]	– 2 757	3 760	39

Notes: a. Includes Northern Territory
b. Net borrowing of $2041 m. approximates gross public sector borrowing requirement.
c. Net financing requirement of $1042 approximates net public sector borrowing requirement

Source: ABS, *Government Financial Estimates Australia 1988–89* (Canberra: 1989, Cat. No. 5501.0). 1987–88 data are still preliminary.

of outlays financed from its own taxation remained stable at around 50 per cent over the 1980s, while its reliance on government grants fluctuated between 20 and 25 per cent. A number of aspects of this vertical fiscal imbalance or revenue gap for the States and for local government should be mentioned.

In the first place, this situation does not accord with the equality between tax revenue and expenditure which the pure theory of public expenditure suggests as an efficiency requirement. It is this lack of power over their aggregate expenditure and concomitant lack of responsibility in spending decisions financed from sources not controlled by the States which the commentators on vertical imbalance in Australia most frequently criticise. The discipline of an effective Budget constraint in the form of matching taxation to expenditure is removed from both levels of government. The Federal Government, with an excess of revenue largely obtained without the necessity of raising tax rates, can spend relatively freely. It is argued that the States similarly do not exercise proper controls over their expenditures because they are largely financed from non-tax sources, and because they can blame any consequent deficiencies on the inadequacies of Commonwealth grants.

The dynamic aspects of the problem should also be appreciated. Changes in revenue bases because of differential growth rates in output and living standards combined with altered expectations about the provision of public services may change the relative size of the revenue gap. This can be clearly illustrated from local government experience. Growing costs and expenditure responsibilities combined with a relatively inelastic revenue base has meant that this level of government has increasingly relied on intergovernmental transfers though, as shown subsequently in Chapter 16, expenditure restraint has come to the fore when grants have been curtailed.

Solutions to the fiscal problems of Australian federalism

In a multi-government system, there are four possible approaches to the problem of vertical imbalance: the transfer of expenditure powers from one level to another; the transfer of tax powers; intergovernmental transfers or grants; and institutionalised revenue sharing. In varying degrees, all four approaches have been utilised in the many attempts to solve the problem of chronic vertical imbalance in the Australian federation.

Transfer of expenditure powers

Although the transfer of powers under certain conditions from the States to the Federal Government is provided for by the Constitution in section 51 (xxxvii), this device has not been frequently used. Some examples include the transfer of the railway system of Tasmania and the country section of the South Australian system to the Federal Government in 1975, and the acceptance, in 1974, by the Commonwealth of the responsibility for funding tertiary education. This is not to say that the Federal Government has not tried to increase its spending powers. It has attempted to amend the Constitution to extend its powers on several occasions; in only one important case, the social security amendment of 1946, was this successful. This extended the Commonwealth power to pay invalid and old-age pensions — section 51 (xxiii) — by including the power to pay "maternity allowances, widow's pensions, child endowment, unemployment, pharmaceutical, sickness and hospital benefits, medical and dental services, benefits to students, and family allowances" — section 51 (xxiiiA). The importance of this amendment is indicated by the fact that for 1989–90 estimated expenditure on these items approximated $19 billion or over one fifth of the total outlays of the Federal Government.

The strategy more frequently used by the Federal Government to extend its effective spending powers is through its power to make grants to the States for specific purposes as part of its wide grants power given by section 96 of the Constitution. Specific Purpose Grants, which were introduced in the 1920s, greatly increased in importance in the post-World War II period, peaking at nearly half of total financial assistance from the Commonwealth to the States in the mid-1970s (as shown in Table 15.2). This type of grant, which is discussed in more detail later in this chapter, gives the Federal Government considerable influence over State programs such as education, social welfare, housing and health.

Transfer of taxing powers

The effective transfer of the major taxing powers from the States to the Federal Government has been the basic cause of the vertical imbalance in Australian federalism. Since 1950 there have been some transfers of relatively minor taxing powers from the Federal Government to the States. For example, during the 1950s the Commonwealth vacated land tax and entertainment tax, thereby allowing the State governments to utilise these tax bases. As shown subsequently in Chapter 16, few States have utilised these tax bases to any extent. A more important tax transfer occurred in 1971 when the Federal Government ceded payroll tax to the States. As shown in Chapter 13, this tax is now a most important revenue-raiser for all States and for the Northern Territory. In 1978 the Federal Government provided an opportunity for States to levy surcharges and to grant rebates on personal income tax by passing the necessary legislation. No States took advantage of this opportunity, and it was abolished in 1989.

Since federation, most of the important tax transfers were in favour of the Commonwealth Government. At federation, the States yielded their major revenue sources — customs and excise — to the Federal Government in return for a fixed share of the net revenue collected for the first ten years of federation. In 1942, as a "temporary" measure for the duration of World War II the States yielded their income tax powers to the Federal Government. Despite subsequent constitutional challenges by the States to the High Court, this income tax power, concurrent with the States by Section 51(ii) of the Constitution, has been effectively retained by the Commonwealth. These federal powers over taxation have been further extended by the wide interpretation given by the High Court to the exclusive federal power to collect customs and excise revenue (section 90 of the Constitution). The business franchise taxes which the States implemented in the 1970s (see Chapter 13) are continually threatened with invalidation on the ground that they contravene the Commonwealth exclusive excise power. The Constitutional Commission in 1987 therefore recommended the deletion of excise from the exclusive tax powers of the Commonwealth to enable the States to levy the retail sales taxes their counterparts in Canadas and the United States use. This, like many of the recommendations of the Commission, has not been placed before the people as a referendum, and even if this were done, such a referendum would be likely to fail.

Intergovernmental transfers: financial assistance grants

The Commonwealth's preferred solution to the problem of vertical imbalance in Australia has been the creation of a system of grants for the States. Such grants have been paid by the Commonwealth from the commencement of federation.

When the States transferred exclusive powers to customs and excise to the Commonwealth at federation, the "Braddon clause" (section 87 of the Constitution) imposed a duty on the Commonwealth of paying no less than three-quarters of the net revenue collected from customs and excise to the States for the first ten years of federation. The Constitution also provided that the *surplus revenue* of the Commonwealth should be transferred to the States but such payments ceased from 1908 onwards. When the Braddon clause expired in 1910, the Commonwealth transformed the grants originally payable under section 87 into per capita grants of $2.50. With the ratification of the Financial Agreement in 1928 which established the Loan Council, these per capita grants were abolished by their conversion into a fixed Commonwealth grant for interest charges and Sinking Fund contributions on behalf of the States. Until 1942, no further general revenue assistance was given to the States by the Commonwealth, except as special grants for equalisation purposes.

When in 1942 the Commonwealth Government obtained exclusive income tax powers under the uniform income tax legislation, the transfer was accompanied by income tax reimbursement grants based on average State income tax collections in the two years immediately preceding the transfer of the taxing powers. These grants were designed to *compensate* the States for the loss of revenue incurred, and were for *general purposes*. In 1946, the arrangement for the distribution of the grant was changed to incorporate factors reflecting special fiscal need and provisions for its gradual increase were introduced. In the years up to 1959, frequent adjustments were made to the total grants payable as tax reimbursement as well as to the distribution of this grant among the various States for equalisation purposes.

In 1959 the system of tax reimbursement grants was replaced by new arrangements of paying financial assistance grants, the change in name indicating the permanence of the income tax transfer. The growth of these financial assistance grants — which incorporated the old tax reimbursement grants and the supplementary grants increasingly paid to the States during the 1950s — was regulated by a formula incorporating population growth and increases in average wages for the State in question as well as a betterment factor. These arrangements were reviewed every five years and marginal adjustments to them were therefore made in 1965, 1970, and 1975.[3] Between 1976 and 1985 financial assistance grants were replaced by what was intended to be institutionalised revenue-sharing. This is discussed in the next section. The new financial grants, introduced in 1985, largely because of financial stringency for stabilisation purposes (see Chapter 18), were to be adjusted initially to ensure fixed percentage real growth (1986–87 to 1987–88) but this was transformed to real declines in the fiscal years thereafter. Ad hoc adjustment has returned to this type of solution to vertical imbalance.[4]

Although by implication the grant system was designed to correct the vertical imbalance in the federation introduced by the income tax transfer, in practice the grants have also been used for both equalisation and other purposes. If vertical imbalance correction was the only objective, a fixed per capita grant, as that which applied in Australia from 1910 to 1927 would have been the appropriate instrument. However, differences in per capita general revenue allocations to the various States have characterised post-World War II financial assistance. The fact that they embodied ad hoc equalisation components until the mid-1980s is the explanation. Since then, their distribution to individual States has embodied per capita relativities as assessed on the principles of the Grants Commission. This is discussed in more detail in the section on remedies to horizontal imbalance.

Revenue sharing

A fourth solution to the vertical imbalance problem is provided by a system of institutionalised revenue sharing. Such a system of revenue sharing provides for the assignment of a fixed proportion of a nationally collected tax (or taxes) to other levels of government, the proportion decided on generally being subject to review among the parties to the agreement after a number of years. This system has been the basis of federal financial relations in West Germany, where the yield of the major taxes is shared among the Federal and State governments.[5]

From 1976 to 1985 Australia adopted a variant of institutionalised revenue sharing, initially in terms of a fixed proportion of federal income tax collection; from 1982 to 1985 in terms of a fixed proportion of all federal taxes. However, unlike the German arrangements, these proportions of revenue were not constitutionally guaranteed, and were in fact largely determined by the Commonwealth Government. The States therefore felt no real loss when the previous arrangement of financial assistance grants was restored in 1985.[6]

HORIZONTAL FISCAL IMBALANCE IN THE AUSTRALIAN FEDERATION

Horizontal fiscal imbalance was defined in Chapter 14 as a revenue deficiency for a unit of a level of government arising from fiscal disabilities. Such fiscal disabilities in turn were described as arising from differing taxable capacities — measured globally or specifically in terms of the tax bases to which the level of government in question has access, or from cost differentials in unit costs of delivering services arising from demographic, climatic or more general geographic factors.

The most casual observation suggests that horizontal imbalance is present among the States, for there is great diversity in such matters as resource endowment, size, population characteristics, climate, industrial development, and degree of urbanisation. Table 15.2 illustrates some of these characteristics and some of the economic indicators relevant to cost disability calculations and taxable capacity estimates. However, in the Australian federation such differences are far less pronounced than elsewhere.[7]

Local government units also have differentials in the cost of providing services arising from size, population density, geographical location, resource endowment, and degree of urbanisation. In addition, they have substantially different taxable capacities reflected in the variations of the per capita value of their tax base. It is not as easy to tabulate these differences because of the large number of local government units involved, but the studies carried out on this subject provide considerable evidence of their existence.[8]

As indicated already in Chapter 14, the existence of horizontal fiscal imbalance raises theoretical questions about the extent of equalisation with respect to both the services provided by the different governments and the tax burdens to be paid by residents. Such equalisation procedures are advocated because they increase the equality of opportunity for all members of the nation. But the equalisation procedures have an impact on the use of resources; by subsidising low income and high cost States, they may inhibit the movement of their resources to areas where their productivity is higher. Such factors are offset by the social and economic reasons for equalisation. Who, for example, would endure the harsh life of an outback mining settlement or a cattle station, if special provision for essential public services were not made? The degree of equalisation to be aimed for is a matter of difficult social and political judgement and this decision is not made easier by the fact that the precise efficiency effects of such equalisation policies are still a matter of dispute among economists.

The degree of standardisation of services implied in many equalisation policies runs counter to one of the alleged advantages of a federal system: the degree of diversity in the provision of goods and services by public authorities in a multi-unit government system. Equalisation procedures may also be misused to give grants to disadvantaged States for political purposes. In Australia, this possibility is greatly reduced by the fact that equalisation is conducted on the basis of assessment by an independent authority, the Commonwealth Grants Commission.

Correcting horizontal imbalance in a federation

Financial assistance through a system of special grants to the more disadvantaged States or local government units in a federation is one method of making equalisation arrangements for the purpose of correcting horizontal fiscal imbalance. This was the method used initially in the Australian federation for a substantial period. In addition, equalisation

Table 15.2 Selected demographic and other State disparities 1980

			NSW	*Vic.*	*Qld.*	*SA*	*WA*	*Tas.*	*Australia*
1.	Size distribution of population	%	36.10	27.48	15.48	9.12	8.85	2.97	100.0
2.	State population growth (annual average since 1977)	%	0.9	0.3	1.3	0.4	1.4	0.7	0.9
3.	Population density (persons per km^2)		6.48	17.37	1.29	1.33	0.50	6.31	2.27
4.	Urban* population as % of total	%	67.9	71.3	48.4	68.9	63.9	32.6	64.5
	Rural	%	11.2	12.2	19.9	15.2	16.3	25.5	14.0
5.	Age distribution 0–4	%	7.76	7.68	7.59	7.23	8.30	8.07	7.72
	5–18	%	24.01	24.85	24.46	24.07	25.49	25.98	24.50
	19–64	%	58.34	58.00	57.86	58.62	57.65	56.59	58.04
	64 and over	%	9.89	9.47	10.39	10.08	8.56	9.36	9.74
6.	Non-English speaking persons as % of population	%	11.58	14.68	5.12	10.30	10.70	3.87	11.00
7.	State Aboriginal population as % of total population	%	0.86	0.41	2.01	0.89	2.24	0.76	1.04
8.	Labour force as % of population	%	44.6	45.7	44.3	45.6	46.4	42.7	45.1
9.	Household income per capita	$	6,792	6,686	6,392	7,479	6,306	5,969	6,605
10.	Personal income tax paid per capita	$	924	927	780	817	872	833	886
11.	Private consumption per capita	$	5,044	4,620	4,515	4,423	4,583	4,226	4,726
12.	State taxation per capita	$	508	514	360	400	414	384	463
13.	State expenditure on goods and services per capita	$	1,098	1,173	1,144	1,181	1,402	1,530	1,205

* In town with population excess of 100,000 persons.

Source: Commonwealth Grants Commission, *Report on State Tax Sharing Entitlements 1981*, vol. II, Appendix D; ABS, *Government Financial Estimates 1982–83*; ABS, *Taxation Revenue Australia*, 1981–82.

arrangements can be made through adjustments in revenue-sharing entitlements by lowering the per capita entitlements of the more fiscally and advantaged units relative to the fiscally disadvantaged ones. This method of obtaining fiscal equalisation is now used in Australia. Fiscal equalisation can also be achieved through specific purpose payments adjusted for fiscal disadvantages in particular States.[9]

In Australia, grants to correct for horizontal imbalance were paid since the early years of the federation. Western Australia and Tasmania applied for and were given special financial assistance from 1910–11 and 1912–13 respectively. In 1929–30, South Australia joined the "claimant States" (as they were called) after a Commission of Inquiry into that State's finances. With the involvement of three States and considerable growth in the size of special grants, it was decided to institutionalise and rationalise the arrangements for the recommendation of such grants through the creation of a special Commonwealth Grants Commission.

Although the Grants Commission was created as a temporary body in 1933, it is still in existence and various States have obtained special financial assistance through its recommendations. Western Australia remained a claimant State from 1910–11 to 1967–68, Tasmania from 1912–13 to 1973–74, South Australia from 1929–30 to 1950–60 and again for a number of years during the 1970s. When these three States withdrew from their claimant status, a substantial sum was added to the base of their financial assistance grant thereby further widening per capita relativities in financial assistance grants. From 1971–72 to 1982–83 Queensland was a claimant State seeking special financial assistance. In addition, the Grants Commission in 1973 was granted legal powers to recommend a special financial assistance to the Northern Territory on the same basis on which it made recommendations for such assistance to the States. In 1978 it was given responsibilities for undertaking a systematic review of State tax-sharing entitlements for the purpose of integrating equalisation payments with general and specific revenue assistance, responsibilities since then periodically renewed.

For much of its more than half-century existence the Grants Commission was an independent statutory body composed of a chairman (initially part-time but now full-time) and two other members appointed for three-year periods. Additional responsibilities given to the Commission from the early 1970s have on occasions expanded its membership. For the initial tax-sharing entitlements review, for example, the Commission was expanded to six members, the additional three being appointed on the recommendation of the States. In spite of these alterations in its composition, there has been a remarkable continuity in the principles of its operations. These principles were first outlined in detail in its *Third Report 1936* and their continued acceptance has been reiterated on numerous occasions in subsequent reports from the Commission. For example, forty years later, the Commission's *Forty-third Report 1976* stated them as follows:

> To enable a claimant State to function at a standard not appreciably below that of other States without having to levy taxation and other charges of greater severity than those in other States, its revenue needs to be supplemented because of:
> (a) its lower capacity to raise taxes and other revenue; and
> (b) its need to incur costs in order to provide comparable government services.[10]

Two basic policy issues are involved in this statement of principle on equalisation grants by the Grants Commission. In the first place, it provides an answer to whether the equalisation grants should be large enough to allow the poorer States to provide the same standard of services as more wealthy ones, that is, whether they should aim at complete equalisation or whether the grants should only be sufficient to allow the disadvantaged States to provide services at a minimum acceptable standard. Secondly, the quoted principle indicates the criteria which it uses to assess the size of the special grant for the disadvantaged State.

The first of these policy issues is the more important. Initially, the Grants Commission decided on a principle of financial need which implied that the claimant States would be brought to a level where they could provide a minimum standard of services but which was appreciably below those provided by the more wealthy States. Over the years this approach was gradually changed to one which approached full equalisation, and those parts of its assessment procedure which implied merely achieving minimum standards have been gradually abandoned.

The other changes that have occurred in providing financial assistance for disadvantaged States are concerned with the method of assessment of the size of the grant. In the early years of the federation, Tasmania and Western Australia based their claims for special financial assistance on the ground that they had suffered special financial disadvantages arising from federation. In particular, they lost their own low tariffs, and were disadvantaged by the higher tariffs imposed nationally to protect the manufacturing sector of the more industrialised States. As a result, the price of their imports rose. This approach was never accepted by the Grants Commission, which argued that grants should be based on the comparison of the budgetary position of the claimant States with those of the non-claimant States. From the beginning of the 1970s this budgetary comparison has been changed by the Commission into one of direct assessment of the supplementary revenue needs of a claimant State.

In this method of direct assessment of the size of the recommended grant, the emphasis is on estimating the revenue and expenditure disabilities of the disadvantaged States. The recommended grant, G_c, is seen as consisting of the sum of two parts: R, the revenue component or the amount needed to compensate the State for its lower revenue-raising capacity, and E, the amount needed to provide compensation for its higher relative cost of providing services.

The revenue disability of a State can be calculated by using the following formula:

$$R = P_c \frac{T_s}{Y_s} \cdot \frac{Y_s}{P_s} \cdot r$$

where T_s/Y_s is the average tax rate of the standard States, P_c is the population of the claimant State, P_s is the population of the standard States, Y_s/P_s is the per capita tax base of the standard States and r is the percentage deficiency in revenue-raising capacity of the claimant States relative to the tax base of the standard States.[11] This formula illustrates the importance of the choice of a standard in equalisation procedures. If the national average is taken as the standard; the percentage deficiency in revenue-raising capacity (r)—and hence the revenue component of the assessed grant (R)—will be smaller than if the standard is based on the wealthier States in the federation. To take an Australian example derived from the data in Table 15.2: because the per capita tax base of New South Wales and Victoria exceeds that for Australia as a whole, using the former rather than the latter raises the value of both r and R as calculated by the respective formulas.

This standard has changed over the years. Prior to 1959 the standard employed by the Grants Commission was based on the performance of New South Wales, Victoria, and Queensland, the three non-claimant States. When South Australia abandoned its claimant status, the Commission had to choose whether it would continue to use the standard provided by the performance of non-claimant States, that is, the three States mentioned with the addition of South Australia, or whether it would adopt a new standard. In the event, it decided to change the standard to the performance of New South Wales and Victoria, the States which were effectively prevented from becoming claimant States at the 1959 Premiers' Conference. As an examination of the formula shows, this change raised the standard and thereby the grants payable to the claimant States. For the purpose of its State tax-sharing relativities review, the Commission has adopted a six-State rotating standard.[12]

To calculate the expenditure component of the grant, E, a similar formula is used:

$$E = P_c \cdot \frac{E_s}{P_s} \cdot c$$

where P_c and P_s as before, are the population of the claimant and standard States respectively, E_s/P_s, is the per capita expenditure of the standard States and c is the cost disadvantage of the claimant State expressed as the percentage increase in costs required to provide equivalent services in the claimant State. The estimation of the cost disadvantage component is one of the more difficult aspects of the Grants Commission's work. By careful analysis of a number of selected services provided by both the claimant and the standard States, the Commission attempts to arrive at a figure for this factor in respect of these services. This procedure involves a great deal of judgement and the use of a neat formula gives a misleading impression of objective precision.

In practice, the recommended grant, $G_c = R + E$, is further adjusted to take account of the equalisation elements contained in the financial assistance grants paid by the Federal Government. As shown earlier, these grants over the years have increasingly included equalisation components and in order to avoid duplication these are allowed for in arriving at the special financial assistance grant recommended. Although this procedure is conceptually simple, the Commission itself acknowledges many practical difficulties in estimating cost and revenue disabilities.[13]

State tax-sharing relativities review

As mentioned earlier, general revenue sharing to redress vertical fiscal imbalance problems can be combined with equalisation procedures through adjusting per capita revenue assistance for the fiscal disabilities applicable in particular States. This was the approach of the Grants Commission when it investigated the State tax-sharing relativities in order to see whether an alternative distribution among the various States was desirable on the basis of its generally accepted equalisation principles.

This approach taken by the Grants Commission can be explained as follows. In the absence of fiscal disabilities leading to horizontal fiscal imbalance, equal per capita grants are the most equitable manner of distributing the aggregate tax share among the individual States. As mentioned previously, the principle of equal per capita revenue assistance has not been followed in Australia in order to correct for identified horizontal fiscal imbalance. Taking actual Victorian per capita grants as its numeraire (= 1.00000) because they were the lowest in that year, per capita tax-sharing relativities were then simply reflected in the relative departure from this index of the other States' per capita grants. For 1975–76 these were estimated as 1.02740 for New South Wales, 1.30985 for Queensland, 1.52676 for South Australia, 1.66516 for Western Australia and 1.00188 for Tasmania. The Commission then interpreted its task as discovering whether these actual relativities in per capita payments frozen into the revenue-sharing arrangements reflected the real fiscal disabilities of the individual States. In short, was Tasmania's receipt of twice the per capita grant of Victoria matched by the fact that Tasmania had twice the cost and revenue-raising disabilities as compared to Victoria?

To test this proposition, the Commission employed its principles of assessing cost disabilities and revenue disabilities and discounted these for the degree to which they had already been compensated for through other financial assistance from the Commonwealth such as specific purpose payments. On the basis of its investigations of actual cost and revenue disabilities, a matter which involved the making of a number of specified assumptions about the treatment of certain items, the Commission reached the conclusion that the actual tax-sharing relativities were not justified on the basis of its equalisation principles. Taking again the Victorian per capita grant as the numeraire (= 1.000) the relativities in the tax shares on the basis of the Grants Commission's equalisation principles were 1.048 for New South Wales, 1.487 for Queensland, 1.319 for South Australia, 1.284 for Western Australia, and 1.549 for Tasmania. In short, this meant that the existing tax-sharing relativities over-compensated Tasmania, South Australia, and Western Australia for their real fiscal disabilities, and under-compensated New South Wales, Queensland and Victoria with respect to theirs.[14]

The actual revenue losses for the States which had been over-compensated for their fiscal disabilities were so large that the Federal Government did not alter the tax-sharing relativities on which it distributed the 1981–82 tax shares. Instead it asked the Grants Commission to recalculate the relativities on the basis of different assumptions, some of which were justified by the alterations in health funding which the Government had introduced in 1981. However, the still substantial changes in relativities of tax shares suggested by the Commission on the basis of these recalculations, have meant that the Commonwealth argued for their gradual phasing-in over a period of five years. Only in 1985 did a new Commonwealth Government accept the relativities as assessed by the Grants Commission as the basis for determining the distribution of financial assistance grants to individual States.[15]

The adoption of the principles of equalisation in revenue assistance which the Grants Commission had gradually evolved since the 1930s came under concerted attack during the 1980s. A review of fiscal federalism arrangements in Australia by a visiting American expert[16] in 1983 queried the high degree of equalisation in which the Federal Government was involved, largely on resource allocation efficiency grounds. This criticism was repeated by Treasury in submissions it made to the Grants Commission and in a review of the fiscal equalisation component in general revenue assistance in the 1988–89 Budget Paper on Commonwealth Financial Relations. The latter concluded that the considerable fiscal redistribution implied should be reversed to "complement efforts in recent years to increase efficiency through structural reforms."[17]

Others[18] have attacked the validity of the partial measure of State taxable capacity, traditionally used by the Grants Commission, suggesting the superiority of a global measure such as per capita income, because it more clearly measures the "true" taxable capacity of a State or local government unit. The proponents of the global measure argue their preference on the grounds that it is to be preferred on all counts, since it either outperforms the partial measure or yields similar results. The global measure appears preferable to deal with taxable capacity measurement problems from inter-State differences in industry structure, interdependence of State tax bases, and particularly significant, by removing possibilities of States influencing taxable capacity measurement by their own policy changes, by including potential as well as actual taxes and by its capacity to acknowledge individual horizontal equity considerations. In addition, the global measure is simpler and generates fewer data problems given the improvements from the early 1980s in State national accounting estimates.

The long-standing methodology of the Grants Commission to allow all States (and Territories) to provide more or less equivalent standards of services without unduly high taxation for their residents is now under attack. Internal criticism of its methodology, such as that on the merits of the global versus the partial measure of taxable capacity, do not question the importance of equalisation in federal financial adjustment. The critiques emphasising the detrimental resource allocation consequences of equalisation attacks the principle of equalisation itself.

Special financial assistance for local government

The Grants Commission has also been involved in recommending equalisation grants for local government. As shown in its reports on this subject for 1974 and 1975, it made such recommendations on the basis of detailed assessment of financial disabilities of individual local government units incorporating the principles it had used in its determination of special financial needs for States. Because these grants were for equalisation purposes only, a significant number of more "wealthy" local government units were not given grants under this scheme, a factor which led to some significant alterations of the scheme.[19]

These changes arose in the context of the introduction of personal income tax revenue sharing in 1976. This was also applied to local government in a rising proportion of income tax revenue — it was gradually lifted from 1.56 per unit to 2 per cent — but like institutionalised revenue sharing with the States, this too was abandoned in the interest of curtailing public expenditure growth. Local government's share in federal financial assistance is divided among the States on the basis of recommendations from the Commonwealth Grants Commission. For 1976–77 these provided the following proportions for each State: New South Wales, 36.6 per cent; Victoria 25.3 per cent; Queensland 17.3 per cent, South Australia, 8.5 per cent; Western Australia, 9.4 per cent; and Tasmania, 2.9 per cent. The Commission arrived at these proportions from its detailed analysis of the revenue and expenditure disabilities of individual local government units aggregated on a State basis. The Grants Commission also recommended that at least 30 per cent of this sum should be used by the States to make weighted per capita grants to all local government units (element A) and that the remaining 70 per cent should be used for equalisation purposes (element B).[20]

The final recommendations for the actual size of the grant to each local government unit within a State are now made by State Local Government Grants Commissions within the guidelines of the Commonwealth recommendations. For 1976–77, for example, the New South Wales Local Government Grants Commission recommended that 87.5 per cent of element A should be divided on a per capita basis and the remaining 12.5 per cent should be used to give additional grants to those local government units with a population density of less than 25 persons per square kilometre. Element B was to be allocated to each council on the equalisation principles of the Commonwealth Grants Commission.[21]

An aspect of these changes in financial assistance to local government which should be especially noted is that these new arrangements have removed the *direct* participation of a federal government authority in the assessment of financial needs for local government authorities. As shown, this is now the task for State Local Governments Grants Commissions. The National Inquiry into Local Government Finance, which reported in 1985, recommended continuation of federal funding on the basis established in the 1970s, stressing a continuing need for equalisation in the distribution of these grants to individual local authorities.[22]

Specific purpose grants

In the post-war period, the Federal Government has increasingly resorted to *specific purpose payments* or *tied grants* which, as their names imply, have to be used by the States for purposes designed by the Commonwealth, sometimes with the additional condition of matching revenue in a predetermined ratio provided by the States for the same purpose. The history of road grants in Australia provides examples of these types. Matching revenue conditions were imposed initially; from 1930–31 to 1949–50 the road grants were paid without any other condition but they had to be spent on roads; after 1949–50, the spending of the road grant was combined with more detailed instructions as to how much of the money was to be allocated to various types of road, such as rural roads and arterial roads, for example.

Matching grants, it will be recalled from Chapter 14, may be closed or open-ended. In 1976, an important open-ended grant was introduced with the Medibank arrangements for financing State hospital expenditure on a fifty-fifty basis. With the rising health bill in Australia, particularly because of rising hospital costs, this arrangement was subsequently changed to a less open-ended commitment, thereby reducing this rapidly increasing expenditure item in the Commonwealth Budget. Apart from this important example, open-ended grants have rarely been used in Australia, unlike the position in the United States.[23]

Specific purpose grants have a long history in Australia. Grants for roads have been paid continually from 1923–24 and grants to meet sinking fund contributions on the national debt have been paid since 1927–28 consequent to the Financial Agreement. The more frequent use of these grants did not start till the 1950s and accelerated particularly in the 1970s.[24] Table 15.3 illustrates the growth of specific purpose grants in the post-war period.

Table 15.3 also illustrates the degree of substitution of specific purpose grants for general revenue assistance which occurred in part of the post-war period, especially during the early 1970s. Such a substitution implies a substantial change because it indicates the substitution of cost sharing for revenue sharing in federal financial adjustment and the replacement of State priorities in spending by priorities established by the Federal Government.

The significance of this substitution is not adequately measured by the aggregate of specific purpose grants relative to general revenue grants since not all of these grants have the same effect on the ability of the States to make independent budgetary decisions. The

Table 15.3 Specific purpose payments to the States classified by function: selected post-war years

	1948–49 $m	1958–59 $m	1968–69 $m	1975–76 $m	1982–83 $m	1988–89 $m
Social services						
Education	—	13.8	105.3	1,461.2	3,100.7	4,472.9
Health	—	14.9	18.2	1,082.8	254.7	3,269.8
Social security and welfare	—	b	1.3	182.4	83.8	368.3
Cultural and recreation	—	—	—	12.0	9.2	15.2
Sub-total	—	28.7	124.8	2,738.4	3,448.4	7,794.2
Economic services						
Roads	13.8	77.8	176.1	442.1	662.0	1,217.2
Other transport	—	3.1	11.4	52.7	327.2	76.5
Industry assistance	0.3	2.2	4.3	109.6	214.9	110.5
Water resources	—	1.1	12.4	46.3	79.0	49.4
Other	—	1.0	0.9	6.2	164.9	137.1
Sub-total	14.1	85.2	205.1	656.9	1,448.0	1,590.6
Other						
Debt charges	18.9	25.9	36.8	47.3	58.9	50.7
Housing	—	—	2.2	362.9	459.4]	
						917.7
Urban and regional					]	
development	—	—	—	263.3	55.1]	
General public services	—	0.5	3.4	7.9	1.2	89.8
Natural disaster relief	—	0.5	11.8	25.0	131.8	29.8
Unclassified[a]	—	—	—	34.4	179.9	689.4
Sub-total	18.9	26.9	54.2	740.8	886.3	1,687.6
Total specific purpose grants	33.0	140.8	384.1	4,136.1	5,782.7	11,162.2
Specific purpose grants as a percentage of:	%	%	%	%	%	%
Total grants to the States	21.2	23.8	26.8	49.3	36.3	46.4
Gross domestic product	3.6	4.8	5.3	5.9	3.6	3.4

Notes: a. Includes defence.
b. Less than $50,000.

Source: For 1948–49 to 1968–69, W.R.C. Jay, "The Shift to Specific Purpose Grants", in R.L. Mathews, *Responsibility Sharing in the Federal System* (Canberra: Centre for Research on Federal Financial Relations, Research Monograph No. 8, 1975), Table 1, p. 44.

For 1975–76, *Payment to or for the States and Local Government Authorities 1976–77* (Canberra: AGPS, 1976), esp. Table 4; *National Income and Expenditure 1975–76, 1976–77*, Budget Paper No. 9 (Canberra: AGPS, 1976), p. 6.

For 1982–83, *Payments to or for the States, the Northern Territory and Local Government Authorities* (Canberra: AGPS 1983), esp. Table 1; *National Income and Expenditure 1982–83*, Budget Paper No. 10, 1983–84, Table 1.

For 1988–89, 1989–90 Budget Paper No. 4, *Commonwealth Financial Relations with Other Levels of Government 1989–90* (Canberra: AGPS 1989), ch. 5, esp. Table 29.

grants made for sinking fund contributions in conjunction with the Financial Agreement are really in the nature of general revenue grants, because the States have to provide for these contributions in any case so that the specific grants made by the Commonwealth for this purpose frees State revenue for other purposes of their choice.

There are other grants which do not affect State priorities in expenditure decision-making. These are the grants paid in respect of a Commonwealth function which is administered by the States; many of the minor grants for social welfare and health fall into this category. Secondly, there are grants paid in respect of activities which are jointly planned by the Commonwealth and some of the States for their mutual benefit. Finally, there are the grants similar to revenue sharing, such as the road grants from 1930–31 to 1949–50 which were based on a share of excise collections, which had no matching conditions and which could be spent on roads as the States saw fit.

Many specific purpose grants in the post-war period do, however, directly interfere with States' responsibilities and functions. Matching conditions and more specific conditions for spending the grants have become more frequent while some of the specific purpose grants after 1974 can be better described as de facto transfers of expenditure functions to the Commonwealth. From 1950–51 onwards, for example, the road grants included conditions for the allocation of a fixed proportion of the grant for rural roads, and after 1960 even more stringent conditions were applied which conformed to Commonwealth formulated priorities in road planning. In connection with the grants made for primary and secondary education, Commonwealth intervention was even more pronounced for some time as States had to follow the national plan laid down by the Federal Schools Commission and had to undertake not to reduce their own relative expenditures on this function from their own general revenue resources. Although the latter principle was accepted by the States, it is difficult to ascertain whether this condition was actually met by them and whether expenditure on education was actually much greater than it would have been in the absence of specific purpose payments.

The funding of tertiary education since the early 1950s provides further examples of federal intrusions into State responsibilities. Under the arrangements which existed till the end of 1973, tertiary education grants had a matching condition (of $1.85 of State revenue, including university fees for each $1 provided by the Commonwealth for current expenditure, and on a dollar-for-dollar basis for capital expenditure). This meant that the Commonwealth, by deciding the total revenue it would make available in grants for this purpose in accordance with its priorities, also decided a substantial appropriation from State funds. Such matching conditions place a considerable constraint on the State's freedom of action in expenditure planning.[25]

From 1974 the Commonwealth took over the responsibility for university and other tertiary education funding, and consequently, has reduced the general revenue assistance and loan funds payable to the States. Although the legislation governing tertiary education institutions is still enacted in State parliaments, the aggregate resources devoted to this function are, in practice, completely determined by federal policies and funding. Like the transfer of the non-urban part of the South Australian railway system and the whole of the Tasmanian railway system, this policy amounts to an effective expenditure power transfer from the States to the Commonwealth. During the late 1980s it enabled the Federal Government to introduce major changes in tertiary education to improve its efficiency: these include the abolition of the binary system which distinguished universities and colleges of advanced education; forced amalgamations between institutions to make the new national system more manageable, and greater influence on syllabus and courses than earlier government administrations had tended to exert.

Specific purpose payments need not imply increased centralisation because they can be reversed. Table 15.3 illustrates a substantial relative decline in specific purpose payments to the States in the years after 1975–76 which, in some cases such as health, social security and welfare, culture and recreation, and urban and regional development, is reflected in absolute reductions in the money size of the grants in more recent years. These changes arose from the general aim of the Fraser Liberal government to wind back the importance of specific purpose payments and return a number of original State responsibilities in this way to the States. The Hawke Labor government elected in 1983 reversed some of these priorities once more.

The discussion of specific purpose grants in Australian practice illustrates the rationale for such grants outlined in Chapter 14. Use of such grants has a variety of important roles in federal fiscal adjustment as the varying nature of such grants over the post-war period in Table 15.3 clearly illustrates.

Whither Australian fiscal federalism?

The 1970s and 1980s were volatile decades in Australian federalism with change following change. The discussion in this chapter indicates that similar change is likely to occur in the 1990s. Changing perceptions of vertical fiscal imbalance, for example, may imply a shift from the grant solution to one relying more on change in function assignment, including tax power reallocation. Likewise, traditional views on equalisation seem likely to be altered over the coming decade. Irrespective of the nature of such alterations in direction, changing circumstances will in any case necessitate adjustments to Australia's fiscal federalism arrangements.

SUMMARY

1. Functions assignment in Australia's federation is by the Constitution, particularly s.51 which outlines federal powers, the States generally speaking having residual powers. Local government powers derive from State legislation.

2. Constitutional assignment of functions in Australia has little resemblance to theoretically predicted assignment, except occasionally at the national (central) and local extremes.

3. Australia's substantial vertical fiscal imbalance has been solved in practice by:

   (a) expenditure transfers to federal government;
   (b) tax power transfers to State governments;
   (c) grants;
   (d) attempts at institutionalised revenue sharing.

   The third solution is, historically, the most important.

4. Horizontal fiscal imbalance in Australia's federation has been remedied by equalisation procedures developed by the Commonwealth Grants Commission since the 1930s. These attempt to equalise fiscal capacity by compensating for cost disabilities in the provision of services and differences in taxable capacity.

5. Prior to the 1980s, equalisation was achieved by making special grants to fiscally disadvantaged States; equalisation now proceeds via the per capita relativities reviews regularly conducted by the Commission, which determine the distribution of general revenue assistance to individual States and Territories. There are also equalisation procedures attached to the financial assistance granted to local government.

6. The equalisation procedures of the Grants Commission have been criticised because of their detrimental resource allocation consequences and for their non-use of a global taxable capacity measure like per capita income.

7. Specific Purpose Grants also play a significant role in federal fiscal adjustment for the reasons suggested by theory: internalising externalities through cost sharing, meeting national priorities and inducing States to undertake the provision of particular services. Both matching and non-matching grants have been used in Australia; the former, however, have rarely been open-ended.

NOTES

[1] As indicated in Chapter 2, most economic functions are specifically assigned to the Commonwealth by Section 51 of the Constitution, including a general concurrent power of taxation. Section 90 exempts customs and excise from this, making the imposition of such taxes an exclusive Commonwealth power. In addition, Section 96 gives the Federal Government the right to make conditional grants to the States, which has effectively prevented the States from resuming income tax powers since World War II. Section 105 as amended enabled federal borrowing arrangements to be institutionalised through the Loan Council (as discussed in Chapter 17). See Attorney-General's Department, *The Australian Constitution Annotated* (Canberra: AGPS, 1980), pp. 44–166 (on Section 51), pp. 297–307 (on Section 90), pp. 352–4 (on Section 96), pp. 366–9 (on Section 105 as amended); Report of the Advisory Committee to the Constitutional Commission, *Distribution of Powers* (Canberra: AGPS, 1987), for a general discussion of the need to review these powers; and *Trade and National Economic Management* (Canberra: AGPS, 1987) for a special discussion of redistributing the economic powers including tax powers.

[2] See Peter Groenewegen, "Tax Assignment and Revenue Sharing in Australia", in C. E. McLure Jr. (ed.), *Tax Assignment in Federal Countries* (Canberra: ANU Press, 1983), ch. 12 and the commentary thereon by P.B. Musgrave and J.G. Head.

[3] See *Payments to or for the States and Local Government 1975–76*, pp. 158–60. This formula worked as follows. If the base grant is \$100 million, population increased by 5 per cent in the preceding year, wages rose by 5 per cent, and the betterment factor applied to wage increases was 10 per cent, next year's grant would be \$100m x 1.05 x 1.055 = \$110.9 million. In 1965 the betterment factor was applied to the grant rather than to wage increases. With the same data, next year's grant under this system would be \$100m x 1.05 x 1.05 x 1.1 = \$121.3m.

A detailed history of these arrangements is provided in Commonwealth Grants Commission, *Report on State Tax Sharing Entitlements*, 1981, vol. 2, Appendix A, pp. 1–30.

[4] See *Commonwealth Relations with Other*

Levels of Government 1989–90, Commonwealth Budget Paper No. 4 (Canberra: AGPS 1989), pp. 35–6.

5 For a discussion see Ewald Nowotny, "Tax Assignment and Revenue Sharing in the Federal Republic of Germany and Switzerland", in C.E. McLure (ed.), *Tax Assignment in Federal Countries*, esp. pp. 261–6.

6 For a discussion of these arrangements, see Peter Groenewegen, "Federalism", in Brian W. Head and Allan Patience (eds.), *From Fraser to Hawke* (Melbourne: Longman Cheshire, 1989), pp. 250–2, 261.

7 See R.L. Mathews (ed.), *Regional Disparities and Economic Development* (Canberra: Centre for Research on Federal Financial Relations, 1981), especially the chapters by Russell Mathews and Benjamin Higgins.

8 For a discussion, see National Inquiry into Local Government Finance, *Report* (Canberra: AGPS, 1985), chs. 8–10.

9 A detailed history of the work of the Grants Commission was issued on its 50th birthday, under the title *Equality in Diversity. Fifty Years of the Commonwealth Grants Commission* (Canberra: AGPS, 1983).

10 See Commonwealth Grants Commission, *Forty-Third Report 1976 on Special Assistance to States*, p. 4. For a similar statement of principles which is less precise, see Commonwealth Grants Commission, *Third Report 1936* (Canberra: 1936), p. 75.

11 r is calculated by the formula

$$r = \frac{Y_s / P_s - Y_c / P_c}{Y_s / P_s}$$

where Y_c/P_c is the per capita tax base of the claimant State.

12 The matter of equalisation standards was exhaustively discussed by the Commission in its *Main Report on State Tax Sharing Entitlements* 1981, vol. 1, pp. 53–71.

13 For a detailed discussion of the methodology of the Grants Commission in theory and practice see its Report on *State Tax Sharing Entitlements 1981*, vol. 1, esp. chs. 2–7, and for a detailed defence of that methodology, Commonwealth Grants Commission, *Report on General Revenue Grant Relativities 1988* (Canberra: AGPS, 1988), vol. 1, ch. 7.

14 The more favourable treatment suggested for Victoria by these calculations can be seen if Tasmania's per capita payments are taken as numeraire (= 1.000). In 1975–76, Victoria's relative per capita share then equals 0.49953; as calculated in the 1981 tax-sharing relativities report, it equals 0.64578 — a considerable improvement relative to Tasmania, which is now the standard of comparison.

15 1985–86 Commonwealth Budget Paper No. 7, *Payment to or for the States, the Northern Territory and Local Government Authority 1985–86* (Canberra: AGPS, 1985), ch. 2, esp. pp. 22–4.

16 E. Gramlich, "'A Fair Go': Fiscal Federalism Arrangements", in R.E. Caves and L.B. Krause (eds.), *The Australian Economy: A View from the North* (Sydney: Allen and Unwin, 1984), ch. 6, esp. pp. 246–52, 273.

17 See Grants Commission, *Report on General Revenue Grant Relativities 1988*, ch. 7, esp. pp. 128, 132–148; Commonwealth Budget Paper No. 4, *Commonwealth Financial Relations with other levels of Government 1988–89* (Canberra: AGPS, 1988), pp. 24–8. The quotation in the text is from p. 28.

18 For a detailed discussion see David Collins, *Partial and Global Measures of State Taxable Capacities* (Sydney: Australian Tax Research Foundation, Occasional Paper No. 4, 1987); New South Wales Tax Task Force, *Review of the State Tax System* (Sydney, 1988) ch. 30.

19 See Commonwealth Grants Commission *Report 1974* and *1975* on *Special Assistance for Local Government*. (Canberra: AGPS, 1974, 1975).

20 See Commonwealth Grants Commission, *Special Report 1976 on Financial Assistance to Local Government* (Canberra: AGPS, 1976), esp. pp. 6–19.

21 See Local Government Grants Commission, New South Wales, Report 1976–77 on *Financial Assistance to Local Government*, ch. 2.

22 See National Inquiry into Local Government Finance, *Report* (Canberra: AGPS, 1985), esp. ch. 14. Ch. 5 provides an interesting analysis of the operation of State government Grants Commissions, as does D.V. Moye, "The Work of State Local Government Grants Commissions" in Geoffrey Brennan (ed.), *Local Government Finance* (Canberra: Centre for Research on Federal Financial Relations, 1987), Occasional Paper No. 41, pp. 15–29.

23 For a discussion of the latter, see J.A. Maxwell, *Specific Purpose Grants in the United States*, Centre for Research on Federal Financial

Relations, Research Monograph, no. 12 (Canberra: ANU Press, 1975), esp. pp. 88–90.

24 No detailed history of specific purpose grants is presented. Those interested are referred to J.A. Maxwell, *Commonwealth-State Financial Relations in Australia*, ch. 3; Robert Jay, "The Shift to Specific Purpose Grants", in R.L. Mathews (ed.), *Responsibility Sharing in a Federal System*, ch. 2; and 1975–76 Budget Paper No. 7, *Payments to or for the States and Local Government Authorities 1975–76*, Appendix 4 (which should be updated by more recent issues of this Budget Paper now called *Commonwealth Financial Relations with Other Levels of Government*).

25 For details of the history of education grants see Robert Jay, "The Shift to Specific Purpose Grants", pp. 50–9 and Andrew Spaull, "Education", in Allan Patience and Brian Head (eds.), *From Whitlam to Fraser* (Melbourne: Oxford University Press, 1979), ch. 7; Don Smart, "Education", in Brian W. Head and Allan Patience (eds.), *From Fraser to Hawke*, ch. 12.

FURTHER READING

The standard history of Australian fiscal federalism is:

R.L. Mathews and W.R. Jay, *Federal Finance* (Melbourne: Nelson 1972).

This can be updated from the annual surveys of federalism provided for the 1970s and early 1980s by the Centre for Research on Federal Financial Relations edited by its Foundation Director, R.L. Mathews. Other sources for official information on fiscal federalism are the annual Budget Paper, *Commonwealth Financial Relations with other levels of Government.*

Brief surveys of Australian fiscal federalism are:

Peter Groenewegen, "Federalism" in Brian Head and Allan Patience (eds.), *From Whitlam to Fraser* (Melbourne: Oxford University Press, 1979), ch. 3;

and in:

Brian Head and Allan Patience (eds.), *From Fraser to Hawke* (Melbourne: Longman Cheshire, 1989), ch. 10.

A useful collection of readings is:

W. Prest and R.L. Mathews (eds.), *The Development of Australian Fiscal Federalism* (Melbourne: Melbourne University Press, 1980).

The work of the Grants Commission is historically reviewed in *Equality in Diversity* (Canberra: AGPS, 1983).

A critical outside review of Australian federalism practice is:

E. Gramlich, "'A Fair Go': Fiscal Federalism Arrangements" in Richard Caves and Lawrence Krause (eds.), *The Australian Economy: A View from the North* (Sydney: Allen and Unwin, 1984), ch. 6.

A useful review of local government's share in federal fiscal adjustment is:

National Inquiry into Local Government Finance, *Report* (Canberra: AGPS, 1985), esp. chs. 3–5, 7–12, 14, 15.

16

State, local and regional government finance

State, local and regional finance issues have been discussed at various points throughout this text. Issues of State and local expenditure, as well as State and local taxation, were addressed when relevant in Chapter 2–5, 11 and 13; State and local borrowing issues are covered in Chapter 17. More important, the impact of the Federal Government on State and local finance was examined in Chapter 15, while the role in public finance of sub-national jurisdictions (State, regional and local) was theoretically reviewed in Chapter 14. The purpose of this chapter is to look comprehensively at some issues of State, local and regional government finance which do not fit so easily in this framework and therefore require separate treatment. Such issues include recent initiatives in State financial reform, with special reference to taxation; reassignment of functions and tax powers, both between the Federal Government and State governments and between State and local governments; and the potential for more far-reaching reform involving the creation of regional government. More variety in service delivery units conforms, after all, to the drive towards greater allocational efficiency encouraged by federal and State governments, and the principles developed by fiscal federalism theory.

STATE FINANCIAL REFORM

State financial reform issues from the mid-1980s were induced by fears that State spending was growing too strongly and that its growth was directed more towards public consumption than to the capital spending required for much needed infrastructure. Relative to GDP, the State and local sector raised its share of national output by 1.5 percentage points from an average of 15.3 per cent in the 1970s, to an average of 16.9 per cent for the ten years ending 1988–89. However, initiatives from the Federal Government in curtailing financial assistance grants to both State and local government (discussed in Chapters 15 and 18) as well as initiatives by State and local governments themselves, have lowered the State/local's share of GDP from a peak of 17.6 per cent in 1986–87 to 15.6 per cent in 1988–89, thereby virtually reversing the trend of the 1980s. However, much of this decrease came from capital account, which declined from an average of 3.3 per cent of GDP in the 1970s to 2.4 per cent for the 1980s, and more disturbingly, falling steadily from 2.7 per cent in the decade ending 1979–80 to 1.9 per cent in that ending 1988–89. Consumption spending by the State/local sector rose considerably in relative terms (from 8.3 per cent in the 1970s to 10.4 per cent for the 1980s), a trend being gradually reversed from the mid-1980s, undoubtedly the result of the sharp reduction in federal finance assistance which became a regular event from 1984–85.[1]

Much of the increased State/local consumption expenditure flowed into education and health. Table 16.1 compares real per capita spending on these items for the six States between 1961–62 and 1984–85. Education spending enabled significant reduction in class sizes; health spending growth reflected the rapid rise in health costs which outpaced general cost levels. In New South Wales, where the real growth in education spending was among the lowest relative to other States, this real growth occurred despite a substantial shift away from government schools towards the private school sector, while the rapid growth in health spending was explained by an aging population, technological change in the health sector and little reliance on private sector health care.[2]

Table 16.1 Real State per capita outlays on education and health: 1961–62 and 1984–85

	Education			Health		
	1961–62	1984–85	Growth*	1961–62	1984–85	Growth*
NSW	231	662	287	108	383	355
Victoria	230	775	337	112	393	351
Queensland	173	651	376	120	357	298
SA	267	744	279	98	432	441
WA	244	734	301	148	484	327
Tasmania	259	782	302	158	442	280

* Growth expressed in terms of 1961–62 figure (= 100).

Source: David Chessell, "State Finances: Lifting the Veil", *Business Council Bulletin*, No. 34, May 1987, p. 24, Table 4.

Rapid growth in spending was combined by growth in public indebtedness for the State governments, involving a growing proportion of outlays to finance interest and other debt charges. This was particularly the case for the State/local public trading enterprise sector which during the early to mid-1980s had a deficit (borrowing requirement) of from 2 to 3 per cent of GDP, invariably much greater than the borrowing requirements of its general government functions. Debt reduction by expenditure curtailment became the policy of State/local governments during the second half of the 1980s irrespective of the real requirements there were for public service expansion, particularly those involving public investment. State financial reform was equated with expenditure restraints, debt reduction and, where possible, tax reductions to coincide with elections.[3]

The changes in State finances for the four years from 1983–84 are graphed in Figure 16.1. These show the sharp declines in relative outlays which have taken place in the States over this period, the rise in own-source revenue which occurred to compensate for declines in federal financial assistance as well as the reduction in net borrowing requirements. Whether a continuing policy of relative public sector reduction is feasible was partly

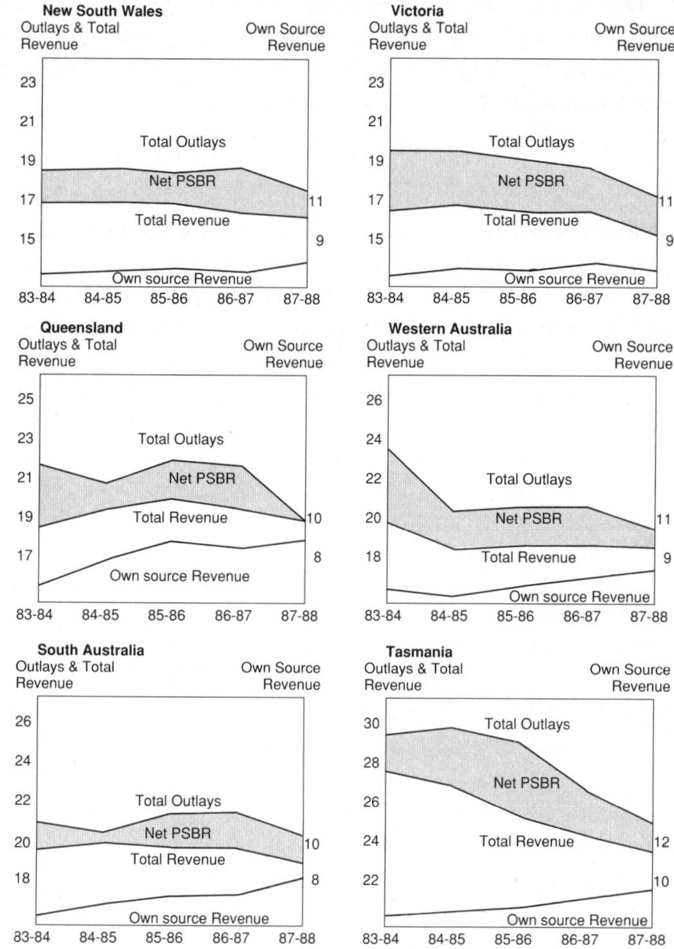

Figure 16.1 Outlays, revenue and net PSBR as a percentage of GSP*

Notes:

* The charts show total outlays, own-source revenue (including the increase in provisions), total revenue and the net PSBR as a share of GSP. The net PSBR is the shaded area shown as the vertical difference between the outlays and total revenue lines. The scales in each chart are the same, the levels, however differ between States. For example, outlays in 1987–88 as a proportion of GSP were around 17.5% in NSW and VIC and around 25% in TAS. Such differences in large part reflect the impact of fiscal equalisation. The change in the ratios for individual States provide the best guide to the stance of State financial policies.

The level of net Commonwealth payments is not represented by the vertical difference between the total revenue (plotted on the lefthand scale) and own-source revenue (plotted on the righthand scale) lines. However, because the two scales are identical the slope of the revenue lines shows the relative trends in the components of total revenue as a proportion of GSP (for example, in TAS the total revenue line declined by 0.9 percentage points of GSP between 1986–87 and 1987–88 while the own-source revenue line increased by 0.4 percentage points of GSP in this period. Therefore, net Commonwealth payments declined by 1.3 percentage points of GSP).

Source: 1989–90 Budget Paper No. 4, Commonwealth Financial Relations with other Levels of Government 1989–90 (Canberra: AGPS, 1989), p. 26. Commonwealth of Australia copyright, reproduced by permission.

addressed in Chapter 3, and is further examined in Chapter 20. Part of the change in State finances was driven by a desire to achieve greater efficiency and productivity in a leaner public sector, an aim which also informs much of the debate on improving fiscal balance and tax revenue independence in the Australian federation.

Alterations in tax assignment for the States

Marginal income tax powers for the States. In Chapter 15 it was indicated that in 1978 the Commonwealth legislated to enable States to impose a surcharge or grant a rebate on personal income tax for their residents. Such surcharges and rebates were to be expressed as a percentage of individual tax liability. This effective provision of marginal income tax powers for the States, while leaving the advantage of uniform income taxation in collection and assessment, was repealed by the Federal Government in 1989, thereby eliminating an avenue of extended State tax powers which two reviews of State revenue-raising during the 1980s had recommended as appropriate.[4]

More radical proposals for State tax re-assignment.[5] These would enable the States to levy personal income taxation in their own right, with the Federal Government making room for the States by cutting its own personal income tax rates. The last can be financed from the revenue savings in abolishing general financial assistance grants. Alternatively, a constitutional referendum removing the exclusive excise power of the Commonwealth in Section 90 would enable the imposition of State retail sales tax. Both these reforms, although radical in the context of Australia's traditional fiscal arrangement for more than fifty years, conform fully to the accepted principles of tax assignment discussed in Chapter 14.

Expansion of existing State tax structures[6]

Less radical but nevertheless useful reform leading to greater State tax revenue independence can be achieved through more intensive State utilisation of their existing tax bases, or by introducing tax bases left free when the Commonwealth ceased to use them. It was suggested in Chapter 11 that land tax was one candidate for expansion in this way, while, provided they retain constitutional validity, business franchise taxes could be expanded into a general sales tax on goods and services. This is one way by which States can use such currently unexploited tax bases as entertainment, personal services and tourist accommodation. Similar initiatives can be suggested in the financial transactions area with a substantial rationalisation of stamp duties by the introduction of an instrument like a broad-based duty on loans and credit of 0.075 per cent. There is also still room for the reintroduction of capital transfer taxes such as probate and succession duties, and the extension of land tax to cover the ownership of a wider variety of assets, perhaps in the form of the general net wealth tax which was discussed in Chapter 11.

Tax uniformity versus tax competition

An inevitable consequence of expanding the States' tax base, no matter how this was done, is a reduction in the high degree of tax uniformity which currently exists in the Australian federation. It would also open the door to considerable tax competition, a tendency which, in any case, is already growing. Examples of such competition are the absence of financial institutions duties in Queensland and the Northern Territory, as well as substantial differences in stamp duties, payroll tax exemptions and rates, as was indicated in Chapter 13. There is still relatively little Australian evidence on the costs and effectiveness of tax competition in stimulating regional economic development. However, those who characterise the benefits of a federal system in terms of diversity, including diversity in tax systems, would not mind this cost.[7]

PROBLEMS OF LOCAL GOVERNMENT FINANCE AND REGIONAL DEVELOPMENT

One of the problems in Australian federalism which so far has not been systematically discussed is local government finance. From the 1960s cries of "crisis in local government finance" were frequently raised by local politicians and responded to by State government inquiries into local government financing. The reason for these concerns was the combination of rising public demands for the provision of local services, particularly those devoted to recreation and community services (libraries, baby health centres, senior citizens centres), requiring higher local expenditure growth and more stable taxation revenue from local rates. Suggested solutions to this problem were generally speaking twofold: access by local government to other tax sources and financial assistance from the Federal and State governments. As shown earlier (Chapter 15) in the discussion of vertical and horizontal fiscal imbalance, the second solution was accepted and local government has increasingly relied on intergovernmental revenue transfers.

A problem less directly related to local government finance but very important in the context of intergovernmental financial relations was that of securing constitutional recognition for local government as a genuinely independent and equal third partner in the federation. As shown earlier, local governments' existence as the creatures of the State governments prevents such constitutional recognition. Attempts have been made by several federal governments to alter this situation through referendum proposals, but all these were unsuccessful.

By way of background to the discussion of local government financial problems, Table 16.2 presents data on the sources and uses of local government funds for 1973–74, 1980–81 and 1987–88. These data reflect the fluctuating importance of intergovernmental grants in local government finance, particularly noticeable in those from the Commonwealth government. Table 16.2 also crystallises the financing problems raised in the first paragraph of this section.

The differing taxable capacities and differences in the cost of providing services which give rise to horizontal imbalance among local government units have already been described in Chapter 15, as has the preferred solution to this problem by means of equalisation grants. The problem of vertical imbalance in local government was ascribed to the fact that it has only one tax source, the rate on land values. The rapid growth in the value of the local government tax base has not been accompanied by a similar rate of increase in revenue from rates, because often there is not a commensurable increase in income to match the increased property value. However, State controls over local rate increases, which New South Wales has used on occasion, also bear responsibility for this. It is also difficult to raise more revenue from this tax for political and social reasons, some of which were discussed in Chapter 11.

Table 16.2 Australian local authorities: revenue and expenditure 1973–74, 1980–81 and 1987–88

	1973–74		*1980–81*		*1987–88*	
	$m	*%*	*$m*	*%*	*$m*	*%*
Revenue						
General taxes, fees, fines	583.9	51.8	1,566.1	50.0	3,334.3	51.8
Other current revenue	131.7	11.7	313.1	10.0	892.9	13.8
Grants — State government	159.0	14.1	383.6	12.2	1,431.6	22.2
Commonwealth direct	2.7	0.2	23.4	0.7	105.4	1.6
Tax share grant [a]			300.8	9.6	—	—
All other [b]	249.3	22.1	545.2	17.4	688.2	10.7
Total revenue	1,126.6	100.0	3,132.1	100.0	6,452.4	100.0
Expenditure						
General public services	192.8	17.1	579.1	18.5	894.1	13.9
Education	3.6	0.3	13.6	0.4	26.4	0.9
Health	28.9	2.6	65.6	2.1	133.6	2.1
Social security and welfare	9.8	0.9	66.9	2.1	229.1	3.6
Housing and community services	114.7	10.2	373.2	11.9	1,134.7	17.6
Economic services						
Road systems	394.2	35.0	841.6	26.9	1,671.1	25.9
Other	135.1	12.0	378.9	12.1	541.1	8.9
Interest	128.5	11.4	342.3	10.9	839.3	13.0
Recreation and culture	115.6	10.3	446.1	14.2	1,014.9	15.7
Other	3.6	0.3	25.2	0.8	–32.9	–0.5
Total outlays	1,126.6	100.0	3,132.1	100.0	6,452.4	100.0
Outlays						
Current	459.8	40.8	1,502.1	48.0	3,964.3	61.4
Capital	666.8	59.2	1,630.0	52.0	2,488.1	38.6

Notes: Figures may not add due to rounding.

a. Tax share grants paid indirect to local government grants commissions (for 1987–88 included with State grant).

b. Includes borrowing of $144.8m (12.9%)) in 1973–74 and $374.9m (12.0%) in 1980–81 and $249.9m (3.9%) for 1987–88 as well as other financing transactions such as movements in cash balances and financial asset holdings.

Source: ABS, *State and Local Government Finance Australia 1980–81* (Canberra: 1982, Cat. No. 5504.0); *State and Local Government Finance Australia 1987–88* (Canberra: 1989, Cat. No. 5504.0).

For example, incomes of the aged do not rise as fast as the value of their homes, so that they find it increasingly difficult to meet rising rate commitments.

At the same time, expenditure by local government has been rising. This rise in expenditure can be ascribed to two factors. In the first place, local government services are particularly labour-intensive and this, in a period of inflation, raises the cost of providing these services at a faster rate than the general rate of price increases. Secondly, many local government areas have introduced new services in the fields of health, welfare, and education, such as baby health clinics, women's shelters, senior citizens centres, youth recreation centres, and public libraries. This trend is reflected in Table 16.2 in the steadily rising relative share of expenditure on social security and welfare.

Grants have offered one solution to provide the additional revenue required by local government. This solution was investigated in Chapter 15 which indicated in that context that fiscal stabilisation requirements from the mid-1980s have reduced the rate of growth of this revenue source. As part of the general drive to reduced public indebtedness, but also for more specific fiscal policy purposes, local government borrowing has also been severely constrained and is now a fairly insignificant source of local funds.

Other solutions to the problems of vertical and horizontal imbalance in local government have concentrated on the expenditure side. Committees of inquiry into local government finance and administration have found that local government units in Australia are far too small to take full advantage of economies of scale and that substantial cost savings could be made if local government units were amalgamated. Such amalgamations would also decrease the problem of horizontal imbalance by reducing cost disabilities caused by the small size of some councils. Unfortunately, experience has shown that such amalgamations are rather difficult to achieve because of local opposition, especially in rural areas. This solution of expenditure reduction through the cost savings by increasing the size of council areas has therefore not proved to be very successful.[8]

Expanding local government functions[9]

The advantages of decentralised expenditure decision-making plus the analysis of optimum community size given in Chapter 14 suggest that local government functions should be enhanced to take advantage of such efficiency opportunities from greater decentralisation. This would move Australian function assignment to local government closer to international practice, particularly that of the United States and the United Kingdom. British local government takes considerable responsibilities in education, housing, police and fire protection. In Australia these public services are preserved for the State level and are hence considerably more centralised. The regional government initiatives, pioneered by the Whitlam Labor government and briefly discussed in the final section of this chapter, were partly geared to widen local participation in public service delivery and decision-making.

Expanding local government revenue sources

Although local rates remain a very useful local government tax, for reasons discussed in Chapter 14 in the context of tax assignment principles, any extension of local government functions would mean either considerable extension of the grant system or expansion of the local government tax base. The last has been an issue of considerable discussion going back to the New South Wales Royal Commission into Local Government Finance which reported in 1967, the work of the Advisory Council on Inter-government Relations in 1981 and the Report of the National Inquiry into Local Government Finance.[10] Both the Royal Commission and the Advisory Council saw merit in expanding the range of local government taxes to include a poll, community or resident tax, tourist and other entertainment taxes, general sales taxes or selective taxes on petrol, fuels and motor vehicles via licence fees. The National Inquiry, on the other hand, was less enthusiastic about such tax initiatives, partly because of the increased possibility of tax competition from such wider local tax powers —

not only between local government units but also between State and local government. It stressed the need for rating reform as an alternative to a wider local tax base, including abolition of exemptions from rating for government property and that used for education, religious and charitable purposes, as well as more adequate compensation to local government for rate relief given to pensioners.

The poll or community tax issue[11] has taken on greater relevance in Australian local government finance discussion following its introduction in the United Kingdom to replace domestic rates. A new inquiry into Local Government Finance established in New South Wales during 1989 has had submissions from farming and other business interests in favour of such a switch, or more simply, to use revenue from a poll tax as a device to substantially lower rate burdens. The regressive nature of the tax, plus the differential impact it would have on households of varying compositions, makes the tax even less desirable from the vertical equity perspective than rates. In addition, the tax is difficult and costly to collect, despite its apparent simplicity. In its report, the New South Wales Committee rejected the introduction of a poll tax but advocated many local financial reforms. These included greater reliance on user charges at the local level where applicable, a proposal in line with the assignment rules presented in Chapter 14.

Regionalism: a fourth tier of government?

The relative smallness and ineffectiveness of Australia's local government and the relative largeness of Australia's States with their highly centralised bureaucracies concentrated in the capital cities has led to demands for the introduction of regional government, possibly as a fourth tier in the federation. Many of these proposals were rather ambiguous about the nature of such new regional bodies. Some preferred elected regional authorities with decision-making powers about matters given to them by either the Federal Government or the States. Such authorities would have constituted a genuine fourth tier of *government*. Others, more modestly, proposed regional organisations as decentralised *administrative* units with some regional autonomy but the major decisions to be made by the central government. Part of this became effective Labor Party policy in the charter for a new federalism prepared by Whitlam in the late 1960s and early 1970s.[12]

Regionalism was never effectively established as a genuine fourth tier of government, during the period of the Labor government (1972–75). What was done was to utilise the concept of regions in various ways and for a variety of purposes, which in general, but not always, were associated with urban and regional development. Three developments stand out in this connection: the development of regions (at least on the map) in connection with financial assistance to local governments; the utilisation of different regions as administrative and decision-making units in connection with the Australian Assistance Plan, and the development of regional growth centres as a form of decentralisation.[13]

The amendment of the *Grants Commission Act* in 1973 provided for the creation of regions for the purpose of making payments of financial assistance to local government. The department of Urban and Regional Development (a creation of the Whitlam government, abolished in 1976) was instructed to put forward such a system of regions, a task which it carried out and reported on in 1973. Its proposals divided Australia into 68 regions initially: 16 in New South Wales, 18 in Victoria, 10 each in Queensland and Western Australia, 11 in South Australia and 3 in Tasmania. In spite of the Act's intentions, these financial assistance grants were in practice paid to existing local government units because no regional authorities capable of receiving these moneys, let alone spending them, were ever created. The *Grants Commission Act* in 1973 in this respect remained a dead letter. These regional provisions were repealed in 1976 during the "new federalism" policy of the Fraser government. A major reason for this policy reversal was the suspicion of the States, particularly those with conservative governments, that these regional bodies were only a device of the Commonwealth Government to destroy the State local government power and thereby to reduce State "sovereignty" even further.

A quite different concept of regions was developed by the Social Welfare Commission (abolished in 1976) in connection with the Australian Assistance Plan. This concept was based on notions of participatory democracy, which was considered to be particularly relevant to the provision of social welfare and social amenities. These regions, unlike the regions proposed by the Department of Urban and Regional Development for Grants Commission purposes, were not generally amalgamations of local government areas, though local governments had representation on most of them, together with interested parties from existing government social security personnel, private social service organisations, and other groups. This combination of individuals formed itself into a Regional Council for Social Development, and this Council would then put forward proposals for social welfare projects and other forms of social amenities, which were to be financed by Federal Government grants. Although these organisations had a strong degree of regional autonomy in decision-making, the way they were set up made it difficult for them to become a separate tier of government in a federation, largely because their creation depended on State legislation and not on an independent charter.

The final creation of regional bodies was in connection with the growth centre program for the economic development of certain country towns (for example, Albury-Wodonga, Monaro, Bathurst-Orange) in order to turn them into large urban centres and thereby effective vehicles for decentralisation. Most of these programs were started under the auspices of the now defunct Department of Urban and Regional Development, but they invariably required State and local government co-operation so that the regional commissions created to administer the development never achieved genuine independent status. The funding was to be largely provided by the Federal Government, as indeed it was by the Labor government; substantial cut-backs in these programs were made in the first two Budgets of the Fraser government in 1976 and 1977 and never restored. As Professor Sawer has put it, "no attempt was made to create a joint general-purpose regional government body, directly elected, to replace local government ... and these developments do not provide a credible example of Mr. Whitlam's new regional partners to the federal compact".

The regional innovations of the Whitlam government, although inspired by the grand idea of fundamentally restructuring the federation, did not reach this ideal in practice, largely because of State obstruction and local government hostility to the diminution of their authority implied by the creation of an additional tier of government. The idea of regional government nevertheless has considerable merit for rejuvenating the federal system. As was indicated earlier in this chapter, some of the advantages of federalism have been lost in Australia because the States are in some ways too large and too centralised, while local government is too small to realise these advantages completely. The creation of regional government between these two entities would have improved this situation, particularly if they were created as elected bodies with decision-making powers about the provision of services with a high regional content. This may have provided a better way of achieving the ideals of a federal system of supplying a diverse range of services, meeting the wishes of the community, providing closer contacts between representatives and constituents, and some participatory democracy.[14]

To conclude these chapters on fiscal federalism, it is useful to reiterate the limitation of the theory, and the principles derived therefrom, as compared with the actual practice of federal systems like that in Australia. These limitations have been amply demonstrated in this and the previous chapters. This is not to say that the principles are therefore useless: they inspire suggestions for reform towards greater decentralisation, the yield of which could be considerable in terms of political, social and economic benefits.

SUMMARY

1. State financial reform in the late 1980s has been prompted by rapid State expenditure growth, particularly in State final consumption spending, combined with borrowing and public indebtedness growth in the mid-1980s.

2. Health and education spending explain much of this State consumption expenditure growth.

3. Alterations in the assignment to the States have focussed on:

   (a) marginal income tax powers;
   (b) repeal of the exclusive excise provision in the Constitution to enable imposition of a retail sales tax or other broad-based consumption taxation.

4. There are various other ways to expand State tax structures from existing taxes or without major constitutional change: these include land tax, wider sales and services taxation including entertainment, personal services and general retail sales; a rationalised stamp duty on loans and credit; and the introduction (or reintroduction) of general wealth taxes.

5. All such extensions enhance the possibility of harmful tax competition but raise the diversity in fiscal systems which federalists prize.

6. Expansion of local government functions, perhaps by creating regional government as a fourth tier in the federation, may be a good method of obtaining efficiency gains from greater decentralisation in public service delivery. This implies either greater grants to local government or an extension of its tax powers.

7. A poll or resident tax, suggested as a supplement or substitute for local rating, tends to be regressive and expensive to administer.

NOTES

[1] Data for this section derives from 1989–90 Budget Paper No. 1, *Budget Statement 1989–90*, Statement 6, especially Tables 2, 3 and 4; Budget Paper No. 4, *Commonwealth Financial Relations with other Levels of Government 1989–90*, ch. 2.

[2] New South Wales Commission of Audit, *Focus on Reform* (Sydney, 1988), ch. 2, pp. 14–17.

[3] This is best illustrated by the report of the New South Wales Commission of Audit, *Focus on Reform*, p. vii, which recommended "significant down-sizing of government" to be partly achieved by privatisation, debt level reduction and cessation of borrowing for non-productive purposes as well as better balance sheet and property management, including disposal of surplus property. For an alternative view, see Evatt Research Foundation, *State of Siege. Renewal or Privatisation for Australian State Public Services*? (Sydney: Pluto Press, 1989), especially chs. 1, 3 and 4.

[4] *Report of the Committee of Inquiry into Revenue Raising in Victoria* (Melbourne, 1983), ch. 9, New South Wales Tax Task Force, *Review of the State Tax System* (Sydney: 1988), ch. 25.

[5] National Priorities Project 1989, John Freebairn, Michael Porter and Cliff Walsh (eds.), *Saving and Productivity: Incentives for the 1990s* (Sydney: Allen and Unwin, 1989), ch. 13; Constitutional Commission, *Summary of Final Report* (Canberra: AGPS, 1988) pp. 70–71; Evatt Research Foundation, *State of Siege*, ch. 6, esp. pp. 117–25.

[6] New South Wales Tax Task Force, *Review of the State Tax System*, chs. 24–6; Peter Groenewegen, "Innovation Possibilities in State Business Taxation" in New South Wales Tax Task Force, *Commissioned Studies* (Sydney, 1989), esp. sections 4.2 and 5.1; Evatt Research Foundation, *State of Siege*, pp. 111–16; National Priorities Project 1989, *Saving and Productivity* , ch. 12.

[7] For a general discussion of the advantages and disadvantages of tax decentralisation, see Peter Groenewegen, "Taxation and Decentralisation: A Reconsideration of the Costs and Benefits of a Decentralised Tax System" (University of Sydney: Department of Economics Working Papers No. 104, March 1988), esp. pp. 10–28. For Australian analysis in the State context, see *Report of the Committee of Inquiry into Revenue Raising in Victoria*, ch. 7; New South Wales Tax Task Force, *Review of the State Tax System*, ch. 29.

[8] For data on local government boundary changes and amalgamations, see Advisory Council on Inter-Governmental Relations, *Local Government Boundary Changes and Amalgamations, An Historical Overview*, Paper 12 (Hobart, 1983).

[9] Peter Self, "The Federal Government's Role in Local Government", in Geoffrey Brennan (ed.), *Local Government Finance* (Canberra: Centre for Research on Federal Financial Relations Occasional Paper No. 41, 1987), esp. pp. 10–14; and see National Inquiry into Local Government Finance, *Report* (Canberra: AGPS, 1985), ch.17.

[10] See *Report of the Royal Commission of Inquiry into Rating, Valuation and Local Government Finance* (Sydney: NSW Government Printer, 1967), ch. 7; Advisory Council for Intergovernmental Relations, *Additional Revenue Sources for Local Government* (Hobart: Advisory Council for Intergovernmental Relations, Occasional Paper No. 4, 1981); National Inquiry into Local Government Finance, *Report* (Canberra: AGPS, 1985) ch. 16, esp. pp. 358–60, 361–4; John Howard "Local Government Revenue Raising", in National Inquiry into Local Government Finance, *Research and Consultancy Reports* (2), (Canberra: AGPS, 1985), chs. 7–10, 13.

[11] A poll tax is a flat money sum levied on adult residents irrespective of capacity to pay. Applications of the tax in practice generally make provision for low-income groups such as social security recipients.

[12] For a discussion of some of these proposals, see M. Neutze, "Local, Regional and Metropolitan Government", in R.L. Mathews (ed.), *Intergovernmental Relations in Australia* (Sydney: Angus & Robertson, 1974); E.G. Whitlam, "A New Federalism", *Australian Quarterly*, vol. 43 (September 1971), esp. pp. 10–11.

[13] This and the following three paragraphs draws heavily on G. Sawer, "The Whitlam Revolution in Australian Federalism", *Melbourne University Law Review*, vol. 10, no. 3 (1976), pp. 315–29.

[14] For a discussion of the advantages and practice

of regionalism see R.J.K. Chapman, "Regionalism, National Development and Government Institutional Arrangements, Regions as Moderating Institutions", Centre for Research on Federal Financial Relations, Occasional Paper no. 24 (Canberra, 1982); C.P. Harris, "Local Government and Regionalism in Queensland" (Canberra: Centre for Research on Federal Financial Relations, 1978); John Macmillan, et al., *Australia's Constitution,* pp. 143–7.

FURTHER READING

J.E. Stiglitz, *Economics of the Public Sector*, 2nd edn. (New York: W.W. Norton, 1988), ch. 17, contains a useful perspective on United States State and local finance.

A useful discussion of the State sector in Australia is:

Evatt Research Foundation, *State of Siege, Renewal or Privatisation for Australian State Public Services* (Sydney: Pluto Press, 1989).

State tax reform issues are discussed in:

Report of the Committee of Inquiry into Revenue Raising in Victoria (Melbourne: Government Printer, 1983).

New South Wales Tax Task Force, *Review of the State Tax System* (Sydney, 1988) and *Commissioned Studies* (Sydney, 1989).

See also:

National Priorities Project 1989, John Freebairn, Michael Porter and Cliff Walsh (eds.), *Savings and Productivity: Incentives for the 1990s* (Sydney: Allen and Unwin, 1989), chs. 11–13.

On local government finance reference should be made to:

National Inquiry into Local Government Finance, *Report* and *Research and Consultancy Reports* (Canberra: AGPS 1985), especially John Howard's report on local government revenue-raising.

Geoffrey Brennan (ed.), *Local Government Finance* (Canberra: Centre for Research on Federal Financial Relations, Occasional Paper No. 41, 1987).

Evatt Research Foundation, *Breach of Contract: The Future of Local Government in Australia* (Sydney: Pluto Press, 1990), esp. ch. 2.

New South Wales Government, *Report of Committee of Inquiry into Local Government Rating and other Revenue Powers and Resources* (Sydney: 1990).

17

Financing government: the public debt

FINANCING GOVERNMENT

In much of the discussion so far, government finance has been implicitly treated on the assumption that taxation revenue matches the government's expenditure needs. In practice, this is never the case. Expenditure by the government may exceed taxation and other current revenue, so that there is then a *Budget deficit*; or there may be a *Budget surplus* because current revenue exceeds government expenditure. In either case, issues of debt policy are involved; a deficit implies an increase in government indebtedness and a decision about the form of borrowing, a Budget surplus implies an effective decrease in government indebtedness and the retirement of some of the many forms which government debt can take. The choice of *where to borrow*, the *cost of borrowing*, and what *forms of debt to retire* over the Budget cycle is part of the art of *debt management.*

Until 1987–88, when it started to generate surpluses, the Federal Budget sector has been in deficit. In addition, for much of that time, Commonwealth Public Trading Enterprises have been net borrowers or drawers on the resources of capital markets. State governments and local and semi-government authorities have also been strong borrowers over this period, largely to finance their capital works, but they too have tended to lower their borrowing requirements relative to GDP from the mid-1980s. The trend over the 1980s in the public sector borrowing requirement is indicated by the fact that relative to GDP net public sector borrowing requirement peaked at 6.7 per cent in 1983–84, but by 1989–90 this had turned into a surplus position with the State/local sector's net borrowing requirement of 0.7 per cent of GDP offset by a massive Commonwealth sector surplus of 1.9 per cent of GDP. The Federal Government's return to a position of net saver from the growing Budget surpluses it is generating is altering the debt management problem significantly, since the problems raised by disposing of the surplus are quite different from those raised by deficit financing.[1]

Irrespective of whether it is in surplus or deficit, this description of the public sector borrowing requirement or aggregate deficit of the total Australian public sector over current receipts focuses attention once again on the federal nature of Australian government and on the importance of this for students of public finance. Public debt is created in Australia by three levels of government and by their instrumentalities within or without their Budget sectors, so that apart from securities issued by general government and their marketing problems there are also semi-government and local government securities. Much of this borrowing on aggregate is under the control and co-ordination of the Loan Council.[2]

Broadly speaking, the various levels of governments can obtain their borrowing from the following sources:

1. Overseas borrowing, limited under the Loan Council global borrowing arrangements.
2. Domestic loan raising through the sale of long-term government securities issued on behalf of Commonwealth and States, or for particular semi-government authorities.
3. Short-term borrowing, of less than one year's duration, by the sale of Treasury notes.
4. Changes in cash and bank balances, including overdrafts, with the government bankers.
5. Other borrowing arrangements such as credit purchases, leasing and so on, by governments and their instrumentalities.

In what follows, the discussion concentrates on the first three items of sources of government borrowing.

These various sources of government borrowing can be usefully considered in another way by looking at the *lenders* rather than the *debt instruments*. The government can raise its loan finance from the public both domestically and abroad. From the point of view of debt management and monetary policy, this source of funds is too broadly defined: loan raisings from the non-bank public and from the banking sector must be carefully distinguished because they have different implications for the money supply. The government can also borrow from its bankers (the Reserve Bank in the case of the Federal Government) by increasing its overdraft against the security of Treasury bills issued to the bank. The government can even "borrow from itself", through its various trust accounts or from departments with surplus funds for the whole or part of the financial year. Such departmental surplus funds and the balances of trust funds are invariably invested in long-term or short-term government securities. Finally, one level of government can borrow from other levels of government.[3]

Financing the Budget is a *continual process*, since the outflows of expenditure are rarely matched by the inflow of taxation and other current revenue during the financial year. In the first part of the financial year there is generally a net outflow of government revenue and in the final quarter of the year a substantial net inflow of revenue into the government sector. Table 17.1 illustrates the seasonal fluctuations in the government deficit on a monthly basis for 1988–89. It should be clear that State governments face similar problems, because their revenue inflows are also more irregular than the outflows caused by government expenditure.[4]

Even if there were no temporary surpluses or deficits in the Budget, there would still be a major debt problem. Portions of the existing debt are continually maturing and this debt must be either retired or refinanced. In connection with these aspects of debt management the state of the loan market has to be investigated, the interest rate implications have to be considered and the maturity of the debt instrument to be issued has to be determined. Such decisions are made in the light of economic circumstances for they influence the liquidity of the economy and the general interest rate structure. In making these choices, the Treasury is also always concerned with keeping interest liability for the Federal Government as low as possible. These issues of debt management are discussed further after aspects of the anatomy of Australia's public debt have been examined.

Table 17.1 Monthly budget surplus/deficit: Commonwealth Government 1988–89

	Expenditure		*Revenue*		*Surplus (+) Deficit (–)*
	$m	*%**	*$m*	*%**	*$m*
July 1988	7,020	102.6	6,026	85.6	–993
August	7,209	105.4	7,615	103.8	+406
September	6,413	93.7	5,813	79.3	–600
October	6,600	96.4	5,643	76.9	–958
November	6,254	91.4	6,847	93.4	594
December	6,699	97.9	6,310	86.0	–389
January 1989	7,764	113.4	6,778	92.4	–986
February	6,299	92.1	7,145	97.4	846
March	6,749	98.7	6,826	93.1	78
April	6,147	89.9	8,963	122.2	2,817
May	7,858	114.9	10,544	143.8	2,687
June	7,083	103.5	9,487	129.4	2,409
Total 1988–89	82,095		87,999		+5,904
Monthly average	6,841	100.0	7,333		
Quarterly average	20,524		21,999		

* Percentage of the monthly average (= 100). The sums of individual figures do not necessarily add due to rounding.

Source: Reserve Bank of Australia, *Bulletin*, September 1988 to August 1989.

THE ANATOMY OF AUSTRALIA'S PUBLIC DEBT

The anatomy of Australia's public debt illustrates a variety of issues which are relevant to the discussion of the economics of the public debt. In the first place, such an analysis discloses the distribution of the total debt outstanding among the various securities, that is, whether they are long-term or short-term securities, or whether the debt is domestically held, or external. Much of this information can be obtained from the annual Budget paper, *Government Securities on Issue*, but this frequently has to be supplemented from other sources.

Information about public indebtedness by levels of government can be presented in terms of their gross indebtedness as measured by securities on issue. A better way of measuring indebtedness is in terms of net debt position. This reduces gross debt by eliminating the debt held either by government itself, as well as the loans it has made to other governments. Table 17.2 gives the net debt position as a proportion of GDP for federal, State and local authorities.

Table 17.2 shows the variability to which both relative and absolute debt positions are prone for the various levels of government. Keeping in mind the popular fear of public indebtedness shared by many sections of the community, Table 17.2 shows how small relative indebtedness has been in the 1980s as compared with the 1920s, 1930s and 1940s, and how rapidly Australia managed to reduce its substantial World War II public debt.

Table 17.2 also shows the generally favourable debt position of the Commonwealth Budget sector, likely to be improved further from the substantial and growing surpluses

Table 17.2 Net debt of public authorities as a percentage of GDP by level of government as at 30 June: 1927–1987 (selected years)

	Federal Budget [a] %	*Authorities total* [a] %	*State authorities* %	*Local authorities* %	*All public authorities* [c, e] %
1927	–22.3	33.5	88.0	10.9	132.4
1935	–30.2	36.6	147.1	13.1	196.7
1939	–22.2	29.9	125.6	10.4	165.9
1946	81.0	113.4	80.3[g]		193.7
1956[b]	0.0	13.3	50.9	3.6	67.8
1966	–20.5	–7.2	48.3	5.5	46.6
1971	–21.3	–9.5	40.5	5.4	36.4
1976	–9.6	–0.4	24.8	4.0	28.4
1978	–4.4	4.2	24.1	3.9	32.2
1980[d]	–0.6	6.7	23.3	3.8	33.8
1981	–0.5	6.5	22.8	3.6	32.9
1987[f]	11.2	15.7	23.1	1.5	40.3

Notes:

a. – (minus) indicates an excess of financial assets over liabilities.
b. National income data prior to 1948–49 not strictly comparable to later data.
c. Public financial enterprises including the Reserve Bank are omitted.
d. Northern Territory included in State sector from 1978–79.
e. Some public authorities have been reclassified from one level of government to another after 1927.
f. Figures not strictly comparable because of different source — also do not add across column because of difficulties in consolidating State aggregate debt position.
g. No separate data for State/local debt available in 1946.

Source: J.P. McAuley, *The Structure of Australian Public Debt* (Canberra: Centre for Research on Federal Financial Relations, 1980), p. 8, updated by J.P. McAuley, "Public Indebtedness and Economic Activity in Australia", paper presented at the 1982 ANZAAS Congress, Section 24, Appendix 2. For 1987, 1989–90 Budget Paper No. 1, *Budget Statements 1989–90*, Statement No. 6, p. 6.25.

Commonwealth Budget has produced since 1986–87. Apart from periods of war, this favourable debt position contrasts favourably with the position of the States and their authorities; a source of friction between these levels of government. In 1975 this led to the transfer of $1 billion of State debt to the Commonwealth (reflected in Table 17.2), a performance which premiers in 1989 suggested should be repeated in the light of the large budget surpluses the Commonwealth was achieving, partly they noted, from substantial reductions in financial assistance grants.

To illustrate the complexity of the net debt concept, the following can be noted. The data shown in Table 17.2 can be said to understate debt position because they fail to fully reflect unfunded liabilities of the States, Commonwealth and local public sectors. A New South Wales Report on the State's Finances [5] showed assessed liabilities (for superannuation, long service, annual and sick leave, workers' compensation and other compensation payments) of $14.7 billion, compared with an official State net debt position for that year of $20.1 billion. Whether to include liabilities which the government incurs as employer and service provider with the conventional debt in terms of public securities issued, depends to a large extent on the purpose of the analysis.

Table 17.3 Government securities on issue classified by holder as at 30 June

	1970		*1980*		*1989**	
Holder	*$m*	%	*$m*	%	*$m*	%
Reserve Bank	1,190	10	5,217	19	3,441	7
Major Commonwealth Trust Funds	2,518	22	3,462	13	2,251	5
Total official	3,708	32	8,679	32	5,692	11
Savings banks	2,229	19	3,119	11	6,862	14
Trading and other banks	1,280	11	4,431	16	14,367	29
Money market dealers	597	5	1,325	5	1,991	4
Life assurance offices	1,195	10	2,798	10	1,795	4
Pensions and provident funds	426	4	1,608	6	1,144	2
Insurance companies	277	2	500	2	727	1
Public authorities	317	3	346	1	385	1
Other	1,596	14	4,580	17	16,881	34
Total non-official	7,917	68	18,707	68	44,152	89
Total	11,625	100	27,386	100	49,844	100

* Preliminary estimate.

Source: Budget Related Paper No. 1, *Government Securities on Issue* (various years).

Table 17.4 Local and semi-government securities by major holders as at 30 June

	1973		*1977*		*1983*		*1987*	
Holder	*$m*	%	*$m*	%	*$m*	%	*$m*	%
Savings banks	2,437	37.6	4,461	43.9	7,008	23.4	6,441	11.3
Trading banks	33	0.5	43	0.4	123	0.4	542	0.9
Life offices and pension funds	2,276	35.1	2,945	29.0	5,463	18.2	9,505	16.6
Non-life insurance	299	4.6	821	8.1	3,117	10.4	4,201	7.4
Building societies	123	1.9	63	0.6	625	2.1	763	1.4
Authorised dealers & money market corporations	24	0.4	94	0.9	160	0.5	469	0.8
Other holders[a]	1,293	19.9	1,727	17.0	13,483	45.0	35,277	61.7
Total[b]	6,485	100.0	10,154	100.0	29,988	100.0	57,148	100.0

Notes: a. Includes householders, corporate sector and overseas holders.
b. Includes securities maturing abroad negligible in periods shown.

Source: Reserve Bank of Australia, *Bulletin*, August 1983, Table 1.14; December 1988, Table 1.13.

Other aspects of the anatomy of Australia's public debt can be illustrated by examining the holders of that public debt. This information is regularly published and is summarised in Table 17.3 for Commonwealth securities and in Table 17.4 for securities issued by local and semi-government authorities. The main use of this information is for monetary policy purposes but Table 17.3 also sheds light on the substantial, and fluctuating, proportion of

Table 17.5 Government securities on issue by type of security as at 30 June 1989

	$m	%
Treasury bonds	33,917	57.3
Treasury indexed bonds	836	1.4
Australian savings bonds	2,745	4.6
Other securities[a]	805	1.4
Treasury notes	9,533	16.1
Other loans[b]	13	—
Internal Treasury bills	1,996	3.4
Total maturing domestically	49,845	84.2
Total repayable overseas[c]	9,388	15.8
Total securities on issue	59,232	100.0

Notes: a. Includes income equalisation deposits, overdue securities and tax-free stock.
b. Includes loans taken over from Canberra Commercial Development Authority.
c. Australian dollar equivalent at 30 June 1989.

Source: Amalgamated from Budget Related Paper No. 1, 1989–90, Government Securities on Issue at 30 June 1989 (Canberra: AGPS, 1989), p. 9, Table 2.

government securities held by the government sector itself. This is important in calculating the government's net debt position.

A further aspect of the anatomy of the public debt is the division of the public debt into various types of security on issue. Table 17.5 gives the details of this division and indicates the relative importance of the various types of securities offered. The nature of these securities should be briefly discussed because this information is useful for the later discussions of debt management problems.

The first four items in Table 17.5 are all long-term securities, that is, securities issued with a life of more than one year's duration. The first of these, which is by far the most important, includes what is generally known as Treasury bonds, which are issued by the Federal Government with a life (maturity) ranging from over two years to over twenty years. The changing maturity structure of these bonds and the term structure of interest rates are examined at a later stage, as is the manner in which these bonds are marketed. These bonds constitute the major form in which government debt is held, largely (as was shown in Table 17.3) by the institutional investors from the financial sector.

Treasury indexed bonds (introduced in 1985) and Australian savings bonds (introduced in 1976) are securities designed to appeal to special segments of the market, and are now both relatively insignificant parts of outstanding government securities. Both were designed to assist the financing of what were then very large Commonwealth budget deficits. Indexed bonds appeal particularly to the life insurance and superannuation segment of the market; savings bonds were designed to tap a substantial household savings market.

Finally, there are the short-dated securities, that is, those with maturities of less than one year. These include Treasury notes, issued either for thirteen, or twenty-six, weeks. These are mainly held by financial institutions, particularly banks and dealers in the short-term money markets. For example, in June 1989, trading banks accounted for 50.1 per cent, short-term money market dealers for 7.8 per cent, savings banks for 26.4 per cent, and the Reserve

Bank for 9.0 per cent of the Treasury notes on issue. The other short-dated security, Treasury bills, are not offered to the public. Public Treasury bills are three-month securities issued to the Reserve Bank with an interest of 1 per cent per annum as a security for government short-term borrowing. Internal Treasury bills are held by the Commonwealth Trust Funds, for example, as security for money lent to the Federal Government. Although not very large in relation to the total debt, Treasury notes are of great importance in the financial system as are other short-term government securities such as bonds with less than two years before maturity. This is because these short-term securities play a special role in the asset structure of the banking system and other financial institutions (the official short-term money market, for example) as a source of short-term liquidity and part of their prudential Prime Reserve Asset requirement.

Maturity structure of the debt

In the discussion of the type of securities offered, the different maturities of the various types of debt instrument were referred to. Over time this maturity structure changes; as bonds get closer to their maturity dates the debt becomes gradually more short-term unless the maturity structure is maintained by the replacement of maturing issues with longer-term debt. The resulting maturity structure therefore depends partly on the types of securities offered by the government and partly on the preference of investors about maturity expressed in the market. The latter, in turn, are determined by expectations about movements in interest rates and by the desire of investors to include in their asset portfolios securities with specific maturity dates. Table 17.6 presents data about the changing maturity structure of non-official holdings of the public debt for selected years from 1966.

The influence of interest rates on the demand for specific maturities by investors is briefly discussed in the next section when the term structure of interest rates is examined. Other influences on this demand arise from the particular requirements of various types of

Table 17.6 Maturity structure of non-official holdings of Commonwealth securities quoted on Australian stock exchanges as at 30 June

Securities maturing in:	*1966*	*1971*	*1976*	*1981*	*1986*	*1989* [a]
		Percentage of total holdings				
	%	%	%	%	%	%
Up to 5 years	36.9	35.8	35.7	58.9[b]	46	61
From 5 to 10 years	24.6	15.4	28.8	20.2	37	29
Over 10 years and up to 15 years	6.5	21.1	16.9	11.2	13	9
Over 15 years and up to 20 years	24.5	16.7	10.4	5.0	3	2
Over 20 years	7.4	11.0	8.2	4.6	—	—
Average period to maturity (years)[c]	9.39	10.82	10.58	5.50	6.7	5.5

Notes: a. Preliminary
b. Includes 19.1 per cent of securities maturing in less than one year in 1981, 18 per cent in 1986 and 30 per cent in 1989. These data exclude holdings of the Reserve Bank and major Commonwealth Trust funds.
c. Covers Treasury Bonds and Indexed Bonds only for 1986, 1989.

Source: Budget Related Paper No. 1, *Government Securities on Issue* (various years).

institutions. Some investors, for example, want to maintain a balanced portfolio of government securities including Treasury notes which mature continuously and which thereby provide a continuous inflow of cash. Other investors may want to balance the maturity structure of their asset portfolio with their expected cash requirements, which may be unevenly spread. Other investors, for example, dealers in the short-term money market, basically deal with securities with maturities of less than two years. A detailed discussion of these matters falls outside the scope of this book. Enough has been said, however, to indicate that the maturity structure of the debt is only partly controlled by the government's debt policy, and that a significant part of it depends on the preferences of investors. The importance of the maturity structure for debt management policy is discussed later.

The term structure of interest rates

Over much of the post-war period in Australia, the yield on long-term government securities has been well above the yield of the short-term securities such as Treasury notes. This period also showed a general upward trend in interest rates in Australia, reversed on only a few occasions when interest rates on government securities declined from substantially reduced demand for private securities in the capital market. There are exceptions to the tendency mentioned previously that long-term rates (yields) are generally above-short-term rates (yields) and in recent years such exceptions have tended to become the rule. For example, on a quarterly basis, 1988–89 saw Treasury notes and bonds with less than two years to maturity offering yields far in excess of those applicable to longer term bonds. These yield curves for 1988–89 are graphed in Figure 17.1.

Economists explain the relationship between short-term and long-term interest rates — what is called the "term structure" of interest rates — on the basis of expectations about changes in the rate of interest. This explanation is as follows. If no changes in interest rates were ever expected, there would be no need to have different rates on long-term and short-term securities and the yield curve — which shows interest rates for various maturities at a particular point of time — would be horizontal. If there is an expectation about rising interest rates, which has been the general long-term expectation in Australia for much of the post-war period, the yield curve slopes upwards. Lenders (demanders of debt) will then hesitate to commit themselves for long periods, because they expect to lend long at more favourable terms later on. The demand for debt therefore shifts to the short end of the market in order to borrow as long as possible while the favourable low rates last. The supply of long-term debt therefore increases. These shifts in demand and supply affect the prices and yields of the securities offered. Prices rise and yields decline at the short end of the market, while at the long end the opposite occurs. This shifts the yield curve upwards. If expectations suggest that interest rates will fall, the yield curve will slope downwards: lenders will then want to commit themselves for as long as possible at the rates favourable to them while borrowers, who expect to fund their debt at more favourable rates when interest rates have declined, will want to borrow as short as possible.

This traditional analysis does not explain the yield curves shown in Figure 17.1. Their slope is much more easily explained in terms of the conditions of monetary policy pertaining over the period. Progressive tightening of monetary policy from April 1988 onwards, raised short-term rates; however, longer term bond rates — a rapidly declining segment of the market as shown in Table 17.6 — followed more slowly, largely because few

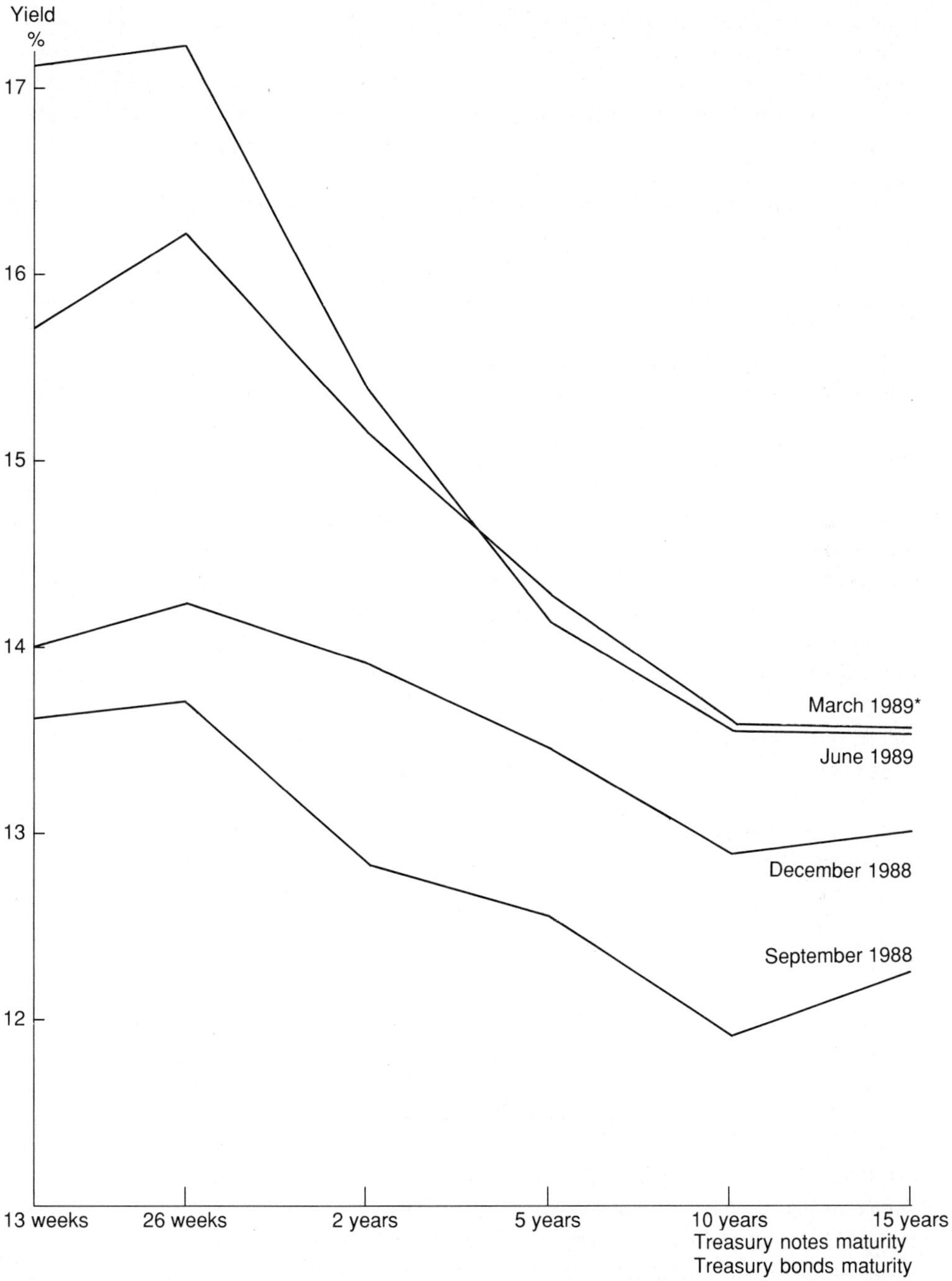

Figure 17.1 Yield curves showing yield to maturity of government securities at selected dates in 1989

Notes: March 1989, 26-week yield for April, no yield given for March.

Source: Reserve Bank of Australia, *Bulletin.*

lenders were willing to commit themselves to long bonds unless there were specific reasons to do so. The small number of bond tenders (three in 1988–89 at July, November 1988 and March 1989) of a total value of $1.2 billion and in fairly longish maturities ($0.8 billion in bonds with 10 to 15 years to maturity, the other $0.4 billion in bonds with 3 to 5 years to maturity) involved gradually rising yields from 11.8 to 13.6 per cent and a coupon (face value) return of 12 per cent. The later tenders reflected falling demand for longer-term bonds, an indication that investors regarded high short-term rates as something unlikely to be a temporary phenomenon.

Some further points on interest rate determination of relevance to the public debt must be made. A major factor which explains the general rise in interest is the inflation rate. Inflation drives up interest rates because lenders wish to protect their claims against a loss in their real value as the value of money falls. For example, if the real rate of interest is 3 per cent, and the inflation rate is 10 per cent, an interest rate of 13 per cent is required to maintain the real value of the claim and to earn the real interest rate on the debt. When the rate of inflation is increasing and is expected to continue, there is an increasing preference for short lending, which allows for more frequent renegotiation of the terms of the loan. In this way expectations about the rate of change in inflation as well as the rate of inflation itself affect interest rates, the term structure of interest rates, and the maturity structure of the debt. The importance of this for debt management is discussed later in the chapter.

In addition public debt interest rates have been influenced by external factors. Increased capital mobility has meant that Australian interest rates have been rather sensitive to rates ruling in other countries, particularly those in the United States. This also introduces foreign exchange consideration into the picture because shifts in international currency values affect real yields. In addition, the bond market has sometimes been influenced by substantial overseas demand. An example is the first half of 1983 with large purchases of Australian bonds by Japanese institutional investors. It should also be noted that the market-oriented approach to government security selling applicable from the early 1980s has increased the volatility of bond yields. These changes are discussed later in this chapter.

THE GROWTH OF THE PUBLIC DEBT

One final matter which should be looked at in the discussion of the anatomy of Australia's public debt is the growth of that debt over time and the relative importance of the interest burden which accompanies the growth of the debt. One way in which the growth of the debt can be shown is by looking at per capita public indebtedness in the post-war period the way in which the matter is often presented in popular discussion. The measures employed in discussing the growth of the public sector can also be utilised. The data for net public debt and interest charges as a percentage of GDP for various years since the end of the 1920s is shown in Table 17.7. As indicated earlier, the growth of Australia's public debt up to the mid-1970s has been largely due to the increase of State indebtedness but the federal contribution to the national public debt also increased for some time during this period as did that of local and semi-government.

Table 17.7 shows the changing relative interest burden of Australia's public debt, but it does so on aggregate only. It is also important to examine the relative importance of interest payments and other debt charges for the various levels of government in Australia. Table 17.8 provides the relevant information in absolute terms and also relative to total government

Table 17.7 Net debt and interest payments as a percentage of GDP: selected years from 1927

Year	*Net debt* %	*Interest payments* %
1927	132.4	6.2*
1939	165.9	5.8
1947	181.3	5.3
1957	63.0	2.5
1967	45.3	2.5
1977	29.0	2.5
1981	32.9	3.2
1987	40.3	3.7

* Interest as a percentage of GDP for 1929.

Source: Net debt: as for Table 17.2.
Interest 1929–57: R. Mathews, *Public Investment in Australia* (Melbourne: Longman Cheshire, 1967) Table 1.1.
1967–87: Australian National Accounts, *National Income and Expenditure*, various years.

Table 17.8 Interest on public debt: Commonwealth, State and local government authorities: 1962–63 to 1987–88 (selected years)

	1962–63	*1967–68*	*1972–73*	*1977–78*	*1982–83*	*1987–88* [a]
Net interest paid ($m) [b]						
Federal	34	34	12	564	1,441	5,323
States	375	555	671	1,210	4,348	8,729
Local	42	66	117	253	522	803
Interest paid as percentage of consumption spending (%) [c]						
Federal	1.3	0.7	0.5	10.8	14.6	32.4
States	29.9	27.6	24.4	34.4	26.1	32.1
Local	30.2	30.7	44.8	34.9	27.6	27.0

Notes: a. Preliminary.
b. Federal net interest is paid *less* interest received from States and Northern Territory.
c. For 1962–63 and 1967–68 percentage of current outlays.

Source: ABS, Public Authority Estimates, 1975–76; ABS, Government Financial Estimates, 1982–83, 1987–88.

consumption spending. The liability to interest payments and debt charges provides an important constraint on government borrowing: a large public debt with the high debt charges it entails pre-empts a great deal of freedom of choice in future expenditure decisions because the contractual obligation of the government to pay these charges ranks among the first items of essential government expenditure.

ISSUES OF DEBT MANAGEMENT POLICY

Following the examination of some of the basic features of Australia's public debt, the problem of debt management can now be discussed, that is, the choices which have to be made about the issuing of debt with respect to interest rates and the maturity of the securities to be issued. At the beginning of this chapter it was indicated that those choices depend on the state of the loan market, the general economic situation, and the Federal Government's desire to keep interest charges as low as possible in order to minimise the Budget constraints which these outlays impose on other expenditure.

As a starting-point it may be assumed that one of the aims of debt management policy is the minimisation of interest charges. At first sight, this suggests a policy of short borrowing because short rates are usually below long-term rates. This would be a most short-sighted policy if interest rates are expected to change. If they are expected to rise, long borrowing at the still prevailing low rates would be the better policy of long-term interest cost minimisation; if rates were expected to fall, short-term borrowing would be adopted. Debt management from this point of view alone would be a delicate skill which requires careful analysis of future market prospects including interest rates in the years ahead.

Interest cost minimisation is not the only issue in debt management, however. After all, if the government wanted to borrow as cheaply as possible, it would finance its activities by issuing interest-free debt, that is, by resorting to cash creation through the printing press or through borrowing from the central bank. This is not a satisfactory solution to the debt management problem, because such monetisation of the debt greatly increases the liquidity of the economy; this generally leads to rises in aggregate demand and to inflation. Because the above example of pure monetisation of the debt is not very usual in government finance, the argument contained therein can be more generally restated as follows. The more short-term the securities issued by government, the greater their impact on the liquidity of the economy, on the level of aggregate demand and the rate of inflation. One of the major tasks of debt management policy is therefore to regulate maturity structure so as to achieve the desired level of liquidity in the economy.

The selection of the maturity of the debt to be issued therefore also reflects choices about the degree of liquidity desired in the economy, which in turn depends on the desired stance of short-term economic policy as a whole. A policy of borrowing long, which reduces the liquidity of the economy, tends to reduce aggregate demand. There is, then, a close interrelationship between debt management and monetary policy; inevitably there will be conflicts between the principle of "economy" (or minimising interest charges) and short-run stabilisation policy.

The interest rates at which public debt can be issued depend on market conditions and, as indicated earlier, these rates are often related to the maturity of the security offered. The market determines these rates through periodic tenders of Treasury notes and Treasury bonds at various maturities, at which investors bid for the quantity of securities on offer, the highest bidders obtaining the quantities they desire. This system of marketing securities by tender means that interest rates are higher, *ceteris paribus*, the greater the amount of government spending to be financed by borrowing.[6]

Debt management therefore constitutes an attempt to balance delicately the desire to keep interest charges as low as possible to raise the necessary funds and to fulfil the requirements of short-run economic policy (which may be either contractionary or expansionary, and which is affected by both the maturity structure and the interest rates associated with the new debt). This problem is particularly difficult in circumstances of "stagflation" that is of inflation, unemployment, and low economic activity such as Australia experienced in the decade after 1973–74. To avoid the inflationary consequences of short-debt financing or financing from the banking sector, longer-term debt has to be sold to the non-bank public. This implies rising interest rates which in turn imply a contractionary impact on the share market, on investment spending including that on building and construction, and thereby on economic activity in general. In this way, a debt policy which is anti-inflationary also reduces opportunities for increased employment.

One way of reducing this conflict is to issue debt instruments which tap sections of the public who do not generally enter the government loan market, thereby reducing the upward pressure on the long-term interest rate. The introduction of the Australian Savings Bond was designed to achieve this result by attracting household savings which generally do not seek an investment outlet in public loans. Another way to reduce the conflict is to make long-term securities more attractive by offering better terms other than higher interest rates and yields. This could be done, for example, by exempting part or whole of the interest payable on government securities for income tax purposes which increases the effective yield of such securities without affecting nominal interest rates. Income tax rebatable bonds were issued in Australia up to 1968. Another way is to index the face value of the bond thereby making it inflation-proof; relatively small quantities of such indexed bonds have been offered on tender to institutional investors and, on application, to individual investors from 1986.

The success of issuing public loans can also be ensured by the creation of a captive market for government securities among large institutional investors. In Australia, savings banks, trading banks, life insurance companies, and superannuation funds are institutional investors whose investment in government securities was partly circumscribed by legal means for this purpose. In addition, the definition of trustee investments has tended to favour investment in government securities, including those issued by semi-government authorities. Banks continue to be required to hold government securities as part of their prescribed prudential Prime Assets Ratio, a matter of some concern in 1989 when suitable assets supply was diminishing as Treasury bond stocks fell from the substantial debt redemption induced by Commonwealth Budget surpluses.[7] Most of the other regulations were abandoned as part of the financial deregulation which took place in the 1980s.

Further aspects of government finance and monetary policy

In addition to these general effects of debt management policy on interest rates and the overall liquidity of the economy, government finance — as measured by changes in securities on issue and in the balance sheets of the banking system — is an important determinant of the money supply, a further important variable in monetary policy. This interrelationship between budgetary policy, fiscal policy, and monetary policy was referrred to in Chapter 2. It poses a difficult demarcation problem for the student in public finance; should the monetary problems associated with financing the Budget be included or not included in a discussion of the subject? Usual practice will be followed here, and only a brief discussion of the monetary aspects of debt financing will be made.[8]

As indicated above, government finance together with the balance of payments, the loan policy of the banking system, and the changes in the balance sheet of the Reserve Bank, are an important influence on the money supply in Australia. If the government adopts a policy of a target growth rate of the money supply, as the Federal Government did between 1976 and 1983, there is an implied constraint on either the amount of bank advances or the quantity of deficit financing to be taken up by the banking system. This follows from the combined bank balance sheet identity which indicates that increases in the money supply (M3) are the result of increases in the banks' holdings of government securities, increases in advances by the banking system, increases in its other assets, and increases in the gold and other foreign exchange holdings of the Reserve Bank. There is therefore no such constraint if the deficit is financed from the non-bank public through the issue of securities, though in that case (as was seen in the section on debt management) there is the danger that interest rates may rise as a result of this policy and this may detrimentally affect other objectives of government policy.

The changes induced by financial deregulation have created greater emphasis on interest rates in monetary policy. The influence of public debt on interest rates has already been mentioned, and debt management in that context remains an important tool of monetary policy as well.

THE LOAN COUNCIL AND GOVERNMENT BORROWING

Australia is unique among other federations because for a period of over 50 years it has co-ordinated the loan programs and loan raisings of both the Federal Government and the various States as well as the larger loan raisings of local government and semi-government authorities. The institution through which this process is co-ordinated is called the Loan Council, which was initially set up on a voluntary basis in 1924 and on a formal, constitutional basis in 1928 when the Federal and State governments ratified the Financial Agreement. This arrangement has been rightly described as a landmark in Australian federal financial relations. During the 1980s financial deregulation altered the functions of the Loan Council, but its determination of a global approach to public borrowing, setting ceilings on aggregate domestic and overseas borrowing, implies a continuing importance for this instrument of federal fiscal relations.[9]

As constituted by the Financial Agreement, the Loan Council consists of the Prime Minister of the Commonwealth (or a Minister nominated by him, generally the Treasurer), the six State Premiers, who frequently are also the State Treasurers (or Ministers nominated by them) while frequently other Ministers attend as observers together with government officials from the treasuries and other departments. The Commonwealth has two votes and, as chairman of the Council, a casting vote as well, so that with the support of two States it can control the meetings. All the important decisions other than the allocation of the loan money between the States are decided on by majority vote. The allocation of the aggregate loan funds among the States has to be agreed to unanimously, in default of which the allocation is decided on by formula, where the aggregate allocation is divided according to the ratio of an individual State's net loan expenditures over the past five years to the aggregate State net loan expenditures over the same period. This formula has never actually been used.

The meetings of the Loan Council take place in June, unless a special meeting is requested by the members. The proceedings of these Loan Council meetings are confidential to its members, and information on the Council's proceedings is generally confined to data on the borrowing program approved during its deliberations and any other major policy changes.[10]

Changes in Loan Council responsibilities

The intention of establishing the Loan Council was to control the whole of public borrowing except for the following: defence loans of the Federal Government, loans for temporary purposes, and loans for local and semi-government authorities defined as small, fixed in 1982 at those which annually borrow less than $1.5 million. As a result the Loan Council during the 1930s and 1940s controlled the greater part of total State and local borrowing requirements and spending for capital purposes — a useful instrument for curtailing capital spending in a period of excess demand on resources such as that of World War II. From the 1950s to the 1970s the Commonwealth dominated Loan Council proceedings and hence could easily control public works programs from the States and local government sectors for fiscal policy purposes. This dominance was achieved through its offers to support State and local works programs by partly financing them from its own current revenue. Such financial support was first given on an ad hoc basis. From 1971 onwards, the Commonwealth has provided one-third of the loan program from its own sources. As one former member of the Loan Council has put it, this has allowed the Commonwealth to run the Loan Council as part of its overall economic management.[11] This constituted an effective policy instrument for economic management purposes when the Loan Council approved 80 per cent of the State/local capital works programs, as occurred in the early 1950s and to a lesser extent in the following decade. However, from the mid-1970s this proportion declined until in 1984 the global approach to public borrowing was adopted by the Loan Council for implementation in the following year.[12]

The global approach to borrowing in force from 1985 (though modified in subsequent years) rests on four propositions. The first is an agreement to voluntarily limit the level of new money borrowings each year from all sources to a global limit agreed to by the Loan Council. This global limit is set on an annual basis and includes a ceiling on public authority overseas borrowings (in 1989 of 22 per cent on all new borrowing). Secondly, all government authorities are included (public financial institutions excepted) and only borrowings to cover unexpected fluctuations in outlays and receipts are exempt. New borrowing is widely defined, including the various types of arrangements by which States and their authorities had subverted Loan Council Control in the late 1970s and early 1980s. Last, government authorities subject to the global limit can refinance maturing debt outside the global limit provided there is no net addition to the total level of outstanding debt.[13]

FURTHER CONSIDERATIONS ON THE PUBLIC DEBT

There are several other theoretical issues considered to be genuine public finance issues in discussions of the public debt. The first of these concerns determining when governments should finance their expenditure by taxation and when by borrowing. This brings in issues of resource allocation, and more important, of stabilisation policy. A second issue concerns the burden of the public debt, especially the question of whether public borrowing can transfer a burden to future generations. These two issues are not unrelated; the answer to the second question, for example, influences the solution to the problem of the tax/borrowing choice.

Financing by taxation or by borrowing?

This used to be considered a classical question because it occupied many of the public finance theorists of the nineteenth century. Since then, its relevance has once more been acknowledged, largely in discussions about the role of the public debt in stabilisation policy, and partly in arguments about the relationship between loan finance and public investment. During the 1980s, the issue has been discussed in the context of a twin deficit theory where high public borrowing is linked to an adverse current (foreign) trade balance.

Prior to the 1920s and 1930s, the question about the tax/borrowing choice was easily answered. Governments should have balanced Budgets in normal times, that is, revenue from taxation should meet the government's expenditure requirements. If governments were borrowing it was a sign that they were living beyond their means which, as in the case of households, was regarded as a contravention of the virtue of thrift. In addition, government borrowing reduced the investible funds available to the private sector and thereby slowed down the rate of growth. The latter is based on the explicit assumption that taxation reduces private consumption and public borrowing reduces private investment. Although the validity of this assumption is difficult to prove, it plays a leading role in much of the economic theory of the public debt.

Two exceptions were allowed to this general rule. The first of these related to extraordinary or war expenditure. War finance could be partly met from borrowing since the large expenditure required in such a national emergency could not be provided from taxation alone. Secondly, borrowing was allowed for genuine government investment where such investment created a long-lived asset with a net return sufficient to service the debt. The last view was adopted as a suitable borrowing principle by the New South Wales Commission of Audit which reported in 1988.[14]

During the 1920s and 1930s other matters were introduced in the discussion of the determination of the tax/borrowing choice. In the first place it was realised that government borrowing as compared with taxation was far more demand-creating because the securities created by the government through its loan raisings became part of the credit base of the financial system and in this way provided a much smaller reduction in the spending power of the public than did taxation. The shorter the maturity of the securities issued, the greater their expansionary demand-creating impact.

More important, it was also realised during this period that in the case of unemployment the classical argument that government borrowing impeded economic growth could no longer be sustained. Resources which were unemployed in the private sector could be safely taken up by the public sector — preferably through cash creation by borrowing from the central bank — without thereby hindering the development of the private sector. Indeed, the public works started with the borrowed funds would encourage the recovery and future growth of the private sector through their multiplier effects.

With the discussions about the effectiveness of monetary policy as against fiscal policy that have taken place especially since the 1970s, many of these conclusions have once again become controversial. It is now argued that when deficit financing of public works for job creation is financed by money creation, no real fiscal policy is involved. What occurs in such a situation is an addition to the money supply and it is this that creates the expansionary and possibly inflationary effects. If deficit financing is carried out by borrowing from the non-bank public, that is, without the creation of additional money, then an expansionary effect would follow only if the funds borrowed were held as idle balances by the public. If the government has to compete for loanable funds in the loan market, it will place upward pressure on interest rates — which has contractionary effects — and by attracting funds away from private sector use, it will reduce private expenditure including investment spending. In this case, it is argued, a pure fiscal policy of demand creation financed by *borrowing* may not be expansionary because of this "crowding out" effect. These issues are further discussed in Chapter 18.

When during the second half of the 1980s Australia's current trade account turned unfavourable (raising external debt), public borrowing was seen to aggravate this outcome by adding to the demand for foreign savings. This is nothing but a simple explanation in terms of the capital market (savings/investment) identity, where:

$$X - M = I - [S + (G - T)]$$

where X is exports, M imports, I private investment, S private domestic savings, G–T the budget balance. An increased deficit, *ceteris paribus*, aggravates an unfavourable trade balance (or reduces a favourable one) to secure the supply of foreign saving needed to bring aggregate saving and investment into balance.[15]

In conclusion, it can be said that a number of considerations are important in determining when to borrow and when to tax in normal times. In abnormal times, such as wars, borrowing is fully justified, subject to considerations about the post-war stability of the economy which can be greatly influenced by the liquidity and other effects of the war debt. The state of the economy, with respect to price stability, employment, and the balance of payments, is a prime consideration. Various parts of this chapter have indicated the effects of debt management and borrowing on the level of economic activity via the maturity structure of the debt, the effect of government security yields on the term structure of interest rates, and, briefly, the possible effects of borrowing as distinct from money creation on the impact of an expansionary fiscal policy. These issues will greatly influence the taxation/borrowing choice but a more detailed discussion of them, including particularly the interrelationship between fiscal and monetary policy is best postponed to Chapter 18, which deals with stabilisation policy.

When there is full employment, price stability, and balance of payments equilibrium, the choice is very largely influenced by the view held on the transferability of the burden of the debt to future generations. If the burden of the debt can be transferred to future generations, it is possible for the present generation to increase its current consumption and thereby its living standards at the expense of later generations. If such inter-generational transfer is not possible, then the choice between taxation and borrowing, on the assumption of a stable economy, is much less important from the point of view of public finance.

Two further points relevant to the taxation/borrowing choice in a stable economy should be noted. The choice is still very important if it is assumed that taxation reduces private investment less than borrowing does, and a high priority is placed on growth and capital accumulation. Also, if the taxation required to meet debt charges becomes very large because there is already a large public debt in existence, this may cause adverse output effects.

There may also be large adverse distributional consequences of a substantial public debt, if it is assumed that the interest payments largely go to wealthy bondholders while the taxes to meet these debt charges fall more or less proportionately on the community as a whole.[16] As Table 17.4 shows, debt holdings of private individuals are relatively small in Australia.

The burden of the public debt

The question of the burden of the public debt is a complex one since it involves questions about the nature of the burden and its inter-temporal incidence. These questions have been increasingly discussed in the literature of public finance since the late 1950s.[17]

The first question that must be answered relates to the nature of the burden of the public debt. Is the capital sum borrowed the burden or are the future interest payment and other debt charges incurred through public borrowing? During the 1940s and 1950s it was generally agreed that neither constituted a burden on future generations in the case of an internal debt. When the government borrowed to finance a capital project, the resources required for its construction were drawn from the present generation in a manner similar to taxation. The interest and debt charges on internally held debt could not be called a burden because they are transfer payments from the taxpayer to the bondholder.[18]

In the case of external debt, the position is different. Here the resources borrowed for use in the public sector are not obtained from the present generation — they are imported from other countries; in addition, the future debt charges and interest payments are not simple transfer payments but require the transfer of real resources from the domestic taxpayers to the foreign bondholders. The conclusion was clear: domestic debt could not, but external debt did, impose a burden on future generations.[19]

A possible burden on future generations in the case of internal borrowing is, however, implied in the different effects of taxation and borrowing on growth and on the capital endowment passed to future generations. Here the burden of the debt is measured in terms of future consumption. If governments borrow when full employment prevails, thereby reducing the investible resources available to the private sector, and if the return on the public investment made from the borrowed funds is less than the return which would have resulted if they had been invested in the private sector, the future income will have been reduced and, with it, the potential consumption of future generations. In short, if public borrowing reduces private investment more than does taxation, and if the rate of return on these funds is less in the public than in the private sector, internal borrowing can impose a burden on future generations.[20]

The issue of intergovernmental transfer of the burden of the public debt has relevance to some practical issues: the borrowing policy to be adopted by State and local governments and the national choice of the debt/taxation financing mix. In the case of State, but more especially, local borrowing, much of the borrowing can be regarded as "external debt", thereby making the transfer of a burden to future generations more easy. Where the construction of a long-lived asset is contemplated by the State or the local government unit, and this asset will yield services for a long future period, inter-generational equity on the benefit principle demands debt financing so that the future beneficiaries of the project will also pay part of the costs.

For the national government there are also some implications from this analysis. If tax finance is largely drawn from private consumption whereas borrowing reduces private investment, current government expenditure should be financed from taxation and not from loan finance. Only capital projects whose benefits extend far into the future should be financed from loan funds. If, as has been the case in Australia, a large part of public capital formation has been financed from current revenue, this policy can largely be justified by the high priority which past governments have placed on capital formation and economic growth to the benefit of future generations.

SUMMARY

1. Borrowing and like financing and debt management issues are involved when expenditure flows and current revenue flows fail to match.

2. Borrowing measures can be subdivided into:

   (a) overseas borrowing;
   (b) domestic loan-raising by issuing longer-term securities (in Australia, Treasury bonds);
   (c) Short-term borrowing, of less than one year's duration (in Australia, generally by Treasury notes);
   (d) changes in cash and bank balances, including overdrafts with government bankers;
   (e) credit purchases, leases and like forms of borrowing.

3. The continuous nature of the Budget process with seasonal fluctuations in expenditure and revenue flows creates the need for short-term financing.

4. Net debt is often defined in terms of securities on issue at a point of time less debt held by the government itself (in its trust funds, for example) or, for the Australian public sector as a whole, loans made to/or from, other levels of government.

5. Another concept of net debt takes government liabilities as employer and service provider into consideration. These include unfunded provision for superannuation and leave, as well as workers and other accident compensation.

6. The maturity structure of the debt is continually changing, as old debt is redeemed, new debt is issued and all debt moves closer to maturity. This has implications for monetary policy and debt management.

7. The term structure of interest rates associated with government debt instruments (and reflected in the yield curve) is explicable in terms of expectations about interest rate changes, which in turn are influenced by expectations about the stance of monetary policy, inflation rates, overseas interest rates and exchange rates.

8. Debt management has several objectives and tasks:

   (a) as a starting-point, it seeks minimum interest cost for governments;

(b) this policy is constrained by the demands of monetary policy, either in terms of interest rates or money supply;
(c) appropriate marketing techniques may secure borrowing targets at satisfactory interest costs.

9. The Loan Council co-ordinates aggregates of government borrowing (the global limit approach) as an exercise in co-operative federalism. It likewise enables central control over borrowing, and hence public sector demand, for stabilisation purposes.

10. The tax/borrowing choice is influenced by extraordinary circumstances like war, the demands of stabilisation policy, and the capital works programs of the government concerned. It can also be influenced by distributional considerations including inter-generational burden shifts.

11. Whether the burden of public debt can be transmitted to future generations depends on various circumstances. One is whether the debt is external (that is, repayable abroad), the other factor concerns the impact of borrowing on the capital stock endowment for future generations. It should be noted that State/local borrowing within Australia has the characteristics of external borrowing for this purpose.

NOTES

[1] 1989–90 Budget Paper No. 1, *Budget Statements 1989–90*, Statement No. 6 (Canberra: AGPS, 1989), pp. 6.19–6.20; Statement No. 5 provides a detailed historical discussion of the financing of the Budget balance, including a statistical table of Budget balance since 1953–54 (ibid., p. 5.13).

[2] The operation of the Loan Council is investigated later in this chapter.

[3] The relative importance of these types of lenders are shown in Tables 17.3 and 17.4 with respect to government securities and local and semi-government securities.

[4] A detailed analysis of these seasonal flows, and their unpredictability as well as variability from year to year is in 1989 Budget Paper No. 4, *Budget Statements 1989–90* (Canberra: AGPS, 1989), Statement No. 5, pp. 5.5–5.7. Spreading revenue collections and expenditure flows has reduced these seasonal impacts, thereby reducing instability in the short-term money market and interest payments for the Federal Government incurred for short-term borrowing by Treasury notes.

[5] New South Wales Commission of Audit, *Focus on Reform. Report on the State's Finance* (Sydney, 1988), pp. 53–5. The conventional net debt figure of the State derives from 1989–90 Budget Paper No. 4 (Canberra: AGPS 1989), Table 16, p. 33.

[6] Surpluses on Commonwealth Budgets have induced reverse tenders from the end of 1989, in which offers of bonds to the Commonwealth will be accepted from registered investers. For details see Reserve Bank of Australia, *Bulletin*, November 1989, pp. 31–2.

[7] For a discussion see K. Davis, "Australian Monetary Policy: a Decade of Change", *Economic Papers* 7(1) March 1988, pp. 13–14. In early January 1990, the Reserve Bank announced a phased-in reduction in the Prime Assets ratio to overcome this problem.

[8] A useful source of reading on contemporary monetary policy issues in Australia is the selection of papers from a "Conference on Australian Monetary Policy Post-Campbell" in *Economic Papers* 7(1), March 1988, pp. 1–108.

[9] The Loan Council was set up in the 1920s as the result of a growing awareness of the need to co-ordinate loan raisings on a national basis. Such co-ordination was required to eliminate the competition by the individual States on the international (especially the British) loan market as well as on the domestic capital market, which tended to raise interest rates on

these loans. It also aimed at improving the efficiency of loan-raising in general. In the context of the then accepted canons of financial prudence, it was also felt desirable to make provisions for debt redemption by creating a national debt sinking fund to which both the Commonwealth and the States would contribute. For a detailed history, see R.S. Gilbert, *The Australian Loan Council in Federal Fiscal Adjustment 1890–1965* (Canberra: ANU Press 1973), which can be updated from Russell Mathews, "Fiscal Federalism in Australia: Past and Future Tense" (Canberra: Centre for Research on Federal Financial Relations, Reprint Series no. 74, 1986), pp. 38–44.

[10] These are invariably detailed in Budget Paper No. 4, *Commonwealth Financial Relations with other Levels of Government.*

[11] R.J. Hamer, "Australian Federalism: A View from Victoria", in Allan Patience and Jeffrey Scott (eds.), *Australian Federalism Future Tense* (Melbourne: Oxford University Press, 1983), ch. 4, pp. 55–6. Cf. the account by Sir Robert Menzies, *Central Power in the Australian Commonwealth* (London: Cassell, 1967), pp. 105–10.

[12] The decline in Loan Council responsibility for (and federal control over) public borrowing particularly by the State and local government sector can be explained by a number of factors. In the first place, the drive towards deregulation of financial markets led to a substantial removal of the public borrowing program from the ambit of Loan Council control. The second factor arose from the States' response to Commonwealth control over their public works spending for fiscal policy purposes, especially when this was particularly tightly applied after 1976. This consisted in devising forms of borrowing which do not fall within the ambit of the Loan Council as traditionally conceived, such as leverage leasing, purchases on extended credit, and other borrowing devices not resulting in marketed securities. In part, the States' strategy in this followed Commonwealth example of using the exemption of temporary borrowing and defence loans for purposes not contemplated by the Financial Agreement.

[13] Budget Paper No. 4, *Commonwealth Financial Relations with other Levels of Government* (Canberra: AGPS, 1989), pp. 49–53, esp. p. 51 of which the paragraph in the text is a paraphrase.

[14] New South Wales Commission of Audit, *Focus on Reform*, p. 8.

[15] For a discussion of this "twin deficit argument", see Hans Gensberg, "The Fiscal Deficit and the Current Account: Twins or Distant Relatives?" (Sydney: Reserve Bank Research Discussion Paper, RDP8813, December 1988), Evatt Research Foundation, *State of Siege* (Sydney: Pluto Press, 1989), pp. 23–9.

[16] For a detailed discussion of these problems in connection with the tax/borrowing choice, including some analysis of the incidence of debt, see C.S. Shoup, *Public Finance*, ch. 18.

[17] This topic was revived largely as the result of the publication of J.M. Buchanan, *Public Principles of the Public Debt* (Homewood, Ill.: Irwin, 1958) to which reference should be made. See also J.M. Ferguson (ed.), *Public Debt and Future Generations* (Chapel Hill: University of North Carolina Press, 1964), R.W. Houghton (ed.), *Public Finance*, Readings 12–14 and A.W. Hooke, *The Burden of the Public Debt* (Brisbane: University of Queensland Press 1975), ch. 2, which provides a useful evaluation of the whole debate.

[18] As indicated previously, such transfer payments may have important output and excess burden effects.

[19] For a discussion of this orthodox position on the burden of the public debt see A.P. Lerner, "The Burden of the National Debt", in R.W. Houghton (ed.), *Public Finance*, Reading 12.

[20] See R.A. and P.B. Musgrave, *Public Finance in Theory and Practice*, esp. 706–11. The other, and rather more esoteric ways in which debt burdens can be passed to future generations will not be discussed here. For a discussion of these see A.W. Hooke, *The Burden of the Public Debt*, chs. 3–7 and the references there cited.

FURTHER READING

The standard texts once again provide a useful starting-point.

See R.A. and P.B. Musgrave, *Public Finance in Theory and Practice* (New York: McGraw Hill, 1984), ch. 33.

J.E. Stiglitz, *Economics of the Public Sector* (New York: W.W. Norton, 1988), ch. 28.

An Australian discussion is:

The INDECS Economic Special Report, *State of Play 6* (Sydney: Allen and Unwin, 1990), ch. 10, esp. pp. 203–5.

See also:

I.R. Harper and G.L. Lim, "Financial Implications of the Commonwealth Budget Surplus", *Australian Economic Review*, 4/88, pp. 19–25.

An evaluation of the burden of the public debt debate is in:

A.W. Hooke, *The Burden of the Public Debt* (St. Lucia: Queensland University Press, 1975).

A useful discussion of the terminology of public debt in the Australian context is:

1989–90 Commonwealth Budget Paper No. 1, Budget Statements 1989–90 (Canberra: AGPS, 1989), Statement No. 5, Statement No. 6, pp. 6.19–6.27.

18

Fiscal policy for stabilisation

A final important function of budgetary policy is its use as an instrument for macro-economic stabilisation through the effects of the government's budgetary transactions on the volume of *output*, the level of *employment*, the rate of change of the *price level*, and the *balance of trade*. After 1945, Commonwealth governments of all political persuasions have accepted responsibility for the regulation of the economy by adjusting the policy instruments available to them to push the system towards more desired outcomes. From the mid-1970s, however, economists have substantially changed their views on the government's role in stabilisation and its ability to influence in any systematic manner the four objectives of general economic policy stated above. In contrast to the 1960s, there is less agreement over which policy instruments should achieve these objectives and over how far these objectives should be pursued by government intervention. Underlying these policy disagreements are differences of a theoretical as well as empirical nature.[1]

Of particular relevance to the discussion represented in this chapter are the disagreements on the efficacy and usefulness of fiscal policy exercised by the manipulation of taxation and expenditure instruments through the Budget. It should be understood at the outset that the events of the 1970s and 1980s have demonstrated that much of the demand management approach derived from the Keynesian income determination models which proliferated in the 1950s and 1960s is far too simple an approach to the difficult issues raised by stabilisation policy. Budgetary policy is therefore at best considered as only one arm of economic policy for stabilisation, leaving aside for the moment how important that arm might be. For this reason, fiscal policy remains an important topic for students of public finance, though studying it in isolation from other macro-policy instruments becomes increasingly dangerous in the light of the complexities of the operations of an actual economy.

A brief guide to the contents of this chapter is therefore particularly relevant in order to emphasise its limitations. The starting-point is the specification of the desired objectives and the policy instruments available to government to influence these objectives (particularly those associated with the Budget). Their interrelationship in theory and practice in Australia forms the concluding subject-matter of this chapter.

THE OBJECTIVES OF STABILISATION POLICY

Foremost among the desired outcomes is the objective of sustainable economic growth. This is required to satisfy expectations about rising living standards *and* to provide adequate employment opportunities for a growing workforce. Growth is therefore a primary objective, but it is not the only one. Growth *and* stability were generally regarded as *the* twin objectives in all the Budget speeches delivered in Australia in the 1950s and 1960s. More recently costs of growth have also been recognised, particularly those associated with the environment. Growth is also desirable because it can facilitate the achievement of distributional objectives. It is much easier for governments to gain control of the resources needed for income maintenance schemes, to aid underprivileged and low-income groups, and for assistance to the developing world when output is growing. However, as shown in earlier chapters, there are also many possibilities for conflict between the distributional objectives and economic growth.

In the previous paragraph, stability was described as an important co-requisite to economic growth. Broadly speaking, the requirement for economic stability includes the maintenance of satisfactory levels of employment and low rates of inflation. However, it is now generally agreed that the achievement of these objectives requires the close co-ordination of all branches of economic policy relating as they do to incomes and wages, money, international trade and, of course, the budgetary instruments of expenditure and taxation. Since the word "satisfactory" is rather a vague term when used in the context of levels of employment and rates of inflation to be aimed at, some more detailed specification of these objectives is necessary.

The full employment objective

The "full employment" objective was described as the "fundamental aim of the Commonwealth Government" in the White Paper, *Full Employment in Australia*, prepared for the Chifley government in 1945. This objective is also incorporated in the three statutory policy objectives of the Reserve Bank in Australia.[2] Full employment is often defined in terms of acceptable levels of unemployment. This can be described either by community standards which have tended to shift over time, or, analytically in terms of the unemployment rate compatible with price stability. The statistical meaning of full employment is therefore not a settled matter, and the full employment target to be aimed at is a social and political as well as an economic issue.

Unemployment has a number of dimensions. First, a distinction has to be made between *voluntary* and *involuntary* unemployment; only the involuntarily unemployed, that is, those wishing to work at the prevailing wage rates, fall within the category of unemployment susceptible to economic policy. Involuntary unemployment constitutes by far the greater part of the unemployed, and it reflects an inadequate level of demand for labour. Involuntary unemployment can be further subdivided into *cyclical* unemployment, *seasonal* unemployment, *regional* unemployment and *structural* unemployment, and each of these types of unemployment may require a distinctive demand management policy. In the formation of economic policy to reduce the level of unemployment, the authorities also will have regard to the characteristics of the unemployed persons, that is, they will distinguish between youth unemployment, female unemployment, unskilled unemployment, and so on.

The objective of price stability

An acceptable rate of price inflation is desired by governments because of the undesirable consequences of high rates of inflation (or high rates of deflation), although excessive deflation of the price level has not been a problem since the 1930s. High inflation rates adversely affect the less organised economic and social groups and are detrimental to a fair income distribution. They may also inhibit growth, investment, and employment opportunities, undermine the efficiency of an economic system regulated by market forces, create social tensions, and foster anxiety and uncertainty in the economic behaviour of all social groups. What is an acceptable rate of inflation is once again difficult to specify; in Australia during the 1960s a rate of inflation which exceeded 2.5 per cent per annum was a cause for alarm and likely to invoke substantial policy response. Higher inflation rates during the 1970s and 1980s has induced an increasing demand for a completely free inflation-free economic environment as the most desirable way of specifying the policy objective.[3]

THE INSTRUMENTS OF STABILISATION POLICY

Because it is generally agreed (notable exceptions in the last two decades being the "monetarist position" and the new classical economics based on "rational expectations") that economies have no inbuilt *automatic* mechanism which ensures economic stability in the medium period, governments now invariably intervene in the economy to offset undesired movements in the level of output and employment and in the rate of inflation by using a number of regulatory instruments.

Chapter 2 briefly discussed the distinction between *budgetary policy* and *economic policy as a whole*, arguing that budgetary policy was one of five areas of economic policy. In connection with *stabilisation policy*, a distinction is frequently made between the instruments of "pure fiscal policy" as well as other stabilisation instruments such as those of monetary policy, incomes and prices policy, and so on. Although such a division can be defended on pedagogic grounds (or for limiting the scope of textbooks) it is an exceedingly dangerous practice; experience points to the interdependence of *all* the instruments and the dangers of looking at particular areas of policy in isolation.

The discussion in Chapter 2 identified the instruments of budgetary policy as *expenditure* and *taxation* policy instruments. Following the analysis of Nevile,[4] this means that the effective instruments of budgetary stabilisation policy or pure fiscal policy in the first instance can be divided into the following seven categories:

1. Current expenditure of public authorities on goods and services excluding military imports.
2. Capital expenditure by public authorities on building and construction.
3. Capital expenditure by public authorities on machinery and equipment.

4. Gross operating surplus of public enterprises (a negative expenditure).
5. Cash benefits to persons.

On the taxation side, an additional two major instruments of immediate fiscal impact are:

6. Personal income tax rates.
7. Rates of sales tax and excise and other indirect taxes (and discretionary changes in the bases of these taxes).

It should be stressed that it is the *rates* of tax which are the instruments and *not* the tax receipts. Tax receipts are not only influenced by changes in tax rates (that is, by discretionary action) but changes in receipts also follow upon (that is, are *induced* by) changes in economic activity (income and expenditure levels). Company tax rate changes are generally excluded from the instruments with *immediate* fiscal impact because their impact is not felt until after a lag of at least a year due to the institutional arrangements for company tax collections. A 1989–90 Budget change to the timing of company tax collections modifies this conclusion, and company tax rates are now a more immediately significant fiscal policy instrument. Changes in the company tax *base* (such as accelerated depreciation, investment allowances and so on) generally have a quicker impact.

Chapter 17 showed that budgetary policy is not simply a case of taxation and expenditure instruments, but also involves debt policy. Because expenditure is not usually matched by current revenue, Budget financing decisions add a further dimension to budgetary policy. Debt policy affects interest rates and the money supply and spending decisions; it is therefore also an important part of stabilisation policy, and so the distinction between *pure* fiscal policy and other policy is even more difficult to sustain.

A further point must be made in this context about the impact of federalism on the instruments of fiscal policy. In Chapter 14 it was seen that economic stabilisation policy is the responsibility of the national government but it was also argued that successful stabilisation policy implementation involves some degree of intergovernmental co-operation. This is because the States maintain a considerable degree of independence in expenditure decision-making (particularly in connection with the first four expenditure instruments distinguished by Nevile) and through control of payroll tax, one of the five major Australian taxes. The extent of federal government control over the seven fiscal instruments is therefore incomplete.

The discussion of these budgetary instruments — tax, expenditure, and debt policy — in connection with stabilisation policy is the major concern in this chapter. This does not mean that other arms of economic policy — monetary policy, wages or more general incomes policy — are completely neglected. In this assessment of fiscal policy in Australia in theory and practice, the interdependence of the policy instruments is continually stressed.

Targets and instruments

In Australia, the planning for stabilisation policy involves setting values for those policy instruments, that is, tax rates, expenditure levels, debt structure, interest rates, money supply, wage growth, and so on, which will yield an overall policy stance to produce the most desirable package of outcomes in terms of sustainable growth rates, levels of employment, and prices. There is a conscious linking of the instruments under government control and the policy targets they are designed to influence.

A considerable body of economic theory specifies this interrelationship between instruments and targets. In this way, for example, the macro-economic policy task of fiscal policy for Australia has been defined in terms of facilitating lower interest rates from an easing of inflationary pressures through a firm fiscal stance.[5]

AN ELEMENTARY VIEW OF FISCAL POLICY

The theory of fiscal policy which dominated the views of Australian economists and Treasury officials up to the early 1970s flowed from the Keynesian theory of income determination in which aggregate demand determines the volume of output and the level of economic activity. Since employment is a function of the level of output in the Keynesian system, rises in aggregate demand will raise the level of employment, *ceteris paribus*. Once full employment has been reached, so the conventional theory went, further increases in aggregate demand would accelerate the rate of inflation rather than stimulate further production. The manipulation of aggregate demand would therefore influence two of the economic stability policy objectives in a more or less non-conflicting way.

In a *closed* economy the components of aggregate demand are private consumption expenditure (C), private investment expenditure (I) and government expenditure (G). That is aggregate demand (Y) can be expressed as $Y = C + I + G$. In an *open* economy the net contribution of the foreign sector to domestic demand, that is, the difference between exports (X) and imports (M) is a further component of aggregate demand. Because imports are regarded as an increasing function of aggregate demand via the marginal propensity to import (m), that is $M = mY$, manipulation of aggregate demand via fiscal policy influences the volume of imports and hence the balance of payments.

This text cannot discuss the theory of income determination and inflation. Its scope is confined to looking at the fiscal policy instruments under government control which can be used to manipulate aggregate demand and thereby influence the policy objectives.

Government expenditure

Government expenditure is largely under the direct control of public authorities, that is, it is therefore largely a *discretionary* instrument of policy. In this context, three points should be noted which limit this general proposition. First, as was seen in Chapter 4, a substantial part of government expenditure is made up of unavoidable *Budget commitments* such as interest on the national debt. Secondly, Chapters 15 and 17 showed that State and local governments, which account for just over half of total public expenditure, have little responsibility for aggregate economic management, but that the existing governmental financial relations do give the Commonwealth Government control over the Loan Council. Thirdly, and most important in this context, is the fact that there are some *induced* elements in Budget expenditures of which unemployment benefits are the most important example.

Induced expenditures illustrate the point that although the government has full discretionary control over its policy instruments, it can nevertheless *not* completely control the actual Budget outcome. Take the simple case of a government Budget where all tax revenue is raised by *poll taxes*, so that the level of economic activity exerts no influence on the revenue side; the existence of *induced* items of expenditure still means that the Budget outcome is influenced by the level of economic activity. If unforeseen private decisions which reduce private consumption and/or investment expenditure lower GDP and raise the level of unemployment, the actual Budget outcome will be a smaller surplus (or larger deficit) than the government had originally planned because of rising unemployment benefits.

This fundamental point may be illustrated by means of a simple algebraic model, which will later be expanded to take account of induced changes in tax receipts. Budget outcome B, is the difference between G and T (tax receipts). Where all tax revenue is obtained from poll taxes, T = T; tax revenue is fully determined by government *discretionary action*. G is divided into government discretionary expenditures (G_d) and induced expenditures (G_i). The latter, which in this simple case we confine to unemployment benefits, is a function of the *rate of benefit* (U_b) which is a discretionary policy instrument and N, the level of unemployment, which is a function of all the determinants in the system, that is T, G_d, U_b, I, C and X–M. This means that B, the Budget outcome, is *not completely* under government control because it partly depends on the private components of aggregate demand, C, I, and X-M. That is, because

$$\begin{aligned} B &= G - T \\ &= B_i + G_d - T \\ &= f(U_b, N) + G_d - T \end{aligned}$$

where, since $N = f(C, I, G_d, T, X\text{–}M, U_b)$, B depends on C, I, X–M, which are not under government control as well as upon G_d, U_b and T, which in this simple expository case are directly set by the authorities.

The implication of this is that the magnitude of B cannot be taken as a measure of fiscal policy stance although this is frequently asserted in popular discussions and in many statements by members of the government, including treasurers. For example, if the government makes no change in its fiscal policy (that is, U_b, G_d, and T remain constant), B can nevertheless increase or decrease because of induced effects following C, I, and X–M. In order to obtain a measure of fiscal policy stance which is purged of such induced effects, a variety of methods can be used.

One method, pioneered for Australia by Artis and Wallace,[6] is to use only discretionary changes (which, in the above example, would be deliberate changes by the government in G_d, U_b and T) to indicate the thrust of economic policy. Increases in G_d and U_b and reductions in the rates set for T are then taken as signs of expansionary fiscal policy which will stimulate aggregate demand. In a more realistic model, the determination of G_d in total increases in G is far more difficult as is the assessment of the induced components in changes in tax receipts (as a study of the Artis and Wallace analysis will reveal).

A second method to remove induced items from the Budget outcome is that developed by American economists during the 1960s which requires the hypothetical exercise of estimating a standardised GDP at the full employment level and then to calculate the Budget outcome applicable to this hypothetical full employment situation given the stance of existing budgetary policy. This method in effect separates out the government's discretionary actions by the device of assuming that private sector decisions are not volatile but are always such as to produce full employment. In the simplified expository model given above, a full employment Budget outcome would only isolate discretionary government action because the assumption of constant full employment eliminates the induced effect upon the Budget via unemployment benefits.[7]

Taxation

So far this discussion has not confronted the realistic situation that taxation receipts are a mixture of discretionary and induced elements, because of the *assumption* that tax receipts are not influenced by the level of economic activity. In reality, tax receipts (T) are a function of the tax rates (t), which are a discretionary policy instrument interacting with the tax base which can be summarised by the level of economic activity, Y, and which is determined by private expenditure decisions by households (C), by firms (I), together with the level of imports and exports and government action on tax rates and expenditure. The changes in tax base by means of legislation can also be described as *discretionary* policy instruments. Tax receipts (T), even more than G, are sensitive to induced changes via Y, the level of economic activity. So the Budget outcome (B = G – T) must be accepted as a mixture of deliberately chosen government actions (the choice of t and G_d for example) and of the volatile decisions of the private sector.

The general argument can be illustrated by a simple example. The introduction of video recorders has caused an upward shift in the consumption function as people have taken advantage of consumer credit facilities in order to obtain access to this new consumer durable. This increase in aggregate spending causes an induced inflow of tax revenue directly from the sales tax revenue received on the sales of video recorders and the necessary accessories such as tapes. General tax revenue will also increase because the upward shift in the consumption function has an expansionary impact on the level of economic activity. The introduction of video recorders therefore resulted in an increased Budget surplus (or reduced deficit) but this is entirely due to induced revenue effects and cannot be used in an indication that the fiscal policy stance of the government has changed. If the government wished to prevent this increase in aggregate demand, it could, of course, take discretionary fiscal action, for example, by increasing the rates of personal income tax. Such actions would also affect the Budget outcome.

Automatic stabilisers and fiscal drag

Induced changes in revenue and expenditure instruments provide the basis for the notion of automatic stabilisers — that is, that some of these instruments operate to dampen the level of economic activity over the course of the business cycle. Most of the taxes in the Australian federal tax system have this property because their base is related to the level of income and expenditure. Unemployment benefits provide the only major automatic stabiliser on the government side; as unemployment increases and the level of income from wage and salary earnings consequently falls, the rising outlays on these benefits provide compensatory income increases. This effect should not be over-rated. Unemployment benefits, even in periods of high unemployment, constitute only a small fraction of disposable income, because the rate at which the benefit is paid is approximately a quarter of average weekly earnings and few unemployed are immediately eligible for benefits.

The more important stabilising effects operate on the revenue side in particular through personal income tax. (The automatic stabilising effects of various tax instruments were discussed in Chapters 9–13.) In times of boom, income rises are automatically reduced with a restraining effect on the level of demand but in the upswing from a recession to recovery the automatic rising share of tax revenue, particularly from personal income tax, operates to slow the pace of recovery. The government, of course, by discretionary action, can compensate for this effect (which is known in the literature as "fiscal drag") by increasing its own level of expenditure or by deliberate changes in the tax schedules.

FURTHER ISSUES IN THE THEORY OF FISCAL POLICY

This simple model of aggregate demand manipulation by varying G_d and t formed the foundation for much of the fiscal policy discussion of the 1950s and 1960s. Lowering G_d and/or raising t to reduce aggregate demand was the remedy for controlling inflation and for curing an unfavourable trade balance by reducing imports: raising G_d and/or lowering t was used to stimulate economic activity and to raise employment levels.

One of the difficulties arising from this simple model can be mentioned immediately. The model assumes that *both* the expenditure and the tax instruments can be quickly adjusted in an upwards and downwards direction. For most of the post-war period expenditure components were seen as only flexible in an upward direction, tax instruments were the preferred tools of fiscal policy, a policy instrument preference illustrated by Australian experience particularly whenever demand had to be constrained. This facet of fiscal policy therefore lent an expansionary bias to the public sector as a whole, and was undoubtedly one reason why fiscal demand management fell into disfavour as compared with monetary and other economic policies. From the mid-1980s strong public dislike of tax increases has meant an upgraded role for expenditure restraint in securing a tight fiscal policy in Australia—as shown, for example, by the falls in outlay relative to GDP the Federal Government has achieved since then, partly by cuts in federal financial assistance to the States and local governments.

Subsequent experience with the operation of fiscal policy produced theoretical refinements which cast considerable doubts on the usefulness of the simple model of demand management set out in the previous paragraphs. Some of the more important modifications to fiscal policy theory can now be briefly mentioned.

1. *Differing impacts of different types of government expenditure*. These may arise from three circumstances. First, the import content of spending may differ, leading to differential effects on domestic aggregate demand from equivalent amounts of government spending. Secondly, because of the lags involved, the length of the period selected for the analysis influences the size of the "impact multiplier" as has been shown by econometric evidence. Thirdly, the impact of government expenditure on goods and services is greater than that of transfer payments because the former has a direct impact on national income as well as the secondary effects of the spending decisions of the recipients. Such differential effects of types of government expenditure have been quantified by econometric research which has estimated government expenditure impact multipliers for various classes of government expenditure.
2. *Inflation and the Budget outcome*. In the earlier discussion it was assumed that induced changes in government expenditure and taxation receipts arose only from changes in

economic activity and the level of employment. Such changes can also occur as a result of changes in the rate of inflation. The indexation of social security benefits links that component of government expenditure directly to the rate of inflation. Similarly, inflation will affect the yield of income and other taxes without any discretionary tax changes. In short, the Budget outcome may also be affected by the rate of inflation, which is, at best only partly under government control.

3. *Perverse effects of tax changes.* In the early theory of demand management, only the income effects of tax changes were discussed: tax rate increases lowered income and aggregate demand; tax rate reductions raised it. This neglected the substitution or relative price effects of tax changes, a matter of importance in an inflationary situation. From the demand management point of view, the control of inflation required rising tax rates. However, as was mentioned in the discussion of the incidence of taxation, rising taxes, particularly in a situation of high demand, lead to price and wage rises thereby partially or perhaps totally offsetting the anti-inflationary effects on the rate of change in prices expected from the reduction in aggregate demand. Hence, contrary to the simple aggregate demand model, tax cuts have been put forward as an important element in a macro-economic policy package designed to reduce, if not eliminate the problems of inflation and unemployment together.
4. *The effect of aggregate tax changes depends upon their impact on the components of aggregate demand.* There is now also considerable controversy about the effects of particular tax changes on the components of aggregate demand; it is sometimes argued that such tax changes may produce unintended effects. An example may explain this further. Income tax cuts designed to stimulate domestic consumption may have distributional consequences more likely to stimulate imports or savings. Discussion of income taxes in Chapters 9 and 10 showed that the effect of these taxes on saving, investment, and consumption expenditure are difficult to determine. A particularly important example in this context is the effect of changes in the company tax on investment spending.
5. *Fiscal policy implementation: The question of lags.* The impact of fiscal policy measures involves consideration of adjustments through time. Three lags relevant for fiscal policy are usually identified in the literature; the recognition lag, the implementation lag, and the response lag. The *recognition* lag measures the time taken to recognise that fiscal policy is required because of changes in the economic situation; its length depends largely on the time taken to diagnose changing trends, which in turn depends on the time taken to compile statistics for the major policy indicators, and so on, and the sophistication of forecasting techniques. The *implementation* lag measures the time taken to implement policy changes after the need for such change has been recognised; its length largely depends on institutional factors, such as the time required to pass tax legislation through Parliament and that required to implement the new law by the Taxation Department. Finally, there is the *response* lag which refers to the time it takes before the private sector responds to the fiscal policy initiatives. For example, taxpayers might respond only slowly to a reduction in their pay-packets caused by increased income tax rates by maintaining their consumption expenditure and reducing their customary level of saving.
6. *The interdependence of monetary, fiscal, and debt policy.* In the simple model given, the Budget outcome, B, was simply described as the difference between government

expenditure (G) and taxation receipts (T). As was seen in Chapter 17, the Budget outcome is financed by changes in the debt holdings of the non-bank public (D) or by changes in the money supply (M). In other words,

$$B = G - T = dD/dt + dM/dt$$

where dD/dt is the change in non-monetary public debt in the hands of the non-bank public and dM/dt is the change in the money supply directly related to government financing. This statement expresses the interdependence of a fiscal policy (reflected through the impact of discretionary government expenditure (G_d) and changes in tax rates (t) on G and T) and monetary and debt policy (the influence of B, the Budget outcome, on D the size (and composition) of the debt and M, money supply).

Some implications of this interdependence for the efficacy of fiscal policy need to be mentioned, though no rigorous demonstration of them will be given. These implications are important because it is now frequently argued that these monetary effects may counteract the contractionary or expansionary objectives of fiscal policy and thereby reduce if not eliminate its efficacy. The following examples provide some illustrations:

(a) A discretionary increase in real government expenditure raises aggregate demand, thence output, the demand for real money balances, and thereby exerts upward pressure on interest rates. Because consumption and investment spending are interest elastic, the rise in interest rates operates to constrain aggregate demand.
(b) An expansionary fiscal policy may raise prices as well as economic activity. These price rises in turn may operate to constrain aggregate demand by various routes such as lowering real money balances and thereby raising interest rates, by increasing income tax yields in a tax regime with money tax bases, by stimulating imports and reducing exports, and by lowering the real wealth in the hands of the public in the form of government bonds and money balances, which may also reduce consumption and investment expenditure.
(c) An expansionary fiscal policy financed by bond issues to the non-bank public may raise interest rates (deterring private consumption and investment expenditure which is interest elastic) and reducing the supply of loanable funds for financing such spending. In this case increased government spending "crowds out" some private spending.
(d) Where inflationary expectations are geared to changes in the money supply and/or changes in the Budget outcome, the announcement effects from what is diagnosed as expansionary fiscal policy (a greater deficit, a smaller than expected surplus, "excessive"' real spending growth) may generate expectations of accelerated inflation, thereby adversely affecting confidence and dampening private spending and aggregate demand.

The importance of these various monetary effects as counter-forces to an expansionary fiscal policy is not precisely known; as in so many cases of economic controversy, the empirical evidence is conflicting. The debate over the "crowding out" effect (mentioned in point (c) above), illustrates this problem. Some economists argue that the effect of an expansionary fiscal policy financed by bond issues to the non-bank public may "crowd out" private investment expenditure by raising interest rates and reducing the supply of loanable funds. Other economists deny that this effect is of great practical importance.

7. *Announcement effects of the Budget.* In the context of the relationship between inflationary expectations and the Budget deficit, the "announcement effects" of the Budget were mentioned without clarifying its meaning. With the general acceptance by the public of the government's ability to intervene in the economy for stabilisation purposes, the announcement of either expansionary or contractionary policy by the Treasurer can affect both consumer and business expectations. For example, the announcement of an increase in the sales tax on motor vehicles to restrain demand may lead to a postponement of their purchase on the expectation that as soon as the short-run difficulties are overcome the tax rate will be reduced. The announcement that demand has to be drastically curtailed in the interest of economic stability may cause changes in the planning of business for future levels of output both in the consumption and investment good sectors. In these examples, the expectations tend to *reinforce* the stabilisation objectives, but this is not always the case. The contrary result could follow from the sales tax example: consumers may anticipate future car purchases on the expectation that things can only get worse and that buying now is better than buying later because even harsher measures may be introduced. Anticipations of likely government policy can also be important in this context. If there are strong expectations in the business community that the government is likely to introduce an investment allowance, firms may postpone investment spending until the allowance is actually introduced, thereby increasing the need for the introduction of such an allowance. Although it is difficult to assess with any precision the specific impact of these considerations, they further illustrate the difficulties and uncertainties associated with the effectiveness of fiscal policy.

In a variety of ways, these seven points all create difficulties for the assessment of the effectiveness of fiscal policy and they have widened the range of views on this effectiveness among economists. These opinions now cover a wide spectrum from those who argue that fiscal policy is virtually ineffective to those who state that fiscal policy is the most important and effective of policy weapons. The implications of this diversity of views for the future of fiscal policy are discussed at the end of this chapter.

AUSTRALIAN FISCAL POLICY EXPERIENCE

The more general, theoretical discussion of fiscal policy so far can be applied to the more recent Australian fiscal policy experience often described as the debate between contractionist versus expansionary fiscal policy. The latter has been consistently espoused by traditionalists in fiscal policy such as John Nevile and Jim Perkins. On the other hand, official views espoused by the Treasury, and accepted elsewhere by a substantial number of other economists see a role for fiscal policy which is different from its traditional demand management task. Some have even argued that expansionary fiscal policy not only is largely impotent in the longer run but that it is positively detrimental to sustained improvements in economic performance. Underlying these views are differing perspectives on the degree of automatic adjustment a market economy is capable of and on the benefits of government intervention and regulation.[8]

This position on Australian fiscal policy debate requires a number of important warnings and qualifications at the outset. The first of these was presented at the opening of this chapter when it was noted that many differences on policy arise from substantial and irreconcilable differences in theoretical and empirical perceptions of the adjustments involved. These cannot be comprehensively dealt with here. Secondly, and as indicated in the previous paragraph, differing philosophical perspectives on the role of government intervention and the efficacy of the market mechanisms also play an important part in the positions taken in this fiscal policy debate. That issue, of greater direct relevance to public finance, is further pursued in Chapter 20. Finally, within the two broad groupings described in the subheading of this section there are also considerable differences of opinion. For example, there are substantial differences between the expansionist approach taken by Nevile as compared with that of Perkins while there also are differences in the contractionist camp on both the role and the extent to which fiscal policy should be practised.

The expansionist viewpoint

The expansionist viewpoint is invariably based on the fact that fiscal policy as measured by its income effects has been excessively contractionary relative to the high levels of unemployment and low levels of economic activity experienced. This is argued to have been the case from 1975–76 onwards. From the point of view of its effect on levels of economic activity and employment, fiscal stance on these arguments has been inappropriate and more expansionary policy would have improved the employment situation by producing more growth in economic activity.

However, because of growing constraints from the balance of payments and the rate of inflation, the desired degree of expansionary impetus and the method of achieving it have been considerably modified as compared to what would have been recommended previously. Current expansionists recognise substantial modifications to the trade-off between inflation and unemployment. Reductions in unemployment brought about by stimulus to the economy now require a higher cost in terms of inflation consequences. In short, there has been an alteration in the "Phillips Curve". Since there is also greater recognition of the costs of inflation in terms of reduced levels of economic activity (examined later in the discussion of the restrictionist view) the inflationary impact of expansionary activity encouraged through the Budget has to be countered by other suitable policy.

Several types of policy mix have been suggested; one of these relies on the specific mix of expansionary Budget policy selected, the other two rely partly on non-budgetary policy instruments. The policy mix which seeks to curtail inflationary effects while expanding economic activity suggests that the appropriate manner to raise aggregate demand is through indirect (commodity) tax cuts which have an immediately favourable impact on the price level as measured by the Consumer Price Index while in the usual manner it expands economic activity through their income effects. The two variants of this expansionary policy seek to curtail its inflationary consequences either by an incomes or wages policy which seeks to restrain cost inflation and/or a tight monetary policy. In fact, combinations of these actions are generally put forward because of the complex consequences flowing from expansionary fiscal action which are now fully admitted.

The Labor government elected in 1983 initially adopted part of this approach to stabilisation policy. It sought to reduce the very high unemployment rate it inherited by some stimulatory fiscal action, combined with real wage restraint through an incomes policy, supplemented by tax reductions, and a firmer monetary policy to promote an environment with sustainable lower inflation and accelerating real activity levels. However, the conjunction of financial deregulation effects on monetary policy together with a floating exchange rate, a substantial deterioration in the terms of trade and a worsening trade account with associated growth in overseas debt levels induced increasing recourse to tighter fiscal policy from the mid-1980s onwards. This policy change is reflected in the transformation of substantial deficits into increasing Budget surpluses and a similar reversal in the aggregate net public sector borrowing requirement, partly achieved by real reductions in public spending.

The restrictionist approach

Broadly speaking, the restrictionist position on fiscal policy is based on the proposition that although the multiplier and income effects of stimulatory Budget action are not denied, the overall effect of such stimulatory consequences of fiscal expansion have now probably become non-existent. Some argue this is the case because the quantitative importance of income effects has been exaggerated as demonstrated by more satisfactory econometric analysis. The effectiveness of stimulatory fiscal action may therefore be less than formerly assumed and may, furthermore, be of shorter duration. When this argument on the income effect of expansionary fiscal policy is combined with its monetary and other effects, contractionary rather than expansionary effects may flow from increasing government spending.

The non-income effects of expansionary fiscal action through tax cuts or increased spending have been concisely spelled out by a former permanent head of the Treasury.[9] These effects are regarded as contractionary and operate via the monetary, the confidence, and the wage reactions from the enlarged Budget deficit which is argued to be a necessary consequence of expansionary fiscal policy. It must be emphasised that such indirect effects of fiscal policy are seen as *additional* to the traditional income effects.

The monetary effects of an increased deficit are associated with its necessary financing transactions. These in turn may either be indirectly inflationary through money supply effects or may depress the level of economic activity through interest rate effects or through other consequences of an offsetting tight monetary policy. The external financial consequences through foreign capital movement and effects on the exchange rate altered considerably after the 1983 decision to float the exchange rate. Permissive stabilisation policy influences international and domestic financial policy much more quickly, yielding rapid exchange rate and interest rate adjustments, which can likewise counteract the objections of the proclaimed fiscal policy stance.

More important in the analysis are the expectations and confidence effects of the variations in Budget outcome and other signals of an expansionary fiscal policy. Experience of the 1970s suggests that a sharp increase in the deficit fuels inflationary expectations and that such expectations are either realised in actual inflation rates or induce contractionary responses for the economy by curtailed private spending plans. In addition, the various policy responses possible to the immediate effects of an increased deficit create uncertainty and loss of confidence with further detrimental consequences for economic activity. These effects are concisely summarised as follows:

> In reality, fiscal policy can affect the economy through a variety of channels in addition to direct income/expenditure effects. It can influence interest rates, exchange rates, the money supply, the balance of payments expectations — notably, inflationary expectations — confidence and uncertainty. These additional transmission mechanisms are, for the most part, extremely inconvenient to handle analytically, and often impossible to quantify. They are, however, no less real for being empirically and often even theoretically intractable.[10]

A defence of expansionary policy based on the measurable effects of recession on the deficit cannot be sustained on this viewpoint, since the effects of a deficit from its financing are there irrespective of whether its size has been influenced by the budgetary consequences of a recession or by discretionary policy measures. In short, as a result of the detrimental consequences on private sector behaviour via a growing deficit, monetary, wages, or expectational effects, expansionary fiscal policy irrespective of its income effects cannot lead to sustained economic recovery and reductions to the unemployment rate. However, unlike the case presented by the expansionists, much of the restrictionist argument is not susceptible to empirical testing by econometric analysis.

In practice, the restrictionist approach has meant a more balanced role for fiscal policy as its protagonists put it. The Budget is still seen as a central policy instrument, both in its own right, and through its contributions to achieving the objectives of monetary and wages policy. In this manner, attitudes to fiscal policy can be said to have become wider. At the same time, this approach gives a narrower perspective on the scope of fiscal policy because it has eliminated its more traditional role of fine tuning the economy in order to achieve economic stability. This narrowing of the scope of fiscal policy makes redundant an examination of the annual budgetary stance in the manner in which this was traditionally done during the 1950s and 1960s.

As indicated at the end of the previous section, restrictionist perspectives on fiscal policy have been winning in Australian policy debate from the mid-1980s onwards. In addition to the arguments about the inappropriateness of deficit financing for curing unemployment which were canvassed in the preceding paragraphs, this move towards a restrictive fiscal policy arises from a growing desire to reduce the role of the public sector for general efficiency reasons. As shown in Chapter 20, such arguments are gaining wider acceptance in Australia and elsewhere and are frequently seen as an important part of the micro-economic reforms designed to raise Australia's international economic performance.

Curtailment of the public sector to ensure greater efficiency implies restrictive fiscal policy, irrespective of the merits of the argument which links such reductions to the efficiency objective. A number of features of the implementation of this restrictive policy need to be mentioned. First, it has been achieved with real expenditure reductions yielding a relative decline in Australia's public sector from the mid-1980s, a feature of Australian experience which, as Chapter 3 indicated, is virtually unique in the industrialised world. Secondly, as was mentioned in the context of Chapters 15 and 17, Australian fiscal federalism arrangements have meant that public sector size reduction in relative terms can be spread to all levels of government. Sharp real reductions in financial assistance to the

States and local government, together with the introduction and enforcement of global borrowing controls at the Loan Council, are the mechanisms by which the Federal Government has achieved this. This success rate has been undoubtedly assisted by the growing political difficulties in raising taxes to finance expenditure growth in a climate where the tax paying public is demonstrably less willing to tolerate this, no matter how laudable the objectives on which the new revenue is to be spent.[11]

Restrictive fiscal policy from this perspective takes on an even less Keynesian flavour, since it tacks micro-economic objectives on to the broad policy requirements informed by the macro-economics of demand management. From the macro-economic view, public demand curtailment and tight fiscal policy of the type Australia has experienced from the late 1980s especially, can continue to be defended on conventional grounds such as curtailing inflationary pressures and demand for imports while freeing resources for exports and private investment growth. However, the potentially detrimental micro-effects of a tight fiscal policy, particularly if mainly directed at productive public investment in infrastructure and human capital creation through education, make assessment of its appropriateness much more complex over the longer term. Fiscal policy's interdependencies with other policy instruments have become more complicated and hence even more difficult to assess.

What is the future of fiscal policy?[12]

The increased openness of Australia's economy from the early 1980s (other aspects of which are examined in Chapter 19) has had major impacts on the manner in which fiscal policy is currently perceived in Australia. Its role in short-term demand management remains unquestioned but its effectiveness for securing sustainable output and employment growth is far less frequently accepted. This scepticism of its long-term worth arises not only from its now widely perceived interdependence with domestic and external financial policy variables, not to mention that with wage and other income determinants; increasingly micro-economic or supply-side consequences of fiscal policy have to be taken into consideration in assessment of its long term effectiveness. Further consideration of this issue is postponed until Chapter 20.

Even on the demand side, fiscal policy is still questioned, if only because it is an instrument of active government policy intervention in the operations of private markets. Such distrust of fiscal policy can become even greater when combined with poor forecasting performance by government agencies. Destabilisation of economic activity rather than a more stable economic environment may then be the actual outcome of government intervention, heightening the case for abandoning the approach to policy. However, the "monetarists" and "rational expectations" school, who actively suggested this type of response to the future of fiscal policy during the late 1970s and early 1980s, are now rarely listened to in this context.[13]

Discretionary fiscal policy for stabilisation purposes does not therefore have to be abandoned. The argument of this chapter emphasised that greater care should be taken in implementing the appropriate policy mix, and this in fact has happened in Australia. It also stressed the greater complexity of assessing the appropriateness of fiscal policy from its interdependence with other policy variables including micro-economic ones. One thing is certain, discretionary fiscal policy is unlikely to be abandoned in the 1990s because use of this policy instrument is inherently destabilising. Better understanding of its complex longer-term consequences requires further research effort and study, hence emphasising a need for public finance students for continuing interest in the wider impact of the Budget on economic activity.

SUMMARY

1. Despite criticism of its effectiveness, fiscal policy for stabilisation, that is, the manipulation of expenditure and tax instruments to influence aggregate demand, remains an important aspect of budgetary policy.

2. Full employment objectives are now generally stated in terms of either socially acceptable unemployment rates or sustainable employment rates with respect to growth and price stability.

3. Price stability is seen as an increasingly important stabilisation objective in itself because of the wide ranging detrimental consequences of inflation.

4. The instruments of fiscal policy are:

   (a) current expenditure of public authorities on goods and services excluding military imports;
   (b) capital expenditure by public authorities on building and construction;
   (c) capital expenditure by public authorities on machinery and equipment;
   (d) gross operating surplus of public enterprises (a negative expenditure);
   (e) cash benefits to persons;
   (f) personal income tax rates;
   (g) rates of sales tax, other indirect taxes and discretionary changes in tax bases.

5. Budget outcomes reflect project discretionary policy changes as well as the impact of economic activity levels on expenditure items (unemployment benefits) and tax collections.

6. Automatic stabilisers dampen the level of economic activity over the course of the business cycle. Examples are taxes whose revenue yield is sensitive to the level of economic activity.

7. Simple demand management techniques (lowering tax rates/raising expenditure to raise demand; raising tax rates/lowering expenditure to lower demand) are modified by:

   (a) variations in impact for different types of expenditure;
   (b) inflation effects on revenue and outlays;
   (c) supply-side or other output effects of tax changes;
   (d) the varying impact of instruments on components of demand;
   (e) lags in recognition, response and implementation ;
   (f) monetary/debt implications of fiscal policy.

8. Debates about the effectiveness of fiscal policy continue but its appropriateness for short-period demand management purpose is invariably accepted.

NOTES

[1] It should be noted that most of these areas of disagreement relate to the theoretical and empirical foundations of modern macroeconomics and cannot be really discussed here. For a good theoretical survey, see Malcolm Sawyer, *Macroeconomics in Question* (Brighton: Wheatsheaf Books, 1982); for some Australian indication of disagreements in this area, see The Indecs Economics Special Report, *State of Play 6* (Sydney: Allen and Unwin, 1990), esp. ch. 1; and for a review of changing attitudes to fiscal policy from a specific public finance perspective, see R.A. Musgrave, "The Changing Image of Fiscal Policy" in R.A. Musgrave, *Public Finance in a Democratic Society* (Brighton: Wheatsheaf, 1986) vol. I, pp. 377–85.

[2] See Commonwealth of Australia, *Full Employment in Australia* (Canberra: AGPS, 1945), para 1. The Reserve Bank's policy objectives are summarised at the beginning of its *Annual Reports*. The gradual alteration of the full employment objective in Australia is documented in Barry Hughes, *Exit Full Employment* (Sydney: Angus & Robertson, 1980), esp. ch. 5, which can be updated from *State of Play* 6, ch. 4.

[3] See *State of Play 6*, ch. 2; cf. Chris Higgins, *The Australian Economy Entering the 1990s*, opening address at Consult Australia Annual Forum, Canberra, November 1989, esp. pp. 1, 20.

[4] J.W. Nevile, *Fiscal Policy in Australia* (Melbourne: F.W. Cheshire, 1970), p. 99.

[5] 1989–90 Budget Paper No. 1, *Budget Statements 1989–90* (Canberra: AGPS 1989), Statement No. 2, p. 2.56. This annual statement is an invaluable official indicator of where economic policy has been and where it is going in the near future.

[6] That is, M.J. Artis and R.H. Wallace, "Assessing the Fiscal Impact", in N. Runcie (ed.), *Australian Monetary and Fiscal Policy* (London: University of London Press, 1971), esp. pp. 378–99.

[7] For a detailed survey of the early American literature on this, see A.S. Blinder and R.M. Solow, "Analytical Foundations of Fiscal Policy", in *The Economics of Public Finance* (Washington DC: Brookings Institution, 1974), pp. 13–36; Australian estimates are published on a regular basis in the *Australian Economic Review*. See Louise Barton, Beatrice Derody, and P.J. Sheehan, "Some Estimates of the Full Employment Budget Position in the Australian Economy", *Australian Economic Review*, first quarter, 1976, pp. 53–8, updated in *Australian Economic Review*, third quarter 1983, pp. 13–14, esp. Table 8. For an alternative approach see J.W. Nevile, *Monetary and Fiscal Policies against Stagflation* (Sydney: University of New South Wales, Centre for Applied Economic Research), paper no. 19, June 1983, pp. 3–5.

[8] See J.O.N. Perkins, *Australian Macroeconomic Policy 1974–85* (Melbourne: Melbourne University Press, 1987), J.O.N. Perkins, "'Some Empirical Evidence about the Macroeconomic Policy Mix", paper presented to the 17th Conference of Economists, Canberra, August-September 1988; J.W. Nevile, "What's Wrong with the Australian Economy?", paper presented to the 17th Conference of Economists, Canberra, August-September 1988.

[9] A clear discussion of Treasury views and the intellectual climate which generated them is G. Whitwell, "The Triumph of Economic Rationalism: The Treasury and the Market Economy", *Australian Journal of Public Administration* (2) June 1990; see also the perspective on stabilisation policy offered in Neil Johnston, David Harrison, Mylinh Hardman and Robert Brooker, "'The Role of Fiscal Policy in Post-War Australian Economic Growth", in Bruce Chapman (ed.), *Australian Economic Growth*, (Melbourne: Macmillan, 1989), ch. 6, esp. pp. 140–59.

[10] 1983–84 Budget Paper No. 1, Budget Statements 1983–84, Statement No. 2, p. 57.

[11] Most public opinion polls taken during the 1980s suggest a growing unwillingness from taxpayers to accept tax increases to pay for improved public services such as social security, education, health, and cultural and recreational activities. Exceptions to these

findings include tax rises earmarked for road improvement and highway construction, or improving the environment, at least if New South Wales experience in 1989 is a guide.

12 This section draws particularly on the paper by Neil Johnston et al., (cited in Note 9 above) and evaluations of Australian fiscal policy given in Statement No. 2 of the Annual Budget Statements from the mid–1980s.

13 For a fascinating account of the growing difficulties in forecasting, see John Llewellyn, Stephen Potter and Lee Samuelson, *Economic Forecasting and Policy. The International Dimension*, (London: Routledge and Kegan Paul, 1985), esp. chs. 1, 3, 6, 11–13.

FURTHER READING

A detailed discussion of stabilisation policy is presented in :

R.A. and P.B. Musgrave, *Public Finance in Theory and Practice*, 4th edn. (New York: MaGraw Hill, 1984), chs. 27–32, which remains by far the most comprehensive treatment of stabilisation from a public finance perspective.

A less detailed treatment is :

J.E. Stiglitz, *Economics of the Public Sector*, 2nd edn. (New York: W.W. Norton, 1988), ch. 28.

An interesting perspective on recent changes in fiscal stabilisation policy is:

R.A. Musgrave, "The Changing Image of Fiscal Policy", in R.A. Musgrave, *Public Finance in a Democratic Society* (Brighton: Wheatsheaf, 1986), vol. 1, pp. 377–85.

For Australian evaluations of recent fiscal policy experience see:

The Indecs Economics Special Report, *State of Play 6* (Sydney: Allen and Unwin, 1990), esp. chs. 1, 2, 4, 8.

J.O.N. Perkins, *Australian Macroeconomic Policy 1974–85* (Melbourne: Melbourne University Press, 1987).

Neil Johnston, David Harrison, Mylinh Hardman and Robert Brooker, "The Role of Fiscal Policy in Post War Australian Economic Growth", in Bruce Chapman (ed.), *Australian Economic Growth*, (Melbourne: Macmillan, 1989), ch. 6, pp. 133–61.

Kevin Davis, "Managing the Economy", in Brian Head and Allan Patience (eds.), *From Fraser to Hawke* (Melbourne: Longman Cheshire, 1989), ch. 4, pp. 66–109.

An official view of fiscal policy on an annual basis can be obtained from Budget Paper No. 1, Budget Statements, Statement No. 2.

19

International public finance aspects

The impact of an open economy on public finance conclusion has already been noted on several occasions in this book. A good example is Chapter 17 which distinguished between external and internal debt on the grounds that burdens associated with the former are more difficult to transfer to future generations than is the case with external obligations. More strikingly, many issues in income taxation raise international questions, particularly in the context of business taxation. In Chapter 10, company tax was partly justified as a separate tax on the ground that it facilitated the taxation of income from overseas investment generated in Australia. The general introduction to income tax in Chapter 9 postponed discussion of interest and dividend withholding taxes to this chapter because of the foreign tax implications they raised. Just as non-residents can be taxed in Australia with respect to the income produced here by firms in which they have invested, so Australian taxpayers when paying tax on foreign source income may have already paid tax in the country where this income originated. These last aspects of income taxation raise intricate questions of equity and efficiency which need to be discussed. Such questions become even more important when certain Australian tax rules are not applicable to non-resident taxpayers. The exclusive benefit to resident shareholders of imputation credits from company tax is a prime example (see Chapter 10).

The impact of such external considerations on public finance has always been important in Australia because of its substantial reliance on overseas investment from the beginnings of European settlement. From the early 1980s a number of factors have increased the importance of these external considerations, hence justifying a separate chapter on this topic. One of these is the impact of floating the Australian exchange rate on the international mobility of capital flows arising from the associated deregulation of foreign exchange transactions. Deregulating international capital flows has been a worldwide phenomenon, hence greatly increasing the integration of Australia in the world economy. A second, not unrelated factor, is the rapid growth of transnational business, with firms operating in more than one nation state and frequently regarding the world as a whole as their approp-riate market. Changes taking place in the countries of Eastern Europe are extending opportunities for such global enterprise even further, while enormous communication improvements have greatly increased the speed of adjustment as one section of the world market reacts to events in another. Foreign exchange markets, stock exchanges and financial and commodity markets in general, can now virtually be described as never closing.

International co-operation has grown likewise over this period, including increasing international coordination of economic policy formulation. The regular meetings of the leaders of the world's major economies are one example of this; the influence of international organisations like the OECD and the IMF is another. The 1992 integration of the market of the European community is a third example of this trend towards greater internationalisation in business and economic activity. Developments like those mentioned in this and the preceding paragraph have particular importance for the ability of a small open economy like Australia to conduct independent stabilisation policy. In addition, they have implications for the conduct of independent national tax policy, in particular within the area of business taxation.

Open economy aspects of public finance are also reflected in the overseas outlays by Australian governments. The importance of government imports, the overseas deficit and variations in the pattern of foreign transfers from the government sector is a further international aspect of public finance examined in this chapter, and a feature of budgeting not really stressed in previous chapters.

EQUITY PROBLEMS IN AN INTERNATIONAL SETTING[1]

In a closed economy setting, taxation raises questions of equity which were discussed in Chapter 7. Such equity problems were only discussed in individual terms: dealing with the equal treatment of taxpayers (tax units) with equal capacity to pay taxes, although as indicated in Chapter 7, there are plenty of difficulties in applying equity principles in practice. For taxation in an open economic environment, difficulties in such equity applications are far greater.

These greater difficulties arise from a variety of factors. First, the notion of equal capacity to pay tax becomes more complex when foreign source income is involved. This arises from the fact that such income usually will have paid already some tax abroad (at the rates applicable to the overseas country's tax regime) hence on equity grounds adjustments need to be made to that income before it can be aggregated with domestic source income to form a single measure of taxable capacity. An open economy complicates inter-individual equity considerations. In addition, units other than individuals or households are involved in equity considerations arising from the use of tax bases with international implications. Governments (that is, countries) exploit such tax bases in domestic situations, so that where the tax base is explicitly shared between more than one jurisdiction, inter-nation equity issues become involved, concerned with which jurisdiction is entitled to exploit which specific part of the shared tax base. Such inter-jurisdictional equity issues have already implicitly arisen in the context of discussing fiscal federalism issues; particularly when considering the most appropriate ways of sharing the revenue from a specific tax base, where the imposing jurisdiction initially pockets the whole of the revenue. Australian fiscal equalisation practice inherent in such revenue sharing is an attempt to distribute that revenue in such a way as to secure inter-state equity in terms of fiscal capacity.[2]

To discuss these equity considerations in international taxation systematically, three types of country must be distinguished. The first is the country of residence of owners (of the source of income); the second is the country of source (of income); the third is the country of incorporation, relevant when ownership is mediated through incorporation of the business entity in question.

Inter-individual equity

When income is received from various countries tax will be payable to various authorities. X, an Australian resident, receives dividend income from the United Kingdom on which tax is paid additional to X's Australian income on which tax is also paid. To ensure horizontal equity, should X's total tax burden (United Kingdom and Australian) be equal to that payable on the same amount of income if obtained purely from Australian sources? If the answer is yes, then inter-individual equity is contemplated globally, if the answer is no and tax is claimed at normal rates on aggregate income of all sources (net of foreign tax already paid), a national equity standard is applied. From 1987–88 Australia has applied the global inter-individual equity criteria to the tax treatment of foreign source income to resident individuals by aggregating that income with domestically sourced income and permitting a full tax credit for tax paid abroad on the foreign source income. This replaced the horizontally inequitable system which exempted all foreign source income on which *some* foreign taxation had been paid, irrespective of the rates at which that tax was collected.[3]

Inter-nation equity

A further international tax equity question arises from how the tax revenue from foreign sourced income is to be divided between the Treasuries of the countries associated with that income. Two rules can be applied in this context: residence, or source, both of which can be discussed. Take first the rule of "source". Any country where income is produced can of course tax such income at source: this applies to the labour income of guest workers as much as to the property income from overseas investment. If taxing at source is the rule adopted, then equity requires equal treatment of that income irrespective of the residence of the owner, a rule which is not always applied. For example, imputation credits with respect to company tax paid are not generally provided to non-resident shareholders, as was noted previously.

The residence rule is more complicated to apply because this varies with the entity having rights to the income. Individual residence can be fairly easily established: non-individual (for example corporate) residence can be defined in terms of place of registration (incorporation) or place of effective management. Substantial tax advantages can arise for both countries (and companies) depending on the criteria of residence established. The OECD's *Model Double Taxation Convention on Income and on Capital*,[4] preferred place of effective management as the suitable criteria for establishing residence. The United States and Canada prefer place of registration (incorporation).

The importance of this issue can be illustrated as follows. In the mid-1980s, a number of American states, of which California was the most important, began to levy proportional taxes on the worldwide profits of multinational companies registered within their boundaries. This applied national United States' State corporate tax practice based on residence in terms of incorporation on a world scale. This unitary approach to business taxes in terms of worldwide earnings was widely protested by affected countries — particularly the United Kingdom and France, but also Australia — and under pressure of the United States Federal

Government it was dropped by most states in the USA which practised it. Subsequently in 1986 a court ruling invalidated the Californian tax from which that state was claiming to obtain $US300–$US400 million in additional revenue in that year. Although California's breach of international equity rules in business taxation was outlawed after some years, this example demonstrates one set of public finance problems arising from the existence of multinational business enterprise, in this case concerning a potential tax base, the exploitation of which needed to be regulated.[5]

EFFICIENCY CONSIDERATIONS IN INTERNATIONAL BUSINESS TAX ARRANGEMENTS

The potential for different tax rates on income from investment spread over different jurisdictions clearly has efficiency implications. Investment decisions are made on the basis of after-tax rates of return, and if advantage can be taken of low-rate income tax countries, few investors will want to miss such an opportunity, *ceteris paribus*.[6] Tax wedges in rates of return relevant to international investment opportunities have the potential to distort international resource allocation efficiency. These non-neutrality aspects of the international taxation of factor income, like the equity considerations, require rules to ensure minimal efficiency losses from their existence.

International income and profit tax co-ordination

Earlier discussion of individual foreign source income taxation measures adopted by Australia in 1986 suggest two principles. Individuals should be taxed on the whole of their income, including that from foreign sources, on the basis of the rates of tax applicable to their country of permanent residence. Tax credits should be given with respect to income tax paid on that income in other countries. This conforms to the global interpretation of inter-individual tax equity, even though it may be costly to the revenue of the country of permanent residence.

These rules are relatively easy to apply to income from personal exertion though there are some exceptions to this proposition from both their application and the ease with which this can be done. For example, Australia continues to exempt foreign source wage and salaries income on which appropriate[7] income tax has been paid in the country of source for periods over twelve months, while it enables pro rata exemption for periods of less than one year. Difficulties in applying these rules arise in some West European countries with social security contributions levied directly on all employees, including guest workers, because such contributions entitle those paying them to specific cash benefits in circumstances such as illness, unemployment and retirement. Australia's practice of not charging directly for social security benefits, eliminates this problem for Australian tax administration.

More substantial difficulties arise in the context of the treatment of property income, although in principle the same rules can apply. Australian corporations should be taxed on the whole of their income at the appropriate company tax rate (in 1989 of 39 per cent) with credits applied to overseas company tax actually paid. However, in the case of companies and other non-individual business entities a number of special difficulties arise. Unlike income from exertion which is invariably received within a short period from when it was actually earned, the timing of property income payments, including business profits, are subject to manipulation by the management of the business or its owners. This discretion over timing enables considerable tax deferral (the value to taxpayers of which was raised in the context of discussing depreciation in Chapter 10). Accrual procedures in assessment of foreign source income can ensure fair (and efficient) tax treatment of foreign source income for Australian business entities.[8]

Given the complexity of the sources of business income and the various ways they can be paid, not to mention the various types of entities through which they can be passed before reaching the Australian company under whose effective management these activities are conducted, a detailed discussion of these issues falls outside the scope of this book. The manner of transforming business income from country to country may involve the payment of that income as royalties, other franchise or licence fees, interest on loans, dividends, capital transfers, many of which categories in themselves are subject to a wide variety of sub-categories. Entities through which this income can pass include subsidiaries, branches, trusts and controlled foreign companies. With different tax treatment accorded to types of business income receipts and sometimes to different types of business entity, it is not difficult to grasp that for all company income to be aggregated in the year in which it accrues is an exceedingly complicated task, and that calculating the appropriate tax credits to offset against Australian tax liability is likely to be far from straightforward. Some specific examples drawn from Australian experience illustrate some of the principles involved.

The Australian source income of a wholly or partly foreign-owned company is systematically taxed through the company tax which applies to all companies operating in Australia. In addition to this tax, which applies to both distributed and undistributed profits in the hands of the company concerned, Australia has imposed since 1959 a dividend withholding tax on dividends paid to non-resident shareholders in Australian resident companies. The rate of this tax is 30 per cent, but in the case of countries with which Australia has a double taxation agreement (now including virtually every relevant country within the ambit of Australia's economic relations), the rate of taxation on dividends is reduced to 15 per cent. In 1968, an interest withholding tax was imposed on interest transmitted from Australia to non-residents. The rate of this tax is 10 per cent and this rate in the case of many countries cannot be varied by the Australian government because of double taxation agreements with those countries.

Although it might appear that these measures ensure that foreign investors in Australia contribute substantially to Australian tax revenue, this may, in fact, not be the case. In 1975 the Taxation Review Committee commented on the anomaly contained in the low rate of interest withholding tax which, when combined with the general interest deductibility for company tax purposes, provided a considerable incentive for foreign investors to *lend* to their companies in Australia and thereby to minimise their tax liability. Once the company was established, it would pay the foreign owners to raise additional capital by way of loans (from themselves) abroad; the interest payable on these loans would reduce taxable profits liable to Australian company tax, and when repatriated would attract a lower rate of withholding tax than if they had been repatriated as dividends. On company tax rates applicable in 1989, this strategy would give a tax saving of 44 per cent (39 per cent of avoided company tax plus the 5 per cent differential between dividend and interest withholding tax in the case where there was a double taxation agreement).[9]

A further anomaly in the taxation of foreign-owned business disclosed by the Taxation Review Committee was the exemption from dividend withholding tax of dividends repatriated by foreign companies operating *branches* in Australia. Nothing was done about the committee's recommendation to close this loophole but the issue became important when the Utah Development Corporation paid out $130 million in dividends in the first nine months of 1977 which, because it operated as a *branch* in Australia, were exempt from dividend withholding tax. Subsequently, the loophole was closed.[10]

Another method by which foreign-owned companies can reduce their tax liability in Australia is through pricing policies which reduce taxable profits. This can be done by charging higher prices on inputs sold by the foreign company to its subsidiary in Australia and by charging lower prices on the output sold by the foreign-owned Australian company to its owners abroad. The Australian *Income Tax Assessment Act* contains a number of provisions against such pricing practices, which state that such prices on inputs and outputs should be the amount paid by the purchaser to the vendor as if they "had been dealing at arm's length".[11] Other avoidance schemes of foreign-owned companies involve tax havens such as the use of Nauru and Norfolk Island as the domicile of the company.

These examples relate to practices of overseas owned companies in Australia. With the general deregulation of capital transactions which coincided with the floating of the dollar, Australian-based companies with multi-national business activities have likewise used tax havens, transfer pricing, overseas borrowing arrangements and other tax minimisation opportunities open to companies investing overseas, to a considerable extent. A report presented to a Parliamentary Inquiry into International Profit Shifting in April 1989, suggested that many leading Australian-based companies earned a substantial part of their total profits in tax havens in 1987–88. The research report surmised a corporate tax strategy for the companies in question of substantial losses on operation in their major centres of business with profits being permanently shifted to tax havens where company tax liability was minimal.[12]

The foreign tax credit system which Australia is implementing in 1990–91 is designed to remove the attractiveness of arrangements involving tax havens. The transfer of profit mechanisms on which they rely are also being scrutinised more closely by an Australian Tax Office much better equipped to the task. As in all cases of tax avoidance, the estimated costs to the revenue from these practices are enormous, but the complexity of the remedies in the form of tax law amendments, plus the lobbying power of the major companies involved, makes it doubtful that these avoidance opportunities will ever be completely removed.

Capital import/export neutrality[13]

Such practices disclose the tax advantages of overseas investment and associated opportunities for international business income transfers. These drive wedges between the pre- and after-tax rates of return hence distorting overseas investment decisions and ensure sub-optimal capital resource allocation both nationally and worldwide. The foreign source tax rules discussed in the previous section were partly designed to enhance investment neutrality but in some cases may not yield such a result. Discussion of the concepts of capital import and export neutrality clarifies this further.

The tax credit system on foreign source income Australia is introducing from 1990–91 results in tax neutrality so long as foreign tax liability credited (that is, company tax plus withholding taxes when appropriate) does not exceed Australian company tax liability. Tax influences on investment choice appear to be neutralised provided all tax deferral opportunities are eliminated by a proper system of accrual assessments. The credit device, if generally adopted, secures this on a worldwide basis, hence preventing distortions to efficient capital allocation from international tax differences.

However, Australia's government revenue loss involved in extending tax credits for foreign tax paid means that there is no such neutrality with respect to the national benefit Australia reaps from overseas investment. This lowers the national after-tax return of the investment relative to domestic investment before tax returns, hence a lower level of capital export than is appropriate under the criterion of world efficiency. National interests are involved since the lower volume of domestic investment under the credit adjustment for foreign tax liability affects domestic productivity levels and living standards of wage-earners. If deduction of foreign tax liability from foreign source income was the only adjustment allowed, a tax preference results in favour of domestic investment as compared to the situation where foreign tax liability results in a full tax credit. This proposition can be explained as follows: Australian investors will invest abroad until after-tax rates of return on domestic and foreign investment are equalised. With arrangements enabling credit for foreign tax paid, this occurs when

$$(1 - t_{aus})\, r_{aus} = (1 - t_{aus}) r_f$$

or

$$r_{aus} = r_f$$

but, with deductions of foreign tax liability only permitted, this condition becomes:

$$(1 - t_{aus})\, r_{aus} = (1 - t_{aus})\, (1 - t_f) r_f$$

that is,

$$r_{aus} = (1 - t_f)\, r_f$$

where r_{aus}, r_f, are before-tax rates of return in Australia and abroad; t_{aus} and t_f, the appropriate tax rates in Australia and abroad.

Global tax neutrality is ensured when equalisation of rates of return before tax is required for optimal investment choice at home and abroad; national tax neutrality requires a preference to domestic investment which requires a lower pre-tax rate of return to compete effectively with overseas investment.

Is neutral taxation possible in an open economy?

Given the theoretical problems in reconciling the rules for tax neutral investment behaviour when national interests are distinguished from global considerations, as well as the difficulties of operating a comprehensive tax credit system on a full accrual basis to ensure satisfactory foreign source income taxation, neutral taxation in the business tax area seems to be a far from plausible objective.

Overseas aspects and conflicts between global and national concepts of efficiency drive further wedges between aiming for, and achieving, neutral business taxation. Two ways in which these tilt the balance in favour of interest borrowing rather than equity financing in the overseas owned segment of the Australian corporate sector should be mentioned in this context. First, the non-application of imputation benefits to non-resident shareholders does little to remove the tax bias in favour of interest borrowing for companies predominantly owned by non-residents.[14] Secondly, the tax minimisation benefits from interest-bearing financing methods for overseas-owned companies to which the Taxation Review Committee drew attention in 1975, continue to hold. In short, when its international aspects are taken into consideration, a tax bias in favour of interest-bearing debt financing continues to exist after the 1987 introduction of tax imputation which reduced this bias for domestic investors.

FURTHER ISSUES IN INTERNATIONAL TAXATION: TAX COMPETITION AND TAX HARMONISATION

The interdependence between international taxation and investment decision, particularly if viewed from the national rather than the international perspective as they generally are, means that tax competition remains important in the battle for attracting the benefits of foreign capital inflow and securing the best possible tax benefits for national investors investing offshore. Some basic forms of such tax competition may be briefly mentioned.

Frequently used strategies to attract foreign investment invariably imply low tax rates, either by adopting a low rate structure or by providing specific tax breaks including the temporary waiver of tax liability altogether (the so-called tax holiday) for foreign investors. These simply raise after-tax rates of return to foreign investors to attract capital inflow.

The raised importance of tax in international investment decision matters, when other barriers to capital movements have been (or are being) removed, a growing inducement for countries is to follow the tax initiatives in business taxation of major investing and/or investment attracting countries. The income tax rate reductions introduced by the United States in 1986 were rapidly followed by many other countries in varying degrees: only West Germany has not followed the substantial rate reductions which the United States initiated. It indicates the growing interdependence of national markets from their incorporated form into the world market, and the gradual reduction in policy-making independence which this implies.[15] The domino effect in income tax rates reductions resembles that of inter-State tax change reactions in a federation discussed in Chapter 15, with particular reference to the Queensland abolition of death duties from 1976. Tax rate harmonisation may therefore be a consequence of tax competition.

Tax efficiency considerations also arise with commodity taxation. Although not yet discussed in this context, distortions in trade flows may result from the imposition of both partial and general taxes on commodities, depending on whether they are levied on an origin or destination basis, for reasons discussed in the earlier chapters on taxation (particularly Chapters 12 and 13). Destination taxes levied on a single product or specific set of products do not, however, interfere with the location of industry, as origin taxes do. This can be illustrated as follows.

Take two countries A and B which specialise and trade respectively in two commodities, X and Y. Suppose B levies a tax on Y, its export good. Consumers of Y in A will substitute domestically produced Y, the fall in exports of Y reduces the value of B's currency in terms of A's, making imports of X from A into B more expensive. A new equilibrium involves less trade and more production of Y in A and of X in B than suggested by production possibilities in the absence of the tax. This tax policy resembles the effect of imposing an import duty on Y in country A. If B's tax on Y had been rebated on exports (turning it into a destination based tax), the distorting consequence for the location of production would have been avoided.

Given these consequences, GATT permits export rebates for product taxes but not for taxes like payroll and corporation tax which are supposed to fall on profits. In its tax harmonisation negotiations before 1992, when fiscal frontiers are intended to be largely abolished, the European Community is restricting the VAT rates charged by its members to a narrow range of rates for necessities (4–9 per cent) and luxuries (14–20 per cent). Fiscal frontiers are therefore not completely eliminated. Excises, where wide disparities reign in the Community are to be harmonised for regional areas only (enabling Southern Europe to retain low alcohol excises) so that the impact of fiscal frontiers will be reduced rather than eliminated as the original founders of the Community had intended.[16]

STABILISATION IN THE OPEN ECONOMY

In an open economy, stabilisation policy is constrained by the effects of demand management on the trade balance. In terms of the simple Keynesian analysis presented in Chapter 18, this was depicted in terms of an import leakage from the multiplier income effects of a demand stimulus. More important, it was argued that fiscal policy initiatives are constrained by reactions of the international financial community via exchange rate movements. Such movements may in turn induce adverse effects on inflation, the trade balance hence in part counteracting the effectiveness of the original fiscal policy change. In addition, increased openness of many of the world's economies has made forecasting accuracy far more difficult to achieve.[17]

Domestic and overseas balance or Budget outcome[18]

A further aspect of external influences on fiscal policy stance is the impact of overseas payments (the overseas balance) on the overall Budget outcome. Table 19.1 shows the relative importance of the Commonwealth Government's overseas transactions in their actual Budget outcome, while Table 19.2 indicates the seasonal variations in the major overseas outlay items responsible for the overseas balance. Table 19.2 shows that defence (largely purchases of defence equipment), foreign affairs (expenses of diplomatic representation, contributions to overseas agencies, overseas aid) and public debt interest on external debt are the major contributors to the overseas balance, with other overseas outlays relatively insignificant. The importance of these overseas outlays and their seasonal variation arises from their direct impact on the balance of payments, while their stable overall relative importance suggests that the total Budget outcome fairly accurately reflects the direction of the domestic Budget outcome and broad income effect of overall fiscal policy.

This account of overseas impact on public finance issues is particularly important in considering taxation effects enables two general conclusions. First, the growing complexity of assessing tax consequences in an increasingly, internationalised business environment. As briefly illustrated here, this is not only relevant to the very difficult area of business

Table 19.1 Domestic and overseas balances

	Domestic balance		*Overseas balance*		*Overall balance*	
	$m	*% of GDP*	*$m*	*% of GDP*	*$m*	*% of GDP*
1979–80	–528	–0.4	–1432	–1.2	–1960	–1.6
1980–81	553	0.4	–1539	–1.1	–986	–0.7
1981–82	945	0.6	–1453	–0.9	–508	–0.3
1982–83	–2537	–1.5	–1975	–1.2	–4512	–2.6
1983–84	–5579	–2.9	–2408	–1.3	–7987	–4.2
1984–85	–3668	–1.7	–3029	–1.4	–6697	–3.1
1985–86	–2035	–0.9	–3595	–1.5	–5630	–2.4
1986–87	1325	0.5	–3956	–1.5	–2631	–1.0
1987–88	4911	1.7	–2847	–1.0	2064	0.7
1988–98	9023	2.7	–3124	–0.9	5899	1.8
1989–90	12008	3.3	–2886	–0.8	9122	2.5

Source: 1989–90 Budget Paper No. 1, *Budget Statements 1989–90*, Statement No. 5, p. 5.5

Table 19.2 Major overseas components of overseas deficit by quarters 1986–87 to 1988–89

	September $m	*December $m*	*March $m*	*June $m*	*Total $m*	*%*
Overseas Budget deficit			*1986–87*			
Defence	273	524	262	649	1708	43.4
Foreign Affairs and Trade	156	147	219	190	712	18.1
Loan flotation expenses	8	20	9	2	39	1.0
Public debt interest	321	397	328	229	1275	32.4
Other*	53	52	52	40	202	5.1
Total overseas deficit	811	1140	875	1110	3936	100.0
			1987–88			
Defence	170	276	360	397	1203	42.2
Foreign Affairs and Trade	129	153	244	200	726	25.5
Loan flotation expenses	—	—	—	—	—	—
Public debt interest	262	456	348	246	1312	46.1
Other*	49	54	48	–541	–390	–13.7
Total overseas deficit	609	938	1000	302	2849	100.0
			1988–89			
Defence	264	295	226	363	1109	35.5
Foreign Affairs and Trade	142	141	209	280	773	24.7
Loan flotation expenses	—	—	—	—	—	—
Public debt interest	219	337	249	171	977	31.3
Other*	68	67	67	64	265	8.5
Total overseas deficit	694	841	751	838	3124	100.0

* Includes positive (surplus) foreign contribution of overseas asset sales of $16m in March Quarter 1988, $607m in June Quarter 1988, turning the outflow negative and hence into a positive inflow.

Source: Budget Papers No. 1, Budget Statements, Statement No. 5, various issues.

income taxation; it also applies to product taxation matters. The tax competition and tax harmonisation implications of such international tax aspects resemble those raised in fiscal federalism theory in the context of sub-national tax assignment consequences. Secondly, growing internationalisation of factor movements has reduced the degree of policy independence of small open economies, not only in the area of tax policy as demonstrated by the influence of United States tax reform on the rest of the world, but in the area of stabilisation policy as well. Grasping such international aspects of the subject will therefore be increasingly important for the public finance student attempting to understand the impact of domestic budgetary policy.

SUMMARY

1. An open economy alters some conclusions from public finance. Examples include the public debt where external debt differs in its consequences from domestic debt; taxation is another major area where international impact is particularly important.

2. Increasing deregulation of international capital movements and other forms of interacting national economies into the world economy make this an aspect of study of growing importance for public finance students.

3. In taxation, inter-nation equity and inter-individual equity have to be distinguished in an international setting.

4. Inter-individual equity implies that foreign source income should be aggregated with domestic source income for tax purposes with relief given for the tax already paid. Full credit against domestic tax liability ensures global neutrality as well as equity; deductibility of foreign tax liability against foreign source income is a domestically preferable means of securing inter-individual equity.

5. Inter-business equity creates problems from determining residence of the business, those of income receipts and precise tax credit/deduction to be provided. Hence investment neutrality is often distorted by international business tax arrangements.

6. Non-neutralities in investment decisions also arise from differing tax treatment of non-resident shareholders with respect to imputation, and the attractiveness of fixed interest borrowing for foreign owned companies for withholding tax reasons.

7. Likewise, destination product taxes can distort investment choices in the form of business location.

8. Tax harmonisation by equalisation tax rates through international co-operation is one method to redress these problems; international tax competition in rates has meant effective co-ordination in personal income and company tax rates trends.

9. International transactions can also be usefully distinguished in the Budget setting, leading to separation of domestic and international Budget outcomes.

10. Many international public finance problems resemble those raised by fiscal federalism, since the last study the impact of "external" fiscal relations for sub-national jurisdictions just as the former accommodates international impact on domestic fiscal arrangements.

NOTES

[1] The major theoretical contributions to this subject have been made by R.A. and P.B. Musgrave: see their classic 1972 paper, "Internation Equity", in Richard Bird and J.G. Head (eds.), *Modern Fiscal Issues* (Toronto: Toronto University Press, 1972), ch. 4; and their more recent textbook treatment, *Public Finance in Theory and Practice*, 4th edn. (New York: McGraw Hill, 1984), pp. 760–1.

[2] Fiscal federalism issues are therefore analogous to international public finance issues: recall the relevance of external debt theory to sub-national jurisdiction borrowing in the context of inter-generational burden shifting opportunities.

[3] See Draft White Paper, *Reform of the Australian Tax System* (Canberra: AGPS, 1985), ch. 20, esp. p. 230, and Appendix 20–A; R.L. Deutsch, "Foreign Tax Credits", *Australian Tax Forum* 4(2), 1987, pp. 161–96.

[4] OECD, *Model Double Taxation Convention on Income and on Capital* (Paris: OECD, 1977), pp. 26, 57–8.

[5] The unitary company tax system, as this type of taxation was called, derived from the United States' State practice in sharing corporate profits for corporations which do business in more than one State. Such a distribution needs to determine residence either by place of effective management or registration. Central assessment of corporate tax in Australia makes this a non-problem for Australian fiscal federalism. For a discussion of the difficulties potentially involved if this was not the case, see Peter Groenewegen, "Innovation Possibilities in State Business Taxation", in New South Wales Tax Task Force, *Commissioned Studies* (Sydney: 1989), pp. 188–9, 307, 329–30.

[6] Investment decisions are of course not only driven by tax considerations: investment in foreign countries depends on the economic environment of the country in question (infrastructure, availability and cost of requisite labour force, degree of regulation) as well as the political stability of the area. Factors impinging directly on rates of return such as exchange rates also influence the overseas investment decision.

[7] Appropriate income tax is difficult to define where State and local income taxes exist in addition to the centrally imposed income tax, particularly where such sub-national income taxes replace other imputs (like local rates) to which Australian income taxpayers are liable. Another problem arises in the case of parts of income tax classifiable as benefit taxes: social security contributions levied on employee income are an example relevant to most OECD member countries (see Chapter 6); the Medicare levy and Higher Education Contribution (see Chapter 9) fall into this category in Australia.

[8] For a detailed discussion of Australia's official initiatives on this very complex matter, see *Taxation of Foreign Source Income*, An Information Paper, April 1989 (Canberra: AGPS, 1989), esp. ch. 1. See also Phillip Anderson, "Economic Policy Considerations in the Taxation of Foreign Source Income", *Australian Tax Forum*, 5(4), 1988, pp. 395–417.

[9] See Taxation Review Committee, *Full Report* (Canberra: AGPS, 1975), pp. 251–2. Although the Australian Finance System Inquiry, *Final Report* (Canberra: AGPS, 1981), pp. 267–71, discussed the use of interest- withholding tax in a critical manner, it did not analyse such tax avoidance possibilities. The impact of interest-withholding taxes is crucial for financial institutions engaged in offshore banking and like financial transactions, an activity financial deregulation was designed to encourage.

[10] Taxation Review Committee, *Full Report*, pp. 269. This issue was widely reported in the *Australian Financial Review*; see for example, 17 October 1977, pp. 1 and 6; 2 November 1977, pp. 1 and 3. Legislation introduced in 1978 amended the law by imposing a tax on such branches.

[11] See Taxation Review Committee, *Full Report*, pp. 266–9. Some of the weaknesses of s. 136 referred to there have been removed by

s. 31c inserted into the Act by the stock valuation adjustment legislation introduced in 1977. For a discussion of an important court case on this subject, see G. Crough, *Taxation, Transfer Pricing and the High Court of Australia* (Sydney: Transnational Corporations Research Project, Faculty of Economics, University of Sydney, 1981). A Parliamentary Inquiry into International Profit Shifting from 1988–89 reported on the matter during 1988 and 1989; while from 1988–89 the Australian Taxation Office is increasingly investigating this type of practice in its extensive company audits, often with assistance from other tax administrations. See House of Representatives Standing Committee on Finance and Public Administration, *Shifting the Tax Burden?* November 1988; *Tax Payers or Tax Players*, May 1989.

12 As reported in the *Sydney Morning Herald*, 17 April 1989, 6 May 1989 and 12 October 1989. The last referred to a report on the subject prepared for the Australian Taxation Office which estimated that related-party international transactions (many of which associated with profit shifting) amounted to $22 billion a year and involved some of Australia's leading corporations.

13 This and the following section draw heavily on the account in R.A. and P.B. Musgrave, *Public Finance in Theory and Practice*, ch. 36, esp. pp. 763–4, 766–9.

14 See Richard Vann and Daryl Dixon, "An Examination of the Imputation System in the Context of the Erosion of the Company Tax Base", *Australian Tax Forum* 4(1) 1987, pp. 63–93; Richard Bird, "Imputation and Foreign Tax Credit: Some Critical Notes from an International Perspective", *Australian Tax Forum* 4(1), 1987, pp. 1–34.

15 F. Vanistendael, "Trends of Tax Reform in Europe", *Australian Tax Forum* 5(2), 1988, pp. 133–179; Vito Tanzi, "Tax Reform in Industrial Countries and the Impact of the US Tax Reform Act of 1986", Washington, IMF Working Papers 87/61, September 1987. The following data indicate the changes that have occurred in major industrial countries in the period from 1979 to 1987.

Top tax rates %

	Personal		*Corporate*	
	1979	*1989*	*1979*	*1989*
Britain	83	40	52	35
Italy	72	50	36	36
US	70	28	46	34
France	60	57	50	39
Australia	60	50	46	39
Japan	75	50	40	42
West Germany	56	53	56	56
Canada	43	29	46	28

Source: (OECD) International Bureau of Fiscal Documentation, as given in *The Economist*, 23 December 1989, p. 88.

16 See Sijbren Cnossen, "Harmonisation of Indirect Taxes in the EEC", in C.E. McLure Jr. (ed.), *Tax Assignment in Federal Countries* (Canberra: ANU Press, 1983), ch. 7; A. Razin and E. Sadka, "International Tax Competition and Gains from Tax Harmonization", National Bureau of Economic Research Working Paper No. 3152, Cambridge Massachusetts, October, 1989.

17 For a discussion of this difficulty see John Llewellyn et al., *Economic Forecasting and Policy. The International Dimension* (London: Routledge and Kegan Paul, 1985).

18 Details provided annually in *Statement No. 5* of Budget Paper No. 1, from which Tables 19.1 and 19.2 derive. States also have international outflows, particularly from international debt exposure but clearly not from the major sources of Commonwealth overseas outlays on defence and foreign affairs, both exclusive federal powers.

FURTHER READING

The classic treatment of this subject are by the Musgraves, see especially:

R.A. and P.B. Musgrave, *Public Finance in Theory and Practice*, 4th edn. (New York: McGraw Hill, 1984), ch. 36; and their "Inter-nation Equity" in R. Bird and J. Head (eds.), *Modern Fiscal Issues* (Toronto: Toronto University Press, 1972), ch. 4.

For Australian discussions see:

Draft White Paper, *Reform of the Australian Tax System* (Canberra: AGPS, 1985), ch. 20.

And for responses to this see:

Richard J. Vann and Ross W. Parsons, "The Foreign Tax Credit and Reform of International Taxation", *Australian Tax Reform* 3(2), 1986, pp. 131–221.

Phillip Anderson, "Economic Policy Considerations in the Taxation of Foreign Source Income", *Australian Tax Forum*, 5(4) 1988, pp. 395–417.

Taxation of Foreign Source Income, An Information Paper April 1989 (Canberra: AGPS, 1989).

For the economics of taxation with respect to global investment decisions and multinational companies see:

Julian S. Alsworth, *The Finance, Investment and Taxation Decisions of Multinationals* (Oxford: Blackwells, 1988), esp. chs. 2, 4, 6, 8, 9.

Gerry van Wyngen, "Impact of International Tax Changes on Australian Investments", *Australian Tax Forum* 6(1) 1989, pp. 89–97.

For some specific Australian applications see:

Michael D'Ascenzo, "Developments in Transfer Pricing Enforcement and Complex Audit Strategy in the Australian Taxation Office", *Australian Tax Forum* 5(4) 1988, pp. 471–492.

House of Representatives, Standing Committee on Finance and Public Administration, *Shifting the Tax Burden*, November 1988 (Canberra: AGPS, 1988); *Tax Payers or Tax Players*? May 1989 (Canberra: AGPS, 1989).

20

Whither public finance?

The previous chapters have investigated many of the principles of public finance and have studied them in the light of Australian institutions. Some general impressions which have emerged are as follows. First, much of the theory of public finance is still imprecise, and on important topics such as the theory of public expenditure determination and tax incidence, its conclusions continue to be matters of dispute among economists. Secondly, the study of public finance is continually in a state of flux because some views on theoretical issues change, and also because of the changing political and institutional framework and changing economic circumstances.

Such changes particularly became more important during the 1970s and 1980s as a result of the more volatile economic situation of these two decades. Much of this during the 1980s was imparted by the growing interdependence of the world's economies, aided as this was by financial deregulation and removal of restrictions on capital movements. These came on top of the instability of the 1970s caused by the world oil price shocks and other dislocative factors, some of which were induced by the policy-makers themselves. The impact of these factors was particularly noticeable in stabilisation policy discussion and the growing impact of international considerations on taxation.

Volatility in public finance debate in Australia was ensured by several issues. Overriding was the increasing concern over the appropriate size of the public sector, reflected in controversy over privatisation, deregulation, the growth of expenditure, taxation and indebtedness, as well as the direction of public spending. More emphasis is placed on securing efficiency and effectiveness particularly in spending decisions, but more generally to affect all aspects of public sector activity. Underlying this matter is the broader, often ideological question, about whether government has exceeded its proper role and in doing so has generated failures exceeding those from the market which provided the inspiration for the original government activity and intervention. Tax reform remained a big issue during the 1980s, scoring its successes as in the case of capital gains and other income base broadening measures; and failures, of which the 1985 consumption tax fiasco is the prime example. In intergovernmental fiscal relations the upheavals of the 1970s were followed by new solutions to redress vertical and fiscal imbalance simultaneously in a way which also enhanced Federal Government control for stabilisation purposes. The global borrowing limitations guiding Loan Council decision-making from the mid-eighties have had a similar result. This has brought this federal institution into line with additional changes in debt management and marketing by replacing price with quantity control.

These changes illustrate that new problems and issues continually appear on the public finance horizon, many of which were designed to ensure continuing public finance debate during the 1990s. Foremost is the issue of appropriate size and scope of the public sector, of which privatisation has become a very important part. Others are the importance of comprehensive consumption taxation as a tax reform issue; social welfare policy in which guaranteed minimum income schemes through negative income tax remains an option and fiscal policies to protect the environment.

This final chapter raises some of these issues partly to illustrate that public finance is a dynamic study, subject to continuous change. The backdrop to this discussion is provided by the ongoing debate over the role of the public sector and the merits of deregulation and privatisation. After an evaluation of some of the more important issues raised in this debate, this chapter demonstrates a continuing important role for the public sector, hence implying that the topic of public finance will go on to be a challenging subject for students of economics.

IS LEVIATHAN COMING?

The rapid rise in public spending during the first half of the 1970s as a result of the implementation of the social programs of the Whitlam Labor government (1972–75) and the lack of success by the subsequent conservative Fraser administration (1975–83) to reduce the relative size of the public sector have suggested to some that Leviathan — that old-fashioned term for the State coined by Hobbes in the mid-seventeenth century, implying big government, and Big Brother[1] — has arrived in Australia. The major policy task for the libertarians of the Right (a term briefly discussed in Chapter 1 of this book) is to lead a concerted assault on the size of the public sector in order to preserve living standards, economic welfare, and personal freedom. The rationale for this critique of the public sector and of the beneficient role of the modern State deserves serious evaluation and analysis by the public finance student. This is all the more important since its popular acceptance in Australia was boosted by the continuing electoral victories of Mrs. Thatcher's Conservative Party after 1979 on anti-public spending platforms in the United Kingdom and by the equally conservative Republicans under President Reagan and his successor President Bush from 1980. Many other developed countries with large public sectors, including those in Scandinavia, are stepping up their attempts to lower the relative flow of resources going to their public sectors if only to meet their residents' aspirations for lower tax burdens.

Chapter 3 indicated that Australia has been one of the few OECD countries successful in reducing the size of the public sector relative to GDP. This was graphically illustrated in Figure 3.1. Likewise, as shown in Chapter 16, State governments are critically examining the growing size of spending on various programs and have sought to curtail the size of their public sectors. Stabilisation purposes — reduction of government contributions to aggregate demand — combined with lowering public indebtedness and public sector demands on the capital markets have played an important part in these moves; there has also been a growing desire to enhance efficiency in, and effectiveness of, government service delivery.

However, Chapter 3 also indicated that measures of public sector growth such as outlays relative to GDP were not free of ambiguities. Examples included the productivity or relative price effect which tends to overstate the relative growth of the public sector. It was also pointed out in that chapter that some of the statistical measures are clearly deficient because they fail to capture the impact of government regulation and control. Some[2] see government regulatory proclivities as far more important a problem than excessive public sector growth as conventionally measured.

The critique of government as regulator sees government intervention not as a means of improving efficiency through correcting distortions in resource allocation caused by imperfect markets or other market failures, or alternatively, as the benevolent despot attempting to maximise a social welfare function through its expenditure and other policies, but exclusively as a redistributive agency. This contradicts the positive role for government budgetary activities summarised in Chapter 2 as the work of the allocational, the distribution, and stabilisation branches of the Budget. Instead, this view depicts regulation as safeguarding sectional interests for largely selfish reasons. Its consequences are invariably described as reductions in general welfare. This argument against regulation is supported by interpretations of the superiority of a market mechanism in generating outcomes and bases itself on estimates of the enormous welfare losses from government regulation arising from the private costs on business flowing from the implementation of social policies. The growth of the anti-regulation lobby has combined with a scepticism about "big government" because it can often be shown to have carried out its tasks inefficiently if not perversely with respect to desired outcomes. The generally perceived failure of interventionist fiscal policy to achieve full employment and price stability has further encouraged such views.[3]

Although aspects of the debate over regulation have considerable relevance for students of public finance (as was demonstrated, for example, in the earlier discussion of company taxation, stamp duties, and financial transaction taxes from the perspective of the efficiency objective of tax neutrality) a detailed discussion of deregulation and its costs and benefits falls outside the scope of a book on public finance. The same can be said in the context of privatisation which largely concerns the efficiency of public trading enterprises, the consideration of which has been explicitly excluded from the contents of this text.[4] However, part of that debate covers the merits or otherwise of contracting out the production of particular government services, a growing practice in Australia at all levels of government. The aim of contracting out is to enhance the efficiency of government service delivery by gaining more services for the same outlay (cost). There is substantial evidence that cost reduction is a major consequence of shifting from public to private production in specific services, sometimes secured by a reduction in quality of service provided or by worse employment conditions for the actual providers of these services.

Many of the arguments in favour of privatisation of government trading enterprises are also being applied more generally to the benefits which can in theory be reaped by transferring service delivery traditionally performed by the public sector (in areas such as education and health, but also public housing and public transport) to the private sector. The examples given are all of services where the community service aspect or other distributional considerations prevent dominance of private provision because such wider provision would not be profitable. Voucher systems, explicit government subsidy to cover community service components of this type of activity and alterations in the provision of health financing are methods by which greater private initiatives in these services can be encouraged without eliminating their social and distributional objectives.[5]

Improved accountability and public spending efficiency

Public sector growth from the mid-1970s (the extent of which was shown in Chapter 3) has also led to a greater awareness of a need to make public spending more cost-effective and efficient. Some significant developments in public financial administration indicated that this has gained wider acceptance but still has much further to go. One way of curtailing too rapid public sector growth is to ensure redundant programs are abolished. This means ongoing evaluation of priorities in spending combined with more specific periodic reviews of public expenditure as a whole. Chapter 5 in particular discussed aspects of techniques designed to achieve greater efficiency and accountability but also noted the many problems they can encounter.

Public sector size and economic growth

In Chapter 3 the impact of economic growth on public sector size was examined as a major explanatory variable of public sector growth. That chapter also commented on potential detrimental impacts of public sector size on economic growth. In Australia, research on the last topic has accelerated in the context of rapid public sector growth in the 1970s and 1980s combined with relatively poor overall economic performance. In Chapter 16 the trend towards increased consumption spending by government and relative decline in capital spending was documented, a factor of relevance to this discussion because public investment can be expected to affect economic growth performance positively. Empirical analysis is not conclusive on this issue, with some studies finding a negative effect of a rising public consumption share in GDP on growth in per capita income, and others the opposite. Poor economic growth performance is in many respects more easily blamed on factors other than government size, such as monetary disturbances and high anticipated inflation rates. In Australia, rigidities in the product and labour market, low rates of capital formation, low educational participation rates and deteriorating terms of trade have been far more significant variables for explaining poor growth performance.[6] Needless to say, this type of discussion quickly becomes prone to ideological flag-waving.

Micro-effects of a large public sector and its underlying institutional arrangement need also to be assessed. Excess burden estimates for particular tax systems impose a significant dead-weight loss from the size of the public sector per se. Disincentive effects from particular tax regimes, such as those from income taxes on labour supply, saving and investment, can further link public sector size adversely with economic growth, since the effects of such disincentives tend to increase more than proportionally with the height of the rates at which taxes are imposed. Disputed misallocation consequences from fiscal equalisation arrangements (see Chapter 15) have also sometimes been blamed for poor growth performance as is the impact on productive capital formation from excessive investment in housing services, in part stimulated by substantial tax preference for this form of investment.

A number of aspects of this issue can be investigated further in this chapter. One of these is much reduced public capital formation which is demonstrable here and overseas and its implications for future economic growth. The second is the growth of the welfare state and various methods of providing effective income maintenance. The third is the role of taxation in economic growth, particularly the potential of broad-based consumption taxation to assist in achieving higher growth rates.

The importance of public investment in infrastructure

Like private investment, public investment is important for lifting productivity levels and increasing economic growth. Particularly important is infrastructure investment (for transport, water conservation, communication, education and health). Infrastructure, as the name implies, is not an end in itself but is indispensible for supporting economic and social ends, which are generally regarded as important for maintaining or securing growing living standards. Infrastructure investment requires relatively high initial capital costs (think of the cost of a new railway track, airport, highway), has a relatively long life, and can therefore be financed over the longer term by borrowing (as suggested in Chapter 17). Much of Australia's infrastructure has existed for long periods, and in many cases its age entails its imminent replacement or higher maintenance costs. New infrastructure investment is also required for demographic reasons (hospitals, schools, roads, transport in general), and for general developmental reasons which disclose gaps in existing infrastructure provision (for example, transport facilities in areas with new mineral developments). Although Australia is a young country in terms of European settlement, much of its infrastructure is old by world standards, in part because Australia's economic development coincided with much of the infrastructure-intensive development in transport, communication, public health and education, which took place everywhere else in the developed world during the nineteenth century.

The rapid decline in resources made available for public investment over the period from 1975 suggests a coming infrastructure crisis, because it implies that what is worn-out is not being replaced when necessary, new infrastructure is not provided when needed for development, structural change, or demographic reasons. Such a policy is clearly uneconomic as uncorrected obsolesence raises operation costs, and imposes additional costs on users through time loss, and deterioration (if not total loss) of more perishable goods in transit. The extent of such costs are difficult to estimate simply and unambiguously, but the quest for micro-economic reform in the transport and communication areas in general suggest that the benefits in terms of higher productivity from better infrastructure are undoubtedly significant.

A parliamentary inquiry on the subject in 1987[7] suggested that some of these problems in public infrastructure provision were institutional. Public capital spending was largely residual after necessary public consumption needs had been provided for, and, given the revenue constraints, appropriate Budget outcomes had been determined. From its basic characteristics, infrastructure development is in some way the easiest form of spending to postpone, and expenditure restraint for stabilisation purposes has invariably fallen more heavily on capital account from the mid-1970s. Priority setting is therefore particularly important in this area. Given overall Budget constraints, this can be done by using accepted techniques like cost/benefit analysis (see Chapter 5). On a national basis with federal-State co-operation, the Loan Council works program allocations and global borrowing limits offer scope for improved public investment decisions, the potential benefits of which have as yet not been realised. Although the extent of the infrastructure problem in Australia is debatable,[8] there is little doubt that public investment trends over the last two decades are creating a growing infrastructure problem, which can duly be resolved by utilising the tools and institutions of public investment planning discussed in previous chapters. A shift in public resource use, not necessarily involving an increase in aggregate publicly used resources towards public capital formation would positively associate public spending growth with economic growth in general.

The growth of the Welfare State[9]

One of the major causes of public sector growth in the past two decades is the increase in social welfare spending whether broadly conceived to include that on health, education, and housing or whether more narrowly confined to outlays on social security benefits. Although spending on housing and to a lesser extent on education has fluctuated, that on health and particularly on social security has continued to grow at generally above average rates. Many of these issues cannot be examined here in any detail because they belong to the more specialised and rapidly growing literature on the economics of welfare, health economics, and the economics of education. However, the phenomenal growth of social security and welfare relative to other Budget outlays of the Commonwealth Government should be examined in the context of public sector size and economic growth.

Three issues stand out for particular examination. First, effects of the ageing of Australia (that is, the expected increase over the coming decades of the proportion of the over-65s in the population) on the rate of increase of welfare spending which may make the achievement of other government priorities more difficult. A second and very much interconnected issue is that of the means test raised by the perennial debate about universality versus selectivity in social welfare provision. A third issue, the manner in which social security is best delivered, is left to a subsequent section of this chapter, though some of the relevant issues have been canvassed earlier in the context of superannuation tax issues in Chapter 10.

The public finance problems induced by an ageing population through increased welfare spending are many. As so often in economic discussion, these can be reduced to a set of choices between various alternatives. One alternative is to do nothing, by continuing paying aged pensions in the current manner, that is, indexed for changes in the cost of living and subject to a means test. This implies (other things being equal which they may not be) reduced outlays on other priorities or increased taxation. A second alternative is to increase the stringency of eligibility requirements for the payment of age pensions by tightening income, assets, residence and other eligibility tests. Thirdly, and not unrelated to the second alternative, active steps may be taken through tax or other concessions to encourage greater private provision for retirement through the sale of annuities and other forms of superannuation by private insurance companies. Finally, but not because the many possible alternatives have been exhausted, a national superannuation scheme (earnings related or with flat rate benefits) could be introduced to replace the present system of benefits financed from current general taxation revenue. Because such a move implies separate social security contributions from the working population, it would make Australia's revenue system also more comparable to that of other OECD countries (see Chapter 6).

A number of the alternatives in the previous paragraph raised means test issues. The first left the selectivity of the present social security system unaltered, the second made it more selective by combining an asset test with the current income test. The fourth alternative of nationally provided superannuation indicates a more universalist approach to social welfare provision. Such a system can be extended to one of national social insurance which covers contingencies like unemployment, sickness, and permanent disabilities as well. It can be designed to pay either earnings related or flat rate benefits. Such a system is a drastic departure from the traditional Australian social welfare system largely based on means-tested benefits. Even family allowances and Austudy are means-tested, only the provision of health care under the Medicare scheme which commenced in 1984 is open to all, irrespective of income levels. Means-testing of benefits is generally supported as being more vertically equitable (recall the evidence on the incidence of these benefits in Chapter 5) and also requires less public expenditure. Whether or not it involves a greater or lesser use of resources depends on the incentive and other output effects from having a means test as against a universal welfare system. Further discussion cannot be provided, but welfare spending is clearly a subject to which public finance economists can be expected to make further contributions.[10] The effects on saving of public provision for the aged link this aspect of public sector size closely to economic growth performance.

Comprehensive consumption taxation and economic growth

In Chapters 12 and 13 the advantages and disadvantages of comprehensive and selective consumption taxation were discussed. Conclusions reached in this discussion were that although selective outlay of transaction taxes had their uses in a tax system, there was considerable benefit from moving towards broad-based consumption taxation on both horizontal equity, and economic efficiency (neutrality) grounds. The more general the tax (few exemptions and a single rate) the greater these advantages, and the smaller the costs of administration and compliance. Finally, it was concluded that the best instrument for achieving such broad-based consumption taxation was the indirect multi-stage sales tax or value added tax of the consumption type. This was preferable to a retail sales tax on administative grounds, particularly if substantial amounts of revenue were to be raised from its use. The last point links this issue to public sector size, since the constraints on raising revenue from a retail sales tax are seen by some as a valuable brake on public sector growth.

Comprehensive consumption taxation is linked directly with economic growth through its potential impact on saving. If this reform is part of a tax mix switch in which personal income tax is to be reduced from part of the revenue raised by the new consumption tax, then saving is likely to be positively affected. The extent of the savings increase is more difficult to assess. A direct consumption expenditure tax (also discussed in Chapter 12) demonstrates this explicitly since that after all is nothing but an income (receipts) tax in which outflows in the form of savings or investment are fully deductible, in order to eliminate the "double taxation of saving" effect inherent in an income tax. Although the saving incentive effects of the direct expenditure tax are certain to be positive, the links with investment and growth are likely to be more tenuous.[11]

Irrespective of its impact on saving, introduction of broad-based consumption taxation can be supported on its reform potential in removing current defects in Australian consumption taxes; likely to yield substantial horizontal equity and efficiency benefits. Detrimental vertical equity consequences can be redressed by appropriate distributional measures compensating those disadvantaged from the move. At the same time, adverse macro-economic consequences can be neutralised by compensatory policies of demand management and income policy, as experience in a variety of countries has shown.[12]

In this context it may be reiterated that tax policy, like public sector size, is difficult to relate precisely to economic growth. The mechanisms linking specific tax regimes to incentives to work, save, invest and take risks are too difficult to quantify to place great reliance on the effectiveness of particular policy conclusions. This aspect of economic growth economics, like that of the general association between the public sector and economic growth, requires considerably more research and even then there can be no certainty of establishing precise causal propositions in this area.

SOCIAL WELFARE, MINIMUM INCOME SCHEMES AND NEGATIVE INCOME TAXES

A further potential controversy in Australian public finance is the proposal to remove the *direct* assistance to the socially disadvantaged provided through the various social security benefits by replacing it with some form of guaranteed minimum income scheme or with a system of negative income taxes. Schemes of this sort have been considered in many countries, including Australia, and it is appropriate to consider some aspects of them here (although a review of the Australian social security systems falls outside the scope of this book).[13]

At present, Australia's system of social welfare and income maintenance largely administered by the Federal Government, is based on what is called the "categorical approach" — that is, certain categories of the population such as those over 60 or 65, children under 16, invalids, and the unemployed receive a certain benefit from the government appropriate to their status. Most of these cash benefits are subject to a means test. For this system to work well, the categories must be clearly defined; people within these categories must be aware of their entitlements; and people should not be able to make themselves improperly eligible for benefits. On this criterion, aged pensions and family allowances score well, but eligibility for unemployment and sickness benefits can often be manipulated by the individual recipient.

Supplementary assistance is frequently given in recognition of differing needs within the category of welfare recipients — for example, home-owning and rent-paying pensioners, pensioners with and without dependants. In addition, many fringe benefits are given to pensioners by local government and statutory bodies and by some private businesses: pensioner rate schemes, meals-on-wheels, senior citizen centres, subsidised public transport, free medical services, and theatre and cinema concessions are some of the better-known examples. The welfare system now has a patchwork-quilt aspect with assistance by agencies of the federal, the State, and local governments, not to mention private welfare agencies often actively encouraged by government. This has led to anomalies, the more important of which is a sharply varying income retention rate in means-tested pensions as private income rises by small amounts. An example from the current system illustrates this. As a result of the concurrence of an income test and liability to income taxation, many pensioner groupings at low levels of income and those in unemployment benefits face extraordinarily high marginal "tax rates" (so-called poverty traps) which in some cases exceed the maximum marginal tax rate of personal income tax. For example, sole parents with two children faced effective marginal rates varying from 75 to 120 per cent including income tax for a weekly wage of $284.20 in December 1987 and flexible hours of work.[14]

These problems in the present social security system have led to suggestions to replace it with a negative income tax or a guaranteed minimum income scheme. The 1974 *Henderson Report*[15] listed the advantages of such schemes as follows:

1. To emphasise that the right to a minimum income and the obligation to pay tax are but two sides of the same coin.
2. To reduce the emphasis placed on special categories in the determination of entitlements and obligations.
3. To provide minimum income levels so that Australians do not find themselves in poverty.
4. To assure all citizens of a logical sequence of income retention rates as private income increases.
5. To favour neither those whose private income fluctuates nor those whose private income is steady.
6. To lighten the administrative load of social security and taxation.
7. To achieve all this without markedly worsening the position of any persons compared with the present system.

How do these systems work? In their simplest form, all systems of tax credits and negative income taxes work with a set of regular minimum income payments plus a tax on private income which may be proportional or progressive. The relationship between the minimum income payment, 'm', the tax rate, 't', and private income, 'p', can be expressed in the following equation:

$$s = m - t\,p$$

where s is the next income subsidy paid by the government which may be positive or negative. The subsidy is positive when the guaranteed minimum income is greater than the income tax paid in private income, it is zero when $m = tp$ and negative when $tp > m$. The important variables in such a scheme are m, the guaranteed minimum income, t, the tax rate, b, the break-even point when $s = 0$ and C the total cost of the scheme or the Budget constraint.[16]

The interconnection between these variables is as follows. With two of the three variables, C, m, and t, being known, the third can be calculated. For example, the acceptance of a Budget constraint by the government set by the total cost of the present system, together with the setting of m relative to some estimated poverty line, will determine the tax rate. Alternatively, the cost of the system can be minimised with a low level of m and a relatively high tax rate, which yields a low break-even point and therefore a small number of recipients of the income subsidy. For maximum redistribution to the needy or those below the poverty line, "m" should be relatively large and "b" small. However, this arrangement involves high marginal tax rates after the break-even point and these may affect incentives to work. This conflict is one of the major problems of the scheme.

It can be easily shown that many of the advantages of guaranteed minimum income schemes as listed earlier from the *Henderson Report*, will follow on its introduction. The right to a minimum income and the obligation to pay taxes are clearly connected; the emphasis on special categories appears to be eliminated; if the mimimum income is set sufficiently high, all Australians will be above the poverty line; income retention rates will have a logical progression (unlike the case of sole parents mentioned earlier) because the average tax rates, even with a proportional tax, will rise smoothly from negative to positive values; if the appropriate value of "m", is adopted no one needs to be worse off as compared with the present system; while finally, if the Taxation Office administers the scheme, large administrative savings appear to be likely from the virtual abolition of the Social Security Department.

Several contrary arguments must be considered. First, because the income requirements of the socially disadvantaged will continue to be different, there will be many, not one, levels of "m", because, as the Henderson Report itself recognised,[17] variations in "m" will be required to take account of home ownership, the number of dependants, and variations in the cost of living. It is, of course, obvious that the more "m's" there are, the greater the administrative difficulties and costs of the scheme. Secondly, the value of "m" initially adopted must be varied either with changes in the cost of living (as is present practice with pensions) or with changes in average weekly earnings (as was practised by the Government until 1975). Such changes and adjustments are relatively easy to make when separate cash benefits are provided to different categories of the needy; they become far more difficult to make when the whole tax system is involved, because changes in "m" are interrelated with tax rates and with the total cost of the scheme. The tax administrators may well be tempted to delay such adjustments as long as possible to save themselves the task of frequent changes in the personal income tax structure.

The *Henderson Report* asserted that the system would achieve substantial savings in administrative costs, but this is open to doubt. As Professor Henderson argued four years prior to the presentation of his *Report*:

> It has been claimed that the scheme would enable most of the administrative apparatus of the welfare services to be swept away, thus achieving great economies. But these claims seem exaggerated, for a social dividend or negative income tax is bound to be rather inflexible, determined probably on an annual basis although paid weekly. Sudden loss of income through bereavement, desertion, accident, sickness or unemployment will need immediate help for which a social service organisation must be retained. It will not be good enough to make an adjustment at the end of the tax year.[18]

In addition to these difficulties listed by Professor Henderson, there are the private compliance costs for social welfare recipients who will suddenly be required to submit annual tax returns.

In short, there are far more problems with such a reorganisation of social welfare than its supporters have pointed out. Most of these assume rather than demonstrate the perceived benefits from their proposals. It is also interesting to note that although such schemes have been advocated in various forms since the early 1960s, no government has implemented this type of policy.[19]

PUBLIC FINANCE, POLLUTION, AND PROTECTION OF THE ENVIRONMENT

Another topic which has been added to the literature of public finance is that related to fiscal policies for the prevention of pollution and protection of the environment. Such problems are regarded as "market failures" and hence are frequently argued to fall within the scope of public finance.[20] They either involve resources such as waste or the atmosphere, for which no prices are charged, or they involve resources similar to public goods. Consequently, they are seen as problems which may be solved by the tools of public finance, in particular, by taxes or government subsidies. This section is not concerned with an analysis of environmental economics as a whole; rather, it is concerned with the question whether market solutions — through the imposition of taxes or the granting of subsidies — are superior (or inferior) to legislative controls. Some of the public finance by-products of such legislative measures will also be examined. The immense environmental concern expressed worldwide at the end of the 1980s, partly in the context of "the greenhouse effect" or global warming, has placed public finance solutions to such problems even more firmly on the agenda.[21]

An illustration will make the issue more intelligible. Take, for example, the classic case of the firm which, in producing its output, inflicts marginal social costs, because of smoke and other effluents emitted from its chimneys and its disposal of waste into the nearby river. These costs are not reflected in the price because both the atmosphere and the river are treated as costless amenities from the point of view of this firm. For the nearby residents, these actions do have a cost: the stench of the smoke, the soiling of washing, the higher incidence of respiratory diseases, and the gradual elimination of water sports such as fishing and swimming. The classic remedy to this problem is to place a tax on the firm's product, equal to the social cost of that output, thereby internalising the social costs. As a result, output will be diminished and the degree of pollution reduced.

Depending on the slope of the cost curve, including that of marginal social cost, and the elasticity of demand for the product, the output effect will be large or small. If it is small, the effect on the neighbouring residents may be hardly noticeable. A practical shortcoming is the measurement of the social cost of this pollution which is a prerequisite for the correct formulation of the tax. As R.A. and P.B. Musgrave point out,[22] these costs are almost impossible to estimate. Environmentalists who want pure air and clean water would not be satisfied with this solution; for them the desired output of the firm is zero.

If the example is varied slightly, a superior policy alternative can be reached. Legislative control may either curtail production, or enforce a change to a technique to eliminate these undesirable by-products. Such alternative techniques are usually available, although they are frequently more expensive for the operating firm. These additional costs can be paid for in three ways: by the consumers in the form of high prices for the products; by the shareholders through lower profits; or by the government through a subsidy which finances the technical alterations. In the final analysis, who pays will depend on the nature of, and market for, the products, as well as on the judgement about the distributional issues involved.

Virtually all pollution problems and those of the environment's destruction raise similar issues. Whether it is logging in State forests or national parks, mining development in national heritage areas, tighter emission controls on motor vehicles and more generally, on all emitters of fluorocarbons in a world conscious of global warming effects, or the noise pollution caused by low-flying aircraft near airports or juggernaut trucks on freeways at night.

All regulatory actions impose costs, which raises the question of who is to pay for them. This involves distributional issues. Sometimes these issues can be solved through the price mechanism. Often they require either legislative controls or direct prohibition, such as constraints upon production (for example, the night curfew applying to Sydney airport), or an enforced change of technique or location. The solution adopted for each problem will depend largely on the relative bargaining strengths of the parties involved.

One aspect of environmental policy of particular importance is the distributional aspect of the environmental control vis-à-vis the unregulated pollution. Unfortunately this aspect has received little recognition in the economic literature of the subject, despite the fact that pollution has deleterious effects on the poor. If nothing is done about pollution it is the less well-to-do who suffer because they live in the worst areas — near factories, airports, and expressways. The rich protect themselves and their residential area by zoning and planning regulations. If action is taken against pollution, whether by tax policy or legislative control, this will affect the cost structure of the industries affected, and result in rising prices with the usual regressive effects of taxes on goods and services. These distributional effects pose some of the hardest problems in environmental economics.

For those concerned with environmental issues *and* equity, the dilemma is that many of the solutions put forward by economists either do not adequately solve the problems (the factory example) or the solution gives rise to unfortunate distributional consequences. Environmental policies are best pursued by direct government controls, and the consequence of such controls should be very carefully investigated for their effects on the poorer sections of the communmity.

The costs involved in controlling fluorocarbon emissions in order to reduce the impact of global warming are expected to be so large that tax policies on energy users responsible for such emissions are likely to be part of the fiscal controls. When Australia's contribution to a 20 per cent reduction of greenhouse emissions by the year 2005 is estimated to require a 40 per cent increase in electricity bills and a substantial reduction in the use of internal combusion engines on current technology, adverse distributional consequences are not difficult to imagine. Additional revenue from pollution taxes can cushion the more detrimental distributional consequences of such reductions in living standards. Fiscal measures of pollution control may therefore generate important external benefits in the form of additional tax revenue, making them more attractive to environment-conscious governments than they have been in the past.[23]

The continuing role for the public sector

In spite of all the talk about deregulation, privatisation through the sale of government assets and enterprises, tax cuts and curtailment of public spending, action on these fronts has been rather limited. Substantial privatisation in the United Kingdom has not been matched by reduced public spending; a smaller public sector in Australia has not been as yet accompanied by much privatisation though there has been considerable deregulation as well as asset sales. Irrespective of whether such initiatives will accelerate in the 1990s, this chapter suggests that there is going to be a continuing and, in the longer run, expanding role for the public sector. Infrastructure requirements, environmental factors and factors inherent in public sector growth itself (such as the "productivity lag" or "relative price effects") are responsible for this conclusion, even if it appears to fly in the face of recent facts. It will therefore become all the more important to ensure that the efficiency of government spending be continually watched and improved, and that tax reform and tax change discussion will remain important topics for debate and analysis. This is, broadly speaking, what public finance is all about. It provides the tools with which to carry out such investigations even though many of these tools are imperfect and therefore need handling with a great deal of care. This is what makes public finance such an exciting subject. The exact path of its future developments cannot be easily predicted but one prediction can safely be made: the skills of the public finance economist are likely to be in as much demand by the twenty-first century as they are now.

SUMMARY

1. Public finance studies are continually changing to keep pace with changes in the underlying theory, in perceptions of the role of the public sector, and in institutions.

2. The integration of the world's economies has altered perspectives on the impact of policies: examples are taxation and stabilisation policy.

3. Issues likely to be of particular interest for the public finance student in the 1990s are the size of the public sector and methods of reducing it such as privatisation and the contracting out of services, tax reform in the consumption tax area, social welfare policy and fiscal policy to protect the environment.

4. Continuing debate on the appropriate scope for government action is one indication of the evolving nature of public finance debate. Manifestations are the analysis of the relative merits of privatisation and the impact of public sector size in economic growth.

5. Part of this evolution is inspired by a search for greater efficiency and effectiveness in public spending and general resource allocations, for which many techniques are available even if they are sometimes difficult to apply.

6. There is little precise evidence on how public sector size affects economic performance, partly because the latter depends on so many other factors as well.

7. Infrastructure spending on transport, communications, education, and water conservation, have clear positive impacts on growth; micro-economic effects associated with large excess burdens and disincentive effects from excessive tax rates and inappropriate fiscal equalisation procedures are associated with consequences detrimental to public sector size and economic growth.

8. Social welfare financing, particularly for retirement purposes, influences national economic performance through its impact on saving, but the precise nature of these interdependencies, particularly the quantitative aspects, remains controversial.

9. Taxation policy, perhaps by greater reliance on general consumption taxation, can likewise favourably influence economic performance by freeing resources for capital formation, another area where quantitative outcomes are difficult to predict.

10. A further important public finance issue for the 1990s is fiscal policy for the environment, particularly in the context of global warming from the greenhouse effect where tax instruments are likely to be used more intensively than are current government measures for protecting the environment.

NOTES

[1] See Thomas Hobbes, *Leviathan*, first published in 1651. Its connotations of all-powerful government and authoritarianism have been exploited in the public finance literature by those seeking constitutional constraints on government spending. See, for example, G.H. Brennan and J.M. Buchanan, "Toward a Tax Constitution for Leviathan", *Journal of Public Economics*, vol. 9, 1977, pp. 301–18; an argument expanded in detail in their subsequent *The Power to Tax: Analytical Foundations of a Fiscal Constitution* (Cambridge: Cambridge University Press, 1980). The reference to "Big Brother" is to the symbol for authoritarianism developed by Left libertarian author George Orwell in his important novel, *1984*, first published in 1949.

[2] This argument is put in N.G. Butlin, A. Barnard, and J.J. Pincus, *Government and Capitalism* (Sydney: Allen and Unwin, 1982), introduction; D.A. Aitkin, "Where Does Australia Stand?" in Glenn Withers (ed.), *Bigger or Smaller Government*? (Canberra: Academy of the Social Sciences in Australia and ANU Press, 1983), ch. 2.

[3] For a comprehensive survey of the literature on regulation in Australia, see J.J. Pincus and G.A. Withers, "Economics of Regulation", in F.H. Gruen (ed.), *Surveys of Australian Economics* (Sydney: Allen and Unwin, 1983), vol. 3, ch. 1. See also R. Parish, "Government and Economic Management", in Glenn Withers (ed.), *Bigger or Smaller Government*, ch. 4.

[4] For comprehensive discussions of privatisation see Simon Domberger and John Piggott, "Privatisation Policies and Public Enterprise: A Survey", *The Economic Record* 62(177) June 1986, pp. 145–62; David A. Henscher, "Privatisation: An Interpretative Essay", *Australian Economic Papers* 25(47), December 1986, pp. 147–74, Evatt Research Centre, *State of Siege* (Sydney: Pluto Press, 1989), ch. 5. A State Perspective is given by the New South Wales Commission of Audit, *Focus on Reform* (Sydney, 1988), esp. ch. 8.

[5] See John Freebairn, Michael Porter and Cliff Walsh (eds.), National Economic Priorities 1987, *Spending and Taxing* (Sydney: Allen and Unwin, 1987), chs. 6,7; New South Wales Commission of Audit, *Focus on Reform*, pp. 14–21, ch. 3, pp. 85–6. A critical discussion of these suggestions is provided in the detailed State case studies, in Evatt Research Centre, *State of Siege*, for example, pp. 186–212 (New South Wales), 242–54 (Victoria), pp. 342–62 (Western Australia).

[6] See Neil Johnston, David Harrison, Mylinh Hardman and Robert Brooker, "The Role of Fiscal Policy in Post War Australian Economic Growth", in Bruce Chapman (ed.), *Australian Economic Growth* (Melbourne: Macmillan, 1989), pp. 133–40; F.H. Gruen, "How Bad is Australia's Economic Performance and Why?", *Economic Record*, 62(177) June 1986, pp. 180–93; Phillip J. Grossman, "Growth in Government and Economic Growth: The Australian Experience", *Australian Economic Papers*, 27(5) June 1988, pp. 33–43; National Priorities Project 1989, *Savings and Productivity Incentives for the 1990s* (Sydney: Allen and Unwin, 1989), esp. ch. 1.

[7] *Constructing and Reconstructing Australia's Public Infrastructure*, Report of the House of Representatives Standing Committee on Transport Communications and Infrastructure (Canberra: AGPS, 1987).

[8] For a contrary view, see EPAC Council Paper No. 33, *Economic Infrastructure in Australia*, (Canberra: EPAC June 1988).

[9] For some recent literature see EPAC Council Paper no. 17, *Growth in Australian Social Expenditures* (Canberra: EPAC, March 1986); F.H. Gruen, "Australia's Welfare State: Rearguard Action or Avant-Garde?" (Canberra: Australian National University, Centre for Economic Policy Research, Discussion Paper No. 22, June 1989). For a longer-term history see M.A. Jones, *The Australian Welfare State* (Sydney: Allen and Unwin, 1980) and Meredith Edwards and Peter Whiteford, "The Development of Government Policies on Poverty and Income Distribution", *Australian Economic Review*, 3/88, pp. 54–73.

[10] The Reports and Discussion Papers from the Comprehensive Social Security Review conducted on behalf of the Federal Government indicate the many-faceted problems raised by this issue. A survey of the initiatives of the Labor government from 1983 in this area is provided in *Towards a Fairer Australia* (Canberra: AGPS, 1988).

[11] See Peter Groenewegen, "Taxation and Economic Growth", *Australian Journal of Public Administration*, 49(3), September 1990.

[12] A general evaluation of broad-based consumption taxation as a reform policy is in Australian Tax Research Foundation, *Consumption Taxes: Everyone's Guide to the Pros and Cons* (Sydney: Australian Tax Research Foundation, 1989). Many of these issues were raised in Draft White Paper, *Reform of the Australian Tax System* (Canberra: AGPS, 1985), chs. 13, 14.

[13] Those interested in such a review can consult the literature generated by the Australian Social Security Review to which reference was made in Note 10 above.

[14] EPAC Council Paper no. 35, *Income Support Policies, Taxation and Incentives* (Canberra: EPAC, October 1988), Chart 3.5, p. 46.

[15] See Henderson Poverty Commission, *First Main Reports* (Canberra: AGPS, 1974, pp. 72–3.

[16] For more details on these inter-relationships see R.A. and P.B. Musgrave, *Public Finance in Theory and Practice*, ch. 34, esp. pp. 715–17. An example of a Budget constraint would be the current level of spending on income support schemes which the new system would not be able to exceed.

[17] Henderson Poverty Commission, *First Main Report*, pp. 75–80.

[18] R.F. Henderson, "Relief of Poverty", *Economic Record*, March 1971, p. 111, cf. p. 110.

[19] For a detailed discussion of problems with integrating social security and personal income tax, see D.A. Dixon and C.A. Foster, "Integration of the Australian Tax and Social Security Systems by a Linear Income Tax: Problems and Benefits", in J.G. Head, *Taxation Issues of the 1980s* (Sydney: Australian Tax Research Foundation, 1983), ch. 6; Daryl Dixon and Chris Foster, "An Alternative Path to Integration of Social Security and Personal Income Tax Arrangements" (Sydney: Australian Tax Research Foundation Occasional Paper no. 1, 1983); Draft White Paper, *Reform of the Australian Tax System* (Canberra: AGPS, 1985), ch. 10.

[20] Historically, such discussions go back to the writings of Pigou, *Wealth and Welfare* (London: Macmillan, 1912). For a more modern public finance-oriented discussion, see R.A. and P.B. Musgrave, *Public Finance in Theory and Practice*, ch. 35.

[21] See for example, Mark Pearson and Stephen Smith, "Taxation and Environmental Policy: Some Initial Evidence", (London: Institute of Fiscal Studies Commentary 10, 1990); Developing Government Responses to the Greenhouse Effect, *Treasury Economic Roundup*, November 1989, pp. 3–20.

[22] R.A. and P.B. Musgrave, *Public Finance in Theory and Practice*, pp. 745–50.

[23] See *The Economist*, "Money from Greenery", October 21, 1989, pp. 16–17, which, among other things, indicates that Holland's environment-conscious government raises approximately eight times in revenue per head from effluent charges than France and twenty times more than West Germany. The Australian data in this paragraph is from David Clark, "Putting a Cost on the Environment", *Australian Financial Review*, February 7, 1990, p. 28.

FURTHER READING

Once again, the general texts provide useful perspectives on issues raised in this chapter.

See R.A. and P.B. Musgrave, *Public Finance in Theory and Practice*, 4th edn. (New York: McGraw Hill, 1984), chs. 34, 35.

J.E. Stiglitz, *Public Sector Economics* (New York: W.W. Norton, 1988), chs. 1, 2, 7, 13, 14.

On public sector growth and economic performance see:

F.H. Gruen, "How Bad is Australia's Economic Performance: and Why?", *Economic Record*, 62(177), June 1986, pp. 180–93.

Phillip J. Grossman, "Growth in Government and Economic Growth", *Australian Economic Papers* 27(50), June 1988, pp. 33–43.

On social welfare policy see:

Conference Papers on Poverty, Income and Wealth Distribution in *Australian Economic Review*, 3/88.

On taxation and economic growth:

Peter Groenewegen, "Taxation and Economic Growth", *Australian Journal of Public Administration* 49(3), September 1990.

On fiscal policy and the environment see:

"Developing Government Policy Responses to the Threat of the Greenhouse Effect", *Treasury Economic Roundup*, November 1989, pp. 3–20.

Index